Post-Victorian Britain
1902-1951

Post-Victorian Britain 1902-1951

L. C. B. SEAMAN

Routledge
Taylor & Francis Group

LONDON AND NEW YORK

First published 1966
by Methuen & Co. Ltd
11 New Fetter Lane, London EC4P 4EE
University Paperback reprinted five times
Reprinted 1982

Published in the USA by
Methuen & Co.
in association with Methuen, Inc.
733 Third Avenue, New York, NY 10017

Reprinted 2004 by Routledge

Transferred to Digital Printing 2004

ISBN 0-415-03994-0

It is not given to human beings, happily for them, for otherwise life would be intolerable, to foresee or predict to any large extent the unfolding course of events. In one phase men seem to have been right, in another they seem to have been wrong. Then again, a few years later, when the perspective of time has lengthened, all stands in a different setting. There is a new proportion. There is another scale of values. History with its flickering lamp stumbles along the trail of the past, trying to reconstruct its scenes, to revive its echoes, and kindle with pale gleams the passion of former days.

WINSTON S. CHURCHILL
House of Commons, 12 November 1940

Contents

Text Illustrations

Maps

Introduction

The period of United Kingdom history that extends from the death of Queen Victoria to the General Election of 1951 is still too often sharply divided into five distinct parts. The years before 1914 have to be studied in books mainly devoted to the nineteenth century; the two great wars of the period tend to be considered in isolation from their origins and their aftermath, and often in isolation from the political and diplomatic changes which accompanied them; the between-war period has been the subject of many books devoted solely to it and sometimes originating from motives apologetic or denunciatory; and there is an absence of coherent studies of the years 1945–51, even though the many changes, domestic and international, which have since occurred have given those years a psychological remoteness out of proportion to their comparative nearness in time. On the grounds of convenience alone, it seems desirable that an attempt be made to survey the whole period in one volume.

The attempt may also be justified on grounds less utilitarian. The years from 1902 to 1914 were not merely an Edwardian and Georgian autumn, stormy or golden according to taste, significant only as denoting the passing of a long Victorian summer; in affairs foreign, imperial and domestic, they were years of seedtime rather than of harvest. It was only from 1902 onwards that the larger ambitions of Germany and Japan, which constituted the major issues in world affairs during the first half of the twentieth century, began to be clearly visible; the story of Germany's unsuccessful attempt to master Europe, and of Japan's unsuccessful attempt to master the Far East are both completely contained within the period covered by this book. In like manner, fear of Russia, still a major consideration of British policy in 1902, speedily took second place thereafter to fear of Germany and (less quickly) to fear of Japan; but in 1951 it stood out once again as the major factor in world affairs. Between 1902 and 1951, the British Foreign Office had, indeed, traced a full circle from Korea back to Korea; unwillingness to be involved in a clash with Russia over that distant place troubled its thoughts about the Anglo-Japanese alliance in 1902 and about the alliance with the United States in 1951. Thus, the first half of the twentieth century provides a coherent period of study because, during it, the main flow of world history was in one sense halted, and in other senses accelerated, by the ambitions of Germany and Japan.

Emergent in 1902, these ambitions could, by 1951, be regarded with some certainty as having been relegated to the past.

In 1902, the fate of Korea was remote enough to cause only mild, and purely official, concern in the United Kingdom. In 1951, it was a matter which produced dramatic and immediate effects upon the British economy, and helped to destroy the unity of one of its two major political parties. This serves as a reminder of what is perhaps the period's most important unifying factor. Even before it began, the railway and the steamship had widely disseminated those industrial techniques the pioneering of which had given the United Kingdom its spectacular but already fading monopoly of the world's trade and oceans. Between 1902 and 1914, the development of wireless telegraphy and the discovery that the petrol engine could solve the problem of powered flight indicated that, during the first half of the twentieth century, history would at last begin truly to be world history, rather than the history of separated continents and cultures. In 1902, but not much earlier, it could be seen, if only by a few, that science and technology were about to destroy the distances which had kept the Americas and Australasia relatively isolated, Africa relatively primitive, Asia relatively decadent and Russia absolutely backward. By 1951, the process was obvious to all.

By accelerating this development, even in the process of diverting attention from it, the wars against Germany and Japan also accelerated the process by which the United Kingdom was transformed from the wealthiest, and apparently the most powerful, of the Great Powers into but one advanced State among many. Already, in the last quarter of the nineteenth century, other States, with larger populations and greater natural resources than hers, had begun to outpace her in technological progress. The two world wars stimulated industrial and technological growth all over the world; but in the United Kingdom absolute growth was accompanied, inevitably, by relative decline, notwithstanding much social advance and much successful adjustment to changing circumstance.

In 1902, Britain's imperial position seemed to dominate the world; even official doubts about its impregnability derived, in part, from the fear of anti-British combinations that never materialized. But, in the four years before 1951, the British abandoned India, Burma and Ceylon, signalling the start of a wholesale European retreat from Asia. In these same years, it lost also what it had fought two twentieth-century wars to maintain: its hold on the strategic centre of world power, the Near and Middle East. In 1951 itself, the signature of the ANZUS pact between Australia, New Zealand and the United States marked an abdication of power in Australasia also. The great world crisis over Korea in 1950-3 was the first for 250 years in which the United Kingdom played the part, diplomatically, militarily and economically, of a minor power. Nor, by the end of 1951, could there be much reliance on the belief that the shadow of a Commonwealth of Nations was more real than the departed substance of Empire. The function of the Commonwealth idea in the 1950's was to be merely that of one uncertain hope competing with the contrary pulls towards union with Europe and 'special association' with the United States.

Yet to describe the period merely as one in which Britain declined is to over-estimate both the magnitude and the duration of the imperial power that had been lost. The 'Pax Britannica' of the nineteenth century was a peace whose maintenance depended less on Britain's absolute strength than on the absolute weakness of others. This thought was expressed, with characteristic lack of sophistication, by Ernest Bevin, speaking in a Commons debate on foreign affairs on 7 November 1945:

> What astounds me about the history of the Navy is how cheaply we have policed the world for 300 years. I often think, when I read this history, that it is a good job no one called our bluff very often. . . . The world was policed largely by the British Navy with less than 100,000 men.

It is to forget also that the Empire whose liquidation had begun by 1951 had been to a considerable extent the creation only of the second half of the nineteenth century. The dissolution of the bonds that tied so many overseas territories to the direct control of Government in London was, in many instances, the abandonment of much that had been too easily acquired, that was too costly to hold on to, and which had only briefly been enjoyed. The process of adjustment to the changing facts of world power represented a growth in realism as well as a decline in power.

In the purely domestic history of the United Kingdom, unity is imposed on the first half of the twentieth century by the emergence of the Labour Party at its beginning and by the achievements of the Labour Government at its end. Confused though Labour's aims and methods usually were, the policies of the other two parties were already, by 1902, committed to the perpetuation of old creeds and old privileges. The transformation of the Liberal Party into the progressive party the twentieth century needed, and may perhaps be said not to have found, was prevented by Asquith's lack of understanding and Lloyd George's capacity for making enemies. The Conservatives stamped themselves as the party of resistance to social change in the first decade of the period, and remained in that attitude, with only minor adjustments of pose, until the 1950's. But by 1951, having, after fifty years of struggle, at last put into effect a programme which would not have been unduly ahead of its time in the reign of Edward VII, the Labour Party, as it faced the opening of the century's second half, did so having become, in its turn, a party too deeply tied to its past. The result was that a half-century that began with a Tory débâcle was brought to an end by a Tory restoration.

It is therefore appropriate to end this book in 1951 because it was in that year (it was certainly not in 1945) that history emerged from the past into the contemporary. At the time, contemplating the sufficiently unfamiliar pattern of affairs since 1945, men took for granted that the problem that would confront them for years ahead was the world-wide rivalry between the U.S.S.R. and the U.S.A. It was assumed, from the evidence of the Korean War, that the triumph of Communism in China was simply an accession of strength to the U.S.S.R. It was overlooked that the emergence of an independent China represented a limitation, and not an extension, of Russian influence in Asia, and that it would pose altogether new problems in the relations between Asia and the rest of the world. That the political sovereignty of the United Kingdom and France would virtually have disappeared from the whole of Africa within the next decade and a half was also not foreseen in 1951; nor that Europe, while losing so much of its overseas power, would shortly recover so much of its interior vitality. And in the United Kingdom, few imagined that the Tory restoration would continue uninterruptedly for thirteen years; or that a society which had spent the whole of the forties in the restrained and centrally disciplined pursuit of common ends in war and peace would give itself over so generally in the fifties to the pursuit of private affluence. By the mid-sixties, the year of the Festival of Britain had come to seem almost as remote as the year of the Great Exhibition.

Woking, March 1965   L.C.B.S.

Acknowledgements

I have to thank Miss Christine Bowles and Miss Mary Smith for their expert and expeditious typing of my manuscript. I am grateful also to my colleague, Mr. G. J. Talbot, for his careful concern for my punctuation and syntax, for the restraining influence he exercised from time to time upon my tendency to over-confident assertion, for his assistance with the tasks of proof reading and, most of all, for compiling the index.

L.C.B.S.

PART I:
END AND BEGINNING
1902-1914

1 · Conspectus, 1902

In 1902 Lord Salisbury had retired, Edward VII had been crowned and the Treaty of Vereeniging had been signed. The Labour Representation Committee had been formed at Farringdon Street in 1900 and in 1902 had already won two seats at by-elections. 1902 was also the year of the Balfour Education Act and of the Anglo-Japanese alliance. All these circumstances justify taking this particular year as a starting-point.

In political history the retirement of Salisbury was as much the end of an era as had been the retirement of Gladstone or the death of Palmerston. Salisbury was the last Prime Minister to sit in the Lords. He was the last to bring to his office, though in a different and somewhat less excessively publicized manner, that devout awareness of Christianity which had also characterized Gladstone. What had distinguished Salisbury's Christianity from Gladstone's was that Gladstone's was basically Protestant, strenuous and optimistic, whereas Salisbury's was more Catholic and more pessimistic. Thus Salisbury, little though he relished selfishness and irresponsibility when he found it in other noblemen, attached, in contrast to Gladstone, little value to legislation as a means of human betterment. Unlike Gladstone, too, he was on the whole, except for the occasional railway directorship, a long way away from the commercial middle class and further still from the urban working class; Lord Salisbury belonged to that fast-dying era when the aristocratic politician could still think of the labouring poor chiefly as rural tenants. The profound but aloof pessimism of an eccentric other-worldly Christian who had himself never lacked for anything was one of the factors behind the marked lack of significant social legislation in the long years of Salisbury's political domination. There was already much evidence that the new forces in the electorate were not content with this state of affairs, and their discontent was speedily made evident when Salisbury left the political scene. His lightweight nephew, philosophical and sceptical where his uncle had been religious and devout, was equally remote from the realities of a great industrial State. Lloyd George commented on the evidence he saw of this in Balfour during the First World War, relating with sardonic enjoyment Balfour's somewhat glazed astonishment when confronted for the first time with a trade union delegation. Lacking his uncle's experience, his authority and his appearance of toughness, Balfour was unequal to dealing with the increasing political awareness of the lower orders, resulting from the growth of the trade union movement, and the general discredit which the length and difficulty of the Boer War had brought upon the only genuinely popular element in late nineteenth-century Toryism, its Imperialism. When to these were added the rogue-elephant tactics of Chamberlain in launching a Tariff Reform campaign, the stage was set for the election defeat of 1906 which condemned Balfour to spend the greater part of his political career as England's most distinguished former Prime Minister. The party considered itself lucky to have won the so-called Khaki Election of 1900 and, indeed, their victory then is ascribable not merely to their somewhat unscrupulous appeal to patriotism but also to the continued disarray of the Liberal Party. They therefore not surprisingly paid the penalty of an overwhelming defeat in 1906, and were not again undisputed masters of the political stage until the days of Baldwin.

The death of Queen Victoria and the accession of Edward VII were naturally taken then, and have been so considered since, as marking the end of an era. It is possible perhaps at this date to underestimate the effects on the national mind. Even more than Lord Salisbury, the Queen had linked the England of 1900 with the still largely rural England of the age before the Railway Mania; she had also linked England with the continent of Europe in a more personal way than has since been possible. Like Salisbury, and for longer than Salisbury, the Queen, by age and experience and through the marriages of her children and grandchildren, the unofficial head of many of Europe's royal families, in a symbolic way bound England, notwithstanding its notorious insularity, with Europe no less than she had bound it to the colonies. And just as the Conservative Party found itself diminished when Salisbury had been replaced by Balfour, so England was in some ways diminished (since politics domestic and foreign are not to be explained in terms wholly rational) by the substitution of Edward VII for Queen Victoria. William II was in awe of his grandmother but tried to patronize Uncle Bertie; and this was not without its significance in view of the temperaments of the two men. Moreover, Edward VII symbolized and encouraged the growing English suspicion of Germany by his obvious preference for France which, though not without precedent among statesmen, can be paralleled among the King's predecessors only by Charles II. The King was also only the second monarch since Charles II to identify

himself publicly with 'smart' society; and since an important factor of the
years after 1902 was a much increased display of affluence by the rich at a
time when real wages were at best stationary, Edward the Peacemaker
perhaps contributed a little, through his highly convivial personality and
his un-Victorian choice of associates, to that increasing hostility of the poor
towards the wealthy which Lloyd George was to exploit so high-spiritedly
between 1909 and 1911. Edward VII's uniqueness in this respect is all the
more noticeable when contrasted with his successors as well as his predecessors. George V and Queen Mary once again made the monarchy
uncontroversial and, perhaps unwittingly, began the process which, by the
middle of the twentieth century, had compelled the royal family to take
part in an almost continuous ceremonial soap-opera.

The signing of the Peace of Vereeniging in 1902 appeared to have brought
to a satisfactory conclusion, if not to a glorious climax, the age of Imperialism in English history. One of the unnoticed features of British Imperialism,
however, is the short run it had as a dominant political theory. A phenomenon which was spoken of in this country by J. A. Hobson and then outside
it by Lenin, as the arch-enemy of liberty throughout the world, which has
long been used to justify vilification of this country not only in Marxist-
Leninist Russia but also in the United States, was in fact a phenomenon
which barely existed before 1874 and which dominated the English mind
only from 1885 to 1902. It is only in these years that Government and large
sections of public opinion appeared to accept the rightness of a policy of
actively extending the boundaries of Empire; only in these years was
opposition to this idea without really effective political expression. 'Land of
Hope and Glory' could not have been written at any time before the 1880's,
and it could never be taken quite seriously at any time after 1906; and it is
altogether fitting that Elgar himself, who prided himself on his Englishness,
soon found it unbearable to listen to. In the Leninist and American-
Liberal sense of the phrase, Gladstone had been an anti-Imperialist and
so had Aberdeen, Peel, Castlereagh and Pitt. After Gladstone, Imperialism
found full political expression only in the careers of Chamberlain and
Rhodes. Behind them, it is true, had been the subtle mind of Salisbury,
but though his Governments added many square miles to the British
Empire he superintended this process very largely as a matter of political
and diplomatic tactics, in a manner not altogether unlike that in which, in
the early 1880's, Bismarck had also undertaken a colonial policy in pursuit
of a particular domestic policy. The Boer War was seriously damaging to
Imperialism partly by its inefficiencies and partly because of the publicity
given by the Government's Liberal critics to Kitchener's concentration
camps; conditions in these were, of course, the inevitable consequence of
Kitchener's notorious lack of interest in the medical care even of his own
troops. He was hardly likely to show much imagination in his treatment of

enemy aliens even if they were women and children. The Boer War did lasting damage to the British Empire chiefly because it made too many Englishmen as uncritically ashamed of Empire as, before 1899, too many had been uncritically proud of it.

The formation of the Labour Representation Committee had attracted no attention in 1900. But in the 1906 election, the L.R.C. and its T.U. allies were to win about fifty seats, a startling indication of the extent to which both the traditional political parties were felt to have failed the working class. The nineteenth century is widely and rightly thought of as a period of continuous social reform; but it is difficult to point to any reforms passed by Whigs or Liberals which were specifically intended to confer direct benefits on the working class as such. This would have seemed contrary to the Liberal concern to achieve what it considered a proper balance between the classes. To the nineteenth-century mind, laws which conferred exclusive benefits on any one class were bad laws. It was for this reason that the Liberals had set out to destroy the privileged legal position previously enjoyed by the aristocracy and the Church. It was also in this spirit that the Tories had legislated in the 1840's against the undue advantage which the common law appeared to give factory owners over their female and child employees. It was because it was widely held that universal suffrage, by giving numerical superiority to the labouring poor, would lead to governments being conducted solely in their interest that democracy had remained a term of abuse in the nineteenth century and parliamentary reform after 1832 had been so long delayed. By 1900, however, the working class had begun to demand once more what it had demanded hardly at all since the failure of Chartism, namely direct political power. Since 1848 the organized working-class movement had ceased to seek political power, partly because of the general material progress of the country, in which all classes except the unskilled worker had tended to share, and partly because the New Unions believed they could safeguard their special position as the aristocracy of labour industrially by negotiation, and politically by acting as pressure groups, procedures which made less heavy demands on their finances. This state of affairs was already coming to an end when Salisbury became Prime Minister for the second time, in 1886. Bloody Sunday (1887), the Match Girls' strike (1888), the London Dock strike (1889) and the growth of industrial unionism among the unskilled workers, suggested that the political future would be shaped, and perhaps dominated, by the greater political awareness of the working class. This new militancy no doubt resulted in part from the sharp decline in the prosperity of some sections of English agriculture in the last quarter of the century and from uncertainties caused by the so-called Great Depression. There was thus a stirring from the depths in late Victorian society, depths which decades of material progress had hardly touched and which had defied the intense missionary zeal of the churches altogether. Yet, at the beginning of the twentieth century, neither of the traditional parties showed signs of coming to grips with the problems thus posed or even of being aware that they existed.

Disraeli had to some extent foreseen that the party which was the more successful in wooing the working-class electorate could best meet the challenge of the future. It was for this reason that he had invented the idea of Tory Democracy, based on social reform and the Empire. It is true that Disraeli's so-called Imperialism was more an imitation of the foreign policy of Palmerston than an anticipation of the colonial policy of Chamberlain and Rhodes; but, in encouraging pride in Empire, Disraeli showed real understanding of the working classes. For working men, the colonies were not, as they were to Gladstonian Liberals, costly administrative inconveniences, but places to which their closest relatives had emigrated and to which lack of employment in this country might eventually compel them to emigrate also. Disraeli had had the sense to see that blood was not only thicker than water but a more living source of political power than the holier-than-thou counting of pence which so often passed among Liberals for a foreign and colonial policy. He had seen too, ahead of his contemporaries, that the extension of the franchise compelled the political parties to woo the working man more directly; and the social legislation of 1874–80, such as the Trade Union Act, the Public Health Act and the Artisans' Dwellings Act, was a real departure in policy; it represented an appeal, limited though it was, to the daily interests of the working class, which, as the record shows, had not been made by Gladstone even in his prime between 1868 and 1874.

Unfortunately Disraeli's clairvoyance was not shared by his successor. Salisbury served his party ill in the long run by his remoteness from the working class. Tory Democracy, it is true, found an immediate champion after Disraeli's death in Lord Randolph Churchill, but Churchill ruined his career by staking more than was politically justifiable on his personal indispensability and on the value which Salisbury would attach to Churchill's following among the now further enfranchised working classes. The power with which the constitution and the party system combine to endow a Prime Minister makes other members of a Cabinet among the most easily replaceable of public figures; a circumstance which goes far to explain the survival in later years of Baldwin without Winston Churchill, and of Neville Chamberlain without Churchill, Eden, Amery, Duff Cooper and Cranborne. Unfortunately, the graver social problems of a great people cannot ultimately be solved by political adroitness. In this matter of the condition of the people, therefore, Salisbury sowed the whirlwind that Balfour was to reap.

The only other source from which the Tories might have continued to imbibe Tory Democratic principles was Joseph Chamberlain. Chamberlain was, however, largely lost to the radical cause by his espousal of Imperialism, and this was a double disaster for the Tory Party. It produced the psychological shock of the Boer War and it enabled Liberalism in 1906 to capture from the Tories the working-class vote which, on its previous record, it had done so little to deserve. This was made easier for the Liberals because Chamberlain added to his other political errors the greater error of championing the cause of Tariff Reform from 1903 onwards. This, coming as it did after nearly twenty years of Conservative rule during which hardly anything had been done politically to satisfy the social demands of the masses, helped to make more credible Lloyd George's attack on the Tories, and the Tory peers in particular, as enemies of the people. It explains also the size of Labour's representation in the 1906 Parliament. This was, however, more than a working-class judgement on the Tories; it was also a serving of notice upon the triumphant Liberals that they were victors on condition that they served the cause of the working class.

The Balfour Education Act of 1902 is likewise a starting-point. It originated the process which the 1950's and 1960's were taught to think of in disparaging terms as the education of a 'meritocracy'. The most important feature of the Act to contemporaries appeared to be that Nonconformists were now compelled to contribute by way of their local authority rates to the upkeep of the Church schools. They had been contributing to this through the national taxes since 1833, and their opposition was thus illogical; but it is customary to regard Nonconformist anger over this matter as a contributory factor to the Liberal victory in 1906. It was, like Tariff Reform, calculated to give new life to old Liberal shibboleths, and is better regarded as an indication of the quite temporary, not to say illusory character of the Liberal victory; for just as Free Trade was a slowly dying cause so the Nonconformist conscience was well on the way to becoming a small ignored voice. What gave the Act its significance both for good and ill was its creation of State responsibility for secondary education through the education committees of the county councils. The lower middle class were now able to educate their children above the elementary level by the payment of relatively low fees; and the children of even the least prosperous among them could henceforth enter these secondary schools provided they could establish a claim to free tuition and a maintenance grant by success in a stiff competitive 10-plus 'scholarship' examination. The State grammar schools thus created were later subject to continuous criticism. The Labour Party disliked them on the grounds that they turned lower middle-class and working-class children into *bourgeois* snobs; and the Conservatives disliked them on the grounds that they enabled fact-crammed examinees to establish a claim to positions in society for which their lack of public school character-training was alleged to make them fundamentally unsuited. This suggests that the grammar schools were almost the only successful solvent of class divisions which this country evolved during the first half of the twentieth century. It would not be far wrong to say that it was the grammar-school educated who gave Labour its decisive victory in the 1945 election and who, out of discontent with the fruits they obtained from that election, put the Conservatives back into power in 1951.

Where the Balfour Act and its consequences are most open to criticism is that the schools which it created or revived were in fact grammar schools, too ready to assume that a traditional education, taking its spirit and aims from the public schools, was the only possible education to give to the new pool of ability for which they catered. A much greater readiness to respond to the country's obvious need for improved technical education would have been more in keeping with the first decade of the century, let alone later decades. By 1902 it was already nearly forty years since a Royal Commission had first called attention to the inadequacy of English technical education, and already well over a decade since the foundation of the Polytechnic movement by Quintin Hogg had pointed a way to the future which, despite the Technical Instruction Act of 1889, the local authorities and the State tended to ignore. They continued to ignore it when the 1944 Act gave them another opportunity to create secondary technical schools on a national scale.

Nevertheless, the grammar schools, along with the trade unions, provided for the first time since before the Reformation an organized route by which persons of humble birth with no flair for making money could rise to positions of authority. As it turned out, the grammar school quickly outpaced the trade unions as a nursery for new talent. Although the trade union movement produced a Foreign Secretary in Ernest Bevin, it is not likely to throw up a man of comparable type again; the Ernest Bevins of the future will be shaped differently by universal secondary education. The significance of educational expansion in effecting social change in the first six decades of the century is not of course to be exaggerated: a number of plays and novels in the 1950's testify to the durability of the fiction that the grammar school product, even when given a university education as well, remained something of a barbarian.

The signing of the Anglo-Japanese alliance in 1902 used to be regarded as marking the end of England's 'splendid isolation'. There are good grounds for saying that Salisbury's policy had never been one of splendid isolation; and grounds also for saying that if splendid isolation had been his policy the Anglo-Japanese Alliance did not end it. Learned arguments as to the origin and implication of the phrase need not debar its use if it is taken to refer to the evident fact that, whereas by the mid-1890's the continental Powers were joined into rival groups, the United Kingdom was formally associated with neither. It is in this sense and this sense alone that the

British were 'isolated', and since it was an isolation from Europe, an alliance with Japan can hardly be said to have ended it.

The Anglo-Japanese alliance had, however, immediate consequences of far-reaching importance and it was certainly a landmark in the history of the relations between the European and the non-European world. For the first time in the modern period, a European Great Power was treating a non-European Power as an equal. The alliance may or may not have ended England's isolation but it clearly ended Japan's; it raised the curtain on a drama which reached its apocalypse at Hiroshima and proceeded thereto by way of the Manchurian crisis, Pearl Harbor and the fall of Singapore. By a curious twist of circumstance, the fact that the British were the first European Power to treat an Oriental Power on terms of equality was never to redound to their credit; but there is no doubt that British patronage of Japan was a decisive event in the revival of the peoples of the East. There were, within less than ten years of it, a would-be 'Westernizing' revolt in Turkey, the first moves in the long-drawn-out Chinese revolution, and the first stirrings of Indonesian revolt against the Dutch. Nothing more pregnant of future change had happened to Asia since Vasco da Gama's arrival at Calicut in 1498.

The alliance also set in train events which changed the course of European history. Without it, the Japanese would not have risked their war with Russia; and that had for its sequels the abortive Russian revolution of 1905, the Anglo-Russian *entente*, and a renewed if unwilling concentration of Russian policy on the Balkans, which by 1914 had produced a situation from which war seemed the only possible escape. By making a Russo-Japanese War possible it made an Anglo-French *entente* more urgent. The French had been working for this since Fashoda; but it was the French desire to bring the Russo-Japanese War to a speedy end before it disastrously weakened France's one European ally that impelled the French to make haste to sign an agreement with England, the ally of Japan. The Anglo-Japanese Alliance was also the first successful positive step that British Governments had taken in foreign policy since the Cyprus Convention of 1878. After 1878, foreign policy was hesitant, as under Gladstone, or cautiously serpentine, as under Salisbury. Egypt had been acquired inadvertently; in 1898 there had been failure to obtain agreement with Russia, and between 1898 and 1901 successive failures to secure agreement with Germany. Even Fashoda was largely negative and its significance greatly exaggerated. All that Fashoda had done was to recall sharply to the French that it was exactly a hundred years since Nelson's victory at the Battle of the Nile had destroyed the one real chance the French had ever had of controlling Egypt, that it was over fifty years since Palmerston had bludgeoned Louis Philippe out of trying to secure Egypt for France by exalting Mehemet Ali, and nearly twenty since the French had opted out of the expedition to Alexandria in 1882. The purpose of the

Anglo-Japanese alliance was certainly the negative one of restraining Russia in north China; but it is significant that the British had at last taken on a new commitment, by offering support for Japanese ambitions in Korea, just as two years later they took on the new commitment of supporting French ambitions in Morocco. In 1902 the British had thus taken the first step along a path from which they were to find it impossible to retrace their steps.

2 · Conservative Balance Sheet, 1902-05

The defeat which the Conservatives suffered in the election of 1906 was so overwhelming that it cannot be explained solely on rational grounds. Considered as a verdict on the achievements of Balfour's Ministry since 1902 it was unjust; and it would be wrong to take it as implying an overwhelming desire on the part of the electorate for the legislation which the Liberals eventually put on the statute book. There seems little evidence that the electorate either knew that they were voting for a Government which would later be described as 'founding the welfare state'; or that, if they had known this, they would have necessarily voted for it. This is shown by the heavy losses the Liberals suffered in the 1910 elections. Discontent with twenty years of Tory rule was deep-seated but incoherent; and there is much to be said for the view that the Conservatives were defeated in 1906 for good reasons but largely over the wrong issues.

Thus, in the prevailing atmosphere of disillusionment after the Boer War, the public mind was more impressed by the issue of 'Chinese slavery' and by the Elgin Committee's revelations of the incompetence with which the war had been conducted, than they were by the Government's achievements in imperial defence and foreign policy. The 'Chinese slavery' affair was certainly an indication of the political insensitivity of Balfour's Government. Chinese coolies were being imported in tens of thousands into the Transvaal to make good the shortage of Kaffir labour. The terms of their employment involved their compulsory attachment to their new masters by a form of indenture and by their segregation into special compounds. The procedure had ugly associations. A somewhat similar reason, the shortage of native labour, had inaugurated the slave trade in

African Negroes for use in the Americas. Worse still, it was bound to reinforce the more and more frequently articulated view of the Radical Opposition that the Tory Government had launched the Boer War for the
benefit of the mine-owners of the Rand and was composed of men who
treated labour with contempt and were indifferent to the elementary
human decencies. Of course, the agitation was fomented for political gain
and, of course, Winston Churchill was right when in a famous phrase he
said that it was a 'terminological inexactitude' to describe the position of
these Chinese as 'slavery'; but here was a deplorable indication that, for
all their virtues, the Conservatives were blind to the times they lived in.
It is indeed odd that a Government which had allied itself with one Oriental
people should cancel out this act of apparent magnanimity by a policy
towards another Oriental people which seemed to establish a direct resemblance between Balfour and Milner and the most ruthless of the
conquistadores. What made it worse was that as a result of the Peace of
Vereeniging the British Government was now itself responsible for what
was done in the Transvaal.

Against this must be set the Conservatives' solid contributions to imperial
defence. Balfour made the Committee of Imperial Defence a permanent
institution and provided it with a secretariat; and although the Government
did not establish a General Staff it did abolish (at last) the office of Commander-in-Chief, and set up the Army Council. In naval matters, Lord
Cawdor (Balfour's First Lord of the Admiralty) and Sir John Fisher, First
Sea Lord from 1904 onwards, reorganized the Navy so that henceforth it
was concentrated into three fleets: the Mediterranean Fleet based on
Malta, the Atlantic Fleet based on Gibraltar, and the Home Fleet based on
the home ports. More important still, they began the Dreadnought building
programme. All these changes were to be of great value to the nation within
less than a decade, but unfortunately they were electoral liabilities rather
than assets. Any reorganization of the Army after the Boer War could only
be regarded as a case of shutting the stable door after the horse had bolted;
and, given the rising temper of the working classes and the growth of
Radical·pacifism in the Liberal Party, any expenditure on battleships
would seem one more affront to the labouring poor. Similar considerations
apply to the signing of the *entente* with France in 1904. Although initially
hailed as an act of pacification it was soon regarded as the alliance of one
Imperialism with another.

Nor did the Government receive much credit for Wyndham's Irish
Land Purchase Act of 1903. This provided for State assistance, on a more
comprehensive and generous scale than hitherto, to enable tenants in
Ireland to purchase land and to repay the agreed purchase price by
annuities spread over 68½ years. Unfortunately, Wyndham then flirted
with the idea of giving more administrative freedom to Ireland as a whole
and, in the face of the Unionist agitation against him, Balfour allowed him

to resign rather than permit his Government to be accused of flirting with common sense in its Irish policy.

The Nonconformist prejudices which had been at work over the Education Act have already been discussed; like prejudices were also aroused by the Licensing Act of 1904. The reduction of the number of public house licences had long been recognized as necessary, but had been held up because the magistrates concerned were unwilling to withhold licences for so long as the law forbade the compensation of the dispossessed brewer. By the Balfour Act, the brewers were to be compensated for loss of licences out of a fund to which the trade itself had to contribute. This allowed the reduction of licences to proceed, whereas the previous arrangement had obstructed reduction. Since nothing would satisfy the Nonconformist conscience but the virtual abolition of public houses forthwith and without compensation, once again the Government received no credit for a piece of sensible legislation. On the issues of licensing and education, the Liberal Party had little reason to congratulate itself: it received too many votes from voters who had too little regard for minorities of whom they disapproved, on allegedly religious or moral grounds.

It is not surprising therefore that the Unemployed Workmen Act of 1905, giving the Local Government Board power to establish unemployment committees to keep a register of local unemployed and to set up labour exchanges, attracted no credit to the Government either. These committees could not give the unemployed financial assistance, but were allowed to appeal to public charity for funds for this purpose. Thus, on one hand the act can be regarded as setting a legislative precedent for the Unemployment Exchanges Act of 1909, since Beveridge secured the passage of the 1909 Act partly by using the statistics made available to him as a result of the Act of 1905. On the other hand, the reliance on charitable subscriptions which accompanied the Act was a further example of how Tories could resist the idea of State responsibility for unemployment even at the very moment of appearing to yield to it.

Understandably, what loomed larger in the mind of the working class was the complicated legal tangle of the Taff Vale case. In 1900, the Amalgamated Society of Railway Servants held an official strike among its members working for the Taff Vale Railway Company in South Wales. The company sued the Amalgamated Society, first to restrain it from action which might damage the company's business, and second for damages already caused to it by their action. The case went against the union in the High Court; the Court of Appeal found for the union; but the House of Lords, as the final Court of Appeal, gave judgement against the union for £23,000 damages plus costs. This decision compelled the unions to regard the Trade Union Acts of 1871 and 1875, which they believed had protected both their funds and their right to strike, as so much waste paper. Since the case had been decided by the Lords as a final Appeal Court the only way out was the passage of a remedial statute. No such statute was forth-coming from the Government; Balfour took refuge in the appointment of a Royal Commission. There could be no other result of this situation than to make the unions a good deal less lukewarm towards the Labour Repre-sentation Committee than they had been in the past. The political levy by which trade unions subsidized Labour candidates was introduced in 1903. Moreover, it is difficult to explain, even to the educated, that the House of Lords, when sitting as a Court of Appeal, has no connection with the House of Lords which because of its Tory majority was in Mr Balfour's pocket. To explain this to the working man, already surfeited with legal niceties, was even more difficult. The Taff Vale case confirmed the working man in the view that the Conservative Party was using the machinery of law and government to deprive him of his rights. Baldwin later claimed that his own attitude to Labour and the trade unions in the 1920's, which struck many of his followers as 'soft', took its origin from his distress at the consequences of Tory disregard of Labour's needs at this particular time.

The final cause of the Conservative catastrophe was Chamberlain's Tariff Reform campaign which he launched in 1903. As a young man, Chamberlain had seen visions; and now that he was older he was still dreaming dreams. He had begun by making a highly successful business as a screw manufacturer, and continued by making a fortune. He followed this by making Birmingham a great city while its Lord Mayor. Achieve-ments of this sort marked him as a man apart from the other politicians of his time. His activities made of him a Radical because to any self-made man of vision it seemed evident that nothing but a radical change in the social and political system could create a right correspondence between the institutions of society and the industrial and commercial nation which they were now called upon to serve. While a member of Gladstone's second administration, he had attacked the aristocracy in terms not unlike those which were to be used by Lloyd George at the time of the People's Budget in 1909. The cry of 'the Peers versus the People' which Lloyd George raised then had first been raised by Joseph Chamberlain, in the months of the Lords' resistance to the third Reform Bill of 1884. In the same period, he had acquired notoriety by demanding free elementary education, the taxing of the rich to provide social reform for the benefit of the poor, and had even dared to call himself a Republican. It was clear that once Gladstone was removed from the stage Chamberlain was the destined leader of the Liberals. Indeed, if the whole course of English political life had not been distorted by the Irish Home Rule problem, neither the career of Lloyd George nor the rise to power of a Labour Party would have taken place. Over Home Rule in 1886, Chamberlain broke with Gladstone and divided the Liberal Party so that it did not come to-gether again as an effective political force for twenty years. But it might not be amiss to say that over Home Rule, Gladstone broke Chamberlain. Henceforth Chamberlain was compelled to sit in the Commons side by side with aristocratic Whigs who together with him led the Liberal Unionists, and in alliance with Conservatives led by the Tory peers he had all his life attacked. It was this situation of Chamberlain's, created by Irish and Gladstonian obstinacy, which lay at the root of the lack of constructive social legislation in the last two decades of the nineteenth century. But if his imprisonment by the Tories constricted his radicalism it could not permanently fetter his dynamic mind. And so it was that, from 1895 onwards, as Colonial Secretary he became the embodiment in Government circles of the Imperialist idea. He became devoted to the cause of Anglo-Saxon supremacy in Africa and, indeed, the world. Chamberlain the business man, the Radical, the organizer of civilized civic life, once he had turned his attention to what he called the 'undeveloped estate' of the ramshackle overseas empire, could hardly be expected to resist the desire to do with it what he had done to Birmingham and to apply to it those principles of sound organization, radical betterment and dynamic growth which were in fact the essential contribution of nineteenth-century England to human progress. To such a mind, not after all totally unlike that of Beatrice Webb, the Queen of the Fabian Socialists, Kruger was as much an impediment to the onward march of civilization as the mosquito and the tsetse fly. And if business progress and civilized organization required from time to time the exercise of a little sharp practice, the end more than justified the means; even if, when translated into an African context, this meant secret involvement, subsequently denied, in the Jameson Raid, and eventually in the Boer War. But one of the most common features of business men is to overreach themselves; and it seemed that Chamberlain's Imperialism had by 1902 all but gone bankrupt. Johannesburg was not, after all, Birmingham.

Nor was Chamberlain's breadth of vision limited to purely African affairs. Like other men of vision at this period, he thought in terms of world policy; and this characteristic of Chamberlain is evident in his projection in 1900 of the idea of a 'triple alliance' of the United States, the United Kingdom and the German Empire to preserve the world for ordered Anglo-Saxon and Teutonic progress against the Latins and Slavs. Such a plan had not the slightest chance of realization at the time that Chamberlain made it, but this had not prevented him from putting it forward for serious and immediate consideration.

His plan for Tariff Reform was of like character and arose from a similarly broad view of world policy. It was clear that Britain's mid-century monopoly, industrial and imperial, was passing away, and that if there were to be the possibility of continued greatness in the face of United States and German (let alone Russian and French) growth, this could only be achieved by a more effective economic and political organization of the

British Empire. By 1903 Chamberlain was convinced that the only method by which he could achieve a closer union within the Empire was by Imperial Preference; and Imperial Preference could be achieved only by taxing imports from outside the Empire. This meant proposing the abandonment of Free Trade. The firm belief that there had been a 'depression' (which in some senses was true) and that it would continue (an expectation which quickly proved false), as well as the unemployment that followed the Boer War, all directed his mind towards the end of Free Trade in favour of the protection of British manufactures. Protection, by preserving the profitability of industry, would also maintain the rate of employment.

Yet again, Chamberlain showed his obtuseness as a politician by plunging so precipitately into this whirlpool of controversy. It is fair to say also that a less intellectually curious Prime Minister than Balfour might equally have hesitated before slipping into the whirlpool as well. The conducting, by a major Cabinet Minister and his Prime Minister, of a pamphleteering and platform controversy as to the basis on which the country's future fiscal policy should be undertaken was not likely to inspire confidence either in the Prime Minister or his Government. The most elementary considerations of tactics required that the advocacy of Tariff Reform should have been mooted first in private. Instead, Balfour made the mistake of publicly advocating the desirability at least of some kind of retaliatory tariff against the country's chief economic rivals. Such a procedure, pardonable in a party in opposition, casts doubts on the capacity both of Balfour and Chamberlain as Cabinet Ministers. Balfour's public efforts at compromise offended the Free Traders in the party without in any way satisfying Chamberlain, and in a short time Balfour thought it expedient to disembarrass his Cabinet both of the Free Traders and the 'whole-hog' Protectionists. The result was to leave in office a Government whose chief characteristic was that it consisted of men patently unprepared to make up their minds about a major problem of policy. Even when, in January 1905, Balfour produced a formula to prevent his own and Chamberlain's supporters offering entirely different fiscal policies at the next election, nobody believed that its acceptance by the two sides made any difference to the fact of their disagreement. The Conservatives paid dearly for Balfour's attempt to retain votes in the country by saying he did not support Tariff Reform, while trying to retain votes in the Lords and Commons by saying he did not support Free Trade. Even after the 1906 election had been lost, Balfour was still prepared to go to ludicrous lengths in trying to pretend that the problem could be solved by a multiplicity of words. He produced another face-saving formula in a letter written on St Valentine's Day, 1906 which included the following:

Fiscal reform is, and must remain, the first constructive work of the Unionist party; its objects are to secure more equal terms of competition for British trade and closer commercial union with the colonies; and while it is at present unnecessary to prescribe the exact methods by which these objects are to be attained, and inexpedient to permit differences of opinion as to these methods to divide the party, though other means are possible, the establishment of a moderate general tariff on manufactured goods not imposed for the purpose of raising prices or giving artificial protection against legitimate competition and the imposition of a small duty on foreign corn are not in principle objectionable and should be adopted if shown to be necessary for the attainment of the ends in view or for the purposes of revenue.

Balfour's last move was to gamble on the possibility that, divided though the Conservative Party now was, the Liberals might be even more divided. He therefore resigned early in December 1905 without asking for a dissolution. Campbell-Bannerman thereupon became Prime Minister of a minority Liberal Government. Balfour hoped that the divisions which had rent the Liberal Party since Gladstone's time would make themselves sufficiently manifest for the electorate to have second thoughts about confirming them in office. Once again, and for the last time as Prime Minister, Balfour proved himself out of touch with political reality. The Liberals presented the electorate with a Government which gave every appearance not only of being strong but of being united. In the January 1906 election the Liberals gained a majority of 84 over all other parties combined. Ranged against the 157 Conservatives and Unionists were not only 377 Liberals but 83 Irish Nationalists and, most significantly of all for the future, 53 Labour members, of whom 29 were sponsored by the Labour Representation Committee.

It would have taken nothing short of the prospect of a rapid return to power to unite the Liberal Party, which, characteristically in a party of the Left, especially when in opposition, could not help but be a prey to fissiparous tendencies. These tendencies had been encouraged by uncertainties about the leadership. Lord Rosebery had resigned the leadership in 1896 but had kept the party in a state of uncertainty about the degree of finality he intended to be inferred from his action. Apart from the inherited cleavage in the party between the Radicals and the surviving Liberal Whigs, there had developed the division between the so-called Liberal Imperialists who had supported the Boer War and those, such as Campbell-Bannerman himself and Lloyd George, who in their different ways had opposed it. Worse still there had, during Balfour's term of office, developed a new clash over Home Rule. Both Asquith and Campbell-Bannerman had upset others in the party by proclaiming their belief that Home Rule for Ireland should be achieved only 'step by step'. These problems in fact presented no difficulties at the end of 1905 because the Tariff Reform campaign had presented the Liberals with the golden opportunity to unfurl their old, faded Free Trade banner. Once again they could represent themselves as the party that could say 'Hands Off the People's Food', and as the party to save the country from a return to the 'hungry forties' when, according to legend, the English had been starving and the Irish dying because a

Conservative Government continued to prohibit free trade in corn. The Liberals swept into power with sectarian prejudices on their Right flank, an angry trade union movement on their Left flank, and with their centre marching triumphantly into the future behind the ghosts of Cobden and Bright.

Nevertheless, the split in the Liberal Party which Balfour had hoped for as soon as it took office in December 1905 was only narrowly averted. The leading Liberal Imperialists in the party, Haldane, Grey and Asquith, had agreed in September 1905 that as soon as Balfour resigned they would refuse to take office under Campbell-Bannerman unless he agreed to go to the Lords, leaving the effective leadership of the Government to Asquith. They secured the approval of Edward VII, and when Campbell-Bannerman first went to the Palace the King did in fact suggest that he take a peerage. Campbell-Bannerman, always a forthright man, had by that time already made it clear that he disliked Haldane so much that he would refuse to let him be Lord Chancellor as he desired, and would, if necessary, exclude him from the Government altogether. He also showed some willingness to appoint someone other than Sir Edward Grey to the Foreign Office. At this, Asquith called the conspiracy off. He became tardily aware that the imminence of the General Election made the creation of a united Government imperative. He was determined not to prejudice his own position and felt satisfied that, since Campbell-Bannerman was twelve years his senior and in indifferent health, the reversion of the leadership to himself could not be long delayed. He therefore allowed himself to be conciliated by his own appointment to the Exchequer, and by the appointment of Grey and Haldane to the Foreign Office and the War Office, respectively; though Grey, who tended to fuss, and was not good at changing his mind, wanted to hold out against the Prime Minister a little longer. The intention of the conspirators, that there should be continuity in defence and foreign policy after the fall of the Conservatives, was largely fulfilled. The fears of the Foreign Office, that the advent of the Liberals would lead to an irresolute foreign policy, proved unfounded as soon as Grey took over. Campbell-Bannerman took little cognisance of the work of the Foreign Secretary, and Grey made sure that the Prime Minister was told as little as possible.

3 · Indian Summer of the Liberals, 1905-09

The first years of Campbell-Bannerman's Ministry were chiefly occupied, in domestic affairs, with attempts to fulfil the more obvious pledges the party had made before its election. Chinese slavery having been dealt with by forbidding the importing of more Chinese (though existing contracts were allowed to run their term) the Transvaal was given self-government in 1906 and so, in 1907, was the Orange River Colony. In 1908 and 1909, the four South African Governments worked out a constitution for a Union of South Africa and this was brought into being by the Union of South Africa Act of 1909. The apparently happy outcome of this swift repudiation of the Imperialist past was consciously used by the Labour Government of 1945–50 as a precedent for similar acts repudiating the past in India and elsewhere. Not for the first or last time, however, were the men of the Left blind to the pitfalls awaiting those who imagine that the past can be put right by a statutory washing of the hands. There was not one moral issue in South Africa; there were two. In effect the Liberals sought to solve the issue of Anglo-Boer relations by shelving the second issue, that of the relations between white South Africans and coloured South Africans. This was to ignore the fact that all through the nineteenth century an important element in the Anglo-Boer conflict had been differing views on the question of the coloured population. Like the Austro-Hungarian *Ausgleich* of 1867, the Liberal settlement of South Africa was a compromise for the benefit of two 'master' races; and it left the larger problem of the subject peoples for future generations to grapple with.

The most important statute of 1906 was the Trade Disputes Act. In future a trade union was not liable for civil wrongs committed on its behalf. That the Act was as comprehensive as this was due to Government yielding to Labour pressure in the Commons. As passed, it represented a revolutionary departure from the common law. It established finally that peaceful picketing was legal, even when its objects were to incite to breach of contract, and even though it was contrary to the common law principle that a man might work where he could and that an employer had a similar right to earn his living in his own way. The result was to give the trade

union movement what amounted to the status of a medieval 'immunity';
and to depart from the Anglo-Saxon principle of equality before the law.
It is not surprising that Asquith and the other lawyers in Campbell-
Bannerman's Government had grave doubts about the propriety of accepting the Labour members' own version of the Bill; and it was the personal
decision of Campbell-Bannerman to cut through the legal tangle and
accept Labour's proposals which got the Act on the statute book in its
final form.

It is typical of the behaviour of the Conservatives at this time that they
did not modify the Trade Disputes Bill in the Lords. Instead, they chose
to defeat the two other Bills of the year, the Education Bill and the Plural
Voting Bill. The former was designed to amend the 1902 Education Act
in a sense favourable to the Nonconformists. In spite of the fact that many
leading churchmen were not opposed to it, the Lords destroyed it by a
number of wrecking amendments. They dealt similarly with the Bill to
end the right of owners of business premises to additional votes in respect
of those premises. At a time when the total electorate was smaller, the
practice of plural voting was more important than when it was abolished
in 1948. The use by the Conservatives, for purely party ends, of the legislative powers of the Lords against a Government which commanded an
unprecedented majority in the Commons was one which the Conservative
leaders would have been wiser to avoid. A further example of Conservative
obstruction was the Lords' destruction of a non-controversial Liberal
Licensing Bill in 1908.

The Liberals were thus being pressed by the Labour members into
legislative action they did not want, and were being prevented from legislative action which they did desire, by the pressure of the Conservatives in
the Lords; and their need to escape from this situation provides the
clue to the subsequent history of this period of Liberal rule. It was under
Labour pressure, for example, that the Government accepted in 1906 an
act giving permission to local authorities to provide school meals for
necessitous children and to establish school Care Committees; this was
followed in 1907 by the authorization of regular medical inspection of
schoolchildren and the setting up of a medical department within the
Board of Education.

If, at this stage, the Labour Party and the trade unions had been capable
of rather more militancy in the political field, and if the Conservatives had
displayed a little less, the Liberal Government might not have long
survived. In 1908, trade was bad, the swing of opinion towards Tariff
Reform was becoming more marked, and the Government began to lose
by-elections. What saved the Liberals, though at a heavy cost, was that the
death of Campbell-Bannerman in 1908, by elevating Asquith to the
premiership, brought Lloyd George to the Exchequer and Winston
Churchill to the Board of Trade. This not only gave the Government a new

aggressiveness which goaded the Conservatives into a succession of political errors; it also gave it a policy capable of stealing Labour's thunder.

This latter task was made politically more urgent by the damaging effect on Labour's political progress of the Osborne judgement. A branch of the Amalgamated Society of Railway Servants, through their secretary, Osborne, challenged the legality of the political levy. The political levy was the compulsory imposition upon trade union members of a contribution to assist the cost of campaigning for Labour and trade union M.P.s and to help give them a salary at a time when M.P.s were still unpaid. In 1908 and 1909 the case went upwards through the courts to the House of Lords; and at each stage the levy was declared illegal. For the second time in less than a decade the laws of England had deprived working men of the power to organize themselves effectively. The Taff Vale judgement had sought to prevent them acting industrially; the Osborne judgement now prevented them acting politically. The Osborne judgement greatly increased the militancy of the unions in the industrial field and gave brief but alarming prominence to Syndicalism, with its emphasis on the use of the strike, not only as a means of establishing better conditions, but also as a means to disrupt and eventually overthrow the capitalist system.

It was Lloyd George who, intuitively and without preconceived plan, sought for a means to cast off the upper and nether millstones which were constricting the Government and threatening, by 1909, to crush the life out of it. There is no indication that he planned in advance to draw up a Budget in 1909 that the Lords would be bound to reject, thus providing a good reason for destroying their veto. It was rather that, given the situation as it had been developing since 1906, it was sound politics to try to save the Liberals by a dramatic appeal to the masses. Under the spell of Lloyd George's rousing oratory, a purely political struggle between Liberals and Conservatives was dramatized as a fundamental struggle between the Peers and the People, with the Liberal Party as the People's champion. Thus it was hoped that the Conservatives could be routed and the Labour Party outbid. At this stage, the Labour Party was inexperienced, devoid of outstanding personalities and coherent political programme, and debilitated both by the Osborne judgement and by the surviving tradition of co-operation with the Liberal Party. There was thus still time to stifle it in its cradle, while its voice was feeble and muffled. By contrast, Lloyd George's appeals would be all the louder and clearer for coming from a magnetic personality whose oratory and whose actions were uninhibited by regard for principle.

Lloyd George had been the most notably successful member of the Campbell-Bannerman Government. Asquith had been a sound Chancellor; Grey had been an unobtrusive Foreign Secretary, since only by shunning the limelight could anyone conduct foreign policy with a large Liberal majority in the Commons; Haldane had been reorganizing the Army, but without attracting public approval. Lloyd George, however, had startled observers by showing considerable ability at the Board of Trade; he had piloted important reforms relating to merchant shipping and patents, had taken the first census of production, had skilfully averted what might have been the first national railway strike in 1907, and settled a shipyard strike in 1908. He had also implemented a Royal Commission's recommendation that London's docks should come under the control of a single Port of London Authority, an undertaking that required both patience and energy in view of the large number of private and public interests involved. All this showed Lloyd George's skill as a manipulator both of people and of plans.

When Lloyd George took Asquith's place at the Exchequer, he at once ran into a piece of good luck which was of permanent benefit to his reputation. It fell to him to preside over the last stages of the 1908 Budget, which Asquith had prepared before taking over the Premiership; and it was this Budget which contained provision for the initial financing of old age pensions. It was thus to some extent fortuitous that when it came into operation the old age pension was familiarly known as 'the Lloyd George' and that ever since he has been inseparably associated with it. He was quick to see, however, that the introduction of old age pensions provided him with the kind of political publicity he needed if he were to present the Liberals as the true friends of the poor and needy, in contrast to the Tories with their championship of the powers of the Lords.

In relation to the size of the problem of poverty, and to the length of time it had been under discussion, the Old Age Pensions Act was inadequate. The operations of the Poor Law had been criticized by a Royal Sanitary Commission of 1869, and had been condemned not only by persons who might be regarded as propagandist, such as Charles Booth in his *London Life and Labour* of 1886, and Beatrice Webb, but also by a whole generation of Poor Law Medical Officers; and a Royal Commission on the Aged Poor had advocated old age pensions in 1895. Yet despite these soberly statistical criticisms of the administrative chaos and human suffering which attended the operations of the Poor Law, it was still governed essentially by the principles of the Poor Law Amendment Act of 1834. The Royal Commission on the Poor Laws which reported in 1909 had been set up in the hope that it would condemn, not the existing system, but the alleged growth of humanitarian departures from it. The prevailing doctrine was still that the deterrent effects of detention in a workhouse and of the stigma traditionally attached to pauperism should be maintained in order to prevent idleness and thriftlessness. In fact, the majority of the Commission reported in favour of abandoning the deterrent principle in Poor Law administration and demanded that it should henceforth concern itself with preventing and curing destitution and not merely with its relief in the traditionally semi-penal fashion. Both the majority and the minority reports were, in practice, in favour of a complete administrative reorganization of the Poor Law.

The introduction of old age pensions took place ahead of the Royal Commission's report and was the first of various piecemeal substitutes for the comprehensive reforms which the Commission advocated. The Act gave a non-contributory pension of five shillings a week to persons over 70, and 7s. 6d. to married couples, provided income from other sources did not exceed 10s. a week. Where other income exceeded £31 10s. a year there was no entitlement to pension. The emotional excitement which it was possible to generate on account of the Act is a proof of how little the poor had come to expect of their rulers. Public meetings could be worked up to utter fervent cries of 'Thank God for Lloyd George!', and old ladies were reported to be weeping tears of gratitude as they tottered to the post offices to draw their pensions. Lloyd George himself spoke of the Act thus in his Limehouse speech on July 1909:

It is rather hard that an old workman should have to find his way to the gates of the tomb, bleeding and footsore, through the brambles and thorns of poverty. We cut a new path through it, an easier one, a pleasanter one, through fields of waving corn. We are raising money to pay for the new road, aye, and to widen it so that two hundred thousand paupers shall be able to join in the march.

Yet, for all its inadequacy, the Act was as significant in the history of social legislation as the inadequate Reform Bill of 1832 had been in the history of affairs political. For the aged poor themselves it was indeed a milestone, since even this meagre pension might make it easier for them to avoid the grisly fate of final incarceration in the workhouse. Furthermore it was a major breach in the iron Victorian doctrine of 'self-help': the Conservative mind was greatly incensed by the non-contributory basis of the new pensions, seeing in them the first statutory admission that poverty could no longer be treated as the divinely-ordained consequence of a misspent life. They realized this was the beginning of the end of a social system based on the notion that the only way to keep the masses at work was the threat of starvation. When Rosebery said that the Old Age Pensions Act was so prodigal of expenditure that it was likely to undermine the whole fabric of the Empire he was not as wrong as he sounded.

It would be uncharitable to assume that the lack of comprehensive legislation following the Poor Law Report had particularly sinister causes. It was due rather to personalities. Asquith was the sort of Prime Minister who presided over the deliberations of his ministers; he was temperamentally averse from directing their activities on his own initiative. What could be done by Lloyd George at the Exchequer and by Winston Churchill at the Board of Trade was done; hence the establishment of the labour exchanges and the trade boards under Churchill and the introduction of health and unemployment insurance under Lloyd George. The failure to reorganize the Poor Law was due to the administrative feebleness of John Burns, the president of the Local Government Board. Although he expressed himself ready in 1907 to succeed Cromer in Egypt (which he said he would 'rule like a Pharaoh') he lacked the drive and authority required to override the unprogressive permanent officials with whom he had to deal in his particular department. A more dynamic Prime Minister would have seen to it that Burns got on with his job, or would have replaced him. Asquith did neither. There was in consequence little progress in the large field for which Burns was responsible – the Poor Law, housing and town planning and public health.

It was the formidable combination of Beveridge and Churchill, his political chief, which produced the labour exchanges, which were now to be staffed by civil servants. Their introduction was based on the recommendations of the Poor Law Commission and on the operations of the Conservative act of 1905. The available facts indicated that much unemployment was the unemployment of casual workers, and the labour exchange made it easier for such workers to find employment, since it tended to reduce time spent travelling in search of work, which in view of the low standard of living of casual workers was a drain on their energy, initiative and resources.

The Board of Trade also produced the Trade Boards Act of 1909. This set up Boards for the four trades in which, largely owing to the lack of trade unions, 'sweated' labour (i.e. long hours and extremely low wages) was found to be prevalent. The occupations concerned were tailoring and the manufacture of chains, lace and paper boxes. The Boards were to consist of representatives of employers and employed, together with a number of outsiders. They were to fix minimum wages, which then had to be confirmed by the Board of Trade. Here again was a significant departure from nineteenth-century principles, though it affected only a small section of industry. Once more, the action was not taken in response to theory; a social problem had been discovered, its existence acknowledged, and an administrative solution worked out for it. As in the matter of pensions, a new principle had nevertheless been given statutory authority, and the State had declared itself for the employee and against the employer.

A year earlier, in 1908, there had been another break with the past. The Coal Mines Act had established a statutory eight-hour day for the miner; this was the first occasion on which the working hours of adult males had been limited by statute.

The Home Office, under Herbert Gladstone, had also been active. After twenty years' experience of a rudimentary system of probation for first offenders the Probation of Offenders Act of 1907 permitted the probation of all offenders; it led, therefore, to an extension of the probation system, though more slowly than was desirable since the Act was not mandatory. In 1908 the Home Office produced the Children's Act which gathered together a large number of regulations which the experience of many officials and social workers had shown to be desirable. For some time past the Home Office had recommended that cases involving children should be heard separately from those involving adults; the 1908 Act went beyond this and established Juvenile Courts. It was also on the basis of past experience, such as the activities of the N.S.P.C.C. and the working of a Children's Act passed by the Balfour administration in 1904, that there were new regulations concerning the employment of children, and others designed to protect them from fire and tobacco and liquor, and from the hazards of begging in the streets.

4 · Challenge to the Rule of Law, 1909-14

Meanwhile, the Government was compelled to conduct its major operations in the constricting atmosphere created by the Conservative threat from the Lords, and by growing industrial unrest. It was not these circumstances alone, however, which produced the controversial People's Budget of 1909. This Budget was remarkable not merely because it was concerned to raise money for social payments to the lower orders. It was also remarkable as the Budget of a Cabinet which had decided not to make what has since tended to become the normal choice that Cabinets make about budgets. Defence requirements necessitated the raising of large additional sums for the resumption of the full Dreadnought programme, which the Campbell-Bannerman Government had slowed down. At first, Churchill and Lloyd George had opposed this expenditure; but what emerged from their opposition was not a decision in favour of either defence or social reform, but a decision in favour of both. It was a budget which, because of its size, the Conservatives were bound to oppose; but in view of its declared purposes they could oppose it only by doing damage to their political reputation, for it would be easy to condemn them as rich men unwilling to contribute to the defence of their country or to the relief of poverty. From the point of view of the Liberals it had the further political advantage that provision for both Dreadnoughts and pensions would keep the Government united and the Labour Party at least grudgingly co-operative. It can hardly be imagined that Asquith expected the Opposition leaders would allow the Conservative peers to reject the budget, since this would be to violate a long-standing constitutional custom. It was a weakness of Asquith's to expect his opponents to have the same respect for the processes of law that he had himself; and, as for Lloyd George, it is difficult to believe that such a skilful politician could imagine other politicians, even Tory politicians, behaving quite so foolishly.

The Budget proposed to increase income tax from a shilling to 1s. 2d. in the pound and introduced super-tax at 6d. in the pound on incomes over £5,000 a year. Death duties on estates over £5,000 were increased. There were heavier taxes on tobacco and spirits, and the liquor licence duties were raised. There were to be special taxes on petrol and motor-car licences. Stamp duties were increased. There were to be a 20 per cent tax on the unearned increment of land values; a new tax to be paid by lessors when leases were terminated; and a tax on mining royalties. The only concession the Budget contained was the introduction into the tax system of children's allowances.

The Conservatives' objection to the Budget was that it was a 'class' Budget directed against the rich and particularly the landowner. Super-tax was not expected to produce more than half a million a year; but in conjunction with the increase in death duties they saw it, not without justification, as the introduction of a purely confiscatory principle in taxation. They objected to the land-value tax not merely because it involved a complete valuation of the land by Government officials but because, in combination with the taxes on lessors and on mining royalties, it looked like a deliberate tax on the landed interest. The tax on petrol and cars was likewise an attack on the wealthy since at this stage the motor-car was still principally a luxurious toy for the rich;[1] the liquor taxes were a frontal attack on the brewing industry which since Gladstone's days had been an essentially Conservative pressure group. One last reason for Conservative objection was that if the Government succeeded in raising additional revenue by increased direct taxation it would nullify the claim of the Tariff Reformers that tariffs were a necessary source of revenue.

The Conservatives therefore launched a furious attack on the Budget not only in the Commons but in the country; and Lloyd George was quick to exploit the vulnerability of the position the Conservatives had now taken up. Their previous harassing of the Liberal Government had not been on issues which it was electorally worth while to challenge them. In opposing the Education Bill the Lords could claim to be protecting the Church. Their opposition to the Licensing and the Plural Voting Bills had been

---

[1] The character of Toad in Kenneth Grahame's *The Wind in the Willows* (published 1908) obviously derives from the popular Edwardian conception of the typical motorist as a reckless braggart with more money than sense and a total lack of consideration for ordinary folk with their 'common little carts'. The clouds of dust which Toad's various motors created are also a reminder of road conditions before the 1909 Budget set up the Road Fund for their improvement.

minor matters. But when, faced with the unavoidable fact that the Government's majority would get the Budget through the Commons, the Conservatives resolved to mobilize their majority in the Lords against it, they were plainly acting unconstitutionally. Moreover, their language exposed them to violent attacks which Lloyd George was only too ready to deliver. When peers of the realm were prepared to assert that a super-tax of 6d. in the pound and the various small land taxes would be the ruin of them, when they descended, as some of them did, to the pettifogging depths of withdrawing their subscriptions to village footballs clubs on the grounds that the Budget would disastrously diminish their fortunes, they were asking for the kind of language Lloyd George used in his Limehouse and other speeches, and in large measure deserving it. And if the Limehouse speech has tended to rank, if not rankle, in the minds of some as the moment when class warfare was overtly introduced into British political life, it is difficult to avoid insisting that it was the Conservatives rather than Lloyd George who must bear the responsibility. When he said, at Limehouse, 'We have not provoked the challenge, but we welcome it', he was probably representing his own and the Opposition's positions with more than his usual accuracy.

There were three reasons why the Conservative rejection of the Budget in the Lords was ill-advised. The Lords had not rejected a Budget for over two hundred years and their action could properly be regarded as having been made unconstitutional by the mere passage of time and by custom. The claim that the Lords were exercising the functions appropriate to a revising chamber when they rejected the Budget was without substance. It was not as a revising chamber that Balfour had either used or defined the Lords. Shortly after the 1906 election, he had asserted that the function of the Lords was to ensure that whoever won an election the ultimate destinies of the country would be in the hands of the Conservative Party. This was a clear indication that the Lords was a political weapon whose function was to serve Conservative Party ends. There are grounds for saying that majorities are often wrong; but this argument had no relevance to the House of Lords, since it had for nearly a century treated every majority as right if it happened to be Conservative and had invoked the theory of the fallibility of majorities only against Liberal majorities. Thus, when Lloyd George said that the House of Lords was 'not the watchdog of the constitution but Mr Balfour's poodle', he had stated the position precisely.

From the political point of view, the Conservatives' agitation against the Budget and their rejection of it in the Lords were a denial of the true principles of their party. Indeed, there are grounds for saying that, on the basis of the previous histories of the two major parties, the 1909 Budget was based on Conservative principles. It was certainly not a traditional Liberal Budget. Gladstone would have regarded it with horror. It violated almost all the principles upon which Liberals had previously conducted their fiscal policies. It provided large sums for national defence, on which Liberals had in the past been reluctant to spend anything; and it was to provide large sums for social payments to the working classes on which Liberals in the past had hardly ever spent a penny. It had always been a Liberal principle not to interfere with the operation of economic laws and not to use public money to succour the victims of those laws. The classic Liberal statute of the nineteenth century was the Poor Law Amendment Act and the classic example of the Liberal response to destitution was the policy of Lord John Russell's administration towards the Great Famine in Ireland. Sir Charles Trevelyan was allowed to devote months and years of utterly devoted energy to the superhuman task of persuading himself, his political chiefs, and the Irish themselves, that even this vast natural calamity could be dealt with by arranging for the bankrupt, the starving and the dying to organize the distribution of food and money to themselves, more or less by themselves.

In asserting that the principles of the Budget were wrong the Tories were denying their own tradition. There was no future for the party if it now associated itself solely with landlord and employer against worker. It had been the essential link between Toryism and the expanding urban society of the nineteenth century that only the Tory Party had the strength, political and social, to counterbalance the influence of the employing class. This is the key to an understanding of the greatness of both Peel and Disraeli. It was the working people of the land to whom Peel had addressed his ultimate justification for his repeal of the Corn Laws. It was on the basis of working-class discontent with Liberal policies that Disraeli had recreated the party in the 1870's; and the 1909 Budget was the first in history resolutely to serve Disraeli's own principles of social reform and the Empire.

In allowing itself to abuse the constitution to protect the rich and to prevent the State taking action to help the poor, the Conservative Party was betraying itself, and in grave danger of handing over the working classes to its opponents. It may well be that its behaviour between 1909 and 1911 helped to make it so difficult for the Conservative Party to acquit itself of the charge of being 'the party of the rich'.

The third reason for describing the rejection of the Budget as misguided is the evidence of the election results of 1910. They show such a swing away from the Liberals that it is more than likely that if this Parliament had run its full term the Conservatives would have won the election due in 1912 or 1913.

The Budget did not pass through the Commons until November 1909 and in the same month the Lords rejected it. Asquith then asked for a dissolution, appealing to the country on the combined issues of the Budget and the reduction of the power of the Lords. The election results of

January 1910 always surprise the student of this period, since the Liberals lost over one hundred seats. They now had 275 members, only two more than the Unionists. The Labour Party had lost over a dozen seats; the Irish Nationalists had 82 seats. There was, as a result, a majority of 124 against the Unionists; but the specific proposals of the Budget, which were the fundamental issues, and with which the Liberals and the Labour Party had been identified, had lost those parties a combined total of 114 seats. The Labour loss may be ascribed in part to the effects of the Osborne judgement; the Liberal losses to the apparent success of the Unionists in persuading the electorate that Liberalism had now become dangerously revolutionary.

The situation was thus embarrassing for the Liberals. They could now operate successfully only with the support of the Irish Nationalists; and the latter were determined on forcing the Government into an immediate attack on the Lords' veto so that the way could be cleared for the early introduction of a Home Rule Bill. The Government would have preferred to reform the Lords rather than leave it in its existing state as a major political weapon of the Conservatives, even though the weapon were to be blunted.

The Government now sent the Budget to the Lords once more; in view of its vindication by the electorate they let it through without a division. Asquith then prepared the Parliament Act. The problem was now to get it passed through the Lords. Precedent indicated that, as in the case of the 1832 Reform Bill, the Prime Minister would invoke on his behalf the power of the Crown to create peerages. The King would be asked to announce his readiness to create sufficient Liberal peers to swamp the Conservative peers, in the confident hope that this threat would persuade the Conservatives to give way. Edward VII had in fact indicated in advance of the January 1910 election that he would not make this constitutional threat until there had been one more election on this specific issue of the Lords. Asquith suppressed this fact, partly because the constitutional propriety of the King's action was doubtful, and partly because Asquith no doubt hoped the situation would solve itself in due course. In the event, Edward VII died in May 1910, before the issue could be put to the test.

George V, soberly endowed with much down-to-earth common sense, had little liking for political dogfights and no desire to involve himself at the outset of his reign in an acute controversy which might compel his initial constitutional act to be one of apparent partisanship for the Liberals. He suggested a conference between the leaders of the two major parties; it met, but produced no agreement. The decisive obstacle turned out to be the question of Ireland. The Conservatives were unable to accept any solution which did not leave them free to block an Irish Home Rule Bill. To this the Liberals could not agree.

The conference thus foreshadowed the dreadful decade that lay ahead for Ireland. It foreshadowed also the long years during which Lloyd George was to be every other political extremist's greatest enemy: during the conference he mooted the idea of a coalition. It was typical of Lloyd George that, faced with a complicated political tangle, he itched to cut right through it; and that, confronted with a battle between opposing principles, he yearned to discard the principles and get something done.

Nevertheless, the fact that this conference came quite near to evolving satisfactory compromises over both Lords' reform and Home- Rule indicates how unnecessary were the political conflicts which were carried on in public in these years. Britain was not well served by the party political system in these years.

The conference having failed, Asquith sent the Parliament Bill to the Lords; they rejected it. George V then repeated his father's request for a second general election before undertaking to the Prime Minister to threaten to use the Crown's power of creating peers. In accepting the King's request Asquith displayed that detached sense of fairness for which he was famous. He would have been within his rights in declining the King's request. The election took place in December 1910, with results closely similar to those of January. Liberals and Unionists each secured 272 seats, Labour and the Irish Nationalists each gained two seats, and there was now a slightly larger majority against the Unionists than at the beginning of the year. Nevertheless their success in holding their position in the Commons suggests that the electorate took a less censorious attitude both to their policy and their methods than the majority of subsequent historians.

The Unionists, having convinced so many voters that Asquith was planning the overthrow of the Constitution by reducing the Lords' power, continued to behave for the most part as if they had convinced themselves also. Asquith's Bill proposed that the Lords should have no further power over Bills certified as Money Bills by the Speaker and that over other legislation they should have only a two-year suspensive veto. To cope with the hypothetical argument that in its last years of office a popularly elected Government might seek to act against the wishes of those who had elected it, the Bill also reduced the maximum interval between general elections from seven years to five. The Bill thus left the Lords with the power to reduce to a mere three years the effective legislative life of any Government it disliked. In the last two of its five years of office, such a Government could pass no legislation of which the Lords disapproved. This, coupled with the absence of any scheme for reforming the composition of the Lords, meant that the Unionists could still make considerable use of the upper house to thwart the electorate whenever it decided to deny the party a majority in the Commons. Nevertheless, only at a very late stage did there emerge a group of Unionists in favour of giving way. When Asquith announced in the Commons that the King had intimated in writing his willingness to create peers if the Tory Lords rejected the Bill he was deliberately howled down. The uproar was instigated by one of the great Lord Salisbury's sons, Lord Hugh Cecil. There was then, for a brief space, talk of a vote of censure on the King for having the temerity to support the declared wishes of the majority of his subjects against those of the hereditary aristocracy. In July 1911, however, the crisis was resolved. When the Bill went to the Lords, 29 unionists peers voted with the Government. It passed by only 17 votes in a division in which 245 peers cast votes. As a prominent Anglican layman, Lord Hugh Cecil must have been chagrined to observe that both the archbishops, and all but two of the bishops present, voted for the Government.

The failure of the Unionists to prevent the passage of the 1909 Budget and the Parliament Act led to Balfour's resignation from the leadership of his party in November 1911. His rejection by his party was not undeserved. He had, ever since Chamberlain's Tariff Reform campaign, followed rather than led the party. He had made little effort to restrain the wild men, and had allowed too much influence to pass into the hands of Lord Lansdowne, the Unionist leader in the Lords. Yet in the final outcome he had had to summon his party to retreat; and after leading it to defeat in three successive elections. He was replaced by Bonar Law, a Scottish Presbyterian who had been born in Canada. The party had been sharply divided between the two obvious claimants to the succession, Walter Long and Austen Chamberlain. When it became apparent that the supporters of neither would reconcile themselves to the leadership of the other, they fell back on Bonar Law for the uninspiring reason that his leadership would divide the party least. To a much greater extent than Balfour, Bonar Law was a follower rather than a leader. His sole advantage over Balfour was that he was a convinced Tariff Reformer and would not therefore embarrass the party as Balfour had done by having medieval disputations with himself on the subject in public. His lack of intellectual pretensions also made him an acceptable leader to the Unionists at this particular time, though hardly a statesmanlike one. A natural second fiddle, he followed Carson's lead over Home Rule from 1912 to 1914, subordinated himself to Lloyd George for most of the war and was finally pushed into the premiership by Lord Beaverbrook and by Baldwin.

The other important social legislation of the Liberal administration included the National Insurance Act of 1911, the Shops Act of 1911 and the Trade Union Act of 1913. The Shops Act, while evading the question of the daily working hours of shop assistants, gave them a statutory half-holiday. The Trade Union Act treated the demands of the unions less uncritically than the act of 1906. It made the political levy legal only after the holding of a ballot and subject to the right of an individual member to contract out in writing.

The National Insurance Act was the most important piece of Liberal legislation, since it established the basis on which most welfare payments were financed thereafter. By the health insurance part of the Act, workers earning up to £160 were to be insured compulsorily against sickness. The worker contributed 4d. a week, the employer 3d. and the State 2d. The benefits were sick pay at 10s. a week, and free medical treatment under a 'panel' doctor. The unemployment part of the act applied to eight major trades in which unemployment was endemic, and was similarly financed by contributions paid by worker, employer and State. It provided 7s. a week unemployment pay for fifteen weeks in any one year.

It is a curiosity of twentieth-century history that, because this Act laid the foundation of a system of welfare which reached its fulfilment in the Labour legislation of 1945–50, it is therefore regarded as a piece of Socialist legislation, the first step in a vast, not to say hazardous, social revolution. Yet the whole purpose of the National Insurance Act was anti-Socialist. State insurance against sickness and unemployment was invented by Bismarck, to take the sting out of Socialist agitation in the Kaiser's Reich and was imitated by Lloyd George for the same purpose in 1911. The 1911 Act, whatever benefits it may have conferred on the working classes, and however important it may be as a pointer to later developments, was an astute politician's bid to meet the menace of Socialism in Britain by using methods first used by Europe's most ruthless opponent both of Socialism and of Liberalism. That the importation into English social life of methods devised by Bismarck should be held to have initiated a beneficent revolution testifies either to the obtuseness of the public mind or to the extreme political cunning of the man who put it on the statute book. Like anything copied from Bismarck, the most successful political confidence trickster of the nineteenth century, the National Insurance Act was also a confidence trick. The opposition of the Unionist peers to the Act, which (with more justice than they imagined) they described as a form of confiscation of working-class earnings, induced Lloyd George to publicize health insurance as a matter of the worker getting 'ninepence for fourpence'. The truth was that the worker contributed towards his benefits not only through his fourpence a week but also through general taxation. In effect, healthy and employed workers were being forced to subsidize sick and unemployed workers. The total financial contribution made by the Government in 1913 to the cost of pensions, sickness and unemployment insurance and to the labour exchanges, taken altogether, represented one per cent of the national income; and this at a time when the real wages of the working class were less than they had been in the last years of the nineteenth century.

The only specifically English innovation in the scheme (the device of insurance cards was copied from Germany) was the use of what were called 'approved societies' for the actual administration of the scheme and the physical distribution of the appropriate benefits. Approved societies could be working men's friendly societies, trade unions or commercial insurance companies. This was both astute and salutary. It was astute because trade unions and friendly societies gained increased membership and new status as a consequence of the service they were providing as Government agents. It was also a means of bringing in new business to the insurance companies and silenced any objections they might have had to the Government's entry into their business. It was salutary in that it preserved some limitation upon the scheme's tendency to bind the working-class population more closely to the State. The interposition of his approved society between the worker and the State did a little to preserve working-class independence. The disappearance of the approved society in favour of a tidily centralized National Insurance Ministry with the passing of the 1946 Insurance Act was a contraction of an important area of social and industrial democracy.[1]

With the active encouragement of the Unionists, who, now that the Parliament Act prevented them rejecting the Insurance Act, were more determined than ever to oppose for the sake of opposing, the medical profession raised its own noisy objections to the scheme on the grounds that they were in danger of becoming bureaucratized. In fact the doctors did well out of it, and the guaranteed annual flat-rate fee they received in respect of each insured patient on their 'panel' provided many of them for the first time with a steady annual income. Thus the scheme was, as a political manœuvre, a masterpiece. It took the sting out of Socialism to the extent that it was supported by most trade union leaders and most of the Labour Party. It bought off the insurance companies; it bought off the doctors. It created for its initiator and his party a reputation for beneficent social innovation; it contributed something of unquestioned value, though of minimal proportion, to the solution of a major human and industrial problem; it hoodwinked its anti-Socialist opponents and even more remarkably the Socialists themselves into thinking that Socialism was almost synonymous in practice with an increase in State insurance; and it successfully disguised from the recipients of health and unemployment benefit how small a proportion of it came from the wealthy and how much of it came ultimately out of the pockets of their fellow-workers. Instead of the expropriation of the expropriators demanded by Marx, they got instead something very like the further expropriation of the expropriated; and remained convinced all the same that the process was something which though thoroughly English (this was false too) was also Socialism.

It is paradoxical that for all the solidity of this Government's achievements when seen in the perspective of the succeeding half-century, the more immediate impression of the last four or five years of its peacetime life is

[1] See page 443.

of men faced with demands they could or would not satisfy, and forces they did not know how to control. From 1909 onwards there was, contemporaneously with the creation of a considerable bureaucratic machine for the increase of social security, a growing lack of faith in the whole parliamentary system. This was expressed in outbursts of unconstitutional violence by militant suffragettes, by militant trade unionists and by the opponents of the Home Rule Bill for Ireland which the Government introduced in 1912.

It is commonplace that Asquith did not have the stomach for directing the affairs of a nation at war. His dealings with the suffragette movement, with the great strike wave and with the English and Ulster Unionists suggest a lack of capacity for coping even with peacetime crises. Asquith adhered massively, sluggishly, marmoreally, to the classic nineteenth-century tradition that progress should emerge only out of the slow processes of political education and persuasion, and that no new interests or classes should be given legal or political enfranchisement until it was certain that this would harmonize with the protection of interests already entrenched. Worse still, he believed that everybody else had his own calm ponderous faith that change need move only at the majestic pace of a minimally mobile glacier. He believed that the Liberal principle of government based on consent had won universal acceptance, and that dissenting minorities would in the end always accept decisions from which they dissented, provided only that the decisions were those of an electorally sanctified majority. It is this attitude of mind that makes Asquith's political behaviour in these years reminiscent of Louis Philippe at his most smug and of Guizot at his most remotely magisterial.

All three challenges to the constitutional Government came from the passionate depths: they were an irrational response to unreasonable circumstances, all of them in some measure attributable to the Government itself. It was unreasonable that women should not have the vote. It was unreasonable that as industry's profits grew in these years, the real wages of the working class should go down. It was unreasonable that Ulstermen should be forced against their will to cease to be full citizens of the United Kingdom. To all three problems the Government had no constructive answer. The women were to be fobbed off; the trade unionists could be ignored because their political and industrial leaders were in political servitude to the Liberals' parliamentary majority; Ulstermen's clamour could be ignored until they should agree at last to see what Asquith saw from the beginning, that it was being exploited for party political ends by a Unionist Party at Westminster desperate in its search for a means to destroy the Government. The consequence was that the Liberals themselves helped to induce the violence displayed by their opponents and then found that they, on their side, were committed to the use of counter-violence. It is this circumstance which, coupled with the collectivist character of so much of their legislation, makes it possible to say that the Liberals had by 1914 long ceased to practise Liberal policies.

The most violent of the Government's enemies were the middle-class women who wanted the vote; and their violence could have been avoided altogether by the simple process of giving them what they wanted. The really militant phase of the suffragette movement did not begin until after the Liberals had come into power and the formidable Mrs Pankhurst put in a position to exploit the situation created by the Government's evasions. There is little excuse for the failure to grant the suffrage; and there is less for the way in which the Government sustained its refusal. Women, imprisoned for their violent acts against property and public order, would then go on hunger strike. They were thereupon forcibly fed. An alternative device was the Cat and Mouse Act of 1913 by which suffragette hunger-strikers were released from prison in order to recover their health, whereupon they would be re-imprisoned. The attitude of the Government to middle-class Englishwomen demanding the right to vote, and reacting with violence to the Government's provocative and pointless delay, provides a sinister comment on the persistent Liberal claim to stand for a higher morality than other political parties. The Cat and Mouse Act came strangely from a Government which a few years before had been grieved so sorely by the hardships suffered by Boer women and children, and by Chinese coolies in the Transvaal.

The other and more significant outburst of violence for which the Government similarly had no constructive policy was the movement within the trade unions usually described as Syndicalism. Syndicalism was copied from the methods advocated by French trade unions and by the programme of the Industrial Workers of the World organized in the United States; though its aims would not have seemed altogether strange to Robert Owen. To Syndicalists, strikes were not a means of improving working conditions or a last-ditch sanction against employers, but an offensive weapon to be used as often as possible to disrupt the national life and eventually overthrow the existing order of society. It was Syndicalism which brought into this country the idea of a 'sympathetic' or general strike, by which the whole trade union movement would, at need, be mobilized to coerce Government and employers by an unshakeable display of working-class solidarity. The most celebrated names in the movement at the time were Tom Mann, famous as one of the organizers of the London Dock Strike of 1889 and first secretary of the Independent Labour Party, and A. J. Cook, later more celebrated as the spokesman for the mineworkers during the General Strike. The Syndicalists were encouraged by the setting up of a Marxist educational organization in 1909 called the Central Labour College; there was an Industrial Syndicalist Education League from 1910 onwards; and from 1912 there was a revolutionary workers' newspaper,

the *Daily Herald*. The number of active Syndicalists within the trade
union movement was at all times small but they were important because
of their energy; many of them formed the nucleus of the Communist
Party of Great Britain when it was formed in 1920.

The growth of Syndicalism, like that of the militant suffragette movement, was partly a consequence of the dilatory inefficiency of those whose
responsibility it was to advance trade union interests by properly constituted means. The trade union movement was incapable of decision-
making on a broad front because of the multiplicity of unions and the petty
rivalries between them; and the Labour Party had neither policy nor
effective personalities. The Government similarly had a responsibility,
from 1909 onwards, to rectify the apparent bias of the legal system against
the unions revealed by the Osborne judgement. It was not till 1913 that
they did so. The interim saw a wave of strikes, often caused less by specific
grievances than by angry frustration at the absence of any other means of
making an effective impression.

The strike wave began in the summer of 1910. There was a four-day
railway strike in the north-east in July; in September there was a strike
in the cotton industry in Lancashire involving 120,000 workers, and then a
fourteen-week lock-out of boilermakers; in all these cases it was clear that
the strikers were hardly less hostile to their official union leaders than they
were to their employers. In November 1910, a local mining dispute
produced a three-day riot in Tonypandy as a result of which troops were
sent from Salisbury Plain. Churchill, now Home Secretary, was not
forgiven by the miners for allowing the troops to be used; and severely
criticized in other quarters for delaying their dispatch while he waited to
see the effect of a personal appeal to the miners to cease their violence. In
June 1911, the National Sailors' and Firemen's Union called an official
strike which rapidly spread to all the ports and was supported by unofficial
action by other dockworkers when there was an attempt to use black-leg
labour. The strike was successful in securing wage increases and was
quickly followed by a widespread dock strike, made the more effective by
the establishment, in the previous year, of a large new industrial union, the
Transport Workers' Federation. At Liverpool, workers in all forms of
transport came out, the city was in a state of siege, troops were called in,
and two men were killed. The situation led the four railway unions to call a
national railway strike. Though not universal it was disorganizing enough,
and once again there were clashes between strikers and troops, with fatal
casualties. Asquith tried to deal with the strike by appointing a Royal
Commission and by strongly asserting the Government's determination to
prevent the paralysis of the railway system. This did not improve matters;
and he soon allowed negotiations to take place under the emollient care
of Lloyd George, whose first step was to secure the co-operation of Ramsay
MacDonald, the Labour Party leader. The strike was ended after four days.

By the end of the year, a more effective system of consultation was worked out, though the railway companies were still not prepared to give full recognition to the railway unions.

The struggle was resumed by the miners, who early in 1912 adopted the Syndicalist tactic of voting in favour of a national coal strike to force the Government to establish a national minimum wage. A Government compromise was wrecked by the intransigeance of both the Miners' Federation and some of the owners, and for the first three weeks of March 1912 a million miners presented the country with the largest strike it had ever seen. The Government ended the matter by forcing its pre-strike compromise through Commons and Lords despite strong Unionist Opposition; and the Miners' Federation grudgingly called the strike off.

Two months later, in May 1912, 100,000 London dockers came out over a relatively trivial matter, though they had been greatly provoked by the aggressively anti-trade-union attitude of Lord Devonport, the chairman of the Port of London Authority. The strike was defeated owing to the failure of transport workers outside London to support it with a national strike, and because Lord Devonport was vigorously determined not to give way, even though Asquith wanted him to. It was noticeable that the powerful railway union leader, J. H. Thomas, came out publicly against the London strike; this was not to be the last occasion on which he braved the wrath of the extremists in the movement.

It was the coming of the war and not an improvement in the situation itself which accounts for the fact that this unsuccessful London Dock Strike marks the end of this period of extreme unrest. It was resumed on much the same lines in 1919 and continued until the General Strike of 1926. Indeed, during the last two years of peace, the unskilled workers were girding themselves for a renewal of battle at the earliest moment. In 1912, the National Union of Railwaymen was formed, by the fusion of the large Amalgamated Society of Railway Servants and the smaller General Railway Workers' Union and the United Signalmen and Pointsmen. It is significant of the character of this new industrial union that the Amalgamated Society of Locomotive Engineers and Firemen, and the Railway Clerks' Association, held aloof from it. The appearance of the N.U.R. clearly signalled a new phase in the militancy of the less skilled workers. Its membership doubled within eighteen months of the fusion. In 1914 came an even more ominous development, the formation of the Triple Industrial Alliance between the N.U.R., the Transport Workers' Federation (which had been behind the 1912 London Dock Strike) and the Miners' Federation of Great Britain. The object of the Triple Alliance was to coerce employers and Government by the threat that if any one of them was involved in a dispute the other two would concert a sympathetic strike in its support. It was thought that the Triple Alliance would bring about such a strike before the end of 1914.

Thus, by the time war began, the country had seen what looked like the culmination of that revolt by the unskilled workers against the rest of society which had begun with the London Dock Strike of 1889. There is no doubt that, had the issue been put to the test, the Asquith Government would have found it extremely difficult to deal with. A situation would have developed not unlike that which was simultaneously threatening to develop in Ireland; and the Government would have been hard put to it to avoid clashes with the industrial workers not greatly less bloody than those which actually developed in Ireland between 1920 and 1922.

It was Irish Home Rule which occupied the first place in the Government's mind from 1912 onwards. The problem was once again that traditional policies of temporizing delay had been outpaced by events. English procrastination and the declining vigour of the Irish Nationalist Party had led to the growth of the Sinn Fein movement, which was beginning to agitate for an independent republic for the whole of Ireland. The long interval since the earlier Home Rule Bills had led also to the full development in Ulster of a strong sense of its economic and religious separateness from the south. Thus, although by 1912 a Home Rule Bill was for the first time a political possibility, it was already ceasing to be regarded by Irishmen themselves as a desirable solution. It did not go far enough for the South; and the North did not want it at all.

Asquith was once again caught between an upper and a nether millstone. The support of the Irish Nationalists had seen the People's Budget through the Commons; and the passage of the Parliament Act (which had also depended on their vote) had removed the power of the Lords to prevent the passage of a Home Rule Bill. But the very disappearance of this traditional obstacle to Home Rule enabled the Unionists to represent him as abusing the powers he had been at such pains to secure, for the shameful purpose of destroying the United Kingdom with Irish votes, and of subjecting the Crown's loyal Protestant subjects in Ulster to the alien rule of disloyal Catholics in Dublin. Having, despite all their efforts in 1909–10, now lost three General Elections in a row the Unionists were desperately anxious not to lose a fourth; and they set out to exploit Ulster's genuine grievance less out of regard for the susceptibilities of Ulstermen than with the object of discrediting the Liberal Government. In any case, the Unionists were now, as always, primarily interested, not in keeping Belfast Protestant, but in keeping Dublin subject to Westminster.

It was fairly easy to represent the Liberals as in the wrong over Ulster. It could be claimed with justice that Home Rule had no support among Ulstermen; yet the Parliament Act deprived them, and their Unionist champions in Parliament, of any legal means of opposing a Bill which sought to expel them from the United Kingdom against their will. In organizing the Ulster Volunteers to resist the operation of Home Rule by armed force, Sir Edward Carson, an eminent lawyer and a leading Unionist M.P., could rightly be described as reckless, dangerous and unconstitutional. Bonar Law's public support for the Volunteers was a revolutionary departure for one who, as Leader of the Opposition, was therefore an alternative Prime Minister. Yet they could always claim that the passing of the Parliament Act by the Liberals had improperly deprived them of the power to resist Home Rule by constitutional means.

It was because he saw through all this that Asquith's only memorable public contribution to the affair until the spring of 1914 was to utter the grimly minatory but ultimately discrediting words, 'Wait and See'. He knew that the real issue at Westminster was not Ulster, and that the Unionists were trying to bluff him out of his Home Rule policy and, if possible, out of office. He behaved all along like a man supremely confident that he was dealing with opponents who must know in their hearts that he had seen through their bluff and that it could not therefore succeed. It was all part of the political game; and he reckoned himself a more capable operator than the slow-minded Bonar Law and the theatrical but superficial Carson.

Exploiting the situation by highly provocative speeches, and parades and drillings of the Ulster Volunteers, the Unionists went on to urge the King to dismiss Asquith and dissolve Parliament. Alarmed, as was his wont, by any suggestion of civil disturbance, George V told Asquith he thought there should be yet another election before the Home Rule Bill was put on the statute book. Asquith replied firmly that this would create the impression that the Parliament Act was so much waste paper. There was then Unionist talk of obstructing the passage of the Army Act; this would deprive the Government of the right to have an army with which to enforce Home Rule. Meanwhile, arms were being imported into both Ulster and the South of Ireland; an indication that there was an increasing likelihood that the political shadow-fight in London might produce a shooting war in Ireland.

The Unionists' most spectacular success was to secure the support of important elements in the army. Lord Roberts, the darling of the public and the hero of Kandahar and of the Boer War, as well as Sir Henry Wilson, the Director of Military Operations at the War Office, were active partisans of Ulster; and Wilson, though a servant of the Government, was in constant communication with Bonar Law. Awareness of this, together with the fear that the Ulster Volunteers might seize arms depots in Ulster, led to plans to move additional troops from the south of Ireland and from England in order to protect them. In addition, Churchill, now First Lord of the Admiralty, moved destroyers into the Irish Channel; and declared, in a typically pugnacious speech at Bradford on 16 March 1914, that if there were threats to resist the operation of an Act of Parliament by force, the time had come to 'put these grave matters to the proof'.

The immediate response was a dramatic demonstration in the Commons by Carson, intended to convey the (false) impression that he was about to leave immediately to organize a military *coup* in Ulster. This was followed by the so-called Curragh Mutiny. Sir Arthur Paget, Commander-in-Chief in Ireland, caused it to be known to the officers stationed at the Curragh, near Dublin (where the army in Ireland had its headquarters), that Ulster-born officers might 'disappear', and that other officers might resign, if ordered north against Ulster. Paget had no authority from Seely, the Secretary for War, to make a public announcement to this effect. All he had obtained from the War Office (though this was bad enough) was an informal agreement that Ulster-born officers could be excused from taking part in operations in Ulster; and that any other officers who raised objections would be 'removed' but not court-martialled. As a result of Paget's evidently improper methods of procedure at the Curragh something like three score senior officers indicated that they would prefer resignation and consequent dismissal rather than act against Ulster.

The news of what was not technically a mutiny, but could hardly be distinguished from one, caused an immediate outcry against the Unionist Party. To be accused of undermining the loyalty of the army was the last thing they desired. Unfortunately, the tale of administrative and indeed political inefficiency was not yet over. The offending officers were summoned to the War Office, but allowed to extract from Sir John French, then C.I.G.S., and from the Secretary for War, a promise that, in return for the withdrawal of the officers' resignations, the Government would not use the army in Ireland to enforce Home Rule on Ulster. In order to put this right, Asquith had to force the resignations of the Secretary for War and Sir John French; he then took over the War Office himself in a grand gesture designed to restore confidence.

The Curragh affair reflected little credit on the Unionists, whose inflammatory behaviour had helped so much to create the disloyalty that Paget's incompetence had startlingly uncovered. It cast considerable doubts on the intelligence not only of Paget but of Sir John French and of those who gave Paget permission to take any action of any kind favourable to senior officers who did not want to obey orders; and it confirms that Asquith's handling of his Cabinet's affairs was liable to be inefficient. The slovenliness in the highest places of Government was all the more alarming in view of the imminence of the war. Its immediate effect, by no means entirely eliminated by Asquith's assumption of the War Office, was to make the risk that the Home Rule affair would issue in violence seem much more likely.

The situation was worsened a month later by the Larne Gun-Running, when the Ulster Volunteers smuggled in, despite the official ban Asquith had at last imposed, 30,000 rifles and three million rounds of ammunition. The result was an immediate rush to join the ranks of the National Volunteers which had been formed as a counter-measure in the south. But when, in July, a similar smuggling operation to that in the north was attempted near Dublin, the army and the police interfered; three Irish were killed and nearly twenty others seriously injured. The contrast between this and the lack of interference with the Larne Gun-Running was one which Dubliners were not soon to forget.

All this time, Asquith had been quietly conducting behind the scenes what he considered the only real battle, the political war of manœuvre. From the start, the Cabinet had held itself in readiness to exclude Ulster from Home Rule if opinion there seemed to make it unavoidable. In a sense, therefore, the Unionists, by whipping up feeling against the Bill in Ulster, were playing Asquith's game for him. In order to compel the Irish Nationalists to agree to Ulster's exclusion he may almost be said to have needed the grim spectre of civil war; and this was duly conjured up for him by the Unionist agitation. On the other hand, since the Unionists claimed that Ulster was their chief concern, the decision to exclude Ulster would abruptly remove their whole platform from underneath their feet. Asquith's dilatoriness between 1912 and 1914 was certainly complacent; but it was also calculated. It was an exercise of what, writing about himself, he described as his

rather specialised faculty of insight and manipulation in dealing with diversities of character and temperament[1]

In great secrecy, various consultations took place between Asquith and the political opponents who so loudly abused him in public. Unfortunately, the Unionists would not easily give way over Ulster, since they would then have no stick with which to beat Asquith. Hence, by the time the last meeting on the subject took place, at Buckingham Palace in June 1914, no decision could be reached because the Unionists insisted that Ulster's exclusion could not be considered unless Ulster was held to include the counties of Fermanagh and Tyrone, fifty per cent of whose population was Catholic. The Conference bogged down in the problem of whether or not these two counties could be partitioned. Thus, Asquith had finally succeeded in compelling the Unionists, including Carson, to accept that the fundamental issue was not, after all, Home Rule, but Ulster; but a peaceful solution was probably even further away in the summer of 1914 than it had been in 1912. He had used tactics in the interim as devious as any of those later used by Lloyd George when Prime Minister; and it was an ill omen for Asquith's performance as Prime Minister in wartime that he had become so certain that great issues that passionately divided nations and cultures could be adequately handled by the acquired skills of a master of political manipulation and of strategic procrastination. Nor was it valuable training for the problems of wartime to have spent, by 1914, almost five years in continuous political shadow-fighting against opponents most of whose threats had been entirely unreal.

[1] R. Jenkins, *Asquith*, p. 336.

5 · The German Problem, 1905-14

The broad problem which faced British Governments in the early years of the century was that of the adjustment of defence and foreign policy to a world situation which appeared to be rapidly changing to Britain's detriment. The British had, between 1713 and the end of the nineteenth century, acquired world commercial and maritime supremacy and the largest Empire in history. The circumstances which had enabled this Empire to be created and maintained had, by the time the twentieth century opened, begun to pass away. This imperial position can now be seen to have been based on the transient circumstance that Britain had pioneered the industrial revolution and therefore, alone among the Great Powers, possessed the resources to sustain an imperial position which was out of all proportion to its size and population. In the perspective of the half-millennium of European exploitation of other continents, the supremacy of the British can now be seen as an inevitably temporary phenomenon. Portugal, with only a million inhabitants at the time, had pioneered overseas expansion, but had soon lost primacy to the Dutch. They in turn, with their inferior resources in manpower and territory, had been surpassed by the English; and it was, after all, the accidents of French preoccupation with European hegemony and financial and industrial backwardness under the *ancien régime* which ensured that it was to be Britain and not France who replaced the Dutch. England had also been helped by the fragmented character of the European State-system during her rise to world power. This had enabled her always to find continental allies to do a great deal of the land-fighting against France for her. Only after years of war, and for a brief period only, was even Napoleon able to reverse this situation.

In the closing years of the nineteenth century almost all these advantages were ceasing to operate. Britain's industrial monopoly was passing away, and this indicated that both the United States and Germany would sooner or later possess the means, even if they did not acquire the will, to challenge Britain as a world Power. The fragmentation of Europe had been ended by the events of the 1860's, with the emergence of a united German State and a united Italy. The first major consequence of this revolution in the

European State-system was the creation by 1894 of the Franco-Russian alliance as a defensive reaction to the Bismarckian system of alliances. This system, by binding together the German Empire, the Austro-Hungarian Empire, Italy, Roumania (and, for a time, Serbia) had placed Central Europe, from the Baltic to the Adriatic and the Black Sea, under the domination of Berlin.

The formation of the Dual Alliance in reply to this system of German domination was, however, the alliance of the two powers who had traditionally threatened Britain's imperial position. It was the first time there had been a durable peacetime alliance of two major European powers both of whom had interests opposed to those of Britain. Since 1815 Russia had been regarded as Britain's most serious potential enemy because of Russia's expansionist aims towards the Aegean, through Persia and Afghanistan towards the North-West Frontier of India, and through eastern Siberia and Manchuria towards China. The French, for their part, thwarted of European supremacy by Bismarck, were turning more and more to colonial ambitions, and this would sooner or later involve them also with Britain. The alliance of France and Russia thus constituted a potential danger to British Imperialism; and a clash between them was something which any thoughtful commentator on the world situation would have considered likely in the not very distant future.

British reactions to a potential threat of this sort were characteristically cautious and unspectacular. One reaction had been the acquisition, chiefly through the unofficial channels of the chartered companies, of large territories in Africa, under the Salisbury régime. The other was a series of piecemeal precautionary diplomatic moves from 1887 onwards. In 1887 Salisbury had concluded (temporary) Mediterranean agreements with the main Bismarckian *bloc*, the Triple Alliance, to protect the eastern Mediterranean against Russia. In 1898, there had been an attempt to come to agreement with Russia with a view to defining spheres of interest in China. From 1898 to 1901 there were several efforts, chiefly through the initiative of Chamberlain, to secure agreements with Germany, similarly with the object of containing Russia. In 1902 this particular object had been achieved, with unexpected success for the British, through the Anglo-Japanese alliance. In 1904 the Anglo-French *entente* had brought to an end the century-long rivalry of the two powers over Egypt.

Unfortunately for the British, the situation was now complicated by the decision of the German Government, already effective before Grey took over the Foreign Office, to build a High Seas Fleet. Given the size and efficiency of the German Army, the extent of Germany's political and diplomatic influence over Austria-Hungary, Italy and Roumania, and the unpredictable way in which the Germans conducted their relations with other States, this further development looked like enabling Germany to create in time of peace a domination over both Europe and its maritime approaches such as no power in modern history had previously exercised even in wartime. Though Napoleon dominated all Europe at the time of Tilsit in 1807, Trafalgar had lost him the seas two years before. It had needed both British sea-power and Russian military power to overthrow Napoleon; neither would have achieved victory without the other. The building of a German High Seas Fleet, therefore, threatened to cut Europe off from the British sea-power which had preserved European freedom; and to cut Britain off from the land-powers who had preserved British freedom. In the absence of effective British intervention (which depended on sea-power) the rest of Europe had no alternative but to capitulate to the dominant military power on the continent. This is shown by the failure of all the coalitions against Revolutionary France and Napoleon except the fifth, and by the circumstances attending the creation of all five. It is shown by the collapse of all Europe, including Russia, in the face of Hitler's diplomacy up to 1939, and of his armies till 1941. Political, military and naval domination by Germany would mean that England had no allies. Even a circumstance as apparently irrelevant as the Austro-German alliance was a blow to Britain once the Germans had a navy; for the Habsburgs had always been Britain's most useful support against either France (save in the Seven Years War) or, since 1815, against Russia. Nor was the establishment of good relations with France and Russia any necessary guarantee of salvation; it would hardly have sufficed to bring victory in 1918 without the intervention of the United States; and it was manifestly inadequate in the Second World War. Moreover, in the circumstances of the years from 1905 onwards, it was a dubious proposition to pin high hopes on the unstable Third Republic and on the corrupt régime of Czarist Russia. Nor, for their part, could they pin much hope on the British. Not only was the naval supremacy of the British being challenged; by continental standards they were without an army.

Grey thus took over office at what he seems to have felt was a moment of extreme peril for his country. He could not pursue an aggressive policy even had he so wished. He had too few soldiers and, to begin with, too few Dreadnoughts. He had behind him (and sometimes beside him) in the Commons a large number of Radical pacifists; and in the country at large a public most of whom thought that Britain's position would inevitably remain great with little or no expenditure of either money or effort. His policy seemed to him therefore to be less that of increasing the strength of the opposition to Germany, either in his own country or in France and Russia, than of struggling to prevent that opposition collapsing altogether. He had so little that was concrete to offer the French or the Russians against the Germans that it is remarkable that their will to resist had not been undermined long before 1914. The credit for this is not of course Grey's. It was chiefly due to the recklessness of German diplomacy and the foolishness of the General Staff officers in all the continental countries, who all fancied, in August 1914, that they could win a European war in a matter of months.

The character of Grey's policy is revealed at the outset by his handling of the Franco-German dispute over Morocco which had begun, in the last months of the Balfour administration, with the Kaiser's dramatic visit to Tangier. The Germans, on the grounds that they alone of the Great Powers of western Europe had not been consulted about the Anglo-French agreement on Morocco, had sent the Kaiser to Tangier to assert publicly that, whereas the Anglo-French *entente* had implied the replacement of the Sultan of Morocco's sovereignty by a French protectorate supported by England, in Germany's view the Sultan was still completely independent. Moreover, Germany would support that independence. The implication of this, and of the concurrent German demand that Moroccan affairs be submitted to an international conference, was that France was not to be allowed by Germany to have an independent colonial policy. The French Foreign Minister, Delcassé, architect of the *entente*, was for resistance. The only effective resistance could be by war, and this was out of the question. Russia had only just concluded her unsuccessful war with Japan; the British had promised only diplomatic support over Morocco, and were militarily incapable of more. Delcassé, unsupported by his Cabinet colleagues, resigned.

Grey thought the crisis implied the imminent subjection of the whole continent to German diplomatic control; for if France submitted, Russia would submit also, especially as alignment with Germany was much more congenial to most sections of Russian governing opinion than alignment with republican France. Since an accommodation between France and Germany was the only logical consequence of the ditching of Delcassé, Grey intervened at the conference at Algeçiras to prevent it. He supported France in order to preserve the diplomatic independence of France and therefore of Russia as well. The result was that Algeçiras was the first defeat the Second Reich had suffered in foreign affairs. Germany suddenly found herself isolated. The attempt which France had already made to detach Italy from the Triple Alliance made still greater progress, and only Austria-Hungary supported Germany at the conference. Grey had thus won a major diplomatic victory at the start of his career. He took the further step of authorizing Anglo-French military conversations. The purpose of these conversations was the essentially diplomatic one of indicating to the French in the strongest possible way that Britain's support was seriously meant, even though the best the British could do was to draw up mere paper plans for military action.

Grey's next achievement was the *entente* with Russia in 1907 which resulted in the somewhat over-simplified view that thereafter Europe was divided into two opposing power-*blocs*, a Triple Alliance (Germany, Austria-Hungary and Italy) and a Triple Entente (Britain, France and

Russia). The Anglo-Russian agreement of 1907 was much more the logical outcome of British policy towards Russia in the previous decade than an irreversible British alignment against Germany. It was still a necessary British policy to eliminate imperial difficulties wherever possible. The Anglo-Japanese alliance and the Russo-Japanese War had eliminated Russia as a danger to British interest in the Far East, and had allowed reductions in the British Far East Fleet. The weakening effect of the war on Russia had also lessened British fears about the North-West Frontier of India. The Admiralty had come to the conclusion by now that the British occupation of Egypt was effective enough to make it possible to abandon the traditional nineteenth-century fear of a Russian advance on Constantinople. There thus remained no area of conflict between the two powers except Persia. The Russians were ready for agreement because, in their parlous condition after 1905, they could undertake no immediate expansionist plans, and were badly in need of British investment finance. The two Powers therefore divided Persia into spheres of influence. The northern part, which contained the Persian capital, Teheran, was left as a Russian sphere of influence; the area bordering on Afghanistan and India was to be a British sphere; central Persia was to be neutral. This had the satisfactory consequence of leaving the Russians in control of an area from which they could not be dislodged, while preserving from Russian influence that area of Persia which was strategically important for the security of India.

It would be wrong to treat the Anglo-Russian agreement as entirely outside the context of Europe; Grey certainly did not do so. The Russians failed to honour their agreement to abstain from interfering in the central neutral zone, but Grey forbore to complain because, he said, he did not want to throw Russia into the arms of Germany. It was obvious that accommodation between Britain and Russia followed as naturally from the Anglo-French *entente* and from Grey's desire to prevent Germany's diplomatic domination of the continent, as it did from British policy towards Russia during the previous decade.

Grey always realized that the logical consequence of trying to maintain French and Russian independence was likely to be war with Germany; but he felt that this risk had to be taken, and that the responsibility for such an outcome would be Germany's and not his. This is shown by his lack of support for Russia during the Bosnia crisis of 1908 and the consequent crisis in Russo-German relations in 1909. When Austria-Hungary annexed Bosnia in 1908, in breach of private undertakings recently exchanged between the Russian and Austro-Hungarian Foreign Ministers, Grey declined to support the protests of either Russia or Serbia. He contented himself with the routine Liberal device of protesting that the Dual Monarchy had been guilty of a unilateral breach of the Treaty of Berlin of 1878. He would do nothing for Serbia, for all Russia's anxieties, if only because he disapproved of the way in which the Serbian ruling dynasty had achieved its position, by a spectacular royal murder, in 1903. But Germany's action in interfering suddenly, in 1909, to warn Russia off from further protests against the annexation of Bosnia represented a repetition of the tactics applied to France in Morocco in 1905. Germany had not been consulted about the Bosnian annexation and had not hitherto committed herself to Habsburg domination of the Balkans. By 1909 therefore, Germany had tried to deprive France of freedom of action in North Africa and also to deprive Russia of any say in the destiny of the Balkans. This was to leave neither France nor Russia much freedom to manœuvre. If the process were not slackened, they would find themselves pushed to the point where, if they were to preserve their independent status, they had no alternative to using force.

The urgent problem throughout the period, therefore, was to seek agreement between Britain and Germany. Chamberlain had seen this when at the turn of the century he had made his grandiose proposal for a new Triple Alliance between the British Empire, Germany and the United States, to preserve the world for Anglo-Saxon-Teutonic domination. This, like so much else that Chamberlain envisaged, showed a proper appreciation of the tendency of the times towards great trans-continental power *blocs*; and such a combination, if effective, would have been un-challengeable. Its only drawback was that it was impracticable. Even if the Germans had been prepared to make a third in such a triumvirate, the United States had no interest in it. Yet Chamberlain's feeling that the United States and Germany were Britain's real competitors for world-power, and that the proper means to deal with the matter was by a business-man's merger was sound. It would have been the translation into the sphere of power-politics of the classic methods of monopoly capitalism. If it had been practicable it might have made the world a much grimmer place; but it might have made it less bloody than it became through the alternative method of a fight to the death.

The United States was not to be cajoled by the prospect of a merger with Birmingham, because it was not yet ready for world-power. The Germans declined because they felt they were ready. The symbol of this aptly-named 'Weltpolitik' was the determination to have a High Seas Fleet. Support of the naval programme was almost William II's only positive contribution to German policy during his reign. It irritated the German Army; it is asserted that it was pursued to provide a much-needed outlet for the rapidly growing German steel industry. But it would be false to dismiss the German naval programme as the mere Ironclad romanticism of a neurotic Hohenzollern who wanted to go one better than his predecessors by having battleships to play with as well as soldiers; or even as an astute device to satisfy the greed of German industrialists. It was as logical as Chamberlain's proposed new Triple Alliance. That had offered one solution to the problem of world power. The building of a German Navy offered an alternative solution. Once it was achieved, Germany could seize world-power single-handed, given that Germany also had the world's best organized army.

Nor can it be overlooked that in almost every respect Germany was the most advanced and the most dynamic of the Great Powers and yet at the same time the most restricted. Her central European position put Germany at the mercy, or so it seemed, of the numerical superiority enjoyed by Russia and of the apparent military threat created by that country's alliance with the French; and beyond these two Powers, the way out to the world's seas was commanded by the British. Yet all three of these impeding States were, by comparison with Germany, inefficient and backward. The British were manifestly past their zenith, the French politically incompetent and socially unstable, the Russians still primitive. Sensing from their own dramatic rise to political and economic domination during the previous forty years that time would not stand still for them, the Germans saw the opening years of the twentieth century with barely controlled impatience as, at once, the first and the last period of time in which they had the opportunity to achieve ultimate greatness. They saw themselves uniquely equipped to inherit the age of empires whose birth Chamberlain had not long before proclaimed. The war of 1914 was, consciously or unconsciously, a bid to seize the inheritance, while Russia was still backward and the United States still barely awake.

The Germans always protested that the function of their new Navy was not that of invading the United Kingdom. That was true. They thought rather that it would make such an invasion unnecessary. Deprived of European allies by the might of Germany's army, Britain would be isolated. In that isolation, the British would find themselves in a state of permanent siege, and with no alternative to submission. For their part, the British insisted that even though the German High Seas Fleet did not match the overall strength of the Royal Navy, it constituted a serious menace, since the German Fleet was wholly concentrated in the North Sea. In view of its world-wide commitments, the Royal Navy would always be liable to find itself in a position of local inferiority in home waters as against the German Navy. Any agreement between Britain and Germany, therefore, would have to include some measure of restriction on German naval building; for this was the only concession the British had to ask of Germany. It was also the only concession the Germans were not prepared to make. Without the Navy, the Germans were committed to the role of a central European Power only; and given the geo-political ambitions to which William II and so many other Germans had succumbed, this was to be bounded in a nutshell, when, with a Navy, they could be kings of infinite space.

Grey, like Chamberlain before him, was therefore faced, when dealing with the Germans, with no programme that could be discussed, and no set of precise objectives one of which might be temporarily discarded in favour of others. There were no areas of conflict which might be dealt with piecemeal as there had been in dealing with France and Russia. The Germans had no Egypt, Tibet, Madagascar, Persia, or Morocco to concede, gain or divide. Almost the only Anglo-German problem of this sort was how they might eventually share the Portuguese empire in Africa; and over this their relations were almost uncloudedly amicable, right up to 1914.

The first move in the matter of the naval race had been Campbell-Bannerman's. As what he hoped might be the beginning of an agreed programme of naval limitation he cut down the Dreadnought programme which he had inherited from the Conservatives. The Germans merely inferred from this that, having invented the Dreadnought, the British were become converts to naval limitation in order to prevent anybody else having Dreadnoughts. Campbell-Bannerman's policy merely encouraged the Germans to redouble their own Dreadnought programme; by 1908 the British were in some danger of falling behind. It was this that produced the great acceleration of the British programme from 1908 onwards whose outcome was first the People's Budget and, by 1914, Britain's margin of Dreadnought superiority. Later, Haldane (in 1912) and Churchill (in 1913) made naval limitation proposals to the Germans and both were rebuffed. By then the Germans were beginning to fish for a British promise of neutrality in the event of a European war. This would have been to concede to the Germans exactly what they had always hoped to gain by their Navy: the elimination from the defence of Europe of the one factor which had so far always preserved it, namely the British Navy. Britain could no more give the Germans an automatic undertaking to stay out of a European war than she could give France an automatic undertaking to join in.

The year 1911 brought the Agadir crisis. On the grounds that the French were violating the decisions of the Algeçiras conference in their handling of Moroccan unrest, the Germans sent a gunboat (*Panther*) to the Moroccan port of Agadir on the Atlantic, and demanded the whole of the French Congo as compensation for German recognition of Morocco as a French protectorate. (England had given this recognition by asking the French to give up Egypt, which they did not possess; the Germans would do the same if the French would give up something they did possess.) There were few German interests in Morocco, but the French were not financially committed to Morocco to any serious extent either; and there was a distinct possibility that the French might give way to the Germans in 1911 as they had nearly done in 1905. This would seem to be the reason for Lloyd George's sudden incursion into foreign affairs by his celebrated Mansion House speech. In this he insisted that war would be better than to allow 'Britain to be treated, where her interests were vitally affected, as if she were of no account in the Cabinet of Nations'. The 'vital interests' were presumed to be the alleged threat of a German naval base at Agadir; but the reference to Britain being treated as if she were of no account may well have been designed to indicate to France as well as to Germany that they were not to come to terms on the matter without prior reference to Britain. The speech speedily brought the crisis to an end; the Germans hastily withdrew their gunboat, disclaimed all intention of wanting an Atlantic naval base in Morocco, and contented themselves with a small area of the French Congo. Once again, the British had intervened to check a German attempt to downgrade France to the status of a satellite.

The Agadir crisis was more important than that of 1905–6. The intervention of the colourful Lloyd George over Agadir helped to impress the fact of Anglo-German rivalry on the public mind of both countries. Moreover, it was followed by the establishment of Poincaré's government of National Union in France; and, just as the Germans had forced arms-expansion on the Russians by their intervention in the Bosnian crisis, so they had helped by the Agadir crisis to create a government of national resistance in France. Significant redispositions of the French and British Fleets were taken shortly after the Agadir affair. While the French assumed responsibility for the safeguarding of the Mediterranean, the British became responsible for the protection of the Atlantic and Channel; the Royal Navy was now the only means available for the defence of the French coast in the event of a war with Germany. Much has been made of the unwisdom of such an arrangement in the absence of a formal Franco-British alliance. The agreement was accompanied by carefully devised formulas declaring that it did not imply 'an engagement to co-operate in war', though if war took place the two Governments undertook to 'consult'. It is for consideration whether, even if the French Fleet had not been, as it now was, concentrated in the Mediterranean, the British would have sat idly by while the German High Seas Fleet sailed through the Channel bombarding the French coast. Much that the British were being driven to do and say in these years (like their warning to Germany that they could not be automatically expected to be neutral in a land war) they would have done and said even if the Anglo-French *entente* and the Franco-Russian alliance had not existed. The Franco-Russian alliance, the British *ententes* with France and Russia and the co-operation of the Anglo-French Fleets were responses to the dangers of the situation, rather than the cause of them. War came in 1914 not because of the alliance 'system' (such as it was) but because in the end the behaviour of Germany made it seem unavoidable.

Grey refrained from making a formal alliance with France for sound reasons. One was traditional and commanded almost universal support. An alliance would increase the likelihood of Britain being committed to participation in a continental war in advance, and for reasons not of her own choosing. As it was, Grey was criticized then, and was criticized frequently later, for committing this country too far to France by his maintenance of the *entente* and by the 1912 naval agreement. From this arose his second reason for going no farther: the *ententes* with restless 'imperialist' France, the 'hereditary' enemy, and with Czarist Russia, another almost 'hereditary' enemy and an enemy of liberty into the bargain, were unpopular with the Radical wing of the Liberal Party. Liberals were much impressed by the sobriety, technological skill and business acumen of the civilized Germans. Unlike the immoral French and the superstitious Russians, the Germans were enlightened Protestants who were always to be found in what was called 'the van of progress', which is where the Radicals reckoned themselves to be. Grey's final reason for abstaining from an alliance was his determination to avoid, for as long as he could, giving the Germans the impression that Britain was ranged against them without hope of accommodation. The absence of an alliance gave Grey his only freedom of manœuvre. Unfortunately he found little use for that freedom.

He used it a little, however, during the London Conference of 1913, when the ambassadors of the Great Powers worked together to produce a peaceful settlement of the rivalries and anxieties caused by the success of the Balkan League in defeating the Turks in the first Balkan war. The Balkan powers' victories created a serious problem for Austria-Hungary by greatly enlarging Serbia. Grey fully supported the Dual Monarchy's anti-Serbian policy of creating an independent Albania in order to deny Serbia a port and a coastline on the Adriatic. He worked with the Germans to restrain and pacify the Austrians and to leave in the Balkans a situation which in several ways seemed to work to the disadvantage of Russia. The Dual Monarchy was allowed to thwart Serbian ambitions on the Adriatic after having been allowed to thwart them over Bosnia; yet Bulgaria, having been defeated in the second Balkan war by Serbia and deprived thereby of most of Macedonia, would be likely to lean more heavily than before on German support.

Grey was so relieved that war had been avoided over the Balkan issue that he seems to have failed to take note of the graver consequences of the abandonment by Britain of that already all-but-forgotten policy of 'maintaining Turkish integrity'. Defeat in the Balkan wars placed Turkey even more completely under German influence than before; and German control at Constantinople represented a threat to Russia's independence which the latter could hardly tolerate. Indeed, the weakest link in Grey's foreign policy was his apparent acquiescence in the precipitate abandonment of Turkey to German influence; though it is fair to say that he was not well served by Britain's diplomatic representatives at Constantinople at this time. In the event of war, Grey had not merely to consider contact with the French; there could be little contact with Russia except through the Straits. Yet no efforts were made to prevent Turkey passing almost entirely under German influence.

Grey was obviously puzzled later on by the circumstance that a complicated tangle like the Balkan wars was settled by the powers round a conference table whereas the relatively simple issue of the assassination of Franz Ferdinand by a Serbian terrorist in Serajevo in 1914, was not. He ascribed the difference, and indeed the outbreak of war, to the fact that whereas the Germans had come to a conference in 1913, they refused to come in 1914. Hence his advocacy of the League of Nations during and after the war; and hence, in part, the simple faith implicit in the League Covenant that an essential preventive of war was the establishment of regular machinery for the concerted discussion and examination of international disputes. This gave rise to the idea that wars were caused by what were called 'disputes' and could be avoided provided the 'disputes' were always submitted to examination and discussion. There was little understanding of the circumstance that a State might invent a 'dispute' for the express purpose of not letting it be settled; or might agree to discuss it solely in order to delay other people's military preparations; or, as in the case of Hitler, go on inventing 'disputes' simply for the purpose of frightening people into acquiescence.

The 'disputes' arising out of the Balkan wars were settled because in 1913 the German Army was not ready for war. The 'dispute' between Austria-Hungary and Serbia over the Serajevo incident was not settled because neither Austria-Hungary nor Germany wanted it settled. The Habsburgs were faced in 1914 with great Serbian hostility (which had very largely been created by Austria's own policies) and by the defection of Roumania to the Russians. This made the Dual Monarchy feel itself at the mercy of two irredentist movements at once: the Serbian demand for Bosnia and the other South Slav territories inside the Monarchy's territory, and the Roumanian demand for Transylvania, ruled by Hungary. The Habsburg Government, therefore, opted for crushing Serbia before it was too late. The German High Command opted for support of Austria because, although this certainly involved war with Russia, they believed that the successful short war for which alone they were prepared, was possible in 1914 but only doubtfully possible thereafter.

Once there were clear signs that war was almost upon them the Russians ordered the preliminary stages of mobilization. This was a military necessity for Russia, given the much slower pace at which she could mobilize fully. In reply, also as a matter of military tactics, the Germans intimated to the Russians that even this partial mobilization in Russia was a *casus belli*. The Russians rejected this ultimatum, and Germany declared war.

Given the Schlieffen Plan, which required an all-out blow against France as an essential preliminary to full-scale war against Russia, Germany at once arranged to get France into the war. The Germans therefore demanded a promise of French neutrality; when France refused, the Germans invented a tale about French violation of German air space and declared war on France also.

The war had thus become European solely in accordance with military time-tables. Nobody bothered with the terms of the various alliances, for the terms of none of them were complied with. Diplomats and politicians were brushed aside, and everywhere the Chiefs of Staff became the arbiters of policy.

The British position was uncertain, because in Britain alone were the decisions not in the hands of the military. Up to this point no issue seemed to have arisen which could be represented as an obvious threat to British interests. The first impulse of a people who, alone among the great European Powers, still remained not merely civilized but civilian, was to abstain from participation in a precipitate abandonment of almost all the processes by which domestic and international affairs were normally conducted. If the Army in Germany had not been so firmly in the saddle there might have been time for German politicians and diplomats to capitalize the strong neutralist and pacifist elements in British society. Bethmann Hollweg, the German Chancellor, made only feeble efforts in this direction; the Kaiser could merely wring his hands, and write hysterically, once the British were in, that the 'dead Edward' was 'stronger than the living I'.

The German Army was, however, indifferent on the subject of British intervention. They expected it to take place and took it for granted that, in accordance with historic precedent, it would be too little and too late to make any difference to the early stages of war; and since in the German Army's view the war in the west would be won quickly there was nothing to worry about. The belated German attempts to angle for British neutrality were propaganda devices to minimize the possibility that Germany might subsequently be charged with sole responsibility for starting the war. Bethmann Hollweg offered to respect the position of France as a European (but not as a colonial) Power and was finally reduced to accusing the British of going to war for the sake of a 'piece of paper'. Only a political chief struggling in desperation with a situation he had ceased to control could have descended to so describing a major international document.

The 'piece of paper' was the Treaty of London of 1839, providing a collective guarantee of Belgian neutrality. In the end, the Asquith Cabinet stirred itself to the point of deciding to make a German breach of this treaty the decisive issue. There was much consultation of the shade of Mr Gladstone, who had gone to the typically stern lengths of issuing a warning to France and Prussia on the subject in 1870; there was some nice quibbling about whether Britain was legally bound to defend Belgian neutrality unilaterally, given that the treaty provided for a collective guarantee. The matter does not seem to have been discussed in the Cabinet until as late as five days before the eventual British declaration of war on 4 August. By 1 August the British had gone no farther than to inform the French that they would oppose German naval action against the

French Channel coast; and even this was carried through the Cabinet only with great difficulty and at the cost of John Burns's resignation.

The Cabinet was induced to make up its mind only when the German invasion of Luxembourg on 2 August made it certain that Belgium would be invaded also; a resolution which was stiffened by an offer of support from the leaders of the Unionist party. On 3 August the King of the Belgians refused Germany's demand for the uninterrupted passage of its armies, and Grey, with a united Cabinet behind him at last (though Morley had also resigned by now) put the case for intervention to the Commons and received the support not only of the Unionists but also of the Irish Nationalists; Redmond, their leader, offered the full co-operation of the Irish, and thus released the British from the necessity of retaining large forces in Ireland.

In view of its culmination in war, any consideration of Grey's policy must be overshadowed by doubt. He has been accused of deliberately keeping his colleagues in the dark; but this is a reflection on the nature of Asquith's Premiership as much as on Grey. He has been accused of deliberately encouraging the French against the Germans, as when he vetoed a suggested Franco-German compromise about the administration of Morocco during the Algeçiras conference; and of pursuing a fussily rigid policy, as when he tried to insist that the band of the Coldstream Guards should not pay an official visit to Germany on the grounds that it had not yet paid one to France. Moreover, whereas Balfour and Lansdowne had concluded the Japanese alliance and the French *entente* exclusively with the Empire in mind, Grey concentrated, to the exclusion not only of the Empire but even of Turkey, on the balance of power in western Europe. He could therefore be represented, more truthfully than English historians are inclined to admit, as a resolute opponent of that Franco-German reconciliation which alone could guarantee the European peace; and he opposed it because in his view it would lead to a German domination of the continent which was inimical to British interests.

The great flaw in Grey's policy, however, was that to go to war in 1914 could not maintain the balance of power in Europe; it could only destroy it. In advocating war in 1914 Grey was dooming his own policy as effectively as, in sending its ultimatum to Serbia, the Habsburg Empire was dooming itself. Like everyone else, Grey anticipated a short war and spoke of Britain as likely to suffer little more from entering the war than she would by staying out. Yet it had taken something like two hundred years of repeated warfare to preserve the European balance against France; and it was contrary to all the evidence of history to suppose that the existence of the Royal Navy made it possible quickly to defeat a great continental land power with the minimum military effort by Britain. Thus, in Britain even more than in Europe, war was seen as likely to constitute a brief interlude of glory for the few, of sadness for some but of mere inconvenience for the many.

It may therefore be said of Grey's foreign policy that it willed the end without willing the means. The only way in which war might have been avoided would have been to make it clear well in advance to the Germans that there would be an immediate British military contribution effective enough to make the Schlieffen Plan obviously unworkable; and to have made it abundantly clear that the whole resources of Britain and its Empire in manpower, industry and finance would swiftly be invoked. Only in this way could the civilian elements in Germany be provided with a strong enough basis for opposing the military leaders. Indeed, it would probably have given the military themselves to pause. The German High Command was by long tradition deeply concerned with the preservation of its Army. This, indeed, explains its techniques of the *Blitzkrieg* and of *Schrecklichkeit*, both of which were designed to combine the maximum of achievement with the minimum of casualties; it also explains much else in German history, including Ludendorff's surrender in 1918 and the Bomb Plot against Hitler in 1944.

Any vast programme of imperial resistance to Germany might have done no more than postpone the struggle for a generation; yet it might have given time for the development of a more civilian state of mind in Germany and it would certainly have given time for the industrialists and financiers of Germany to acquire an economic domination of Europe so great that military conquest would have seemed pointlessly wasteful.

Whether the British could have followed such a policy is doubtful. The British were too civilian-minded to grasp the extent of military domination in Germany and perhaps too civilized to place themselves in advance in a position of total opposition to the German nation. They would have been unwilling to face the cost, which would have meant peacetime conscription and all that that involved in the diversion of men and resources; it would have increased the armaments race; it might well have involved the hostility of the United States; and it would have foundered on the quicksands of Dominion independence.

In the moment of victory, Haig remembered Haldane. Historically speaking, however, it is best to recall his work at the moment of decision in 1914. For it was Haldane's army reforms, carried through during the Campbell-Bannerman administration, which in the last resort made the question of immediate British intervention worth considering at all. Haldane had created the General Staff and the British Expeditionary Force of six divisions for immediate dispatch to continental soil; he had provided a pool of non-regulars with some military training by setting up the Territorials;· and a pool of potential officer-material through the Officers' Training Corps in the schools. It was because of these and other reforms initiated by Haldane that the British were able speedily to mobilize at least six regular and fourteen territorial divisions in 1914.

PART II:
FIRST WORLD WAR
1914-1918

---

6 · The Generals' War, 1914-16

The Germans' expectation that the war would be decided in a matter of weeks was in fact fulfilled, though not in the sense they had intended. By 13 September 1914, their attempt to effect the total elimination of French military resistance in six weeks had ended in abrupt failure. The establishment of a static German line on the River Aisne, and the later extension of that line north-eastwards to the Channel coast, marked what proved the irreversible defeat of the attempt at the military conquest of all Europe. All subsequent German policy, and most of Europe's history until 1945, were to be concerned with the refusal of the Germans to accept the verdict of the Battle of the Marne as final.

The Schlieffen Plan, on which the Germans based their hopes of destroying French military power in six weeks, had been completed by 1907; and because of the feebleness of German civilian authority it had become the only fixed element in German policy. It had not subsequently been discussed or criticized; and since it was less a plan than a desperate gamble it says much for the morale and technical skill of the German Army that it adjusted itself as well as it did to the Plan's failure.

The idea was that the greater part of the German Army should wheel through Holland and Belgium and right round the west of Paris and then pin the whole French Army against the Moselle fortresses, the Jura and Switzerland. It was a gigantic gamble with time. It presupposed a degree of strategic and tactical control so great, and a system of communications so efficient, as to raise doubts about its practicability in even the most unreflecting mind. Only a Government dominated by military men conscious most of all of their armies' numerical inferiority to the combined French and Russian enemy, could have allowed itself to be committed to it.

For their part, the French were committed to what was called Plan 17, which involved a great offensive in Lorraine, where it was assumed the bulk of the German forces would attack. This German invasion would be resisted by a heroic dash into its midst by an army whose qualifications for such an operation were limited to its belief in its ability to achieve it.

At the outset, the Schlieffen Plan was modified. Moltke, the German Chief of Staff, rejected the idea of an invasion of Holland, a circumstance which necessitated even faster movement through Belgium. He also diverted, to the assistance of the armies facing the French in Lorraine, divisions which might have added decisive weight to the main advance. In the last week in August he withdrew six corps from the Western Front (unnecessarily) to assist the defence of East Prussia against the Russians.

It did not follow that it was necessarily a bad thing for the Germans that Moltke lacked faith in the plan and was prepared to modify it. The real drawback was that he lacked faith in his own capacity to make correct decisions swiftly, and lacked that technical control during the advance which alone could have given him accurate information on which to base his changes of tactics. He directed the battle first from Luxembourg and then from Coblenz, all the time in a state of nervous anxiety. The lack of adequate liaison between his army commanders, their often inadequate intelligence, and his own imperfect knowledge of what was going on, are sufficient in themselves to explain why the great gamble failed in the end. The fact that in the first days of September Moltke abandoned the attempt to swing round west of Paris and envelop the whole French Army need not have resulted in the retreat from the Marne which followed. What failed at that moment was the morale of the German High Command. The French were allowed to recover the initiative and to exploit, to the full extent of the (very narrow) limits available, the advantage they now derived from the shortness of their lines of communication. Paris was saved and so was the French Army.

In the nature of things, the British contribution was a small one, involving at this stage less than 100,000 men. Since, however, the miscalculations of both the Germans and the French were so great, and the margin between defeat and victory at this stage so slight, the participation of the British in this opening campaign must not be underestimated. The quality of the fighting troops in the B.E.F. was probably the highest in Europe; unfortunate, therefore, was the inexperience of its staff officers and its shortage of heavy guns and shells.

The British were run into by the advancing Germans at Mons, in Belgium, on 23 August. The terrain was difficult, the meeting unexpected, the German attack disorganized and their advance held up. The British were heavily outnumbered, but greatly impressed the enemy by their rapid musketry fire; their performance was immeasurably better than might have been expected, given that this was the first battle the British had fought on west European soil since Waterloo.

Nevertheless, Mons was followed by a retreat, since the whole French

Army was retreating on the British right; and the only other noteworthy British action in this period was the engagement at Le Cateau (26 August) when one tired British corps stood and fought the Germans off, because their commander feared retreat would otherwise become a rout. As it was, the British might well have been encircled if Kluck, the German commander opposing them, had not failed to gauge British intentions. He did not move forward against them the day after the battle of Mons because he assumed their successful defence would be followed by a renewal of the battle; and thereafter the Germans continued to operate under the impression that the British were retreating westwards towards their bases on the coast when they were, in fact, retreating southwards to maintain contact with the retreating French. Nevertheless, Sir John French, the British C-in-C, was increasingly conscious of the smallness of his army, of the casualties it had suffered, and of the depressing effects on morale of its almost continuous retreat. He was on the worst possible terms with Lanrezac, the French commander on his right, since Lanrezac added to his justifiable pessimism a less justifiable boorishness which was aggravated by Sir John's contemptuous ignorance of the French language. Sir John concluded by 30 August that the French were retreating so fast that he would be left in the lurch. He therefore sought permission to do what the Germans had expected him to do earlier, namely retreat to his Channel base at St Nazaire, at the mouth of the Loire. He was only prevented from doing so by the personal intervention of Kitchener, Secretary of State for War since the outbreak. Kitchener disconcertingly chose to put on his Field Marshal's uniform for the purpose of overawing Sir John.

The British maintained contact with the French, therefore, and retreated south of Paris (near Melun) and not west of it. The British move forward from Melun thereafter, to take part in the Marne battle, was extremely hesitant and Sir John was loth to believe that the French were intending to make a real counter-stroke against the Germans. As it turned out, the B.E.F. found itself facing a gap between the German 1st and 2nd Armies. They advanced into the gap with greatly revived morale, but at a sluggish pace because of Sir John's fear that he was moving into a trap. It seems, however, that it was the nerve of the German commanders that gave way; after earlier regarding the B.E.F. as a defeated force they now regarded it as a much greater danger than the facts justified. After much indecision, Moltke ordered a retreat to the Aisne. His resignation followed in due course, a fitting comment on the fact that the retreat was due at least as much to technical and operational failures on the German side as to the crude toughness of the French commander, Joffre.

In the north-east, the Germans had not yet abandoned hope of turning the Allied flank. They succeeded in capturing the great fortress of Antwerp in October 1914, partly because there had been a touching faith in its impregnability and partly because the Allies sent assistance to the Belgians too late. Although the bulk of the Belgian Army managed to escape, the city capitulated on 9 October. For the next month, the Germans engaged in a furious battle to turn the flank between Arras and the Channel coast. The Belgians, though suffering the loss of 35 per cent of their strength, managed to hold on in the extreme north-east, and the flank was, after all, held against the sea.

The B.E.F. had now been moved up to concentrate around Ypres. Even though Sir John French was as sanguine now as he had earlier been dejected; although Foch was as devoted as ever to the idea of attack; and although the Germans were likewise still confident of an early break-through; the defence of Ypres by both French and British troops saved the situation. The battle died out in stalemate with the onset of winter.

There was now at neither end of the battle-front, from the sea to Switzerland, a flank that could be turned. Although, therefore, the final verdict of 1914 was that the Germans had failed in their grand design, the balance sheet still showed in their favour. One-tenth of France, 80 per cent of her coal, 90 per cent of her iron, and large areas rich in timber were in German hands, as also were Luxembourg and almost all Belgium. The Germans were able to exploit these areas to the full and to counteract for some time the effects of the British naval blockade, which in any event would be relatively slow to take effect. On their side the Allies, however, had gained the one strategic element on which ultimately the Germans had pinned their hopes, and that was time. Much of the tragedy of the succeeding three and a half years arose from the failure of almost all the Allied commanders to realize that this was all that 1914 had gained for them.

The situation on the Western Front by the end of 1914 gave rise to problems which neither side was able to solve. The competing armies were both devoted to the doctrine of the attack; yet the events of 1914 had shown that armies lacked the technical means for successful large-scale attacks against armies of comparable size. Once an army had solved the problem of resisting the effects of shrapnel and high explosive by the primitive expedient of digging trenches with spades, artillery tended to lose its value to the attackers, particularly artillery which fired with too shallow a trajectory. The defence was also strengthened by the development of the magazine rifle and the belt-fed machine-gun. Against these, frontal assault became suicidal. Nevertheless, the High Commands continued to be obsessed with the idea that frontal assault, sustained by an artillery barrage, would achieve a great break-through and thereafter restore mobile warfare; the preponderance of cavalry officers on the Allied side in particular meant that commanders sacrificed thousands of lives in an ultimately unsuccessful effort to turn the war they had to deal with into the kind of war they wanted to deal with. Even when frontal attacks did achieve local success

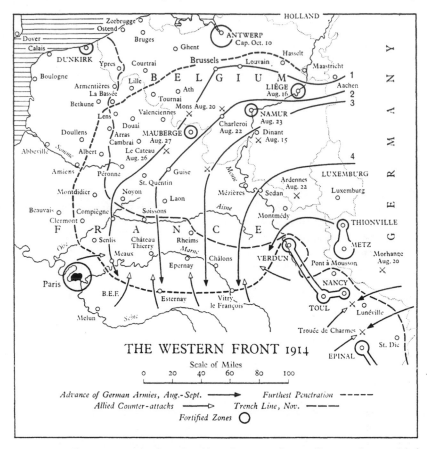

THE WESTERN FRONT 1914

Scale of Miles

0   20   40   60   80   100

Advance of German Armies, Aug.-Sept. ——→   Furthest Penetration ----
Allied Counter-attacks ——▷   Trench Line, Nov. ———
Fortified Zones ◯

they usually worsened the situation by creating salients whose chief
characteristic was their vulnerability; they became pockets which the
defenders could squeeze at the throat. Armies could not advance fast
enough against complicated trench systems because their speed at the
point of battle was limited to that of the heavily encumbered infantryman.
Even when advancing in 1914 in the most favourable circumstances
enjoyed by either side during the war, the Germans, for all their careful
planning, eventually lost their impetus for this reason. In addition, the
farther an army advanced, the farther it moved from its railhead; but as the
other side retreated, it moved nearer to its railhead. Thus it was possible,
at critical stages in the war, to stem an advance the nearer it approached
the defender's railheads. Armies could, in short, be concentrated quickly,
thanks to the steam locomotive; but they could only be deployed in battle
at a rate that was too slow to overrun a reasonably well-organized defence.

The only Allied plan that was consistently adhered to from 1915 to the end of the war, however, was the mounting of large frontal attacks in order to achieve a break-through. The cost in men's lives created a memory that outlasted the second, and greater, war of 1939–45.

The situation required immediate and expert examination of the technical problems involved. It required a bold acceptance of the inadequacy of existing methods of attack and a well-informed determination to find alternative methods of waging the war. This was not forthcoming. It is significant that although Kitchener had two insights into the nature of the war, he acted upon only one of them. He was the first to see that there would be a long war; and he recruited volunteers to fight it. In 1915 he said that the German lines must be looked on as 'a fortress that cannot be carried by assault and also cannot be completely invested'. This insight, however, led to no such decisive action as the first. It posed problems which were beyond his capacity to solve.

The first moves, not unexpectedly, came from the Germans, who faced virtually the same problems as their enemies. They were not only much swifter than the Allies to adapt themselves to trench warfare; they also used two technical devices for overcoming its handicaps. One was poison gas, which was a failure. The other was the use of the submarine as a weapon against British commerce and shipping. It was in May 1915 that the Germans sank the *Lusitania*, causing 12,000 casualties, among whom were 100 United States citizens. They did not develop the U-boat campaign to the full as yet, however, and the most noteworthy endeavour to get round the deadlock came in fact from the British side.

Throughout the war, Lloyd George and Churchill were strongly critical of the many unsuccessful attempts to achieve a great break-through on the Western Front. Churchill was, as always, impatient for action, but intelligent enough to see that it could not be achieved by frontal assaults against a good trench system, while Lloyd George had an instinctive distaste for the military mind and for the whole crude business of land warfare. They therefore sought, by using naval power, to mount a diversionary or outflanking movement in south-east Europe. The Russians had already suffered heavily at the hands of the Germans and, at the end of 1914, the Turks had entered the war and sent an army into southern Russia. A diversion in south-east Europe might therefore prevent a Russian collapse, and compel the Germans to send troops to help Austria-Hungary. From the point of view of British imperial security it also seemed desirable to attack the Turks, since their support of the Central Powers constituted a potential threat to Egypt and to the Persian Gulf.

The obstacle to any such action by the British was the French insistence that no troops should be made available from the west; for just as the British were nervous about the possibility of the war in Europe being won entirely by the French, so the French were nervous at the prospect of seeing the British revert to their traditional habit of using great European wars as an opportunity to extend their power outside Europe. In consequence, Kitchener vacillated. At times he favoured the idea; when it came to details he was lukewarm and indecisive. In the end, at Sir John Fisher's suggestion, warmly supported by Churchill, a fleet of obsolete battleships was sent to force the Dardanelles and to capture Gallipoli and then Constantinople. It was some time before it was realized that battleships could hardly fulfil this programme without military support; and matters were made worse when the Russians vetoed an offer of military help from the Greeks on the grounds that it might lead to Greece laying claim to Constantinople.

The naval bombardment of the forts which blocked the passage through the Dardanelles began in mid-February 1915 and continued till mid-March, when a full-scale attempt was made to force a way through. It was called off, within sight of victory, because of the fear of undetected mines, which at a critical moment sank three British ships. The naval attack might still have been resumed but for the fact that, by now, a military force of 75,000 men was at last being got together under the command of Sir Ian Hamilton. The Navy therefore decided not to resume the attack and to do nothing while Hamilton's army was assembled. The army landings could not begin, however, until nearly the end of April and the Turks made excellent use of the respite to strengthen their defences under the German general, Liman von Sanders, who took over as supreme commander.

The delay was due to the absence of preliminary planning of the military operations. Hamilton had only one division of regulars, and neither they, nor the colonial and territorial troops who made up the rest of his force, had previous experience of landing on a hostile coast. Not even the weather conditions had been studied in advance; when Hamilton discovered that suitable landing-craft for the operation actually existed he was told by Kitchener they were not available; and the arrangements for transporting both the troops and their supplies to the area were chaotic.

Hamilton's landings on 25 April 1915 were well organized and initially successful; but his powers of leadership in the field were limited by his diffident nature and his habit of exercising overall command from a battleship off-shore. The landings were soon seen to have achieved no more than perilous beach-heads, vulnerable to Turkish shelling from the heights above, and devoid of shade, cover or water. There was a shortage of shells and of medical supplies. It was a situation which might well have been avoided if some of the commanders at Hamilton's disposal had been more resolute.

Throughout the summer there was no alternative but to hold on. The shortness of the nights, and the requirements of the political situation, made a withdrawal unthinkable. In August, having now been greatly reinforced, Hamilton planned renewed landings at Suvla, to the north of the already established beach-heads. Again Hamilton was badly served by his commanders, in particularly by General Stopford, who was sent out by Kitchener solely on the grounds of his seniority; he had never previously commanded a force in battle. Stopford, and his hardly less senile subordinate officers, allowed the Turks time to concentrate in force and to render the Suvla landings as ineffective as the spring landings had become. The troops, having endured dysentery all the summer, were left to face blizzard and frostbite in the winter. Between mid-December 1915 and 9 January 1916, they were evacuated, and the campaign written off.

The failure at Suvla had been followed by Bulgaria's entry into the war on the side of the Central Powers. Greece refused to join the Allies; and to keep some sort of foothold in the Balkans at all the French and British found themselves compelled to lock up large numbers of troops in the fruitless occupation of Salonika.

The Gallipoli disaster had the unfair result of damning Churchill as an irresponsible amateur strategist. Yet, if it is possible to condemn the commanders on the Western Front for their obstinate habit of studying maps and not the ground when planning their doomed offensives, the difference between them and the advocates of diversionary enterprises in the east is perhaps only in the maps they looked at. The soldiers looked at maps of France; the amateurs looked at maps of the world. It is not certain that the forcing of the Dardanelles and the capture of Constantinople would have had the startling results which it is still sometimes asserted would have ensued; the fact that the capitulation of Bulgaria in 1918 signalled the end of the war in the west is irrelevant. Nor does the evidence suggest that had success at Gallipoli resulted in the acquisition of Balkan allies this would have been of great value. The diversion of men and materials for the comfort of Russia in 1916 might have greatly weakened France and Britain without decisively stiffening the Russians. A military effort large enough to threaten Austria-Hungary while holding the Germans on the west would likewise have produced a serious dissipation of limited resources. The poor showing of the British in two other military sideshows, in Palestine and Mesopotamia in 1916, hardly suggests that the easterners' larger notions were necessarily sound.

Nevertheless, Gallipoli failed, not because of the amateurs, but because of the experts. Kitchener had no idea how to plan or provide for a campaign of this or, indeed, any other sort. The Navy had shown itself timorous, the Army commanders hardly less so; on more occasions than one the break-through to Constantinople might have been achieved. The failure of leadership was almost complete; even Hamilton's intelligence was vitiated by his diffidence. In the end the only thing to do with Gallipoli was to romanticize it, by concentrating, justly enough, on the bravery and tenacity of the men who suffered in it, and by borrowing from ancient history a sufficient number of classical allusions, to clothe modern incompetence in the garments of Greek tragedy.

The Western Front during 1915 produced in fact ample evidence that the Army leaders were incapable of dealing with the problems confronting them. In March, Joffre, now French C-in-C, ordered two unsuccessful attacks against the Germans, and Sir John French launched the Battle of Neuve Chapelle in the same month. Although the preparatory staff work was competent enough, the British gained little ground, all of it in the first three hours of a battle that was persisted in for three days. April saw the Second Battle of Ypres when, using poison gas for the first time, the Germans attacked the Ypres salient. The ground lost by the British had no value, but Sir John French insisted on trying to defend it, for the not very comprehensible reason that if men retreated their morale suffered, whereas if they held their ground for no sound strategic reason and got killed in the process, morale was maintained. Sir Horace Smith-Dorrien was dismissed from his command by Sir John French for questioning this theory. The British suffered 60,000 casualties, and this, combined with the serious depletion of ammunition, meant that the next main attack, the Battle of Festubert, on 9 May, failed within an hour of its launching. The débâcle prompted Sir John French to blame everything on the shortage of shells and this had important political repercussions at home, involving the establishment of a Coalition Government and Lloyd George's appointment as Minister of Munitions. The greatly improved shell situation on the Western Front in the autumn of 1915 was not, however, due to these changes, but to increased shell production under the War Office system which Lloyd George criticized and eventually superseded.

Since nothing was supposed to be wrong except a shortage of shells, no change was made in the general strategic view that attacks must go on. Kitchener did not like them, but Joffre insisted, and the bad situation of the Allies in general made it seem out of the question to stay on the defensive in the west. In September, Joffre attacked in Champagne and insisted on the British attacking at Loos. The French gained about eight miles at a heavy cost; but Sir John French mismanaged affairs at Loos, making bad worse by allowing the battle to drag on till early November. British and French casualties approached a quarter of a million. Joffre's consolation was that a lot of Germans had been killed too: about 150,000 of them.

In December 1915, Sir John French was replaced as British Commander-in-Chief by Sir Douglas Haig. It is perhaps too easy to criticize Sir John. He was given assignments throughout 1915 which his judgement told him were unwise, but he was overborne by Joffre; and this was usually because Joffre overbore Kitchener too, and against these men Sir John could do little. He was fighting a war for which his previous experience had provided no training. As the commander of a relatively small army he could not talk to his French allies on terms of equality any more than Kitchener could; and if he was temperamentally unsuited to the strain of it all, so were other more celebrated generals – including Moltke, Nivelle, Pétain, and, in the end, Ludendorff.

What Haig brought to his new position was precisely this quality of steady nerve. He was possessed of a tireless resolve to carry out his divinely ordained duty of engaging the enemy. Obstinately and soberly, he clung to the simple notion that ultimate victory would not elude the just cause he had been appointed to serve. Since the war in the west continued to be the sort of war in which little counted but a grim resolve to go on attempting the impossible Haig was perhaps what the British Army needed. Those who attacked him appear to have been singularly unwilling to name the commander who might have replaced him.

Nineteen-fifteen was thus a year of disaster. There had been costly failure in the west, the Dardanelles campaign had proved a fiasco, and the Russians had been driven from Poland and Galicia, yielding a million prisoners. In the Balkans, the Central Powers had destroyed the Serbian Army and overrun Albania; and Bulgaria had entered the war, thus immobilizing a substantial Allied force in Salonika. Yet the Germans were still not in sight of victory. It was increasingly evident that England was the most dangerous of their enemies, and that time was on England's side, since it would enable the naval blockade to take effect and also conscription, introduced in March 1916. The new German Chief of Staff, Falkenhayn, decided that he lacked the resources to overwhelm the British armies in France at this stage, and decided instead to attack the great French fortress of Verdun. This was less in the hope of gaining ground than of 'bleeding the French Army to death'. Verdun he believed, correctly enough, was of such symbolic value to the French that they would defend it at whatever cost, and despite the fact that its defences had been seriously neglected.

The battle, begun by a fierce bombardment on 21 February 1916, lasted until July; the French saved Verdun, at a cost of nearly half a million men, the Germans suffering very little less. The hero of the defence was Pétain, almost the only senior French commander not wholly devoted to the doctrine of the offensive. In the latter part of the campaign, however, he was replaced by Nivelle, whose tactical skill earned him the reputation he was so speedily to lose in 1917.

On balance, Falkenhayn had perhaps wasted his forces less than if he had sought an all-out blow against Russia: victory there could be waited for. He had probably wasted them a good deal less than if, like his opponents, he had ventured an all-out offensive to break the enemy lines. Moreover, after Verdun the French Army was never again quite the dominating military partner in the alliance it had been before. Yet, once more, and at heavy cost in casualties, the Germans had achieved less than they hoped. They had pursued the attack beyond the limits of the militarily justifiable, and their morale had suffered. By contrast, and this counted for most in the end, the morale of the resolutely optimistic Joffre was quite unshaken, while, to the north-east, Haig was as confident as ever that, whatever the immediate facts, the Lord of Hosts was still with him.

As far as the Allies were concerned the main business of 1916 was to be a great Anglo-French offensive on the Somme. The Somme was selected by Joffre purely because this was where the French and British fronts adjoined: it was a bad choice of area for an attack, since the German positions there were quite exceptionally strong. Owing to their losses at Verdun, the French shared less than a third of the twenty-five mile front. At first, Haig had not wanted the Somme offensive, but later became enthusiastic, probably because of the enormous weight of the preparations; the artillery in particular looked so formidable as it gradually assembled. In the event, co-ordination between artillery and advancing infantry broke down. Worse still, the seven days' preliminary bombardment failed to smash the German positions as expected; the new Minister of Munitions had got shells produced in quantity, but their quality was sometimes poor. On the first day of the offensive, the British losses were 60,000 men. The only response by the staff was to renew the attack.

The battle dragged on slaughterously, on both sides, from the beginning of June until 13 November 1916. At the end, the Germans had been pushed back about three to seven miles over a thirty-mile front. The British and the Germans each lost about half a million men, the French 200,000. The only evidence that one of the partners on the Allied side had once been ingenious enough to pioneer a technological revolution was the brief, bungled appearance on 15 September of forty-nine tanks, only eighteen of which actually made contact with the enemy. They nevertheless played their part in depressing German morale. For, despite the appalling disparity between the Allies' casualty list and the useless territory they had gained, the Somme demonstrated to the Germans the weight of the material that could be employed against them; Allied air superiority was another instance of this. It was, after all, the Germans, not the Allies, who had committed themselves, and were being increasingly committed, by their vast territorial gains, to total victory. The Allied staffs were certainly profligate of men's lives on the Somme, and doubtless it was here that the British soldier lost his last illusions about war. But it can hardly have encouraged the Germans. For them, every battle not decisively won was a battle lost; each failure to snatch victory left the Allies still in possession of time.

Nineteen-sixteen was also the year of the naval battle of Jutland. The German High Seas Fleet had already served Germany well; the mere fact of its existence had prevented the Grand Fleet from acting as an offensive force. The High Seas Fleet knew itself incapable of defeating the Grand Fleet; but it was sufficiently large for the British to be hardly less chary of risking an open battle. Fear of mines, and inadequate defences against submarines, also inhibited in the admirals the mystical faith in the offensive that characterized the generals.

Unfortunately for the Germans, if they were not to take some action against the Grand Fleet, there was little else for their surface ships to do; and, for the time being, submarine warfare was in suspense for political reasons. In 1916, Admiral Scheer decided to try to lure part of the Grand Fleet into isolated action. Jellicoe, the British admiral, knew of the plan in advance, because of British knowledge of the German wireless code. Admiral Beatty was sent off with the British battle cruisers to lure Scheer in his turn towards the Grand Fleet. Scheer realized his danger and broke away; Jellicoe did not follow him. Scheer then unaccountably turned up again. Contact was made between the fleets and again broken off. At this point, the British were between Scheer and his North Sea base, and Jellicoe knew that Scheer had two possible routes to take home. He guessed the less likely of Scheer's routes and guessed wrong; with the result that the High Seas Fleet got back safely. The British had lost three battle cruisers, three cruisers and eight destroyers, the Germans one battleship, one battle cruiser, four other cruisers and five destroyers. The High Seas Fleet did not emerge effectively from its bases for the rest of the war.

It is impossible to examine any account of Jutland without being impressed by the extent to which naval warfare of this sort had passed beyond the capacity of fallible human beings to control it. The possibilities of error in manœuvre and communication in a huge vulnerable armada covering about 400 square miles of sea were too numerous for finite human intelligence to apprehend. The great size of the Grand Fleet, itself a consequence of German building, is a striking example of the unimaginative megalomania which explains so much in the 1914-18 war. The Grand Fleet was too big for the professional capacity of the naval officers serving in it; it was big beyond the capacity of many officers, and of the Admiralty, to make accurate observations or send correct signals. Its size was greater, too, than the capacity of naval architects or the Navy's ballistic engineers; in significant respect the armaments and the design of the Grand Fleet were inferior to those of the High Seas Fleet. On the evidence of the half-blind, half-deaf, blundering behaviour of this armada of mastodons during the time when it was only partially engaged with the enemy, it is possible to suggest that Jellicoe's extreme caution, even if pushed, as perhaps it was, to the point of miscalculation, was something of a crowning mercy for his fleet and his country.

7 · The Generals' War, 1917-18

By the end of 1916, many on both sides felt sufficiently frustrated to see that the deadlock must soon be broken either by a dramatic new offensive device or by a compromise peace. The second alternative was favoured by those who feared, correctly enough, that to continue the war would destroy the whole of European society as it had existed before 1914.

For Germany, the chance of making a separate peace with France had been lost by the failure of the Verdun offensive. The chance of a separate peace with Russia had been lost by the scope of German gains in 1916 and, worse still, by a German promise of independence for Poland. Nevertheless Bethmann Hollweg, the unwilling political prisoner of the generals ever since 1914, did make the gesture of offering peace negotiations in December 1916. He did so because he knew that submarine warfare was about to be forced on him and that this would lead to United States intervention and thus to eventual German collapse. For his part, President Wilson, was anxious for peace because although he had been elected to the Presidency expressly to keep the U.S. neutral, he realized that if the war continued he would almost certainly be unable to stay out of it; obviously it suited his political situation to try to force an end to the war by extracting the last ounce of influence out of United States' neutrality before it was too late. His diplomatic *alter ego*, Colonel House, was sent to Europe with, in effect, a promise of armed U.S. intervention on the side of the *Entente* if the latter accepted the U.S. proposals and the Central Powers rejected them. However, since the Allies thought the U.S. would soon be forced into the war by German action, House's mission aborted. Sir Edward Grey was not unfavourable; and Lord Lansdowne, in 1916 and in 1917, appropriately expressed the traditional High Tory distaste for war *à outrance* which, like his behaviour over the Parliament Act and Home Rule, marked him as a relic of an age long dead. However, at this precise moment (December 1916), Asquith fell from power, to be replaced by Lloyd George, determined upon 'the Knock-out Blow'.[1] A further attempt by Wilson to get both sides to state their aims produced little but anger on the side of the *Entente* and indifference on the side of Germany. The

[1] See Chapter 8.

Entente resented Wilson's assumption that they were little better than the Germans; and the latter preferred, in accordance with precedent, to gamble with time. Unrestricted submarine warfare would compel the British to sue for peace on Germany's terms before the United States' intervention had time to take effect. Indeed, given the extent of European territory in their hands at the end of 1916, the Germans could hardly be expected to yield it, except under threat of imminent defeat; and they clung to the illusion that they were on the verge of victory. To talk of a 'compromise' peace in 1916 and 1917 is to misuse the word; any peace arrived at by negotiation at that time could not have been a compromise. If the Germans had been allowed to keep any French, Belgian, Russian, Serbian or Roumanian territory it would have been a victory for Germany. If the Germans had given up all of it (or even some of it) it would have seemed a victory for the Allies.

The Germans, therefore, concentrated hopefully on the task of using unrestricted submarine warfare to such an extent that in six months Britain would be forced to sue for peace. They launched the campaign on 1 February 1917 and expected it to have achieved its object by 18 August. The U-boats had instructions to sink at sight all vessels, neutral or Allied, sailing in the seas around the British Isles, the French Atlantic Coast and the Mediterranean. Two hundred and sixty ships were sunk in February 1917 and 338 in March; in April 1917, 430 ships were lost, representing a total tonnage for that one month of 886,610. It was out of the question to build new ships at the rate required to make good such loss; and, more serious, the crews of the lost ships were often lost with them. Jellicoe, now First Sea Lord, declared he could see no solution for the problem; and already the corn reserves in the country were down to about six weeks' supply. Well before this, Lloyd George had already been reacting strongly against what he called the 'stunned pessimism' of the Board of Admiralty and demanding a trial for the convoy system as an anti-submarine measure. Merchant ships sailing together under the protection of escorting warships would prove a more elusive target than ships sailing singly; all the existing anti-submarine devices, such as guns, depth charges, wireless and hydrophones would be concentrated and made available to the escorting warships, whose protective activities would also be facilitated by the circumstance that they would not be ranging the seas in search of the U-boats.

The Admiralty opposed the scheme for months, and implemented it as grudgingly and gracelessly as possible. They declared that merchant seamen would be unable to keep station in a convoy, believing, apparently, that holders of a master's 'ticket' in the mercantile marine were mere navigational amateurs. They misread their own statistics, and said that 2,500 ships entered and left British ports every week and that they had insufficient warships to protect so many vessels. A relatively junior naval staff officer discovered that the correct number of ships needing protection was not 2,500 but 140. They said convoys would be too slow, their speed being dictated by that of the slowest vessel in the convoy, apparently believing that it was better for merchant ships to be sunk than to be slow. Fortunately, by zestful manœuvre, irregular consultation of serving naval officers, the introduction of new blood into the Admiralty, and occasional downright bullying, Lloyd George got his way and the situation was saved. By the end of 1917 the British were sinking submarines at a faster rate than the Germans could build them. Out of 88,000 vessels convoyed up to the end of the war only 436 were lost; the rate of sinking among vessels sailing singly was 25 per cent.

More was needed than skilled organization to see the country through its most dangerous crisis. There had to be a ruthless restriction of civilian imports and rationing of meat, sugar and butter. There had to be a great increase in the rate of shipbuilding. Nor were all merchant ships convoyed. The percentage of deaths in the mercantile marine was higher than in the Royal Navy.

Lloyd George's intervention in military affairs in 1917 was less happy than his timely intervention in the submarine crisis. He had a supreme lack of confidence in both Kitchener and Haig. A submarine had eliminated Kitchener by torpedoing the vessel on which he was travelling to Russia, in June 1916. With Asquith also out of the way, only Haig remained; and Lloyd George was desperately anxious to remove this last obstacle to a complete change of control. Lloyd George's experience of England's political leaders, her civil servants and her defence chiefs had engendered in him lifelong contempt for their brains and a barely concealed scorn for their methods. The only men he would willingly use were those whom he chose himself or who, for whatever reason, followed him and forsook all others. In the matter of military strategy his whole mind and spirit were, to his credit, appalled by Haig's dogged adherence to the frontal attack. Alone among the leaders of the British war effort, he did not regard the horrifying casualty lists as a matter for no more than a mournful wringing of the hands; alone among them he sought information from junior serving officers about the nature of the war in its reality—the mud, the stench and the blood. At this stage, however, he lacked the authority necessary for so drastic an act as the displacement of Haig, and worse still, there was, as he realised himself, a shortage of candidates to take his place. Moreover, Lloyd George's revulsion from the horrors of the Western Front was, like the objection of his former Liberal colleagues to conscription, partly a revulsion from war itself. Yet, after Verdun, the burden of holding off the Germans in the west fell more and more on the shoulders of the British Army; the diversion of troops and resources to other fronts in 1917 might well have led to the war in the west being lost.

Indeed, Lloyd George seems to have wanted Haig eliminated very largely in order to get the main war effort transferred from the west to somewhere else; early in 1917, his favourite brainchild was a substantial offensive against Austria-Hungary on the Italian front. In a paradoxical way it was therefore fortunate that he lost interest in this idea when he allowed himself, like so many others, to fall victim to the personal magnetism of the new idol of the French, Nivelle. Nivelle, for reasons which defy analysis, now convinced almost everybody that he could achieve the final break-through in the west. Lloyd George was converted to Nivelle's plan partly because, unlike Kitchener and Haig, Nivelle was articulate; and since the Welsh tend to be both loquacious and intelligent, Lloyd George was always ready to assume that all loquacious persons were intelligent and that all inarticulate ones (like Kitchener and Haig and, later on, Neville Chamberlain and Baldwin) were fools. Moreover, the nature of Nivelle's offensive appeared to require unity of command; and this would realize Lloyd George's dearest wish, the reduction of Haig to a subordinate status. Lloyd George succeeded only partially in this object: and by seeking to achieve it in an underhand way, he poisoned the relations between Haig and Nivelle, and made worse, if that were possible, Haig's loathing for all politicians in general and for Lloyd George in particular. Thus, Lloyd George, who had protested against the Somme and was to protest about Passchendaele later in the year, became a party to the most unsuccessful Western offensive of all.

Nivelle's plan was to smash through the not very secure lines the Germans held after the Somme offensive of 1916. Before he could attack, however, the Germans had withdrawn to elaborate new defences, the Hindenburg Line, devastating the intervening area as they did so. By the time Nivelle launched his offensive nobody in the French Army and few French politicians believed in its chances, but all had committed themselves too deeply to it to afford the risk of calling it off. Not even Haig believed in it.

Within its limits, the British offensive on the Somme in April 1917, at Arras and Vimy Ridge, was a tactical success, and the ground gained proved of great value in holding off the Germans in March 1918; but as a contribution to the campaign of 1917 it was of less value. The advance was pushed too far, and ground to a stop: naïvely, cavalry were sent forward into the crater-ridden areas won by the infantry and, like the inefficiently used tanks, reduced all to confusion. Casualties on both sides were over 100,000.

The first day of Nivelle's advance a week later, which was planned to gain six miles, gained 600 yards. As usual, there seemed nothing to do but to persist and to widen the attack. After a fortnight, however, the offensive was abandoned and Nivelle was replaced as Commander-in-Chief by Pétain. There had indeed been gains: prisoners and guns had been captured in quantity. But French casualties had been high and, above all, the promised miracle had not been worked. The French Army became **a prey**

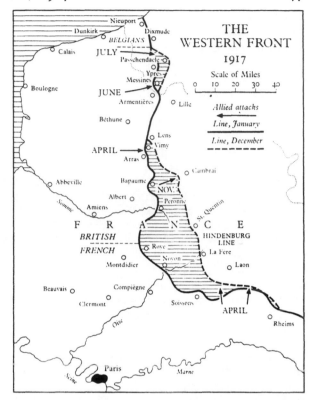

to mutiny, and throughout the summer it needed all Pétain's majestic combination of firmness and sympathy to restore order. With a cautious realism uncharacteristic of the commanders of 1914–18, he determined to remain on the defensive and to wait for the Americans.

Haig, however, was less disposed to wait for others to gain credit for winning the war; and he used the temporary incapacity of the French as an excuse for planning a new British offensive. A preliminary success at Messines in June 1917 preceded a battle whose alleged object was to carry British forces from the Ypres salient on to Ostend. Once again, an immense quantity of artillery was assembled and its ten-day bombardment destroyed all the surface drainage of the area over which the British were to attack. This, and the exceptionally heavy rainfall, made the battlefield a sea of mud. Tanks were unusable and artillery immobile. Officially known as the Third Battle of Ypres, but more usually referred to by the name of the ruined village of Passchendaele, captured at the end of the campaign in November, this new display of unimaginative incompetence was less expensive in casualties than the Somme, but more horrible, and even

emptier of strategic significance. Late in November, the moral of it was
pointedly drawn. South of Passchendaele, at Cambrai, a massed attack
by nearly 400 tanks, operating over firm ground and without the usual
preliminary artillery bombardment, tore a four-mile gap in the German
lines to a depth of five miles. Nothing came of it, however; the infantry
and cavalry sent in to exploit the gap were poorly handled by their commanders, and in two days the Germans regained as much'territory as they
had lost. Fortunately for the campaign of 1918, the Germans did not think
to devise anti-tank measures.

Elsewhere, the onset of winter in 1917 was marked by an Austro-
German offensive against the Italians, who had long been fruitlessly
attacking in the Julian Alps. The Italians retreated in disorder to the line
of the Piave. Nearly 300,000 Italians were made prisoners and 400,000
deserted; the dead and wounded numbered 40,000. Once again, as on the
Marne, however, there was national recovery. On a rational calculation the
Italian Army should have disintegrated. In fact, the necessity of at last
defending the soil of Italy itself revived Italian morale and perhaps made
the war popular for the first time. Another effect of this disastrous Battle of
Caporetto was to hasten the establishment of a Supreme War Council by
the Allies. For the moment, however, it merely helped to add to the catalogue of 1917's failures. Compared with them, the capture of Jerusalem
by British forces under General Allenby counted for little.

In the wider sense there were two events in 1917 which may, with
more than usual accuracy, be described as epoch-making. With a great
roll of propagandist drums the world stage was at last entered, Left by
the Russians and Right by the United States. It is of course an exaggeration
to describe European history as 'finished' at some point in the twentieth
century. It is equally false, however, to pretend that events occurring
within the western peninsula of the Eurasian land-mass can have, in the
future, the determining influence on world affairs they had in the eighteenth
and nineteenth centuries; and it was in this respect that 1917 is a turning-
point. Wilson's declaration of war against Germany, and the Russian
Revolution, gave notice that Europe's future would be decided by her great
eastern and western 'colonia': the one the product of the English political
tradition and of the eighteenth-century Enlightenment, the other the
offspring of the theocratic bureaucracy of Byzantium and of nineteenth-
century Socialism.

At the outset, however, there was no time for long-term considerations
of this sort. The collapse of Czarism in the spring of 1917 and of Kerensky's
fumbling Provisional Government in the autumn was followed by the
Bolsheviks' separate peace with the Germans at Brest-Litovsk in April 1918.
This, by ceding vast areas of European Russia to Germany, appeared to
prelude not an era of Russian influence but Russia's elimination. Thus,
the Germans had won on the Eastern Front; and given the confusion

amid which the Bolsheviks endeavoured to rule, and their widespread unpopularity, the most likely outcome was that Russia would become a German colony. Nor for some time would the United States be effective in the field. They had neither sufficient trained men nor weapons of war.

It was perhaps inevitable, therefore, that both the United States and the Bolsheviks, lacking in 1917 and early 1918 the material resources for waging war, bent their energies the more feverishly to the battle for men's minds; and, in doing so, rehearsed the tactics of the larger battle they waged in mid-century. Conceiving themselves outside the Franco-British struggle with the Germans, and fundamentally opposed to it, Lenin and Wilson, caparisoned with slogans, appeared on the scene like two apocalyptic horsemen proclaiming that the former things had passed away and that all things were to be made new. The Russian revolutionaries, before Brest-Litovsk, had proposed to the belligerent powers a peace without annexations or indemnities, based on 'the self-determination of all peoples'. The purpose of these demands was, of course, propagandist: they were designed to turn the general war-weariness into revolutionary repudiation of all war-mongering capitalists and above all of that particular group of them which represented Germany at Brest-Litovsk. From the Bolshevik point of view, their propaganda failed: the Brest-Litovsk treaty which the Germans imposed on them was one of the most severe in the history of Europe.

Nevertheless, from February 1917 onwards, the Russian people's revolt against the bestiality of the war roused some sympathetic echoes in the west. Some (but only some) of the French mutineers seem to have believed themselves to be inspired by Russian example. There was an attempt to hold a meeting of Socialists from all belligerent countries, including Russia, in Stockholm in August 1917, but the conference was not held, in particular because of the implacable opposition of both the English and French Governments.[1] The sabotaging of the conference increased the hostility of the working-class movement to the war and, as a demonstration of the wickedness of capitalist Governments, helped Lenin's anti-war propaganda.

Self-determination was thus for Lenin, once he took it over, a recipe for the defeat of all European Governments so that Russia might be saved the losses she eventually suffered at Brest-Litovsk. When Wilson appropriated the same slogan he used it as a nostrum to save Europe simultaneously from the falling-sickness of revolution bred by war-weariness, and from the convulsive collapse likely to result from the obsession of all the belligerents with the idea of a Knock-out Blow. Naturally, Wilson's line was more attractive: to tell people they could have a new world by going on doing exactly what they were doing already, unpleasant though it was, appealed more tellingly to the ingrained inertia of the human mind than Lenin's insistence that they had to stir themselves to make a revolution first.

[1] See also page 99.

The trouble was that, when Lenin spoke of self-determination of peoples, the words were at least intended to mean that peoples should decide for themselves, within the framework of an international Socialist fraternity. When Wilson used the phrase he did not know what he was talking about. It can now be seen that Wilson's world-wide dissemination of a meaningless catch-phrase was one of the great disasters of modern history.

In between the Russian invention of the phrase and Wilson's enunciation of the Fourteen Points on 8 January 1918, Lloyd George astutely intervened on 5 January with his own version. Significantly, it was contained in an address to the trade unions, summoned for the specific purpose of informing them of what the Government's war aims really were. The Prime Minister was in a happy position. The British and French Governments had never had time or opportunity, like those favoured non-participants, Wilson and Lenin, for the framing of large schemes for world-regeneration. With more than justifiable modesty they had thought that defeating the Germans was the biggest war aim they were capable of. By the end of 1917, however, beating the Germans seemed to necessitate a special effort to placate both the organized working class and the President of the United States; and since both wanted to be told that the war would bring more delectable prizes than a German surrender, Lloyd George was happy to oblige. Kerensky, Lenin, Wilson had all indicated clearly enough the phrases that people wanted to hear. Earlier still, in October 1916, largely as a helpful intellectual exercise for the benefit of his colleagues, Balfour had produced a thoughtful memorandum about peace terms; and, for good measure, the indefatigable Mr Sidney Webb had produced, in December 1917, a version of his own, called *Labour's War Aims*, which the party had accepted as recently as 17 December. With his customary skill, therefore, Lloyd George stated precisely the nature of people's feelings after over three years of a war to which, in January 1918, there seemed no prospect of an end:

'When men by the million are being called upon to suffer and face death, and vast populations are being subjected to the sufferings and privations of war on a scale unprecedented in the history of the world, they are entitled to know for what cause or causes they are making the sacrifice.'

He then went on with equal skill to say more or less exactly what all other high-minded people had been saying for a twelve-month. Germany was not to be dismembered; the future form of Germany's government was for the German people to decide. Belgium was to be restored and reparation made to her. Occupied territories were to be freed, Alsace and Lorraine were to be restored to France, Poland was to be restored, Italian and Roumanian national claims were to be satisfied. Indisputably Turkish territories would remain Turkish; and an international organization would be set up.

Interspersed with these unexceptionable pronouncements were others, less precise. There was an obscure hint about 'reparation for injuries done in violation of international law', which was vaguely linked with the sufferings of the merchant navy. Austria-Hungary was to be preserved but at the same time its nationalities were to receive 'genuine self-government on true democratic principles'; it would be pointless to speculate what this misty notion could mean in practice. The Germans were not to get their colonies back because they had treated the natives badly; and these unhappy victims of German wickedness were to be 'placed under the control of an administration acceptable to themselves'. This was said to be a process of 'national self-determination'. The non-Turkish areas of the Middle East were 'entitled to a recognition of their separate national conditions'. Lloyd George was careful to say that what this really meant 'need not here be discussed' since the one British aim outside Europe which had been pursued through thick and thin since Turkey's entry into the war had been that of establishing British power in the Middle East. Significantly, although Lloyd George several times used the phrase 'self-determination' he did not once add the vital words 'of peoples'. He clearly preferred the traditionally British phrase, 'government by the consent of the governed'; it was safer. Self-determination of peoples sounded too much like a claim to government by dissenting minorities – such as Sinn Fein in Ireland, the Nationalist Party in Egypt, or Congress in India.

The pacification of the British trade union movement and the utterance of the right phrases for the comfort of President Wilson were long-term devices, designed mainly with a view to an eventual victory in 1919. The defeat of the Russians, however, gave the Germans the opportunity to stage one more attempt to invoke the lightning. They had tried this tactic unsuccessfully in 1914. They had tried it unsuccessfully with the U-boat campaign in 1917. Now, Ludendorff was to try it again; and just as a German decision started the war in 1914, so a German decision ended it in 1918.

Ludendorff approached the task of attempting a break-through in sober awareness that this was the last throw. The Army's morale was sound but there were no reinforcements. Civilian morale was low: 1918 had begun with anti-war strikes in the big cities, and though the Royal Navy had failed to destroy the German High Seas Fleet, its blockade was by now sapping the health and will of the German people. Only victory could save the Germans now: and if it were long deferred the Army's morale would sink to the civilian level. Since there was still no effective political leadership in Germany, Ludendorff, with his driving will, became the sole arbiter. The task he set himself was made the more urgent and the more overwhelming by his awareness that Germany's allies were all clearly at the end of their tether.

Throughout the winter of 1917–18 he prepared for his offensive. He was to adopt the tactics of infiltration by storm troops of various arms, who would seek out and flow over weak points in the defences and round the

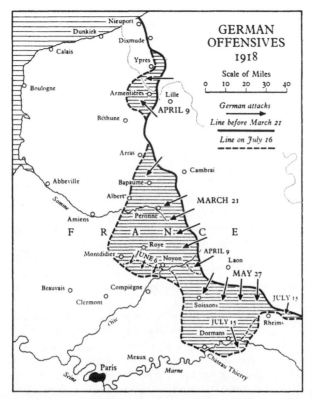

strong ones. Rigidity of objective, inflexibility in the chain of command, the old unhappy emphasis on the infantryman as the sole principal element in an attacking force were abandoned. That the new tactics achieved such success in the spring of 1918 showed how relatively little German Army morale and efficiency had been weakened by the Allied offensives of 1917.

Pétain had prepared for the expected offensive by training troops in the carrying out of delaying manœuvres; but Haig was unprepared to deal with an offensive, being under the impression that German morale had been too badly shaken in 1917. Nor does there seem much evidence for the claim that, when the Germans attacked, Haig had insufficient troops. The extent of the British retreat in March 1918 was due rather to the unsatisfactory nature of the defensive positions they adopted, and to the fact that they were incomplete. Haig misread German intentions and strengthened the British left wing in the north, around Ypres, under the mistaken impression that his right wing, south of Arras, was in no great danger and that, if it were threatened, there would be adequate time to reinforce it.

The scale, thoroughness and speed of the German attack towards the

Somme smashed through the inadequate British defences in the first two hours of the battle. The brunt was borne by General Gough's Fifth Army and the Third Army, both composed of divisions whose best soldiers had been lost in the Passchendaele offensive of the year before.

Haig blamed the fog, and claimed that he had too few troops; but any additional troops sent out to him would have been as raw as those he already had. By 23 March 1918, the Germans, having smashed through a gap six miles deep and forty miles wide, seemed in sight of finally separating the Allied armies. Haig would have to retreat to cover the Channel Ports, and Pétain would have to do likewise to cover Paris. Having asked Pétain for the assistance of three French divisions on 21 March, Haig now asked for no less than 20. Pétain in fact sent seven; but gloomily looked on Haig's cause as lost; there are grounds for saying that the war itself would have been lost had Pétain sent as many divisions to Haig as Haig now asked for.

The vital requirement, therefore, was swift action to maintain morale on the Allied side: for, as in 1914, neither the German Commander-in-Chief nor his armies could survive the mental and physical strain of a succession of victories that still left the enemy unconquered. The Germans were beginning to fall short of their best expectations owing to the sheer fatigue imposed by an advance that lacked motor transport. Ludendorff began to multiply his attacks and therefore dissipate the still great but unreinforceable energies of his armies.

By contrast, Lloyd George flung himself with concentrated determination into the task of retrieving the situation. Convinced, on the basis of past experience, that Haig's first reports of the crisis understated the dangers, he descended upon the War Office in 1918 much as he had descended on the Admiralty in 1917. On the critical day of 23 March he personally arranged for the rapid dispatch to France of all the available troops stationed in the United Kingdom. He commented unfavourably on the large number of men on leave from the front even though a German offensive had been expected: he ordered the dispatch of boys of under nineteen. He ordered divisions to France from Egypt and Palestine, and later on went to the politically dangerous lengths of ordering conscription in Ireland. He also saw to it that shipping was made available.

By 26 March the battle was beginning to stabilize, as the British recovered some semblance of order and the Germans began to lose momentum. Haig quickly recovered his nerve, too. The bitterest of his detractors have to admit that, after the first shock of Ludendorff's offensive, Haig's stature as a general greatly increased. He was well aware that he had made mistakes in the early days of his command; but he had not let this awareness of his fallibility unman him, so that he was able to learn from his mistakes. His steady confidence at last began to look like virtue, and his calm resolve now was to gain time so that he could be reinforced by the French. By contrast, Pétain became convinced that the Germans were about to beat, first the British, and then the French. It was because of Pétain's pessimism that Haig at last accepted Foch as 'co-ordinator' of the Allied Armies; and by mid-April as 'Commander in Chief of the Allied Armies in France'. Foch now controlled the reserves, though not the actual operations of battle. Nevertheless, the whole outcome of the campaign depended on covering the moral gap that had developed between Haig and Pétain and Foch's new position achieved this. By the first days of April, despite fierce and often critical fighting, Ludendorff's break-through had reached its limit. The Germans had failed to reach Amiens; the line they now held was a third longer than the one from which they had attacked; and it had gravely exposed flanks. Foch continued to hold back the reserves while the Germans grew more and more exhausted and undisciplined. They were demoralized too, it is said, by discovering how well-stocked were the British food and supply depots.

Ludendorff could not afford to give up, and on 9 April 1918 attacked south of Ypres. The result was an advance of five miles over thirty miles of front, due chiefly to the overwhelming of an unfortunate Portuguese division. The whole line had been thinly defended and many of the British troops were either battle-weary, or were mere eighteen-year-olds. A break-through to the coast at Calais seemed not impossible. Once again, dogged resistance was sustained long enough to confine the German attack within limits that were, after all, short of catastrophe.

Ludendorff attacked again on 27 May, this time against the French. Attack here, he thought, would fatally weaken the British front by drawing reserves from it. His Chemin des Dames offensive, in the same area as Nivelle's fiasco of 1917, gained ten miles in the first day, and once more took the Germans to the Marne. But yet again all that had been gained was a dangerously exposed salient. Another attack was launched, east of the salient thus gained, on 15 July. It failed. Moreover, on 18 July the French launched a successful counter attack against the exposed Chemin des Dames salient and drove the Germans back four miles.

This was the beginning of the end. Ludendorff, about to launch his 'final' attack on the British, ordered a retreat instead. On 24 July, at Haig's suggestion, Foch at last gave his agreement to an Allied offensive east of Amiens. On 8 August, the British advanced six miles, and for the first time used tanks effectively. Ludendorff's frenetic zest had prevented his realization that 18 July was the turning-point: he called 8 August 'the black day for the German Army', because only then did he at last admit to himself that his great offensive had proved no more than a prelude to defeat. A series of sharp, limited attacks by the British and Americans from then until early September deprived the Germans of all the salients they had gained by Ludendorff's offensives. But the German line still held, and the Allies expected not to break through until 1919.

Ludendorff, however, had exhausted his store of optimism. He believed the war lost and the German line liable to be broken at any moment. An Allied advance from Salonika had produced a prompt Bulgarian request for an armistice. There was now no possibility of the customary German rescue-operation on behalf of crumbling allies. Ludendorff therefore tempestuously demanded on 29 September 1918 that the German Government secure an immediate armistice.

Like Moltke in 1914, though in a more spectacular and melodramatic fashion, Ludendorff lost his nerve. Both had attempted to achieve the impossible and both had failed; both had won great victories in the course of their failure; both, when confronted at last with the fact of failure, took wrong decisions in consequence. Moltke had ordered a general retreat in September 1914 not because the German Army was in danger but simply because it had not won the war. Ludendorff likewise insisted on an armistice at the end of September 1918 not as the result of a defeat but because of the prospect of defeat in the following spring. There was nothing in the military situation to justify assuming an Allied victory before then. At two critical moments, therefore, the German cult of military might had resulted in placing the nation's destinies in the hands of broken men. Nothing so justifies the determination of Lloyd George and the French politicians not to leave the conduct of war in the hands of the generals as does the fate of Germany, whose generals had control from first to last, and which, in the end, was deserted by them.

For only a man devoid of political sense would have assumed, as Ludendorff seems to have done, that once an armistice had been asked for, and a nominally democratic Government had been set up in Berlin to secure favourable treatment from Wilson, the war could be resumed if the terms offered to Germany were unwelcome. Germany was in fact defeated by Ludendorff rather than by the Allies; his action in seeking for an armistice destroyed morale in the Army, led to a mutiny in the Navy, and to the destruction of the entire German political system.

By appealing to Wilson, Ludendorff hoped either to gain a pause during which his Army could recover or else to obtain some sort of idealistic peace of justice and mercy in which everyone would instantly forget the war and forgive the Germans. The first hope proved unrealizable; but so did the second. The only use Wilson's Fourteen Points ever had was that they existed, that Ludendorff had heard of them (but allegedly never read them) and therefore believed that the armistice could be achieved by an offer to accept them. In practice, neither Ludendorff nor Wilson had any choice. A peace which in large measure satisfied the wishes of the French and British Governments was inevitable because their forces and not those of the United States had done the fighting in the war and because France and Britain had not officially accepted the Fourteen Points and were determined not to. Nor would the Germans have necessarily got an idealistic peace had they waited till 1919; by then the U.S. army would have contributed much more to victory and, to judge from the attitude of the U.S. Commander, Pershing, would have favoured terms hardly less Carthaginian than those of 1945. It is thus an illusion to believe that the Germans were ever within sight of the benevolent peace terms they later claimed to have been cheated of.

Five weeks of fighting took place before the signature of the armistice itself on 11 November, 1918. The British and French Governments pressed Wilson to stiffen his demands while anxiously consulting their generals as to the likelihood of the Germans accepting them. Haig was convinced that the Germans would not accept terms, chiefly on the not unreasonable, but largely irrelevant, grounds that their immediate military situation did not warrant their doing so. (In Ludendorff's position, Haig would certainly not have sought an armistice.) The South African, General Smuts, whom Lloyd George had brought into the Imperial War Cabinet, was gloomier still. In his view, any terms in excess of Wilson's bare Fourteen Points would demand of Germany the equivalent of unconditional surrender; Germany would resist this; and the result would be wholesale European disintegration. Foch thought the Germans would not sign but, more realistically, believed he could now defeat them in six weeks.

Lloyd George would have none of this. The armistice terms must be of a sort to prevent a German resumption of the war. The Fourteen Points said the Germans were to evacuate and restore conquered territories: the Allies insisted there should be compensation and, in addition, the immediate evacuation of German territory west of the Rhine, the surrender of supplies and material, a denunciation of Brest-Litovsk and the handing over of the Fleet. The notion that Wilson's Fourteen Points had, when it came to it, any closer connection with the armistice and the peace than that of a series of vague premature suggestions is an illusion. Well before the armistice, Wilson had been forced by the Allies and by the equivocations and blunders of the Germans to accept that the Fourteen Points would be modified or abandoned in order to impose, first, an armistice from which Germany could not recover militarily, and then a peace from which it was hoped she could not recover at all.

Lloyd George and Clemenceau did not have quite such a struggle with Wilson over this as their critics maintained. Wilson's idealism was dominated by a liberal–puritan belief in justice; and by the end of 1918 he thought of himself as commissioned not only to remake the Old World but to impose a just punishment on the Germans for their wickedness.

With Ludendorff gone, the Kaiser in flight, a revolution of the masses on their hands, and starvation in sight, the Germans signed what was, in effect, an unconditional surrender.

8 · The Politicians' War: Asquith in Decline, 1914-16

By training, experience and temperament, Asquith was not well suited to lead a nation committed to a war whose prosecution required the full mobilization of its manpower, its industry and its morale. By 1914, his deficiencies might have been more plainly visible had his followers been less idolatrous and he himself less adept at concealing those deficiencies behind a mask of magisterial superiority.

The two major charges against his wartime rival, Lloyd George, were that he was 'rooted in nothing'[1] and that he was consumed by personal ambition. Yet Asquith is not much less vulnerable to the first charge and equally vulnerable to the second. Asquith had little to sustain him but a classical education and a legal training, and yet his classical education did not make him a great classical scholar and his legal training did not make him a great lawyer. Outside these two fields he knew little. He had no links with the aristocracy and, although his origins were in the Yorkshire woollen trade, he disliked business-men and was more rather than less ignorant of the industrial and commercial worlds than many of his rivals and colleagues. As for the working class, his contacts with them were limited to the several occasions when he invoked the coercive power of the law against them. What, therefore, he possessed, at his best, were the qualities a study of the classics and the law were traditionally supposed to provide and which, in Asquith's case, were defined by his wartime friend and subordinate, Edwin Montagu: an

incomparable capacity for mastering a particular case at once, detecting the vital considerations, discarding the bad arguments, and giving a clear and right decision.[2]

Unfortunately, this power of clear analysis was subject to a disastrous flaw, perceived by the least critical of his admirers, his second wife, Margot Tennant. She wrote:

The Asquiths – without mental flurry and with perfect self-mastery – believed in the free application of intellect to every human emotion; no event could have given heightened expression to their feelings. . . . I have hardly ever seen the saint or hero that excited their disinterested emotion.[3]

[1] See page 150.
[2] Jenkins, *Asquith*, p. 432.
[3] Margot Tennant, *Autobiography*, i, p. 270.

This absence of emotional involvement in the outside world certainly enabled Asquith to examine political problems with detachment; but the conviction from which the detachment ultimately sprang was that the problems themselves did not really matter.[1] They arose, in his view, from the prejudice and folly of his intellectual inferiors; and few indeed were those whom Asquith did not regard as his intellectual inferiors. Thus, problems could always be solved by the steady application of his capacity to distinguish the good argument from the bad, and by his masterly habit of giving time for the passions to burn themselves out and the prejudices to collapse under the cumulative pressure of irresistible facts.

His lack of belief in the political convictions of others derived in part from the lack of conviction he had observed in his Unionist opponents when Prime Minister, and in part from his own lack of conviction in much else save the maintenance of legally constituted authority. Never in his career had he done anything that might prejudice his determination to secure, and thereafter keep, the leadership of his party. When in opposition in the 1890's he had spoken in the House only when he thought it would enhance his reputation to do so. He had taken inordinate pains never to espouse an unpopular cause, never to lose an opportunity to trim his sails amid the squalls that afflicted a party distracted by divisions between such diverse persons as the querulous John Morley, neurasthenic Lord Rosebery, choleric Harcourt, down-to-earth but hypochondriac Campbell-Bannerman, talkatively philosophical Haldane, and fussy Sir Edward Grey. Asquith was a Gladstonian Liberal who hedged for nearly twenty years over Home Rule and pursued a Home Rule policy in the end only because he had to. His attitude to the South African War had been the strictly legalistic one that it was fully justified by the fact that Kruger had sent the British an ultimatum; and when Campbell-Bannerman had accused the Balfour Government of adopting 'methods of barbarism' in the war's closing stages, Asquith wrote him a letter of courteous disapproval; but, even when being as definite as that, he took care to make the letter read like a complaint, not against Campbell-Bannerman, but against John Morley. In like manner, his endeavour to shunt Campbell-Bannerman into the Lords in 1905, so remarkably like Lloyd George's effort to reduce him in his turn to a Prime Minister *fainéant* in 1916, was bought off at the price of high office for himself and Grey, and at the expense of Haldane's desire to be Lord Chancellor. By 1914, he was so conscious of his acknowledged excellence in the conduct of government business and the out-manœuvring of his political rivals that he tended to inhabit a closed world of adoring women-friends and relations, and sentimentally loyal subord-

---

[1] The well-known story of the Featherstone colliery strike illustrates this. When Home Secretary under Gladstone in 1893, he had ordered the use of soldiers against miners on strike at Featherstone in Yorkshire, as a result of which two men were killed. When later heckled with the question, 'Why did you murder the miners at Featherstone in '92?' his reply was, simply, 'It was not '92, it was '93.'

inates. He had become, for too many Liberals, a political chieftain who could do no wrong; every account of him gives the impression of a man insulated from reality by the hothouse atmosphere of almost swooning admiration with which he chose to surround himself. The chances that he would succeed in leading the nation to victory in a gigantic war were remote.

On 5 August 1914, Asquith appointed Lord Kitchener as Secretary of State for War. This was not only because it was good for morale and for the Government's somewhat shaky reputation. It represented accurately the attitude that Asquith and, with the possible exception of Winston Churchill, most politicians in those days might be expected to take on the outbreak of war. War was a specialized undertaking, like going to law or going to hospital; and from the point of view of soldiers and politicians alike, the soldier was the expert whose advice and competence no politician was qualified to question. It would be like arguing with a surgeon while lying on an operating table. Certainly, Kitchener's attitude in Cabinet indicated to some members of it that he clearly wished they could be anaesthetized for the duration. This basic problem of whether war should be left to the Army commanders to conduct in the way they thought best or whether they should be subordinated to close criticism and control by politicians was at the back of most of the war's political crises. Asquith clearly adhered to the former view. To him, the management of war on land and sea merely created additional departmental activities over which he would exercise merely supervisory and co-ordinating functions. He would accept what the military experts told him without seeking to tell them how to do their job, exactly as he would accept the figures of crime presented by the Home Office without venturing to tell Scotland Yard how to deploy the Metropolitan Police.

Unfortunately, it turned out that there were no military experts in 1914; and though Kitchener was not greatly worse than other military chiefs he was certainly not much better. He had won the battle of Omdurman in the Sudan in 1898; he had shown no great tactical skill during the Boer War and had been Commander-in-Chief in India. He did not know Europe; he did not know England; he did not know how to work side by side with civilians; and he resented being questioned by his colleagues in Cabinet. Throughout his career he had worked in aloof isolation attended by a small group of favourite military subordinates; with the result that the techniques of delegation and co-ordination essential to the running of a great Government department were beyond him. He lacked the administrator's gift of seeing the connection between one thing and another. Thus he saw that the war would be long and therefore recruited volunteers into what came to be called Kitchener's Army; but it needed others to remind him that these additional soldiers needed a greatly increased output of ammunition. He saw that the German flank on the west could not be turned, but obstructed attempts energetically to develop new technical inventions; and when invited to see tanks first demonstrated, shortly before his death, omitted to tell the department concerned what he really thought of them. It is true that in 1915 the British were suffering almost as much from Sir John French's poor generalship as from lack of shells, and that much of the later profligacy in artillery bombardment was tactically inadvisable: but Kitchener did not impede shell manufacture for reasons of tactics but through lack of imagination. There seems little doubt that Kitchener's secretiveness, and his unsuitability for the tasks of organization did much to create the impression that Asquith's Government lacked initiative and decisiveness in the conduct of the war; to this extent, therefore, it is a little unjust that Asquith, in the end, took most of the blame. Nevertheless, it was in itself a mistake on Asquith's part to rely so heavily on a bronzed colonial soldier whose capacities were largely a matter of myth and whose chief effectiveness was as a model for a recruiting poster.

Having got Kitchener, Asquith had to keep him; and it was the combination of a Prime Minister who shrank from making forceful decisions and a Secretary for War with a dull passion for obstruction that produced the long and involved process by which Lloyd George eventually took control. His dissatisfaction with the handling of munitions and supply dated from the second month of the war when he noted that though, as Chancellor of the Exchequer, he had made ample finance available to the War Office it showed little disposition to use it, refusing, chiefly because of the extra work involved, to make use of firms outside its traditionally small circle of contractors. These, in consequence, became overburdened with contracts they could not fulfil. The result was that Kitchener worried more about the expenditure of shells in a battle than the high number of casualties; and when French complained of shortages Kitchener kept the complaints to himself. When Lloyd George proposed, in September 1914, the establishment of a Cabinet Committee to deal with matters of supply, Kitchener at first refused and, even when he did give way, the Committee was wound up after three months. Lloyd George continued to complain, and acquired the support of Balfour. A new Munitions Committee to deal with supply was set up in March 1915; but this, too, made little progress in the face of continued War Office obstruction.

The expected crisis came when Sir John French chose to let it be known both to Lloyd George and to *The Times* that the failures of the British in May 1915 were in his opinion due to the shortage of shells. Lloyd George's response was to threaten to resign his chairmanship of the Munitions Committee. Simultaneously, Sir John Fisher, First Sea Lord, decided that the lack of success of the Dardanelles venture justified his precipitate resignation. He could, he said, 'stand it no longer'. The failure of the Western Front offensives and the Dardanelles expedition, the desertion of his post by Fisher and Sir John French's attack on Kitchener and the War Office over the shell situation, produced a crisis of political confidence and the end of the Liberal Government.

Not unexpectedly, a crisis created in the last resort by Service chiefs failed to produce satisfactory results or to bring down true culprits. Asquith remained Prime Minister and Kitchener Secretary for War, but the Cabinet now contained the Conservative leaders, Bonar Law, Lord Lansdowne, Balfour, Sir Edward Carson and Lord Curzon; and, as a sop to the working class, the Labour Party leader, Arthur Henderson, was made President of the Board of Education. The persons selected to receive the burden of punishment for the failures of the Government were Winston Churchill, First Lord of the Admiralty, and Haldane, the Lord Chancellor. Churchill was sent 'to polish the brass' as Chancellor of the Duchy of Lancaster for having been in favour of the Dardanelles expedition; Haldane was replaced because he had described Germany as his 'spiritual' home, had somehow contributed to the outbreak of war by failing to warn the Government of Germany's preparations, and was alleged for good measure to have become woolly-headed. Asquith's treatment of these men showed yet again that his abiding political concern was the maintenance of his own personal position. Haldane was his oldest friend, but Asquith, though expressing his regrets to Grey, who doubtless passed them on, wrote no word of apology himself to Haldane. One man, however, had his way – or nearly. A Ministry of Munitions was established and Lloyd George was to be its Minister.

The creation and operation of a Ministry whose functions were vital to the effective conduct of the war on the battlefield was a task for which Lloyd George was peculiarly suited. As the evidence of his early career indicates, he was at his best when faced with the problems, however complicated, of one particular task. When confronted with too many problems at once, as he was from 1918 onwards, his energy and his mental agility quickly got out of control and he tended to operate untidily in too many directions at once. As Minister of Munitions, he was free to gather staff from whatever source he chose and to organize without that regard for precedents and orthodoxies which had so clogged the War Office. He went outside the Civil Service for many of his principal subordinates: partly because these new men from the world of business would owe their positions entirely to him and also because they would possess that quality of decision-making which Civil Service procedures tended to inhibit. Nevertheless, he had a many-sided battle to fight. Every task performed by his Ministry, whether in design or production, was a function subtracted from the War Department and was impeded accordingly; and not merely from professional or departmental jealousy but because there was potential danger and confusion in the existence, side by side, of two ministries both concerned with the invention, design, production and supply of weapons of war.

Munitions production was also hampered by the deeply entrenched conservatism of the trade unions. After much discussion, the Munitions of War Act of 1915 provided for Government control of munitions factories; after considerable difficulty the unions were won over, by the lure of high and guaranteed wages and a tax on excess profits, to 'dilution' – especially the employment of women – and the abandonment of many craft union rules about the demarcation between one skilled job and another. It was largely to resist these inroads on trade union rights, for the prosecution of a war that was never popular with the working class, that shop stewards first became a prominent feature of industrial life.

These problems were tackled not only by legislative action, but by frequent personal appeals to the workers and trade union movement by the persuasive Munitions Minister, whose appearances on these occasions were usually supported by the presence of Arthur Henderson. Success was not painlessly achieved. There were prosecutions of malcontents, and tribunals were set up to enforce the regulations limiting munition workers' freedom to change their jobs; and Beatrice Webb, the Fabian Cassandra, was acidly convinced that it was all a plot devised by 'the Welsh conjurer', not to beat the Germans, but to cheat both the workers and the stupid leaders of their trade unions.

Lloyd George also brought about a series of enactments designed to combat drunkenness. These included drastic reductions in licensing hours and the punitive taxation of alcoholic beverages. The most spectacular device employed to encourage sobriety among munition workers was a royal pledge from Buckingham Palace. By it, the King established Prohibition throughout his household. Lloyd George regretted that the House of Commons reduced the effectiveness of 'the King's Pledge' by refusing to apply it to the Palace of Westminster; he would clearly have preferred to establish Prohibition everywhere.

Many of the regulations by which Lloyd George brought about the detailed control of the munitions industry were derived from the celebrated Defence of the Realm Acts. The first of these had been passed in August 1914 and had given the Government power to issue regulations 'as to the power and duties of the Admiralty and the Army Council for securing the public safety and the defence of the Realm'. The later Acts extended the Government's power to legislate by regulation over most areas of the national life in wartime; their application to munitions factories and the drink trade led to the long-nosed interfering female 'DORA' becoming as frequent a character in newspaper cartoons as Colonel Blimp was to be a generation later.

There were more serious problems, however. Many Liberals were alarmed at the increase of Government interference and by the increasing determination to equip the country for the prosecution of a fight to the finish. These developments were seen as threatening to destroy individual liberty and the essentially civilian character of English life. To plan for the total defeat of Prussian militarism seemed likely to involve the Prussianizing of England itself, if national bankruptcy did not take place first.

These fears crystallized during 1916 round the question of conscription. Conscription had first been discussed in Cabinet in June 1915 and produced such controversy that the issue had been evaded by the 'Derby Scheme', administered by the Earl of Derby, the Director of Recruiting. It involved voluntary registration for Military Service, on the understanding that married men who registered would not be called up until after all the single men on the register. By the end of 1915 the scheme had failed; married men had registered in large numbers but not the bachelors. In January 1916 the conscription of bachelors was therefore introduced; but it was not until May 1916 that conscription was applied to all males from eighteen to forty-one.

It was only with the utmost difficulty that Asquith carried his Cabinet and party with him on this. 27 Liberals voted against the conscription bill in May, and Sir John Simon, the Home Secretary (more famous as Foreign Secretary from 1931 to 1935) resigned over the issue in January 1916. At one stage Asquith faced the resignations also of Sir Edward Grey, who was still Foreign Secretary, Walter Runciman, the President of the Board of Trade, and McKenna who, as Chancellor of the Exchequer, believed the country could not afford the expense of calling up so many men.

It is symptomatic of the weakness of the Cabinet that so many of its most influential Liberal members should hesitate so long and obstinately on this issue. In effect, they were insisting that the country should be defended only by such persons as felt temperamentally inclined to do so, or who were too headstrong, or too ignorant, for more civilized employment. Perhaps they were worried by the essentially democratic nature of conscription; but in the main they took their stand on the objection that it would militarize the nation, strike a blow at personal freedom, and imply a resolve to a fight to the bitter end that could only produce the destruction of the European State-system. Yet their objection was probably at heart an objection to war itself. As things stood in 1916, however, they had the choice between continuing the war (which necessitated conscription) or losing it. It is possible over the conscription issue to sense the mounting Liberal dislike of Lloyd George: if he had not been making such progress in the matter of munitions, conscription would have been pointless.

Nineteen-sixteen was, however, the year of Jutland, Verdun and the Somme, and of the surrender of a besieged British force at Kut, in Mesopotamia, after a campaign characterized by quite outstanding incompetence. In June, after the death of Kitchener, Lloyd George became Secretary of State for War; having by that time exhausted the opportunities for initiative open to him as Minister of Munitions, his chief anxiety thereafter was the relative powerlessness of his new position as the civilian head of a Service ministry. In particular, he feared the power of Sir William Robertson, the Chief of the Imperial General Staff. At first, Lloyd George committed to paper a vigorous condemnation of the way the war was being conducted and of the lack of civilian control over the military, adding that he proposed to resign so as to be free to put the facts of the situation to the people at large. He was careful to show this document to particular cronies such as Bonar Law and Lord Beaverbrook, and to refrain in fact from sending it to the Prime Minister. His next move was to suggest sending Robertson on a mission to Russia; but Robertson refused to fall into so obvious a trap. Trouble then arose with the military over Lloyd George's decision to appoint a number of civilian experts to control military railways and transportation.

It was, therefore, with a growing sense of exasperation that Lloyd George viewed the various vague peace moves in the latter part of 1916; in a widely publicized interview with a United States Press correspondent on 28 September he described President Wilson's peace feelers as unwarrantable 'outside interference' and tartly pointed out that Wilson had made no peace move in 1914 and 1915 when the Germans seemed so certain of victory and the Allies so ill-prepared to resist them. From this time onward, Lloyd George became generally associated with the policy of 'the Knock-out Blow'. Grey protested at this cavalier treatment of the possibility of United States mediation; Lord Lansdowne protested even more strongly, and demanded to be told in effect whether the Knock-out Blow was a practical policy. Haig and Robertson, however, abruptly insisted that victory was in fact attainable. This converted all the Cabinet, at least in public, to Lloyd George's point of view. It did not, however, convert Haig and Robertson into allies of Lloyd George; for he was by now convinced that many of his colleagues did not want to fight the war, and that Haig and Robertson did not know how to fight it. The last straw was the total failure to attack in the Balkans from Salonika, which Lloyd George was convinced (with the sort of baseless optimism which he found inexcusable when Haig and Robertson applied it to the Western Front) would deliver Bulgaria and Roumania, destroy Austria and preserve Russia.

In collusion with Bonar Law and Sir Edward Carson and with the energetic assistance of Max Aitken, the future Lord Beaverbrook, Lloyd George therefore began, at the end of November 1916, to agitate for the creation of a small War Committee with full power to control the day-to-day business of the war. Of this Committee, Lloyd George was to be the chairman, and its remaining members were to be Carson and Bonar Law. In his usual devious fashion, Lloyd George seems to have relied on Aitken to drive Bonar Law to make the first overtures to Asquith; and the confusion of consultations, dinner-parties, button-holings and letter-writings that ensued was carried on against the background of a mounting Press campaign (which nobody believes to have been spontaneous) against Asquith's alleged weakness and in praise of Lloyd George's dynamism. Since the political consequences of these happenings were so dramatic and long-lasting, and the personal feuds engendered were so bitter, the affair is encompassed about with a cloud of witnesses few of whom can be regarded as disinterested. The view that Asquith was the noble victim of a base intrigue engineered by a consumingly ambitious and treacherous Lloyd George may, however, be ascribed to family and dynastic loyalty and relegated to the status of political hagiography. Winston Churchill, whose literary references to the politicians of the period are distinguished by their magnanimity, long ago poured gentle scorn on the notion that, in the last weeks of 1916, Asquith was

a kind of Saint Sebastian standing unresisting with a beatific smile, pierced by the arrows of his persecutors.[1]

In fact, Asquith seems to have viewed the affair at the outset with his customary Olympian detachment from everything save the need to preserve his own position. Mr Lloyd George, he thought, had many of the qualities of a Prime Minister, but he 'did not inspire trust'; and the great drawback of the plan for Lloyd George's chairmanship of a War Committee was that it would look like an attempt to undermine 'my authority'. When it became apparent that Lloyd George wanted Balfour to be excluded from the Committee, and removed from his position as First Lord of the Admiralty, Asquith's manner became even more like that of a revered Head Master expressing disapproval of a tentative list of new school prefects. He despised Bonar Law and detested Carson; and he was not prepared to let Lloyd George do to him what he had himself tried to do to Campbell-Bannerman in 1905.

Nevertheless, Asquith appears to have agreed, by 3 December 1916 (under the impression, which may or may not have been true, that all the Conservatives were against him on the issue), to the setting up of the War Committee, subject to his own 'supreme and effective control of war policy' and to reservations about personnel.

On the following day, however, The Times, then owned, like the Daily Mail, by Lord Northcliffe, a more megalomaniac and less likeable newspaper proprietor than Beaverbrook, published one article excessively critical of Asquith and another interpreting the previous day's Asquith–Lloyd George agreement about the War Committee (an agreement which was supposed to be known only to the two men concerned) as involving a complete and highly desirable surrender of authority by Asquith to Lloyd George. Asquith at once assumed that the existence of the agreement, as well as the false interpretation put upon it, had been passed on to The Times by Lloyd George, and that Lloyd George was deliberately whipping up a Press campaign against his own Prime Minister. Asquith

[1] W. S. Churchill, Great Contemporaries, page 123.

therefore indicated that he was reconstituting the Government and that, although there would be a War Committee, he himself would be its chairman. Lloyd George replied in ringing phrases that he would not in that case serve in the new Government. To Asquith's astonishment, Balfour then indicated that he was wholly in favour of a War Committee under Lloyd George's chairmanship. This led to a Conservative refusal to serve in any Asquith Government which contained neither Bonar Law nor Lloyd George; and Asquith thereupon resigned.

Asquith conferred next day with Balfour, Bonar Law, Lloyd George and Henderson. The first obvious alternative Prime Minister to Asquith was Bonar Law, as Conservative leader. There was a unanimous wish that Asquith would agree to serve under Bonar Law, but that, if he would not, Lloyd George should try to form a Government. Asquith then consulted all the Liberal Ministers (except Lloyd George) and they unanimously advised him to serve under neither Bonar Law nor Lloyd George. This was the end of the matter and by the following day, 7 December 1916, Lloyd George had succeeded without difficulty in forming a Government. Not one of the Liberal Ministers in the Asquith Coalition was invited to join, and the members of the National Liberal Club hastened to reaffirm their unswerving loyalty to their displaced chieftain. But Lloyd George and his associates might well have said in 1916 what Lloyd George was to say in a similar wartime crisis in 1940: 'It is not a question of who are the Prime Minister's friends; it is a bigger issue.'[1] There is little available evidence that Asquith thought in terms of this bigger issue of how to revitalize the war effort. All he saw was a challenge to his authority as Prime Minister; and his sensitivity about the contacts between members of his Cabinet and the Press arose to a great extent from his ingrained belief that his capacity as Prime Minister should be accepted as unquestioningly by others as it had, for over twenty years, been accepted unquestioningly by himself.

The Labour Party was reluctant to give the new Government their support, but eventually agreed to Arthur Henderson taking a seat in the small War Cabinet. Labour M.P.s were also placed at the head of two new Ministries, one for Labour and the other for Pensions. Beatrice Webb was very gloomy. The Lloyd George administration involved, she thought, 'the supremacy of all I think evil and the suppression of all I think good' and the continuance 'to the bitter end, not only of the war, but of faith in war as the universal solvent'.[2]

In a sense, Beatrice Webb had stated not only her own but the Liberal case against Lloyd George. When Lloyd George told the Labour representatives at this juncture, 'I hate war; I abominate it', he clearly sounded as if he was in fact thoroughly enjoying it. Asquith, Grey, McKenna and

[1] See page 322.
[2] Beatrice Webb, *Diaries*, 1912–24, page 71.

Runciman, the Liberal Ministers, really did abominate war; but since they also hated prosecuting it, and were manifestly not very good at it, their elimination from the seats of power was not the merely sordid intrigue they claimed but a logical consequence of their unsuitability. They still inhabited, at the end of 1916, an illusory world in which men could choose between good and bad: peace and war. In the real world at that moment the choice was between the bad and the worse: between a regimented national war effort and national defeat. It was Lloyd George's justification that he realized this and the Liberals' condemnation that they did not.

It was nothing so simple as mere ambition that elevated Lloyd George at this moment. It was rather his belief that the great tasks of war called urgently for the kind of dynamic energy that he alone could provide. Past experience validated his belief. Great feats of organization and persuasion came naturally to him: the Port of London Authority, Old Age Pensions, the People's Budget, National Insurance, the financial arrangements of 1914, the creation of the Ministry of Munitions, all provided ample evidence of the truth of Churchill's later assertion that at getting things done Lloyd George was incomparable; and if the support he received in 1916 from Bonar Law and Carson is not necessarily corroborative evidence, the support he also received from Balfour is more convincing. To the end of his life, Balfour insisted on the paramount quality of Lloyd George's contribution to the winning of the war.

The political consequences of Asquith's displacement were greater than those which flowed from any other political manœuvre since the revolt of Joseph Chamberlain against Gladstone. It ended Asquith's effective career immediately; limited that of Lloyd George to only six more years; and destroyed the Liberal party. Its only long-term beneficiary was the Conservative Party, which it transformed into the only coherent, nationwide political organization the country was to possess for almost the whole of the next thirty years. This meant that those whose opinions were to the Left of traditional Conservatism were without the means to effective political action throughout that period. Some, through dislike of Socialism, made do with the Conservatives *faute de mieux* and this, though the process was barely visible until 1950, tended to shift the Conservatives somewhat to the Left, and explains Baldwin's desire in the 1920's to be the leader of the people without a party of their own. Others gravitated towards the Labour Party; but since its ideological and social roots were so deep in the organized working class, this process, too, was slow to take effect.

9 · The Politicians' War: Lloyd George, 1917-18

Asquith's obstinacy and Bonar Law's abnegation served Lloyd George ill in the long run and planted the seeds of his eventual downfall. Lloyd George was probably truthful when he claims that he did not seek the Premiership; and accurately, if rather naïvely, self-revealing when, regretting Bonar Law's refusal he wrote, 'I felt confident that Mr Bonar Law would give me a free hand and extend to me *the support of a loyal chief* which was all I desired.'[1] It is a curious definition of the proper function of a Prime Minister, but the history of the next six years is a commentary on the problems created by a Prime Minister whose essential quality was the ability to get things done. As time went on, Lloyd George became so occupied with getting things of all sorts done that the business of government dissolved into chaos.

The Liberal ministers' boycott also made Lloyd George the prisoner of a Conservative Party whose rank and file never wholeheartedly accepted him. The extent of his dependence on the Conservatives was at once revealed to Lloyd George when he proposed to take Churchill into the new Government. So fiercely did the Conservatives object that it was eight months before he got his way. Moreover, a strong Conservative group made their support dependent on there being no commitment over Ireland and no immediate change in the command of the Army.

The new Government was notable for certain constitutional innovations not many of which survived the war itself. A War Cabinet was created which, at the outset, consisted solely of Lloyd George, Lord Curzon, Lord Milner, Bonar Law and Arthur Henderson; but Balfour, who took Grey's place at the Foreign Office, was also frequently called in, and Carson became an additional member in July 1917. Of these, only Bonar Law, who was Chancellor of the Exchequer and Leader of the Commons, had serious departmental duties. Lloyd George also invited Dominion Prime Ministers to Cabinet meetings from time to time, and General Smuts of South Africa was a member of the War Cabinet itself from 1917 to 1919. He took further advantage of the extraordinary elasticity of the constitution by appointing a considerable number of other men to office who were outside the par-

[1] Lloyd George, *War Memoirs*, Vol. 1, p. 596. (Author's italics)

liamentary political parties. H. A. L. Fisher was summoned from the University of Sheffield to become President of the Board of Education. Sir Albert Stanley, later (as Lord Ashfield) the head of London Transport, went to the Board of Trade, and to the new Ministry of National Service came the Lord Mayor of Birmingham, Mr Neville Chamberlain, who thus attained ministerial rank in 1916 though he did not enter the Commons until 1918. Lloyd George rapidly developed a poor opinion of Neville Chamberlain's abilities and replaced him after eight months.

The important permanent innovation was the establishment of a Cabinet Secretariat, headed by Sir Maurice Hankey. Until this time no minutes had been kept of Cabinet discussions; no written report of Cabinet decisions affecting them were sent to the relevant Departments of State; and in the absence of a Cabinet Secretary there had been nobody to ensure that the Cabinet systematically remembered to find out whether its decisions were implemented. It is strange to recall with what lordly amateurism the politicians had hitherto controlled the nation's affairs.

In the last two years of the war Government controls were multiplied. Shipping, like the railways and the mines, came under almost complete Government control, as part of the comprehensive resistance to the submarine menace. To conserve shipping space, imports were controlled and restricted. Food production was increased by the Government's power to force landlords to cultivate additional land and by guaranteed prices and minimum agricultural wages. Rationing of meat, sugar and butter was introduced, less because of real shortage, than because of the depressing effect of food queues on public morale. By the end of 1917 the Ministry of National Service was empowered to order men from inessential work into the Services and to draw up a list of reserved occupations. The Servile State had arrived, said the Government's critics. It was, for the most part, the price to be paid for survival; and many progressive persons who objected to controls in wartime were among the first to complain at their speedy cessation when the war was over.

By comparison with this tremendous activity, the affair of the proposed Stockholm Conference in 1917 doubtless seemed relatively trivial.[1] Unfortunately, it led to Henderson's resignation from the Government, and had political consequences probably greater than those usually ascribed to the Maurice Debate of twelve months later. It was a striking example of Lloyd George's capacity for strewing his path with irreconcilable enemies. The War Cabinet was at no time well-disposed to the proposal of the Kerensky Government that a conference of Socialists from all the belligerent countries should meet at Stockholm to discuss ways of bringing about peace. Nor did it approve of Arthur Henderson, a member of the War Cabinet, joining with Russian Socialists, whose support of the Allied cause was uncertain, in fraternizing with Germans at such a meeting. The

[1] See page 79.

Cabinet did agree, however, that Henderson should visit the Russian
Provisional Government, and he spent six weeks in Petrograd in June and
July. On his return he accepted the Labour Party executive's proposal
that he should accompany Ramsay MacDonald, the party's treasurer, but
a presumed pacifist, to Stockholm. The War Cabinet protested to Henderson, Henderson offered to resign, and Lloyd George temporized. Henderson then went off to Paris to help plan the Stockholm conference. When
Henderson returned to London, Lloyd George kept him waiting outside
the Cabinet Room for nearly an hour before communicating with him.
The precise physical circumstance in which Henderson did his waiting
acquired political and historical importance from Henderson's subsequent
furious assertion that he had been kept on 'the doormat'. Lloyd George
says the vigil took place in 'my Secretary's room'. Other sources speak of
it as being largely spent 'in a passage'. Since, however, Henderson was a
member of a War Cabinet of only five members it is difficult to see why
he should have been kept waiting at all. The upshot was that, this time,
Henderson challenged the Prime Minister to dismiss him and yet again
Lloyd George temporized. It then became apparent that the U.S., Italian
and French Governments would refuse to allow representatives to go to
Stockholm and the Cabinet decided to do likewise. Henderson nevertheless
persisted in strongly recommending participation to his colleagues in the
Labour Party. After being denied Cabinet papers as a result, Henderson
himself resigned and Lloyd George sent him (and passed on to the Press)
an exceptionally unpleasant letter conveying to the world at large the
impression that Henderson had been disloyal to his Cabinet colleagues.

As a result of this incident, Lloyd George, having already made an
enemy of Asquith and most of the Liberal Party, now made an enemy of
Henderson and most of the Labour Party. Lloyd George handled Henderson too gingerly to start with and too contemptuously at the end; he wanted
Henderson to stay, hoped he could be jollied or bullied out of his scheme,
and then finally gave way in public to an explosion of anger at Henderson's
refusal to change his mind. The incident determined Henderson to build
up the Labour Party as a fully independent body, with the result that Lloyd
George was denied the support of organized Left Wing opinion for the
rest of his life. The importance of this fact overshadows the consideration
that, in supporting the Stockholm plan to the point of resigning from the
Cabinet, Henderson showed a lack of political common sense.

In the operational field in 1917, Lloyd George's greatest achievement
was in getting the convoy system into operation, and his greatest error was
in backing Nivelle's disastrous offensive: he sought to exonerate himself
by saying that the military left him no alternative once they had rejected
his idea of a joint offensive on the Italian front. He consequently saw
Nivelle's failure as yet further evidence of the futility of western offensives,
and he therefore had grave doubts about Haig's ambitious Passchendaele

offensive. It seems, however, that Lloyd George felt incapable of challenging in detail the claims of Haig and Robertson that the campaign had every prospect of reaching its long term objective of capturing Ostend and Zeebrugge. Had Lloyd George, as he had originally intended, been able, under Asquith, to establish himself at the head of a War Committee he might have pressed Haig more vigorously. As it was, he was still deeply involved in the submarine problem and all the multifarious problems of the home and economic front, and not even Lloyd George could fight the Admiralty and the Commander-in-Chief and C.I.G.S. as well. Worse still, once the campaign had started and was obviously not going to achieve its objectives, he did not dare order a halt. G.H.Q. fed the home front with reports that all was well, and, despite the pessimism of his most experienced commanders, Haig was as confident as ever. To add to the Prime Minister's sense of frustration, Passchendaele was followed by the Italian defeat at Caporetto. As far as Lloyd George was concerned, both disasters were the consequence of his failure to override Haig.

In November 1917, a Supreme War Council, composed of representatives of all the Allies, was established by a conference at Rapallo, largely at Lloyd George's insistence. In January, the Council decided to create a central Allied reserve under an inter-allied Military Committee presided over by Foch. In March 1918, as a result of the pressures created by the German offensive, Foch became responsible for co-ordinating the Allied armies and in April became Commander in Chief of the Allied armies in France, though his power was exercised almost entirely through his control of the reserves. Nevertheless, his careful husbanding of them till the last moment contributed greatly to the German defeat.

As has been noted in the previous chapter, Foch's final role was Haig's doing and resulted from his justifiable dissatisfaction with Pétain; so that 'unity of command', in so far as it ever existed, was not Lloyd George's work, but Haig's, and was not accompanied, as Lloyd George seems always to have wished, either by the dismissal of Haig or by his subordination to the French Commander-in-Chief in the field, which might have had disastrous consequences. The only major step Lloyd George was able to take was to make Sir Henry Wilson C.I.G.S. instead of Robertson when, in February 1918, Robertson objected to being denied an effective place on the Military Committee of the Supreme War Council. Once Haig saw that he had either to submit to the civilian power or suffer the same fate as Robertson, he chose the former course. Nevertheless, Haig and Robertson stirred up a fierce Press campaign against Lloyd George and secured the full support of Asquith in the Commons; and Haig had appealed to George V.

Those who sought to bring down Lloyd George's Government over this issue gave the impression of having become obsessed with two ideas. One was that the business of fighting Germany was being conducted by Lloyd George for purely personal ends: the other that the conduct of operations in the field ought to be the purely personal concern of Sir Douglas Haig and Sir William Robertson. Asquith endorsed this opinion in the Commons on 12 February 1918, with the words 'There are no two men in the whole of Europe whose military judgement I would more unhesitatingly accept.'

Hatred of Lloyd George flared up again in May 1918 with the so-called Maurice Debate, which arose out of figures presented to the House by Lloyd George in April to rebut the charge that he had weakened the army in France by keeping troops in this country. Haig had offered this as an excuse for the German break-through in March 1918.

The responsibility for providing the figures on which Lloyd George had based his contention was that of General Sir Frederick Maurice, Director of Military Operations at the War Office, who had shortly afterwards been removed from his post. On 6 May 1918, Maurice wrote to *The Times* asserting that Lloyd George's claim that the army in France was stronger in 1918 than in 1917 was untrue, and that it was in fact weaker. Maurice demanded a parliamentary inquiry.

To the accompaniment of a violent anti-Government Press campaign, Asquith moved the setting up of a Parliamentary Select Committee to examine Maurice's allegations. Lloyd George got the proposal defeated by 293 votes to 106, chiefly by insisting that the figures he had given to the House had been supplied by Maurice himself while he was still D.M.O. at the War Office. Asquith and his supporters were thus branded as factious opponents of the Government at a time of maximum military danger in France, and General Maurice was retired on half pay.

The incident involves three separate problems. First, is the general one of whether the army in France had been dangerously deprived of troops by the spring of 1918, and by whom. This would seem still to be a matter of argument. The second is that even if Haig's forces in March 1918 were, for whatever reason, inadequate for an offensive, it is now considered that, properly handled and properly deployed, they were numerically adequate for sustaining a much more tenacious defensive than they did against Ludendorff's first onslaught. The third point is that there is some evidence that the figures given by Lloyd George were supplied by Maurice's department and were wrong. Maurice, however, had subsequently amended them; but the papers containing the amended, and presumably correct, figures were overlooked in Lloyd George's office, not discovered till afterwards; and then by his secretaries, who promptly burned them. If this story be true, a remaining problem is why Maurice did not at once recognize Lloyd George's statistics as his own unamended ones, and make his case stronger by accusing Lloyd George of deliberately suppressing the amended figures.

Basic to the issue, however, was not whether the War Office, the Prime Minister or Haig had done their sums wrong, but whether or not here was a chance to get Lloyd George out of office. Over this, as over the matter of a

Supreme War Council and an inter-Allied Military Committee, there were doubts and difficulties which, however critical the military situation, were deserving of discussion. Yet the manner in which the discussions were conducted precluded any real examination of their merits and reduced all to the level of personal intrigue. Much of the blame for this must be ascribed to Lloyd George. Over-engaged as he was, politically vulnerable as he felt himself to be, he tended to follow more and more assiduously the spirit of his favourite scriptural quotation, 'There is a path which no fowl knoweth and which the eye of the vulture hath not seen.' He thus created, as Asquith had said in 1916, a perpetual atmosphere of distrust: no man discarded by Lloyd George seems ever to have forgiven him. Thus, in 1917, he discarded Neville Chamberlain and Arthur Henderson; they became his enemies for life. With the solitary exception of Churchill, not one of his senior ministerial colleagues among the Asquith Liberals ever worked willingly with him again. Lloyd George had as little respect for persons as he had for institutions, so that nobody felt safe in dealing with him. Yet in descending, as they did, to dubious counter-intrigue, his opponents of 1917–18 can hardly be said to have deserved well of their country; and the contrast between the fighting soldiers' devotion on the blood-soaked mud of the battlefields, and the jealous rivalries of the generals and the politicians, is one of the most distasteful features of the war.

It is, of course, an exaggeration to attach much political importance to the Maurice Debate as the start of a Lloyd George–Bonar Law vendetta against the Liberals who voted against the Government on this occasion. All the damage that needed to be done to the relations between the Coalition Leaders and the Asquith Liberals had been done before May 1918.

Nineteen-eighteen witnessed two major pieces of legislation, the Electoral Reform Bill and the Fisher Education Act.

The Representation of the People Act of 1918 emerged slowly out of initially modest proposals to modify electoral procedures so that Service personnel would not be denied the vote through lack of the necessary residential qualifications. As eventually passed, the Act provided for a redistribution of seats with a view to making constituencies approximately equal in size and it increased the number of M.P.s to 707. It established universal male adult suffrage, by establishing a simple six-months' residential qualification. The principle of women's suffrage was conceded by the grant of a vote to women over thirty. In future, polling in a General Election was to take place on one day; and the rule was established that candidates polling less than one-eighth of the total votes cast should forfeit their £150 deposit. Plural voting was not abolished, but no voter might in future vote in more than two constituencies; and men of 19 were enfranchised if they had served in the war. Conscientious objectors, however, were disqualified from voting for five years. The Act more than doubled the electorate.

H. A. L. Fisher's Education Act became law in August 1918. It raised the school-leaving age from 12 to 14, and abolished all fees in elementary schools. It also provided for compulsory day-continuation classes for children between 14 and 18, though this provision was largely negated by post-war economies; nursery schools for children under five were also authorized, but financial restriction and the lethargy of local authorities obstructed this development also. Here and there, the better local authorities used the powers conferred on them by the Act to establish Higher Elementary or Central Schools for the benefit of children who did not or could not proceed to Secondary Education. Fisher was also responsible for improving the financial status of the teaching profession through the Teachers' Superannuation Act of 1918 and the establishment of the Burnham Committee to negotiate a national salary scale. Secondary Schools received increased grants, and State Scholarships to enable Secondary School pupils to proceed to Universities were established. The Universities received increased Government grants also, and £8,000,000 was made available to allow ex-servicemen to receive a University education.

PART III:
THE WIZARD MERLIN
1918-1922

10 · Politicians and Proletariat, 1918-22

Three days after the armistice of 11 November 1918 the Government announced that a General Election would take place on 14 December. It is usual to regard the decision of the Government to appeal to the country as a Coalition on the basis of its ultimately successful war record as peculiarly Lloyd George's. It would, in the light of hindsight, be equally appropriate to say that it was the result of a free but mistaken choice by Bonar Law. His, and his principal colleagues', view that their sole electoral asset was Lloyd George's great popularity in the country ignored the fact that if the Conservatives had gone to the polls as a separate party in 1918 they would have been without effective, organized rivals. At that moment a Lloyd George–Asquith reconciliation was out of the question (though it was attempted) and on its dubious war record as a whole the Liberal Party could hardly have commanded much support. Labour could also have been discounted at this stage. The Conservative Party had been the largest in the House since the spring of 1911; and its electoral chances would perhaps have been no more impaired by a break with Lloyd George in 1918 than were Labour's by its break with Churchill in 1945. The morale of the rank and file would also have been strengthened if the party had set itself free from the Lloyd George connection. Bonar Law, however, a sort of political Jellicoe, refused to risk his fleet in an all-out engagement, shirked the obligations of his position as a party leader and preferred to shelter behind 'the little man'.

Conservative and Liberal candidates acceptable to Bonar Law and Lloyd George received an official letter signed by both leaders, as a means of ensuring that Conservatives would not vote against approved Coalition Liberal candidates and that Lloyd George-Liberal electors would vote for approved Conservatives. It was this letter that Asquith described (in topical allusion to food rationing) as a 'coupon', and the election became

known as the 'coupon election'. Much was made of the allegation that
sitting Liberal M.P.s who had voted against the Government in the
Maurice Debate did not receive the 'coupon'. This was untrue.

The Coalition won; 338 Conservatives were elected and 136 Coalition
Liberals. Together with 10 other Coalition supporters, this gave the
Government a total of at least 484 members. In addition, 48 other Con-
servatives who had not received the coupon were also elected and most of
these in fact supported the Government. In opposition were 63 Labour
M.P.s and 26 Asquith Liberals; 73 Sinn Fein M.P.s were elected from
Ireland, but refused to take their seats at Westminster.

The desperate position of the Opposition Liberals was the consequence
of the arbitrary character of the British electoral system and the ruthless
tactics of the Coalition bosses. The Asquith Liberals gained 12 per cent
of the total votes cast in the election but only just over 4 per cent of the
non-Irish seats, the wastage of their votes being due to the fact that
everywhere they were opposed. Of the 136 Coalition Liberals, 27 were,
by arrangement with the Conservatives, unopposed, so that their 13·5 per
cent of votes gave them just over 21 per cent of the seats in the House.
So relentless had been the pressure on the Liberals that not one of their
leaders was elected; even Asquith was not spared and did not return to the
House until he won a by-election at Paisley in 1920. The party had to be
led in the House by Sir Donald Maclean, who had been deputy-speaker
since 1911. No wonder Asquith's intensely loyal supporters felt that Lloyd
George had been guilty of political assassination.

As soon as the election had been announced the Labour Party had withdrawn from the Coalition, though one or two minor figures in the party
continued to support it. In the new House, the Labour Party could count
on 63 M.P.s, a considerable rise on its 1910 figure of 42; the number of
Labour voters rose from the 1910 figure of 376,581 to 2,385,000 and its
percentage of the total votes cast was 22·2 in 1918, compared with under
8 per cent in the 1910 elections.

No doubt much of this increase is ascribable to the operation for the
first time of adult, as distinct from household, suffrage; but it was due to
the absence of any other anti-Coalition party organization which could
appeal to the working classes. The Asquith candidates were Whigs rather
than Radicals and carried with them an undoubted air of political failure,
if not of senility. Apart from these negative considerations, the Labour
Party had a better organization than in the past. Henderson, under the
tutelage of Sidney Webb, had organized it for the first time as a national
party with local branches to which individuals might belong; previously
it had been a loose association of trade unions, socialist groups, the Independent Labour Party and the Fabian Society, and had no individual party
members. It also went into the election for the first time with a programme,
Labour and the New Social Order, also compiled by Sidney Webb. The

declared aim of Labour was now to secure to workers by hand and brain 'the full fruits of their industry' on the basis of the common ownership of the means of production. It proposed the nationalization of coal, electricity, railways, the drink trade and the land, and a levy on capital. It would be rash to assume that the Labour vote increased because of the attractiveness of these proposals, or that the various elements in the party were very enthusiastic about them. For most voters (and, indeed, for Sidney Webb) *Labour and the New Social Order* was a forecast of a distant future. Votes cast for Labour in 1918 were cast by trade unionists for tradition's sake, by some purely as a protest against the old social order, and by others rather grudgingly, since the new programme seemed, by its cautious vagueness, to preclude the revolution they believed to be needed.

The immediate consequences of Labour's new position as the largest Opposition group in the Commons were not inspiring. Ramsay MacDonald lost his seat, as did Snowden and Henderson. Labour was led in the Commons by William Adamson until 1921 and by J. R. Clynes thereafter; neither was particularly distinguished. Although Henderson returned to the Commons in 1919, MacDonald and Snowden did not return in the lifetime of the Coalition. In her usual fashion, Beatrice Webb thoroughly disapproved: the Parliamentary Labour Party after the election was 'a very sham lion'; its twenty-five miner M.P.s were 'for general political purposes dead stuff' and its leader, Adamson, was 'dull-witted'.

It had, of course, been difficult for the Coalition leaders to find anything very purposeful to say to the electorate; and there was a low poll. Despite the appointment of innumerable reconstruction committees from 1917 onwards, there was no agreed post-war programme, partly because of inadequate co-ordination, and partly because the armistice had caught the Government unprepared. Since, therefore, all that the Coalition leaders wanted was to stay in power, they adopted what they hoped were vote-catching slogans as they went along. Lloyd George promised 'a country fit for heroes to live in'; and as the campaign proceeded use was made of the idea of hanging the Kaiser and of the even better one of demanding from Germany 'the whole cost of the war'. Much was made also of 'the menace of Bolshevism'. Only the Conservatives and their Coalition Liberal allies were said to be capable of resisting this threat. The Asquith Liberals were too feeble to resist it, the Labour Party's programme was indistinguishable from it, and the trade unions were riddled with it. These simple notions were to constitute a great part of Conservative electioneering tactics for nearly half a century after 1918 and must, on the evidence, be adjudged highly effective.

An examination of the years from 1918 to 1922 gives the impression of a journey through chaos. The rulers of England were as unprepared for the problems of a sudden reversion to peace as they had been for the problems of sudden war in 1914. The Coalition Government contained men of great ability but had neither a coherent policy nor effective machinery of planning and co-ordination. Balfour, who was Foreign Secretary till October 1919, and Lord Curzon, who then replaced him, were immensely gifted; Churchill, as Secretary for War and then as Colonial Secretary was resourceful and energetic; Lord Birkenhead, the Lord Chancellor, was both brilliant and eloquent; Lord Milner, for two years at the Colonial Office, was the ablest of the small but formidable group of minds which espoused the imperial idea. Bonar Law, Lord Privy Seal and the second man in the Cabinet until March 1921, was a solid master of detail, and Austen Chamberlain, whatever his intellectual limitations, was admired for his integrity and was an experienced Chancellor of the Exchequer. Less influential, but still more than average politicians, were H. A. L. Fisher the historian, and Christopher Addison, who became the first Minister of Health in 1919 and later a distinguished figure in the Labour Governments of 1945–51. Other Government members included the experienced administrators, Sir Robert Horne and Sir Auckland Geddes, and the industrialist Alfred Mond. Yet, for all its ability, the Government gave the impression of lurching from expedient to expedient, from ill-considered adventure to ill-considered adventure, until in the end it seemed to become an inextricable confusion of rival ambitions, rival corruptions, rival superficialities and rival opportunisms.

The clues to the mystery lay in the intractable nature of the problems that faced the Government and in the character of Lloyd George. He faced simultaneously the problems of demobilization; of brief boom and rapid slump; of whether or not, and how, and how fast, to dismantle wartime controls; of how to cope with the intellectual and social ferment stirring in the Labour movement and among the industrial workers; of violence in Ireland, Egypt and India; and the complex tasks of reconstruction in Europe and the Middle East after the simultaneous collapse of all the world's greatest land-empires. Like the wartime generals, Lloyd George and his ministers were confronted with problems beyond their capacity to master within the time at their disposal. Every study of the period indicates that, though much was achieved, the Government's reputation was disastrously compromised by the Prime Minister's inspired lack of method, his irresistible and often magnetic personal dictatorship, and his self-confident inability systematically to delegate.

In its dealings with the organized industrial workers the Government's policy was dictated by its prejudging of the issue. They saw it as a straight fight between the employing class, which it deemed to be patriotically devoted to the cause of national prosperity, and the workers, who were unpatriotically undisciplined, monstrously acquisitive, and liable, owing to their innate stupidity, to be led into ways of revolutionary violence by socialist and trade union 'agitators' in the pay of Moscow. The Prime

Minister was far too occupied with the problems of the peace conference, far too unsympathetic personally to the organized working class and far too dependent on the Conservative Party to try to develop an alternative approach. He merely saw to it that the desired aim of countering labour unrest should be achieved by outflanking manœuvres and by bluff rather than by a head-on collision.

The militancy among the workers which faced the Government was in part a swift return to the mood and the semi-revolutionary objectives which had given birth to the Triple Alliance in 1913.[1] The mood was angrier and the objectives more openly defined as a result of the war and its uncertain and inglorious aftermath. The doubling of T.U. membership in

Strange Outlandish Creatures of Sinister Aspect have been found in the Vale of Health Pond at Hampstead.

OUR CONTAMINATED POND. John Citizen explains to the bewildered authorities that the *real* cause of industrial unrest is the influence of Moscow. *Evening News,* 3 November 1926.

the war years provided not only a sense of power but also a sense of anxiety, because wartime dilution and the suspension of restrictive practices threatened both jobs and hard-won union rights. The pre-war lack of faith in the Labour and T.U. 'establishments' continued: even the publication of *Labour and the New Social Order* underlined the disparity between ultimate aims and the feeble showing of the parliamentary party: and the T.U.C.'s support of the war and its continued inability to co-ordinate a

[1] See page 41.

policy increased the rank and file's sense of frustration. The Bolshevik revolution and the greater publicity given to ideas of nationalization and 'workers' control' sharpened the feeling that there was much to do and that by united resolute action it could be done quickly. In these immediate post-war years men's lives seemed more than ever the playthings of social injustice and irrational hazards. In the early months of 1919, demobilization was sufficiently slow to provoke demonstrations among sóme soldiers, and the drafting of others to fight in the war of intervention against the Bolsheviks added to the fears and uncertainties. Wages rose, but prices outpaced them; a boom and a galloping inflation occurred in 1919, to be followed by a slump and a rapid deflation in 1920. Some men (and by no means did this exclude all the working class) had done well out of the war; others had been killed or maimed, and some had survived the hardships of war to die from the epidemic of 'Spanish influenza' which killed altogether 150,000 people in 1918 and 1919. War profiteers and boom-time speculators flourished (or were widely believed to flourish) while the workers lived in daily expectation of a frontal assault on their wages and working conditions.

Less than three months after the armistice there was an isolated but violent strike in Glasgow, primarily in the cause of a forty hour week for Clyde engineers and shipworkers. It was led, among others, by William Gallacher (who became prominent in the Communist Party of Great Britain after its foundation a year later), Emmanuel Shinwell (later a member of the Attlee Labour Cabinet), and David Kirkwood who, after twenty years as a Labour M.P., was elevated to the peerage as Baron Kirkwood in 1951. The Red Flag was run up, troops with machine-guns and tanks were brought in, and both Gallacher and Shinwell received prison sentences. In the more colourful histories of the working-class movement the event came to be regarded as an occasion on which 'the workers' revolution' nearly happened.

Of greater moment, however, was the problem of the coal industry. Even before the 'Battle of George's Square' in Glasgow, the Miners' Federation had demanded a six hour day, a 30 per cent wage increase and nationalization of the mines through workers' control, and had backed its demand with a strike threat. Even worse from the point of view of the Government, which under wartime regulations was still in control of the mines, the other Triple Alliance Unions looked like advancing demands of their own, and this at a time when London had only three days' supply of coal.

The Government simultaneously let it be known that they would use troops if a strike took place, and that, if it did not, they would establish a Royal Commission on the mines. The miners agreed to postpone the strike on condition that Lloyd George appointed as spokesman for the miners' cause three men known to favour nationalization: Sir Leo Chiozza Money, a wealthy convert to the Labour Party, R. H. Tawney, the Socialist economic historian, and Sidney Webb, the author of *Labour and The New Social Order*.

Lloyd George's reputation suffered heavily from this concession. The miners' president, Robert Smellie, the aggressive Sir Leo and the persistent Sidney Webb turned the inquiry into a public arraignment of private enterprise in coal. As early as 20 March 1919 the Sankey Commission (its chairman was Sir John Sankey, a judge who became Lord Chancellor in the second Labour administration) made an interim report recommending a reduction in hours, and a levy on the owners to improver miners' housing and welfare. It condemned 'the present system of ownership', as well as demanding for the miner 'an effective voice in the direction of the mine'. By June, the Commission reported by a majority of one in favour of nationalization; the owners on the Commission naturally dissented from this. Using the owners' dissent as his excuse, Lloyd George declined to adopt the majority's decision. Worse still, the miners had finally called off their strike after the interim report in March, on the strength of a written undertaking by Bonar Law 'that the Government are prepared to carry out in the spirit and in the letter the recommendations of Sir John Sankey's report'.

There was thus justification for regarding the Government's conduct over the Sankey Commission as a manœuvre to raise false hopes and to play for time until the worst of the coal shortage was over and the issue had lost its appeal. It was also held, subsequently, that talk of using troops (which had alarmed Smellie very much) had been a piece of unscrupulous bluff. The spectacle of a powerful Government, in open alliance with reactionary employers, trading on the miners' leaders' hatred of violence and on their belief in the good faith of the country's elected rulers was an unpleasant one. Hardly less distressing in this period, therefore, was the repeated readiness of the trade union movement to try conclusions with hostile Governments without systematic examination of strategy and tactics. The British worker was as loyal to his trade union leaders in peace as in wartime he had been to his officers; in both cases he allowed himself, far too often, to be led straight to defeat.

The other stalling operation of 1919 was the summoning simultaneously with the Sankey Commission of a National Industrial Conference in Central Hall, Westminster, attended by representatives of the unions (the Triple Alliance abstaining) and the employers. Lloyd George himself spoke at the inaugural session, looking, so Beatrice Webb wrote, 'more than ever the actor-conjurer . . . he might have been the Heavenly Father of the World of Labour'. The function of the conference was to advise the Government on how to avoid industrial unrest. It produced recommendations in favour of a forty-eight hour week, a public works programme and increased pensions and insurance payments. It set up a joint National

Industrial Conference which lasted till 1921; but, for all practical purposes, it served, like the Sankey Commission, to enable energies hostile to Government and employers to be dissipated in fruitless talk and resolutions.

These diversionary tactics were accompanied by others more robust. A police strike in September 1918 was hastily appeased by a pay increase; but a second strike in London a year later against an official ban on membership of the National Union of Police and Prison Officers was unsuccessful, and was followed by the dismissal of the strikers; and when nearly 1,000 police struck in Liverpool in August 1919 troops were called in.

By the end of September 1919, a resolute attempt by the Government to impose wage reductions provoked a national rail strike. The appearance of a head-on clash between the Government and the powerful N.U.R. was underlined not merely by the fact that the Government retained its wartime control of the railways but by the peremptory attitude of Sir Eric Geddes, the Minister of Transport, and by the Prime Minister's description of the strike as an 'anarchist conspiracy'. *The Times* called for 'a fight to a finish', troops were called out, lorries were requisitioned and every effort was made to create the impression of a nation being organized to resist revolution. On this occasion, however, the Government overplayed its hand. The N.U.R. showed unexpected initiative by conducting an effective publicity campaign which included full-page newspaper advertisements and a propaganda film for the country's 'picture palaces'.

The strikers soon won a temporary victory. Within a week the Government had agreed to maintain existing wage rates and gave guarantees for full reinstatement of strikers without victimization. It was the most successful trade union achievement of the period; the credit was largely due to the N.U.R's general secretary, J. H. Thomas, M.P., for his astuteness in combining with the unprecedented publicity for the railwaymen's case a studied abstention from asking the other Triple Alliance unions to launch a sympathetic strike. This would have given substance to the Government's case that it was dealing with a nation-wide 'conspiracy'. By confining the contest strictly to the merits of the issues in dispute and by getting them expounded with so much success, Thomas, later to be so maligned, had rendered his followers a signal service.

If, as Beatrice Webb believed, the outcome of the railway strike was a defeat, not only for the Government, but also for the extremists who had looked to a great strike to signal the 'revolution', the affair of the *Jolly George* gave a contrary impression. In the spring of 1920, the Poles invaded Russia and in May captured Kiev in the Ukraine. Dockers at the East Indian Dock refused to permit the sailing of a freighter, the *Jolly George*, on the grounds that it was loaded with munitions for Poland; immediately thereafter the Dockers' Union, led by Ernest Bevin, later to be Attlee's Foreign Secretary, banned the loading of all munitions for use against the U.S.S.R. By the end of July, however, it was Warsaw that was in danger, owing to the Red Army's swift recovery from near-débâcle in the summer. On the face of it, it looked as if Central Europe's only military bastion against Bolshevism was about to be overrun; the British Government therefore sent the Soviets an ultimatum, demanding a halt to their advances. Promptly, the T.U.C. and the Labour Party threatened a general strike against 'any and every form of military and naval intervention' against Russia. A Council of Action was established to be in readiness to implement this policy, and local Councils of Action appeared in most large urban areas with the same object. Lenin later expressed the opinion that these Councils of Action had been Soviets in all but name.

The fact that there was no British intervention against Russia was widely believed to be the result of this dramatic working-class protest. In reality the halting of the Bolsheviks by the so-called 'Miracle of the Vistula' was due chiefly to the military skill of the Polish leader, Pilsudski, and the French General Weygand. Moreover, the readiness of the Bolsheviks to cede large tracts of Russian territory to Poland at the subsequent treaty of Riga suggests that their purpose in fighting the war was defensive.

Nevertheless, the whole affair was fraught with dangers. Lloyd George and Curzon were recklessly (and unnecessarily) over-playing the diplomatic game, given the intense war-weariness of the nation as a whole; and Lloyd George made matters worse by appearing to concede victory to his working-class tormentors by announcing, at the very last moment, that he had never intended to go to war at all. This merely reinforced the impression that 'direct action' had won a notable victory. It was indeed fortunate for the Government that the Councils of Action quickly disappeared from the scene.

While these heady gestures of defiance were being made on behalf of the Russian workers, the miners were once more arrayed for battle. They demanded wage increases, and a cut in the price of household coal, went on strike in October 1920, appealed for help from the Triple Alliance, and not for the last time failed to get it; once again, J. H. Thomas preferred to advocate conciliation rather than to thrust his N.U.R. forward into the firing-line. Disengagement seemed to him all the more urgent in view of the Government's swift passage of an Emergency Powers Act, which gave the authorities power to declare a state of emergency, to rule by decree (i.e. by Orders in Council) and to dispense with trial by jury. The miners ended the strike after a fortnight, on terms which gave them limited wage increases over an interim period of five months.

Before the five months were out, the brief post-war boom had collapsed, and the coal industry in particular faced a sharp fall in prices, aggravated by first deliveries by the Germans of reparations coal. The compulsion on the industry to demand wage decreases was so great that the Government evidently decided that it was politic to try to disentangle itself. It precipitately announced its intention to abandon State control of the mines before the end of March 1921. At the same time, the owners demanded that miners accept wage rates which, in real terms, would be below the 1914 figure, and the replacement of national wage regulations by the pre-war system of wage-fixing by districts. This would involve proportionately greater wage reductions for miners working in the less profitable pits. The miners' answer was the most widespread coal strike on record, and an appeal to the Triple Alliance for a sympathetic strike. The Government at once invoked the Emergency Powers Act. Troops were moved to mining areas, reservists were called up, and volunteers were embodied into a Defence Force which, if it had gone into action, might well have proved a home-based version of the Black and Tans operating at the same time in Ireland.

The coal strike had begun on 1 April 1921 and, after one postponement, the 'general' strike of railwaymen and transport workers was announced for midnight on 15 April. But on the afternoon of that day, thereafter known in trade union history as 'Black Friday', the Triple Alliance yet again drew back. There was no general strike; the miners were left to struggle on alone for two months and were then forced very largely to accept the owners' terms. A Government subsidy enabled the reductions to be a little less severe than those originally planned.

Since a general strike did in fact take place in 1926 there was a disposition to regard the leadership as courageous in that year but chicken-hearted in 1921. There are grounds for the opinion that its decision in 1921 was a good deal more sensible than that of 1926. At the last minute, the miners were offered by Lloyd George a temporary wage settlement pending further discussion on the subject of their objection to district wage-fixing. They had rejected it, in part because their secretary Frank Hodges had not consulted his executive in advance. This narrowed the issue to the point where a general strike seemed unjustified, not only to public opinion in general, but also to J. H. Thomas of the N.U.R., and Ernest Bevin of the Transport Workers, who accordingly made the miners' rejection of compromise an excuse for calling their sympathetic strike off. If the evasiveness of Thomas was perhaps characteristic of the only union leader to approach Lloyd George in deviousness, the objections of the formidable Ernest Bevin were grounded in the common-sense argument that the movement as a whole lacked the coherence of organization and purpose that were needed to challenge effectively a Government armed with the power and the will to resist.

The defeat of the miners marked the turn of the tide for the Government: the onset of the slump as well as the retreat on Black Friday meant that the morale of the unions was debilitated by fear of unemployment and their finances depleted by unemployment payments to out-of-work members. Engineering workers, shipyard workers, dockers, railwaymen and textile operatives all suffered wage reductions after Black Friday; yet, though in 1921 nearly 86,000,000 working days had been lost in strikes, in 1922, the last year of the Coalition, only 19,850,000 were lost, despite the fact that 1922 also saw a steady drop in real wages.

From the summer of 1921 onwards, the major industrial problem ceased to be the battle between organized employees and their bosses and became instead that of large-scale unemployment. By June 1921 there were over two million unemployed and throughout 1922 the figure hovered around 1½ million. It was never to fall lower (though it often rose much higher) for the remainder of the inter-war period.

The problem was seen by Government as primarily one of public order. Its task was in one sense made easier by the fact that the more spectacular organization of unemployed protests tended to be the work of the National Union of Unemployed Workers; but Wal Hannington, the leader of the N.U.U.W., was an avowed Communist. This deprived it of trade union support, so that although its demonstrations were frequently violent, its lack of funds prevented it from ever being much more than a propaganda movement throughout the 1920's and 1930's; and its Communist affiliations, together with the embattled indifference of the general public, doomed it even as a propaganda force.

The Coalition's chief response to the problem, however, was to create, on the limited and actuarially well-based foundation of the unemployment insurance scheme created in 1911, the elaborate, vexatious and pauperizing system of unemployment payments which came to be memorably, but not always quite accurately described as 'the dole'.

A number of new Unemployment Insurance Acts was passed between 1920 and 1922. The Act of 1920 extended unemployment insurance to all manual workers and non-manual workers (except agricultural labourers and domestic servants) earning under £250 a year. The 1920 Act proved inadequate for the long-term unemployment which first appeared in 1921. Both the 1911 and the 1920 Acts had been designed to deal with temporary unemployment, and the duration of the benefit was largely determined by how many stamps a man had on his insurance card: that is to say, unemployment benefit was actuarially related to contributions. When entitlement to unemployment insurance ceased (after a maximum of twenty-six weeks by 1921) the unemployed then became a charge on the local Poor Law Guardians, who got their funds from local Poor Law rates. This ceased to be possible once the unemployment figures rose: for there would be the greatest unemployment in precisely those Poor Law areas which, being hardest hit by the slump, could levy only the smallest poor rate. Moreover, the entire working class regarded going on poor relief (this was the legal sense of the phrase 'becoming a pauper') as an ultimate degradation.

In 1921, therefore, two fundamental changes of principle were introduced. By various Acts of that year it was established that the unemployed

could obtain from the labour exchanges (which handled all unemployment
insurance payments) what were called 'extended' or 'uncovenanted' benefits. These were financed by Treasury loans to the national unemployment
fund, and were thus poor relief 'doles' legally disguised as unemployment
benefit and financed not out of Poor Law rates but by national taxes.
This principle of disguised pauperization was further extended by the
introduction of additional payments for the dependants of the unemployed. The actual figures for 1920–21 are given below:

		in respect of:	
Benefit payable	to man	wife	each child
Nov. 1920	15s.	Nil	Nil
Mar. 1921	20s.	Nil	Nil
June 1921	15s.	Nil	Nil
Nov. 1921	15s.	5s.	1s.

The introduction of uncovenanted benefits and dependants' allowances
by no means eliminated recourse to the Poor Law; the total numbers
compelled to seek allowances from the Guardians varied in this period from
a quarter of a million to about a million. The scales varied from place to
place. The Labour-controlled council of the Metropolitan Borough of
Poplar insisted on the high outdoor relief payment of 33s. for a man and
wife; with the result that 'Poplarism' became for a time a vogue-word to
denote wasteful 'pampering' of the unemployed out of 'other people's
money'. The Poplar councillors achieved further notoriety by claiming
that the cost of this poor relief prevented the council from paying its
legally due quota of money to the L.C.C. This resulted in the councillors,
whose leader was the well-known Labour M.P., George Lansbury, being
sent to prison.

Thus early, therefore, Government policy had achieved the result of
diverting the attention, both of the general public and of the unemployed,
from the problem of unemployment itself to the altogether less socially
explosive issue of how much or, more accurately, how little, the unemployed
and their families needed to keep them from starvation. Twenty years of
social and political controversy were devoted to this basically sterile
matter. For bold constructive thinking about the fundamentals of economic
theory and practice there was substituted the dreary to-and-fro of charge
and counter-charge about the significance of an ever-increasing number of
technical terms and nice distinctions. Unemployment became an accepted
element in the national way of life, with a dreary but constantly changing
vocabulary of its own such as 'genuinely seeking work', the 'gap' and
'transitional benefit'; and it acquired academically nice distinctions like

those between unemployment benefit, unemployment assistance, and public assistance. And, with the coming of the 'means test' in the 1930's the real character of the problem was finally lost sight of in a bitter and unending controversy about a mass of petty regulations and major and minor inquisitions designed to measure with bureaucratic exactness the precise 'needs' and the precise 'means' of every unemployed workers' household. It is a commonplace that the dole staved off revolution; but it did not do so only by deadening the anger of the unemployed with small weekly injections of financial sedative; it did it also by diverting, to the insoluble and ultimately irrelevant problem of what was a 'just price' to pay a man who had no work, minds which would have been more fruitfully engaged in trying to discover how society could be so organized as to abolish long-term unemployment altogether.

The worsening condition of the economy in 1921 provoked a further step towards 'disciplining' a people who, in the current mythology, had enjoyed excessive wages during the war, and were demanding their continuance in peace and a lot of social services as well, despite the slump. The idea was sedulously encouraged in the popular Press that the employing class and the country faced bankruptcy owing to the 'squandermania' of the Government departments. Financial experts saw salvation only in 'remorseless' economy; and a committee of business-men under Sir Eric Geddes reported early in 1922 on the detailed implications of 'remorseless'. The Army, Navy and Air Force were to be reduced and so were war pensions. Education was to be cut, the State's contribution to unemployment benefit reduced and employment exchanges abolished. State help for the local authority maternity and child welfare services set up under the Coalition's own Maternity and Child Welfare Act of 1918 was also to be curtailed. Fortunately, the panic subsided and the Government blunted the force of the so-called Geddes 'Axe' before actually wielding it. Nevertheless the episode set the tone of much average thinking in the inter-war period, firmly establishing the idea that any expenditure on social welfare of any sort or on any kind of Government planning was certain to plunge the country into immediate bankruptcy. Rarely have wealthy people pleaded poverty with such monotonous and unjustifiable regularity as the well-to-do classes in England between the two wars.

The industrial and financial policies of the Coalition thus set the scene for a twenty-year 'cold war' between the rich and the poor in Britain; and in these respects, whatever changes it ushered in others, the fall of the Coalition was to make little fundamental difference. After 1922, more lip service was paid to the possibility, or at any rate desirability, of a kind of peaceful co-existence between the employed and the employing; but it remained the standard practice till after 1939 that every economic difficulty should be met by an attack on the economically weak and the socially under-privileged; and the philosophy of the Geddes Axe, that since

Government action always cost money there should if possible be no positive Government action at all, was rarely departed from and then only grudgingly or for electoral purposes.

The latter years of the war had, as has been shown earlier, been accompanied by a great increase in the number of Government departments, boards and commissions. Potentially even more important, perhaps, were the innumerable committees reporting to the Ministry of Reconstruction established in 1917. Composed of large numbers of social workers, public officials and politicians of all parties, they were busily engaged in reporting on the future of local government, education, housing, electricity and agriculture. One committee, under Lord Haldane, proposed a complete reorganization and streamlining of the main Government departments. There was thus available when the war ended an ample supply of blueprints for that systematic 'modernization' of the management of the nation's affairs for which more energetic minds in all political parties continued to call throughout the succeeding half-century. Little emerged, however, chiefly because full implementation would have involved both nationalization and an increase in the power of the Civil Service; and the moment the war ended there sprang up (or was worked up) a violent hatred of all forms of Government control, reaching its climax, as has been shown, in the Geddes 'Axe'. The agitation was so great that the Government rapidly abandoned most of its schemes and in this, as in so many other respects, established the main pattern of policy for the whole inter-war period. A rigidly doctrinaire cleavage was artificially created between those who wanted more State control and those who opposed it; and since the Labour Party made nationalization its official policy, and State direction of industry was most noticeable in the emergent Communist régime in Russia, all advocates of fairly similar techniques in Great Britain were willy-nilly labelled Socialist and vulnerable to the charge of being crypto-Communists. Even those whose social or political affiliations made such labels inappropriate usually found themselves excluded from major participation in national affairs. In consequence, a problem of public administration became a matter for political passion regardless of the fact that in practice the Labour Party liked nationalization less than it pretended, while its opponents put a good deal of State control into practice while vehemently preaching against all forms of it.

Thus, the Coalition's flight from bureaucracy and planning was not complete. Five new Government departments survived: the Ministries of Air, and of Pensions were not disbanded after the war, and the Ministries of Health and of Labour were set up in 1918; 1919 and 1920 saw the permanent establishment also of the Forestry Commission (1919) and the Medical Research Council (1920); and in 1919 the Electricity Commission was set up, though complete nationalization of supply and distribution throughout the country had seemed certain. Equally certain had seemed railway nationalization, a policy which by this time had already received the blessing of such unimpeachable anti-Socialists as W. E. Gladstone and Winston Churchill. What emerged instead was the abandonment of wartime Government control in 1921 and an amalgamation scheme under the Railways Act of 1921, sponsored by the Ministry of Transport. This created the four great systems which survived as private companies until nationalization in 1948: the Great Western, the Southern, the London Midland and Scottish and the London and North-Eastern.

In spite of the best efforts of the opponents of 'squandermania' and 'bungling officialdom' the Civil Service in the 1920's was just over twice as large as before 1914. In the same way, quasi-theological detestation of State welfare services also failed to gain all its objectives, and just as the Coalition failed to prevent the growth of 'the servile state' so did it fail to prevent the growth of 'the eleemosynary state'. This was most clearly to be seen in the Unemployment Insurance Acts, which increasingly became a matter of subsistence payments to the unemployed out of public funds. It was seen also in the establishment of State Scholarships to the Universities by the Board of Education under Fisher in 1920, although these were withdrawn under the Geddes Axe and not resumed until the advent of the first Labour ministry in 1924.

The most striking example, however, was seen in housing. The new Ministry of Health, under Christopher Addison, produced the Addison Housing Acts of 1919. Local authorities were encouraged by Government grants or subsidies to build 'council houses' to be let at less than the 'economic' rent. The financial arrangements by which the Ministry assisted the local authorities proved unsatisfactory and Addison was removed from his post, though not from the Government, as a 'failure'. Nevertheless, despite, the economies which resulted from the Geddes Axe, about 200,000 council houses were built in the four years after the war and the principle thus established became a permanent feature of social policy. Like the dole, council houses were greatly resented by the classes who did not need them but were compelled to help pay for them through increased local rates and through Government taxation: two recurrent axioms about the working class in the small talk of the more well-to-do were that many of the unemployed were unemployable, and that if bathrooms were put in council houses the tenants would use them to keep the coals in. Council houses were also criticized, often justifiably, as poky, and even more justifiably as too few in number. They were also criticized on aesthetic grounds by persons too concerned with external appearance (i.e. their effect on the sensitive beholder) to recognize the superiority of council-house interiors to anything previously available to those who actually lived in them. They were unhesitatingly condemned as 'the slums of the future'; a verdict for which forty years later there was little justification. A state-subsidized housing policy, whatever its limitations and incidental injustices, was the only way of meeting the fact that private enterprise could not then provide housing of a socially acceptable standard for the large section of the population who could only afford to rent its living accommodation. In this field, therefore, the Coalition once again set in motion trends which, though unpopular with its supporters, were not to be reversed by its successors.

The involved history of statutory rent restriction had been begun by Rent Acts in 1915 and 1920; in general, these Acts either protected existing tenants of working-class homes against rent-increases by their landlords, or set a limit to the increases. Like subsidized local authority housing, rent restriction on certain types of property continued through the next few decades, and no major incursion into the system was made until the Rent Act of 1957.

The Coalition also made a tentative move towards a protective tariff, though the issue of Free Trade and Protection remained a politically explosive one for a Government with Coalition Liberals in its ranks. Accordingly, the Safeguarding of Industries Act of 1921, which imposed duties of 33⅓ per cent on imports from countries outside the Empire, applied chiefly only to chemicals and certain electrical products. Once again, however, future tendencies were being revealed.

Among other legislative enactments of the Coalition was the Act of 1919 disestablishing the Anglican Church of Wales, and an Act of the same year setting up the Church Assembly of the Anglican Church. At the end of 1919 the Sex Disqualification Removal Act allowed women to stand for Parliament.

11 · Terror in Ireland, 1916-23

When war began in 1914 Asquith's Government had sought to put the problem of Ireland into cold storage. The third Home Rule Bill had been put on the statute book, but its operation postponed for the duration of the war. Redmond's acceptance of this on behalf of the Irish Nationalist Party, and the immediate concentration of the Unionist Party on the issues of the continental war, appeared on the surface to hold promise of a period if not of peace at least of suspended animation in Ireland.

Unfortunately the appearance in the North of the Ulster Volunteers and in the South of the Irish Volunteers had deepened the abiding Irish conviction that Irish issues could be decided only by the use of force. There were grounds for the view that it had been the threat of force by Ulster rather than the outbreak of a continental war that had postponed Home Rule for all-Ireland; and for the view that Redmond had committed a tactical error in capitulating to the English at the moment of England's maximum weakness. Since, therefore, Redmond and his parliamentary followers had behaved as patriotic members of a United Kingdom they lost the support of those whose aim was to end Ireland's participation in that unity. With traditional Irish leadership in abeyance and with large numbers of the least fanatical Irishmen enlisting in Kitchener's armies, power in Ireland itself passed into the hands of what at the outset was a fanatical minority dominated by Sinn Fein, a group founded by Arthur Griffith in 1904, and determined on a more thorough separation of Ireland from England than was implied by a Home Rule Bill. In 1916, Sinn Fein and the Irish Volunteers staged the Easter Rebellion, originally intended to follow the successful landing of German arms. The landing was prevented, and Sir Roger Casement, a former British Consular official who had been active in securing German support, was captured and later executed for treason. Notwithstanding Casement's capture, the Easter Rebellion took place in Dublin, the rebels proclaiming an Irish Republic. Although the rising failed, it led to hundreds of casualties and thousands of arrests. Fifteen of the leaders, mostly young men, were subsequently tried and shot. Eamonn De Valera, one of the most successful officers in the rising, was imprisoned instead of being shot, owing to his possession of a United States passport.

To the English, the issues in the Easter Rising were simple; citizens of the United Kingdom had committed an act of rebellion and Casement had been guilty of association with the King's enemies in the middle of a terrible war. The facts that only a handful of the rebels had been executed, and that the majority of those captured had been imprisoned, testified to England's moderation and humanity. The only complicating issue for Englishmen was United States opinion, which was notorious for its high moral tone on the subject of British Imperialism and above all over Ireland, if only because of the large Irish element in the eastern states of the U.S.A. It was for this reason that De Valera escaped execution and that somewhat questionable tactics were adopted by the British legal authorities to denigrate Casement's moral character in order to disqualify him, if possible, for the martyr's crown he so clearly desired.

Fewer consequences for evil might have flowed from the events of Easter 1916, and the deaths of these pitiable young martyrs might have been less futile, had it been found possible to resist Unionist obstruction at home. With creditable courage, Asquith made one more attempt to get reason to prevail and, adopting his favourite expedient in time of trouble, authorized Lloyd George to work for a settlement. Lloyd George proposed to the Unionists and the Irish Nationalists a compromise by which there should, as a temporary measure, be Home Rule for the South, no change in the status of Ulster, and a continuation of full Irish representation at Westminster. The question of a permanent settlement should be left to a post-war Imperial Conference. The proposals were as ingenious as might have been expected of their author, and although Sinn Fein would not have accepted them, Carson did. The majority of Unionist leaders would not, however. They preferred to advocate repression in Ireland and the continued denial of Home Rule. The last opportunity of winning over moderate Irish opinion and of detaching the Southern Irish from Sinn Fein was thus let slip. In famous words, the Irish poet, W. B. Yeats, said of the Easter Rising, 'a terrible beauty is born'. In the years that followed the terror was real enough; the 'beauty' was chiefly a poetic fiction.

Unionist extremism did much to obstruct a renewed attempt at compromise with the Irish Nationalists, and was in part responsible for the belated attempt to impose conscription on Ireland in 1918. Instead of drawing young men away from Sinn Fein, as the Unionists had expected, it drew them into it. If patriotism was the right thing for the able-bodied youth of all other European nations it was equally right for the youth of Ireland. To join the Irish Volunteers combined the two great advantages: it made a man a patriot and it enabled him to avoid the horror of the Western Front. To put matters even more in the hands of extremists, the Government imprisoned most Sinn Fein leaders in May 1918.

In the 'Coupon Election' only six Irish Nationalists were elected to Westminster; the 73 other seats in Ireland outside Ulster were won by Sinn Feiners. They refused to take their places at Westminster and instead constituted themselves as an Irish Parliament or Dail Eireann. They proclaimed an independent Irish Republic and appealed to the peacemakers at Paris to give them the national recognition that was being so freely accorded to Poles, Czechs and Jugoslavs (but which was, they might have noted, being withheld from the Egyptians, and being withdrawn from the Arabs).

During the first half of 1919 Sinn Fein prepared for the task of destroying British authority in Ireland. After his escape from Lincoln jail had been contrived by Michael Collins, Sinn Fein's master of escapology, intelligence and sabotage, De Valera went on a propaganda tour of the United States. Although he was soon involved in a fierce quarrel with some sections of Irish American opinion, he secured much American financial support and roused anti-English feeling in the United States to an exceptional degree. In Ireland itself, Collins and Griffith raised funds, trained and organized terrorists, and undertook widespread acts of violence and sabotage; and by irresistible pressure made it impossible for the Irish police (the Royal Irish Constabulary) to secure local recruits.

In August 1919, Sinn Fein and the Dail were both declared illegal by the British Government. The Metropolitan Police Commissioner was made Commander-in-Chief in Ireland. The R.I.C. was reinforced by well-paid volunteer ex-soldiers from England, known, from their black belts and khaki uniforms, as 'the Black and Tans'. An Auxiliary Division of the R.I.C. was also recruited from British ex-army officers. Both the Black and Tans and the Auxiliaries were ill-disciplined and irresponsible. There followed a bitter struggle between British troops and the R.I.C. on one side, and the I.R.A. on the other, which was at its worst from the spring of 1920 until the summer of 1921. There were many acts of brutality both by the Black and Tans and by the I.R.A., though the excesses of the Black and Tans were much more widely publicized in Ireland, England and overseas than those of the I.R.A. This was inevitable in the mental atmosphere of the times; self-determination of peoples was the fashionable principle of all political thinking outside the rarefied regions of official diplomacy, and the war only recently won had been fought for the rights of small nations. No action more likely to outrage the public conscience of the civilized world could have been undertaken than the Coalition's attempt violently to put down what almost everybody, outside the ranks of the extreme sections of the Unionist Party, regarded as the legitimate desire of the Irish for national independence.

Only the multiplicity of Lloyd George's preoccupations at this time can provide an excuse for his Irish policy. There was, of course, still one valid principle for which the Coalition was perforce sole trustee, namely the safeguarding of the Ulster minority in the north; and ultimately the Imperial Government alone had sufficient power to protect that minority. Yet, during 'the Troubles', as they were called, very little was heard of the need to protect Ulster, and it would be difficult to sustain the plea that in its operations against the South, the Government's agents were solely, or even principally, actuated by concern for Ulster. Nor was it a matter of the maintenance of law and order; what was manifestly at issue was the maintenance of British sovereignty.

While the fighting continued, however, the Coalition took the first steps in the direction of reason. The Government of Ireland Act, 1920, provided for Irish Home Rule, with two Irish Parliaments, one for the South at Dublin and the other, at Belfast, for the six most Protestant counties of the historic province of Ulster. The possibility of eventual unity was to be provided for by a Council of Ireland in which both Parliaments would be represented. Both parts of Ireland would remain within the United Kingdom and continue to have representation at Westminster.

The Bill satisfied nobody, since Ulster had never wanted separation from England. Nevertheless, with a bad grace, Ulster accepted; but only after a ruthless communal war against the region's Roman Catholic minority, to make certain that Sinn Fein would have no 'fifth column' north of the border.

Sinn Fein and the I.R.A. ignored completely an Act which partitioned Ireland and kept both parts of the country inside the United Kingdom. Sinn Fein wanted complete independence of the British Crown, and complete control, not only of the South, but of Protestant Ulster as well. In the months after the passing of the Act, British civil authority virtually ceased to operate in Southern Ireland; but armed action by the English continued, and Lloyd George declared publicly, 'we have murder by the throat'.

By the spring of 1921, however, pressure was being brought to bear on the Government from all quarters. The Press, including, for a variety of reasons, both the *Daily Mail* and *The Times* as well as the Liberal dailies, was increasingly hostile to the policy of repression; the Archbishop of Canterbury, as well as many influential Conservatives, also pronounced against it, as did a Labour Party commission on Ireland; and these elements were reinforced by General Smuts. Consciousness of the damage being done to Anglo-United States relations was also growing. At this time, too, George V felt called upon to remind the Government that Irishmen were also his subjects and ought not to be ill-treated by undisciplined Black and Tans. (This royal concern was to be paralleled later in the year when, with staggering common sense, he informed the Prime Minster that what the unemployed really wanted was neither charity, nor the dole, but work.) Over the Irish issue the King acted eagerly on a suggestion made to him by Smuts that he use his State Opening of the first Northern Ireland Parliament under the 1920 Act as the opportunity for an appeal for sanity and reconciliation. After a certain amount of prodding, Lloyd George saw to it that the King was duly provided with the sort of speech Smuts had suggested. It made a considerable impression, not least, perhaps, because of George V's manifest sincerity and good will; and he urged the Government not to miss the opportunity apparently provided by this possibly brief moment of relaxation. In his most soothing manner Lloyd George replied (truthfully) that the matter was in hand. In fact, secret negotiations for a truce had been going on through various intermediaries since the end of 1920; and a cease-fire was eventually arranged in July 1921.

In order to obtain a settlement, Lloyd George had to get the partition of Ireland accepted both by Sinn Fein and by the Conservatives, even though both groups were still officially committed to the unity of Ireland. Sinn Fein wanted all of it to be an independent State ruled from Dublin, the Conservatives wanted all of it to be ruled from Westminster. Quite apart from political considerations, both parties thought that the division of Ireland was ultimately impracticable. Lloyd George, however, was determined to make Sinn Fein forgo control of Ulster and to make them accept Dominion status, and thus abandon their aim of an independent, undivided Irish republic; and he would make the Conservatives agree to the abandonment of British rule over Southern Ireland as the inescapable price for safeguarding the rights of Ulster. Since neither Sinn Fein nor the majority of rank and file Conservatives had so far shown any disposition to compromise, this was a major undertaking. Lloyd George proved equal to it.

In the first place, the methods adopted by the Black and Tans in Ireland had discredited the policy of repression even among those who had advocated it. Sir Henry Wilson, still the most ardent of Unionists, was greatly angered by the use of the Black and Tans, and insisted that unless the Government used the regular army in a properly conducted military campaign against Sinn Fein, it should abandon repression altogether. It was necessary, he said, to 'go all out or get out'. But, by the summer of 1921, it was no longer possible to 'go all out' in Ireland. By accident or design, Lloyd George's policy during the 'Troubles' had discredited the use of force altogether, and had pushed things to the point where all that the Conservatives had left to save from the wreck of their Irish policy was the separate status of Ulster and the unity of their own party. In the outcome, Lloyd George saved Ulster for them; but the unity and morale of the Conservative Party were shattered in the process, and for this Lloyd George was never forgiven.

His method of breaking Conservative resistance to a settlement was to suborn its leaders. This task had already been facilitated by the retirement of Bonar Law from the Government in March 1921. The official reason was his failing health: but there were suspicions that his real reason had been to avoid involvement in the inevitable compromise over Ireland. Leadership of the party had then passed to Austen Chamberlain, and his loyalty to Lloyd George was such that the latter was able freely to manœuvre for the support of the other important Tories. Principally, he secured the support of Lord Birkenhead, the Lord Chancellor, who played a major part both in securing Tory acquiescence and in the negotiations for the final 'treaty' with Sinn Fein.

To complete his team, Lloyd George won over his only outstanding Liberal Cabinet Minister, Winston Churchill, whose relations with the Prime Minister had been growing more and more acrimonious over a wide variety of domestic, colonial and imperial issues. Churchill had been a strong advocate of coercion in Ireland, but the prospect of joining Birkenhead and Austen Chamberlain in the execution of a major act of policy proved irresistible. Lloyd George also had the uncovenanted boon of Lord Beaverbrook's support on this issue. This not only gave the Prime Minister valuable Press backing but a useful intermediary for dealing with the still obdurate Bonar Law, over whom Beaverbrook had a great personal ascendancy. Bonar Law was not, however, to be moved from his opposition; and this gave Lloyd George the opportunity to play his most formidable card, a threat of resignation. This would have caught the Tories so hopelessly divided that the threat was enough both to disarm the Prime Minister's enemies and to stimulate his supporters.

In his negotiations with Sinn Fein, Lloyd George probably served the cause of the unrepresented Ulstermen more successfully than any of its accredited spokesmen. He browbeat Collins and Griffith into accepting an agreement which gave Northern Ireland the option to withdraw from the proposed Irish Free State (this, of course, happened at once) and which left the definition of the consequent boundaries for subsequent discussion. Lloyd George unscrupulously promised that the proposed Boundary Commission would so limit the area of Northern Ireland that it would be economically incapable of separate existence. But, in the strain of the final stages, all that Sinn Fein got out of him was a formula of conspicuous ambiguity, which by 1925 had been interpreted in a manner entirely favourable to Northern Ireland, whose 1920 boundaries were then made permanent.

Sinn Fein had lost on this issue not only because of Lloyd George's final dramatic threat of all-out war. It was also because they were entangled to the very end in their forlorn struggle to secure the principle of a republic. It was against this that Lloyd George had all along been fighting, using all his skill to persuade the Irishmen that acceptance of Dominion status, for all that it involved an oath of allegiance to the Crown, gave them the reality of independence. Collins and Griffith might have been less obstinate had 'Dominion status' and the phrase 'British Commonwealth of Nations' not then been relatively novel terms. As it was, over a quarter of a century later, when it was already clear that these terms were indeed compatible with genuine independence, they were still unacceptable to Indians. In 1921, however, the British Government appeared ready to impose its choice of terminology by force and Lloyd George beat the Irish because he made them believe that force would in fact be used. Collins and Griffith had, therefore, to give up Northern Ireland and accept both membership of the British Commonwealth and an oath of allegiance to the Crown. They were also committed to Britain's use of certain 'treaty' ports; and there was no concession, therefore, to the original Sinn Fein demand for the right to be neutral in time of war.

The Anglo Irish 'treaty' of 1921 was regarded as Lloyd George's most remarkable personal achievement. His handling of the affair certainly revealed many of his most characteristic qualities: the astute combination of bluff and charm, cunning and threats in difficult negotiations. Moreover, for all its imperfections and dubieties the 'treaty' provided a fair and reasonable settlement, which guaranteed the independence of the South without sacrificing the rights of the North. If Lloyd George's methods of getting it, like his original recourse to violence, are open to question the quality of the achievement itself is not. All the tendencies of the previous seventy-five years had been towards either a crude nationalism that suppressed minorities or a crude imperialism that ignored nations. The Irish 'treaty' achieved a fair balance between the claims of a nation, the rights of a minority and the pride of an empire: it would be difficult to say as much of most other settlements of national issues.

Naturally, therefore, those who made the settlement were soon repudiated. Collins and Griffith, and other Irish supporters of the treaty, faced civil war at the hands of those who still demanded a republic and the right to coerce Ulster. In less than a year, Griffith was dead, Collins murdered and Lloyd George driven from office.

12 · Peace Making in Europe, 1919-22

Those who represented Britain at the peace conference were united by one idea, consciously or unconsciously held: that Britain's responsibilities to the Empire and Commonwealth made military involvement in Europe wholly undesirable. The close ties with France, developed since 1904, were outside the traditions of British policy, not because that policy had previously been characterized by hostility to France, but because they were a departure from the principle that Britain should not be committed to any continental Power. The total military commitment against Germany, which had cost the Empire nearly a million lives between 1914 and 1918, was something the British wished never to resume. In that conviction they were supported by the Dominions, whose independent stature was attested by their separate representation at the Paris conference. The real desire of Britain and the Dominions in 1919 was to reverse the trend of British foreign policy since 1904 and to return to the days of splendid isolation; and it is worth repeating that, for all Salisbury's dislike of that phrase, its popular success had indicated how well it expressed the deeper wishes of the nation at large. Nor is it without significance that its first public utterance had come from a Canadian. The provenance of the phrase was a reminder that the Dominions, as they advanced towards independent international status, would inevitably desire to pull the United Kingdom away from Europe.

This awareness of imperial responsibilities, or at least the dislike of European commitments which those responsibilities implied, explains the apparent weaknesses and contradictions of British policy at the Paris peace conference, and throughout the period between the wars. It is true that this awareness was not often given public expression. Those politicians and Service chiefs who adhered to it, like the one or two popular newspapers that proclaimed it, were either not listened to, or were laughed at, by thoughtful people of most political affiliations. Yet Liberal ideas of international co-operation, whether through free trade in the nineteenth century, or through collective security in the twentieth, took deep root neither among official policy-makers nor in the minds of Englishmen in general. To believe otherwise is to ignore the evidence. The only important ceremonial spectacle put on for the British public in the 1920's was a British Empire Exhibition, held at Wembley in 1924 and 1925; true, it made very little money and its only permanent legacy was a football stadium; but it expressed an attitude very different from that expressed when, also six years after a great war's end, the authorities arranged the exhibition of 1951, as part of what was called, so much more modestly, the Festival of Britain. Students of the between-war period ought not, like the serious people of the time itself, to derive nothing but a sense of superiority from the fact that the best-selling mass-circulation newspaper of the 1920's was the *Daily Mail*, which constantly railed at supporters of the League of Nations as 'lovers of every country but their own'; or from the fact that, by 1939, the circulation race had been won by the *Daily Express*, which continuously preached Empire Free Trade and which carried the idea of isolation from Europe to the limits of promising its readers in 1939 'there will be no war in Europe this year'. Perhaps the most important piece of evidence is the strong popular support for the Eden Government's attack on Egypt in the Suez crisis of 1956, by which date all enlightened people had supposed, in their blinkered way, that this sort of thing had died out, if not with Palmerston, at any rate with Sir Garnet Wolseley.

The desire for a return, if possible, to isolation from Europe had become almost an imperial necessity by 1919. Henceforth, the United Kingdom Government could mobilize materially and morally for war only with the consent of the now effectively independent Dominions. More than that, the responsibilities of Empire were increased by the war. The growth of national sentiment was already evident in Egypt and in India, rendering the British position in both less easy to maintain. The collapse of Germany and Turkey, and the potential enmity of Bolshevik Russia, led to the acquisition by the British of new power and responsibilities throughout that area of the Middle East from which they had driven the Turks. In these circumstances, it was a matter of elementary prudence for the British to seek a settlement of Europe that minimized, if it could not eliminate, the possibility of future British involvement. These considerations, strong in the minds of the Empire's leading representatives at the peace conference, were reinforced by another, becoming ever stronger as time went by. This was a revulsion from the mere thought of another war like the one just ended.

There was thus, at bottom, a coincidence of aim between sections of the community who on the surface seemed bitterly opposed. Those M.P.s who tried to force Lloyd George's hand by calling for 'Hanging the Kaiser' and by insisting on impossibly exorbitant reparations were demanding a Carthaginian peace so that never again would Britain be called aside from her true imperial destiny by the bloody necessities of European war. When, less than twenty years later, men, most of them of like political allegiance, cheered the appeasement of Hitler at Munich, they were not being inconsistent. Wanting to 'Hang the Kaiser' or 'Squeeze the Germans' and wanting to mutilate Czechoslovakia were different manifestations of the same desire to secure peace in Europe at any price that Europeans could be made to pay. It would be difficult to find in the period between the wars any section of the British community, outside the Churchill entourage and a small group of Foreign Office Francophils, that was not, as far as Europe was concerned, almost entirely pacifist. In 1933 the Oxford Union Society voted against fighting for King and Country (i.e. against volunteering for another Kitchener's Army); in 1938 almost the whole country, by a great plebiscite of applause for Neville Chamberlain, voted in exactly the same way.

Britain's 'real' interests at the end of the war (the interests, that is, of Britain as an imperial power) were, as Clemenceau frequently took angry pleasure in reminding Lloyd George, fully satisfied. Germany handed over her fleet and lost all her colonies, most of them coming under the control (through the mandate system) of member-States of the British Empire. In Europe itself, as the Foreign Office firmly asserted, Britain had no territorial interest. There was only the negative aim of helping to achieve a settlement that would be not only stable but self-perpetuating: the nature of the new Europe must be such that it would not require British action to preserve it.

To assist him in his approach to peacemaking Lloyd George suffered from no lack of advice. Balfour had been Foreign Secretary since 1916, and he and his advisers had given long and at times profound thought to the European problem. There were also many committees of civilian and military experts, arming themselves with data on every aspect of each of the many problems that called for attention. The leading Dominion statesmen also formed part of the British Empire delegation, and Smuts of South Africa was always at hand with advice, most of it impressively pessimistic. In addition, Lloyd George had a staff of personal advisers of his own for foreign affairs, led by Philip Kerr, later Lord Lothian. These were attached to the Prime Minister's personal secretariat, which was known to his enemies as 'the garden suburb', from having its London headquarters in temporary huts in the garden of 10 Downing Street.

There were, as always among those working in association with Lloyd George, bitter complaints about the Prime Minister's failure to co-ordinate these many sources of information or to consult those who, by virtue of their appointments or their expert knowledge, expected to be consulted. The result has been to create an impression of levity and irresponsibility in Lloyd George's handling of the great issues of the conference which is probably unjust, above all if it is remembered that policies suggested to him from United Kingdom or Dominion sources could only be implemented after they had been submitted to the almost invariably hostile scrutiny of President Wilson and Clemenceau. At no time, whether in small things or great, was Lloyd George the man to be confined by a system; and he was often so much more mentally agile than his advisers that his thought-processes were too swift for them. Moreover, the subject-matter of the conference, wide-ranging as it was, was of immense complexity and had to be handled at speed and with extreme skill. Lloyd George never adhered to the almost sacred English principle that nothing may be done except after long committee meetings, 'where,' as Churchill later wrote, 'everything is settled for the greatest good of the greatest number by the common sense of most after the consultation of all'.[1] By contrast, Balfour said of what happened in Paris, 'at this conference all important business is transacted in the intervals of transacting other business'. Perhaps this was inevitable. Mountains of advice had to be cut through, chasms of misunderstanding had to be bridged, crevasses of disagreement were for ever requiring to be jumped or circumvented. If, in coping with these hazards, Lloyd George used unorthodox methods without pausing to defer either to all the experts or to all his colleagues this is perhaps due less to his wickedness than to his ability.

Before and during the conference there was long and searching examination of the kind of Europe that would best meet the overriding imperial requirement that it could maintain and defend itself without active British assistance or ultimate British military intervention. The Foreign Office had been in the forefront in the planning of a League of Nations, and there was no dissension with the United States on this issue, though it has to be remembered that while the peace was in the making it was envisaged as a League of Nations of which the United States would be a member. It was recognized, however, that the League's authority in its infancy would not be strong. Unless and until it could prove itself, it seemed essential to base the European system either on the balance of power or on the principle of nationality. Whichever principle was adopted, the object would be to prevent Germany dominating western Europe, since this was likely to involve the British in a war to preserve the independence of France and Belgium. It was also necessary to set limits to German pressure on south-eastern Europe, since this would, in the long run, con-

[1] W. S. Churchill, *The Gathering Storm*, p. 404.

stitute a threat to Asia Minor, Egypt, the Persian Gulf and the route to India.

Before the implications of the Russian revolution became apparent, expert British opinion had tended to favour a revival of Russian power as a counter to Germany in the east. The threat of Bolshevism produced an emphasis instead on the principle of nationality. This could be invoked to justify the establishment of a group of independent nations – Poland, Czechoslovakia, Jugoslavia and German-Austria – to bar the way to a future German *Drang nach Osten*. Some of these States, together with Roumania and the newly liberated States of Finland, Estonia, Latvia and Lithuania, would also be what the French called a *cordon sanitaire* protecting Europe from Bolshevism. Some of Lloyd George's Foreign Office advisers also considered that a Europe based on the nationalities would be more stable than the old pre-war empires, each of which had been made unstable by its own minorities or restless by their sympathy with kindred minorities outside its borders.

Generally speaking, the French and United States delegations were enthusiastic about setting up the new small States, the French because they would weaken the Germans, the United States on moral and ideological grounds. By contrast, both Balfour and Smuts were hostile to what the latter rather foolishly called the 'Balkanization' of Europe. Both feared that the new States would be badly governed and be an incitement to Germany to attack them. Lloyd George inclined more to the views of Balfour and Smuts than those of Clemenceau and Wilson, but for a severely practical reason. He seems to have felt that what really mattered was whether or not the new system was compatible with the eventual re-establishment of reasonable relations between the victors and the Germans. Accordingly, he clung with quite unusual persistence to the view that the peace settlement must not impose on Germany terms that were manifestly unjust, lest the other Great Powers (and the British Dominions) found it morally and politically impossible to enforce them if Germany, at some future date, decided to break them. Thus, over the size of the new Poland, over the Saar, the Rhineland, and the scope of reparations, Lloyd George intervened repeatedly and sometimes successfully, to secure modifications in Germany's favour. He several times warned his fellow-peacemakers against imposing terms so severe that the Germans would refuse to sign them; when the Germans were presented with the terms and protested about them, he continued to warn; and more than once he put to his allies the question which sums up so many of the dilemmas which were to come: when the passions of this present time have receded can you imagine your people marching against Germany to maintain these terms?

He could not, however, pursue this policy too far. What if, in spite of everything, the new European States-system failed to be self-perpetuating? Peace, and the restraint of Germany, could then be secured only by obtaining permanently the co-operation of both France and the United States. For this reason he could not exceed certain limits in opposing the wishes of either. He could not consistently support France in an anti-German policy without alienating the United States; but he could not consistently support the United States against France because of the gnawing possibility (so soon to become fact) that the United States would revert to isolationism. The Welsh juggler had to try to keep all three balls in the air. If he dropped one, the whole enterprise would collapse. But it is not surprising that even close observers of the Prime Minister were too bewildered by the juggling to see the principles upon which it was based.

Two factors prevented Lloyd George acquiring at Paris the ascendancy to which his percipience perhaps entitled him. One was, as so often with him, the personal factor. Lloyd George never acquired that stock-in-trade of the normal politician, *gravitas*. When Castlereagh had said of the peacemaking of 1814–15, 'It is not our business to collect trophies of war but to bring the world back to habits of peace,' he commanded respect because the words were uttered by an austere English *milord* whose whole bearing and manner of life clothed them in sincerity; whenever Lloyd George said anything, sophisticated persons instantly suspected him of trying to fool somebody. So it is that Balfour and Smuts emerged from their equivocal careers, and from the peace conference in particular, as men of profound wisdom; but Lloyd George ended both with a reputation for charlatanism.

The second factor is more important: no British statesman could now dominate the world stage as a Castlereagh or a Palmerston had done. Naval supremacy, financial supremacy and industrial supremacy, the essential equipment for world-domination were now at the command, not of a British statesman, but of Woodrow Wilson; but Wilson lacked the ability to use them. He was deficient in understanding, not well served by his experts, and about to be repudiated by his country. Yet Wilson's personal deficiencies could not disguise the reality: if the United States did not take charge of the conference, and the system it created, nobody else could. Much breath and much ink were wasted in England from 1919 onwards by persons, by no means all of them on the Right, who failed to recognize that there could no longer be such a thing as a *Pax Britannica*. True, Lloyd George had one asset which he seems have exploited less than he might have done: the magnitude of the British military and naval contribution to the defeat of Germany, to the salvation of France and the preservation of the United States. This entitled the Empire to more influence at the conference than Lloyd George in the end obtained for it; but he had little or no sense of the past and took no pleasure in the pomp and circumstance of war. He quickly put both behind him and tried only to chart a tentative course for an uncertain future.

This attitude is seen in his co-operation with the United States to cut down French demands on Germany's western frontier. He would have nothing to do with the demand of Foch that the French frontier should be extended to the Rhine by the annexation of German territory. He rejected also the French demand that an area east and west of the Rhine be detached from Germany to form an independent buffer state regardless of the wishes of the area's inhabitants. He insisted that neither Britain nor the Dominions would fight to preserve such a buffer state. When the French next demanded a long-term Allied occupation of the Rhineland, Lloyd George joined with Wilson in demanding a limited occupation and eventually secured to the Germans their control of the zone's civilian affairs. Not to press the French too far, he then proposed a British-United States treaty of military guarantee. Thus, it seemed, he could avoid giving the Germans the legitimate battle-cry of 'Give us back the Rhineland', but yet face them with the permanent obstacle to aggression of a threefold military alliance. Even here, Lloyd George reinsured himself against over-commitment: the British guarantee was contingent upon the United States guarantee, and when the latter failed to materialize, the British offer lapsed also. Yet, in securing Wilson's agreement to the guarantee in

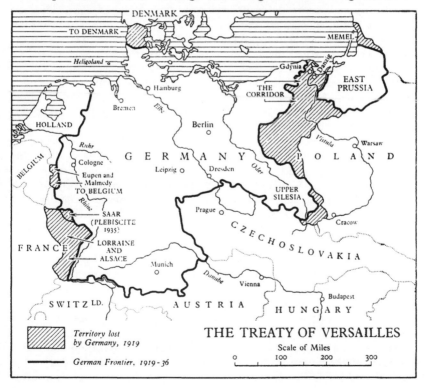

THE TREATY OF VERSAILLES

Territory lost by Germany, 1919

German Frontier, 1919-36

Scale of Miles
0   100   200   300

the first place, he had achieved what might well have been a major diplomatic victory and a revolution in world politics; but the manœuvre was a warning that without United States co-operation, Britain would be unlikely to intervene in continental affairs again. It was significant also that, as drafted, the British guarantee provided that no Dominion would be associated with its implementation without prior consent.

On the matter of reparations, Lloyd George also endeavoured, in the end, to leave the problem open for decision by his proposition that the final assessment of Germany's liability be postponed to a later date. This was, of course, an ultimately unsuccessful attempt to make the best of a badly-bungled job. Lloyd George had failed to resist exaggerated ideas about the amount that Germany could pay, and faced hostility at home whenever it seemed apparent that the conference was trying to set limits to its demands on Germany. Worse still, the conference prefaced the relevant section of the treaty with articles justifying reparations on the grounds of Germany's 'war guilt'. The result was to obscure the issue with years of embittered argument.

Over the Saar, some members of the British delegation approved the original French demand for its full cession to France but, reacting to Wilson's steady opposition to this, Lloyd George came round to favouring the eventual solution which placed the Saar under the League of Nations and its coal mines in French hands for only fifteen years, after which its ultimate destiny would be decided by plebiscite. Over Poland, he fought both Clemenceau and Wilson. He insisted that the limits of the Polish corridor should be drawn so that it contained as few Germans as possible. He also prevented the inclusion of Danzig in Poland. Even though economically necessary to Poland as its only outlet to the Baltic, it was unquestionably a German city and it was due to Lloyd George that Balfour's plan of making it a Free City under the League of Nations was written into the peace treaty. He had a disproportionately lengthy struggle to ensure that the future of Upper Silesia, an important industrial region of mixed Polish and German population, should be the subject of plebiscite and not of outright annexation to Poland. On these topics he clashed with the French, who wanted Poland to be as big as possible in order to weaken Germany, and with Wilson, who conceived it his duty to put right in 1919 the wrong done to Poland by the eighteenth-century partitions. Lloyd George insisted, against both men, that the settlement with Poland had to be of such a nature that the Germans would accept it and the Allies would be ready in future to defend it. He used the principles of self-determination to restrain Wilson, and considerations of military feasibility to restrain Clemenceau.

In sum, therefore, Lloyd George did much to moderate the terms imposed on the Germans, and in this he resisted not only Clemenceau but some members of his own delegation. Because, however, he feared the withdrawal of the United States into isolation, he felt precluded from preaching moderation as a principle because this would have involved a breach with France. The results of his efforts were therefore not commensurate with the time and energy he devoted to them. The Germans were not mollified, and the French believed themselves cheated of the security they demanded; even so, the causes of failure are to be found in the mental condition of the French and Germans rather than in the activities of Lloyd George. His pursuit of moderation arose from his conviction that German power would inevitably revive and that the settlement must be one to which Germany might reasonably be expected to become reconciled. His effort at an Anglo-United States military guarantee for France arose from a clear understanding of the real price that would have to be paid if the settlement was to be preserved. On both counts, Lloyd George failed to achieve the results he desired. It was a not ignoble failure.

All through 1919 the Allies were also involved with Russia, the one European Great Power which was not to attend the peace conference. Since 1918, the British, together with the French, had been giving assistance to the various counter-revolutionary armies conducting a civil war against the Bolsheviks. At various times, British forces operated in the Ukraine, around Murmansk and Archangel, and in Vladivostok. The question of more extensive intervention against the Russians came up for discussion at Paris, but Lloyd George and Wilson were opposed to this, and by the end of 1919 most Allied troops had been withdrawn from Russia; in 1920 it was Poland who played the leading part in attacking the Bolsheviks. With the Poles' tardy victory in the battle of the Vistula in 1920, Western military interference in Russia came to an end. The refusal of the Western Powers either to intervene effectively or to come to terms with the Bolsheviks sowed the seeds of much future trouble.

The years 1921 and 1922 were largely taken up with conferences devoted to the twin problems of reparations and of the security of France, now greatly prejudiced by the collapse of Wilson's power in the United States. In the spring of 1921, the Germans, who were already in default over their initial reparations payments, wanted the Allies' further demands scaled down, and tried to make their payments dependent on the withdrawal of the armies of occupation. The Allied reply, which had Lloyd George's full support, was the occupation of certain west German industrial towns. Two further conferences fixed Germany's total liability at £6,600 millions, but by the end of 1921 the Germans once more threatened default, and Britain and France again met to deal with the problem at Cannes in January 1922. Plans for closer Anglo-French unity were prepared by Lloyd George and Briand; but at the critical moment Briand was the victim of a French political crisis and was replaced by Poincaré, a rigid anti-German. The negotiations quickly collapsed. Nothing would satisfy Poincaré except a precise military undertaking by the British to send a given number of troops in a stated number of days in the event of France being involved in war. Lloyd George rejected this firmly. Worse still, Poincaré wanted precise guarantees of intervention in the event of a German infraction of the treaty terms as they applied to Germany's eastern neighbours. Lord Curzon, now Foreign Secretary, made it clear that Britain, though ready to support France in the event of a German invasion of French soil, would not, except as a signatory of the League Covenant, take action in the event of an attack on Poland.

From Cannes, the diplomatists moved, in April 1922, to Genoa. Lloyd George hoped this conference would at last provide a Grand Design for the pacification of Europe, and for the final vindication of his reputation at home and abroad. Most European States were represented, including both Germany and Russia; so also were the Dominions. A notable but threatening absentee was the terrible Poincaré; and Lloyd George was threatened with the angry resignation of Churchill, irreconcilably hostile to any recognition of Bolshevism. Churchill could be ignored, but not Poincaré. The latter helped to sabotage the conference by making a violent anti-German speech in France, and by encouraging the Belgians to oppose any recognition of Russia. The Germans and the Russians made their contribution to failure by signing the treaty of Rapallo. By this, the two pariah Governments of Europe resumed full diplomatic relations and reciprocally renounced all claims to reparations. All that Lloyd George gained from the conference therefore was an enhanced reputation as a dynamic source of disruption: by endeavouring to bring Russia into the European concert he had widened the rift between Britain and her allies and had acted as matchmaker for a sinister *mariage de convenance* between the two most dangerous enemies of the European order.

Once again, however, he had failed largely because those with whom he tried to work lacked his percipience. If both Germany and Russia were not reconciled to the West, they would become reconciled to each other: contempt for Russia at Genoa led to Rapallo in much the same way as contempt for Russia at Munich led to the Molotov-Ribbentrop agreement of 1939. If France demanded too much from Britain, France would get next to nothing. If Britain undertook directly to intervene to preserve every territorial arrangement in Europe she would default on that undertaking; if France wanted British support it must be limited to support for the defence of France. It could not be support for the domination of Europe by France regardless of the reasonable feelings of Germany. That Germany revived and made unreasonable demands on the rest of Europe in the 1930's is a reflection much less on the policies of Lloyd George than on the policies of those who opposed him at home and abroad at this time.

The last and most damaging of the many foreign foes with whom Lloyd

George wrestled after the armistice was Mustafa Kemal, the post-war leader of the Turks.

At the peace conference, the Greek Government of Venizelos laid claim to the port of Smyrna and its hinterland in Asia Minor. This was felt by the Italians to conflict with ambiguous promises made by Britain and France during the war that Italy should receive gains in this area. The Italians, who were already occupying Adalia, farther south in Asia Minor, therefore began to extend the area of their occupation in the Smyrna direction. Britain and France tried to prevent one *fait accompli* by another, and sent a Greek force to Smyrna in May 1919 to forestall the Italians. From Smyrna, Greek forces went on to occupy a considerable part of Asia Minor.

By the treaty of Sèvres, which the Allies forced the Sultan to sign in 1920, Turkey, as well as losing her Arab territories, was to yield up Constantinople, the Straits and the Dardanelles to Allied control and to give Smyrna to the Greeks for five years. The treaty was at once repudiated by the Turkish Nationalist leader, Kemal, who, with Ankara as his capital, had already begun to create the nucleus of a modern Turkish State and an army capable of resisting Allied attempts to rob Turkey of purely Turkish territory. In the hope of getting a great deal out of the venture, the Greeks offered to bring Kemal to heel by marching against him from Smyrna. During the next twelve months the Greek Army got to within forty miles of Ankara but no farther.

Lloyd George, supported by Balfour but opposed by Churchill, had been pro-Greek from the outset, and remained pro-Greek in spite of the declining prospects of Greek success in 1921 and of a change of régime in Greece which gave it a pro-German king. Lloyd George seems to have been persuaded that the Greeks were capable of establishing a strong pro-British empire in the eastern Mediterranean and of eliminating Turkish rule altogether. It was a project more characteristic of Napoleon III than of Lloyd George, but as Turkish resistance hardened, the Prime Minister switched to emphasizing the necessity for Allied solidarity against Kemal's open defiance of one of the major peace treaties.

By the end of 1921, however, he was almost entirely without support in his persistence. The Italians had every reason from the start to dislike the Greek venture, and the French, already infuriated by the extension of British control in the Arab Middle East, made haste to negotiate a secret peace with Kemal when, in September 1921, it became evident that the Greeks were likely to be defeated. Soon, Kemal was receiving arms from both the French and the Russians. By September 1922, the Greeks had been driven from Asia Minor, and Smyrna was in Turkish hands.

Kemal's forces now moved on the Straits, guarded only by a few Allied battalions at Chanak and the guns of part of the British Mediterranean Fleet. The first of the post-war dictators now faced the victors of 1918 with their first test. Whatever follies had been so far committed in encouraging the Greeks had now been purged (though only by the unfortunate Greeks) and what was at stake at Chanak was the fate of the whole European system so recently brought to birth. Here, as on so many other occasions between 1918 and 1922, Britain, the Dominions and Europe rehearsed the attitudes they were to adopt so frequently in the succeeding seventeen years.

Precipitately, the Cabinet, with both Balfour and Churchill now supporting the Prime Minister, published a communiqué indicating the likelihood of war. It reached the Dominions before they had officially received news of the Government's proposals for military action, and this offended their sense of independence. It enraged Poincaré, who at once ordered the withdrawal of French troops from Chanak; and the subsequent meeting in Paris between Lord Curzon and Poincaré seems to have been devoted to an exchange of offensive remarks, from which Curzon emerged in tears. They did, however, manage to agree on offering Turkey new peace terms; and Curzon salved his vanity by informing the Cabinet that he had been very firm indeed with Poincaré.

The combination of Cabinet aggressiveness, of cool-headedness by the British Commander-in-Chief, General Harington, and of caution at the last by Kemal, ensured that the crisis was settled by negotiation. A new treaty was drawn up at Lausanne in 1923, after the fall of the Coalition. By it, Turkey regained Constantinople and Adrianople, and sovereignty over all Asia Minor. Reparations and disarmament, both demanded in the Treaty of Sèvres, were omitted from the Treaty of Lausanne. Thus, Kemal's use of force had compelled the Allies to moderate their demands, and Lloyd George's show of force had compelled Kemal to make peace. It was a more reasonable and a more lasting conclusion to a tangled international problem than most of the conclusions arrived at in subsequent years.

13 · Reshaping the Middle East; India; The Pacific

At the peace conference and after it, Lloyd George and his ministers were also concerned with the major problem of creating a completely new Power-structure in the Middle East. The task was complicated by the tangle of ambiguous and contradictory commitments into which the Government had entered during the war.

From the moment of Turkey's entry into the war, the British were bound to consider ways and means of regaining a secure hold on the short route to India. In the nineteenth century this had been maintained, first by Britain's predominant influence at Constantinople and then, after 1882, by control over Egypt and the Suez Canal. The alignment of Turkey with Germany was thus a major threat to Britain's imperial position, and it is only in relation to the struggle for control of Europe that the Dardanelles campaign and Britain's operations in Mesopotamia and Palestine may properly be called 'sideshows'. If Britain is thought of as a world Power, which is what she really was, rather than a European off-shore island, which she had not been for several hundred years, her military activities in the Middle East were not sideshows at all.

Britain's determination to acquire the bulk of the Turkish Empire was thus a major war aim; and the moment Turkey entered the war, Egypt, then still nominally part of the Ottoman Empire, was declared a British protectorate; and Cyprus, technically held only on lease from Turkey since 1878, was formally annexed. At an early date, Kitchener, whose experience of India, Palestine and Egypt was lifelong, had indicated to an influential Arab leader, Abdullah, a son of the Hashemite prince Hussein, Sharif of Mecca, that Britain's beneficent attitude towards Islam, hitherto expressed in support of Turkey, might well express itself in support of Arab freedom, should Turkey join the Germans. Attitudes in London were too vaguely defined as yet, and the situation on the Western Front too grim, for immediate action, and the two factors together helped to concentrate anti-Turkish policy on the Dardanelles campaign in 1915, except for an equally unsuccessful attack on Bagdad in Mesopotamia, launched under the auspices of the Government of India.

The year 1915 had also brought the French more fully into the picture. To bolster up Russian morale the British had accepted Russia's demand for Constantinople and the Straits after the war. This at once produced a French claim for what was rather vaguely called 'Syria'; in the French view the term was capable of applying to the whole area from the Taurus Mountains to Egypt and of including both Damascus and Palestine.

The French demand led to much ambiguity, some of it intentional, some of it accidental, in all subsequent British dealings with both the Arabs and with France. Arab freedom and British security were not necessarily compatible in the first place; Arab freedom and French colonialism were even less compatible. Worse still, the British, particularly after the advent of Lloyd George to the Premiership and of Balfour to the Foreign Office, were increasingly determined on acquiring Palestine, and without making this clear either to the French or to the Arabs.

British interest in Palestine arose from an amalgam of motives, and was expressed at an early date in the war. In 1914, Herbert Samuel, a member of Asquith's Cabinet, and a prominent figure in British Jewry, proposed the formation of a Jewish State on the grounds that it would create an area of goodwill of great value because of its proximity to Egypt. Early in 1916, Grey sounded France and Russia about making plans for Palestine which would persuade Jews in America and the East to look more favourably on the *entente* cause. More persistent than this, to begin with, was the view that since Palestine was of such significance to so many religious faiths it would be better if its custodianship were in the hands of the British rather than in those of either Islamic Arabs or the Catholic French.

When, therefore, in June 1916, Sharif Hussein began the Arab revolt he was setting off on a long march to disappointment and disillusion, whose consequences for ill were still not worked out half a century later. At the time, however, circumstances were all against precise definition of aims or clear territorial demarcation – 1916 was no year in which to draw boundaries in the Middle East, for they might so easily have been written in sand in more senses than one. In 1915 and 1916, the British entered into one agreement with the French, the so-called Sykes-Picot agreement, and another with the Sharif, through the McMahon correspondence of the latter part of 1915. These agreements were ill-defined and were incompatible both with each other and with the evolving intentions of the British Government. Given the war situation as it then was, and the confusion amid which the British were conducting their negotiations, this is not altogether surprising, and is to be regarded less as an indication of original imperialist sin than of traditional British muddle. There were three sources of policy at the time, Westminster, Cairo and Delhi, and there was little liaison between them; and the Government of India with its authoritarian traditions did not like the Arab revolt at all. Furthermore, there was little systematic control over the various men on the spot (of whom T. E. Lawrence was the most picturesque) who were working with and for the Arabs.

Lloyd George's accession to the Premiership was the prelude to more action. He wanted a British advance on Palestine from Egypt; he wanted Palestine to be British; he wanted favours for international Jewry in Palestine; and he wanted no pledges to the Arabs that conflicted with this programme. It was, of course, too late to hope to implement a policy as specific as this without incurring charges of bad faith, but in substance Lloyd George got his way in the end.

In 1917, however, existing confusions were confounded by even greater incompatibles. British forces entered Bagdad in March 1917 and the Cabinet promptly announced to the 'Arab race' that Hussein, having driven the Turks from the Hejaz, was now King of that area and an ally. It then called on the Arabs of Mesopotamia to join with the British in 'uniting your kinsmen in the north, south, east and west in realizing the aspirations of your race'. This reckless reference to all points of the compass could not be squared with the Sykes-Picot agreement.

Worse was to follow, in November 1917, with the Balfour 'declaration' of the Government's intention to work for 'the establishment in Palestine of a national home for the Jewish people'. This was the crowning achievement of the energetic group which had been hard at work encouraging the Cabinet to support the Zionist idea. Herbert Samuel, Balfour, Lord Robert Cecil and Lloyd George himself proved particularly receptive, and so were a number of the young men in the 'garden suburb'. The most celebrated propagandist was the Zionist leader, Chaim Weizmann, who was particularly successful in wooing both Lloyd George and Robert Cecil.

One object of giving the promise at this particular moment was the hope that it would inspire the Jews in Russia to keep Kerensky in favour of continuing the war; but a Jewish National Home was a blunt propaganda weapon with which to impress the Russians. Lenin seized power on the day the Balfour Declaration was issued.

In the turmoil of hopes, fears, propaganda, revolution, desert fighting in the east, and trench warfare in the west, the Declaration made less impression than knowledge of subsequent history might suggest. Yet already, Syrian Arabs were protesting that Palestine was an essential part of their promised inheritance, and already some Englishmen on the spot felt compelled to try to exorcise the whirlwind of Arab anger by nice attempts to distinguish between 'a Jewish State' and 'a Jewish national home'.

A third complication was created by the entry of the United States into the war. This called in question the whole business of annexations in the Middle East, for the simon-pure Wilson wanted to touch the pitch of war without being defiled by its tar-stained implications. To soften the shock of hearing that, having conquered Mesopotamia, the British were presumptuous enough to want to keep it, the President was given the impression that Palestine was to be under international control.

With Wilson, also, came the Fourteen Points. The slogan of self-determination naturally swelled Arab hopes; not to be outdone, the British and French Governments issued a joint proclamation, just before the armistice, promising the Arabs free Governments of their own choice.

It is against this background of inflammatory phrases and contradictory promises, of divided counsels and reckless propaganda that the Coalition worked to bring some order to the Middle East between 1918 and 1922. The wonder is that it produced in the end a structure which, though obviously unlikely to be permanent, was far stronger than it might have been, and broke down in the end less because of its inherent faults than because of the shocks of a second world war.

When the Arabs entered Syria and Damascus in 1918, as fighting allies of the British Army under Allenby, their leader Feisal, the most splendid of the sons of Hussein, fully expected, as did his many British friends, that he would become the ruler at least of Damascus and part of its hinterland.

The French, however, demanded direct rule for themselves over both Syria and Damascus, and by the middle of 1920 had driven Feisal into exile. The arguments at Paris were bitter, but Lloyd George and Balfour were too entangled in the web of past errors and present controversies to be able to resist Clemenceau. True, the Sykes-Picot agreement had been understood to provide for Arab rule in Damascus; but it also provided for the internationalization of Palestine, and this, with lamentable consequences to themselves, the British were determined to prevent. Nor could the British deny to France the right to the kind of direct rule over Syria that Britain was at that moment trying to establish in Mesopotamia. There were enough quarrels with the French over the settlement of Europe without making matters worse by a chivalrous stand on behalf of Feisal.

In August 1920, the Middle East was divided between France and Britain: Syria and Lebanon went to France; Palestine and Mesopotamia (Iraq) to Britain. All four territories were to be held as mandates under the supervision of the Permanent Mandates Commission of the League of Nations. These arrangements were in contradiction to wartime promises to the Arabs, and to the wishes of the inhabitants.

Not unexpectedly, the result was unrest and violence in 1919 and 1920 throughout the Middle East. It is perhaps true to say that only a Government with Lloyd George as its Prime Minister could have got itself into such a tangle; but it is perhaps also true that only a Government with Lloyd George at its head could have extricated itself so dexterously. Lloyd George was so lacking in principle in the accepted sense that he was always open to fresh arguments and always ready for fresh devices; and in 1921 and 1922 he was bombarded on all sides by men determined to give British power in the Middle East a surer foundation than ambiguity backed by military force.

Those who knew the British most intimately, the Egyptians, had burst into rebellion as early as March 1919, when the British deported the Egyptian Nationalist leader, Zaghlul. Zaghlul and his followers had rashly dared to assume that if self-determination was to apply to Czechs and Poles it should apply also to Egyptians; and that if Governments of their choice were to be offered to the Turks' former Arab subjects, the Egyptians, who legally came in the same category should be treated likewise. More relevant to the rebellion was the anger of the Egyptian population at the way they had been treated by the British during the war. There had been much requisitioning of land and animals, and something very like forced labour in the service of the British Army. Although the revolt was quickly suppressed, General Allenby, who took over as High Commissioner, still faced many sporadic outbreaks of disorder, and at the end of 1920 a commission under Lord Milner reported in favour of giving Egypt independence, and of basing Britain's special interests in Egypt on a treaty of alliance between the two countries.

The Conservatives in the Coalition were hostile to what they deemed to be highly dangerous proposals, and the new régime was established only because, in the end, Allenby virtually threatened the Cabinet with his resignation. Lloyd George was quick to see that if Allenby could not guarantee to hold Egypt if the protectorate was continued, the protectorate would have to end. In 1922, Egypt was granted at least a form of independence, though the British Army remained, and so did many restrictions on effective Egyptian sovereignty. Egyptian Nationalists were never to be reconciled to a legal independence that gave Egypt a status hardly distinguishable from that of a mandated territory; but the Coalition had at least turned British policy in Egypt towards the right direction.

Discontent flared up in Mesopotamia simultaneously with the announcement of the British mandate, and long and costly military operations were required to deal with it. The Iraqis were not disposed to accept a situation by which, after their liberation under British auspices, there were fewer Iraqis in positions of authority than in the days of their servitude to the Turks. Resentments were fanned by the news of the flight of Feisal from Damascus, and by echoes of Arab plaints against the Jews in Palestine. In Palestine itself the announcement of the mandate was likewise followed by anti-Jewish riots.

The change that enabled the British to ride out the storm was largely the consequence of Churchill's move from the War Office to the Colonial Secretaryship in February 1921 and of the transfer to Churchill, from the Foreign Office, of responsibility for the Middle East. Although there is evidence that Churchill at one point toyed with the idea of inviting the United States to take over both Palestine and Mesopotamia, he quickly swung to the view that if Anglo-Arab relations were to be resumed on a tolerable basis, something must be done to repair the damage done by so many broken promises. Among those who accompanied Churchill to Cairo to examine the problem at close quarters was T. E. Lawrence. Lawrence, a strange combination of archaeologist, tough guerrilla tactician and romantic, had taken a prominent part in the desert struggles of Feisal and his men against the Turks, but had retired from public affairs in disgust at what he conceived to be Britain's disgraceful betrayal of Feisal. Churchill, who had met Lawrence in Paris during the peace conference (which Lawrence attended, in Arab dress, as a partisan of the unlucky Feisal) now managed to lure him back from All Souls', Oxford, from which he had from time to time issued attacks on British policy.

Churchill and his advisers produced an ingenious compromise which, as it turned out, solved most of Britain's more immediate problems. Iraq would become a kingdom, and the disappointed Feisal would be its first king; part of the Palestine mandate would become the autonomous Kingdom of Transjordan, under Feisal's brother, Abdullah; and British security in Iraq would in future be the responsibility, not of soldiers thick on the ground and at the mercy of lurking tribesmen, but of the at once more mobile, less ubiquitous and less vulnerable Royal Air Force. There were cries of pain from the Army and the War Office at the transfer of its duties in Iraq to the upstart R.A.F., and the French were much upset by the new position of Feisal who, as far as they were concerned, was an anti-French rebel in exile. The settlement was, however, a tribute to the flexibility, not only of Churchill, but of men such as Milner and Balfour who had also helped to salve so many of the wounds inflicted by so many broken pledges.

The British thus emerged from the war and its aftermath with a pre-dominance over the Middle East outside French-controlled Syria that lasted, though not without incident, for a quarter of a century. Its attainment had been something of a *tour de force*, and it had been conducted in an atmosphere which provided the romantic schoolboy feelings of a certain type of imperialist-minded Englishman with the only outlet they found in the grimly unromantic decade that opened in 1914. The strange tendency of upper class Englishmen to hero-worship Arab chieftains found its fullest expression in Lawrence's desert fighting and in his partnership with Churchill at the story's end. Like all schoolboy romances it was inadequately connected with reality. There was always something immature about the English notion that the best products of the English public schools could be accepted as big, wise blood-brothers to the sheikhs and emirs of the Arab world; allotting territories to the sons of Hussein would not in the long run solve the problem of the Jews in Palestine, of the subjection of the Egyptians, or of the growing desire of more and more Arabs to throw off the control, not only of the English, but of Arab rulers who were Englishmen's friends.

In India during the Coalition period, the authorities were much embarrassed both by the increased agitation of the Hindu National Congress, and by Muslim agitation against the anti-Turkish policy of the Government at Westminster. In accordance with tradition, the British pursued their Olympian way, offering slow progress towards greater self-government with one hand and swift suppression of disorders with the other. By the Morley-Minto reforms of 1909 Indians had been admitted to membership of the Councils advising the Viceroy and the Provincial Governors, and in 1917 the Government had proclaimed its ultimate object for India to be that of responsible government within the British Empire. The Montagu-Chelmsford report of 1918 led to the Government of India Act of 1919. This set up a Legislative Council with a large elected Indian majority and eight provincial legislatures, also with elected Indian majorities. Unfortunately, from the point of view of the Indian Nationalists, these bodies had no control over justice, internal security or even finance, and by now a benevolent attempt to give Indians training in aspects of administration such as education and sanitation was regarded merely as renewed manifestation of Englishmen's conviction that they were a superior race. In an atmosphere of disorder and sedition came the episode at Amritsar, in April 1919, when General Dyer opened fire on an unarmed crowd who, after the murder of four Europeans, refused an order to disperse. Ten minutes' firing led to the death of 379 persons and to over 1,000 other casualties. Like the suppression of the Easter Rebellion, the Amritsar incident passed into legend. The 'terrible beauty' born of this affair was Gandhi's 'non-violent' campaign for Indian independence. Inevitably it led to a good deal of violence; and when the Coalition fell Gandhi began a six-year prison sentence.

The Washington naval conference took place in 1921 at the invitation of Woodrow Wilson's successor, President Harding, Balfour being the leader of the British delegation. Its purposes were to limit the ambitions of Japan, and to deal with the problem of the balance of power in the Pacific. The United States could outbuild the British in capital ships, but were unwilling to face the possibility of having to outbuild Japan as well, which they would have felt bound to do if the Anglo-Japanese alliance were renewed after its expiry in 1921. For their part, the British, particularly in view of the Geddes Axe, were anxious to cut down naval expenditure now that the German Navy had disappeared, provided this did not leave the Pacific entirely in Japanese hands. By the treaty, the ratio of capital ships between the United States, Britain and Japan was to be 5:5:3. At the same time, a Four-Power Treaty between these three powers and France (also an interested party in view of her possessions in Indo-China) guaranteed the Pacific *status quo*, so that the British could eliminate the need for the Anglo-Japanese alliance, which then lapsed.

It was a much applauded event, and for his part in it Balfour received the Order of the Garter and was raised to the peerage. It was perhaps appropriate that Balfour should have presided over the ending of a policy with whose initiation he had had so much to do. The abandonment at Washington both of the two-Power standard in naval building and of the Japanese alliance, followed as it was less than a year later by the almost complete breakdown of Anglo-French co-operation at Chanak, clearly marks the end of a chapter in British foreign policy. Unfortunately it can hardly be said to have begun a new one, and after the fall of the Coalition it is difficult to assert with conviction that there was a coherent British foreign policy at all.

14 · The Downfall of
Lloyd George, 1922

Judged dispassionately from afar, the post-war Coalition had substantial achievements to its credit. It disembarrassed English politics at last of the *damnosa hereditas* of Ireland. It took the first small unwilling steps in the direction of greater self-government for Egypt and India. It shaped the history of the Middle East for a quarter of a century. It shared in the creation of the least unjust territorial settlement that Europe had known since the fall of Rome, a settlement which, in its essentials, survived even the Second World War. It had started new trends in housing policy and in the relief of poverty. Yet hardly any of these achievements could be seen as such at the time; they were judged to be little more than cunning devices, mean expedients, crafty compromises and shoddy betrayals. And if, by the last months of 1922, there seemed at last to be peace at home and abroad, it looked to be a peace without victory. The trade union movement was for the moment exhausted, and working-class morale was being slowly sapped by unemployment and pauperization; while employers felt little security in a world of falling prices and contracting markets. The Irish treaty reaped an immediate harvest of bloodshed in the Free State, fear in Ulster and political resentment at Westminster. Meagre concessions in Egypt were seen as the first step in the undoing of the great work of Cromer; and the Government's treatment of General Dyer after the Amritsar affair produced almost as much criticism as had Dyer's treatment of the Indian rioters. It would have been almost impossible to find a single Englishman to say a good word for the peace treaties, or an expert or official who was not angered by Lloyd George's part in the making of them. Anglo-French relations were bad and, with the imminent French occupation of the Ruhr, were about to become worse. Naval supremacy had been abandoned for ever at the Washington Conference; yet even such precarious peace as had been achieved, proved, as late as October 1922, to be balanced on the hair's breadth of Chanak.

If the public at large seemed sunk in apathy, the politicians were seething with discontent, unanimous only in their conviction that the situation at Westminster was no longer endurable. From that particular opinion, Lloyd George himself would hardly have dissented in the autumn of 1922;

but whereas the great majority of M.P.s at Westminster were anxious that Lloyd George should cease to be Prime Minister, a small but powerful minority (which, of course, included Lloyd George himself) wanted him to continue. The difficulty was that Lloyd George, by virtue of his position, had power and patronage but only a handful of followers, whereas his enemies, though greater in number, were without a parliamentary leader.

More than any other Government, Lloyd George's was a personal one. His breach with Asquith in 1916 and the 'Coupon Election' of 1918 made him, for all practical purposes, a leader without a party; for the 136 Coalition Liberal M.P.s were a purely personal following, many of whom owed their election in 1918 to Conservative votes, as a result of their having been recipients of the joint Lloyd George–Bonar Law 'coupon'. To the bulk of the Conservative Party, Lloyd George was detestable on account of his personal character, his devious methods and his frequently un-Tory policies. The only reason he survived was that he had the unwavering support of Bonar Law, who in turn commanded the loyalty of the Tory back-benchers. But in March 1921, Bonar Law resigned from the Government and announced his withdrawal from politics. From that time onwards, Lloyd George's position was perpetually in danger. Although he was thereafter supported by Austen Chamberlain, who succeeded Bonar Law as Conservative leader, for all disgruntled Tories Bonar Law was henceforth a king over the water. At first he was obstinately deaf to the cries of 'Will ye no come back again?' but in the end he succumbed and Lloyd George was at last overthrown.

It was a long process, however, and during most of 1921 and 1922 all the Tories could do was writhe in impotent rage while the Welsh wizard continued his now increasingly knavish tricks. The devices he used to preserve the special influence of his small group of Coalition Liberals were particularly objectionable to the Tories. He secured for his followers a disproportionately large share of Government offices and patronage, and saw to it that men who were useful to him, particularly as contributors to his personal party funds, were freely rewarded with titles. There was so little decent discretion about it that it came to be widely believed that titles and honours were obtainable for cash payments. Lloyd George seems also to have exercised his charms upon the Conservative Party treasurer with remarkable effect: large sums of money were missing from Conservative funds when the Coalition came to an end, and it appeared that some of the missing money (£80,000 was mentioned) had been diverted by the Conservative treasurer to Lloyd George. He received an earldom in Lloyd George's last Honours List.

Lloyd George employed other dubious stratagems. When the position of Lord Chief Justice became vacant early in 1921 the obvious candidate was one of Lloyd George's abler supporters, Sir Gordon Hewart, the Attorney–General. Not wanting to lose Hewart from the Commons, the

Prime Minister hit on the device of appointing an elderly substitute as Lord Chief Justice on the understanding that he would resign the moment the Prime Minister found it expedient to release Hewart from the Government. When Lloyd George felt compelled to dismiss Addison from the Ministry of Health, on the grounds that his housing policy had failed, he instantly appointed him as Minister without Portfolio at a salary of £5,000 a year. There was such an uproar over this that the Prime Minister was reduced to suggesting that Addison's new appointment and salary should continue only until the end of the parliamentary session – a period in fact of only three months. Addison felt so humiliated by this incident that he shortly afterwards resigned and joined the Labour Party.

What enraged the average Tory member most was that the whole business of government was in the hands of a 'court' Party over which they, the 'country' members, had no control. Lloyd George lasted as long as he did because he turned the Cabinet into a kind of political Versailles from which none of his favourite courtiers, however aggrieved, could risk expulsion, because it would be like consigning themselves to a political grave. Thus, when the negotiations for an Irish treaty began, Lloyd George was on the worst of terms with both Birkenhead and Churchill. Birkenhead, as Lord Chancellor, was outraged by the appointment of a temporary Lord Chief Justice, since he correctly regarded it as a breach of constitutional law. Churchill was enraged by Lloyd George's lukewarmness over intervention in Russia, by his failure to tackle unemployment, and by his encouragement of the Greeks. After his successful distribution of territorial consolation prizes to the Hashemite family in the Middle East he was furious, on returning home, to find that he was not promoted to the vacant post of Chancellor of the Exchequer. Yet Lloyd George won both Churchill and Birkenhead over to his Irish policy by the simple process of promising to take them into his full confidence during its implementation. The reason was clear. Without Lloyd George's favour, their talents would have found no employment. Churchill made this clear in a letter to Lloyd George when the latter dramatically threatened to resign owing to Tory opposition to his Irish policy. Churchill warned Lloyd George (not that he needed the warning) that resignation would mean, in effect, political extinction:

'Mr Bonar Law will be invited to form a Government. Why should he not do so? . . . Why should he not succeed? Most men sink into insignificance when they quit office. Very insignificant men acquire weight when they obtain it. . . . The delusion that an alternative Government cannot be formed is perennial. Mr Chamberlain thought Sir Henry Campbell-Bannerman "would be hissed off the stage". Mr Asquith was confident that you could not form an administration.'

It was a sound prognosis of the political dilemma both of the Prime Minister and of all his chosen courtiers. When Bonar Law replaced Lloyd

George, Lloyd George went into the wilderness for ever and Churchill until, in 1924, he purged his offences by rejoining the Conservatives.

The Irish settlement was the beginning of the end for Lloyd George. The treaty and the partition tore the heart out of the Unionist Party, leaving it without a cause to defend. The fiasco of the Genoa conference and the apparently irresponsible attempt to bustle the country into war with Turkey over Chanak were the final straws. When the Prime Minister announced, in October 1922, that the Coalition would shortly appeal to the electorate for a renewal of its power, all those Tory members who were not of the 'Court' party burst into revolt. Under great pressure from many quarters, Bonar Law was persuaded at last to return to politics and lend his support (in effect his leadership) to the rebellion. He was already more than half on their side as a result of having made a public attack on the Government's policy over Chanak; but now, as always he shrank from having greatness thrust on him. Not even the tardy conversion of the brilliant Lord Curzon to the rebel cause gave him much encouragement, even though it meant that at least one of the really famous Conservatives would be at his service. In the end Bonar Law gave way to a sense of duty; and for the first time since Lloyd George took over the reins of government a major political decision was made out of simple loyalty to others.

When the party leaders met the rebels at the Carlton Club on 19 October 1922, the mere presence of Bonar Law was enough to decide the issue.[1] Chamberlain, as party leader, advised continuance of support for the Coalition and so did Balfour; but when Bonar Law haltingly, and without histrionics, said he thought the real issue was not whether they won or lost the next election but whether or not the Conservative Party was to survive, the matter was decided. An alternative leader to Lloyd George had emerged. There were 187 votes for ending the Coalition and only 87 for continuing it. Immediately after the meeting, the Conservative ministers resigned from the Coalition and Lloyd George's own resignation followed at once. Bonar Law was sent for, formed an administration without difficulty, as Churchill had prophesied, and was duly elected leader of the Conservative Party in place of Chamberlain. Parliament was dissolved a week after the Carlton Club meeting, and the General Election of November 1922 gave the Conservatives a majority of 88 over all other parties.

The most famous speech at the decisive Carlton Club meeting was made by Stanley Baldwin. Although he spoke before Bonar Law, it is wrong to suggest that it was Baldwin who made up Bonar Law's mind for him. It was rather that Baldwin was more successful in putting into words what both Bonar Law and the Tory rebels were thinking. Baldwin had been a

---

[1] If there is substance in Mr A. J. P. Taylor's view that Lloyd George was a British Mussolini, then, in view of his behaviour in 1916 and 1922, Bonar Law clearly qualifies as Lloyd George's Victor Emmanuel III.

back-bench Conservative M.P. from 1908, a junior Treasury minister from
1917 to 1921, and thereafter a Cabinet Minister as President of the Board
of Trade. His role had been inconspicuous, his remarks in Cabinet few;
and when he heard that Baldwin was working for the downfall of the
Coalition, Lloyd George had said, 'What does little Baldwin think he can
do to us?'. The answer was that Baldwin in a few quiet but convincing
words switched off the current of Lloyd George's power at its Conservative
source. Lloyd George, he admitted, was a 'dynamic force';

'but a dynamic force which had already shattered the Liberal Party and
which was well on the way to doing the same to the Conservative Party.
The result of this dynamic force is that [Mr Austen Chamberlain] and I
stand here today, he prepared to go into the wilderness if he should be
compelled to forsake the Prime Minister and I prepared to go into the
wilderness if I should be compelled to stay with him'.

More was at stake, however, at the Carlton Club meeting than the future
of the Conservative Party; more even than Baldwin's keenly-felt desire
for a return to what he called 'clean government'. In breaking free from
Lloyd George, Baldwin and his fellow-rebels restored political power once
more to its traditional place, namely into the hands of a political party
with an elected majority in the Commons. If the one indisputable achievement of the British in the period between the wars is that they preserved
their parliamentary institutions, then the credit must go first of all to the
Carlton Club meeting of 1922. Lloyd George had displayed many of the
characteristics of the demagogue-dictators who were to proliferate on the
Continent after his fall: the persuasive platform oratory, the deft personal
charm, the contempt for traditional parties whether of the Left or of the
Right, the ability to confound the experts by bringing off occasional
triumphs while disregarding them or overruling them, and the mysterious
capacity, found in Napoleon, as in Mussolini and Hitler, to secure the
loyalty and admiration of men of ability, breeding and culture who
nevertheless recognized that, by their standards, he was a vulgar upstart.
Above all, he had that capacity for 'getting things done' which many
Englishmen (while themselves supporting Baldwin or MacDonald) later
regarded as a sufficient justification for the continental dictators.

When Maynard Keynes wrote of Lloyd George that he was 'rooted in
nothing' he was probably as near to the truth about him as anyone is likely
to get; the phrase helps to explain the difficulty of arriving at a consistent
opinion about him. Lloyd George's origins were in the rural Radicalism of
Nonconformist west Wales, and this is enough in itself to explain his lifelong indifference to English traditions and institutions. He passed his
childhood and youth in a remote and foreign land, untouched by industrialism and ruled by an alien Church and aristocracy. There was no common
ground between him and other politicians, and almost all his private con-

fidants were Welsh; his failure to achieve durable friendships during his political career was almost complete. As a rural Radical, he hated the English governing class and disliked and feared the industrial working class. The more primitive Radicals had always tended to regard industrialism as ugly and degrading, and this feeling was strengthened in Lloyd George by the contrast between the quick mind of the rural Welshman and the slow inarticulacy of the English working class. His Radicalism did not, of course, constitute much more than a state of mind once he had arrived in politics. He had little then but his capacity to speak and to act; but with few real values to give coherence either to what he said or to what he did. Lloyd George rarely saw anything but given problems and the need to solve them; for him, a problem had no history and no context but the immediate situation. Bonar Law saw everything in the context of Presbyterian Ulster and the Unionist Party; Churchill would see it against the great sweep of history; MacDonald would see it as a growing point in the struggles of a new political party striving towards maturity after a difficult birth; Curzon saw everything in the context of an aristocratic tradition; Asquith in terms of the measured growth of ordered liberty; even J. H. Thomas thought in terms of the trade union movement and Birkenhead, whatever his other faults, never quite forgot that he was a servant of the law. None of these things meant much to Lloyd George.

Not only was he rooted in nothing; he refused even to be grafted. Almost all rebel politicians who work within, or indeed against, the English tradition, become in the end assimilated to it, whether their origins are in Clydeside, Lossiemouth, Lambeth or Allahabad. But no man seems to have been more thoroughly insulated against the subtle attractions of the English way of life than Lloyd George. MacDonald obviously loved the graces of political life, but Lloyd George refused, in his own phrase, 'to be a flunkey'. He evaded visits to the Palace or to Windsor; he did not care if his subordinates put up peerages for sale; and he was always liable to retreat to a country hide-out where, guarded by an old Welsh housekeeper he could dine off cold rice pudding. He wanted the reality of power; for its trappings he cared nothing. For this, he was never forgiven; to men brought up in the English public school and university tradition to be careless about the trivialities of public ritual was to be sacrilegious.

Equally un-English was his passion for speed. The pitch and moment of his acts were not to be sicklied o'er with the pale cast of official or expert dubieties. He always sought the fastest means to the quickest decision. The Civil Service tradition, of slow consultation and careful co-ordination before taking action, was outside his experience, as was the academic discipline from which it derived. If there had to be advisers, they must be quick-witted, highly articulate people of his own choice. This explains why he was opposed with such malevolence not only from the Tory back-benches but from the clubs where Civil Servants and academics congregated.

It explains also the controversial problem of his various interventions in the conduct of the war, such as his almost fatal infatuation with Nivelle, his resolution over the question of convoys, his long nagging battle with Haig and Robertson. He could hardly help hating both of them. To him, the Army was the most traditional and therefore the least admirable element in a tradition-bound society. Combining demagogy with humanity, he attached no value to the proud regimental histories, the battle honours, the intensely in-bred loyalty and professionalism without which the Army could not have held together at all; instead, he saw the Western Front simply as a matter of brave common soldiers being butchered by the folly of the English upper class. As War Prime Minister, he had two major achievements to his credit: he saved the principle of civilian control, and by his intuitive and unshakeable buoyancy he infused his colleagues and the nation with a confidence in victory that a sober examination of the facts might not have justified. His actions in detail will always be matters for intense disagreement; and those who conclude that his capacity for error might have been fatal are always likely to be fewer than those who conclude that without him the war might have been lost.

---

15 · Signs of the Times

When Bonar Law announced in 1922 that his aim would be 'tranquillity, and freedom from adventures and commitments both at home and abroad' he summed up the desires of the whole nation. Ever since 1909 there had been ceaseless political controversy at home, and since 1914 the intolerable burdens of fighting a great war and of grappling with the world-wide chaos which had followed it. Yet, whatever sense of achievement men had felt at the end of 1918 had been dissipated by 1922. Europe was distracted; India, Ireland and Egypt in ferment. Peace had brought not prosperity but shrinking wages and unemployment to the working class, and falling profits to the industrialist. The political scene, as Lloyd George left Downing Street for ever, was one of confusion; the most gifted of the Conservatives were estranged from the new Conservative Government, the Liberal Party cleft into two bitterly quarrelling halves, the Labour Party a dumping ground for working-class protests rather than a source of inspiration or of hope for the immediate future. Since the struggles of the past decade had availed so little, the country was swept by a desire to ignore social and political problems altogether. People wanted a rest; as one of the bright young men of the period said in a radio debate in 1927, 'This is an age of aspirins rather than of aspirations.'

The intellectual atmosphere of the 1920's was therefore one of clever or angry disillusionment. Attitudes towards the war among the educated had passed rapidly from innocent romanticism through stunned despair to angry disgust. Rupert Brooke had greeted the outbreak in 1914 with lines of schoolboy immaturity:

Now, God be thanked Who has matched us with His hour,
    And caught our youth and wakened us from sleeping,
With hand made sure, clear eye, and sharpened power,
    To turn, as swimmers into cleanness leaping,
Glad from a world grown old and cold and weary,
    Leave the sick hearts that honour could not move,
And half-men, and their dirty songs and dreary,
    And all the little emptiness of love!

By 1917, Wilfred Owen had already provided an answer in a harrowed poem about the victim of a poison gas attack:

In all my dreams, before my helpless sight,
    He plunges at me, guttering, choking, drowning.

If in some smothering dreams you too could pace
    Behind the wagon that we flung him in,
And watch the white eyes writhing in his face,
    His hanging face, like a devil's sick of sin;
If you could hear, at every jolt, the blood
    Come gargling from the froth-corrupted lungs,
Obscene as cancer, bitter as the cud
    Of vile, incurable sores on innocent tongues, –
My friend, you would not tell with such high zest
    To children ardent for some desperate glory,
The old Lie: *Dulce et decorum est*
    Pro patria mori.

The sense of mental and spiritual exhaustion which lay behind the social and political apathy of the twenties was expressed in T. S. Eliot's *The Hollow Men*:

We are the hollow men
We are the stuffed men
Leaning together
Headpiece filled with straw. Alas!
Our dried voices, when
We whisper together
Are quiet and meaningless
As wind in dry grass
Or rats' feet over broken glass
In our dry cellar

Shape without form, shade without colour,
Paralysed force, gesture without motion;
Those who have crossed
With direct eyes, to death's other Kingdom
Remember us – if at all – not as lost
Violent souls, but only
As the hollow men
The stuffed men.

Disillusionment was more generally expressed in derisive contempt for the values and standards of a society that was alleged to have led the young into war by exploiting their nobler impulses, and to have cheated those who survived of the promised benefits of peace. All who could afford the luxury of an intellectual life entered into a gleeful competition to see who could be the most brilliantly cynical. At the most successful level was Lytton Strachey, whose two books, *Queen Victoria* and *Eminent Victorians*, turned the Queen into a joke and some of the most famous of her subjects into guys. Less esteemed, but even more successful in finding the nineteenth century hilariously funny, was Philip Guedalla. Bridging the gap between the intellectuals on one hand and the matinée audiences and circulating library readers on the other were Noël Coward who wrote 'daring' plays, and a temporarily fashionable Armenian expatriate called Michael Arlen, who wrote one or two smart novels. The women created by these writers tended to give the impression that, in addition to smoking in public, they drank a great deal, probably took drugs and were certainly unchaste.

Nineteenth-century values had been under fire long before 1914; but on the whole the critics had been as soberly high-minded as those they attacked. The 1920's, however, were disillusioned even with traditional forms of rebellion. Earnest critics of the old order were by now attracting less attention; although Bernard Shaw and H. G. Wells were still the unofficial educators of intelligent young men in the provinces, such serious advocates of radical change as the Webbs and R. H. Tawney were relatively little known because they appealed, in nineteenth-century fashion, to reason, whereas the intellectual tendency of the twenties was to revolt against reason. This was partly attributable to popularized versions of the hypotheses of Freudian psychology, emphasizing the influence of the irrational subconscious mind on human behaviour and insisting that all human drives were fundamentally sexual. It was in the 1920's that it first became fashionable to talk sagely of the dangers of sexual 'repression' and of the undesirability of 'inhibition'. Many writers of the time also argued that the emphasis on intellectual and scientific advance which had characterized European thinking since the eighteenth-century Enlightenment had distorted and crippled both the individual and society as a whole. After all, the most highly intelligent and highly organized society in the history of the world had plunged into the cruelty and irrationality of the 1914–18 war. In the impatient mood of the 1920's few stopped to inquire whether the world that produced the 1914–18 war had really been rationally organized; in the 1920's H. G. Wells was almost the only important literary figure who retained his faith in the saving virtue of organized scientific intelligence, and his writings on this topic were unpopular. More representative of the intellectual mood of the times was the contributor to the 'advanced' literary periodical, *The Adelphi*, who wrote in 1930:

The modern Renaissance is the discovery of a road to life through Intuition. Words are the vehicle of Intellect; and of Intellect the modern Renaissance has resolved to beware.

The flight from reason was international, and was even more observable in painting than among the 'advanced' writers. On the Continent it quickly reached its logical conclusion in Fascist nihilism; both in Mussolini's Italy and Hitler's Germany rational and scientific attitudes to life were regarded as equivalent to sedition. Goebbels assured a visiting Cambridge historian in 1932 that National Socialism was to be understood not with the head but 'with the heart'; and Göring announced belligerently, 'When I hear the word culture I reach for my revolver.' In England, however, only a few intellectuals preached anti-intellectualism, and it failed to elicit the response it achieved in Italy and Germany. The most celebrated anti-intellectual in England was D. H. Lawrence, whose novels and poems often derive such coherence as they possess from a passionate faith, vividly expressed, in the validity of direct intuitive awareness of the physical world. Lawrence had considerable influence over the most brilliant of the intellectual nihilists of the period, Aldous Huxley. His novel *Point Counter Point* provides not only a bitter commentary on the sexual morality of the leisured classes of the twenties, but contains a large number of conversation-pieces on the risibility of man's claim to be a rational creature and of the hollowness of life when spontaneity is crushed by the disciplines of a scientifically organized society. This theme found its fullest expression in Huxley's *Brave New World*, a vision of a future in which scientific conditioning of human behaviour had become so efficient that the one 'normal' spontaneous character in the book is driven to a violent death as the only means of either escape or (futile) protest. Huxley's own personal escape proved to be by way of religious mysticism; and, with his conversion, anti-intellectualism died out as a highbrow fashion in England.

With so many diverse influences at work to mock established values, the 1920's provided a lively interlude of genuine intellectual freedom in European history. Before 1914, writing had been inhibited by the sheer weight and achievement of tradition. In the 1930's, writers were required to commit themselves *for* Democracy and *against* Fascism; in the 1940's, they were mobilized either by the Government or by the pressure of opinion into the service of the war effort; in the 1950's, it was necessary to say nothing that might label one a fellow-traveller or a crypto-Communist. In the 1920's, however, the big war was over and another big one was not in sight and British politics was a meaningless game played by undistinguished players. Fascism was an Italian eccentricity, Germany was where interesting experimental films and plays were being produced, and Communists were either a handful of disgruntled agitators, or a distant tribe on civilization's remote borders. Intellectual life, like the social life of the upper classes, was a gay irresponsible holiday.

In consequence of this, and many other social factors, the 1920's were much taken up with the problem of 'youth'. Ever since the stable values of the mid-Victorians had first been seriously challenged in the 1880's, the rate of social change had been steadily increasing; and after the 1914–18 war it accelerated rapidly. The war ended the old order (or so it seemed) and now the war itself was over. Two sorts of restraint were felt to have been removed: the restraints of the pre-war social pattern, and the restraints of wartime gloom. In consequence, the gap between the young and old was wider than usual in the 1920's; and the death of many men who would otherwise then have been in their late twenties and early thirties made the gap wider. Other factors contributed: the growing influence on the young of the modes of the United States, the social emancipation of women, and the intellectual trends already referred to. In the 1930's and 1940's the pace of change slowed down again, but was resumed in the late fifties; and only then did the gap between the generations once more become a talking point.

Youth also tended to be a cult because young men seemed to have been the war's sacrificial victims. Youth had to celebrate its survival, and assert its right to existence by proclaiming its independence of all the older generation's values. The alleged shortage of young men in the twenties helped to accelerate the social emancipation of young women. The traditional female tactics were apparently felt to be inadequate to the times. The typical young women of the twenties took care neither to frighten young men by too much flaunting of feminine curves nor to lose too many chances by an excess of shrinking modesty. The female shape became flat-chested, and the female head was shorn of its long hair which, with monotonous iteration, had been called 'woman's crowning glory'. This created a so-called 'boyish' look. It was boyish only in the sense that it was not feminine in the way that Edwardian fashions had been. These had emphasized the curves of the female body to the extent of amplitude if not of caricature. The ideal Edwardian female was referred to as 'a fine figure of a woman'. This was apparently felt to be too overpowering for the allegedly scarce young men of the twenties; and so they were offered tubular-shaped girl-friends with one or other of the current short-haired styles: bobbed, shingled or 'Eton-cropped'. Until this time young girls had worn their hair long, and when they were considered nearly grown-up they 'put their hair up' and wound it into 'buns' and other coiled shapes. The day when the daughter of the house announced that she was going to have her hair 'bobbed' was a sad one in many homes, and a stormy one in some.

The compensation to the male for the loss of femininity involved in the short hair and the tubular torso was the rapid shortening of the skirts. To the Edwardian young man the sight of so much as a female ankle was an almost pulsating experience; but in the twenties the female knee was revealed to all. The social theorist's explanation for short skirts was that they were more convenient than long ones for climbing into and out of trains and buses, and were thus a symbol of woman's new mobility as a wage-earner. A more telling explanation is that they were the fashion trade's device for making sure of the immediate success of silk and artificial silk stockings in the new, and rather shocking, flesh-pink colours. Thick or black stockings vanished from the scene, and for forty years were regarded with distaste as symbolic of the sexual taboos of the nineteenth century.

With the short skirt, too, came the dancing craze of the twenties; and the leg-kicking 'Charleston' dance. It was ridiculous, ungainly and undignified; but it was high-spirited and extrovert, and, by the popular dancing standards of both previous and later generations, energetic. It expressed release from old restraints and from the burden of recent tragedy with a gay cock-a-hoop self-confidence. The combination of the two moods was not to be possible much after 1929, so that what seemed so daring to contemporaries seemed, thirty years later, artless and naïve.

The music for the dancers (who in fact normally preferred waltz, fox-trot, one-step and tango to the quite ephemeral Charleston) was of a sort rather loosely called 'jazz'. This kind (or rather these kinds) of music traditionally originated, as a popular phenomenon at any rate, with the enormous success of 'ragtime' in the United States just before the 1914 war; the honour of being the first real 'hit' or 'pop' tune of the twentieth century probably belongs to 'Alexander's Ragtime Band'. In the early stages, performers of the new 'syncopated' music were spoken of as forming 'jazz bands'; then 'dance bands'; and then, by the late twenties, 'dance orchestras'. Each label represented the stages by which jazz was merged into large-scale commercial show-business. The typical instrument was, in the first stages, the banjo; the ukulele had a brief vogue also; but by the end of the twenties it was the saxophone or the muted, or otherwise-strangled, 'hot' trumpet that symbolized 'jazz'.

The popularity of 'jazz' widened the gap between young and old by giving the young, perhaps for the first time in history, a musical 'culture' of their own. The middle aged knew only the Victorian and Edwardian romantic ballad (of which 'Love's Old Sweet Song' was the most insidiously lasting) or the music hall comic song typified by 'Any Old Iron'. The romantic ballad could be sung (and often was) by professional singers of the highest pretension; but the 'jazz' lyric required for its performance an entirely different technique, and one which orthodox musicians could despise but not acquire. The music hall song, like the music hall itself, was a doomed attempt to perpetuate the social atmosphere of the Old Kent Road as it might have been at the time of the London Dock Strike of 1889. In consequence, both forms of popular entertainment swiftly declined and the gulf between the generations was liable to become acrimoniously obvious every time a younger member of the household put on the gramophone or switched on the wireless.

There were other gulfs, too. In cultural matters, people in the twenties were parcelled off, in the vogue words of the period, into highbrow, middlebrow and lowbrow. Intellectual writing seemed a deliberate affront to an older generation, which still 'loved' Dickens and Tennyson. Here was the gap between highbrow and middlebrow. To the lover of classical music, jazz was a sacrifice of form and melody to improvization and rhythm. Here was the gap between highbrow and lowbrow. It was thus in the twenties that there first appeared signs of what later came to be referred to as the divorce between culture and the masses. It was, of course, nothing of the kind. It was a matter of the creation, side by side with the normal evolution of cultural forms among the privileged minority, of a new mass-culture quite different from what is sometimes still treated as a precious heritage: the old urban culture, represented by the street ballad, or the old rural culture, represented by the folk song and folk dance. Mass culture was, to begin with, largely an American importation, but in time it was to become international; so that, parallel to the highbrow absorbing the influence of French painting and the Russian film, was the lowbrow learning song and dance rhythms from West Africa by way of Louisiana.

These developments were due to the new techniques of dissemination, chiefly the cinema and wireless broadcasting (not universally referred to as 'radio' till the Second World War). The cinema was overwhelmingly American in the twenties, and by far the most potent influence in the creation of a mass culture. Not until 1928 were there 'talking pictures'; till then the absence of sound necessitated extravagant gestures and banal sub-titles of the 'Came the Dawn' variety. To a generation still not as far away from pre-war sentimentality as it pretended, these were acceptable enough; and, for the masses, film stars became idols. It is a reminder that the young were still not the true arbiters of fashion that the successful film stars of the twenties appealed mainly to adults. Rudolph Valentino, the screen's great lover, was adored to the limits of hysteria by women of riper years, and Mary Pickford, though advertised as 'the world's sweetheart', exploited a little-girl charm which did not mean much to the younger generation. Greta Garbo, likewise, was always a strictly adult favourite, if she ever was a favourite at all; her austere style caused her to play a larger part in the history of the film than she did in the minds of contemporary audiences. The young in the twenties lavished their affection on the heroes of the westerns, and on the comedians. The great age of screen comedy was almost over by the mid-twenties; Chaplin's best work had been done, and he was about to fall victim to delusions of grandeur. Similarly, the riotous slapstick 'shorts' with their calamitous falls through ceilings, their vertiginous motor-car chases and their squads of grotesquely jerking policemen were mostly earlier than the 1920's.

Experimental broadcasts of speech and music had taken place intermittently in England under private auspices from 1920 onwards and it was

soon clear that the Post Office, which was officially responsible for communication by wireless telegraph, would have to intervene to prevent a
multiplicity of competing broadcasting concerns. At the end of 1922 the
Post Office gave an interim licence to a British Broadcasting-Company
(consisting of the Marconi Company and other firms) to start operations
from eight broadcasting stations. In 1926 the Company was converted into
a public corporation, known as the British Broadcasting Corporation, and
controlled by a board of governors appointed by the Postmaster General.
Its first director-general, Sir John Reith, had been managing director of
the British Broadcasting Company. A man of determined character and
strong views, he established the tradition that the B.B.C. was primarily a
public service and not just a monopolistic purveyor of 'show-business'.
Since wireless sets were inexpensive, they rapidly became indispensable
pieces of household equipment, giving instant access to much new
experience. Thanks to Reith's emphasis on the idea of public service,
B.B.C. programmes catered for, and encouraged, a wide range of tastes
and interests. It is untrue that Reith made the B.B.C. priggish and reactionary, though it was careful to avoid both the ultra-violet of excessive
intellectualism or the infra-red of the music hall, night club and cabaret.
It tried not to be vulgar, and it insisted on being the cultural arm of Anglo-
Scottish Protestantism. Within these limits it immensely increased the
public stock of harmless pleasure and useful knowledge. Popular dance
music was broadcast daily, and this no doubt ensured that 'jazz' established
itself permanently instead of being the merely temporary craze it might
have been had it emerged in another age. Classical music, too, acquired a
larger audience, and this was important in a country in which central and
local government were, as they still are, largely in the hands of persons
indifferent to culture and hostile to its financial encouragement. The wireless also made available, to most of the homes of the country, regular book,
film and theatre reviews; there were occasional setpiece debates in which
might be heard the voices of Bernard Shaw and G. K. Chesterton; light
entertainment was forced to devise other aids to expression than the red
nose, baggy trousers and loud voice of the music hall comic transporting
two or three acts from music hall to music hall with only rare changes of
routine. Radio drama developed a high level of competence by the end
of the 1920's, Tyrone Guthrie's *The Flowers Are Not For You To Pick* in
particular attaining the status of a minor classic by its skilful employment
of radio's technical devices. Broadcasting was thus a beneficent instrument
of social and cultural melioration; and it is perhaps not without significance
that it was the one major social institution of the period which kept itself
free from the interference either of big business or of politicians.

Since much that the cinema offered was rubbish and much that came
out of the early loud-speakers was trivial, noisy or innocuous, both inventions were suspect to the intellectuals and those who had reached maturity

before 1914. D. H. Lawrence expressed what were felt to be the dangers of these mechanical means to passive entertainment:

> For God's sake let us be men
> not monkeys minding machines
> or sitting with our tails curled
> while the machine amuses us, the radio or film
>   or gramophone.
> Monkeys with a bland grin on our faces.

Headmasters denounced the cinema on speech days with some regularity, and it was asserted that the radio would result in people losing the capacity to 'make their own entertainment'. Children would no longer learn to play the piano. There was a great rush (after careful Bowdlerization) to preserve old English folk songs before they were lost for ever in a tidal wave of blues and hit tunes from across the Atlantic. There thus began in the twenties the long struggle to perpetuate the class war by the use of cultural weapons. Culture had been for so long the preserve of the well-to-do that it became an axiom that culture that was disseminated *ipso facto* ceased to be culture. By the 1930's this was beginning to produce an equally reactionary counter-attack on behalf of what was (and is) sometimes described as 'true' working-class 'culture'; this was a rather sloppy attempt to be patronisingly enthusiastic about brass bands, pigeon-fancying and fish and chips. Both factions were misguided. The new techniques had made inevitable the emergence of a mass-culture that was bound to be different from the segregated class-cultures of the past. Much that was disseminated by the new processes was ephemeral or bad; but the hostility to mass culture so frequently expressed from the 1920's onwards was often the result of a narrow educational system, a too early hardening of the spiritual arteries and, above all, of an ingrained distaste for the masses as such.

---

16 · MacDonald and Baldwin Arrive, 1922-23

In the 1922 election, the Conservatives gained 347 seats, the Asquith Liberals 60, the Lloyd George Liberals 57, and Labour 142. 71·3 per cent of the electorate voted, compared with only 58·9 in 1918, and all parties thus increased their total votes. 5,500,000 Conservative votes were cast,

4,249,000 Liberal votes and 4,241,000 Labour votes; but owing to the fact that 42 Conservatives were returned unopposed, these figures underestimate the number of Conservative supporters. The large increase in the number of Labour M.P.s (from 59 to 142) was mainly the result of an increase in the number of candidates put forward. The lack of close correlation between a party's total vote in the country and the number of its M.P.s in the Commons was more noticeable than usual in the 1920's. With three parties contesting many seats from 1922 onwards a high proportion of M.P.s was returned on a minority vote. Many Liberal votes were not reflected in the Commons because so many Liberal candidates obtained second place in three-cornered elections, and Labour votes were often 'wasted' in building up large majorities in particular constituencies. These circumstances aggravated the normal tendency of the British electoral system to impose on the country Governments of which a majority of voters have expressed their disapproval. On only three occasions during the first sixty years of the twentieth century did the political party forming the Government receive a majority of the total votes cast: the Conservatives had 51·1 per cent in 1900, 55·2 per cent in 1931, and 53·7 in 1935. The view therefore that the British parliamentary system tends to produce stable Governments ought to be qualified by the reflection that they are nearly always minority Governments.

Perhaps this is a virtue. Safe Governments with a majority in Parliament but a minority in the country are probably less inimical to democracy than safe Governments with an absolute majority, and less productive of anarchy than minority Governments with no Parliamentary majority; but in the 1920's the situation was fraught with dangers because all three political parties were themselves divided. In 1922 the Conservatives were divided between the majority who had made Bonar Law leader and the influential minority who had wanted to maintain the Coalition; the Liberals were two rival factions; and Labour was not in any coherent sense a party at all.

That some degree of stability emerged from these unpropitious circumstances was almost entirely the personal achievement of those much maligned men, Baldwin and MacDonald, both of whom were thrust into effective power for the first time by the 1922 election and its aftermath.

MacDonald arrived first. When the greatly enlarged Parliamentary Labour Party met to elect a new chairman, all were conscious that this time they were electing the Leader of His Majesty's Opposition. It was not, however, as a tribute to his resemblance to an upper-class politician, but to his reputation as a wartime pacifist, that MacDonald was chosen by the Parliamentary Party as its leader. MacDonald had been chairman of the Parliamentary Party from 1911 to 1914 and had led it well; after that, his opposition to the war, and his failure to obtain a seat in 1918, had still left him with the important position of treasurer of the Labour Party's National Executive. The party was led in the Commons by Arthur Henderson from 1914 to 1918 and, during the post-war coalition period, first by Willie Adamson and then by J. R. Clynes; the leadership of both had been undistinguished. By contrast, MacDonald had appeared as a martyr to capitalist vindictiveness during the election and by-election campaigns he had unsuccessfully fought in 1918 and 1921; and at the party conference of 1921 he had taken care to speak sympathetically about the party's Left wing. A further point in his favour in 1922 was that, in his usual fashion, Arthur Henderson, the real architect of the post-war Labour Party's fortunes, had not won a seat in the General Election.

Discontent with Clynes, the absence of Henderson, and the support of Left-wingers among the new M.P.s resulted in the election of MacDonald, not merely as chairman of the Parliamentary Party, but as 'chairman and leader'. The overthrow of Clynes was not in accordance with such precedents as the party could look back to, and was an illustration of the way the fraternal spirit on which the party prided itself in theory tended to evaporate in practice. It is conventional to view MacDonald's election as the result of a misunderstanding of his aims and outlook. True, the Left soon decided that from their point of view he belonged to the far Right of the movement; but once he became leader of the party nobody seriously attempted to unseat him until he unseated himself by forming the National Government of 1931. Perhaps Beatrice Webb summed up the feelings of the movement in general when she recorded in her diary:

And looked at impartially and without considering the way it was done, MacDonald's chairmanship has much to recommend it. He is abler than Clynes: he is free to devote his whole energy to being Parliamentary leader; he has a greater hold over the Scottish contingent,[1] and his chairmanship prevents him from depreciating the Parliamentary Party in the country which he would have done if he had been passed over. If he is not the best man for the post, he is at any rate the worst and most dangerous man out of it! He has now the opportunity of his life, and it remains to be seen whether he is a big enough man to rise superior to his personal hatreds and personal vanities and sectarian prejudices and do what is wisest for the cause in its largest aspects.[2]

What Mrs Webb was forgetting in writing this, so typical of her own and other people's evaluation of MacDonald then and afterwards, was that although MacDonald had perhaps more than his fair share of 'personal hatreds and personal vanities' he had fewer 'sectarian prejudices' than most other prominent figures in the movement. In trying to help his followers to rise above those prejudices as he did until 1931, he did much that was 'wisest for the cause in its largest aspects'. Clynes was a nice man, and Henderson a kind of working-class Austen Chamberlain with a flair like his for always playing the game and always losing it. MacDonald was a *grand seigneur manqué*: not an ideal leader, perhaps, for the motley

---

[1] A reference to the Clydeside M.P.s (Shinwell in particular) who worked most prominently for MacDonald's election.

[2] B. Webb, *Diaries*, Volume I, p. 231.

collection of misty idealists, semi-professional revolutionaries and moribund trade union officials that filled the benches behind him, but the only one who could create the impression that he was familiar with the techniques of parliamentary government.

Baldwin's advent was even more circuitous but hardly less adventitious. Balfour, Birkenhead and Austen Chamberlain were not available for employment in the Bonar Law administration because, although they did not oppose it after the election, they had opposed its formation. In consequence, after assuring the continuance of Lord Curzon at the Foreign Office, Bonar Law had little choice but to make Baldwin Chancellor of the Exchequer. While holding this office, Baldwin increased the public awareness of him created by his Carlton Club speech by bungling, to the full accompaniment of a great deal of mismanaged publicity, the negotiation of a British war debt settlement with the United States. The proposals were far from generous, but Baldwin had no success in obtaining modification of them and, in the end, a weak Government grudgingly accepted what he had done; he made the chance of a better settlement worse when he antagonized United States opinion by making caustic remarks to the Press about the narrowmindedness of certain members of Congress. Negotiating in a tight corner on matters of complexity was one of the several political skills which Baldwin never acquired.

A few months after the 1922 election, Bonar Law fell victim to the illness which killed him by the autumn. As a result, while Curzon presided over Cabinet meetings during the Prime Minister's illness, Baldwin deputized for him in the Commons. When, in May 1923, Bonar Law resigned, the issue of the succession clearly lay between the two men. The choice of Baldwin rather than Curzon became a *cause célèbre* in constitutional history for reasons which, on the whole, may be deemed insufficient.

Two constitutional principles were allegedly involved. One was whether or not a Prime Minister retiring from office in mid-term for reasons other than loss of political control does or does not advise the Crown on the choice of his successor. According to one version, an outgoing Prime Minister could not 'proffer' advice; according to Bonar Law himself it was 'not customary for the King to ask his Prime Minister to recommend his successor'. According to the King's private secretary, Bonar Law's health was too bad for the King to have the opportunity of consulting him; according to L. S. Amery, Bonar Law declined to make a recommendation. Quite obviously nobody knew what the rules were; the most useful hypothesis therefore is that no constitutional principle was involved at all, but only the fact that, whether in sickness or in health, Bonar Law did not like making unpleasant decisions. He disliked the unpleasant responsibility, when more or less on his deathbed, of denying Curzon the Premiership he knew Curzon coveted and which, on his record, Curzon could be said to deserve.

The reason neither Bonar Law nor, very significantly, anybody else who has been named, wanted Curzon to succeed had little to do with constitutional principles and much with the fact that nobody liked Curzon. He was notoriously arrogant, touchy and pompous, and once provoked his own coachman to describe him to his face as 'the damnedest cad in England'[1] He had quarrelled with almost everybody in his time and was widely regarded as unprincipled. His desertion of the Coalition at the last moment was regarded as the action of a man who deserted the ship just when he became certain, not only that it was sinking, but that there was another ship to jump on to. Thus, the stated objection to his succeeding to the premiership was not the real one. Balfour, who was ill with phlebitis, nevertheless promptly left his sickbed in the country when summoned to the Palace for his advice. It was apparently he who found the saving formula, that Curzon was ineligible because of his peerage; Balfour carefully said no more than this, but it seems that he subsequently displayed the complacency of one who had cleverly spiked someone's guns, not the sorrowful righteousness of one who had downed a brilliant colleague in the interests of the British Constitution.[2]

Curzon thus had the odious task of presiding over a meeting of the Conservative members of the two Houses for the purpose of electing as their leader a man who, though now Prime Minister, he had described in the throes of his disappointment, as 'a man of the utmost insignificance'. The tone of his speech indicates that Curzon knew that the choice had been made on personal and not constitutional grounds. It is worth recalling that the so-called precedent of 1923 did not prevent the suggestion in 1940 that Neville Chamberlain's successor should be Lord Halifax; similarly, when Harold Macmillan resigned from the Premiership in 1963 on the grounds of ill-health, nobody pretended that the Crown should not consult the outgoing Prime Minister. The invocation of the constitution over Curzon's rejection in 1923 sprang from the desire of everyone concerned to by-pass Curzon without actually telling him to his face that nobody wanted him. The absence of suitable devices of this sort made the rejection of R. A. Butler in 1957 and 1963 both more obvious and more painful.

Thus, like MacDonald, Baldwin rose to the first place in his party because a rival candidate, though entitled to pre-eminence, was not personally acceptable; and just as MacDonald was made leader because Henderson was out of Parliament, so Baldwin was made Prime Minister and leader because Austen Chamberlain was not in the Government.

.   .   .   .   .

[1] Beaverbrook, *Decline and Fall of Lloyd George*, p. 46.
[2] When late that night Balfour returned to his sickbed at Sheringham after his fatiguing journey, he was asked by some of his most cherished friends who were staying with him, 'And will dear George (Curzon) be chosen?' 'No,' he said placidly, 'dear George will not.' Winston Churchill, *Great Contemporaries*, p. 234.

There were many other resemblances between these two men, who were
to occupy 10 Downing Street alternately from 1923 to 1937. They were
more successful in winning votes in the country than in securing the undivided loyalty of their respective parties in the Commons, since both found
party polemics distasteful. Both hankered in a sentimental way after a
scheme of things in which all honest men of limited vision but unlimited
goodwill would lie down together like lambs. Both were masters of the
well-turned platform speech that gave audiences a cosy feeling that, if
everybody was very kind to everybody else, political strife would cease
and industrial and economic problems would solve themselves. Mac-
Donald talked of socialist brotherhood, and Baldwin, even before becoming
Prime Minister, had informed the House of Commons that the unemployment problem was not to be solved by actually making plans to deal with
it, but by the use of words:

Four words of one syllable each are words which contain salvation for this
country and for the whole world. They are 'Faith', 'Hope', 'Love' and
'Work'. No Government in this country today which has no faith in the
people, hope in the future, love for its fellow-men, and which will not work
and work and work, will ever bring this country through into better days and
better times. . . .

After years of Lloyd George, the Commons was much moved by this,
particularly as Baldwin's voice and manner gave a strong impression of
sincerity and because during the long quiet years since he had entered
the House in 1908 he had acquired (in contrast to MacDonald) the genuine
affection of the average member. But there was much in Baldwin's moving
and well-composed political sermons that foreshadowed MacDonald at
his worst and vaguest.

Both men paid heavily in their last years for their inability to do more
about 'work and work and work' than talk emotionally in public. By 1940,
the average Labour supporter looked back on MacDonald as a leader
who had betrayed his party, and the average Tory looked back on Baldwin
as a leader who had betrayed his country by failing to rearm it against
Hitler's Germany. Even at the time it was obvious that their combined
effect was to dampen the fires of the nation's energies and passions; under
their influence, England seemed so stagnant that it requires a real effort to recognize the signs of progress that are to be found in the Baldwin–MacDonald
era. Even so, much of the progress went on in spite of them, and they did
not call attention to it because they were themselves hardly aware of it.

Perhaps the basic reason for the dislike with which their memories
have been pursued lies in their determination to prevent party strife
becoming an irreconcilable war of classes. Baldwin was determined not
to let the Tories degenerate into an employers' party, just as MacDonald
was determined to make Labour something more than the party of the
industrial employee. Baldwin once memorably said,

I sometimes think, if I were not leader of the Conservative Party I should like to be the leader of the people who do not belong to any party. At any rate I should like to feel I had got them behind me. . . .[1]

And MacDonald, on the eve of becoming Prime Minister, told his own constituents that he did not care to be called a Socialist and preferred to be looked on 'as a sort of non-party Party leader'.

In perspective, they were, following the prescription written by Bonar Law in the 1922 election campaign, the Great Tranquillizers. By holding in check the extremists of their respective parties, they saved English society from being torn in pieces; by their skill as political leaders they succeeded for a time in putting back into working order the classical English political system by which the country is governed by alternative parties neither of which is bound exclusively to the interests of one class. By their persistent appeals to the kindlier emotions of men, to the feelings which united a community, rather than to those which divided it, they saved their country the political anarchy which demoralized France and from the frenzied dictatorships of action for the sake of action which demented Italy and Germany. The rule of Baldwin and MacDonald was the price the English paid for preserving their political freedom and their political stability at a time when everywhere else in Europe these things were fast disappearing.

Baldwin became Prime Minister on 22 May 1923 at the head of a Conservative Government with a comfortable majority. Yet, on 16 November 1923, Parliament was dissolved and, at the General Election on 6 December, the Conservatives lost 86 seats.

This unexpected development was due entirely to Baldwin. In October he announced to a large Conservative meeting that he had become convinced after thinking about the problem of unemployment 'day and night for long past' that the only long-term solution was a tariff to protect British industry against foreign competition. Since Bonar Law had given a pledge that the Government would not introduce tariffs, Baldwin proposed an appeal to the country on the issue. The words he used illustrate Baldwin's ability to make everything seem honest and heart-warming:

I have come to the conclusion myself that the only way of fighting this subject (i.e. unemployment) is by protecting the home market. I am not a clever man. I know nothing of political tactics, but I will say this: Having come to that conclusion myself I felt the only honest and right thing as the leader of a democratic party was to tell them, at the first opportunity I had, what I thought and submit it to their judgments.'[2]

Baldwin's references here to his lack of cleverness and his ignorance of political tactics need to be set against his subsequent claim that the whole thing was a political manœuvre:

[1] G. M. Young, *Baldwin*, p. 188.
[2] Quoted, *Britain Between the Wars*, Mowat, p. 166. Somewhat different wording is quoted in *British Political Parties*, McKenzie, p. 111.

The dissolution was deliberate and the result of long reflection. Rightly or wrongly I was convinced you could not deal with unemployment without a tariff. On political grounds the tariff issue had been dead for years, and I felt it was the one issue which would pull the party together, including the Lloyd George malcontents. Lloyd George was in America. He was on the water when I made the speech and the Liberals did not know what to say. I had information he was going Protectionist and I had to get in quick. I got the Cabinet into line. But for this move Lloyd George would have got Austen Chamberlain and Birkenhead and there would have been an end to the Tory Party as we know it. Bonar Law had no programme and the only thing was to bring the tariff issue forward.[1]

This is not necessarily mere hindsight on Baldwin's part. He was exceptional in the amount of time he devoted to ruminative study upon personalities and groupings in the Commons; in his quiet way he was a much better manager of men than Lloyd George, because he always saw others as persons whereas Lloyd George saw them only as props to be used, or not used, in his lifelong political conjuring act. Baldwin was fully aware in 1923 of his personal limitations; he felt it an urgent duty to heal the rift in the higher ranks of the Conservative Party that he himself had made so manifest at the Carlton Club meeting; he knew that Lloyd George was the most gifted personality on the political stage and that he had it in him to gather round him some of the best brains in both the Liberal and the Conservative Parties and fashion them into the Centre Party he had wished to create as long before as 1910. Basic to his policy at the end of 1923 was Baldwin's desire to 'dish the Goat'. By making Protection a Tory plank, Baldwin forced Lloyd George to stay a Free Trader and created once more that clear distinction between Tories and Liberals that Lloyd George's methods had obscured. Perhaps too, he reverted to the theme of the Carlton Club meeting; the real issue was not whether the next election was lost or won but the preservation of the Conservative Party. With a still-divided Liberal Party and an ineffective Labour Party, the only real hope of a stable political future for England lay between a united Conservative Party and a strong Centre Government under Lloyd George; and Baldwin, having served in the Coalition, felt he knew which alternative would best serve England's interests.

The election results were the immediate disaster for the Conservatives which Baldwin's critics had predicted. The country decisively rejected Protection; and, instead of their 1922 majority of some 75 over all other parties, the Conservatives found themselves, after the 1923 election, in a minority of almost 100. The Liberal party had reunited, with Lloyd George campaigning under Asquith's banner for Free Trade, and had secured 159 seats, an increase of about 40; while Labour, which denounced Protection as a cause of higher prices, gained roughly 50 seats and now had a total of 191 M.P.s.

[1] The Times, *Lord Baldwin, A Memoir*, 1947, p. 8.

Baldwin did not at once resign, but waited until Parliament reassembled in January 1924, when his Government was defeated on a vote of confidence. In the three weeks that thus elapsed, it was settled that there could be no Conservative–Liberal Coalition Government, because it would look like an anti-Labour conspiracy, given that the two parties had just fought the election on contrary economic principles and given also that Baldwin and Neville Chamberlain would not serve in a Government which would have to contain Lloyd George. A Liberal Government was out of the question since it would not get Conservative support; so was a Liberal-Labour Coalition because too many in the Labour movement would regard it as treachery to the working class, and because MacDonald would have been as little inclined as Baldwin to sit in Cabinet with Lloyd George. The only way out, therefore, was for Labour as the larger of the two Free Trade parties to form a Government, with Liberal voting support in the Commons. Thus, the architects of the first Labour Government were Asquith and Baldwin, assisted, one might say, by George V, who took the constitutionally and mathematically correct line that, when the Conservatives were defeated in the Commons, he would have to send for MacDonald because he led the next largest party in the House.

17 · Dilemmas of the First Labour Government, 1924

The Labour movement was taken aback by the election result and its unexpected outcome. It seemed to many that Baldwin's resuscitation of the tariffs issue must inevitably revive the Liberals as the chief Opposition party, and produce an Asquith Government with Lloyd George and Winston Churchill as its principal members, and with the Labour Party supporting it once more as in the days before 1914. The mythology of the Labour movement had not prepared it for the eventuality of the two 'bourgeois capitalist' parties urbanely standing aside to make way for a Labour Government they were alleged to be united in wanting to prevent. In consequence, to some, the Webbs in particular, the advent of a Labour Government so much earlier in time than had been expected seemed 'slightly ludicrous'. Many others, however, saw it as a moment of heart-warming triumph. Disillusion was swift.

It was in fact disastrous for the well-being of Britain in the twenties and thirties that, largely as a result of the political career of Lloyd George, the country was now without an effective political party of the Left. The 1923 election showed that the Liberal Party had continued to decline in strength over the country as a whole. Most people recognized that its unity at the time was, as Asquith bitterly described it subsequently, 'a fiction if not a farce'. Asquith and Grey belonged to a distant past, Lloyd George was associated with a war and a peace settlement that everybody wanted to forget, and Churchill was mistrusted. Yet, if the Liberal Party was failing, the Labour Party was incapable of effectively replacing it, and remained so until 1945. It was MacDonald's misfortune that though he wanted to make Labour look like a progressive party to suit electors of all sections of the community, he never found the way to do it.

The obstacles to making Labour a truly national movement capable of sustaining a broadly-based alternative Government were considerable, and it would be premature to assume that the obstacles had all been overcome by the 1960's. Its organization was extremely cumbersome. It had begun as a loose federation of working-class or vaguely Socialist societies, and, although after 1918 there were also constituency Labour parties with individual members, it remained fundamentally an uneasy federation of conflicting interests and ideologies. Technically, final authority in the party lay with the Annual Conference, which defined policy and elected the party's National Executive Committee for the ensuing year. The trade unions and other affiliated organizations nominated thirteen members out of the twenty-three on the Executive Committee, and the constituency parties nominated five; of the remaining five members, four had to be women and the fifth was the party treasurer. When it came to the actual voting for the Committee, however, nominees were voted upon by the entire Conference; and in view of their large membership, the trade unions had by far the largest number of votes at Conference. They had far more votes than the other affiliated societies, such as the Co-operative Society, the Independent Labour Party and the numerically very small Fabian Society, or the constituency Labour parties, whose total of paid-up members was nearly always small. The trade unions thus had a decisive voice in determining both the composition of the Executive Committee and the policy formulated by Conference.

The Parliamentary Labour Party, however, consisted solely of those persons within the movement who had contrived to get themselves adopted by a constituency party and then elected to Parliament. Many would-be candidates were sponsored by trade unions; others could usually claim membership of one or other of the affiliated societies; a few might well be middle-class ex-Liberals whose chief virtue from the point of view of their constituency was that they could themselves foot the bill for their election expenses. There was thus always something slightly fortuitous about the relationship in ideas and affiliations between the Parliamentary Party and the movement as a whole. Almost the only common factor between Conference, Executive Committee and Parliamentary Party was likely to be the strong influence of trade unionists.

It was this particular factor which militated against Labour's claims to be a national and not a class party. The Conservatives were an industrial employers' or a shareholders' party only by comparatively recent adoption; and few people hesitated to vote Conservative on the grounds merely that they were not employers of labour or did not own stocks and shares. Labour, on the other hand, had always proclaimed itself the party of the industrial workers, and, however much some of its leaders might seek to broaden this view, the preponderance of the trade unions in the movement was its only indisputable characteristic.

The Labour Party thus had to campaign under the disability of appearing to be the political arm of a sectional interest to which the majority of the electorate did not belong, and which pursued the sectional aim of securing for its members a larger share of the national wealth in the shape of shorter hours and higher wages, regardless of other sections of the community. The trade union movement could be accused with justice of caring little either for the professional classes or for the small shopkeeper, for example. There was no reason why it should, any more than one would expect the R.I.B.A. to concern itself with the hours and conditions of doctors, or the F.B.I. with the economic status of midwives; but by the same reasoning doctors would not be expected to vote for a political party dominated by architects, or midwives to vote for one dominated by steel magnates.

Labour's dependence on trade unionism was inescapable because without it it would have had little or no money, and because without a powerful sectional interest behind it a political party has no true basis. (This has been the insuperable obstacle to the revival of the Liberal Party). Nevertheless, it was undoubtedly an electoral handicap to the Labour Party that it so obviously depended for its existence not even on a particular class but on an organized section of that class, representing, even when membership was at its peak, no more than two-fifths of the working population. Much of the work of the Webbs, and much of the personal tragedy of MacDonald, were the outcome of their realization that for Labour to become a real alternative party to the Conservatives it had to acquire a broader base than that provided by the industrial manual workers.

Trade union domination contributed to the party's chronic lack of unity. Trade union leaders recognized only one loyalty: to the particular needs of their union members, measured in terms of immediate working conditions. They had no political philosophy, and were solely concerned with the struggle to squeeze economic advantage out of their employers. It would not be inaccurate to say that the sole contribution of the trade unions to the political movement consisted of money and votes – the votes of most of its rank and file at election times, the votes of its delegates at the annual conference and the votes of its sponsored M.P.s in the House of Commons. In the realm of political ideas it contributed almost nothing. The trade union leadership was almost always, for all its vast voting power, isolated from its own rank and file and from the political theorists and idealists in the political movement. Its isolation from its rank and file was due to the indifference of most union members, and the reckless revolutionary fervour of the energetic minority among them. Its isolation from the political theorists was due partly to the inveterate jealousy felt by established working-class leaders for all potential rivals, and partly to the deep-rooted suspicion of ideas characteristic of men who, having attained to positions of responsibility without the aid of formal education, regarded its disciplines and theories as irrelevant or nonsensical.

If trade unionism condemned Labour to disunity so did the parallel division between the Parliamentary Party and the Independent Labour Party. The latter had preceded the Parliamentary Party in time, having been one of the principal bodies which had brought it into being. True, most members of the Parliamentary Party belonged to it, but it held its own conferences, sponsored its own candidates and laid down its own policies, which it usually regarded as embodying the true faith which the Parliamentary and trade union leadership were neglecting or betraying. The I.L.P. was almost as hostile to the party's intellectuals as were the trade unionists. In their view, Keir Hardie alone was the true prophet and, like the Communists, they looked on the working class as a peculiar people who must be roused to an unremitting struggle against the forces of capitalism, and who were to be instructed to be ever-vigilant against bourgeois corruption and infiltration. To them, therefore, the Webbs, like their young protégé from Oxford, G. D. H. Cole, then coming into prominence, were always slightly suspicious characters; on the other hand, they were as little in love with MacDonald as the Webbs were.

In these confusing and intimidating circumstances cohesion could be attained only by dominating leadership of the Parliamentary Party, and this MacDonald provided as soon as he began to form a Labour administration. In theory, he and the Parliamentary Party were the servants of the Annual Conference and of the National Executive Committee; in theory, the Parliamentary Party was the political arm, principally, of the trade union movement; in theory, too, it was a loose alliance of M.P.s representing a variety of semi-Socialist ideas and interests. In practice the Parliamentary Party and the Labour Government were dominated by MacDonald as Prime Minister. His first service to the political Labour movement, therefore, was to impose on it the kind of leadership from above which characterized the Conservatives, and for the lack of which the Liberals had already nearly perished. MacDonald exploited, with aloof selfishness, the autocratic powers which the constitution places in the hands of the Prime Minister. He took little advice, even from senior members of the Parliamentary Party, when forming his Government; and, after forming it, he consulted some of them even less. He tried to exclude Arthur Henderson, of all people, from the Cabinet and gave him the Home Office only grudgingly; he refused to have the venerable George Lansbury, the East End's favourite Labour leader, in the Government at all. He appointed Haldane as Lord Chancellor, and another Liberal, Lord Parmoor, as Lord President of the Council; Lord Chelmsford, a Tory ex-Viceroy of India, was appointed to the Admiralty; and, with a final gesture of disrespect to the movement in general, MacDonald combined in his own person the office of Prime Minister and Foreign Secretary. The only Left-wing Socialist in the Cabinet was John Wheatley, who became Minister of Health.

MacDonald was not forgiven for the patrician contempt with which he conducted himself as Prime Minister in 1924. His reasons seem clear. Churchill had sneered that Labour was 'not fit to govern', and MacDonald believed that, in the long run, everything depended on proving – not to the Labour movement, but to voters outside it – that the gibe was untrue. MacDonald was concerned to establish a Government that accepted the situation as it really was. By a series of unpredictable accidents, Labour was in office long before it possessed the degree of support which would make possible the implementation of a characteristically 'Labour' policy, long, indeed, before the movement had grasped what 'Labour' policy involved. He needed, therefore, men who would accept the unavoidable circumstance that a minority Government, whose duration was certain to be limited, could not suddenly purge the Civil Service, dissolve the British Empire, disband the Army, Navy and Air Force, compel industry to grant all-round wage increases, and draw up a scheme of nationalization, for which, in any case, no clear blueprints existed.

Naturally, this policy created disgruntlement among the leaders and disillusioned the rank and file. From the intellectual Right, Beatrice Webb wrote,

MacDonald wants 8 million voters behind him and means to get them even if this entails shedding the I.L.P., the idealistically revolutionary section who pushed him into power.[1]

And from the far Left the Communists claimed at the 1924 annual conference that the movement faced the alternatives of 'a new Liberal Party – or a more vigorous Workers' Party.[2]

Yet such was the movement's intellectual and organizational confusion that there was no serious effort to dethrone MacDonald. Nothing could quite dim the lustre of the central fact that he was the first Labour Prime

[1] B. Webb, *Diaries*, Vol. II, p. 4.
[2] A. Hutt, *Post War History of the British Working Class*, p. 180.

Minister, the first leader of the party of the people to attain the highest office of State and to be treated on terms of equality by the great ones of the earth. If, in the end, he became a scapegoat, he had a good run as an archetype first. One of his most consistent critics, Emmanuel Shinwell, the Clydeside I.L.P.-er, who was given only junior office in the Mines Department in 1924, went so far as to say of him (though not without qualification)

he was at this time and for the rest of the nineteen-twenties the best-admired political leader ever appointed in peacetime.[1]

It is difficult to reconcile this assertion, however qualified, with the almost complete lack of support from the trade union movement that faced MacDonald. Ernest Bevin, general secretary of the Transport and General Workers' Union, which was almost his personal creation, called a dock strike in February 1924 which paralysed every port in the country with the object of securing an increase of two shillings a day. The strike lasted ten days and achieved its object; but not before the country and the Labour movement had been presented with the anomalous situation of one of the country's largest unions refusing the mediation of a trade unionist who held the office of Minister of Labour in a Labour Government; and of a Labour Government making plans to use troops to keep supplies going if the strike continued. In March, the London tram-drivers and conductors, also members of Bevin's T.G.W.U., came out on strike for more pay, and Bevin summoned the London busmen to sympathetic strike action. This called attention to the piquant fact that the Labour Government's Minister of Transport was the T.G.W.U.'s president. Once again, conciliatory action by a Labour minister came to nothing. MacDonald wrote a personal appeal to Bevin, but received nothing in return but a threat to bring the London underground railways to a halt as well. MacDonald retaliated by proclaiming a state of emergency under the Emergency Powers Act drawn up by the Coalition in 1920.[2] This brought protests from the General Council of the T.U.C. and from the National Executive. A way out was found when the Government introduced a Bill to inject some kind of order into the competitive chaos of London transport, and when the employers at last made a wage offer which the men could accept. Thus, Bevin had won, and the Government had been greatly discomfited.

During at least five of its ten months of office the Labour Government was harassed by other strikes: in shipyards and ship repair shops, among railway shopworkers and builders. There was an unofficial strike among the workers at the Wembley Empire Exhibition and on the London tube railways; and there was nearly another coal strike.

Bevin's own justification for what, on the face of it, seemed an eccentric

---

[1] E. Shinwell, *The Labour Story*, p. 124.
[2] See p. 113.

reaction to the advent of a Labour Government, underlines the anomalous position of a vested interest which is also the patron of a political party:

The bulk of the unions want something done in their own time and they are right in their demand. . . . There is work to do on the industrial field as well as in the political arena. While it is true that the two are to some extent part of the same effort we must not lose sight of the fact that Governments may come and Governments may go, but the workers' fight for betterment of conditions must go on all the time.[1]

Bevin's contention was reasonable as far as it went; but it did reveal a lack of preparatory thinking that no agreed plan of action between the political and industrial wings accompanied the operation of a Labour Government. The Labour movement had fervour; it could appeal to basic moral values; it had the sinews of industrial organization. But it had no co-ordinating brain. G. D. H. Cole had the temerity to suggest, in the light of the events of 1924, that this problem ought to be examined. Bevin brushed him aside with the contempt of the hard-headed union boss for new-fangled notions from outsiders. He sneered at 'the continual popping up of new factions' with ideas for attaining Socialism by

a set of rules based upon such knowledge of the working class as has been gleaned from the theoretical treatises in the University library. . . . To understand the workers one must live with them and work with them.[2]

It was as progressive an attitude as that of a firm of city financiers refusing to install telephones or typewriters.

Meanwhile, in fields other than those of industrial relations, the Government did what it could to prove it was fit to govern. 'The great and manifold tasks of Empire must in the end subdue these new forces to their purpose,' *The Times* had written, and so it came to pass. The Labour Government would not introduce an era of pacifist harmony by scrapping the Navy; they planned to provide it with five new cruisers (though not eight as the Tories had proposed). True, they stopped work on the Singapore naval base; but they took a firm line with Egyptian nationalists, and the Prime Minister informed the Indians that Great Britain would not be 'cowed' by acts of violence. The air estimates were increased, and the use of R.A.F. bombers to maintain order in Iraq was defended from the Government front bench. The critics on the Left did not stop to ask how long the Liberals would have supported a Government which pursued radically different policies; but the shock to the evangelical, pacifist and anti-imperialist feeling in some parts of the movement, on being confronted with the realities of government, was considerable.

In domestic affairs, improvements were made in unemployment benefit, old age pensions were increased, state scholarships were rescued from the oblivion into which the Geddes Axe had consigned them, £28 millions

[1] A. Bullock, *Life and Times of Ernest Bevin*, Vol. I pp. 243–4.
[2] Bullock, *op. cit.*, p. 256.

was allotted to public works, and the duties on sugar, tea, cocoa and coffee were cut. The Wheatley Housing Act is regarded as the most durable of the Government's achievements. It granted a State subsidy of £9 millions a year for the construction of council houses, and was combined with negotiations with the appropriate unions to increase the building labour force. Under the Wheatley scheme 500,000 houses were built in the next ten years.

In foreign affairs, MacDonald set about improving Anglo-French relations, which were bad by the beginning of 1923, chiefly owing to British dislike of the French occupation of the Ruhr. Fortunately for MacDonald, the futility of French policy in the Ruhr and the runaway inflation which German resistance to it had caused, induced a more sensible mood in both countries. The ferocious Poincaré gave way to the more internationally-minded Herriot; and in Germany, a new Foreign Minister, Stresemann, determined on a policy of 'fulfilment', attempting to restore his country's status by co-operation with France and Britain rather than by continued passive resistance. The outcome of these changes was the London conference in August 1924 at which the Dawes Plan for tackling the reparations problem was accepted by Germany and its ex-enemies. It included arrangements for assuring a stable currency in Germany, a scaling down of annual reparations payments and for the raising, chiefly in the United States, of foreign loans to tide the Germans over. The French were to evacuate the Ruhr.

Although he was lucky to have taken over the Foreign Office at a time when things were working together for his good, MacDonald gained much prestige for his handling of the London conference; it was also bad luck on Curzon who would, for all his prickliness, probably have done at least as well had Baldwin's intuition not put the Tories out and Labour in. Nevertheless, MacDonald deserved some good fortune and in at least one important sphere of international relations he was able to show a Labour Government (or rather its Prime Minister) to advantage.

MacDonald also led a strong British delegation to the League of Nations Assembly at Geneva in 1924. Although the Government refused to support a proposed Treaty of Mutual Assistance which would have made military assistance to victims of aggression automatic, it did produce the Geneva Protocol, in the drawing up of which Arthur Henderson and the pacifist Parmoor had a considerable share. This aimed at making arbitration of international disputes compulsory; but before it could be ratified the Government fell. Nevertheless, MacDonald could justly claim that Labour had produced the first serious efforts made by a British Government to turn the League into a reality.

Like Lloyd George, however, MacDonald ran into trouble when he addressed himself to the task of trying to bring the U.S.S.R. into the European system. He accorded official diplomatic recognition to the

U.S.S.R. almost immediately on coming into office, and in August 1924 signed a commercial treaty. After much haggling, a further treaty was signed, foreshadowing, subject to satisfactory Russian payments to the British bondholders whose investments had been confiscated after the Revolution, a British loan to Russia. The prospect of the Government being defeated when these treaties came before the Commons for ratification may have contributed to MacDonald's decision to resign in October over the comparatively trivial issue of the prosecution of a Communist journalist.

In August, the acting editor of the Communist *Workers' Weekly* was charged with publishing an article calling on the military not to fire on their fellow-workers. The prosecution was dropped on the grounds that the article had been no more than a protest against the use of troops in industrial disputes. MacDonald was criticised, as usual, from several quarters. The Left wing of the Labour Party treated the original charge (accompanied as it was by a raid on the *Workers' Weekly* offices) as one further example of the Government's hostility to the working class movement; and the Liberals and the Conservatives treated the dropping of the prosecution as further evidence (after the treaties with the Bolsheviks) that the Government was either a friend of the Communists or the tool of its quasi-Communist Left wing. When the Conservatives put down a motion of censure, and the Liberals demanded a committee of inquiry, MacDonald chose to treat the matter as one of confidence and, as soon as the Government was defeated, asked for a dissolution. The Conservatives so contrived matters that the motion which brought the Government to defeat was not theirs but the Liberals'. This helped to ensure that in the imminent election some Liberals would lose votes because the party had put Labour in and others would lose votes because it had put Labour out.

Fear that the Government might be thrown out later over the Russian issue is not the only reason offered to explain MacDonald's impetuous haste to dissolve over the Campbell case. Another suggestion is that he was mentally and nervously exhausted by the constant attacks of his enemies in the Tory and Liberal Parties and of his professed friends in the Labour movement. His personal methods of carrying out the burdens of both the Premiership and the Foreign Office also strained a temperament that was at no time robust. Yet another is that he made haste to synchronize the dissolution with the party's Annual Conference. He would then be able to present himself and his Government as victims of capitalist wrecking tactics in the Commons and of Communist wrecking tactics outside. Both notions would – and in fact did – provide a means of rallying the great bulk in the centre; MacDonald, who was the year's party chairman, had the Queen's Hall in a state of euphoria not unlike that which filled it at other times of the year when Sir Henry Wood was conducting the Promenade Concerts. Moreover, at a time when the popular Press was ringing with blood-chilling warnings that a vote for Labour was virtually a vote for the institution of the Soviet system in Britain, this Annual Conference of 1924 rejected the affiliation of the Communist Party to the movement, and forbade both the adoption of Communists as parliamentary candidates and the admission of individual Communists as members of the party.

The sensation of the election campaign was the so-called Zinoviev Letter. This purported to be from Zinoviev, the member of the Soviet Government who presided over the Communist International, which controlled Communist propaganda outside Russia. It was addressed to the Communist Party of Great Britain, and called upon its members to work for ratification of the proposed Anglo-Soviet treaty because this would provide greater opportunities for Communist infiltration in Britain not only among the workers but also among the armed forces. A copy of this letter (the original has never apparently come to light) was sent by the Foreign Office to *The Times* four days before polling day. A letter of protest to the Soviet representative in London by a Foreign Office official was also published.

The fact that the Zinoviev letter contained the contemptuous references to the Labour Party usual in Communist polemics went unnoticed. It was seized on, both by *The Times* and the *Daily Mail*, as evidence that the Labour Cabinet had been on the verge of committing the country to treaty relations with a Government resolutely determined to destroy the British people by subversion from within. It was thus the patriotic duty of every true Briton to vote for the Conservatives and the Union Jack and not for the Labour Party and the Red Flag.

Whether the letter was a forgery or not has not been determined. MacDonald, still Foreign Secretary at that moment, was busy in the country with his election campaign; the letter's substance had been communicated to him, and he had instructed that, if its authenticity were proved, a protest should be made and its contents published. It was in fact published by the Foreign Office before its authenticity could be established because the *Daily Mail* also had a copy and was apparently threatening to reveal it in its own columns first. There was thus the further element in the affair of a patriotic newspaper forcing the hand of a dilatory pro-Bolshevik Government because ever-vigilant news-hawks had found out that it had something to hide.

It was an unsophisticated tactic and there is no evidence that it had much effect; but if it did not sway the electorate in 1924 it served to embitter the Labour movement against their opponents for a generation. It became a cardinal belief in the Labour Party that at every election campaign the Conservatives were liable to think up another 'trick' like the Red Letter, and in the long run it redounded to the Conservatives' discredit. It might also be suggested that it helped to exacerbate that feeling of having to deal with inherently unscrupulous opponents which produced the General Strike of 1926.

The 1924 election returned 415 Conservatives to Westminster, 152 Labour M.P.s and 42 Liberals. In the largest turnout of any election between 1910 and 1950, the Conservative vote rose by 2,500,000, and the Labour vote by just over a million, whereas the Liberal vote had fallen by 1,382,000 (i.e. by over 30 per cent in ten months). Thus, Baldwin was back, with a record number of Conservative M.P.s behind him (a record which only he himself among Prime Ministers subsequently exceeded) and the Liberal Party was now of the parliamentary dimensions of the Labour Party of 1910.

18 · Conservative Achievement, 1924-29

The 1924 election vindicated the skill (or intuition) with which Baldwin had handled the Conservative Party's affairs since taking over from Bonar Law. It was now, thanks to him, united in personnel and triumphant at the polls, and had at last recovered from the disruptive effects upon it of the acts of Joseph Chamberlain and Lloyd George. Baldwin's second Government contained all Lloyd George's former Tory supporters. Austen Chamberlain became Foreign Secretary, Birkenhead went to the India Office, and, when Curzon died in 1925, Balfour joined the Cabinet also.

The biggest fish Baldwin landed, however, was Churchill, who at last realized that, now it had had to drop Protection, the Conservative Party offered him the only chance of continued political usefulness. He contested Epping as a Conservative and returned to the House for the first time since 1922. Baldwin not only took him into the Government, but made him Chancellor of the Exchequer, the Government post which Churchill was least qualified to hold. There could be no clearer illustration of how exclusively Baldwin saw politics in terms of managing other politicians. Outside the Government, Churchill would either be a rebellious back-bencher or become an ally of Lloyd George; if brought inside it and under-employed in a minor department he would make himself a nuisance by trying to interfere with most of his colleagues' departments. Baldwin gave Churchill the Treasury because it would give him enough to do to keep him quiet; and, with Churchill too busy and Lloyd George too powerless to cause trouble, Baldwin felt that both he and the country could sleep peacefully at night and be all the better for it.

In choosing his chief colleagues, Baldwin was living on the political legacy of the past; except for Churchill, they were all at the end of their careers. The newer men in the· Government consisted almost entirely of the frustrators and the frustrated of the next decade and a half. Neville Chamberlain was at Health, as he had been in 1923; the future Lord Halifax, as yet still the Hon. E. Wood, was at Agriculture, Sir Samuel Hoare was at the Air Ministry and Sir Thomas Inskip was one of the Law Officers. All these were to play a large and not usually glorious part in the politics of the 1930's. Others were to be the much baffled opponents of these men: among them were Lord Robert (Viscount) Cecil who left the Government in 1927 over its lack of support for the League of Nations, to which he devoted his life; Leopold Amery, a doughty Imperialist who held no Government office from 1929 to 1940 and whose speech from the Tory back benches in May 1940 did much to sweep Neville Chamberlain out of 10 Downing Street and Churchill into it;[1] and Duff Cooper, who resigned after the Munich agreement. The Government had, as its leading figure of fun, Sir William Joynson Hicks, known in affectionate derision as 'Jix' who contrived to make the Home Office ridiculous on a number of occasions. It is safe to say, therefore, that not only was it a Government without a policy; it was a government without new talent. The one exception to this was, perhaps, Sir Douglas Hogg; but he entered the Lords, as Viscount Hailsham, on becoming Lord Chancellor in 1928, and contributed little to political life in consequence.

The first task of Austen Chamberlain at the Foreign Office was to inform the U.S.S.R. that the treaties negotiated by the Labour Government would not be proceeded with. Next, he informed the League Council that Britain would not accede to the Geneva Protocol. Thus, the two props on which European peace might have been built, a stiffening of the League's peace-preserving procedures and an attempt to woo the Russians out of their Slavo-Marxist isolationism, were smartly kicked aside. Neither prop might have served; but the alternative device now invented certainly did not.

In October 1925, the Locarno Treaties were signed. The frontiers between France and Germany, and Belgium and Germany, were guaranteed by the three Powers concerned and by Great Britain and Italy; Germany and Poland, and Germany and Czechoslovakia undertook to submit disputes between them to arbitration; and France signed treaties of mutual assistance with both Poland and Czechoslovakia in the event of aggression by Germany.

These arrangements were hailed as a triumph for all concerned: Austen Chamberlain for Great Britain, Briand for France and Stresemann for

[1] See p. 321.

Germany. When Chamberlain described them as marking 'the real dividing line between the years of war and the years of peace' he was not altogether exaggerating: one further agreement made at Locarno was that Germany should enter the League. The atmosphere at Locarno had been genuinely cordial and, taken in conjunction with the Dawes Plan for reparations drawn up the year before, presaged a new era of European harmony. Yet the value of Locarno was limited strictly to the fact of its being agreed upon; intrinsically, the various promises said little and omitted much. In regard to the German problem, Britain undertook at Locarno to do what she knew very well she would have to do: i.e. defend Belgium and France against a German attack. Similarly, the French undertook to do what they knew very well they would have to do if they were to survive: i.e. defend Poland and Czechoslovakia against Germany. More important were the omissions: if Germany attacked either Poland or Czechoslovakia neither Great Britain nor Italy was committed to doing anything. The basic problem, therefore, that France by itself might not be strong enough to defend Poland and Czechoslovakia against Germany, was written out of existence.

Moreover, the mere signature of the Locarno agreements implied that the League Covenant, to which Germany was about to become a full party, was null and void. Already, under Article 10, every signatory of the Covenant guaranteed all other League members against external aggression. Already, under Article 15, every League member had undertaken to submit every international dispute either to arbitration, judicial decision or to examination by the League Council. Consequently, the States concerned said, at Locarno, that they would do what they intended to do anyway, but that they would not do certain things they had already promised in the Covenant that they would do.

Thus, though it was a badly needed gesture of reconciliation, Locarno was little more than the enshrinement in an international agreement of the adage that courtesy costs nothing. Unhappily, both the Covenant and Locarno set the fashion for meaningless gestures in international affairs. Before Baldwin's Government fell it had also signed the Kellogg-Briand Peace Pact of 1928 in which almost all States undertook to renounce war 'as an instrument of national policy' while still being allowed to fight wars of self-defence. The public at large, unfortunately, mistook these displays of ritual politeness for reality, and entered the 1930's convinced that, provided more and more politicians signed more and more pieces of paper, peace was assured. This process reached its culmination when Neville Chamberlain returned from Munich with a piece of paper in 1938.

Perhaps no member of Baldwin's Cabinet was more relieved by the settlement of the political scene in 1924 than the Minister of Health, Neville Chamberlain. He was a priggish man, quite without personal magnetism and resentfully aware that this put him at a disadvantage both as a debater in the House and as a competitor with livelier rivals for public notice and affection. He was also conscious that although, like his father Joseph and his brother Austen, he had been Lord Mayor of Birmingham, he had not been much of a success as a businessman and had failed to give satisfaction when called in by Lloyd George to serve for a short period as Minister of National Service. When he first entered the Commons in 1918 he was already in his fiftieth year and never developed much interest in party politics, which were the breath of life to men like Lloyd George, Churchill, MacDonald and Baldwin. But if he lacked the skills for playing the political game he did possess a capacity for quiet persistent work. The opportunity to exercise this modest but useful gift was presented for the first time when in 1924 Baldwin won for him the more or less certainty of four or five years of office. His awareness, in his years of service under Baldwin, and then in the National Government from 1931 onwards, that he was almost the only Cabinet Minister of the time who had a consistent record of jobs successfully accomplished probably helped to harden him in the view that he could always do a good job if he were free to do it by himself in his own fashion. He was a political tortoise; and because he had outrun so many of the prancing hares of the 1920's he developed a carapace so hard that by 1940 it was almost impossible to get through to him.

Whereas Austen may be said chiefly to have inherited his father's Unionist and Imperialist convictions, Neville seems to have inherited the Chamberlain Radical tradition; and this fits in with his personal inability to put on the grand manner, which fitted the be-monocled Austen like a glove. Neville was the sort of middling Tory business-man that Baldwin pretended to be; and though his attitude to the poor was harshly complacent he was as unresponsive to the lure of luxury and high society as Baldwin himself. The result was that Neville Chamberlain was responsible for the only major developments in the history of State-organized social security which took place between the fall of Lloyd George and the issue of the Beveridge Report in 1942. In furthering these developments, he worked in harness with the Chancellor of the Exchequer; and Churchill was as conscious as Chamberlain was of being the son of a Unionist who had also been a Radical.

Although few of them were of major significance, Chamberlain piloted no fewer than twenty-one Bills through the Commons between 1924 and 1929; no wonder he recorded in private his disapproval of the indolence of the Prime Minister. In 1925, Churchill and Chamberlain put through a joint programme of social reform. In his budget, Churchill made financial provision for a new State pensions scheme, which Chamberlain introduced as the Widows', Orphans and Old Age Contributory Pensions Bill. All persons covered by National Health Insurance were now compulsorily insured, not only against sickness and unemployment as before, but also for widows' pensions, with allowances for dependent children and orphans, and for a 10s. a week pension for insured workers and their wives at the age of 65. The non-contributory pension created in 1908 for those over 70 was continued, but insured persons would get the full rate of pension once they were 70, irrespective of their means. The act was thus a milestone in the history of social security legislation; it is characteristic of its author's lack of political flair that, whereas in the folk-memory of the nation the contributions of Lloyd George, of Beveridge, of Churchill and of Bevan are remembered, that of Neville Chamberlain is usually forgotten.

Chamberlain's legislative *chef d'oeuvre*, however, was the complicated Local Government Act of 1929, one of the century's major administrative statutes before 1945. The Act brought about wholesale changes in finance and organization. First, it provided for derating: agricultural land and buildings were freed altogether from local authority rates, and industrial premises were liable for rates on only one quarter of their net annual value. The purpose of these changes was to relieve both industry and agriculture of the burden of paying the local authorities for services from which, in the main, they did not greatly benefit. Furthermore, the system of basing rates solely on the rental value of premises had discouraged improvement, and was open to the objection that it was unrelated to the profitability or unprofitability of the business concerned. To the charge that derating transferred the whole rates burden to residential property, a partial answer was that factory owners and farmers were themselves also owners and occupiers of such premises.

The 1929 Act was also concerned to distribute the financial burdens of local authorities more equitably. It transferred responsibility for the relief of the destitute from the 640 Poor Law Unions established by the Poor Law Amendment Act of 1834 to Public Assistance Committees of the 140 County and County Boroughs; after 1929, the old Poor Law Guardians ceased to function. The purpose of this was to distribute the cost of the poor rate over a whole administrative county. Before 1929 each group of Guardians levied its own poor rate, so that the poorest areas, which could least afford it, and upon whom the demand for poor relief was greatest, had the highest poor rate. This had led to desperate action by some of the more hard-pressed areas. The example of Poplar had been followed by various Boards of Guardians who had insisted on paying very high rates of poor relief on borrowed funds. Chamberlain had already obtained power to supersede such Guardians; he used it in West Ham and the mining districts of Chester-le-Street, in Durham, and Bedwellty, in Monmouth-shire. The abolition of Boards of Guardians in the 1929 Act made the average area of charge for poor relief four times larger than before. In order to spread the burden still more widely the Act also substituted Block Grants from the Treasury for the old Grants-in-Aid. Previously, Government grants to a local authority had been calculated as a percentage of the authority's own expenditure on a given service. After 1929, each authority received a block grant calculated according to a complicated formula, based on the area's needs and population. This had the effect of shifting more of the cost of local services in the poorer areas from the local rate-payer to the Exchequer – i.e. to the whole body of taxpayers.

The Act had therefore much to commend it; but it was open to the criticism that it was an elaborate financial overhaul of a system that was in fact out of date. Derating was designed to help industry at a time when much of it was chronically depressed; but nothing serious was done to find a positive cure for the decline in British exports. Moreover, if there was a case for condemning local authority rates as a regressive tax in their application to industry, there was also the wider problem that they were regressive by nature and might have been replaced by some other form of local authority tax. Nor did the transfer of responsibility for the destitute to the Public Assistance Committees reflect the strong body of feeling which had claimed, ever since the Poor Law Commission of 1905, that the whole Poor Law as such should be replaced by a system which made no distinction at all between a destitute person and any other citizen. Chamberlain, however, held to the traditional Puritan conviction that poor relief must always be kept small enough to deter idleness.

Other useful legislation by the second Baldwin administration included the Act, already noticed, which established the British Broadcasting Corporation, and the Electricity Supply Act; both of these became law in 1926. The latter Act placed the generation and the 'wholesale' distribution of electricity in the hands of a Central Electricity Board, chosen by the Minister of Transport. The C.E.B. was to purchase electric power from the generating stations (the smaller of them were superseded) and distribute it to the electricity supply companies. These were still either municipally or privately owned. It was a strange, if efficient, half-way house on the route to nationalized electricity: the Board did not control supply to the consumer nor did it build or own the generating stations. Its most obvious consequence was the National Grid with its ubiquitous 'pylons'.

Like the B.B.C., but unlike the Port of London Authority, the C.E.B. was controlled by nominees of the central Government. Nineteen-twenty-six is therefore an important landmark in the history of the public corporation as an institution; the non-elective character of those chosen to run a public corporation and their freedom from day-to-day interference by the Ministry which appoints them were their distinctive characteristic. The connection between the public corporation and anything that might reasonably be described as socialistic was thus tenuous from the outset. As a managerial device the public corporation was invented by strongly Conservative Governments and its over-all effect has been to increase parliamentary control very little and popular control not at all.

In 1928, the anomaly by which the franchise had been extended only to women over 30 in 1918 was removed by the grant of female suffrage on the same terms as male suffrage. Joynson Hicks, along with that other not very glowing political luminary, Sir Thomas Inskip, was also prominent in 1927 and 1928 in securing the defeat of a proposal brought before the House, as a result of the deliberations of the Assembly of the Church of England, for the revision of the Prayer Book. Few Anglicans a generation later greatly mourned the failure to make the 1928 Prayer Book the only legal basis of Church of England services; but the circumstances of its rejection long rankled. That a change on which the deliberative body of the Church had agreed should have been rejected by a House of Commons containing members who might be Nonconformists, atheists or Jews, was humiliating. Since the only way out would be disestablishment, so that the Church stopped being ultimately dependent on Parliament, nothing was done. The advantages of establishment were held to outweigh the disadvantages.

The reasons for the book's rejection reflect little credit on either the intelligence, or the historical and religious sense of its opponents. The basic objection of Joynson Hicks and the evangelical party which followed him was that the Prayer Book contained provision for such matters as the reservation of the holy sacrament. This was denounced as Papistical; the book's opponents preferred, to these terrifying innovations, the state of mind which nourished its spiritual roots in such elements in our religious heritage as the Titus Oates plot, the Gordon riots and Lord John Russell's Ecclesiastical Titles Bill.[1]

On its side, Parliament compromised by inactivity also. The new Prayer Book was subsequently published and could be used at the discretion 'of the bishops'. In practice, this meant at the discretion of the parish priest. Such a procedure was illegal, since use of the 1928 book was clearly contrary to statute; but no parliamentary reprisals followed.

The significant contribution to Imperial affairs made by this Government was the setting up of a committee on Inter-Imperial Relations, presided over by Balfour, which reported to the Imperial Conference of 1926. This endeavoured to give a comprehensible legal definition to the relations of the self-governing Dominions with one another and with the United Kingdom. The definition had to try to demonstrate, unequivocally, the equivocal position of the Dominions as independent sovereign States who were nevertheless members of an Empire. Under Balfour's sophisticated guidance it pronounced that the United Kingdom and the Dominions were

autonomous communities within the British Empire, equal in status, in no way subordinate to one another in any aspect of their domestic or external affairs, though united by a common allegiance to the Crown, and freely associated as members of the British Commonwealth of Nations.

[1] 'There was a great deal of feeling on the matter and the protagonists opposed each other rather like a Hindu-Moslem mob' (Earl Winterton, *Orders of the Day*, p. 151).

The formula was much applauded and was indeed ingenious in its use of the survival of monarchy in Britain. In future, the only legal link between the Dominions and the United Kingdom was through the one United Kingdom institution which, though sovereign, was both neutral and powerless in relation to British politics and government.

The formula received legal sanction when it was incorporated into the Statute of Westminster in November 1931. By the statute, the Crown acquired a multiple legal personality; the King acted as King of Great Britain, Canada, Australia, New Zealand and South Africa and (nominally) Ireland. He exercised his kingly functions in each Dominion through the physical presence of a Governor-General, appointed in accordance with the wishes of the appropriate Government, and carrying out in each Dominion the functions, ceremonial and constitutional, which in the United Kingdom were carried out by the King in his own person. As King of Great Britain he conducted his relations with the Dominion Governments through the Secretary of State for the Dominions; as titular head of that part of the empire which was outside the Dominions he acted through the Secretary of State for the Colonies; and as Emperor of India he functioned through the Secretary of State for India and the Viceroy.

The formula served well enough until after the Second World War, though the Irish had made nonsense of it by 1939. By that time they had refused to have a Governor-General, had declared themselves a republic, and had proclaimed their neutrality in the Second World War. Constitutional purists had always regarded neutrality as incompatible with membership of the British Commonwealth owing to the extreme metaphysical difficulty of envisaging a royal personage being simultaneously both belligerent and non-belligerent. Worse was to come after 1945 when successive new candidates for 'Dominion status' objected to the word 'Dominion' because of its association with domination, objected to the idea of being under the British Crown because they wanted to be republics, and compelled the abandonment of the adjective 'British' on the grounds that they were not British. However, in due time, a formula was found to cover these requirements also; by the 1960's Elizabeth II was the 'Head' of a 'Commonwealth of Nations' shorn of its British epithet.

The difficulty of devising a formula to describe the independence-with-association which was the mark of Britain's relations with her Dominions after 1919 and even more so after 1945 reflects chiefly on the inadequate categories of international and constitutional law. These are by tradition dominated by the notion of sovereignty. The definition of sovereignty has proved difficult enough; to define freedom, however, is ultimately impossible, since to define it is to limit it. Yet it is so rare a commodity in the association of States, above all the association of those who were once unfree, that unless it is defined, even confusedly, nobody will believe it exists.

19 · Towards a General Strike, 1922-26

The causes of the General Strike of 1926 are general and particular. Some of the general causes are to be found in the overall failure of British industry to adjust itself to a changing pattern of world trade; others in the out-of-date, unintelligent attitudes of both owners and miners. More particular causes are such specific happenings as the slump in coal exports after the temporary recovery during the French occupation of the Ruhr, and the return to the gold standard in the spring of 1925. Ultimately, however, responsibility lay with the individuals or groups of individuals who made particular decisions (or failed to make them) at particular times. In the last resort, the General Strike was, on the evidence available, an unnecessary and avoidable calamity for which the General Council of the T.U.C. and the Baldwin Government were both to blame.

Discontent among employees in the basic industries in the 1920's was caused by large scale unemployment, a fall in wages since 1920, and fear of further cuts. The existence of so much unemployment made the bargaining power of workers almost entirely dependent upon trade union organization, for, without it, wages would certainly have been depressed still further. If labour, like any other commodity, is over-plentiful, it will not normally command a good price. The workers were thus bound to feel that aggressive union action was essential to preserve their standards of living. The general decline in the profitability of the basic industries created in employers the desire to go on reducing wages. True, the statistics seemed to show that officially the cost of living had also fallen, more or less in line with the fall in wages, so that the real value of the latter was not much less than in 1920. But, since money wages were everywhere low, a quite small deficiency in their real purchasing power mattered much more to the individuals concerned than to an economist looking at the situation on a graph. Furthermore, the standard of living, as measured by general need, was rising all the time. By the mid-twenties it was, for example, not unreasonable already to describe as 'poor' someone who could not afford to go to the 'pictures' or pay for a wireless set and a wireless licence; but to the official mind these were 'luxuries'. Thus, in 1925, Beatrice Webb wrote, with evident bewilderment,

What puzzles me is the gross discrepancy between the alarmist views . . . about the decadence of Great Britain – confronted by the absence of all *signs* of extreme poverty among the people at large. Compared with the eighties, even with the early years of the twentieth century, *there is no outward manifestation of extreme destitution.* . . . What is the explanation of this curious combination of the permanent unemployment of 11 per cent of the population with a general sense of comparative prosperity on the part of the bulk of the population.[1]

Over a century before, in the years of depression after 1815, similar difficulty was found in reconciling reports of distress among the workers with the fact that they were able to buy tea and sugar and cotton clothing which had not been possible forty years earlier. In a civilized country, however, poverty is a relative, not an absolute term. Anyone whose standard of living is well below the general standard is *ipso facto* definable as 'poor'. The fact that, in some other society, or at some other time, he would have been considered 'rich' is irrelevant. The basic facts were that the workers in the heavy industries in the 1920's tended to be badly off in relation to many other sections of the community, and fully expected, to judge from the attitude of their employers, shortly to be made worse off. And perhaps the most tragic fact (which Beatrice Webb seems not to have realized) is that without the large army of unemployed they might have been poorer still. The older industries were able to keep going and to pay reasonable wages to much of their labour force only by dispensing with part of it, and leaving it to be maintained in idleness by the unemployment insurance fund or the Poor Law Guardians.

Had there been signs of hope or of revival in the basic industries the workers would probably have been less eager than they were to follow the call of their leaders for a national strike in 1926. As it was the industries on which British prosperity had traditionally been built and which had hitherto provided employment on the largest scale were either contracting in the post-war period or, at best, making little progress in the face of strong foreign competition. Whereas, by the middle 1920's, the world demand for cotton exceeded the pre-war level by 20 per cent, British cotton exports, particularly of the cheaper qualities, declined. The Indian market had been lost to the Indians themselves and to the Japanese, who had also captured much of the Far Eastern market. Central and South American markets had also been captured by the United States. If there was less unemployment in the Lancashire cotton industry than might have been expected, this was due to the general adoption of short-time working; but this put up production costs.

Productive capacity was also in excess of effective demand in iron and steel and in shipbuilding in the mid-twenties. In 1925 British industry was

[1] B. Webb, *Diaries*, Vol. II, p. 66.

capable of producing more than twice as much pig iron and over 40 per cent more steel than it in fact manufactured. After an extravagant boom immediately after the armistice, British shipbuilding yards, which were capable of satisfying the world's entire annual demand for new vessels, found themselves regularly short of orders.

The uncertain state of world trade in the period up to 1925 was a temporary phenomenon, which a healthy industrial organization might be expected to survive. The development of industrial capacity by other countries was a permanent factor; but a live industrial leadership could have adjusted itself to this also. The economist, Maynard Keynes, surveying the industrial scene in 1926, was provoked, by what he saw, to question 'the suitability and adaptability of our business-men to the modern age of mingled progress and retrogression' He went on,

What has happened to them – the class in which a generation or two generations ago we could take a just and worthy pride? Are they too old or too obstinate? Or what? Is it that too many of them have risen not on their own legs but on the shoulders of their fathers and grandfathers?[1]

Adaptation might have been tackled in a variety of ways. The reduction of over-all capacity by agreed reorganization of these industries was indeed resorted to, but not until later. Even this was calculated to worsen the evils of unemployment; in areas where the social need was for more work, to close shipyards and mills and factories seemed like a final slamming of the door. Improved techniques of production were needed; but progress in this direction was hampered by psychological factors: British industrialists were dominated by the past and too lacking in confidence in the future to accept the financial burdens involved in re-equipment. The long-term cure for the country as a whole was to divert capital and labour to newer industries. The market for the kind of goods produced by the traditional basic industries was expanding at a far slower rate than the market for electrical goods, chemicals, artificial silk and motor-cars, for instance. In fact these new industries did expand in the 1920's and 1930's, but not at a rate to compensate for the decline in the older industries. This was to some extent due to a shortage of capital for domestic investment owing, in part, to the long-standing tradition of investing a large amount of capital abroad. Apart from this, there would have remained the somewhat intractable problem of the immobility (or inadequate mobility) of the surplus labour force. Older men who had spent most of their lives in coal mining, ship-building and cotton were not easily transportable to the south-east where the newer light industries tended to be; and though, over the whole period between the wars, there was a steady migration from the derelict areas of the older industries to the Thames Valley it was inevitably slow, because almost every individual movement had to be an act of unaided private risk and expenditure. Over and above

[1] Quoted R. Harrod, *Life of John Maynard Keynes*, p. 380.

this, there was, perhaps, at the highest levels yet another psychological factor: was Britain, the home of sound workmanship and high-quality production, to descend to making a living by turning out silk stockings, bicycles and radio sets?

The coal industry showed all the characteristics of the other basic industries in an aggravated form. Both the amount of coal exported, and the proportion of the world demand for coal which Britain supplied, were much less than in 1913. Much of the loss of overseas coal markets was to Germany, which instead of being one of Britain's best customers for coal now supplied the bulk of the Italian market and was also exporting coal as reparations. Coal exports to Russia declined sharply with the Bolshevik revolution; there was a further loss of markets due to the increasing use of oil fuel by shipping, and to the competition of countries, such as Poland, which rapidly developed their own coal resources. The home market could not take up the slack, among other things because of the lack of growth in the older industries which depended on coal, and because the expanding electricity industry developed techniques of economizing in coal.

Once again, a new competitive pattern of world production called for improved techniques. The British coal industry suffered from being older and therefore less up to date than the coal industries of other countries; and some seams were beginning to be worked out. But there was less mechanization than elsewhere; whereas output per man-hour increased rapidly on the Continent it increased little in the British coalfields. As in the cotton industry and the shipyards, wholesale reorganization, as well as mechanization, was an urgent need, and all the psychological and financial factors which prevented this happening in the other basic industries were even more strongly at work in the coal industry; it is in the light of these facts that the failure to nationalize the coal industry in 1919 must be considered to have been a major disaster. The great defect of private enterprise in coal was that it showed little or no drive or initiative. The coal industry was certainly 'private'; but it was not enterprising.

Two specific factors outside the industry helped to produce a crisis in 1925. First, although coal exports had increased during the French occupation of the Ruhr because this had dislocated Germany's coal production, the downward trend was renewed at the end of 1924 after the French withdrawal. Second, the Government decided to complete the return to 'normalcy' signalized by the Dawes Plan and the Locarno agreements, by the further step of returning to the gold standard. This was announced by Churchill, as Chancellor of the Exchequer, in April 1925: and the pound sterling would be once more at parity with the dollar as in 1914. The overriding purpose of this move was to restore the position of London as a world financial and banking centre, a not improper objective in itself. Its effects were to increase the value of all foreign investments in Britain (because sterling was now a more valuable currency than before the return to the gold standard) and it reduced the burden of the American debt to the income tax payer because fewer pounds sterling were now needed to provide the United States with the dollars due to it year by year. It also helped to secure stable exchange rates in the next few years.

Unfortunately, going back to the gold standard at pre-war rates of exchange with the dollar increased the cost to the foreigner of all British exports, since sterling was now a more expensive currency. The chief, and almost the only, opposition among economists came from Maynard Keynes who insisted that the pound had been over-valued by as much as 10 per cent and that therefore the price of all British exports had been correspondingly increased. He insisted that, if the exporting industries were to survive at all, they had only two alternatives: to reduce wages or export at a loss. Thus, he declared, the return to the gold standard implied an onslaught on industrial wages, and he prophesied correctly that the first victims would be the miners.

It is perhaps a pity that Keynes lacked a certain singleness of mind and purpose at this period. Had he not, as he did, dispersed his energies over a wide field of interests he might have been able to develop fully and in time the theoretical refinements of the case he was making against the return to gold. He was already held in considerable esteem as an economist, but was suspected of too much brilliance and not a little superficiality. Politically he carried little weight since his allegiance was to the Liberals; so that although, a few years later, his theories were to gain wide acceptance among economists, in 1925 he was rather a voice in the wilderness. It is certainly somewhat bizarre that his attack on the gold standard should have been made in three articles contributed to the *Evening Standard*. They were later published as a pamphlet entitled, perhaps a little unfairly, *The Economic Consequences of Mr Churchill*. The title was a reference to Keynes's earlier polemic against reparations (and Lloyd George) which had been called *The Economic Consequences of the Peace*. This had probably done more than any other piece of writing in the twenties to turn derision of the whole peace settlement into a political and intellectual cliché.

The mine-owners were prompt to fulfil Keynes's prophecy. On 30 June 1925, two months after the return to gold, they gave notice to terminate existing wage agreements at the end of July and demanded immediate wage reductions, together with the abolition of arrangements which had, since 1924, secured, in effect, a guaranteed minimum wage. This was to transfer to the miners, and the miners alone, responsibility for keeping the coal industry profitable. The owners had failed to reorganize and to re-equip; the Government had adopted a financial policy which helped to price British coal out of the foreign market. But the owners insisted on preserving their profits notwithstanding; and at the expense of miners' wages. The miners' answer on 3 July was a flat refusal, unaccompanied by any counter-proposal; and the fiery new secretary of the Miners' Federation, A. J. Cook, announced that the miners would neither accept mediation nor co-operate with a court of inquiry, either on the reduction of wages or the lengthening of the working day.

From this moment the miners were inflexible. Their President, Herbert Smith, was an immovably obstinate Yorkshireman; 'We have nowt to give,' was his most characteristic contribution as a negotiator. A. J. Cook considered that his whole duty as secretary was to tour the mining areas whipping up the men's lust for battle. Compromise and negotiation were as far from their thoughts as from the mind of an army general staff which had ordered general mobilization against foreign invasion. It was this that caused Birkenhead to say that if he had not seen the mine owners he would have thought the miners' leaders the stupidest men in England.

On 10 July the miners placed their problem before the General Council of the T.U.C. which promised to co-operate whole-heartedly with them 'in their resistance to the degradation of the standard of life of their members'. On 30 July the miners' representatives met Baldwin; the Prime Minister told them, 'all the workers of this country have got to take reductions in wages to help put industry on its feet'. This remark did much to justify the unions' claim that the attack on the miners' wages was merely the prelude to an attack on the wages of all industrial workers. Despite subsequent claims that it was a sinister attempt by the trade unions to subvert the constitution, the General Strike was, in the minds of the T.U.C., always a strictly industrial dispute.

On the same day, therefore, the General Council of the T.U.C. gave notice that, from midnight 31 July 1925, the N.U.R. and T.G.W.U. would place a complete embargo on the movement of coal by rail, road and sea.

Baldwin's reply was to capitulate. The Government would give the industry a subsidy until 1 May 1926 (Baldwin having declared only two days earlier that he would not grant a subsidy) and a Royal Commission would conduct an inquiry. With memories of Black Friday 1921 still rankling in the minds of trade unionists, the *Daily Herald* christened this day of Government surrender 'Red Friday'.

This collapse on Baldwin's part well illustrates the combination of indolence and impetuosity in his character. He did not want to give way to the miners because to do so would destroy him politically. Yet he did not want a strike, because such a conflict cut across his whole conception of tranquillity as the nation's most urgent need. He had made this clear when soon after again becoming Prime Minister he resisted a back-bench Conservative demand for a repeal of the Trade Union Act of 1913:[1]

[1] See p. 35.

We, at any rate, are not going to fire the first shot. . . . Although I know there are those who work for different ends from most of us in this House, yet there are many in all ranks and all parties who will re-echo my prayer: Give peace in our time, O Lord.[1]

It was very moving; but he had done nothing subsequently to translate conciliatory words into conciliatory action. He was therefore faced, at the end of July 1925, with a situation he did not want but which he had sought to avert only with mellifluous phrases. His surrender was less a subtle plan to gain time than an admission that he did not know what to do.

'Red Friday' sharpened the resolve of both sides; the miners because they considered they had won, the owners and the bulk of the Conservatives because they thought Baldwin had let them down. On the one side, A. J. Cook announced:

I don't care a hang for any Government or Army or Navy. . . . We have already beaten not only the employers but the strongest Government in modern times.[2]

On the other, Joynson-Hicks trumpeted:

Sooner or later this question has got to be fought out by the people of the land. Is England to be governed by Parliament and by the Cabinet or by a handful of trade union leaders?[3]

Perhaps it is notable that not quite contemporaneously with these utterances Keynes was saying:
The next step forward must come, not from political agitation or premature experiments, but from thought. We need by an effort of the mind to elucidate our own feelings. At present our sympathy and our judgement are liable to be on different sides, which is a painful and paralysing state of mind. . . . There is no party in the world at present which appears to me to be pursuing right aims by right methods.[4]

It was the voice of a twentieth-century Philip Melancthon, totally unheeded by disputants whose only common feature was their ignorance of the fundamental grounds of their dispute.

In the last three months of 1925 and the first three of 1926 the Royal Commission, under Sir Herbert Samuel, conducted its inquiry; the Government made preparations to maintain essential supplies if a national strike were to take place; and the trade union movement's courage slowly oozed out at its fingers' ends without its being fully aware of the fact. The Home Office, under its senior permanent official, Sir John Anderson,[5] divided the country into ten regions, each under a Civil Commissioner, who was to be assisted by a staff of Civil Servants and by local committees which were also set up in readiness. There was also a voluntary body called O.M.S.

[1] G. M. Young, *Baldwin*, p. 91–6.
[2] Quoted, Mowat, Bullock.
[3] Bullock, *Life and Times of Ernest Bevin*, p. 279.
[4] Harrod, *Life of J. M. Keynes*, p. 356.
[5] See also p. 412.

(Organization for the Maintenance of Supplies) which patriotic citizens could join in order to train themselves as strike-breakers by learning to drive locomotives or lorries. By contrast, the T.U.C. did little, hoping against hope that the Royal Commission would produce plans which would make it possible to reopen negotiations.

In March 1926, the Samuel Commission reported. It condemned the owners. Longer hours would lead to the production of more coal that nobody wanted to buy; lower wages would merely enable the owners to evade the industry's need for reorganization. The Commission indicated the various ways in which the owners should undertake this task. It then went on to condemn the Government subsidy. This, too, would enable the owners to evade their responsibility to reorganize; it was also inequitable to subsidize one backward industry at the expense of others. Therefore, as a temporary measure, while reorganization took place, miners should accept a reduction on their 1924 wages, which had been fixed at a time of purely temporary prosperity. It recommended, however, that national wage agreements should continue.

It is difficult to see what excuse now existed for the Government, the owners, the miners or the T.U.C. to allow either a coal strike or a national strike to take place; but of all the interested parties, only the T.U.C. tried to take the Report seriously, because they alone lacked the will to fight. Unfortunately, as well as lacking the will to fight the Government, they lacked the will to fight the miners. The miners – and there is no evidence that their views were misrepresented by the rock-like Herbert Smith or the flame-like A. J. Cook – were determined to fight against any wage reductions and were not fundamentally interested in reorganization either. This would mean the closing down of a number of uneconomic pits, and they took it for granted that nothing would be done for the miners thus rendered redundant except to consign them to the dole queue or the Poor Law.

The owners clearly wanted a showdown and to that end ignored the Samuel Report. They demanded lower wages and district, instead of national, wage agreements. The Government tried to evade responsibility by announcing, in terms of the utmost vagueness, that it would do what it could to implement the Samuel Report, provided both sides agreed to it. This was simply giving the parties concerned full permission to steer straight towards their collision. Nevertheless, the T.U.C. continued to look for formulas which would keep negotiations going, if not between miners and owners, at least between themselves and the Government. No plan of action for a national strike was devised until three days before the miners were due to start the coal strike.

The coal strike began on 1 May, but the T.U.C. struggled through still further attempts at a settlement, since the miners' leaders had formally handed over 'the conduct of the dispute' to the T.U.C. and had then gone off to the coalfields. They were satisfied that further negotiations would lead nowhere. As a result, last-minute attempts by the T.U.C. and the Cabinet to find a saving formula were conducted on 2 May amid much confusion. The miners' leaders could not be referred to quickly because they had left London; the T.U.C. omitted to inform the Cabinet that they had temporarily lost their miner colleagues; the Cabinet was thus kept waiting without knowing why, and eventually became bad-tempered. This upset Baldwin, since, like MacDonald, he had no head for the dizzier heights of a crisis; so that even though the miners' leaders were eventually got to Downing Street, Baldwin abruptly called the negotiations off around midnight on 2 May. His reason was that he had heard by telephone that the printers working on the *Daily Mail* had refused to print a leading article which attacked the idea of a general strike as unconstitutional and revolutionary.

Even when confronted with this bewildering dénouement, the General Council still did not give up. But when, in the small hours, they endeavoured to deliver to 10 Downing Street a letter of protest, they found that the Cabinet had gone home and Baldwin had gone to bed.

The General Strike was in the end forced on the T.U.C. by Baldwin's decision to suspend negotiations for reasons which can hardly be called adequate. His letter to the T.U.C. complained that instructions had been issued 'to carry out a general strike' and that 'overt acts' had already taken place 'including a gross interference with the freedom of the Press'. While it is true that Ernest Bevin had told trade union representatives on 1 May that strike action would begin on 3 May, he had added 'if a settlement is not found'. It was a bit late for Baldwin to complain of this thirty-six hours later, particularly in view of the conditional nature of Bevin's remarks. As for the overt acts, the action of the printers of the *Daily Mail* is the only one that can be traced; the printers concerned had acted on their own initiative and not as the result of any official policy by their union, N.A.T.S.O.P.A. To describe their action as actually having begun the General Strike, a claim that Baldwin reiterated subsequently in the Commons, was false.

Thus, Baldwin's cessation of the talks was the most provocative action taken by any participant in the sequence of events up to that moment; and the readiness of the T.U.C. to go on negotiating even after it, indicates that the General Strike took place because Baldwin forced their hand. The reason usually advanced for his action is that he was tired and overwrought and preferred to provoke the unions rather than those increasingly impatient members of his Cabinet who insisted on a fight to the finish. Conscious even at the best of times of his limitations as a Prime Minister, he was temperamentally and politically unable to hold out against such determined opponents of organized labour as Churchill, Neville Chamberlain, Leopold Amery, Douglas Hogg and Joynson Hicks. There was hardly one of these men who was not his superior in ability or personal drive.

20 · The General Strike and After, 1926-29

At midnight on 3 May 1926, the General Strike began. Literally at the eleventh hour, last-minute negotiations were attempted on the basis of a new formula devised by Ernest Bevin, but not made public, even though he asked Ramsay MacDonald to do so in the Commons that evening. The Cabinet indicated that it would now accept nothing from the T.U.C. except unconditional surrender. On 4 May, therefore, the country faced, in addition to the coal strike, a complete stoppage of work by all road and rail transport workers, dockers, printers, electricity and gas employees, by workers in the building trades, and in iron, steel, metals and chemicals.

The almost 100 per cent support which the organized working class gave the strike is a phenomenon which must be classed with the response to Kitchener's appeal for Army volunteers in 1914 and with the national revival which exploded into life at the time of Dunkirk in 1940. It shares with them the same unthinking unconcern for immediate personal advantage, the same irrational refusal to measure the formidable size of the endeavour so lightly embarked upon, the same sudden illumination of loyalty among a people normally distinguished by emotional and mental lethargy. The Baldwin Government had been right after all in seeing a General Strike as a threat to society. The mass support given to the T.U.C. during the first days of May 1926 revealed how alienated from the governing and employing classes the organized workers of the country had become. The rights or wrongs of the miners' case, the constitutional argument that this was an attempt by a minority to coerce the legal Government—these things were in many ways irrelevant to the deeper issue that the working class felt that, ultimately, its duty was not to 'the nation' nor to 'the constitutionally elected Government' nor to 'the community' but to its own class. The comparative lack of violence during the strike merely reflected the basically civilian character of Englishmen in general and of the working class in particular. But a class war does not cease to be class war because nobody actually gets killed; and if the strike had gone on longer than it did, people probably would have been killed. Fear of this was one reason why the T.U.C. General Council called it off.

There was great rage on the other side at the discovery that the working class had chosen, with something like unanimity, to follow their industrial leaders rather than their duly elected rulers. By supporting the strike, the working class repudiated both Baldwin and the Conservatives and Mac-Donald and the Labour Party. In the events leading to the strike, and those leading to its conclusion, the Parliamentary Labour Party had played little active part, and MacDonald's true feelings had probably been expressed when, in the summer of 1925, he had actually condemned Baldwin's surrender on Red Friday:

The Government has simply handed over the appearance, at any rate, of victory, to the very forces that sane, well-considered, thoroughly well-examined Socialism feels to be probably its greatest enemy.[1]

In consequence, there was no lack of patriotic persons ready to do their bit to 'save the old country from the Reds'; no lack of sober, respectable citizens prepared to do a job of work in the hour of danger, just as fourteen years later their like were to answer Eden's call for enrolment in the Home Guard. Undergraduates worked on the docks and drove trains and buses, and their sisters and their mothers ran canteens for them. Nearly 130,000 men hastened to enrol themselves as special constables, being encouraged to do so by a broadcast appeal from Joynson-Hicks, whose language would have been equally appropriate had he been recruiting officer for the Black and Tans. The Navy kept the docks and the power stations going, and its warships were sent to watch over a number of ports; the Army was much in evidence in London, and was used to escort food convoys from the London docks to Hyde Park, where a supply depot was set up. On 11 May the Cabinet made plans to issue an Order in Council prohibiting banks from paying out money 'to any person acting in opposition to the national interest'. This would have prevented the unions continuing to issue strike pay. George V, who had already protested against more than one action of the Government on the grounds that it was calculated to drive the strikers to more desperate measures, protested against this also:

Anything done to touch the pockets of those who are now only existing on strike pay might cause exasperation and serious reprisals on the part of the sufferers.[2]

It was not the only occasion during George V's reign when common sense was more in evidence in Buckingham Palace than in Downing Street. This particular notion of the Government's was dropped.

Baldwin later averred that more might have been done to provoke the strikers had he not diverted Churchill to the task of editing a Government newspaper known as *The British Gazette*. Having wanted to use warships against Ulstermen, and the whole British Army against the Bolsheviks, Churchill could hardly have been otherwise restrained from plunging noisily into battle against a strike that threatened the authority of the

[1] Hutt. *Post War History of the British Working Class*, p. 113.
[2] H. Nicolson, *King George V*, pp. 418-9.

Parliament and constitution he so greatly revered. As it was, the whole tone of *The British Gazette* was appropriate to a state of war, and offered a preview of how the Dunkirk spirit would be created fourteen years later. Thus, the issue of 6 May contained in well-spaced official print like that used to announce nothing less than the death of the reigning sovereign:

A MESSAGE FROM THE PRIME MINISTER

Constitutional Government is being attacked. Let all good citizens whose livelihood and labour have thus been put in peril bear with fortitude and patience the hardships with which they have been so suddenly confronted. Stand behind the Government, who are doing their part, confident that you will co-operate in the measures they have undertaken to preserve the liberties and privileges of the people of these islands. The Laws of England are the people's birthright. The laws are in your keeping. You have made Parliament their guardian. The General Strike is a challenge to Parliament and is the road to ruin.

STANLEY BALDWIN

On another page, in what bears all the marks of a Churchillian editorial, was a 'we shall not surrender' manifesto:

. . there can be no question of compromise of any kind. Either the country will break the General Strike or the General Strike will break the country. His Majesty's Government will not flinch from the issue, and will use all the resources at their disposal and whatever measures may be necessary to secure in a decisive manner the authority of Parliamentary government.

It is surprising, in the circumstances, that there were not more than about 3,000 prosecutions for violence or incitement to violence during the strike.

The Government was, however, greatly fortified in its propaganda campaign by a speech in the Commons by the Liberal, Sir John Simon. He was, for reasons not accessible to the lay population, greatly esteemed as a lawyer. He told a gravely attentive House that the General Strike was illegal, that the Trade Disputes Act of 1906 did not extend to it, and that all the trade unions leaders concerned were personally liable for damages 'to the uttermost farthing' of their possessions. On the day before the strike ended, a High Court judge also declared, on the grounds that a dispute between the T.U.C. and the Government could not be a trade dispute at all, that the General Strike was not protected by the 1906 act.

The T.U.C. realized, when the strike had lasted a week, that it had done nothing to change the Government's mind. All the signs by 11 May were that the official attitude was hardening. Public opinion outside the trade union movement was at no time favourable to the strike, though still sympathetic to the miners. The Government could stick to its policy of unconditional surrender, because it had the finance and the coercive power to make its policy effective, whereas the T.U.C. could not disburse strike pay for ever and had no intention of resorting to violence. Once again, they pinned their hopes on Sir Herbert Samuel, who now offered himself as a mediator. The initiative in accepting his offer came from J. H. Thomas, the member of the T.U.C. General Council who disliked the General Strike most and who wanted it ended as soon as possible, whatever the objections of the miners. Samuel and the General Council made two more attempts to devise a formula which would ensure that wage reductions in the mines were firmly tied up with reorganization. Herbert Smith rejected both and pointed out (correctly) that the Government had already informed Samuel that they regarded his mediation as strictly unofficial. In the face of Smith's obduracy, the T.U.C. decided to accept the Samuel proposals as a basis for ending the General Strike and for renewing full negotiations on the coal strike.

On 12 May, a delegation of three members of the T.U.C. General Council went to 10 Downing Street. They were Arthur Pugh, the T.U.C. President, who had been a frightened man all along; J. H. Thomas, who had twice backed his N.U.R. out of sympathetic strikes, once in 1912 and again on Black Friday in 1921; and Ernest Bevin of the T.G.W.U. Pugh and Thomas, as befitted their senior positions in the movement, did what talking there was, but neither even mentioned the Samuel proposals. Once they had said they had come to call the strike off, Baldwin merely replied that he thanked God, and would do all he could to bring miners and owners together for a lasting settlement. All Thomas could do was to try to butter Baldwin up:

We trust your word as Prime Minister. We ask you to assist us in the way only you can assist us – by asking employers and all others to make the position as easy and smooth as possible.

This Baldwin said he would do; the exchange of woolly banalities was his métier. Bevin then came near to an explosion; no man was less likely to mistake platitudes for firm undertakings. He asked for Baldwin's good offices in the matter of the reinstatement of strikers, and pressed for some assurance that in fact real negotiations about the miners would now be resumed. Baldwin tried to bounce Bevin: 'You know my record,' he said. Bevin persisted: he wanted to know how soon the Prime Minister would meet the T.U.C. again. Baldwin then snubbed him: 'Whatever decision I come to, the House of Commons may be the best place to say it.'

The T.U.C. made much in the next twenty-four hours of the virtues of the Samuel proposals, which it still pretended to its members were to be the basis of the next moves in the coal dispute; but the miners had rejected the proposals before the General Strike was called off, and they rejected them again the day after. The weakness displayed by Pugh and Thomas in their interview with the Prime Minister was at least realistic; their weakness in letting the miners drag them into the strike in the first place was a good deal more culpable.

Although the strike was officially called off during the afternoon of 12

May, it was resumed unofficially the next day when in many places returning men were faced with attempts to make them accept lower wages, loss
of seniority or even withdrawal from union membership. The Government
had overplayed its hand in proclaiming that it had got unconditional surrender. Local strike committees now took charge in many places and prevented a return to work. This rallying of the ranks helped to cool the
Government's mind. A general strike run by the T.U.C. was a fairly tame
tiger: but widespread strikes in the hands of local extremists behind whom
were 100,000 angry men who felt their leaders had betrayed them was a
different matter. Baldwin at once switched to his most conciliatory mood
and the worst of the many dangers the country had risked since 3 May
was overcome, though the T.U.C.'s negligent failure to obtain safeguards
against victimization before calling the strike off resulted in many workers
getting their jobs back only after much delay, and with reductions in wages.

Any hopes Baldwin may have had that the miners would prove more
pliable after the T.U.C. had abandoned them proved vain. The miners still
refused to accept wage reductions, and the owners replied to efforts to
implement other parts of the Samuel proposals by demanding the end of
'political interference' in the industry. They were so intransigent that
not only Baldwin but even Churchill rebuked them publicly; but, to the
end, the Government preferred to give way to the owners rather than to
the miners. By December 1926, the coal strike had collapsed. District by
district the men went back, to work longer hours than before and for
substantially lower wages.

In May 1927 the Government passed a new Trade Disputes Act. This
made sympathetic strikes illegal, thus implying that Sir John Simon's
interpretation of the law as it stood in 1926 was inadequate. The political
levy was also made illegal unless individual members contracted in writing
to contribute to it (so reversing the procedure laid down in the Act of 1913).
Civil Servants' unions were forbidden to affiliate to the T.U.C. Thus,
Baldwin, having refused 'to fire the first shot' in 1924 by passing an Act
against the political levy, let his Government fire a last shot at an already
defeated 'foe' in 1927. The act was purely vindictive.

The General Strike cost the trade union movement £4,000,000 out of its
accumulated funds of £12,500,000; membership dropped from five and a
half million to less than five in the twelve months after the strike; and the
effect of the Trade Dispute Act was to reduce the Labour Party's income
from the unions' political funds by one quarter. The miners' strike cut the
year's exports of coal by half and the coal shortage put 500,000 men out of
work in those industries that depended on coal. It has been estimated that
the miners themselves lost three-quarters of a million pounds in wages.
These results of the combined follies of Baldwin's Government, the coal
owners, the miners' union, the T.U.C. and the Parliamentary Labour

Party in 1926 showed how easily in peace as in war the English people could give the impression of being lions led by donkeys.

The most succinct expression of the long-term effects of the General Strike was provided by words spoken as soon as it was over by C. T. Cramp, who jointly held the N.U.R. secretaryship with J. H. Thomas, 'Never again!' Frederick Engels had said half a century before, 'There is no power in the world which could for a day resist the British working class organized as one body.' Stanley Baldwin and his undistinguished colleagues had resisted at any rate a great part of the British working class, organized

MOSCOW'S 'ARTIST'S OWN' EXHIBITION A hilarious example of the attitude of the Conservative popular press towards the U.S.S.R. and towards the Miners' Secretary, A. J. Cook, who visited Moscow in December 1926. *Evening News*, 11 December 1926.

as a body, for nine days; and had emerged from the contest unscathed. This did not stop Left-wing members of the Labour movement continuing to quote Engels, but trade union leaders no longer listened to them, and kept steadily to the Right for the next twenty years. Much of this trend was associated with the increasing influence of Ernest Bevin in the movement. Bevin was immensely practical, but he had a more continuously developing outlook than the older generation of union leaders. He fought unpractical theorists and emotional revolutionaries alike with merciless directness, and this, allied with his great capacity for work, helped the movement slowly to regain its morale and widen its horizons.

The effect on the Parliamentary Labour Party was, quite undeservedly, to its advantage. Whereas Lloyd George caused yet another fissure in the

Liberal ranks by sympathizing with the strike, to the great anger of Asquith, who characteristically supported the Government, the Labour front bench devoted their time largely to helplessly wringing their hands. MacDonald relied almost entirely on evasion masquerading as profound emotional involvement. He said in the House of Commons during the strike:

I again ask this House if it cannot do something. I am not speaking for the trade union movement at all. I am speaking for nobody. I have not consulted with my colleagues. I am speaking from my own heart because I believe I know what all this will mean as the days grow into weeks and the weeks (I hope not, but it may be so) grow into months. I am an outsider. I stand apart. I am not a member of a trade union and therefore I am a little freer than some of my colleagues, and, therefore, I can do things for which perhaps I may be blamed tomorrow. But I cannot let pass this opportunity of telling the House what is in my heart.

MacDonald's heart-rending performance as the sorrowing 'outsider' made it easier for the electorate to make a distinction between the party and the trade unions. Its rigid refusal to co-operate with the British Communist Party, and the growing gulf between the Parliamentary leaders and the I.L.P.'s demand for more revolutionary policies when it came under the influence of James Maxton, helped still further to increase the Parliamentary Party's respectability. So did a revision of *Labour and the New Social Order*, which was approved by the Annual Conference of 1928 under the title *Labour and the Nation*. It was fairly widely condemned as vague and timid, both by Left-wing critics within the movement and by the movement's opponents. Its relevance for the future is perhaps that it was the first Labour Party document to advocate State control through the device of the public corporation, which in effect meant an abandonment of the principle of 'workers' control' mentioned in *Labour and the New Social Order*.

Like most Labour Party pronouncements issued *ex cathedra* it was liable to borrow clichés from three distinct fields of thought. Socialism was, it announced,

the practical recognition of the familiar commonplace that 'morality is in the nature of things', and that men are all, in very truth, members of one another. It is a conscious, systematic struggle for political democracy to end the capitalist dictatorship in which democracy finds everywhere its most insidious and relentless foe.

It was a formula which cobbled together the secular moral earnestness of the English agnostic, the sentimentalized cult of human brotherhood which derived from the vestigial Christianity of the movement's chapel-bred element, and an adrenalin-stimulating slogan borrowed from the hated Marxists.

It also helped the recovery of the Parliamentary Labour Party that though the Conservatives had won a complete victory over the trade unions

A SEA OF TROUBLES An indication of an increasingly general view of Baldwin between 1926 and 1929. *Daily Chronicle*, 14 December 1926.

Hamlet (*Stanley Baldwin*): "*The time is out of joint; Oh, cursed spite, that ever I was born to set it right!*"

and the miners, the victory was a prelude to nothing. The Government's policy between 1927 and 1929 seemed vindictive, silly or irrelevant. As if the Trade Disputes Act was not enough, unemployment benefit was reduced, and there was a renewed insistence on the principle that to qualify for it a man must be 'genuinely seeking work', at a time when there was little work for the most genuine to seek. In 1927, Joynson Hicks organized a police raid on the premises of the Russian Trade Delegation in an unsuccessful attempt to find another Zinoviev letter among its papers; frustrated by this failure, the Government then broke off trade and diplomatic relations with Moscow. To set against this there was only the stony administrative edifice of Chamberlain's vast Local Government Bill.

Baldwin appeared to have abdicated. He was at this time diverting himself and select audiences up and down the country with felicitous speeches on the Bible, the *Oxford Dictionary*, the *Boy's Own Paper*, and Mary Webb, and was quoting to his audiences Housman's lines about 'the country of quiet livers, the quietest under the sun'. The Master of the Cutlers' Feast at Sheffield welcomed him as a 'plain, straightforward Englishman', adding 'I wonder if he is at heart a politician.'[1]

[1] The Times, *Lord Baldwin*, p. 13.

Baldwin knew what he was doing, if nobody else did. He could not control his extremists, but he could pretend to be having nothing to do with them. They looked very much like politicians at heart, and were losing the Party support in the country with every reckless move they took. He, by not looking at all the kind of politician they were, was doing his best to ensure that the man at the head of affairs should be seen to be honest, kindly and civilized. He had no rivals for the leadership; in the long run, the storm would die away and he would still be there, plain and straightforward, and still to be trusted.

The immediate impression, however, was of nervelessness. The bulk of his rank and file found only the passing of the Trade Disputes Act to their liking; both the National Union of Conservative Associations and the Women's Unionist organizations passed resolutions in 1927 indicating that they derived more satisfaction from its passing than from anything else the Government had done. On the other hand, a group of 'Young Conservatives', among them the future Prime Minister, Harold Macmillan, began to demand the drawing up of a constructive programme of Conservative reform, and even compelled the Government to withdraw a scheme for reform of the Lords put forward in order to clip the wings of a future Labour Government. Quarrelsome, and lacking in direction, the Conservatives drifted to electoral defeat in the 1929 election. All that Baldwin could offer was the slogan, Safety First.

Into the political vacuosity caused by a programme on one side of 'Safety First' and on the other of 'the morality of the nature of things' there was now projected a volley of Liberal thunderbolts. Asquith had gone to the Lords as the Earl of Oxford and Asquith in 1925, had resigned the party leadership in 1926, and died in 1928. Despite much mental anguish in those party circles which preferred John Simon, Liberals had little alternative but to accept the leadership of Lloyd George, who now at last promised to place some of his large and allegedly ill-gotten Political Fund at the party's disposal in the 1929 election. Taking the advice of many experts, he produced plans for agriculture, for town planning, for the control of public services by public corporations, for more systematic methods of credit control and for a large public works programme, involving road-building, railway modernization, more housing and more electric power, to absorb the unemployed and add to the nation's capital assets.

All this, unquestionably, is what a broadly based, stable 'progressive' party would have put through, had there been such a party. The Labour election programme contained much that was in the Lloyd George programme and this enabled the Labour Party to claim that he had stolen his ideas from them. But the Labour Party lacked the brains and the will to implement these ideas, and the Liberals were fatally compromised by the electoral system which had condemned them to the role of a third party whose existence 'split the vote'. Moreover, not only was Lloyd George now regarded as a somewhat absurd figure; there was a general impression that he was insincere and had devised these programmes solely in order to get himself back into power. The accusation was meaningless; a politician who devises a positive programme in order to get into power is entitled to as much respect as politicians like Baldwin and MacDonald who also wanted power but had no idea what to do if they got it. Moreover, if there is anything in the argument that 1929 was not the right time to put such plans into practice, it is almost as true that the years immediately after 1945 were not much more appropriate. The real weakness of a 'forward' programme was political: nobody believed that the Liberals could implement it or that Labour wanted to. Furthermore, the political education so necessary as the preliminary to such radical change in the management of public affairs was lacking in a nation then outstandingly slow to adapt itself to changing economic circumstance.

The majority of the population refused to go whoring after false Celtic gods, and divided neatly into those who wanted safety first with Honest Stanley and those who thought Ramsay MacDonald was very nearly as safe. Just under 8,657,000 electors voted Conservative, just under 8,400,000 voted Labour. This gave Labour 288 seats and the Conservatives 260; 5,300,000 votes were cast for the Liberals, compared with just under 3,000,000 in 1924, but the increase merely raised their numbers in the Commons from 42 to 59. It was certainly a defeat for the Conservatives: the numbers voting had increased by 6,000,000 compared with 1924; but the Conservative vote had gone up by only 600,000 compared with the Liberal increase already noted and with a Labour increase of almost 3,000,000. Labour thus, for the first time, and, on its record undeservedly, became the largest party in the Commons, and Ramsay MacDonald once again became Prime Minister.

---

21 · Second Chance for Labour, 1929-31

It may well have been true, as has been suggested, that MacDonald was less enthusiastic about becoming Prime Minister in 1929 than either Baldwin or Lloyd George would have been. He did not relish the burden of trying simultaneously to satisfy those whom he called the 'easy-oozey asses' of the movement (chiefly the I.L.P.) and yet carry on the business of government, particularly as Labour still had no majority in the Commons. In the first debate in the new House he showed he understood the realities of the parliamentary situation:

I wonder how far it is possible, without in any way abandoning any of our party positions . . . to consider ourselves more as a Council of State and less as arrayed regiments facing each other in battle . . . so far as we are concerned, co-operation will be welcomed.

After the events of 1931 these words were twisted into evidence that he had all along planned to desert Labour and form a Coalition with the other parties. MacDonald was, however, merely reacting to the fact that the electorate had conspicuously failed to make up its mind in the 1929 election. No party had a mandate to impose its will on any other party. The great trouble with MacDonald's wilder opponents was that they did not understand the significance of the election results. Nearly 14,000,000 of the 22,500,000 electors had voted against even the muffled proposals contained in *Labour and the Nation*; if democracy had any meaning at all, MacDonald therefore had a duty not to implement them. The pledges given in the election campaign had all been contingent upon Labour securing a clear majority; to accuse MacDonald of violating these pledges was to push the doctrine of the mandate beyond all reasonable limits.

MacDonald took no risks in forming his Government. The only Left-wing entrant into his Cabinet was George Lansbury who was entrusted, however, with the harmless post of First Commissioner of Works. This enabled him to provide facilities for swimming in the Serpentine in Hyde Park. 'Lansbury's Lido' was perhaps the Government's only lasting domestic achievement and still further endeared Lansbury to those who like their politicians elderly, benevolent and harmless. Ex-Liberals joined the Government ranks: Lord Sankey became Lord Chancellor, Wedgwood Benn went to the India Office, and Christopher Addison, jettisoned by Lloyd George in 1921, became Minister of Agriculture and Fisheries in 1930; the post of Attorney-General went to Sir William Jowitt who, having been elected as a Liberal, joined the Labour Party immediately thereafter. Sir Charles Trevelyan, member of a famous Liberal family, went to Education, and a rich and handsome new convert from Conservatism, Sir Oswald Mosley, became Chancellor of the Duchy of Lancaster. The old guard were shuffled round a little; though Snowden went back to the Exchequer, Henderson was at last grudgingly made Foreign Secretary. Clynes took the Home Office, and Thomas became Lord Privy Seal with special responsibility for unemployment, one of the less enjoyable political jokes of the century. Sidney Webb went to the Lords as Lord Passfield, and became Colonial Secretary. The future generation of Labour leaders did, however, begin to make their appearance: Herbert Morrison became Minister of Transport, A. V. Alexander went to the Admiralty and Arthur

Greenwood became Minister of Health. Attlee had been promised office by MacDonald, but did not get it until 1930, a few months before Sir Stafford Cripps, another of the wealthy converts, also entered the Government. Emmanuel Shinwell found a small niche as a junior minister at the War Office and was almost the only real Left-winger in the Government. The Government also contained for the first time in history a woman Cabinet Minister, Margaret Bondfield, the Minister of Labour.

In the light of the economic muddle in which the country had existed since 1918 and the crisis into which it was soon to be plunged, the Government's record in domestic affairs was uninspiring. There was the expected tinkering with unemployment insurance. Treasury grants to the Unemployment Fund were twice increased, the allowance for a wife was raised from 7s. to 9s. a week, and the onus of proving that a man was 'genuinely seeking work' was transferred back to the Ministry of Labour. In 1930, a Coal Mines Bill reduced the eight-hour day to seven-and-a-half and provided for districts to fix output quotas so that price- and wage-cutting might be avoided. A Housing Act, introduced by Arthur Greenwood in 1930, provided Government subsidies for slum clearance, and an Agricultural Marketing Act was put through by Addison to enable producers to set up marketing boards to organize their sales and fix prices. Herbert Morrison introduced the Bill to establish control of London's passenger transport by means of a public corporation, which was eventually passed after the Government had fallen. Other proposals did not reach the statute book. The Lords threw out a Bill to raise the school-leaving age to 15, and Conservatives and Liberals combined to wreck a Bill to remove most of the more objectionable features of the Trade Disputes Act of 1927. The chaotic state into which the parliamentary system had fallen was illustrated by the tedious and frustrating manœuvres which were used to prevent the passage of a bill for electoral reform. It would have allowed the alternative vote (which would please the Liberals) but it sought to prohibit plural voting and to abolish university representation, which pleased neither Liberals nor Conservatives.

The truth was that the three-party system was producing chaos. The Conservatives were in great disarray, devoting part of their time to opposing the Government, part of it to quarrelling with the Liberals, and the rest of it to complaining about Baldwin's poor leadership. The Liberals were as disunited as ever: Sir John Simon was coming more and more to the fore, and he and his followers were on the worst possible terms with Lloyd George, who was probably still hankering after somehow capturing the allegiance of the Labour Party.

In foreign affairs, Henderson, always well liked by Continental Socialists, quickly established a reputation. He resumed diplomatic relations with Russia, and co-operated fully with further attempts to strengthen the

peacemaking machinery of the League and to work for a disarmament
conference. He was also enthusiastic about the withdrawal of the occupation
forces from the Rhineland five years ahead of the Versailles time-limit.
This can be regarded, in the light of subsequent events, as a mistake: but
it is not reasonable to criticize politicians for not predicting the rise of

TOO MANY PRINCIPAL BOYS. The Liberal Party in disarray. *Daily Express*,
16 December 1926.

Hitler. At the time, the most strongly criticized aspect of the conciliatory
moves then being made towards Germany was the new reparations programme known as the Young Plan, which further reduced the annual German payments. At a conference at The Hague in 1929 about the implementation of the Young Plan, the British were represented by Snowden.
He insisted, in his most unpleasant manner, on securing a larger share of
reparations payment for Britain. There was nothing in the least disgraceful
in this action of Snowden's: it upset the Labour movement, however,
because his manners made things difficult for Henderson and because his
success made him popular with the Conservatives.

In 1929, MacDonald visited the United States; it was a personal triumph
which must have done much to compensate for the frustrations he endured
at home as a minority Prime Minister leading a Government that did not
like him and a party which perpetually criticized him. The sequel to his
visit was the London Naval Conference of 1930, over which he presided
with the graciousness which had now become second nature to him on such
occasions. The United Kingdom, the United States and Japan agreed to

an approximate 5:5:3 ratio in cruisers, destroyers and submarines; they agreed also to limit the armament of submarines, and to a five-year naval holiday in battleship construction. France and Italy attended the conference, but their participation in the treaty was prevented by Italy's claim to parity with France in cruisers, which the French, reasonably enough, said would produce permanent French inferiority to Italy in the Mediterranean. The treaty was not favourably viewed either in Britain or Japan. It was felt that the Admiralty had gravely underestimated the Navy's needs; and since one of their reasons for accepting a relatively low figure for cruiser tonnage was the recent signature of the Kellogg-Briand pact it hardly seems that their calculations were sound. The Japanese Minister who signed the treaty was invited to commit hara-kiri on his return, and one member of the Japanese Naval Staff did in fact kill himself by way of protest. Italian pretensions and Japanese irrationality were soon to prove more formidable forces in international affairs than the goodwill of Ramsay MacDonald and President Herbert Hoover.

Despite the brave gesture of dismissing Lord Lloyd, the tough British High Commissioner in Egypt (to the great indignation of the Conservatives), Henderson made no progress with the Egyptian Nationalists and therefore failed to regularize Anglo-Egyptian relations; as an ardent and international Socialist, he badly wanted to do so. Nor did the Government fare better in Palestine, where disorders between Jews and Arabs led to a ban on any extension of the areas under Jewish control. Sidney Webb was not a success at the Colonial Office.

The affairs of India were of considerable importance throughout the period of the second Labour Government. The Government of India Act of 1919 had provided that, after the lapse of ten years, a Commission should be set up to examine the possibility of further advance for India. In view of the persistent demand of the Congress movement, led by Gandhi, for complete independence, Baldwin's Government had decided not to wait until 1929 and appointed the promised Commission, headed by Sir John Simon, in 1927. This was also done to anticipate the advent of a Labour Government. The Commission was representative of British opinion only; no Indians were invited to serve on it. On becoming Prime Minister, MacDonald accepted Simon's suggestion that the Commission extend its purview to take in relations between British India and the Indian Princes, so that a blueprint for the future constitutional development of the whole sub-continent might be produced. In the autumn of 1929, after a visit home, the Indian Viceroy, Lord Irwin (as the former Edward Wood and future Lord Halifax was temporarily entitled) endeavoured to soothe Indian opinion by a proclamation that the attainment of Dominion status was 'the natural issue of India's constitutional progress'. The announcement was criticized by some, who disagreed altogether, and by others who realized that it was promising what nobody had any immediate intention of conceding. Moreover, Congress at once launched a civil disobedience campaign to substantiate its demand for total independence.

The Simon Report was issued in June 1930 in an atmosphere of widespread disorder in India, of which the central event was a march to the sea by Gandhi for the purpose of protesting against the Government's monopoly of salt. Once arrived at his destination he and his followers occupied a salt marsh. The Government of India, with Labour in office in Westminster, had recourse to mass arrests; Gandhi and Nehru, the future Indian Prime Minister, were among the leaders who were imprisoned (usually, it should be recorded, in circumstances of no great discomfort).

The Simon Report proposed an enlargement of the powers of the elected legislatures and envisaged the future of India as a federation of self-governing provinces much on the same lines as Canada. There would be a Federal Assembly, but defence, foreign policy and ultimate responsibility for finance were to be reserved to the Viceroy and his Council.

In spite of the lack of enthusiasm for the report, both in India and England, MacDonald summoned a Round Table Conference on India which began its work in November 1930. Again its usefulness was limited by the fact that though the Indian Princes were represented, Congress was not. The Princes agreed with the proposal for an All-Indian federation, however, and MacDonald (who had presided over the conference) next invited the Conservatives to give their support to the idea of proceeding to consultations with Congress. This, after the downfall of the Labour Government, led to the second Round Table Conference which was attended by Gandhi.[1]

This MacDonald–Baldwin *entente* over India was, of course, essential if there was to be any worth-while progress in the matter, since in the nature of things MacDonald's Government was of uncertain duration; but although it did not in fact produce immediate progress in Indian affairs it had one important consequence in domestic politics. It caused a permanent breach between Baldwin and Churchill. Churchill denounced both the Government's proposals and Baldwin's support of them. The 'frightful prospect' had been 'recklessly' and 'wantonly' opened up of our losing India 'in the final result', with consequent 'measureless disasters' for the Indian people. Churchill forthwith resigned from Baldwin's Shadow Cabinet.

Four days before this, Churchill had also made a vicious attack upon MacDonald (over the attempt to change the Trade Disputes Act of 1927) and had described him as 'the Boneless Wonder':

I remember when I was a child, being taken to the celebrated Barnum's Circus, which contained an exhibition of freaks and monstrosities, but the exhibit on the programme which I most desired to see was the one described

[1] For later developments in India see Chapter 51.

as the 'Boneless Wonder'. My parents judged that spectacle would be too revolting and demoralizing for my youthful eyes, and I have waited fifty years to see the Boneless Wonder sitting on the Treasury Bench.

In contrast to this pointless pugnacity on Churchill's part, consistent though it was with his attitude to Ulstermen, to Kemal at Chanak, to the Bolsheviks, to Sinn Fein until 1921, and to the General Strike, Baldwin's words on India had the sound of statesmanship. He was clear as to the nature of the dilemma of this as of most of the nationalist problems which the British faced from the time of Parnell onwards:

The fulness of time means *now* to India and *never* to certain diehards.

And in phrases that look back to the Younger Pitt and forward to Macmillan's words about another continent he also said,

. . . what have we taught India for a century? We have preached English institutions and democracy and all the rest of it. . . . There is a wind of nationalism and freedom blowing round the world and blowing as strongly in Asia as anywhere in the world. And are we less true Conservatives because we say 'the time has now come'? Are those who say 'the time may come – some day', are they the truer Conservatives?

His collaboration with Labour over India was only one of Baldwin's troubles between 1929 and 1930. His control over the Party when in opposition seemed no greater than in the last years of his Premiership; its morale was bad, its attendances lax. Worse still, the issue of Protection returned to plague him. The fact that it had lost the Conservatives the 1923 election did not deter the proprietors of the *Daily Mail* and the *Daily Express*, Lords Rothermere and Beaverbrook respectively, from using their newspapers as media for continuous attacks on Baldwin for failing to adopt the policy they advocated. Both insisted that Baldwin come out in favour, not only of a protective tariff, but of taxes on food imports, for without these there could be no Imperial Preference, an idea most precious to them. In the summer of 1930, Baldwin revealed to a Conservative meeting that Rothermere had written to him saying that his support was contingent on Baldwin agreeing to policies of which Rothermere approved, and on his submitting to Rothermere the names of his principal Cabinet ministers for prior approval. Baldwin declared,

A more preposterous and insolent demand was never made on the leader of any political party. I repudiate it with contempt and I will fight that attempt at domination to the end.[1]

The revelation produced a swing of opinion in Baldwin's favour, but he found it necessary to return to the attack in the spring of 1931. He referred to Rothermere and Beaverbrook at a public meeting in terms which caused great astonishment. He accused them of employing 'direct falsehood' in their newspapers, and of 'misrepresentation, half-truths, the alteration of

[1] See R. McKenzie, *British Political Parties*, p. 136–41.

the speaker's meaning by publishing a sentence apart from the context'; and concluded,

What the proprietorship of these papers is aiming at is power, and power without responsibility – the prerogative of the harlot throughout the ages[1]

Baldwin had thus by the summer of 1931 achieved the remarkable feat of roundly defeating two of the country's most powerful vested interests, trade unionism and the millionaire Press.

When the Labour Government took office in June 1929, the unemployment figures stood at 1,164,000. In January 1930, the figure rose to 1,761,000, and by the end of the year reached 2,500,000. Yet the main issue at the election had been how to conquer unemployment.

The group of ministers to whom MacDonald committed the task of planning this conquest were J. H. Thomas, George Lansbury, Tom Johnston and Sir Oswald Mosley, an ill-assorted and ill-qualified team. Thomas had no stomach for hard work, Lansbury was politically illiterate, Tom Johnston a lightweight, while Oswald Mosley had the useful but disruptive quality of being a young man in a hurry. They produced various ideas, and £42 millions were assigned to public works, chiefly on roads. Their weakness was that they lacked persistence or authority, and were chaff in the wind when reckoned against Philip Snowden, who adhered to the doctrine of rigid economy in public expenditure. Indeed, one of the most remarkable of the Labour Party's many anomalies was that its only financial expert had the mentality of a Poor Law Commissioner of the late 1830's; it would not be an exaggeration to say that in fiscal matters he was more reactionary than Neville Chamberlain, who was almost urbane and humanitarian by comparison.

In February, 1930, Mosley produced proposals which he persuaded Lansbury and Johnston to submit to MacDonald without prior consultation with Thomas, a snub which was not altogether undeserved. The proposals apparently included plans for tariffs, for pensions and allowances to facilitate earlier retirement from industry, and for public control of the banking system. The rejection of the plans led to the break-up of the unsuccessful team. Mosley resigned, Thomas became the first Secretary of State for the Dominions, and the Prime Minister made the inspiring announcement that final responsibility for the unemployment problem was henceforth to be his own.

Mosley pressed his case before a meeting of the Parliamentary Party and at the annual Party Conference in the autumn, in both cases gaining much applause but an adverse vote. He proceeded then, by way of expulsion from the Labour Party and the announcement that he was forming a New Party, to the foundation, a year later, of the British Union of Fascists. It is the

[1] See R. McKenzie, *British Political Parties*, pp. 136–41.

measure of the relatively high standard of living of the British people as a whole, of the relative competence of their parliamentary system, and of their overall emotional stability (or mental sloth) that this development was always regarded solely as the consequence of Mosley's personal ambition, It might better be regarded as indicative of the dangers of the continued frustration of men of ambition and ideas which characterized both the main political parties from 1918 to 1940. Both Baldwin and MacDonald invested heavily in the stability of the English national temperament. The case of Oswald Mosley indicates that this investment proved ultimately sound; and in the end there was a surprising dividend. For the frustration of the only dynamic young man on the political stage in 1930 brought into the Government for the first time, as the new Chancellor of the Duchy of Lancaster, Clement Attlee. That the future was to belong to this small, quiet man and not at all to Oswald Mosley is a comforting illustration of history's unpredictability.

The immediate consequences were of no comfort to the unemployed, however, and once again imaginative plans to tackle unemployment were discredited by being associated with an unstable or unorthodox personality. Keynes, Lloyd George, Ernest Bevin, Oswald Mosley: these were the men whom economists would later regard as having been, by and large, on the side of the angels in the period between 1929 and 1931; but their contemporaries saw them as more or less sunk in original sin. Keynes was too clever, Lloyd George a superannuated political conjurer, Ernest Bevin a social menace and Mosley a spoiled young man. And so, unprepared and uncomprehending, the Government faced, in the summer of 1931, the financial crisis that destroyed it.

PART V:
THE NATIONAL
CONSERVATIVES
1931-39

22 · Labour Breakdown, 1931

The financial crisis of 1931 was the consequence of a slump in world trade which had in part preceded, but which was aggravated by, a financial panic in New York at the end of 1929. This had so upset the insecure monetary foundations of international trade that its repercussions produced a world-wide and deepening loss of confidence; and by the summer of 1931 its effects appeared likely to overwhelm the United Kingdom.

The basic cause of the Great Depression was the maldistribution of the world's gold supply. It was, of course, normal that there should be an alternation of boom and slump in the operations of trade at a time when it was to a large extent unregulated by State control. The United States had expanded its industrial production in the 1920's well beyond the capacity of its own domestic market; it was producing far more goods than its citizens either needed or could afford. Yet its financial policy had made it difficult for it to go on exporting its excess production. Not only did the United States have most to sell; it had a large proportion of the world's gold. Some of this gold reached the United States in the form of interest on war debts; gold also tended to flow towards the United States because New York had been taking the place of London and Paris as an international banking centre. Both factors tended to reduce the purchasing power of the United States' potential customers.

This situation had been mitigated after the Dawes Plan by considerable United States loans to Europe, particularly to Germany. Thus, between 1925 and 1928, United States loans to Germany enabled Germany to pay reparations to her former enemies; these then transmitted money back to the U.S.A. as payments for their war debts. This at least kept gold in circulation; and, overall, United States overseas investments which had been around 2,000 million dollars in 1913, reached 15,000 millions in the late 1920's.

Even this did not remove the inherent imbalance of the situation. By no means all the money lent by the U.S. to Europe had been used for productive purposes; much of it had gone into social projects such as better housing. Moreover, if the rest of the world tried to earn dollars by exporting to the United States it faced the obstacle of the high U.S. protective tariff.

Nevertheless, in the main with borrowed United States money, the volume of world trade increased in the later twenties; but, if the American loans stopped, the system would collapse, and unfortunately the United States engaged in unchecked stock market speculation at this time, convinced that the boom was for ever. By 1928, share prices were being determined not by the trading prospects of the concerns whose shares were being bought, but by the frenetic conviction of investors in general that share values were bound to go on increasing. In the minds of investors, stocks and shares became as detached from the realities of trade and industry as, in the minds of philatelists, postage stamps are detached both from the economics of the postal service and from the face value printed on them. Shares were bought and sold on the American stock market between 1925 and 1929 in the way that, thirty years later, Impressionist and Post-Impressionist paintings were bought and sold in the art-dealing world: their value was related only to the high prices people were prepared to pay for them, and to the firm belief that their value would continue to go up.

It is a matter for argument whether the boom broke in the autumn of 1929 because there were already signs that the volume of world trade was decreasing or because such a boom would have to burst sooner or later. The most dramatic day of the collapse was 24 October 1929, when 12,894,650 shares were sold on the New York Stock Market by people desperate to get rid of them in the belief that if they hung on to them they would soon be worthless. Yet this Black Thursday was only the most spectacular day in the history of the collapse; it was not quite the first day of falling share values and was certainly not the last.

For dealing with the problem, only one technique was resorted to: that of saying, all through 1930, that the worst was over. Since the boom and the crash were to a considerable extent psychological in origin, there was some sense in President Herbert Hoover's repeated utterance of consoling phrases. Unfortunately, there was not only a crash but also a slump, and the crash had made certain that the slump would be a sensational one. The crash deepened the slump by bringing to an end the flow of American loans abroad. The shortage of gold thus became acute, and world prices fell dramatically. To make international trade even less profitable, tariffs against foreign competitors were rapidly introduced everywhere, to protect home manufacturers and producers. By 1933, world wheat prices were 42 per cent of the 1929 figure, cotton 34 per cent, rubber 13 per cent, copper 29 per cent, and timber 55 per cent. Countries producing commodities such as these were thus unable to pay for their imports of manufactured goods; and industrial countries everywhere suffered heavily in consequence. By 1932, industrial production in the United States stood at 54 per cent of the 1929 figure, in Germany it was 53 per cent, in the U.K. 84 per cent; and the unemployment figures in these countries were 13,700,000, 5,600,000 and 2,800,000 respectively.

The most serious repercussions of the financial crisis in New York were felt in Germany, whose economy, bearing in mind its liability for reparations, depended on foreign loans, which between 1924 and 1928 totalled £750 millions. There was no provision in the Young Plan for any adjustment in Germany's annual reparations payments in the event of a drop in world prices. But by 1930 world prices had halved, and thus Germany's load of debt (like everybody else's) was doubled. U.S. loans stopped, short-term loans were called in, and export of manufactures to the U.S. became almost impossible because of the raising of U.S. tariffs to still higher levels.

Efforts to ease the German situation in time (and wherever there is a loss of financial confidence the time-element is of vital importance) were prevented by French intransigence. The death of Stresemann and the fall of Briand did not help matters. France vetoed the request by the new German Chancellor, Brüning, for a suspension of reparations payments, and also his proposal for a customs union with Austria. The failure, in May 1931, of the largest Austrian bank, the Credit Anstalt, which owned 80 per cent of Austrian industry, quickly followed, threatening the loss of almost all foreign investments in Austria. Both Germany and Britain at once gave loans to Austria (to their own hurt) but loss of confidence produced a run on the banks in Germany itself. This might have been prevented had the French acceded more quickly than they did to the United States' proposal for a twelve-month moratorium on reparations payments. In mid-July, all German banks had to be closed for two days, after the important Darmstädter und National Bank failed.

In the same month, the crisis reached the United Kingdom. There were heavy withdrawals of gold from the Bank of England in the second half of July and there was a distinct possibility that by the end of August the Bank would be unable to meet its obligations. The Bank had not only its foreign creditors to think of, but the United Kingdom Government as well; and just at the critical moment an event occurred which was certain to undermine foreign confidence in Britain's financial reputation, and thus to hasten the withdrawal of gold from the Bank. This was the report of the May Committee.

In February 1931, the Conservatives had attacked the Government's 'extravagant' expenditure and the Liberals had moved for a committee to recommend economies. In March, Snowden, who may be said to have been in complete agreement with his Government's critics, appointed a committee under Sir George May, an important figure in the insurance world, to examine the whole matter of national expenditure. Even before the Committee could report, the Government had had to lend more money to the Unemployment Insurance Fund, owing to the rise in the number of the unemployed. As Parliament was rising for the summer recess, Snowden said he had received the May Report, and that it was likely to shock opinion both at home and abroad; and MacDonald announced the appointment of an Economy Committee consisting of himself, Snowden, Henderson, J. H. Thomas and Willie Graham to deal with the Report. It was published just after Parliament had dispersed.

Nothing (except its immediate discussion in the House of Commons, which the Government had astutely taken pains to prevent) could have been more likely to accelerate the flight of gold from London than the picture presented by the Report of the Government's financial position, and the devices it proposed for remedying it. A deficit of £132 millions was estimated for the 1932 budget, and it would surely require, on the part of investors who had, since October 1929, been as irrationally pessimistic as they had previously been irrationally optimistic, a great act of faith to imagine the MacDonald Government wiping out such a deficit. Indeed, the May Committee made such a possibility seem even more unlikely by the very nature of its proposals. The Report proposed what is still liable to be described as 'a general reduction' in salaries. What it in fact demanded was a cut in the pay of all that portion of the community which had made the mistake of entering the public service; and a reduction in unemployment benefit. The Army, Navy and Air Force were to have their pay cut back to the 1925 figure, police pay was to be cut by 12½ per cent and that of teachers by 20 per cent. Pay cuts were also to be imposed on Civil Servants; and as a gesture to the principle of 'equality of sacrifice', of which much was to be heard in the ensuing weeks, the pay of judges and ministers of the Crown was to be reduced also. The reduction in unemployment benefit was to be 20 per cent. The justification for this was eminently reasonable. Compared with the position in 1921, an unemployed man with a wife and two children was getting 36 per cent more in benefit in the summer of 1931, whereas in the intervening period the cost of living had dropped by 29 per cent. Thus was asserted the principle that, because the community could not find work for the unemployed, they were to be denied any share in the community's improved standards of living.

Foreign investors were now convinced that Britain's financial position was thoroughly unsound. Withdrawals from the Bank continued, and its officials campaigned strenuously to get the Government to put the May Report's recommendations into operation. All the party leaders returned to London on 11 August 1931 and MacDonald had meetings with Baldwin and Neville Chamberlain, representing the Conservatives, and Sir Herbert

Samuel, representing the Liberals (Lloyd George was in hospital after an operation). An atmosphere of crisis thus rapidly built up, and nothing was done to calm the now hectic state of international banking. The only voices raised to question the really serious nature of the crisis were from the Left: the two Labour members of the May Committee had refused to sign the Report, the T.U.C. General Council was strongly against it, the Liberal *News-Chronicle* blamed the crisis on 'rumour', and Keynes condemned both the Report and the action it proposed as 'replete with folly and injustice'. These criticisms were dismissed as irrelevant. 'We were on the edge of a precipice' according to the bankers, and just as in 1926 the miners were called upon to preserve the profits of the coal industry so, in 1931, the unemployed, the Civil Servants, the teachers, the policemen and the armed services were called upon to save the financial reputation of the City of London. The Bank of England informed MacDonald that £50 millions, previously borrowed from New York and Paris in July, was already spent and that another £80 millions loan was imperative; but the New York bankers held out little hope that a loan to the United Kingdom would attract nervous American investors unless the Government first took steps to balance the budget. The alternative, of course, was to go off the gold standard and admit that the Bank could not meet its obligations. This was held to be out of the question; for, once the pound was no longer tied to gold, its value would, it was asserted, drop so fast that the country would fall victim to the galloping inflation which had destroyed the savings of the German middle class in 1923. Fear of this had most to do with the decisions which were now taken both by MacDonald and Snowden.

The Labour Government was under great pressure. The Bank was urging immediate action to prevent national bankruptcy. The Opposition leaders were sternly demanding exactly what economies the Government had in mind, and twice insisted that its proposals were inadequate. The state of the parties was such that somehow, and quickly, a solution acceptable to all of them had to be found; otherwise political breakdown would be added to, and accelerate, financial breakdown. Party warfare at this moment would produce the expected bankruptcy more speedily than anything else. MacDonald was assured both by Chamberlain and by Samuel that, if his Government enforced economies which they judged to be adequate, they could guarantee the support of their two parties, or, failing that, that they would support a reconstructed Government.

There were, however, contrary pressures on MacDonald. He was already open to the accusation that he was submitting to the dictation of the Bank of England and, indeed, of New York banking houses. There was also the T.U.C. The Cabinet had various meetings with the General Council in August, its chief spokesmen being Walter Citrine, the General Secretary, and Ernest Bevin. Both had learned a good deal of late, and Bevin in particular had been the only trade union member on the recent Macmillan

Committee on Finance and Industry. This had given him an insight into matters of finance and currency unusual among trade union leaders at this time; moreover, he had already, in the course of the Committee's deliberations, not only listened to some of the heretical notions of Keynes, but had used the opportunity to do some hard thinking about the relation between financial policy and trade and unemployment. He had also come to acquire much of Keynes's lack of respect for the gold standard and a less than idolatrous attitude to the idea of a balanced budget. Accordingly, the T.U.C. infuriated both MacDonald and Snowden by rejecting their claim that the situation threatened immediate catastrophe, and by making counter-proposals. The General Council insisted that if the budget must be balanced there should be genuine equality of sacrifice:

An all-round cut in the form of a graduated levy on the profits, income and earnings of all classes of the community, plus new taxation on fixed-interest securities, the real value of which had been enhanced by the fall in prices.[1]

It was by now a sore point with Bevin that the maintenance of the gold standard and the high international value of sterling preserved the rate of interest on Government and other securities. He saw the Government's plans as a device for protecting the middle class at the expense of the poorest or weakest sections of the community.

Both Snowden and Thomas insisted that the T.U.C.'s proposals were irrelevant to the situation as it actually was, and perhaps they were right. Whether the Cabinet or the T.U.C. liked it or not, it is probably true that confidence abroad would not have been maintained by any of the T.U.C.'s proposals. They would certainly not have secured the support of the Opposition and this MacDonald was determined to get.

Thus, lacking support from the industrial wing of the movement, MacDonald was forced back on his own Government. His nerves were now in a bad state and his manner increasingly that of a man seriously overstrained. If even the mild and equable Sidney Webb could describe the T.U.C. as 'pigs' for their failure to co-operate, the likelihood that Mac-Donald would submit to further rebuffs from his own movement was remote. And on the issue of the cuts in the dole his Cabinet was sharply divided.

MacDonald therefore took steps in anticipation of his Government's collapse. The attitude of the T.U.C. had helped to harden his colleagues' opposition to a proposed 10 per cent reduction in unemployment benefit. MacDonald therefore informed George V that the continuation of his administration was in doubt, and the King sent for Samuel and for Baldwin. Both indicated their willingness to serve under MacDonald if he chose to form a government containing members of all parties.

Finally, MacDonald was told by representatives of the New York banks that the American public would be unlikely to subscribe to a loan unless the proposed economies included the 10 per cent cut in unemployment benefit,

[1] Bullock, *Life and Times of Ernest Bevin*, p. 488.

were on a scale large enough to give full satisfaction to London financiers, and were put into operation before the loan was made. It was thus essential for MacDonald to secure from his colleagues what some of them had so far still refused to give: agreement to the cut in unemployment benefit. He found that, out of his Cabinet of twenty members, nine or ten, including Henderson, Clynes, Alexander, Greenwood and Lansbury, were obdurate. He therefore had no alternative but to end the existing administration; and its members appear to have assumed that, after consultations between MacDonald, Baldwin and Samuel, a Conservative-Liberal coalition would then be formed. When, however, the Labour Cabinet met the next day, for what it knew would be the last time, its members were told by the Prime Minister that he was to remain in office at the head of a 'National' Government. There would, it was announced later in the day (24 August, 1931) be a small Cabinet of nine. It would contain four Conservatives: Baldwin, Neville Chamberlain, Sir Samuel Hoare and Sir Philip Cunliffe-Lister (originally known as Sir Philip Lloyd-Greame and later as Lord Swinton). There would be two Liberals: Sir Herbert Samuel and Lord Reading, who, as Sir Rufus Isaacs, had been Attorney-General in Asquith's Government, and who had served as Viceroy of India from 1921 to 1925. There would be three members of MacDonald's now defunct Labour cabinet: Snowden, who would stay at the Exchequer, Thomas, and Lord Sankey. When all the Government offices had been filled it was seen that the only other Labour members to follow MacDonald at that moment were Lord Amulree, who stayed at the Air Ministry, MacDonald's son, Malcolm, and George Gillett, a banker, who held a junior post. As for the administration as a whole, somebody, with pardonable cynicism, nicknamed it 'The Government of the unburied dead'.[1]

---

23 · Tory Take-over, 1931-32

The ostensible reason for forming a National Government of all parties had been that only by this means could foreign investors be assured that the war of parties would be replaced by a united resolve to prove to the foreign investor that Britain was financially and politically sound. The desired

[1] Earl Winterton, *Orders of the Day*, p. 175.

economies would be implemented quickly and without angry controversy; the budget would be balanced and the gold standard preserved.

The plan worked only partially. Snowden brought in an emergency budget on 10 September. The standard rate of income tax was raised from 4s. 6d. to 5s., allowances for children were reduced, and surtax was increased. There were to be higher duties on petrol, entertainments, tobacco and beer. The appropriation for the sinking fund which provided for the payment of interest on part of the National Debt was reduced by nearly £20 millions. The sections of the community specially selected for victimization by the May Report were duly penalized. On average, Government Ministers, Judges, M.P.s, the police and the armed services suffered 10 per cent cuts. Teachers were chosen for special treatment: their cut was 15 per cent. Unemployment benefit was cut by 10 per cent but, in the interest of further economy, contributions were increased, the benefit period was reduced to twenty-six weeks in a year, and for certain forms of benefit a 'needs' test was to be applied.

By these means, Snowden provided for a saving, in a full year, of £70 millions. Since the Labour Government had committed itself, before its overthrow, to a saving of £56 millions it may be said that from the purely fiscal point of view the National Government came into existence for a task no more herculean than that of reducing Government expenditure by £14 millions (The total national income of the United Kingdom in 1929 was estimated at just under £4,000 millions.) It is difficult to avoid the conclusion that there was something wrong both with international financiers and British politicians that the problem of raising a sum of money so small should have been the occasion for such convulsive and contorted manœuvrings.

Furthermore, the manœuvrings failed either to restore foreign confidence or to save the gold standard. During the eleven days after the announcement of Snowden's economy proposals the drain of gold from London was so heavy that the £80 millions credit which the overthrow of the Labour Government had obtained for Britain was almost all exhausted. On 21 September, Britain went off the gold standard after all; and the runaway depreciation of the pound in the international market which had been regarded as the immediate result of such action failed to take place. The pound soon settled down at about two-thirds of its former value.

A major reason for these developments was the report that naval crews at Invergordon in Scotland had greeted news of the cuts in their pay by starting a mutiny. Nervous foreigners perhaps remembered that the downfall of the Kaiser's Reich had begun with a naval mutiny at Kiel in November 1918, and that a naval mutiny at Kronstadt in 1917 had been one of the most dramatic events in the Russian Revolution. The news from Invergordon was followed by immediate withdrawals of gold from London on a scale exceeding that which had caused the original political crisis.

Although the Invergordon affair seems to have been the politest possible form of mutiny, it involved 12,000 men. They confined themselves to refusing to parade on the quarter-deck and thus sabotaged the intended summer exercises. Almost at once, the Government gave in. In addition to going off the gold standard on 21 September it announced that no pay cuts in the Navy, the other services, the police and among teachers would exceed 10 per cent. (The Government's original plans for naval pay had involved an *average* cut of 10 per cent, and ratings were threatened with greater reductions than that.) The Admiralty, for its part, handled the affair with swift discretion, contenting itself with relatively mild punishments: the dismissal of some of the ringleaders, and the early retirement of some of the officers involved, on the grounds that they had not acted against the offenders with greater vigour.

The Invergordon affair was one of the few events in 1931 which was followed by immediate results. The Navy achieved, in a matter of days, two things the politicians and economists failed to do. It saved the armed forces, the police and the teachers from the worst effects of Government victimization; and it pushed the country off the gold standard. Thus it may be suggested that it was the Navy which, by one of history's more appropriate paradoxes, at last freed its countrymen from the 'economic consequences of Mr Churchill'.

The second reason for the failure of the new Government immediately to restore foreign confidence was that its creation had not ended party warfare, but had made it worse. Snowden's economies had passed the Commons with a majority of only 60; 249 M.P.s, including the whole of the Labour Party except for the handful within the National Government, voted against them. The Labour movement was so incensed by Mac-Donald's desertion of them that all the former Labour ministers attacked Snowden's economies, in complete disregard of their acceptance of most of them before their Government was overthrown. The attempt to secure three-party agreement to the economy programme had come near to success while MacDonald was Prime Minister of a Labour Government. His decision to take office at the head of a National Government caused it to fail utterly. The Labour Party now repudiated the economy programme in its entirety; and the Conservatives began to campaign for an immediate election.

It is possible to detect, indeed, the workings of a subcutaneous Conservative plan, all through 1931, to use, and indeed aggravate, the financial situation for the purpose of displacing and discrediting Labour. The May Committee had been the offspring of Conservative censure of wasteful Government expenditure; and when the May report was issued, the Conservative Press and *The Times* were notably at pains to draw the most alarming conclusions from it. Since this presaging of immediate financial disaster was bound to worsen the lack of confidence abroad, it can only have been undertaken with the objects of breaking the Government's nerve and of emphasizing its unfitness to govern. That the outcome of this campaign was the formation of a National Government was due to the unconventional circumstance that MacDonald and Snowden were all along in collusive agreement with Baldwin and Chamberlain. But the result of their collaboration was that only the Government had been recaptured for the Right wing. Events from 24 August onwards postulated the further necessity of capturing the House of Commons. With something like 260 genuine Labour M.P.s still at large, and the Conservatives still in a minority in the House, the campaign was still not complete. The holding of an early election therefore followed logically from the betrayal of the Labour citadel from within by MacDonald and Snowden. They had given the Conservatives the keys of the kingdom; they could not now prevent them from entering into possession of the whole of it.

Once again, the Conservatives asserted themselves against their leaders. Of the National Government's Inner Cabinet, MacDonald, Snowden and Samuel did not want an election; and neither Baldwin nor Chamberlain was happy about the demand of many of their followers for an independent Conservative appeal to the electors on the issue of a tariff. This would wreck the National Government, owing to the theological adherence to Free Trade of both Samuel and Snowden, and was likely once more to rally the scattered but angry hosts of Labour. The Conservatives were in a strong position, however: Samuel had too small a Liberal following to count, because Lloyd George had recovered sufficiently to begin a campaign against the National Government, and because Sir John Simon led another Liberal contingent which, as time was to show, would support the Conservatives with a disregard for principle which, were it not so unimportant, could be described as staggering; and as for MacDonald and Snowden, they could count on nobody of any consequence at all except for the now merely comical Jimmy Thomas.

Nevertheless, Baldwin and Chamberlain, wiser than their followers, resolved to preserve the National façade. Chamberlain evolved a formula by which the Government should appeal to the country for what MacDonald later called 'a doctor's mandate'. The three parties forming the Government would issue their own separate programmes, and the Government as a whole sought from the electorate unfettered authority to decide, if returned to power, to do what it thought best. Thus, the Samuelite Liberals sought votes for the preservation of Free Trade, the Conservatives proclaimed the virtue of Protection, and MacDonald and Snowden said that the Government's election would merely result in an impartial examination of the tariff question. Baldwin employed the deliberate fuzziness characteristic of him: the Government 'must be free to consider any and every expedient which may help to establish the balance of trade'.

.   .   .   .   .

The election campaign was conducted with little restraint on either side. Labour was fighting for survival, the Conservatives for total victory; so much so that Conservatives were put up to oppose Samuel and four others among the Liberal members of the National Government. Snowden, whose health had not been good in 1931, did not seek re-election to the Commons; freed, therefore, by the prospect of a peerage from risk of defeat he could at last speak his mind. Even before Parliament dissolved he had gloated over what he deemed to be the inevitable defeat of his former colleagues as he gazed at them from his front-bench position:

I have noticed during the last three days I have been sitting here the faces of my old associates. I have admired the way they have cheered to keep their spirits up, and I have admired that, knowing that only a few weeks remain before the place that knows them will know them no more.

Later, he broadcast a description of Labour's policies as 'Bolshevism run mad' and likely to 'plunge the country into irretrievable ruin'. Beatrice Webb paraphrased the contents of his speech thus:

unless the poor consented to remain poor and even to become poorer, the capitalists, abroad and at home, would withdraw their wealth and reduce the country to universal bankruptcy and consequent starvation.[1]

Labour's programme was, of course, calculated to lose them even more votes than the awesome spectacle of their own former Chancellor denouncing them as Bolsheviks. They proposed to solve the country's problems by State control of the banks, of transport, steel, electricity, gas and coal, and by central economic planning, combining all this with pious genuflections in the direction of a balanced budget nevertheless. The idea of the Labour Party, bereft of its most important leaders, carrying into effect a programme as ambitious as this after its sorry performance in the two previous years was risible in the extreme. An electorate which had less understanding of the technicalities of domestic and international finance even than the experts found it much easier to believe that the Labour Party was composed of men who had run away from the crisis and had failed to do their duty in the nation's hour of need. Labour's reply that the whole thing was 'a bankers' ramp' seemed on the other hand an insult to the electorate's intelligence. It stood to reason that all this uproar must have the profoundest causes; there was obviously something so seriously amiss that heroic measures (particularly measures involving a tightening of the belts by the shiftless unemployed) must be absolutely essential. Moreover, it was put about by Runciman that, if elected to power again, a Labour Government would raid the deposits in the Post Office Savings Bank and use the proceeds to keep up the dole. Runciman, who had served under Campbell-Bannerman and Asquith, and was thus another of the

[1] B. Webb, *Diaries*, Vol. II, p. 293.

'unburied dead', was suitably rewarded after the election by being made President of the Board of Trade.

On Tuesday 27 October 1931, the long Conservative domination of the political scene that was to last until 5 July 1945, was duly begun. Just under 12,000,000 of the 21,500,000 voters presented the Conservatives with 473 seats. Two separate Liberal groups (the Liberal Nationals under Simon, and the Liberals under Samuel) who nominally supported the National Government provided the Conservatives with a total of 68 further supporters. Also elected were 13 National Labour M.P.'s supporting MacDonald; so that altogether the National Government could, for the moment, count on the support of 554 out of the 615 M.P.'s in the Commons. On the other side there were four Independent Liberals headed by Lloyd George; and, in spite of obtaining 6,750,000 votes (a drop of nearly 2,000,000 on their 1929 figure) the Labour Party was now represented by only 46 members. There were also 5 I.L.P. members but they did not receive the official Labour Whip. So overwhelming was the result that the National Government could claim to contain more members of the second Labour Government in its ranks than did the Parliamentary Labour Party, which now contained, of senior ministers only George Lansbury, and of the junior ones only Clement Attlee and Stafford Cripps.

Inevitably, the Labour Party blamed everybody but themselves for the catastrophe. Indeed, only the partisan or the naïve could subscribe to the notion that the events of 1931 tell the story of Good Patriots who put Country above Party deservedly routing Poltroons who deserted their posts in the hour of the Nation's Need. And if there were no very firm grounds for Labour's post-election cry that it was all a 'bankers' ramp', there are several to substantiate the view that much of what happened was a Conservative 'ramp'. There is no doubt that all through the year the Conservatives relentlessly exploited the situation for party advantage. The creation of the National Government gave the Conservatives a dominant position in the executive. They then used that position to hold an election which, by virtue of their appropriation of the National label, gave them overwhelming control of the legislature. By the autumn of 1932, they had also driven Snowden and the Free Trade Liberals from office, so that from then until the 1935 election the only sense in which this Conservative Government was National was that it contained MacDonald as Prime Minister, Thomas at the Dominions Office and a body of Simonites whose designation 'Liberal National' meant, in reality, that they were in the National Government because they were not Liberals.

As far as the Labour Party was concerned all was the fault of MacDonald; and here again it is hard to deny that he alone had made the pretence of a National Government possible; and pretence it undoubtedly was. The only basis on which it could have been a truly National Government would have been if it had secured the support in the Commons of a large number of Labour M.P.'s; yet MacDonald made no serious attempt to obtain such support. The greater part of his political activity during the days before 24 August was devoted to consultations with Baldwin, Chamberlain and Samuel. On the evidence available, suspect though most of it must be, MacDonald seems, consciously or half-consciously, to have let the crisis provide him with justification for doing what he had long wanted to do: to cut himself off from a party with whose members he had long ceased to sympathize. It was almost certainly not done as a matter of calculation. MacDonald probably accepted without qualification the orthodox financiers' insistence on the need to restore confidence and on the perils of being forced off gold. Nobody in a responsible position in the world of politics and finance would prefer the advice of the General Council of the T.U.C. Those of his colleagues who resisted the economy proposals seemed to him men who, because of party or class prejudice, were refusing to face facts. Only when he was with Baldwin, Chamberlain and Samuel at this time can he have felt he was with men with whom he could talk a common language. His tendency to slither into self-pitying anger against those who obstructed or criticized him at last got the better of him. He would not be condemned to the humiliating role of a Prime Minister who lacked the courage to save his country. If he were to stay with Labour, the best the immediate future could offer was the degrading position of leader of a discredited Opposition certain to be overwhelmed at the polls. Outside the Labour movement, he was valued as one possessing the stature, the outlook, the graces of an international statesman. Inside it, he was in uncongenial association with men he had outgrown, and continually compelled to defend himself against the surly hostility of trade unionists and the impracticable idealism of the I.L.P.

Given MacDonald's temperament it was almost impossible for him to resist the persuasions to which he was being subjected. George V esteemed him highly, and was an easy convert to Samuel's view that the right solution to the August crisis was for MacDonald to continue as Prime Minister of a reconstituted Government. And if Mr Baldwin could inform His Majesty that he was prepared 'to sink Party interests for the sake of the Country' by serving under MacDonald, nothing was more natural than that MacDonald should similarly 'sink Party' by serving over Baldwin. When MacDonald informed the King that owing to his colleagues' obstinacy the Cabinet must resign,

The King impressed on the Prime Minister that he was the only man to lead the country through this crisis. . . . His Majesty told him that the Conservatives and Liberals would support him in restoring the confidence of foreigners in the financial stability of the country.[1]

[1] Nicolson, *George V*, p. 464.

It was not to be expected that MacDonald would prefer, in the face of this, the contrary opinions of men like Citrine, Bevin, Lansbury, Henderson or Clynes.

If, after the formation of the National Government, the Labour Party as a whole declined to support him, this was because he had neither asked it to nor shown signs of wanting it to. He was subsequently prepared to assert to the nation at large that he had sacrificed none of his Socialist principles; but he deliberately omitted to say so to the Labour Party. Henderson is quoted by Beatrice Webb as saying that MacDonald expected to take 100 members of the Labour Party with him over to the National side of the House; but there is no evidence that he tried to persuade them. Indeed, he seems to have pursued the reverse tactics with some of his junior ministers, advising them, in the interest of their future careers, not to go with him into what, in his usual exaggerated fashion, he called 'the wilderness'. Attempts to defend MacDonald's political tactics at the height of the crisis, and to abuse the Labour Party for its reactions to them, seem to break down over his failure to put the matter before the party whose elected leader he was. Thus, Attlee's verdict, written as late as 1959, when the dust might be thought to have settled, was still that this was 'the greatest political betrayal in our annals'.

MacDonald did not, as is often said, split the Labour Party. He and his few associates first deserted it, and were then formally expelled from it. Henderson took over the leadership and the party simply carried on. It was as a result of the party's solidarity in repudiating the few defectors that the Government MacDonald created was never a National Government. Of the two major parties in the State, one rejected it from the day of its birth.

Much had been wrong with MacDonald's leadership of Labour. He had tried to prove that Labour was fit to govern; all he did in the end was prove that MacDonald was fit to be Prime Minister. The first two Labour Governments were a personal *tour de force* by MacDonald; and, in a sense, the electorate judged rightly that once he was gone, there was little left in Labour to support. The gap between MacDonald and his followers was so wide that both before and after 1931 there were many who claimed that he had all along been planning some kind of 'deal' with Baldwin. Thus, to quote evidence from a source outside the party, Earl Winterton, a Conservative back-bencher, recorded that two I.L.P. members of the House insisted in the early summer of 1931 that MacDonald was 'carrying on secret negotiations with Baldwin':

You can say what you like, Winterton, but I tell you as a fact that those two wily old birds, your leader and ours, have put their heads together and have decided on a Coalition some time in the autumn.[1]

[1] Earl Winterton, *Orders of the Day*, p. 171.

Yet nobody did anything about it. Infuriated by his aloofness, bewildered by the frequent vagueness of his public utterances, affronted by his patrician airs, jealous of his international reputation, and often in despair over his lack of resolute Socialist policy, his followers seem to have regarded his ascendancy over them as simultaneously deplorable and unshakeable. For MacDonald, however, the strain seems to have grown intolerable, and the 1931 crisis compelled him at last to abandon one of the two roles, of statesman and Labour Party leader, which he had tried so hard to combine since January, 1924. He dearly wanted to go on with both; but the obstinacy of his colleagues looked like driving him to sacrifice the greater role to the lesser, and this he could not do. A lonely and emotional character, he saw himself as one who out of unpropitious beginnings and much intractable circumstance had made a Great Man; and, much as he valued the Labour Party, he was prepared to shed the artifact for the sake of its maker. It was not easy; with his highly-strung romantic temperament he could never take difficulties lightly, and in this, as in the lesser crises of his life, he endured great inner tension and at times appeared distraught.

The shocked surprise of his colleagues at what he did in forming the National Government testifies both to his inner isolation from them and their failure to be more than minnows to his Triton. They were revealed at last as small men. If MacDonald loved power too much, they had all along shown the hardly less grievous fault in politicians of being too much afraid of it. Events since 1929, culminating in the crisis of 1931, had proved that the Labour movement had neither the will nor the capacity to govern. In 1926 it had failed disastrously in the industrial field; in 1931 it failed just as disastrously in the fields of politics and finance.

24 · Politics and Economics of Recovery, 1931-39

The Conservative Party was, from 1931 onwards, in an enviable position. Under Baldwin's leadership it had defeated the trade union movement in 1926 and annihilated the Parliamentary Labour Party in 1931. It had turned Lloyd George into an impotent antic, banished the obstreperous Churchill, cowed the Press Lords, and imprisoned the leader of the Labour opposition in 10 Downing Street. MacDonald was too tame a Coriolanus, Baldwin a

much too subtle Tullus Aufidius, for there to be any question of a breach
between the apostate leader and the Tory Volscians; MacDonald was never
one to risk the Tarpeian rock.

The first inevitable consequence of the extinction of effective political
opposition was the jettisoning of Free Trade. Walter Runciman, as
President of the Board of Trade, put through an Abnormal Importations
Bill in November, 1931, giving him power for six months to impose duties
on manufactured articles which could be alleged to be entering the country
in unusually large quantities. A month later, the Minister of Agriculture
obtained similar powers to impose duties on imports of fruit, flowers and
vegetables. In February 1932, Neville Chamberlain, now at the Exchequer, where he was to remain until he became Prime Minister in
1937, introduced an Import Duties Bill. This put a 10 per cent duty on
most imports not already dutiable, but exempted imperial products
pending an Imperial Economic Conference due to meet in the summer in
Ottawa. There was also to be an Import Duties Advisory Committee, on
whose advice the Government, during the next three years, constructed a
comprehensive tariff.

The Ottawa Conference, when it met, proved not much more than an
exercise in bathos after the heroics which had attended the long struggle
for Imperial Preference. The best that can be said for its decisions is that,
since the organization of world trade had apparently collapsed beyond
repair, it was no bad thing to try to organize trade within the Commonwealth. Unfortunately, the original notion that the United Kingdom should
provide a guaranteed market for imperial primary products and the Empire
a protected market for United Kingdom manufactures was out of date. If
it was true by 1932 that the nineteenth century was over, it was equally
true that the eighteenth century was over too. Canada's trade with the
United States, for instance, had increased since 1914 by leaps and bounds;
what Canada wanted in 1932 was an alternative market to the United
States, which had just imposed a heavy discriminatory tariff on Canadian
industrial products. United Kingdom proposals for Imperial Free Trade
would not help Canadian industry and would probably harm Canadian
agriculture. The notion that Imperial Free Trade would automatically
help British manufactures was thus partly out of date. Nor was there any
evidence that Imperial Preference in itself would solve the problems of
the New Zealand butter and meat producer. The conference therefore
produced a series of bilateral agreements which, while increasing preferences to Dominion products, did not reduce the often high tariffs on British
exports to the Dominions. Preference in this direction was to be achieved
instead by raising still further the tariff on foreign goods. Ottawa thus
brought the Commonwealth into line with other parts of the world; its
decisions, like theirs, still further restricted world trade.

.   .   .   .   .

Just as, in its own polite way, Britain had, like continental countries in the thirties, achieved something like a one-party system of government (though not a one-party State) so, in 1932, it had its genteel Night of the Long Knives. Three years before it became necessary to purge the National Socialist Party in Germany of those who imagined its policy would be Socialist as well as National, the National Government had to purge itself of the minority who clung to the notion that National did not mean exclusively Conservative. Even before the Import Duties Bill was introduced, the Samuelite Liberals, as well as Snowden, threatened to resign owing to their continued adherence to Free Trade. The break was avoided by the startling device of abandoning the doctrine of collective Cabinet responsibility. The defenders of Free Trade would accept the tariff advocated by the majority of their Cabinet colleagues, but would remain free to oppose it in Parliament. This they did, Samuel speaking against the Bill in the Commons and Snowden attacking it in the Lords. It was one of the many incidents which illustrate what is learnedly described as 'the flexibility' of British constitutional procedure, but which show that, in reality, a British Cabinet can do what it likes. This particular arrangement was, however, so unusually absurd, not to say cynical, that it was rapidly terminated. Immediately after the Ottawa Conference, all the dissidents resigned their posts. MacDonald was much upset. He told the King:

I cannot hide from Your Majesty my apprehensions of the result of resignations at this time. . . . The new Government will . . . be, to all intents and purposes, a single-party administration, and I think Your Majesty will find that a Prime Minister who does not belong to the Party in power will become more and more an anomaly, and as policy develops, his position will become more and more degrading.[1]

This echoes, rather too late, Herbert Morrison's astute observation to him in the crisis of 1931 that it would be much easier to get into a political combination with the Tories than it would be to get out of it; and the acerbity of the departing Snowden:

They [the Tories] have sacrificed nothing, but have used the enormous Tory majority we gave them at the election to carry out a Tory policy and identify us with it. We have sacrificed our party and ruined the political careers of a score of young Labour M.P.s.

With the Samuelites gone and Snowden with them, the only sense in which the country now had anything but a Tory Government was that MacDonald, Thomas and Sankey were still in it and so were the Simonite Liberals. MacDonald's prophecy that his position would become more and more degraded, at least in the public eye, rapidly became true. He had to endure the added ignominy of public criticism by the acidulated Snowden, who now, like the other ex-members of the second Labour

[1] H. Nicolson, *George V*, p. 498.

Government, firmly went on record as having always disliked and suspected MacDonald.

The last political inconveniences having been eliminated, the Conservative-controlled National Government was thus, from the autumn of 1932 onwards, in uninterrupted command of the nation's affairs until the spring of 1940. The 1935 election, although it increased Labour's strength in the Commons to 154 seats, did not materially alter the situation.

Subject always to the criticism that it was distinguished by a stony indifference to human suffering, the National Government's domestic policy from 1931 to 1939 was often less orthodox than the record of Conservatism in the 1920's might have suggested. In its handling of the issues of economic stagnation and of recovery, the National Government of the thirties anticipated the social, economic and administrative techniques of the Governments of the forties and fifties while appearing to observers to be sunk in lethargic contentment with the system as it was. When it adopted new techniques it seemed to use them for the wrong purpose and never to apply them thoroughly or systematically. Thus, although there was indeed recovery from the Depression, so that, for example, the economy 'cuts' of 1931 were partially restored in 1935 and fully restored in 1936, to the people at large, even the prosperous, it seemed a Government without a sense of purpose; and although recovery took place, there was no sense of revival. It was not merely that the international situation made optimism impossible; it was also that recovery in Germany and the United States seemed to have been achieved more dramatically and more consciously, and that in the U.S.S.R. there was immense economic growth, whereas in Britain, even in areas of rising standards of living, there was a gnawing sense of national economic decline. When the dictators referred to Britain as 'effete' there was a suspicion that they were right.

Britain's slow recovery during the thirties took place without, for example, a co-ordinated effort to deal with the basic problem of the declining older industries. They needed drastic overhaul, and indeed organized contraction, coupled with the vigorous encouragement of newer industries by facilitating the mobility of labour and increasing the availability of capital. These things happened, but haphazardly. There was some reorganization and some controlled restriction of output. There was growth in some new industries, especially the consumer and service industries; there was a boom in private enterprise house building. In each case, Government action can be said to have offered a slight stimulus. But what might have been organized as a concerted national endeavour was allowed to happen piecemeal, and often without regard to unhappy social consequences.

Policy towards the export trade well illustrates the confusion of the Government's actions and its achievement of only partial success. The Ottawa agreements changed the pattern of exports without increasing their volume. Moreover, by limiting the opportunities of European countries for trade with Britain, Ottawa helped to increase the economic dependence of those countries upon Germany. Subsequent attempts to organize overseas trade were hardly less coherent. Agreements were made with Baltic countries for agreed quotas of imports, in return for concessions to British coal exports. This helped the east coast ports and coalfields but did nothing for the South Wales coalfields which suffered heavily from the competition of German coal. Nor did the Baltic agreements accord with what was called 'the Ottawa spirit', since they limited the importance of the preferences given to Dominion imports. The upshot was that the Government's use of tariffs and quotas failed to increase British exports. They were 87·3 per cent of the 1927 figure in 1930, went down to 68·1 in 1932 and had risen only to 86·4 per cent as late as 1937.

The Government's agricultural policy was similarly a hotch-potch, which, beginning as an attempt to protect the farmer against foreign competition, ended as a policy of fairly indiscriminate encouragement of the agricultural interest by Government regulation and subsidy. There was a Government-guaranteed price for wheat. An Agricultural Marketing Board set up marketing boards for milk, bacon and potatoes as well as for sugar beet. Imports were limited by quotas. Prices to the farmer were guaranteed by a subsidy in the case of sugar beet, and by Government purchase, through the Milk Marketing Board, of all milk produced; the object was to raise prices for the farmer without raising them for the consumer. There was, however, a general charge on the Exchequer, rising from about £45 millions in 1934 to around £100 millions in 1939. There was a marked difference, therefore, between the treatment afforded to farming in the thirties and that afforded to coalmining in the twenties. The coal subsidy had been condemned as inequitable because it selected one particular industry out of many similarly hard-hit industries, and on the grounds that it was inconsistent with sound business principles. No such considerations were applied to the farmers; the Exchequer now not only subsidized farming, but accepted the additional costs involved in producing at home foodstuffs it would have been cheaper to import. The concern to keep down the cost of food by disbursements from public funds was a foreshadowing of the policy pursued even more vigorously in the forties; nevertheless the principal object of the National Government was to benefit the farming community rather than the consumer. Output increased in the thirties, but the process must certainly be judged to have been artificial and accompanied by many anomalies.

The Government also took only feeble action to assist the recovery and reorganization of coalmining, the steel industry and shipbuilding. In mining, the quota system, established by Labour's Act of 1930, ensured that production and employment continued in many of the less efficient pits, but it restricted the output of the more efficient. Little or no progress was made towards the voluntary reorganization and amalgamation which was supposed to follow from the establishment (also by the Labour Government) of the Coal Mines Reorganization Commission. The National Government allowed its efforts to be blocked by the owners. However, by the Coal Act of 1938, royalties were nationalized (with compensation to owners) and a belated attempt was made to give added strength to the Reorganization Commission.

The Government's contribution to progress in the steel industry was equally limited. A tariff was put on imported steel, and the Government demanded in return some measure of reorganization. The British Iron and Steel Federation was the result. It followed a policy of closing less economic undertakings, but also constructed new modern plants, notably those of Richard Thomas at Ebbw Vale, and Stewart and Lloyds at Corby. Unfortunately, the most well known of the Federation's activities was its refusal to allow a new steelworks to be built at the Tyneside town of Jarrow, plunged into destitution by the closing down of the shipyard which had employed most of its male population. This produced one of the most celebrated of the various books of protest engendered by the hardships of the 1930's. The story of Jarrow's plight attained wide publicity owing to its fiery Labour M.P., Ellen Wilkinson. Her book on the subject, *The Town That Was Murdered*, was one of the more enduring of the propagandist works of the period; unfortunately it appeared too late (not until the outbreak of war) and like so many Left-wing writings of the period tended to assume that short of 'a planned Socialist economy' nothing could really be done:

The poverty of the poor is not an accident, a temporary difficulty, a personal fault. It is the permanent state in which the vast majority of the citizens of any capitalist country have to live.

Wholly, and in the eyes of the Left luridly, restrictive was the work of the National Shipbuilders' Security, set up in 1930 to buy up and shut down shipyards, regardless of the high percentage of unemployment among shipyard workers. The scale of the problem facing the industry is shown by the fact that, even after the closures organized by the N.S.S., shipyards were still capable of producing 40 per cent more than the normal annual demand. Government intervention in shipbuilding did not come till comparatively late. There was a Government subsidy to tramp shipping in 1936 and 1937, and loans were provided to assist the construction of the Cunard liner, *Queen Mary*.

The Government may also be said to have had a financial policy which superficially looked more modern than it was. It followed a policy of cheap money, by lowering interest rates, which in theory was a spur to the economy. The Bank Rate, which had varied between 3 and 5 per cent during most of the 1920's, had been raised to 6 per cent in the 1931 crisis, but was reduced to 2 per cent early in 1932 and remained at that figure with brief exceptions for nearly two decades. The object was to reduce debt charges rather than to stimulate borrowing for redevelopment and general recovery. Opinion among some economists was already coming to believe that low rates of interest should be used to finance public works as a remedy for unemployment. The Government did not adopt this policy to any substantial degree, though the low interest rates assisted the local authorities to finance some road building. Certainly, low interest rates did not lead to much new capital investment in the period, though they had much to do with the housing boom, by making low mortgage repayments possible. The only major stimulus the Government provided for the economy was the rearmament programme from 1936 onwards.

Yet, for all the impact it made at the time and in subsequent histories, the Depression in the United Kingdom was a temporary phenomenon which had passed its peak by the end of 1933, and which did not seriously interfere with the steady improvement in general standards of living. The major cause of recovery was the general fall in the prices of primary products all the world over. This, itself a consequence of the Depression, reduced the prices of British imports, minimized the effect of languishing exports, and brought down the cost of living. The fall in prices was so considerable during the Depression that even when it was at its worst the real income of the employed working classes declined very little, if at all, and from 1932 it increased steadily. In consequence, there was a diversion of resources to the consumer and service industries, with a consequent increase both in employment and in real standards of living. Prosperity was also promoted by the continuing growth of employment in banking and commerce characteristic of twentieth-century England. In assessing the state of the economy as a whole in the thirties, therefore, the existence of a large army of unemployed has to be offset by the considerable increase in the total volume of employment. For those fortunate enough not to be engaged in the older export industries, the thirties saw the foundation of what was later to be called the affluent society.

Signs of this were manifest, at any rate in the southern half of England. The number of private motor-cars registered rose from just over a million in 1930 to over 1·8 million in 1937; the number of radio sets and telephones went up steadily. Holiday camps appeared, Butlin's first being opened in 1937 at Skegness, a seaside resort whose slogan, 'Skegness is So Bracing' had already achieved nation-wide fame. The Holidays with Pay Act of 1938 gave legal sanction to workers' rights to one week's paid holiday a year. It was the decade of the super-cinema. These plush cathedrals of pleasure were, it was estimated, visited twice weekly by as much as 25 per cent of the population; some of them offered 'matinée prices' as low as sixpence 'in all parts of the house' for three hours' entertainment.

Greyhound racing, which had been begun in the late 1920's, flourished in London, Manchester, Edinburgh and Glasgow, and motor-cycle speedway racing ('dirt-track' racing) now came into prominence in the larger urban centres. Other signs of the time were the building of large dance halls, whose patrons at once defeated attempts to 'posh them up' with the title 'Palais de Danse' by domesticating the term as 'the Pally'.

More striking than these were the concomitant developments in housing and the generation and supply of electricity. In local authority house-building there was a halt during the Depression. The operation of the Wheatley Housing Act[1] was stopped in 1933, and the Greenwood Act for slum clearance was one of the obvious victims of the economy drive. National Government Housing Acts of 1933 and 1935 did, however, follow the Greenwood Act's example and concentrated local authority attention on the problems of slum clearance and overcrowding, with the assistance of a Government subsidy. The development of council house estates and flats was therefore almost as marked a feature of the 1930's as of the 1920's.

More characteristic of the 1930's was the boom in private enterprise house-building for sale to purchasers able to borrow from a building society. From 1930 onwards, the contribution of private enterprise house-building to the total of new dwellings moved rapidly ahead of the contribution of local authority schemes. The reasons for this were largely ascribable to Government policy, though the low cost of living and the large pool of labour helped, by enabling wages to be kept down. More important elements in housing costs were the low cost of materials in the thirties, and low interest rates. Another factor sometimes making for cheapness was the tendency to exploit Government and local authority road building. New private enterprise houses were frequently built along the new roads of the thirties, giving rise to the phenomenon of 'ribbon development' so detested by architects and town planners. This kind of development reduced road, drainage and other costs for builders. As a result, the private enterprise houses of the 1930's were well within the reach of the more prosperous wage earner or the lower ranks of the clerical workers. A three-bedroomed house with bathroom could, by the mid-thirties, be obtained in the south of England for £500 cash, or for £25 down and monthly payments over twenty-five years of from £3 to £4 per month. Elsewhere the cash price could be from £350 to £400. Council house rents, by contrast, ranged from about seven to fifteen shillings a week. These would be the only hope for the lower-paid workers, or those whose employment prospects were such that they could not raise the initial deposit or risk a twenty to twenty-five year commitment.

There was much Left-wing criticism of the private house-building boom, partly on the grounds that it diverted resources from local authority

[1] See p. 176.

building of houses to rent, and subjected housing in general to the profit motive. It was also criticized in intellectual circles, partly on the grounds that the houses were in red brick, that they were box-shaped, tended to stultify traffic improvements by their frequent location along what were intended to be trunk roads, and that they induced a complacently snobbish frame of mind among their occupants. Another complaint was that they were full of bored and idle wives. This reflected two phenomena of the thirties which were peculiar to it: the decline in the number of children per family and the absence of employment for married women.

The least frivolous of these criticisms was that which concentrated on the diversion of resources from the areas of greatest need. By 1939, there had ceased to be a shortage of houses, and by that year also one third of all the houses existing in England and Wales had been built since the end of the First World War; but there were still many slums and much bad housing, particularly in Scotland. But this typified the policy of the time: there was readiness to exploit a new demand for housing which would enrich building concerns and building societies; but there was no readiness to give priority to the improvement of the worst housing conditions, since the finance for this would have to come mainly from classes of society who were chiefly concerned to spend their money on the new affluence. Like Guizot addressing himself to those Frenchmen in the 1840's who wanted the vote, the National Government's slogan was 'enrichissez-vous'. Those who wanted a reasonably appointed dwelling-place could always get one. They had merely to get rich enough to be able to pay the quite modest deposits and the remarkably low monthly repayments. The flaunting of the values of affluence before the eyes of the population at large helps to explain the growing devotion to the football pools in the thirties. The statistically remote prospect of winning a fortune in the pools provided a stay-at-home chance, appropriate to a sedentary age, of doing what, in the nineteenth century, might have been done only by the more arduous exercise of joining a savage gold-rush on the other side of the oceans.

For the electricity industry the housing boom was a great stimulus. In the new houses, electricity replaced gas as a form of lighting and the supply companies pushed the sale of electric cookers with much energy. Between 1931 and 1937 electricity output doubled and the period saw the first wide employment of electric power in the home. Along with the cooker came the decline of the battery-powered radio, and the appearance of such minor aids to domestic living as the electric toaster, the electric iron and the electric hair-dryer. One of the most significant promotion drives of the late thirties was on behalf of the electrically-powered vacuum cleaner. Indeed, the door-to-door salesman seeking to persuade suburban house-wives to enter into hire-purchase agreements to buy vacuum cleaners was a characteristic figure, symbolizing the strange anomalies of the period. He took the job because the large labour surplus made more worth-while jobs hard to get; yet the job was there for him to take because the comparatively new electrical industry was booming, in line with a housing boom. A man had only to fail minimally in some way to find himself unemployed in most parts of the country; it was very much a matter of luck. If he was in an area of high unemployment he had nothing but the dole. If he was in other parts of the country his alternative was nearly always some sort of seedy selling job. He had no weapons with which to resist the ruthless conditions imposed on him by his employers. If he failed to sell his vacuum cleaners, he ceased to be employed; and then he probably sank one stage lower and went from door-to-door trying to persuade householders to buy one or other of the daily newspapers, alluring them, if he could, with offers of the gift books and free insurance policies with which the dailies were trying to outbid one another at this time. The door-to-door salesman of the thirties, clinging to the margins of respectability, was, in his own way, representative both of the constriction of opportunity and of the growth of affluence which went side by side at that time.

The distinguishing feature of the nineteen-thirties in England was that it was a time of resolute non-heroism. Germans and Italians were being turned into heroes whether they liked it or not; everything that happened, whether for the purposes of peace or in preparation for war, was organized as a battle, whether it was to build flats, drain marshes, construct roads, or purify the race of degenerate persons and influences. In the United States, Roosevelt mobilized public opinion behind his various projects of recovery so brilliantly that it was long before it was fully realized that his chief contribution to recovery was his skill in reviving American morale without, like the dictators in Europe, destroying freedom. In Russia, gargantuan feats of capital construction were undertaken, and consumer goods were deliberately withheld, so that a whole generation willy-nilly devoted itself to endowing future generations with the fecund advantages of a planned industrial State. But if one were to seek for a slogan that expressed the state of mind of England in the way that Göring's 'guns before butter' summed up what was desired in Germany, it would probably have to be something like 'ice-cream with everything'; certainly, if Stakhanov, the heroic workman who set the fashion for the over-fulfilling of production quotas, was the symbolic figure of the Russia of the thirties, his counterpart in England was probably the Wall's ice-cream man, trundling through the suburban streets his loaded tricycle with its small cargo of 'twopenny bricks' and bearing the slogan, 'Stop Me and Buy One'. And in large cities, the role of women at work was symbolized, for Russia, by the female street cleaner and, for England, by the 'Nippy', the Lyons' teashop waitress.

25 · The Problem of Unemployment, 1931-39

Three factors determined the attitude to the unemployment problem in the thirties. First was the belief that it was insoluble. Second was the belief that, although the insolubility of the problem necessitated the distribution of unemployment relief, disbursement of that relief must be so contrived that abuses of the system by the unemployed should be reduced to a minimum. Third was the circumstance that mass unemployment was largely confined to specific areas, of which the inhabitants of the rest of the country remained (and preferred to remain) ignorant. From all three factors there developed corollaries: the majority of the unemployed were unemployable, many of them were scroungers, and none of them was quite the same sort of person as the average Englishman in other parts of the country. With the fairly active connivance of the majority of the population, the Government practised a kind of industrial apartheid, with the areas of mass-unemployment as so many economic Bantustans, whose inhabitants could emerge only if they were able, usually by their own unaided efforts, to obtain work, in a new and unfamiliar trade, from an employer in some more fortunate part of the country. Few would, in the first instance, bring their families with them. This was prohibited, not by legal sanctions, which were unnecessary, but by the cost.

The size and shape of the unemployment problem may be judged by the following figures:

Total Unemployment in Great Britain 1927–38 (to the nearest tenth of a million):				
	1927	1·1	1933	2·5
	1928	1·3	1934	2·1
	1929	1·2	1935	2·0
	1930	1·9	1936	1·7
	1931	2·7	1937	1·4
	1932	2·8	1938	1·9

Percentage of Unemployed in certain Trades 1936:	All trades	12·5
	Shipbuilding	30.6
	Coalmining	25·0
	Shipping	22·3
	All textile trades	13·2

Percentage of Unemployed in certain Trades 1936:	Commerce and Finance	3·8
	Printing and Paper	6·2
	Skilled building crafts	6·3
	Chemical Trades	7·9
	Engineering	8·3

Percentage of Unemployed in Various Areas 1936:	S.E. England	5·6
	London	6·5
	S.W. England	7·8
	Midlands	9·4
	N.W. England	16·2
	N.E. England	16·6
	Scotland	18·0
	Northern Ireland	23·0
	Wales	28·5

The first of these tables illustrates the failure to bring down the high unemployment figures of the worst period of the Depression to anything like the level of 1927, itself not the best year of the 1920's. The second shows how high unemployment was confined to the old heavy industries. The third shows the disparity between unemployment rates in London and the South compared with those in the North, in Scotland, and in Wales and Northern Ireland. Even these figures do not pinpoint the problem; for the contribution to the high unemployment figures in the areas badly affected was greatest in particular parts or particular towns in those areas. In 1934, for instance, the percentage of unemployment in Jarrow was 67·8 compared with a national average for that year of 16·6; in Merthyr Tydfil it was 61·9; in Gateshead 44·2; in Motherwell 37·4. By contrast, the percentage for the same year for the Greater London area was 8·6, for Luton 7·7, for Birmingham 6·4, and High Wycombe 3·3. In 1936 there were 89,600 registered unemployed in Glasgow alone, and 84,000 in Liverpool.

Northern Ireland, industrial Scotland, South Wales, parts of Cumberland and the Tyne-Tees area in the north-east were therefore the worst hit

An unusual but revealing announcement in the Situations Vacant columns of a daily newspaper during the Depression. *News Chronicle*, 8 December 1933.

areas, together with parts of Lancashire. These were the areas most closely tied to the older export industries. Few had alternative sources of employment. They had been created in the flood tide of the early industrial revolution; now the tide had ebbed away, and they became deserted islands of misery, living largely on charity.

That little could be done was the common ground shared by politicians of the Left and of the Right. The austerer Tories thought nothing could be done about it because it would cost money. It was, they persuaded themselves, a malady which would somehow, some day, right itself through the slow operation of economic laws. Interference would subsidize industries for which there was a contracting market and whose management was inefficient; positive help to find work for the unemployed elsewhere would perhaps merely transfer unemployment from one area to another, and certainly introduce the dangerous principle that the working class ought always to be cushioned by State action against mass redundancy wherever it occurred. Sir John Simon seems to have been hinting at this, when, in a debate on unemployment on 9 July 1935, he declared that the Government

had resolved to tackle the situation by every measure possible which would not undermine the foundations they had laid. Their responsibility to those in work made it necessary that a policy should not be pursued which would jeopardize their interests.

Those on the Left were no less unimaginative in their attitude. Unemployment to them also was an inevitable characteristic of unplanned capitalism, with its alternation of booms and slumps, and nothing could be done except to await the achievement of planned Socialism. Crises of over-production and unemployment were, according to John Strachey's widely read *The Theory and Practice of Socialism*, published in 1936,

analogous to natural catastrophes. Under the capitalist principles of production for profit, the adjustment of production to need takes place (in so far as it takes place at all) automatically and unconsciously. It is not something which anyone does: it is something which happens. Hence it is uncontrolled and uncontrollable.[1]

G. D. H. Cole's *Condition of Britain*, published a year later, was hardly less pessimistic. He pinned his hopes on the raising of the school-leaving age from 14 to 15, the pensioning off of older workers, and on the eventual decline in the total population, which was expected to occur in the second half of the century. Like most Socialists he fell back, in the end, on the desirability of ensuring as the main contribution to immediate policy.

that the unemployed shall be treated as human beings who are the victims of social disorder and not as either criminals to be punished or 'social nuisances' to be barely kept alive at the lowest possible cost.[2]

[1] Op. cit., p. 65.
[2] Op. cit., p. 235.

This, in practice, meant the generous distribution of charity disguised as unemployment assistance.

If the Government was united with its opponents in a common faith that mass unemployment was a largely uncontrollable phenomenon, it was determined to eschew generosity. Sir John Simon's remark, quoted earlier, indicates the trend of thought: it would be unfair to those in work to do too much for those who were not. Generosity to the unemployed would remove the primary incentive on which the industrial system relied – the fear of the sack and of destitution. If men did not fear these, they would not work. How persistent the idea was may be illustrated by quoting from two such relatively enlightened persons as Beatrice Webb and Harold Nicolson. The former wrote,

The danger in front of the Labour movement is its deep-seated belief that any addition, under any condition, to the income of wage-earners is a good thing in itself. That was why it was so fatal to start State-subsidised insurance, it was bound to end by becoming unconditional outdoor relief – and that 'addition' to the livelihood of the poor was certain to increase the area of unemployment. It is a most demoralizing form of voluntary idleness. Under capitalism the wage-earner's life is so hard, and the wage-earner is so irresponsible, that idleness, with a regular pittance, is comparatively attractive to large bodies of men – they won't accept and won't keep work they don't particularly like or are not accustomed to – and when they do accept it, they are not overkeen to bestir themselves.[1]

Nicolson, though apparently quoting from MacDonald, produces the following insensitive observation when, in dealing with the objections in the Labour Cabinet of 1931 to the proposed cuts in unemployment benefit, he writes:

If a scheme that imposed such grave sacrifices on other sections of the community left the unemployed in a privileged position, the Labour Party might lose moral prestige.[2]

The nature of the 'privileged' position enjoyed by the unemployed may be illustrated thus:

Average Weekly Wages, 1931 (Men)	Unemployment Benefit, 1931		
	Single Man	Married Man	Married Man with 2 children
Coalmining 45s. 11d.	BEFORE THE 1931 CUTS:		
Cotton 45s. 3d.	17s. 0d. 26s. 0d.		30s. 0d.
Shipping 42s. 8d.	AFTER THE 1931 CUTS:		
Agriculture 31s. 4d.	15s. 3d. 23s. 3d.		27s. 3d.

In order to find himself in the 'privileged position' (before the cuts) of being about as well off as the lowest-paid worker in the country, an

[1] B. Webb, *Diaries*, Vol. II, p. 284.
[2] Nicolson, *George V*, p. 463.

unemployed industrial worker had first to acquire a wife and then get her to present him with two children. The cuts in 1931 made sure that an unemployed shipyard employee, for instance, had to have four children before he received as much as an employed agricultural labourer. earned. Most of England's troubles in the thirties are ascribable to its being governed by the kind of person who thought of the chronically unemployed as in danger of enjoying a 'privileged' status by drawing unemployment benefit, and by people who, like Mrs Webb, could not escape the conviction that the working class were a different sort of human being from the rest of society, sharing with Egyptian *fellaheen* a built-in tendency to crowd round middle-class white people clamouring for *baksheesh*.

There was, of course, statistical evidence for the contention that the unemployed were doing pretty well out of the dole. The cost of living went down more than the dole did; and a man on unemployment benefit at the depths of the Depression in 1933 was no worse off than an unskilled labourer in work in 1913. In view of the lack of work at skilled rates in the most depressed areas, the only jobs which the unemployed might take in the thirties were often so intermittent and so badly paid that they really were better off on the dole. In consequence, the authorities engaged in a constant battle to ensure that as few men as possible could evade work on this account. For this would be an affront to the rest of the community, and might, if it spread, lead to more and more people preferring the dole to a starvation wage.

Along with the 10 per cent cuts in 1931 came the insistence on a 'means test' for all those whose claim to benefit was not covered by their contributions to the insurance fund. Since this means test was operated, and the so called 'transitional' benefits distributed, by Public Assistance Committees of the county councils, the Treasury agitated for administration to come under central control. The result was the Unemployment Act of 1934. This established a national Unemployment Assistance Board which, through its local offices, was to be responsible for all able-bodied unemployed as soon as they ran out of their twenty-six weeks' entitlement to unemployment insurance benefit. From this to the centralization of almost all 'welfare' payments in a Ministry of National Insurance was obviously only a relatively small step. While responsibility had been in the hands of the elected local Poor Law Guardians (until 1929) and, thereafter, in those of the Public Assistance Committees of the elected county councils, it could be maintained that it was ultimately under political control. Under the new system, the U.A.B. was a kind of public service, not controlled by elected councillors, and not even subject to day-to-day control by the Ministry of Labour who appointed it. It thus had many of the attributes of the later National Assistance Board or of a Regional Hospital Board.

There were few who saw this new public body as foreshadowing a not-very-distant and different future. It was seen, rather, as 'clamping a new bureaucratic system on the unemployed', so that the Government might shelter behind it. This impression was confirmed when, in its tidy effort to establish a uniform national rate of relief instead of the varying local rates provided by the P.A.C.'s, the U.A.B. announced scales which, in some parts of the country, involved considerable reductions in benefit. There was such an outcry that the Government thought it prudent to postpone the introduction of the U.A.B. system until the spring of 1937. Few of the unemployed were then made to suffer reductions.

It was, however, the means test which caused most bitterness. Officially, this was always described as a 'household needs test' but the kindly implication that the U.A.B. was there to give a household what it needed was never taken seriously by the recipients. The total income of all the members of a household might be such that it could be deemed not unreasonable to ask it to accept responsibility for one unemployed member of it; at least, this would be the view of those who framed the regulations since they would be unacquainted with what it was really like to be unemployed in a working-class environment. The anomalies produced by the means test were, however, probably more demoralizing than the abuses it was intended to remove. It meant that every penny earned by any member of a household to which unemployment assistance was given had to be reported to the local officer so that the amount of assistance could be kept as low as possible. In effect, this meant that a levy was imposed, for example, on a son who was in work, in order to contribute to the maintenance of an unemployed father, or on a daughter who was in work, in order to help support an unemployed brother. And the moment the employed son or daughter had an increase in wages this, too, had to be reported to the U.A.B. so that its payments could be reduced. If the increase were not reported, the unemployed member of the household would be liable to prosecution.

Outside the areas of mass unemployment there was not much understanding of the nub of the matter. Of course it was scandalous that a man might get more money when he was unemployed than when he was working; but the scandal consisted in the fact that though the U.A.B. scales were a minimum, arrived at by a scrupulous bureaucratic calculation of 'need', wages were often lower still. Likewise, it could be regarded as scandalous that two young people on the dole should get married; but the scandal, after all, was not that they married but that they were on the dole, and that frequently it was the wife who might be the quicker of the two to find a job. Finally, what was not realized by those who did not know the facts from personal experience or close investigation, was that the only element in the whole situation that was demoralizing without qualification was the brute fact of unemployment itself. All the other so-called demoralizations followed inescapably: the gradual loss of self-respect, the submission to petty persecution from the means test officer, or, worse still, the liability to tell tales to him about the neighbours, the sense of drift, of pointlessness and, among the older men, of sheer despair. Some young men had never worked, some elderly men would never work again. Yet from the outside, it was criminal of such people if they went to the pictures to save fuel and light, and to obtain an hour or two's escape from the drab tedium of having nothing to do.

In 1934 there were at last signs that the Government recognized that something ought to be done about the areas of high unemployment. In November, by the Depressed Areas Bill, the Government appointed unpaid commissioners to encourage economic and social improvements in South Wales, Tyneside, West Cumberland and Scotland, and armed them with a grant of £2 millions. No doubt for the better sustaining of public morale, the Lords insisted that the word 'Depressed' should be struck from the Bill's title and replaced by the adjective 'Special'. Despite much good will on the part of the Commissioners, little was achieved that was not merely palliative. The grant was too small, and expenditure on public works on any large scale was not allowed, so that only minor improvement schemes were subsidized. A few years later, under the stimulus of concessions about rates, taxes and rents, trading estates were set up in some parts of the areas concerned, but they mainly sustained light industries and employed few workers, most of them female. Attempts to get industries to move into the 'special' areas on any large scale came to little.

It is sometimes alleged, in defence of the Government's failure to embark on a positive policy to relieve unemployment, that the economic theory to justify such a procedure, running contrary as it did to the financial orthodoxy of the nineteenth century, had not yet been produced. It was presented to the world by Keynes in *The General Theory of Employment, Interest and Money*, published in 1936, which provided the theoretical basis for encouraging economic expansion by Government policy whenever the economy appeared to be running down. He demonstrated (among a great deal else) that what was needed in periods of depression was not to 'save' but to 'invest'. Money must be spent at such a time in order to stimulate industrial recovery, since to curtail investment in such circumstances impeded enterprise at the moment when it was most needed.

It is, of course, impossible to defend the principle that politicians must not do things until economists have first found a theory to fit them. There were adequate advice and example for the Government to draw upon had it so minded. Keynes, Bevin, Lloyd George, Franklin D. Roosevelt were all alive, vocal and active during the thirties, and these and many others pointed out that the money and the administrative effort expended on maintaining the unemployed in idleness could be better spent, economically and morally, by providing large schemes of public works. If the Government were afraid of such outlandish and dangerous personalities as these, they could, to take but one example, have followed the advice of Harold Macmillan, who sat as Conservative M.P. for the town of Stockton-on-

Tees and therefore had frequent occasion actually to visit a 'special area'. Together with Sir Arthur Salter and Geoffrey Crowther, he put his signature in the summer of 1935 to a document called 'Peace and Reconstruction', which outlined a programme of national development by means of capital expenditure on electrification, housing, roads, national parks and local authority improvement schemes.

There was, by the mid-thirties, already evidence as to what policies could be used to reduce employment, and there was evidence, too, that the policies worked. All Keynes really did was to explain why they worked. The view that MacDonald, Baldwin, Chamberlain and Runciman could do virtually nothing to cure unemployment because nobody had yet discovered how to do so is a myth.

PART VI: 'WITHOUT GRIP OR GRASP': BRITISH FOREIGN POLICY 1931-1939

26 · Illusion and Reality, 1931-34

Between 1919 and 1931 it was possible to believe that the world was, however fitfully, laying the foundations of an international world order whose twin pillars would be general disarmament and the pacific settlement of disputes through the League of Nations. Between 1931 and 1933 the little that had been achieved was swept away in the gales of the Depression. The machinery for the settlement of disputes was ground into the dust of Manchuria by the Japanese; the Disarmament Conference met from 1932 to 1934 only to contemplate its own coffin, while Arthur Henderson pleaded, Ramsay MacDonald orated, John Simon legalistically niggled, the French sulked and the Germans threatened; and a World Economic Conference opened on 12 June 1933 with a speech by George V and an address by Ramsay MacDonald (again) only to adjourn indefinitely forty-five days later, with nothing achieved.

The international system collapsed in those years at the same time as, and largely on account of, the collapse of the international economic system. The concentration of gold supplies in the United States and France, with its consequent catastrophic effect on world prices, meant that industrial nations could not sell to the primary producers because the primary producers could not afford to sell to the industrial nations. Wheat and coffee were burned because this was cheaper than losing money by paying to transport them to a distant market that could not afford to buy them at a worthwhile price. Nations tried to trade as little as possible with one another because the low prices of foreign imports would either limit still further the domestic market for home products or undercut the home product altogether. Governments everywhere engaged in the kind of nationalist and restrictionist economic policies which the United Kingdom adopted: resorting to tariffs, quotas and, in some cases, barter, in order to protect their own industry and agriculture from the undercutting foreigner, and to develop their domestic markets because foreign markets were congested with too many products chasing too little money. The universal habit of debt-repudiation, and its somewhat politer counterpart, currency devaluation, were both inimical to international investment, since they were measures which, in effect, robbed the foreign investor of his money. Thus, when the pound was devalued in 1931, foreign holders of sterling investments lost about 20 per cent of their money; when the Japanese devalued the yen the aim was to undercut the foreign manufacturer by sweeping reductions in the prices of Japanese products. Everywhere, therefore, in the years of Depression, the States of the world turned to siege economics. Many of their inhabitants were forced to adopt the standards of life and to acquire the psychological outlook appropriate to siege conditions. There was an enforced closing of the ranks, a routing out of traitors within and a frenzied effort to prevent contamination from enemies without. Politics was replaced by racketeering gangsterism, persuasion replaced by terror; and free institutions, appropriate only to nations not under stress, were replaced by one-party dictatorships based on physical and psychological coercion.

Even States whose political systems were well rooted in the past showed similar tendencies; in addition to siege economics, the United States, France and the United Kingdom all had their Fascist or semi-Fascist movements. The United States escaped lightly in this respect because of the personality of Franklin D. Roosevelt, though there was much in his system that did not conform to the normal in United States history; and in France, the republican tradition was strong enough to prevent Fascism doing more than aggravate the creeping paralysis of the national will. In the United Kingdom the malaise was chiefly manifested in nine years of one-party domination; but, significantly, under the label 'National', with its implication, characteristic of the Europe of the thirties, that any individual or group opposed to the party in power was in some way subversive. Organized, broadly-based political opposition to the National Government was slow to develop before 1940. As political forces, the Labour Party was incoherent and the trade union movement gelded. The employed were complacent, and the unemployed demoralized, either by their worklessness or by their just-endurable condition as pauperized pensioners of the U.A.B. The Government consistently supported Fascism abroad, and, for the most part, only a disregarded minority disliked this policy. Such demonstrations of patriotic solidarity behind authority as the 67 per cent vote in favour of the National Government in 1931, and the frenetic enthusiasm for Chamberlain after Munich suggest a frame of mind not altogether unlike that which, in Germany and Italy, had to be elaborately induced.

The Manchurian affair from 1931 to 1933 uncovered all the difficulties of dealing with 'aggression' in the context of the League Covenant. By Article 10 of the Covenant all members were bound to defend the territorial integrity of any one of them against 'external aggression' and, by Article 15, were required to submit 'disputes likely to lead to a rupture' to arbitration, judicial decision or to examination by the League Council. They were forbidden to resort to war until three months after an award, decision or report had been issued. In addition, Japan was signatory to the Kellogg-Briand Pact of Paris which had 'outlawed' war as 'an instrument of national policy', and to the Nine-Power Washington Treaty of 1921, which committed all the interested nations to the policy of the 'open door' in China.

Japan's actions in Manchuria from 1931 to 1933 violated all these undertakings, but, unfortunately, Japan could put up a marginally legal defence, at least for her initial interference. As a result of the Russo-Japanese War, Japan acquired Russia's leasehold rights over part of Manchuria as well as the South Manchurian railway. In 1915, China conceded to Japan the 'Twenty-one Demands', among which was the right of Japanese and Koreans to reside in Manchuria and to acquire land and undertake business operations there. The long civil war in China had led both to a breakdown of Chinese authority in Manchuria and to a growth of nationalistic feeling there; the two developments combined to produce frequent attacks on both Japanese and Koreans. Perhaps more ominous for the Japanese was that the Chinese Nationalist forces (the Kuomintang), under Chiang Kai-shek, had now nominally secured control over all China proper and could legally claim Manchuria as well.

Therefore, in September 1931, Japanese forces in Manchuria used a minor attack on the Japanese-controlled railway at Mukden as an excuse for the immediate military occupation of the city. By the end of the year they had established military control of almost all Manchuria. The promptitude of Japanese military action after the Mukden incident suggested that it had been contrived by the Japanese themselves.

The reactions of the rest of the world followed what was to be a recurrent pattern. China brought the matter to the notice of the League within three days. The League appealed for the termination of hostilities without success, but sent a Commission of Inquiry. In February 1932, the Commission, headed by Lord Lytton, departed for Manchuria and reported back early in October 1932; but by then the Japanese had formally 'recognized' Manchuria as the 'independent' State of Manchukuo. In February 1933, the League Assembly adopted the Lytton Report's finding that Manchuria was unquestionably a Chinese province, and its recommendations that the

Japanese should confine their forces to the railway zone they had policed before the Mukden incident, and that there should be Manchurian autonomy under China, with safeguards for the economic rights of Japan. The Japanese reply was to give notice of withdrawal from the League and to go on to conquer the city and province of Jehol which gave them control of the passes into China proper. The Chinese Nationalists at Nanking then signed an armistice, by which they withdrew their forces from a large area of China south of the Great Wall.

1933 ended, therefore, with every prospect of Japan becoming paramount in China. At Geneva, there had been an infinitude of speech-making and

THE DOORMAT. The anti-Government view of the outcome of the Manchurian crisis. The League's back is broken by the Japanese aggressor, while Sir John Simon produces face-saving devices. *Cartoon by Low*, 19 January 1933.

compromise-drafting, a tortuosity of endeavour to find a peaceful solution. This merely gave the 'aggressor' time to complete his programme without interference. Sir John Simon, as British Foreign Secretary, distinguished himself by expounding the arguments on the Japanese side so fully that he earned the public thanks of the Japanese delegate. He was much criticized for refusing to display enthusiasm for what was pompously described as the 'Doctrine of Non-Recognition', the adopted brain-child of United States Secretary of State Stimson. This attempted to universalize the principle that territorial conquests achieved by aggression should be denied diplomatic recognition: everybody was to pretend that Manchuria was still part of China, just as twenty years later everybody was asked to pretend that 'China' was not really China, but only Formosa.

Thus, while there are parallels between Japan's behaviour in Manchuria and attempts by other Powers to act similarly towards Turkey in the nineteenth century, the closest parallel that occurs to the student of history is Bismarck's successful military operation against Denmark in 1864. This was a parallel violation of a variety of international engagements by a Government which had scotched internal parliamentary opposition in the interests of the military; it was a similar prelude to a long story of aggrand-isement, the one leading to the temporary domination of Europe, the other to the temporary domination of East Asia. In 1864, those whose interest it was to prevent a Prussian domination of Europe stood aside, just as between 1931 and 1933, those who desired to prevent Japanese domination of China also stood aside. By now there is less disposition to blame the British for failing to rescue Denmark than to condemn Palmerston for boasting beforehand that Britain would do so. So, over Japan's aggression in Man-churia, what is perhaps more blameworthy than the failure to do anything is the pretence that something was going to be done. The Japanese militarists skilfully exploited the economic and political confusion in which the world and their own country were then immersed, to impose upon Japan, China and the world a policy it was impossible to reverse.

The Manchurian crisis also exposed the 1919 fallacy about 'the pressure of world opinion'. Unanimous world condemnation of aggression made little impression on those actually conducting the aggression. What was being said to the world from several quarters was, in effect, what Bismarck had said to the Germans in 1862: 'the great issues of our time will be decided not by votes and debates but by blood and iron'. And just as, in the 1860's, civilized people refused to believe their ears, so did they commit the same mistake in the 1930's, and with even more catastrophic results. The world of the 1930's, faced with Japanese militarists, with Mussolini's theatrical aggressions and Hitler's combination of public bullying and private devious-ness, was as baffled and futile as the Danes, the Habsburgs and Napoleon III when trying to cope with Bismarck. To the time-honoured view that war was diplomacy carried on by other means there was now added the corollary that diplomacy was war carried on by other means. The British in particular showed little sign of realizing this until the spring of 1939; and, being bungling amateurs in belligerent diplomacy compared with Hitler, blundered into war against him while hardly aware they were doing so.

Educated people in Britain, both in and out of politics, were slow to understand Hitler and Mussolini. They were ready to admire both of them, much as enlightened people in France and England had admired Prussia in the 1860's. They seem to have thought, as Papen and Hugenburg thought in Germany, that Hitler could be tamed; and that Mussolini already was tamed. It is important to set against the post-1940 view of Hitler and Mussolini as monsters the views actually expressed about Fascism in the middle of the 1930's. One of the more noteworthy examples is to be found in H. A. L. Fisher's widely acclaimed *History of Europe*, published in 1936:

Yet humane Italians were found, even from the first, to applaud a movement which, despite the ferocity of its oppression, brought into the political life of Italy a sentiment of grandeur recalling the Imperial age. The glowing genius of the 'Duce' communicated itself to every part of the body politic. An entirely new standard of efficiency was required of every branch of the Public Service. The trains ran to time. . . . By degrees Fascism which had at first been viewed as the violent dream of a lunatic was received with respect and admiration . . . If the price was the loss of liberty, it was a price the Italians were prepared to pay. Again Italy had produced a man of the Caesarean mould, a tyrant with the *bravura* of an orator, and the broad sympathies of a man of the people.[1]

The clue to the complaisant attitude of so many Englishmen to Mussolini and to Hitler is that, basically, they approved of what these men were doing. The dictators attacked Communists, trade unionists, Social Democrats and pacifists. They made strikes illegal, and they put an end, not only to civil strife, but to political dissension of all kinds. It was possible for a typical English Conservative to disapprove of the methods by which these policies were pursued, but impossible to condemn the policies themselves, since they were policies which, in its own more sophisticated way, the British Conservative Party had itself sought to pursue and not without success. Fascism's violent opposition to liberal-minded intellectuals also found ready sympathy in an England whose chief political personalities were Baldwin and Chamberlain. Both men had such an obsessive distaste for intellectuals that they excluded men with first-class brains from their Governments almost as an act of policy. And though there was general agreement that Hitler treated Jews abominably they were *German* Jews with whom he had to deal and probably either 'profiteers' or Communists. They were therefore quite different from British Jews, many of whom had been to good public schools or even to Oxford and Cambridge. Most important of all, Hitler was Europe's best defence against Communism. Once again, Fisher, the great Liberal historian, spoke for many when he wrote:

The Hitler revolution is a sufficient guarantee that Russian Communism will not spread westward. The solid German *bourgeois* hold the central fortress of Europe.[2]

The fear that to do anything (or at times even to say or print anything) that might weaken Hitler would open the floodgates to Communism was a

[1] Op. cit., p. 1194-5.
[2] Op. cit., p. 1209.

major contribution to the so-called 'weakness' of British foreign policy and a major source of Hitler's strength both at home and abroad.

A further explanation of the British Government's generally accommodating policy towards Germany was that public opinion supported such a policy, above all in the perhaps decisive years 1933–6. From the almost unanimous (but none the less mistaken) conviction that the treaty of Versailles had imposed injustice and hardship on the Germans, was derived the further conviction, among considerable sections of the population, that the war was thereby revealed not only as brutal but pointless; it must never happen again. Hitler's initial seizure of power in 1933–4 coincided with a wave of pacifism in Britain. This was partly a decent revulsion against the public exaltation of brutality and violence which characterized the public utterances of the Nazis, and partly the result of much anti-war propaganda.

Richard Aldington's bitter war novel *Death of a Hero* appeared in 1928. Robert Graves's autobiographical *Good-bye to All That* followed in 1929. Both took the false heroics out of war. Also in 1929 came R. C. Sherriff's play *Journey's End*, which with a moving dignity portrayed life in the trenches as a grey sad tragedy. At the same time came the English translation (and soon afterwards a highly compelling film version) of *All Quiet on the Western Front* by Erich Maria Remarque. Publication of this turgid German novel about the sufferings of men in a demoralized army in retreat is, like Pabst's perhaps more effective film, *Kameradschaft*, a reminder that the ferocity of Hitler's propaganda against pacifist intellectuals was dictated not merely by Hitler's own character but also by the existence in Germany of an anti-war spirit which could be regarded as just as representative of the Weimar Republic as the secret re-armers and blustering Rightists who are perhaps treated as more typical of the Germany of the 1920's than they really were.

In 1933 two more books, uncompromisingly pacifist in tone, attracted unusually wide audiences. *Cry Havoc* was something of a sensation because its author, Beverley Nichols, had made his name as one of the bright impertinent young men of the brittle twenties. He now came forward to expound the pacifist cause with an equally bright sincerity which must have greatly impressed the large public which had hitherto relied on him solely for amusement. Vera Brittain's *Testament of Youth*, an autobiographical lament for a lover and a brother whose deaths in the war were felt by the author, even half a generation later, to have robbed the world of its best meaning, went into nine impressions in just over two years. Since, like *Journey's End*, its mood was sensitive (and for later tastes maudlin) it affected a readership which would have been repelled by anti-war propaganda of the more political variety. Those who preferred their pacifism sour could buy *The Secret International* whose sixth impression was contemporaneous with the appearance of *Testament of Youth* on the bookstalls. Published by the Union of Democratic Control, a Left-wing body founded in the later years of the war to propagate Socialist ideas on international affairs, it was a ferocious attack on armament manu-facturers. Its cover was embellished with a kneeling figure captioned, 'The Munition Maker's Prayer: Give us this day a little war'. The same organiza-tion also published another pamphlet on the same theme, in the autumn of 1933, called *Patriotism Ltd: An exposure of the War Machine*. Its 'Con-clusions' contain the following:

Fascism – the extreme form of organized nationalism – threatens war wherever it develops, and Hitlerism today is a menace to every country on its frontier. Many people today believe that a preventive war against Germany in the near future before she can become a first-class military nation is a probability.

Such a situation produces an atmosphere ideally suited to the interests of Patriotism Ltd., which under various high-sounding slogans, prepares people's minds for war, in the Press, on the platform, on the screen and in the military displays for which 1933 is a record year.

The fight against war must be organized on the basis of the fight against Imperialism, on the fight against the system which leads to Fascism.

It is significant that the action recommended by the pamphlet was not active resistance to foreign Fascism. This would merely serve the interest of the arms manufacturers. Instead there was merely to be a 'fight against Imperialism', in other words opposition to war of any sort. It is thus appropriate that in February 1933 the Oxford Union Society should vote against fighting for King and Country and that, in the celebrated East Fulham by-election in the same year, the issue of rearmament versus renunciation of war by way of the League of Nations took up most of the campaign, resulting in the conversion of a Conservative majority of 14,500 into a Labour majority of 4,840.

The year 1934 saw the foundation of the Peace Pledge Union. This was the creation of H. R. L. Sheppard, the vicar of St Martin's-in-the-Fields, London, who had become well known as a result of frequent broadcasts from his church. He called on all males to send him a postcard stating that they would never support or approve another war, and would persuade others to adopt the same opinion. By 1936 the movement had 100,000 members and had secured the adhesion, among others, of Aldous Huxley. In the course of a closely argued pamphlet justifying complete non-violence he wrote:

In a vague way practically everyone is now a pacifist.

Whether this claim was substantiated by the 'Peace Ballot' organized by the League of Nations Union in June 1934 was open to question. The Peace Ballot was a privately-organized national referendum, and no fewer than $11\frac{1}{2}$ million votes were cast. There were five questions. Almost all voters answered in the affirmative the question 'should Britain remain a member of the League?'; over 10 million votes favoured the 'all-round reduction of armaments' and condemned the private manufacture of arms. A large majority was in favour of the 'all-round abolition of national military and naval aircraft' and for the employment of non-military sanctions against an aggressor. There were as many as 6¾ million votes in favour of the employment of military sanctions.

The only questions of significance in the Ballot were the two parts of the fifth question, about sanctions. So long as the will to peace involved nothing more arduous than continuing membership of the League, or in wanting disarmament or in being afraid of bombers, it was relatively easy to subscribe to it. It was even possible to approve economic sanctions against an aggressor, for, to the private citizen, this sounded like some form of passive resistance which would not greatly inconvenience him. But when it came to military sanctions, those who loved peace, the League and Disarmament were as undecided as His Majesty's Government.

In view of their impregnable position in the Commons between 1931 and 1940 there was, of course, little need for the Conservatives to take much notice of pacifist trends in the country. Indeed, the fashion for pacifism weakened the Labour Party more than it embarrassed the National Government, since it created a disruptive struggle within the party between those who took the view that all wars were wrong, and those who were prepared to justify wars in defence of the League Covenant.

The real cause of the National Government's troubles when trying to deal with the problems of the 1930's in Europe was that it inherited a heaped-up legacy of confusion from the past, dearly wanted to clear it up, but was continually outwitted by the craft of Hitler. Throughout the period from 1933 to 1939 the British Government was at no time opposed to what Hitler did but only to the way he did it. Thus, Sir John Simon wrote to George V in January 1935,

The point which Sir John has been pressing is that the practical choice is between a Germany which continues to re-arm without any regulation or agreement, and a Germany which, through getting a recognition of its rights and some modification of the peace treaties, enters into the comity of nations, and contributes, in this and other ways to the European stability.[1]

The British Government thus repeatedly allowed Hitler to force their agreement to changes which they themselves desired. The British did not like the *status quo* in Europe. They thought it materially and morally too costly to defend. Unfortunately they were repeatedly humiliated when attempting to conciliate Hitler because he was always at least one step ahead of them. A diplomat trained in the orthodox manner would have paid more respect to the rules, and played the conventional game of *détentes*

[1] Harold Nicolson, *George V*, p. 522.

and *démarches* and *pourparlers* and protocols. Hitler, however, was an illbred creature from the gutters of central Europe, to whom civilized procedures were distasteful. His chosen devices were blustering uncouthness, screaming public utterances, the dramatic action taken at the instinctively-chosen right moment – and thereafter the resort to pacific protestations of sweet reasonableness so that the stupid Anglo-Saxons would decide after all that he was a man who could be trusted to keep his word.

Only two doubts existed about giving Hitler what he asked for. One was that every success he gained by these methods strengthened National Socialism at home and extended its evil influence to areas hitherto free from it. About this, the British Government showed no distress; perhaps, accustomed to close contact with uncivilized persons in the course of their imperial mission in Africa and Asia, the British rather assumed that Europeans were also in their way merely a slightly superior sort of backward people.

The second doubt was more serious, and concerned Hitler's ultimate intentions. To begin with, Hitler wanted, it seemed, merely to throw off the disabilities imposed on Germany by the Treaty of Versailles. But these disabilities were already of little consequence by the time Hitler came to power. Reparations had gone already, and since, at the Disarmament Conference, the other powers had accepted the German demand for 'equality of status' well before Hitler was made Chancellor, this presented no serious problem either. There were many signs that in the ordinary course of diplomacy the Germans could expect to secure from the other Powers the right to rearm at a slow pace, and this was all Germany wanted for the time being. There remained the demilitarization of the Rhineland, and (if the Disarmament Conference failed altogether) the Versailles limitation on the size of Germany's armed forces. The former was merely a hurt to sensitive pride, and the moral justification for the latter had disappeared now that the possibility of German rearmament had been discussed at Geneva. If Germany's territorial losses were considered, an attempt to recover Alsace-Lorraine or the Polish Corridor would obviously produce immediate war, and this, in 1934, Germany was incapable of facing. Thus there was, on sober reflection, comparatively little to fear for some time to come. As Sir John Simon soothingly told the King when Germany left the Disarmament Conference in 1933,

'Fortunately time is available, for Germany is at present quite incapable of undertaking aggression. Europe forewarned is, in a sense, Europe forearmed'.

When Hitler later pressed his demand for the inclusion of all Germans within his Reich, this too offered no insuperable difficulties. That an independent Austria could never be a viable State was one of the more celebrated of the false verities of the 1920's; and if the matter of the

Sudeten Germans was raised, it would instantly be recalled that there had been grave doubts about their being included in Czechoslovakia in the first place. Britain had already made it clear enough (to go no farther back than Locarno) that she would not fight to preserve the frontiers of Czechoslovakia, whatever the implications of Article 10 of the League Covenant. As for an attempt to recover Danzig and the Polish Corridor, Danzig was full of Germans and Poles were using Gdynia instead; while, though the number of Germans in the Polish Corridor was small, the Polish Army was large.

There could only be cause for genuine alarm if Hitler was planning something bigger. This the British Government seemed reluctant to believe; and could not undertake to legislate against it in advance. The ghostly voice of Castlereagh echoed through the Foreign Office: 'this country cannot and will not act upon abstract and speculative principles of precaution'. Besides, it seemed that Hitler's real objective was to secure *Lebensraum* at the expense of Russia; but not only was this a long-term objective, it was also one which could hardly alarm the British. Meanwhile, it was far more sensible, in the probably long-lasting interim, to do everything possible to calm Hitler down by not opposing him unnecessarily. By negotiation and appeasement he could be assimilated into the family of the European diplomats.

27 · Four-Power Confusion, 1933-35

When Hitler became Chancellor of the Weimar Republic on 30 January 1933 he was by no means master in his own house. Before this could happen he was preoccupied with the 1933 election, and the Enabling Bill of the same year which gave him the means to put through the Nazi revolution that turned Germany into a one-party unitary State. Even then he had still to cope with his own party enemies by the purge of 30 June 1934, an act which established the domination over the army which Röhm and his S.A. had made so difficult for him. Not until the death of Hindenburg in August 1934 was Hitler in supreme control as *Führer und Reichskanzler*. In consequence, his interventions in foreign policy in this period, though alarming enough, were comparatively cautious. It would be wrong to think of him as being prepared at this stage to do more than exploit the situation as he found it, though always with an eye to laying such foundations for the future as appeared possible. Germany had to be set once more on the road to greatness (whatever that might mean); but he was more concerned in 1933 and 1934 to stamp out the debilitating influence of pacifism and internationalism inside Germany than to create so much alarm outside his frontiers as to provoke a military attack which Germany was in no position to resist. He regarded his psychological battle for the soul of the Germany people as primary; without this, rearmament and conscription would be premature. Before they were given their guns, the Germans must first be washed clean of their pernicious democratic, Socialist, Communist and pacifist ideas, and taught that all who held these ideas were traitors to the Fatherland. The only 'foreigners' he could allow the Germans to fight, for the moment, were the Jews. They were a special kind of 'foreigner' who, by great good fortune, were not citizens of a foreign power which could deliver protests, recall its ambassador, threaten to mobilize, or appeal to the League of Nations. They were citizens of National Socialist Germany and could therefore be attacked with impunity.

Before Hitler's appointment as Chancellor, Germany had withdrawn from the Disarmament Conference in September 1932 but had returned in February 1933 because in December 1932 the other powers had accorded Germany 'equality of rights' in a system of 'all-round security'. The summer of 1933 was taken up with consideration of a disarmament plan drawn up by Ramsay MacDonald. The Germans came within sight of accepting it, realizing that it would allow them troops not greatly fewer in number than they themselves thought it possible to train adequately during the next few years. Eventual rejection of the plan and withdrawal from the Conference in October arose from fear that the French might publish the documentary proof they possessed of Germany's illegal rearmament. Both France and Britain were well informed about this illegal German rearmament, but the British would not support French sanctions on the issue. For this reason, the French demanded that the MacDonald Plan include international supervision of national armaments, and that rearmament of States with limited armaments should follow, and not coincide with, the disarmament of the normally armed powers. It was the news that Britain and the United States were about to adhere to this French proposal that prompted Hitler's withdrawal from the Conference, and from the League of Nations. A plebiscite in Germany in November 1933 duly provided a 95 per cent vote of approval.

It seemed a triumphant manifestation of the new German spirit: no longer would Germany go cap in hand to a world in conference. But what to the Germans looked like a Wagnerian act of defiance was a calculated decision that in future Hitler would deal with his adversaries one by one.

What is more, he had thus early proved that he was right and his expert advisers wrong. They had thought it would be a disaster if Germany came back from Geneva empty-handed, and that French sanctions would be applied if Germany announced her intention to rearm. The German diplomatists of the twenties had really been living in the same illusory world as the French and British. It was Hitler, who screamed most noisily about the shackles of Versailles, who was the first to discover that they were not real shackles at all, but only cardboard imitations; and it is possible that the discovery astonished him as much it astonished every body else.

1934 had barely begun when he made another surprising discovery: that he could do a deal with the most apparently resolute of his armed enemies, Poland. Poland seems to have feared that the most likely outcome of a German resurgence would be a four-power European directorate composed of Germany, France, Great Britain and Italy, a notion already mooted by Mussolini. This would displace Poland as France's principal ally. The other possibility was a Russo-German war; and of this, Poland would be the first victim. It was therefore largely on Polish initiative that the ten-year non-aggression pact between Germany and Poland was formed in January 1934; but its chief gains were Hitler's. He had neutralized the large Polish Army, gravely weakened the structure of French security, and set up an insurmountable obstacle to the effectiveness of a Franco-Russian alliance twelve months before it was drafted. That Hitler could, thus early in his career, put Germany's revisionist claims against Poland so abruptly on one side is either a tribute to the ascendancy he had already acquired in Germany, or else an indication that Germans, while prepared to attend mass Nazi rallies and beat up Jews, were at heart a good deal less bellicose than anybody dared to hope.

In similar fashion, the June purge of the S.A. and the attempted Nazi *coup* in Austria were both clear signs of the inner nature of the Nazi movement and of Hitler's sinister adroitness. The 'night of the long knives' was an organized mass murder whose object was to secure the adherence of the Army to the Nazi cause by eliminating the Army's Nazi rival; and Hitler's repudiation of the Austrian Nazis after their murder of Dollfuss was a sign that he was, as yet, a megalomaniac with a sense of the possible. Austria was Mussolini's sphere of influence, and when Mussolini moved troops to the Brenner during the crisis, Hitler abandoned whatever plans his mind contained for controlling Austria. Ironically enough, Hitler adopted towards Mussolini in 1934 the attitude that Britain and France adopted to him during the Abyssinian affair twelve months later. He wanted to keep Mussolini from going over to the enemy.

Hitler's most important forward move in 1934 was to insist, against his defence experts, that the strength of the German Army should be raised during 1934–5 to the level the generals had planned for 1937–8. But in Britain the chief concern in political circles was fear, not of the German Army, for which it was felt the French were a match as yet, but of the nascent German Air Force. Churchill's lurid reference in a Commons speech of 7 February 1934, to the opening hours of a war, 'with the crash of bombs exploding on London and cataracts of masonry and fire and smoke' might have come straight out of a pacifist pamphlet. Fear of the bombing aeroplane was the common factor shared by all shades of British opinion at this time. One might summarize the reactions of the various parties by saying that Baldwin ('the bomber will always get through') thought it was terrible to contemplate the bombing of our cities and hoped it would not happen; the pacifists were sure it was going to happen and so preferred peace at any price; the Labour Party believed in exorcising the bombs by intermittent chanting of the phrase 'collective security'; and Churchill thought the proper thing to do was to have a large air force to defend our cities and to hit back at the enemy's.

Since in the end Churchill's view prevailed, history (which not only says 'alas' to the defeated but '*Sieg heil*' to the successful) tends to assume that Churchill was right. All through 1934 he hammered away at the National Government for its lethargy and at the Opposition for its evasiveness, but with little result. In the strictly technical sphere, Churchill's thesis was faulty. The German Air Force was not as strong as he made out; like so many others, he was taken in by Hitler's vauntings. The *Luftwaffe* was not designed for bombing cities, but for giving support to the German Army; it was conceived as a tactical weapon, not as a strategic weapon in a total war against civilians. Churchill's misjudgements here were to have grievous consequences when the war actually came, and Britain ended by greatly out-Hitlering Hitler in this respect. Yet despite his romantic's delight in the arts of war, what distinguished Churchill above his contemporaries was not simply his desire for action but the warmth of feeling that accompanied it. Churchill did not merely want something done about the Nazis; he hated them. Churchill could claim, as result of his fierce support of intervention in Russia in 1919, to be the world's anti-Communist Number One; but he did not commit the common mistake of condoning Hitlerism on the grounds that it was saving Europe from Communism. To him, National Socialism and Communism were equally detestable tyrannies and, unlike too many others, he saw that a Europe 'saved' by Hitler would be saved only for psychopaths.

Churchill thus mattered less on account of his specific proposals than for his attack on the pretences both of the Left and of the Right. Unfortunately, the list of his political offences was by now so long that his chances of securing a large following were remote. He had deserted the Tories in 1905, joined with Lloyd George in their attempted strangulation in the Coalition period and had helped to ditch them over Ireland; and, except in name, had deserted them again over India in 1931. He had sent troops against the miners of Tonypandy; he had provoked the Curragh incident by his fleet movements; he had identified himself with Gallipoli, with a reckless war against the Bolsheviks, and with irresponsible bellicosity over Chanak. He had been pilloried by Keynes for restoring the gold standard and himself had pilloried the trade unions during the General Strike. He despised the Labour Party, regarded MacDonald with contempt and Baldwin with bewildered dislike; and, having been cast by the Webbs and by Stafford Cripps for the role of England's future Fascist leader, was generally feared as a warmonger. It was not that the British were feeble in their failure to respond to him in the mid-thirties; it was rather that on his record he was a man greatly to be feared. And in 1936 he made his parliamentary reputation worse by seeking to resist the displacement from the throne of Edward VIII.[1] For their part, not only were MacDonald and Baldwin afraid of Churchill; they were afraid of rearmament too, partly for temperamental reasons and partly for reasons of finance. They were convinced that rearmament could not be embarked on until the country had recovered from the Depression.

Moreover, neither they, nor anybody else, knew how much to rearm, because, pardonably enough, they cannot have known exactly what to rearm for. If they tried to rearm for 'defence' and not for 'offence' this posed the unanswerable question as to where the boundary lay between these two largely metaphysical conceptions. Baldwin, in his customary fashion, stated the problem but did little about it. Our, frontier, he announced, was on the Rhine; but in practice this really meant that the French would have to defend it. Aware (unconsciously, one must at present assume) that 'defence' against Germany could be achieved only by arming for all-out offence, the Government rearmed slowly in the hope that something would turn up. Everything therefore depended on the astuteness of their diplomacy.

1935 opened with two developments of great value to Hitler. In January, the plebiscite held in the Saar under the terms of the treaty of Versailles resulted in a huge majority in favour of its return to Germany. This increased Hitler's freedom of manœuvre by eliminating the possibility that the French might refuse to allow the plebiscite on the grounds of Germany's illegal rearmament.

In the same month, Abyssinia officially notified the League, under Article 11 of the Covenant, that a dispute existed with Italy, arising out of an armed clash between Italian and Abyssinian forces, in December 1934, at a desert place called Walwal. There had been casualties on both sides, and each accused the other of aggression, the Abyssinians claiming that Walwal was in Abyssinia, the Italians that it was in Italian Somaliland. Since, in the circumstances then existing, an appeal to the League by

[1] See p. 279.

Abyssinia was an appeal to France and Britain against Italy, nothing could have suited Hitler better.

The Abyssinian appeal cut across various complicated diplomatic man-œuvres centred upon the problem of Hitler. The French were working to bring about an alliance with the U.S.S.R., involving a subsidiary Russian guarantee of Czechoslovakia. The French Foreign Minister, Laval, was also working to cement an *entente* with Mussolini. This would involve the preservation of Austrian independence, and the transfer to Italy of French shares in the railway connecting Addis Ababa, the Abyssinian capital, with Djibuti in French Somaliland. At the same time, the British were sounding Hitler on whether an agreement on armaments was possible; and MacDonald's pacifist friend, Lord Allen of Hurtwood, was learning for the first time that Germany was prepared to limit her naval armaments to 35 per cent of the British. The Abyssinians were therefore persuaded to let Italy go through the motions of arbitration without involving the League.

No progress resulting, Abyssinia appealed once more to the League, in March 1935. Once again the two parties were told to seek a settlement between themselves. This was because the new Abyssinian appeal coincided with Hitler's abrupt abrogation of the disarmament clauses of the treaty of Versailles, and the reintroduction of conscription.

The object of Hitler's decision to move at this juncture was political. Agreement on the ending of these restrictions on Germany was well in sight and there was no immediate intention to accelerate Germany rearma-ment. But the dramatically illegal way of doing it increased Hitler's reputa-tion in his own country as the courageous Führer who was restoring Ger-man pride by his fearless defiance of the wicked makers of the Versailles *Diktat*; and it shook the nerve of the outside world by giving the impression that Germany was more heavily armed and readier for action than she was.

In spite of Hitler's repudiation, Simon and Eden visited him a week later. The meeting had been planned for a fortnight before; Hitler had postponed it, claiming that he had a cold, but doubtless so that when they did arrive he could face them with a *fait accompli*. He took advantage of their presence to step up his war of nerves. He gave them exaggerated figures about the size of the illegal German Army, and then informed them that Germany had already obtained air parity with Britain. This was untrue. It was also an unnecessary piece of bluff. Upset though they seem to have been by his announcements, Simon and Eden showed signs of being impressed by their first meeting with the Führer, and readily agreed to pursue negotiations about a naval agreement.

The French were somewhat less accommodating. The process of linking France with Russia, and Russia with Czechoslovakia, continued, and, to re-establish the diplomatic encirclement of Germany which the Polish-German Treaty of 1934 had broken, the support of Italy was sought. Accordingly, MacDonald, Simon and Laval conferred with

Mussolini at Stresa in April 1935. The meeting produced little more than words. Germany was reprimanded for her unilateral breach of the Versailles Treaty; the independence of Austria was declared to be the common concern of all three Powers; and they reaffirmed their loyalty to Locarno. The truth was that MacDonald, Simon and Mussolini had their minds on other things: MacDonald and Simon on their forthcoming naval agreement with the Germans, and Mussolini on Abyssinia. The two factors together wrecked what was supposed to be an impressive re-creation of the inter-allied unity of wartime.

That summer, too, the British had other diversions. On 6 May 1935, with a Thanksgiving service at St Paul's Cathedral, there began a week of celebration in honour of the Silver Jubilee of the accession of George V and Queen Mary. The King's official biographer is silent as to what prompted the authorities to organize the celebration of what was only twenty-five years of rule, especially at a time when there was little to be jubilant about, and much to fear. Some thought it a sinister plot by the National Government to induce in the people a mood of joyous togetherness in view of an autumn election. The response, however, was a genuine outburst of affection. Their Majesties were nightly cheered by thousands gathered outside Buckingham Palace to see the Royal Appearances on the floodlit balcony. Royal visits were made during the week to a carefully chosen selection of the more plebeian London boroughs, where the slum-dwellers put up decorations and flags, and cheered and waved with gusto. The strangest thing was that, whether they realized it or not, George V had for some time past been almost the only significant personage in British ruling circles who was worth cheering, and certainly one of the few European heads of State in 1935 for whom any decent person could reasonably feel affection. He had long been indefatigable in bringing his presence into the streets and factories of the land, and, though endowed only with the social and intellectual qualities of a country squire, he was more in tune with the working classes than either his predecessors or his successors. The Hanoverians had been bores, fools or scoundrels; Victoria had been wife, mother, widow, recluse and imperial symbol in turn; Edward VII had been a cosmopolitan *bon viveur*; George V, for all his private irascibility, was a nice old man who worried about the poor and the unemployed, and clearly thought Sir John Simon not a very good Foreign Secretary. He warned the British ambassador to Germany that

we must not be blinded by the apparent sweet reasonableness of the Germans, but be wary and not taken unawares[1]

and even had the temerity, in 1933, to express strong disapproval to the German ambassador of the Nazis' treatment of the Jews; his censures were

[1] Nicolson, op. cit., p. 522.

thought sufficiently noteworthy to be passed on to Hindenburg himself.[1] In April 1934, he had been even more severe, informing Hitler's ambassador that 'Germany was the peril of the world':

'What was Germany arming for? No one wanted to attack her, but she was forcing all the other countries to be prepared for an attack on her part. The ambassador tried to excuse Germany by saying that the French fortifications were impregnable and that Germany had no fortifications on her side. His Majesty ridiculed this idea, and said that in the last war fortifications were useless and would be even more so in the next.'

The Jubilee celebrations were therefore less irrational than they seemed. They were an instinctive counter-demonstration by the British public against sub-human dictators abroad and sub-standard politicians at home, an assertion of the worth-whileness of ordinary human personality. George V realized this himself. 'I am beginning to think they must really like me for myself,' he said, with what was obviously almost as much surprise as pleasure.

The next sensation was provided by Baldwin. On 22 May 1935, as a result no doubt of the Simon-Eden visit to Hitler in March, he announced in the Commons that, when he had denied Churchill's claim in February 1935 that the German Air Force was equal to that of Britain and would be twice as large by 1937, he had been wrong and Churchill had been right. Of the estimate he had then given of the future, Baldwin now said,

There I was completely wrong. We were completely misled on that subject. . . . There is . . . no occasion for panic . . . whatever responsibility there may be – and we are perfectly ready to meet criticism – that responsibility is not that of any single Minister; it is the responsibility of the Government as a whole, and we are all responsible, and we are all to blame.

It would seem that on a strict technical basis, it was Churchill who had been wrong. But this does not exonerate the Government which, apparently, was either unaware of the true situation or was deceiving itself and the public.

Unfortunately, the Government's confusion was masked both by Baldwin's astute public performance as an honest man admitting frankly that he had been guilty of error, and by the attitude of the Opposition. The Labour Party voted against the Government's proposals to treble the strength of the R.A.F. by 1937, to the accompaniment of a declaration by Attlee that

Our policy is not one of seeking security through rearmament but through disarmament. Our aim is the reduction of armaments, and then the complete abolition of all national armaments under the League.

Shortly after this, in June 1935, MacDonald resigned the Premiership to Baldwin, who handed on to his predecessor the post of Lord Privy

[1] Robertson, *Hitler's Pre-War Policy*, p. 15.

Seal. At the same time, Sir John Simon was replaced at the Foreign Office by Sir Samuel Hoare, while Anthony Eden, who had been Foreign Under-Secretary since 1933, was consoled by being appointed to the Cabinet as a Minister for League of Nations affairs. In spite of the Government's belief that on the matter of air defence Churchill was better informed than they were, he was not invited to join them. Nor was Lloyd George, despite a series of meetings he had had with members of the Cabinet earlier in the year about his plans for economic reconstruction. Baldwin did not leave Churchill entirely in the cold; he invited him, in July, to join a secret Committee on Air Defence Research 'as a gesture of friendliness to an old colleague' – and, one may judge, in the hope that any future technical criticisms Churchill might make would be raised, initially at any rate, behind the scenes. It would be less embarrassing.

On 18 June 1935 (the one hundred and twentieth anniversary, it was noted in France, of the Anglo-German victory over the French at Waterloo) an Anglo-German Naval Agreement was signed. The undertaking not to exceed 35 per cent of British tonnage was duly given, along with an irrelevant promise to work with the British for the ultimate abolition of submarine warfare. Sir Samuel Hoare opened his brief career as Foreign Secretary by informing a sceptical world that this was 'in no sense a selfish agreement'. The objection that it condoned a breach of the peace treaty by Germany was quickly shrugged off:

Apart from the juridical position, there seemed to us to be, in the interests of peace – which is the main objective of the British Government – overwhelming reasons why we should conclude the agreement. In the opinion of our naval experts we were advised to accept the agreement as a safe agreement for the British Empire.

It is hardly surprising that, in coping with the Abyssinian affair during the months that followed, the French Prime Minister, Laval, was to show more enthusiasm for co-operating with Mussolini than for co-operating with the British.

The continued postponement of international action about the Italo-Abyssinian dispute was appearing more and more like passive acceptance of Mussolini's obvious preparations for full-scale war against Abyssinia as soon as the rainy season ended in the autumn. In May 1935, the Italian Minister of Finance announced that his Government had already spent £10 millions on military activity in East Africa, and on 24 May Mussolini said,

Let no one hold any illusions in or out of Italy. We are tolerably circumspect before we make a decision, but once a decision is taken we march ahead and do not turn back. . . . Better live as a lion one day than a hundred years as a sheep.[1]

It was in the context of the imminent probability of an Italian attack

[1] Quoted, *Abyssinia and Italy*, Royal Institute of International Affairs, 1935.

on Abyssinia that the Peace Ballot had taken place. So far, indeed, from being the downright pacifist demonstration its opponents claimed, its 6 million votes in favour of military sanctions may be said to mark the beginning of the end of the pacifist era in England. Mussolini was proving a speedier educator of British opinion than Hitler.

The Government, however, had still had something to learn. Eden went to Rome to offer Mussolini a strip of Abyssinian territory in exchange for which England would give Abyssinia an outlet to the sea in British Somaliland. Mussolini rejected this, as he did further 'compromise' suggestions made under League auspices in August.

28 · Sanctions and the 1935 Election

The gravity of the situation was at last beginning to affect the Labour movement. The chief innovation after the disasters of 1931 was the establishment of the National Council of Labour in 1932, to co-ordinate relations between the Parliamentary Party, the National Labour Executive and the General Council of the T.U.C. The result was much greater influence for the T.U.C., through Ernest Bevin and the general secretary, Walter Citrine. Nevertheless, it was difficult to evolve an electorally acceptable domestic policy for the now demoralized party and even more difficult for it to produce a foreign policy. The thin ranks of the Parliamentary Party, led by Lansbury with Attlee as his Deputy, were not very effective in the Commons, partly because Lansbury was so obviously not fitted for the role of Leader of the Opposition (and MacDonald rarely treated him as such) and also because Attlee though farther to the Left than his later attitudes might suggest, was then, as always, unimpressive in manner. Henderson, though secretary of the party until 1934, was preoccupied with his thankless role as President of the Disarmament Conference. As a result, the battle for control of the movement went on outside the Parliamentary Party.

Most of the running was made by the intellectuals in the movement, with Ernest Bevin and Herbert Morrison opposing, unfortunately, both them and each other. The advocates of dramatic measures at home and total pacifism abroad included Sir Charles Trevelyan, Lord Ponsonby and

Sir Stafford Cripps, all wealthy upper middle-class converts to the cause, whose behaviour justified Beatrice Webb's comment that what intellectuals brought to the movement was not their intellect but their emotions. At the Annual Conference of 1932, Trevelyan demanded that the next Labour Government pledge itself in advance to introduce Socialist legislation whether it had a parliamentary majority or not; both Cripps and Attlee demanded that the party nationalize all the joint stock banks, and Cripps, with his fine voice and look of stern and godly virtue, declared there must be no compromise whatever with the capitalists. There was also fierce dissension between Bevin and Morrison about the constitution of the nationalized boards through which Labour now proposed to manage nationalized industries and services. Morrison opposed Bevin's trade unionist insistence that there should be some form of 'workers' control' over the new boards, thus early insisting on the principle that management was not a function in which employees ought to share. It was a strange theory to wish on to a party which claimed, in however vague a way, to be Socialist; and the long-term consequences of its implementation in the years after 1945 are not likely to be regarded by future historians as wholly beneficent.

In 1933 the movement was much distracted both by pacifism and by the increasing vehemence of Cripps. He insisted, in various public speeches, that a Labour Government should anticipate the inevitable capitalist resistance to its Socialist programme by assuming emergency powers and ruling, Hitler-fashion, by decree. The Commons should be 'reformed' to make it easier to pass Socialist legislation; and the Lords, of course, should be abolished. Cripps also thought Labour might have to do something about the opposition it was likely to meet from 'the Buckingham Palace set'.

When the Annual Conference met in 1933, rather more attention was given to a unanimous anti-war resolution calling for 'an uncompromising attitude against war preparations' and for the organization at home and abroad of a general strike 'in the event of war or threat of war'. The subsequent excuse for passing such a resolution nine months after Hitler's accession to office was that it was related, not to Hitler, but to an obscure fear that the Government might provoke a war with the U.S.S.R., which had recently put some British engineers on trial on a charge of spying. Bevin, who fiercely attacked Cripps as well as Morrison, later damned the whole proposal by pointing out that in the Europe of 1933 there were hardly any trade unions left:

Who and what is there to strike? Trade unionism has been destroyed in Italy and Germany; practically speaking it does not exist in France; it is extremely weak in the U.S.A. . . . while there is no possibility of a strike against the Russian Government in the event of war. What is left? Great Britain, Sweden, Denmark and Holland. . . .[1]

[1] Bullock, op. cit., p. 550.

It is false to pretend that Labour, either in 1933 or 1934, was opposed to war only if it was war against Russia. Ideologically committed to the view that war was a product of capitalism, the movement deduced from this that all wars were capitalist wars, foisted upon the workers by the greed of rival capitalist States. (Arising out of the idea that wars were caused by economic factors came the flabby thought that there ought to be a world conference to arrange for a more equitable distribution of raw materials. It was advocated at various times in this period by persons as temperamentally different as Ernest Bevin, Aldous Huxley and Samuel Hoare.) Rather more popular, however, was the demand for resistance to both Fascism *and* War. The apparent illogicality of the slogan may have arisen from the belief in some minds (taking their cue from Cripps) that the real danger of Fascism was in Britain itself and that war was somehow a separate issue which would arise only if capitalist (or Fascist) Britain quarrelled with foreign Fascists, and thus produced what, in accordance with theory, would be a war with which the Labour movement should have nothing to do. The idea that it might be necessary to fight Fascism by war or the threat of war was discounted; but there were, it must be admitted, always good reasons for thinking that the National Government had no particular quarrel with Fascism as such.

During 1934, European events were even more chilling. The forcible suppression of the Austrian Socialists by Mussolini's puppet, Dollfuss, in February, dramatically demonstrated that, throughout continental Europe, all that the British Labour movement believed in was being ruthlessly destroyed. The break up of the Disarmament Conference showed that disarmament was a dead duck too. Yet typical Labour reactions continued to be the wrong ones. The destruction of social democracy and trade unionism abroad was seen, not as a problem involving changes in foreign policy, but merely a more vigorous opposition to the National Government, lest it be tempted to adopt Fascist policies at home. The failure of disarmament was seen, not as creating the problem of German rearmament, but solely as further evidence of the evil intent of the National Government. In Labour's view the real villain of the Disarmament Conference was, not Hitler, but Lord Londonderry, MacDonald's Air Minister, who had opposed the abolition of bombers because of their usefulness for conducting punitive campaigns on the North-West Frontier of India. Almost to the end of the period of peace, Labour had great difficulty in discarding the theory that disarmament was perfectly feasible and that it was being prevented solely by the obstinacy of the British Government.

The 1934 Conference went some way to adjusting policy to facts. Despite Ponsonby and Cripps, the Conference gave its approval to the principle of collective security through the League of Nations, while promising to oppose the British Government in any 'unsupported claim to be using force in self-defence'. Approval of military sanctions under the Covenant was also given.

The uninterrupted development of Mussolini's war preparations against Abyssinia through the spring and summer of 1935 faced the party with the imminent prospect of having to make good this pledge. In July the National Council of Labour intimated to Baldwin that the movement would support a strong League of Nations stand against Mussolini; and the issue was the major concern of the T.U.C. Conference held in the first week of September.

In August 1935, France and Britain had proposed to Mussolini an ingeniously benevolent scheme by which Italy would have 'wide economic opportunities' in Abyssinia; Abyssinian attacks on the frontiers of Italian Somaliland would be eliminated and there would be collective assistance by the three Powers for Abyssinian economic development. All that was asked of Italy was respect for Abyssinia's territorial integrity. The plan was rejected. 'We shall,' Mussolini told two divisions of Blackshirts as they set sail for Africa, 'go forward until we achieve the Fascist Empire'; and the Italian representative later said at Geneva that the Eden proposals did not seem generous to Italy.

For her, only 100 per cent of her demands could be regarded as generous.

The T.U.C. Congress at Margate, therefore, pledged full support of any Government action to restrain the Italian Government and to uphold the authority of the League. Walter Citrine, the general secretary, went as far as saying:

There is no real alternative now left to us but the applying of sanctions involving, in all possibility, war.

A week later, these energetic sentiments appeared to have secured the unqualified support of Sir Samuel Hoare. At Geneva on 11 September he announced:

In conformity with its precise and explicit obligations the League stands and my country stands with it, for the collective maintenance of the Covenant in its entirety, and particularly for steady and collective resistance to all acts of unprovoked aggression. The attitude of the British nation in the last few weeks has clearly demonstrated the fact that this is no variable and unreliable sentiment, but a principle of international conduct to which they and their Government hold with firm, enduring and universal persistence.

The speech made a profound impression; but not on Mussolini. In a high-spirited interview published in the *Morning Post* a week later he said,

There is an Italian Army in Eritrea, and so far the preparations have cost us 2,000 million lire. Do you think we have done that as a joke? No! We are on the march. It's too late to tell us to stop.

Nor did the new-found enthusiasm of the National Government for fulfilling its international obligations meet with the approval of the leader of the Parliamentary Labour Party, George Lansbury. The Labour Conference was held from 28 September to 4 October 1935, its deliberations thus coinciding, in their later stages, with the long-awaited Italian invasion of Abyssinia on 3 October. Hugh Dalton, the most dynamic of the younger intellectuals in the movement, who combined an academic knowledge of economics with a vivid awareness of the realities of Fascism, strongly urged party support for sanctions (a word which did not occur in Hoare's celebrated speech at Geneva). Cripps opposed a sanctions policy and described the League once again as 'a capitalist conspiracy', resigning his position on the N.E.C. in protest, just as earlier, in September, Ponsonby had resigned from the Labour leadership in the Lords on similar grounds. In view of Cripps's known sincerity and intellectual ability this was a greater blow than it perhaps seemed; he was not an uneducated firebrand, a Maxton, or an A. J. Cook, but a man who commanded the loyal admiration of many highly intelligent people. Nevertheless, the defection of Cripps counted for little beside the more dramatic circumstance that Lansbury himself, the party leader, now sought, in these unpropitious circumstances, to make a stand on behalf of Christian pacifism.

To the accompaniment of references to 'the Prince of Peace', to 'the faith I hold' and to the thoughts that had come to him, 'an old man', as he lay sick and on his back, he announced his intention to

stand as the early Christians did and say, 'This is our faith, this is where we stand and if necessary, this is where we will die.'

With all this was admixed a certain saintly cunning. With the kind of careful frankness more usually associated with Stanley Baldwin he admitted that it was 'intolerable' to have a leader who disagreed fundamentally with the party he led, and went on,

I should not consider an expression of opinion hostile to my continuance as leader as anything more than natural and friendly.

Lansbury was unlucky. There was no 'friendly' sequel to his utterances; instead, there was a bulldozing demolition of his whole position from the enraged Ernest Bevin. In a shouted, much-interrupted speech he exposed Lansbury's attitude quite brutally:

Let me remind the delegates, that when George Lansbury says what he has said today, it is rather late to say it.

To this there could be no answer. If Lansbury was a Christian pacifist first and leader of the Labour Party second, his duty had been clear ever since, at least, the Annual Conference of 1934. It is true that he had offered to resign but he had let himself be dissuaded; yet, given that Lansbury took his stand on conscientious scruples, he should not have continued for so long to accept, as party leader, policies he disagreed with.

It was on this particular question of what Lansbury's conscience required of him that Bevin delivered his culminating blow:

It is placing the executive and the movement in an absolutely wrong position to be taking[1] your conscience round from body to body to be told what you ought to do with it.

Four days later, Lansbury resigned the leadership. Even then he was asked to reconsider his decision and Attlee, who had been acting as deputy leader, was pointedly asked to serve only as 'acting leader' for the remainder of what was certain to be a short session. Dalton and Morrison, to name no others, seemed more likely candidates for the substantive post if, as seemed probable, they returned to the House after the autumn election.

The combined effects of Hoare's pronouncement at Geneva and the public quarrel within the Labour Party had an adverse effect on the party's prospects in the 1935 election. Hoare had, in effect, stolen Labour's collective security garments, while the party had lost a leader and found, so it seemed, a nonentity.

Yet, while it made sense for the Labour Party to declare its readiness to resist Fascism, it made much less sense for the National Government to declare a similar resolve. Fascism stood for the overthrow of all that Labour stood for: for the crushing of working-class political freedom and, now, for the extinction of what little was left of native independence in Africa. But the National Government was anxious to secure Mussolini's adhesion to the anti-German *bloc* adumbrated at Stresa and, throughout the Abyssinian affair, was always at pains to insist that it had no quarrel with Italy. In his celebrated September speech at Geneva, Hoare laid considerable emphasis on the state of opinion in Britain. He had assured his listeners that the British people had supported the League because 'they were deeply and genuinely moved by a great ideal':

It is because they cling to this ideal that they would be deeply shocked if the structure of peace to which they have given their constant support were irrevocably shattered

and in his concluding remarks he had referred to 'the recent response of public opinion' and to 'the attitude of the British nation in the last few weeks'. It would seem therefore that the Government let itself be over-persuaded by the signs of determination which could be detected in the Peace Ballot, and in the conversion of the trade unions and the Labour Party. The day after Hoare's Geneva speech, for instance, Morrison, endorsed the Foreign Secretary's claim to be speaking for the whole nation:

There is nothing to be lost in making it known that as a whole and subject to matters of emphasis and detail Sir Samuel Hoare's speech commands the overwhelming support of British public opinion.

[1] Less kindly versions of the word used here include, 'carting' 'trailing' and 'hawking.'

Yet, though Hoare's speech indicated that he had correctly assessed the state of the British mind, events soon proved that he had misjudged the military and the diplomatic situation. He perhaps accepted the view that Mussolini had embarked on a long and difficult war which would sooner or later compel him to see reason. Neville Chamberlain, Jan Smuts, Winston Churchill, the German Army leaders and some Italian military experts all thought Mussolini was running grave risks in Abyssinia, and might well have to yield to economic or diplomatic pressure.

Worse still, Hoare failed to read the mind of Laval. Laval was indifferent to the fate of Abyssinia, being concerned solely with French security. This could be maintained only by keeping Germany isolated. Yet the British were jeopardizing this aim: first by the Anglo-German Naval Agreement, and now by a zeal for collective security which was threatening to drive Mussolini into Hitler's arms. Thus, it soon became apparent to Hoare that, if Mussolini persisted, resistance to him would be collective only in name, and bear more and more the character of a purely British resistance. Therefore, although the League resolved on 7 October 1935 that Italy had gone to war in breach of the Covenant, the most it had done in the way of sanctions by mid-November was to recommend a limited economic embargo. The question of cutting off Italy's supplies of oil was left for later discussion. On 23 October 1935, Hoare had scouted the idea of closing the Suez Canal to Italian vessels, and a day later Baldwin announced,

We have no intention of acting by ourselves or going farther than we can get the whole League to go. We have never had war in our minds.

When, therefore, during the course of the election campaign, which took place in the first fortnight of November, 1935, Baldwin promised that the Government 'would not waver in the policy it had hitherto pursued in Abyssinia' it was difficult to know what the policy was that it was not going to waver in. He also pledged that there would be 'no great armaments'. Both promises were uttered solely because they were what the electorate wanted to hear. They bore no relation to the Government's intentions. The Government had no collective intention in November 1935; it merely wanted to stay in power.

In this aim, at least, it was successful. Though Labour revived to the extent of obtaining 154 seats, the Conservatives, with 387 seats, and their MacDonaldite and Simonite clients with 8 and 32 seats respectively, had a comfortable majority. The Liberals dropped from 33 to 20 seats. Distinguished victims of the election were Samuel, who was replaced as Liberal leader by Sir Archibald Sinclair; and the MacDonalds, father and son. Ramsay was defeated at Seaham by Emmanuel Shinwell, who had a majority of 20,498. The MacDonalds were soon found safe seats, however, and continued in office.

Another near-victim was Clement Attlee. The return to the Commons of many M.P.s who had been prominent before 1931 gave rise to some unfraternal intrigues about the leadership. Dalton conducted a brisk campaign on behalf of Herbert Morrison, a widely known personality because of his vigorous leadership of the highly successful Labour majority on the L.C.C. This helped to create counter-moves on behalf of Greenwood, however, and Attlee was elected, after a second ballot, as the leader who was likely to divide the party least. Dalton claims to have recorded in his diary 'And a little mouse shall lead them!' It could not, however, be overlooked that Attlee had been continuously in Parliament since 1922, had survived the holocaust of 1931, had been quietly on the Left rather than the Right, was less personally unacceptable to the trade union movement than Morrison, and devoid of the prima donna qualities that had made MacDonald so odious, at least in retrospect. The party badly needed a man who could perform the extremely difficult task of leading it without dividing it. This, almost to the end, was Attlee's virtue. His great weakness, so obvious to those who desired an alternative in 1935, was his complete lack of personal magnetism. He made no impact on the public mind and little on the Labour movement.

29 · The End of Collective Security, 1935-37

With the need to consider public opinion now disposed of for the time being, it was possible for the Government to address itself to discovering what its Abyssinian policy really was. The process was hastened by the possibility of the further discussion of oil sanctions. Eden's July proposals for buying Mussolini off with the offer of Abyssinian territory were now refurbished and made more generous to Italy. Hoare visited Paris in December and there discussed the plans with Laval. While Hoare proceeded thence to Switzerland for the winter sports, details were leaked to the French Press. They involved the cession of rich outlying areas of Abyssinia to Italy, and the granting to Italy of rights of economic expansion and settlement in a further large area. In return for all this, Abyssinia would be given access to the Red Sea by the cession of a small strip of Italian Somaliland acidly described by *The Times* as 'a corridor for camels'.

Publication of the Hoare-Laval Plan caused a notorious political uproar in England, though the unkindest Press comment was probably that of the *New York Herald-Tribune*:

A cynic may be struck by the curious exactitude with which the non-Italian portion of Ethiopia would be reduced to the Lake Tana basin and the watersheds of the Nile tributaries. He might conclude that the real meaning of the collective system was one under which the aggressor collects everything in sight except the territories vital to British interests in the Sudan and Egypt.

What caused the flood of letters and telegrams which reached M.P.s, and the almost universal condemnation of the plan in the Press, however, was its apparent determination to reward the aggressor (in advance) by giving him more Abyssinian territory than he had at that moment succeeded in capturing. It was certainly conciliatory, though to one party only; it was certainly not a compromise because, had it become operative, it would have represented a victory for Mussolini's invasion; and it was certainly a violation of the Covenant and of Hoare's public promise of

steady and collective resistance to all acts of unprovoked aggression.

The Government therefore decided upon retreat. Baldwin's version was that the Government had not liked the plan, but had agreed to it out of loyalty to the absent Hoare, and now took full responsibility for it. Nevertheless, in view of public indignation, the plan should be regarded as dead; and Hoare resigned from the Foreign Office.

Hoare's justification of the Plan when speaking in the Commons after his resignation was

that no responsible Government could disregard that Italy would regard the oil embargo as a military sanction or an act of war against her.

This, he implied would have led in effect to an Anglo-Italian war, and thence to the collapse of the League. He hinted strongly that the proposals were Laval's price for considering oil sanctions at all – 'the minimum basis on which the French Government were prepared to proceed':

I felt that the issues were so grave and the dangers of the continuance of the war so serious that it was worth making the attempt, and that it was essential to maintain Anglo-French unity.

He made a further prophetic point:

I have been terrified . . . that we might lead Abyssinia on to think that the League could do more than it can do, that in the end we should find a terrible moment of disillusionment in which it might be that Abyssinia would be destroyed altogether as an independent State.

He then reverted to the growing threat of the whole operation turning into an isolated clash between Britain and Italy:

There is the British Fleet in the Mediterranean, there are the British reinforcements in Egypt, in Malta and Aden. Not a ship, not a machine, not a man has been moved by any other member State.

Hoare concluded a speech delivered with much emotion by saying:

looking back at the position in which I was placed a fortnight ago I say to the House that I cannot honestly recant.

When Baldwin spoke, he said, memorably,

. . . my lips are not yet unsealed. Were these troubles over I would make a case, and I guarantee that not a man would go into the Lobby against us.

It would thus seem that the 'villain' of the piece was Laval, and that the Plan was devised to satisfy his insistence on the re-creation of the Stresa Front. This could only be achieved by a speedy end to the war and to Britain's attempt to involve France in acts of hostility to Italy. It was after Hoare's September speech at Geneva that Laval had begun to press for a firm British promise to support France in the event of a German attack and to underwrite the proposed Franco-Russian alliance.[1] It may also have been known that the poor showing of the Italian forces up to the time when the Plan was drawn up was already causing Mussolini to seek a *rapprochement* with Hitler.[1] The whole Anglo-French involvement in Abyssinia thus cut clean across Laval's policy, and the British must, by December 1935, have fully realized this.

The Hoare-Laval Plan, rejected though it was, ended both the history of collective security and the effective life of the League of Nations. Mussolini sent a new and more vigorous commander to Abyssinia, and the French resisted further attempts to impose oil sanctions. The war ended, in May 1936, with a complete Italian victory and the proclamation of the King of Italy as Emperor of Abyssinia; in July came the abandonment of sanctions.

The death of the League (its official, unnoticed existence continued till 1945) had already been certified by Neville Chamberlain, in June 1936, when he called the continuance of sanctions 'the very midsummer of madness':

The aggression was patent and flagrant, and there was hardly any country which it appeared that a policy of sanctions could be exercised upon with a greater chance of success than Italy . . . That policy has been tried out and it has failed. It failed to prevent war, it failed to stop war, it failed to save the victim of aggression.

This pronouncement was probably the first example of Chamberlain's tendency to pronounce upon foreign affairs without consulting Hoare's successor at the Foreign Office, Anthony Eden. Eden had acquired a reputation as 'a stalwart supporter of the League of Nations and a resolute opponent of aggression'. His particular gifts, however, were for conciliation

---

[1] Robertson, op. cit., p. 64.

and compromise; he had been associated with Simon in the preliminary negotiation of the Anglo-German Naval Agreement, and had twice been the medium through whom attempts had been made to pacify Mussolini with Abyssinian territory. The rejection of these plans may well have led to that dislike of Mussolini which caused him to resign in 1938 when Chamberlain tried to appease Mussolini behind Eden's back. His appointment in December 1935 had no effect on the Abyssinian affair, despite the opinion of the British and continental Press that the result would be a reversion to the policy of sanctions.

Eden's major asset was his personableness. Only 37 years old, he seemed, in a world largely dominated by elderly politicians, to be not only handsome and well-dressed, but young, and a representative of the bravery and idealism of the generation that had served in the 1914–18 war. Even a German newspaper viewed his appointment sentimentally. The *Berliner Tageblatt* benevolently wrote,

It is under the protection of Mr Baldwin that Anthony Eden has grown up so young to such high honours. Mr Baldwin took him to his heart and it is this friendship across the gulf of generations that gives Mr Eden a chance to prove his worth.

Inaction over Abyssinia during the early months of 1936 was, however, mainly due to increased preoccupation with the problem of Hitler. The French fear that sanctions would drive Mussolini towards Hitler was justified. Alarmed by his generals' lack of success, by the British abandonment of the Hoare-Laval Plan, and by the possibility of oil sanctions, Mussolini began courting Hitler (with a promise to disinterest himself in Austria) in December 1935. Ever since November 1935, the French ambassador in Berlin had been warning his Government that Hitler might re-enter the Rhineland in defiance of the Versailles and Locarno Treaties as soon as the Franco-Russian alliance was ratified, and in January 1936 there were Anglo-French conversations about possible counter-action. The British insisted, characteristically, that a German entry into the Rhineland was not a vital interest. Hitler was not to know this and, overcoming his initial suspicion of Mussolini's overtures, asked for support and perhaps parallel action by Italy in the event of a German denunciation of Locarno. In February 1936, Hitler received British proposals for an air agreement, coupled with hints that the British might concede to Hitler the right to phased remilitarization of the Rhineland.[1] Hitler was not much interested in obtaining his objective by slow legal methods, however; he concentrated instead on assuring himself of the support of Mussolini.

On 7 March 1936, therefore, Hitler denounced Locarno, and German forces entered the Rhineland. It was in every sense a diplomatic *coup de théatre*. It was not necessary for Germany to use unilateral action to get

[1] Robertson, op. cit., p. 73.

back into the Rhineland, for only France objected, and neither the British nor the Italians supported French objections. As for the French, though they needed British and Italian support to restrain Hitler so long as it remained a diplomatic problem, once it became a matter of meeting force with force, they were not, at this juncture, in need of military assistance. They had merely to mobilize. They did not do so. This may be treated as a lack of resolution, or as an act of commendable caution. Mobilization in March 1936 might have stopped Hitler in March 1936; but though such action (like oil sanctions against Italy) would have upheld the sanctity of treaties it would probably not have solved the 'German problem' itself. It might perhaps have branded Hitler in the eyes of the German Army as a reckless firebrand. But, equally, it might have proved more successful in arousing German nationalism than anything even Hitler had so far done.

In many ways the denunciation of Locarno was more important for the future. Hitler's argument that the Franco-Soviet pact so distorted the Locarno Pact as to make it practically non-existent gave clear notice that he would break any treaty, even one signed voluntarily, as Locarno had been, on the flimsiest excuse. This added piquancy to the fact that Hitler accompanied his treaty-breaking acts by offers of new non-aggression pacts with all and sundry on both his eastern and western frontiers, and with an offer to return to the League of Nations. He also proposed that there should be a new demilitarization agreement to apply to the French and Belgian sides of the German frontier as well as to the German side. This would have meant the French dismantling the Maginot Line. Understandably, nothing came of these proposals. By the summer of 1936, therefore, all the devices for safeguarding the territorial system established by the Paris peace conferences had been destroyed. The punitive clauses imposed upon the Germans had been torn up, and the collective system of the League of Nations had collapsed also.

It is easier to condemn British and French politicians of the 1930's for their failure to prevent these developments than to appreciate their predicament. The disarmament of Germany that followed the war's end, being only a physical disarmament, was as nothing compared with the disarmament of her enemies which was a psychological disarmament as well. The military power of Russia had dissolved in revolution, that of the United States and Great Britain had been immediately liquidated. The French alone retained, for a time, the will to make victory a permanent reality; but, since they were alone, they lacked the means. It was thus inevitable that the restrictive clauses of Versailles would disappear once a German Government decided it would no longer abide by them. Hardly anybody realized this, except perhaps the British, but they were too lacking in intellectual directness to put their belief into action until they were bluffed into it by Hitler. Both Hitler and his military advisers addressed themselves to the breaking of Versailles between 1933 and 1936 with a trepidation that reveals that they, too, over-estimated the effective power of their opponents. They were afraid of the British, and of the French Army, and participated fully in the delusion that Italy was a Great Power. At the expense of a bloody internal revolution, and in an atmosphere of theatrical brutality, Hitler achieved nothing between 1933 and 1936 that could not have been gained without these methods. As it was, he achieved them without firing a shot outside the frontiers of Germany.

The controversy over British rearmament continued during 1936. In March, increases in all three services were provided for, once again in the face of Labour opposition. In the same month, Baldwin appointed Sir Thomas Inskip as Minister for the Co-ordination of Defence. The news was greeted with amusement and scorn, since it was the general opinion, shared by Inskip himself, that he had no qualifications for the post.

Had rearmament been taken seriously, a Ministry of Defence would have been set up, and Churchill would have been appointed to it. This was not done, partly because it would have been too provocative to the opponents of rearmament, and partly because Churchill's return to the Cabinet might prejudice Chamberlain's right to succeed Baldwin as Prime Minister in the following year. It is over the appointment of Inskip for these dubious reasons that Baldwin came nearest to being 'guilty' in defence matters.

Baldwin blundered even more before the year was out, and to the lasting hurt of his personal reputation. Prefacing his contention with the claim that he was about to speak with 'appalling frankness' Baldwin sought to rebut yet another of Churchill's charges of dilatoriness over rearmament by saying in the Commons in November 1936:

Supposing I had gone to the country and said that Germany was rearming, and that we must rearm, does anybody think that this pacific democracy would have rallied to that cry at that moment? I cannot think of anything that would have made the loss of the election from my point of view more certain.

In his view, the Fulham by-election of 1933 proved that the country would not have given him a mandate for rearmament.

These unhappy words gave rise to Churchill's subsequent accusation that Baldwin was here guilty of 'putting party before country'; yet all he was doing in this speech was ruminating aloud upon the difficulty, within the framework of a political democracy, of trying to act ahead of public opinion. He meant merely to confess to weakness: he would follow public opinion, not lead it. In the event he stumbled into an apparent admission that, when during the election campaign he had given a pledge there would be 'no great armaments', he had not only failed to lead public opinion but for some time had been deliberately misleading it.

Baldwin's foolishness at this particular moment may well have been due to his preoccupation with the love life of the new king, Edward VIII, who had succeeded to the throne on the death of George V in January 1936. By November, Baldwin had already been in touch with the King on the matter of his close friendship with an American, Mrs Simpson, who having already divorced one husband, had finally obtained her freedom from a second at the end of October 1936. Baldwin was alarmed to learn· that the King did not feel able to carry out the duties of his office without a wife, and that that wife must be Mrs Simpson. The suggestion was put forward of a 'morganatic' marriage, by which Mrs Simpson would not assume the title of Queen. This would have required special legislation, and, owing to the Statute of Westminster, similar enactments in all the Dominions. Neither the United Kingdom, nor the Dominion Governments, were prepared to introduce such legislation, and the King therefore decided to abdicate.

The liberty of the Press in the United Kingdom had not prevented news of the King's friendship with Mrs Simpson from going entirely unmentioned in print in this country. As far as the people at large were concerned, the affair began on December 2nd and 3rd with mystifying accounts in the newspapers of a speech by the Bishop of Bradford, criticizing the King's religious practices, or more accurately his abstention from them. This was followed by confusing articles referring to 'A Grave Constitutional Crisis'. Barely a week later, on 11 December, the King's Act of Abdication had been put through both Houses; on the 12th the Duke of York was proclaimed King as George VI, immediately conferring on his brother, who at once left the country, the title of Duke of Windsor.

It was a remarkable operation, almost the only one in his political career in which Baldwin acted with speed; and, despite assertions to the contrary, the majority of the population were little moved by the event. They were sorry the King was going, because they looked on him as likeable and unstuffy; but they were not disposed to make a fuss about it. The prevailing, though unspoken, feeling seems to have been that none of it really mattered much. The Duke and Duchess of York were nice people and they had two charming daughters; they would do just as well.

Only Churchill tried to raise opposition. He protested in the Commons at the 'uncanny facility' with which the King was being disposed of:

If an abdication were to be hastily extorted, the outrage so committed would cast its shadow forward across many chapters of the history of the British Empire.

Churchill's protest met with little or no response, and the affair was soon forgotten. In order to hasten the process of oblivion, the Duke, who married Mrs Simpson in 1937, was given no appointment except that of wartime Governor-General of the Bahamas, and made only rare and strictly private visits to the United Kingdom. The Duchess of Windsor was also carefully excluded from the privilege of being addressed as 'Her Royal Highness'.

.   .   .   .   .

The abdication was the last major event of Baldwin's political career. Six months later, in May 1937, he resigned the Premiership, became Earl Baldwin of Bewdley, and took no further part in politics. MacDonald appropriately resigned at the same time, dying in the following November. MacDonald had already suffered the obloquy of a man who was alleged to have betrayed his party, but there lay ahead of Baldwin the years till his death in 1947 during which he was despised as the man who had allegedly betrayed his country by failing to arm it for war against Hitler's Germany. The contempt in which he was held in the decade after 1937 was itself somewhat contemptible, but there can be no denying that neither he nor MacDonald had much to contribute to the nation once the 1920's had collapsed into the chaos of the 1930's. Soporifics and sedatives had their value during the acute domestic tensions of the 1920's, but the 1930's called for different qualities. Baldwin and MacDonald were deficient in intellectual power, sluggish in temperament and possessed of a squalid dislike of men of drive and personality. Baldwin, in particular, peopled his Governments with men so mediocre that, among them, Neville Chamberlain could rightly be looked upon as his successor 'by undisputed title'.[1] This was perhaps Baldwin's real disservice to his country.

Inactivity over the reoccupation of the Rhineland and the conquest of Abyssinia, coupled with lethargy over disarmament, created an impression of drift and indifference which was heightened by the attitude of the Government to the opposing sides in the Spanish Civil War which began in July 1936. In conjunction with the French Government of Léon Blum, the British organized a non-intervention agreement among the principal European Powers, as the result of which an international Non-Intervention Committee was set up. It soon became apparent that Mussolini, to a considerable extent, and Hitler, to a somewhat less extent, were both actively assisting the Right-wing rebels led by General Franco. France and Great Britain, however, banned the export of arms and materials to Spain, even though this denied to the Spanish Republican Government its normal right to trade freely with other States. The only active protests against Italian and German breaches of the non-intervention agreement came from the U.S.S.R., which then proceeded to give support to the Spanish Republicans. The reaction of the British Government was to throw most of the blame for foreign intervention in Spain on the Russians, who had publicly repudiated the agreement, rather than on the Italians and Germans, who kept on pretending they were keeping it.

The British Government's reason was that, as soon as it became clear that the rebels were a major force in Spain, they wanted Franco to win quickly, so that the matter could be disposed of as soon as possible. Soviet intervention was helping to prevent this desirable. conclusion and was

[1] *Daily Telegraph*, 29 May 1937.

therefore regarded as both inconvenient and sinister. The fact that, without Italian and German assistance, Franco's threat to the Republic might soon have failed was, in the British view, irrelevant. Thanks to his foreign friends, Franco seemed already on the way to victory. Therefore, the only sensible thing to do was for everybody to stand aside and let him get on with it. The British could then turn to the task of re-establishing good relations with Italy.

Since, however, Soviet help and stiff Republican resistance prevented Franco's immediate victory, the British had to pretend that Italian intervention did not exist or that, if it did, this was entirely the fault of the Russians. In January 1937, an Anglo-Italian agreement was signed by which both Powers professed their intention to preserve the international *status quo* in the Mediterranean. The *Giornale d'Italia*, declared:

This gentleman's agreement is above all a voluntary and frank liquidation of a recent stormy past. It is what the English call a handshake after a controversy that is ended.

The label 'Gentleman's Agreement' stuck; but the Italian implication that the gentlemanliness was all English was confirmed by the simultaneous landing of 4,000 Italian troops at Cadiz, by further Italian troop landings in the following months, and by Mussolini's announcement that the establishment of a 'Bolshevik' Government in Spain would violate the agreement. In fact, breaches of the non-intervention agreement by Italy continued throughout 1937, and included attacks by 'unidentified' aircraft and by submarines on neutral (including British) as well as Spanish Republican shipping. These attacks did not cease until the Nyon agreement in the autumn when, after an initial refusal, Italy agreed to share naval patrolling duties against these 'unidentified' submarines. Even so, as late as October 1937, Italy admitted officially to the presence of 40,000 Italian troops in Spain, a casualty list was published, and Mussolini presented medals to relatives of the Italian fallen. All this was accompanied by unceasing anti-British propaganda in the Italian Press and continuous blocking of efforts to make non-intervention a reality.

Hitler had been as instant a beneficiary of the Spanish Civil War as he had been of the Abyssinian affair. Embroilment with Britain in the Mediterranean, and active military involvement in Spain itself, began the process of turning Mussolini into Hitler's vassal. The first sign of this was the signature of an Austro-German treaty in July 1936 (also called a gentleman's agreement) by which Germany recognized Austrian independence; in return Schuschnigg, the Austrian Chancellor, declared that Austria considered herself a 'German' State. This transferred Austria's diplomatic allegiance from Italy to Germany, and ended the likelihood of an Austro-German *Anschluss* such as had nearly been forced upon Hitler by the extremists who murdered Dollfuss in 1934. For this reason, the agreement pleased Mussolini; but his absorption in the Spanish affair left Hitler a

free hand in central Europe. Nevertheless, Mussolini was sufficiently uncertain of his new friend to make great efforts in 1936 to create anti-British
feeling in Berlin. He passed on to Hitler information concerning a number
of anti-German dispatches sent to London by the British Ambassador in
Berlin, Sir Eric Phipps. These had been collected and circulated by Eden
with the over-all recommendation that rearmament must be accelerated to
prevent Germany dominating the continent.[1] By November 1936, Mussolini was able proudly to proclaim the existence of the Rome-Berlin 'Axis'.

The diplomatic position of both powers was further strengthened by the
signing of the Anti-Comintern Pact, also in November 1936, between
Germany and Japan. This, by aligning Japan with the Axis, confronted the
British with the simultaneous hostility of Japan in the Far East and of
Italy in the Mediterranean, a difficulty which was intensified when the
Japanese resumed large-scale warfare against China in July 1937. Although
this new development was originally unwelcome to Germany, Mussolini
and Ciano seem to have converted Hitler by pointing out how difficult
Japan was making things for the British. In November 1937, therefore, the
Anti-Comintern Pact was made a tripartite agreement. Given that Russia
was now held to have weakened herself seriously by the purging of her
most experienced generals, the world could be regarded as divided between,
on the one hand, the three aggressive military dictatorships of Germany,
Italy and Japan, and on the other the politically and socially paralysed
French, the inept British, the enfeebled Soviet Union and the isolated
United States.

30 · Chamberlain Takes Charge, 1937-38

It was in May 1937, when all these developments were in train, that
Neville Chamberlain succeeded Baldwin as Prime Minister. A busy,
efficient man, he was affronted by the drift and disarray in British foreign
policy since 1931, and was convinced that a determined effort must be
made to put matters right. He regarded war as detestable, was as certain
as were the adherents of the League of Nations (whom he despised) that
all disputes could be settled peacefully, and that, if he were allowed to

[1] Robertson, op. cit., pp. 95-7.

operate without interference, he could arrange this. He also had no patience with military weakness; although he was offended by Churchill's bellicosity, he attached importance to rearmament, since he realized, if only because of the events of 1935–6, that it was pointless to threaten a 'strong' line against the dictators if they believed there was no armed strength to make it good. Thus, from May 1937 until March 1939, Britain had a coherent and consistent foreign policy at last.

Of all the principal actors on the international stage in these years, Chamberlain most nearly approached the conventional image of a political dictator. Compared with Chamberlain between 1937 and 1939, Hitler was impulsive and uncertain, continuously engaged in the weighing of pros and cons, and for ever balancing contrary advice from various military and political advisers. Mussolini likewise spent his time in ceaseless manœuvre and deepening uncertainty, and was equally susceptible to military and political advice. Chamberlain on the other hand, though nominally at the mercy of such democratic limitations upon his power as a free Press, unfettered parliamentary debate, the almost unchecked right of public assembly, and the necessity of maintaining unanimity in his Cabinet and an undiminished majority in Parliament, succeeded in virtually ignoring all these inconveniences, at least until the spring of 1939. No Prime Minister cared less for the Press, for public opinion, for the opinions of his colleagues or the advice of his experts. Neither of the dictators was more ruthless in discarding those who offered unwelcome advice than Chamberlain between May 1937 and March 1939. At least Hitler and Mussolini had each other and, in a remote way, the Japanese; but Chamberlain spurned the U.S.S.R., cold-shouldered the U.S.A. and seems to have treated the French as rather tiresome dependent relatives to be kept severely in their place.

As soon as he became Prime Minister, he took steps to try to arrest the tendency for the effective world Powers to divide, in 1937, into the potential aggressors and the would-be resisters of aggression. He rejected absolutely the traditional device of a grand alliance against the aggressors; it had been resorted to in one form or another by such shining names as Elizabeth I, William of Orange, Marlborough, the Pitts, father and son, Castlereagh and, willy-nilly, by Grey; and it was now being advocated by Churchill. Chamberlain dismissed all this. No supporter of the League of Nations was more certain than Chamberlain that alliances caused war; and what his predecessors had tried to do, and his contemporaries wanted to do again, by collaboration with others, he was determined to do by himself. Chamberlain saw himself as a one-man device for the settlement of international disputes without recourse to war. With single-minded devotion and with complete disregard for contrary advice or criticism, Chamberlain set out to bring peace to Europe with all the embattled arrogance of the Victorian public servant he really was. He was a Chadwick come to put the continent's diplomatic drains right, a stern physician come to vaccinate it against war, a dour District Commissioner come to bring peace and justice to darkest Europe. He would civilize the Fascist head-hunters by bringing them into personal contact with himself. By treating them with magnanimity and equity, and by patiently redressing their just grievances, he would lead them to understand, and eventually to practise, the God-given Anglo-Saxon virtue of respect for the rule of law. They would cease to shout, bully or bluster, because they would come to know that such tactics were out of place in civilized society and, when dealing with Englishmen, unnecessary. The English knew instinctively how to do right; they did not need to be told, let alone shouted at. Hitler could have Austria and Czechoslovakia, or even Tanganyika, and Mussolini could install Franco, provided only there was no unpleasantness about it.

Consequently, throughout the second half of 1937, while, as previously described, the Axis and the Anti-Comintern Pact were being constructed, Chamberlain worked with dedicated zeal to prove, at least to Mussolini and to Hitler, that these vulgar displays of hostility to the British were totally uncalled for. He sought the advice of the bearded Count Grandi, the Italian ambassador in London, and at his suggestion sent a personal message to Mussolini, without consulting Eden, the Foreign Secretary. Chamberlain felt he had something with which to lure Mussolini to his side, namely British recognition of Italy's conquest of Abyssinia; all this at a time when Italian submarines were violating the non-intervention agreements about Spain and when every victory of Franco's forces was being hailed in the Italian Press as a triumph for Italian arms.

As for policy towards Germany, Chamberlain's influence was at work even before he became Prime Minister. At the suggestion of Ribbentrop, the German ambassador in London, Sir Eric Phipps, had been moved from Berlin and was replaced as ambassador to Germany by Sir Nevile Henderson in April 1937; and Henderson was given his brief by Chamberlain. Henderson had more than his share of English upper-class admiration for the Nazi system; although he privately condemned the 'excesses' of the régime, he thought it would be a good thing for Englishmen if most other aspects of the Nazi creed and practice were imported into this country. Addressing a Berlin audience shortly after his arrival, in words which, he subsequently wrote, came 'from the bottom of his heart', he said:

Guarantee us peace and peaceful evolution in Europe, and Germany will find that she has no more sincere and, I believe, more useful friend in the world than Great Britain[1]

This was a precise statement of Chamberlain's policy.

In November 1937, the staging of an international hunting exhibition in Berlin was made the excuse for establishing informal contact through Göring, who organized the show, and Lord Halifax, who was then Lord

[1] N. Henderson, *Failure of a Mission*, p. 23.

President of the Council and shared Göring's predilection for killing wild animals. This manœuvre, like Chamberlain's hobnobbing with Grandi, was undertaken without the good will of Eden or the Foreign Office. Halifax met Hitler, on 19 November 1937, and let him know that Britain realized that in Danzig, Austria and Czechoslovakia changes were destined to come, but that all that was worrying his Government was that such changes should be achieved peacefully.

The British were therefore busily confirming Hitler's own hunch that the plans he was currently formulating for an active extension of German influence in central Europe could go forward without Anglo-French interference. This was not a particularly brilliant piece of forecasting; it was a reasonable deduction from known facts and from all the evidence of British policy and intentions since 1920. As it was, Hitler misread into Chamberlain's overtures a subtlety they did not possess: he thought appeasement was a cunning holding action due to the backward state of British rearmament. Chamberlain's apologists share Hitler's error, relying for justification on Chamberlain's public and private insistence on the need for rearmament. They forget that Chamberlain merely thought of armaments as an additional item in the essentially civilian wardrobe of his diplomacy. He had made this point when, speaking to his own constituents in Birmingham in July 1937, he had said that the aim of rearmament was to make Britain so strong that 'nobody should treat her with anything but respect'. The only sense in which this did not represent his policy was that he might more accurately have substituted 'me personally' for 'her'.

These considerations make it possible to put in perspective the views which Hitler is alleged to have put before his chief military advisers in conference on 5 November 1937. An account of Hitler's observations at this conference is contained in a document known as the Hossbach Memorandum, because it is apparently based on an account of the meeting drawn up subsequently by Colonel Hossbach, who had been present as Hitler's adjutant. The significant point which emerges from it is that Hitler proposed a fairly early attack on Czechoslovakia, on the grounds that neither Britain nor France would interfere. Thus, when Halifax had visited the Führer a fortnight later, he can hardly have done anything to change Hitler's mind; he can only have provided him with one more confirmation of his political insight.

In pursuance of the policies of the British and German leaders, the early months of 1938 witnessed the bizarre coincidence of purges in both Berlin and London. Hitler got rid of advisers who wanted less rearmament, just as Chamberlain got rid of advisers who wanted more rearmament; and while Chamberlain was dismissing important British officials because he did not want to run the risk of war, Hitler was dismissing important German officials because he wanted to run this risk. First, Hitler dismissed his chief economic adviser, Schacht, because Schacht did not believe the economy could stand the immediate acceleration of the arms programme that Hitler wanted. Early in February 1938, he got rid of the Reich War Minister, Field Marshal Blomberg, and the Commander in Chief, Fritsch, both on the basis of trumped-up charges about their morals. Hitler became his own War Minister; and the new Commander in Chief, von Brauschitsch, was more subservient to him than his predecessors. Worse still, the Foreign Minister, Neurath was replaced by the Anglophobe Nazi, Ribbentrop. Hitler was now in control both of the Foreign Ministry and of the German High Command, and began, if the evidence available from the period is to be believed, to prepare for action in central Europe, and thereafter against the West.[1]

Chamberlain's purge was concentrated on the Foreign Office. The somewhat impetuous anti-German Permanent Secretary, Sir Robert Vansittart, was removed from his post on 1 January 1938 and made Chief Diplomatic Adviser to the Government. This preserved Sir Robert's pension rights during the last two years of his serving career, but ensured that he had no influence. Before February 1938 was out, Eden had been driven from his place as Foreign Secretary also.

Eden did not like Chamberlain's headlong flirtation with Mussolini. He was greatly affronted by Chamberlain's habit of taking advice from the Chief Industrial Adviser to the Government, Sir Horace Wilson. Wilson had for years been Chamberlain's principal confidant, and perhaps continued to be so after 1937 because he could be relied upon not to embarrass the Prime Minister with advice based on knowledge or experience of foreign affairs; his most important previous role had been that of Chief Conciliation Officer at the Ministry of Labour.

The crisis came, however, over simultaneous differences between Chamberlain and Eden concerning the United States, Austria and Italy. In January, Roosevelt had asked Chamberlain for his views on the desirability of the United States summoning an international conference to seek a relaxation of tension. Chamberlain, without consulting Eden, replied that Roosevelt's proposals would cut across his own plan to secure Italian co-operation by according *de jure* recognition to the conquest of Abyssinia. This greatly upset the United States, which attached much value to the doctrine of non-recognition (the only international weapon they had at the time), and feared that its abandonment in Abyssinia would act as a spur to the Japanese, whose conquests were likewise awaiting *de jure* recognition. Eden protested, but to little avail. Chamberlain preferred Sir Horace Wilson's view that Roosevelt's suggestion was 'woolly rubbish'.[2] No doubt it would have produced little tangible result had it been pursued; but it was illogical of Chamberlain to spurn Roosevelt's proposal on the grounds that the United States was 'isolationist'. It was a fault that diplo-

[1] Robertson, op. cit., p. 113.
[2] Eden, *Facing the Dictators*, p. 562.

matic rebuffs of this sort could only encourage. Chamberlain, however, did not believe he needed help from anyone.

The climax came over Austria. Growing Nazi disturbances provoked Schuschnigg to visit Hitler on 12 February 1938 to get the Führer to restrain the Austrian Nazis, as he had promised to do in the agreement of 11 July 1936. Instead, Hitler demanded, as the price of his future support, the subordination of Austria's economic and foreign policy to Germany, and the appointment of Seyss-Inquart, a prominent Austrian Nazi sympathizer, as Minister of the Interior in Schuschnigg's Cabinet.

This increase of German control over Austria emphasized Italian subservience to Hitler; and Count Grandi made fresh and urgent overtures to Chamberlain less than a week later. Eden insisted that no settlement could be discussed until Italian volunteers had been withdrawn from Spain: no new agreements should be contemplated while old ones were still being broken. After a long conversation between Chamberlain, Grandi and Eden, during which Chamberlain is alleged to have fed Grandi with the replies he should make to Eden's objections to a new agreement, Eden resigned on 20 February. Chamberlain was glad to see him go. The Parliamentary Under-Secretary at the Foreign Office, Viscount Cranborne (who became Marquess of Salisbury in 1947) resigned at the same time. On 25 February 1938, Eden was replaced by Lord Halifax, and Lord Cranborne by R. A. Butler.

In the Commons debate after the resignations, Chamberlain expressed his objectives quite clearly:

We are . . . now engaged upon a gigantic scheme of rearmament which most of us believe to be essential to the maintenance of peace. . . . I have never ceased publicly to deplore what seems to me a senseless waste of money. . . . I cannot believe that with a little good will it is not possible to remove genuine grievances and to clear away suspicions which may be entirely unfounded.

By contrast, Churchill claimed that Eden's resignation caused him a sleepless night, given over to 'emotions of sorrow and fear', and led him to think of Eden (who was forty at the time) as

one strong young figure standing up against long, dismal, drawling tides of drift and surrender[1]

The immediate results of the resignation justified Cranborne's assertion that the readiness to talk with Italy would be regarded 'not as a contribution to peace but as a surrender to blackmail'. The Italians were promised that the talks would end in recognition of Abyssinia; but they had no intention of embarrassing Hitler's position in Austria, and took care to let Hitler know as much.

Encouraged as he already was by the over-all situation, Hitler was now stung into action by a tactical error on the part of Schuschnigg. Irritated by Hitler's treatment of him, Schuschnigg suddenly announced, on 8

[1] Churchill, *The Gathering Storm*, p. 232.

March 1938, his intention to hold an immediate plebiscite in Austria, asking its citizens to register their desire to maintain 'a free and German, independent and social, Christian and united Austria'. This enraged Hitler, whose mind was much more preoccupied with how to eliminate Czechoslovakia than with taking over Austria. He acted at once, however. He ordered an invasion of Austria for the 12th, the day before the plebiscite was due. Even though, by midnight of the 11th, German demands for the cancellation of the plebiscite and the replacement of Schuschnigg by Seyss-Inquart had been conceded, it was too late to stop the German march.

There was nothing anybody could do. The British expostulated, the French had a Cabinet crisis, Mussolini sent his good wishes, and Czechoslovakia decided not to mobilize. Hitler had acted quickly, impulsively and in a bad temper; nevertheless he had won a major victory, and won it on the cheap. His excited message to the Duce ('Mussolini, I will never forget this') indicates how surprised he was at the successful outcome of this unpremeditated and theoretically hazardous operation. In view of the absence of hostile action by the rest of Europe, Seyss-Inquart was then given orders to end Austria's independent existence, and to announce its incorporation in the Führer's Reich.

31 · Munich, 1938

Although the world was not to know that Czechoslovakia had been the first, it was obvious, after the *Anschluss*, that it would be the next, of Hitler's intended victims. The French made the ritual gesture of reaffirming their obligation to defend Czechoslovakia, and Chamberlain likewise conformed to rule by insisting in the Commons, on 24 March 1938, that Britain was under no obligation to Czechoslovakia. Unfortunately, he did not leave it at that, and in somewhat congested phrases assumed, by implication, responsibility for preventing a Czech crisis from leading to war:

The inexorable pressure of facts might well prove more powerful than formal pronouncements, and in that event it would be well within the bounds of probability that other countries besides those which were parties to the original dispute would almost immediately become involved.

This was taken of course, as a warning to Hitler, though a muffled one; but, given the drift of Chamberlain's policy, it was much more of a warning to the Czechs. The logic of having no obligation to the Czechs implied that Britain would do nothing. The logic of saying that if war arose over

HE TOOK WATER AND WASHED HIS HANDS. Low's bitter comment on the Mediterranean Agreement with Italy, which he represents as being achieved at the expense of defeated Abyssinia and the victimised Spanish Republicans. 20 April 1938.

Czechoslovakia other countries would be drawn in implied that Chamberlain would do a great deal more than nothing; he would see to it that war did not arise over Czechoslovakia. Chamberlain thus committed himself in advance to taking the German side against the Czechs.

The first British move after the *Anschluss* was the conclusion, on 16 April 1938, of the long-wished-for Anglo-Italian agreement. Italy was to withdraw volunteers from Spain, and Britain would organize international recognition of Abyssinia. The agreement, as all Chamberlain's opponents had insisted, did not improve relations between the two countries, but,

[1] Save that it led to a reduction of Italy's anti-British propaganda among Arabs and Egyptians.

just to make sure, Hitler visited Rome in May and seems to have dissipated Mussolini's inevitable though disguised and useless annoyance at the *Anschluss*. Hitler did not, however, wish to act precipitately against Czechoslovakia, and for the time being kept in the background, leaving the Sudeten Germans themselves to conduct a campaign for 'self-determination' against the Prague Government. The Sudeten German leader, Henlein, was sent to London in mid-May, where he was to indicate that the Czech State was in such a state of disintegration that intervention to save it would be useless. Since this was what the British wanted to hear, he made a favourable impression.

The restiveness of the Sudeten Germans, together with the violence of the German Press against the Czechs, produced so much excitement shortly afterwards, that on 20 May 1938 the Prague Government ordered partial mobilization, fearing an immediate German invasion. There was no substance in their fears, and a German denial of warlike intentions followed at once.

The incident provoked Halifax to warn Germany of possible British involvement if war took place, but to warn France to count on British support only in the event of unprovoked German aggression against France. The French, for their part, warned the Czechs that, if they were unreasonable, France might withdraw from her obligations. This could only add up to an unwillingness by Britain and France to help the Czechs. Amid all Hitler's shifts of intention during the summer it is difficult to escape the conclusion that he remained convinced almost, though perhaps not quite, to the end, that whatever action he took against Czechoslovakia he could count on Britain and France doing nothing.

The advice he received from his generals at this time was that Germany was not in a fit state to risk war with Britain and France. Hitler, however, weighed the lesser risk of having to fight the West, if he threatened Czechoslovakia in 1938, against the greater risk that, if he postponed action, Britain would gain time to rearm and thus deprive him altogether of his larger aim of European domination; and decided accordingly. There is no escape from the conclusion that appeasement, with its anxious willingness to meet Hitler's demands, was interpreted merely as an unwillingness to resist him and, worse still, an unwillingness based, not on goodwill, but on a grudging awareness of purely temporary military weakness. Hence, even Chamberlain's advocacy of British rearmament served to increase Hitler's 'respect' for Britain only in the sense that it encouraged him to make haste.

There was nothing that could stop Hitler in 1938 except an early and unequivocal announcement that an attack on Czechoslovakia would immediately produce war with Britain and France. This would have made the generals' objections to Hitler's plans unanswerable; and on the evidence of Hitler's previous behaviour it is likely not, as has been suggested, that

Hitler would have been overthrown by the generals, but that he would have yielded to their objections and drastically changed his plans.

Since the British, like the French, were determined not to fight Hitler, they searched strenuously for reasons to justify compelling the Czechs to give way, and went to extreme lengths to distort the truth in so doing. From Hitler's point of view, the most infuriating fact about Czechoslovakia was that the Sudeten Germans were not being persecuted, and that, given time, they might become assimilated into the now twenty-year-old State. The British also knew the Sudetens were not being persecuted; even Runciman, sent over as special envoy to effect a settlement between Prague and the Sudetens, was forced to admit that the worst the latter had suffered was 'tactlessness, lack of understanding, intolerance and discrimination' and that the Czech régime was 'not actually oppressive and certainly not "terroristic"'. Nevile Henderson, however, with myopic pro-Germanism, wrote to the Foreign Office at various times during 1938 as follows:

It is morally unjust to compel this solid Teuton minority to remain subject to a Slav central government at Prague.[1]

. . . the Czechs as a whole are an incorrigibly pigheaded people[1]

There can never be appeasement in Europe so long as Czechoslovakia remains the link with Moscow and hostile to Germany.[1]

This was merely to translate Hitler's own propaganda into English:

Among the majority of the nationalities which are being oppressed in this State there are 3,500,000 Germans. That is about as many persons of our race as Denmark has inhabitants. These Germans are creatures of God. . . . and He has not created the 7,000,000 Czechs in order that they should supervise 3,500,000 Germans[2].

. . . the *raison d'être* of Czechoslovakia was not only to attack Germany. Bolshevism used Czechoslovakia as a roadway to Central Europe[2].

During the summer, the Sudeten Germans negotiated with the Czech President, Benes, with the professed object of securing autonomy. The objective of the Sudetens was to demonstrate, for the benefit of the British, that Benes was unreasonable, while Benes in the hope of compelling Britain and France to come to his aid, strove to prove that it was the Sudetens who were unreasonable. It had thus required much pressure to extract from Benes a 'request' to the British to send out a mediator, who had duly appeared in the person of the otherwise superannuated Runciman.

The ulterior purpose of Runciman's mission, as Benes knew, was to secure evidence of Czech intransigence; but even Runciman was forced, by the astute way Benes handled the Sudetens, to admit that the latter were the real trouble-makers. The discovery doomed Czechoslovakia. On 7 September 1938 *The Times* came forward with the suggestion that the

[1] Quoted, Gilbert, *Britain and Germany Between the Wars*, pp. 109, 110.
[2] Hitler, Speeches at Nuremberg, 12 September 1938, and at Berlin, 26 September 1938.

best course open to the Czechs might be to cede the Sudeten regions to
Germany. Indeed, it was obvious that, if no Czech-Sudeten compromise
were attainable but war was nevertheless to be avoided, this was the only
solution. On 12 September, Hitler, in a violent speech at Nuremberg,
demanded that the Sudeten Germans be given 'self-determination'; and
the Sudeten Germans themselves at once staged a revolt. It was suppressed;
but Henlein then went into hiding and demanded the Sudetenland's
cession to Germany.

As the crisis approached, with everybody convinced, as Hitler intended
them to be, that the Germans were about to march into Czechoslovakia,
Chamberlain was relieved to discover that the French Prime Minister,
Daladier, also had no stomach for a fight. Fortified by French nervelessness,
and assisted by no advice other than that of Sir Horace Wilson, Chamberlain therefore flew to see Hitler at Berchtesgaden on 15 September. He
found Hitler ready to postpone military action (which he was not then
immediately meditating) in order to give Chamberlain time to go back
home again to secure Cabinet agreement to Hitler's demand for Sudeten
'self-determination', i.e. the partition of a Czechoslovakia whose government, as the suppression of the Sudeten disturbances proved, was still in
complete control of its territory.

The Cabinet gave its agreement to the proposal and so did the French,
though they insisted that Britain guarantee what would thereafter remain
of Czechoslovakia. Chamberlain accepted this proposal after only brief
Cabinet deliberation; and the Czechs were informed that they must accept
the cession of the Sudeten areas. If they resisted, they would resist alone.

When, however, Chamberlain returned to Hitler at Godesberg on 22nd September, Hitler told him the transfer of the Sudetenland was 'no longer of any use'. Additional areas not previously mentioned must be transferred, and the Czechs must withdraw from the region within six days. Only after a heated exchange did Hitler agree to postpone his deadline to 1 October. Two reasons are offered for Hitler's sudden raising of his demands. One is that he was determined upon war, the other that he expected the Czech State to disintegrate altogether in a matter of days: the Hungarians were demanding the return of Slovakia, with its one million Magyar minority, and the Poles were also demanding the Teschen area, in order to secure a common frontier with Hungary. If that happened, Hitler could take whatever he wanted, and Chamberlain would be left with no Czecho-slovakia to negotiate about.

Whatever his reasons, Hitler was now pushing Chamberlain rapidly towards a war he did not want and which would be about, not Czecho-slovakia, but the technicality that Hitler wanted quickly, and by the warlike use of troops, what Chamberlain wanted him to have slowly, by an unwarlike use of troops. On 26 September, Hitler announced publicly to the Germans, in a violently anti-Czech speech, that if the Czechs did not hand over the Sudetenland by 1 October, Germany would take 'active steps'. Chamberlain therefore allowed the Foreign Office to announce:

if . . . a German attack is made upon Czechoslovakia the immediate result must be that France will be bound to come to her assistance and Great Britain and Russia will certainly stand by France.

This warning was conveyed by Horace Wilson to Hitler personally on the 27th, while Henderson, through orthodox channels, passed to the Germans a new Anglo-French scheme by which Hitler could have almost all his Godesberg demands except that his entry into the areas to be ceded would be phased over the period from 1st October to the 10th. Hitler replied that he would not compromise over 'immediate occupation' but would guarantee what was left of Czechoslovakia; he then ordered further German divisions to mobilize. Chamberlain replied by assuring Hitler that he could trust the British and French Governments to see he got what he wanted from the Czechs 'without war and without delay'; and he also said he was ready to come again to Germany to arrange it, with French and Italian representatives also present, if Hitler so desired. He simultane-ously asked Mussolini to 'urge the Chancellor to agree to my proposal'.

The next day, 28 September 1938, Hitler agreed to hold the desired meeting. It took place at Munich on 29 September where he was joined by Chamberlain, Daladier and Mussolini. The four men signed an agreement to implement the Anglo-French scheme submitted to Hitler two days earlier. The Czechs were not represented at the meeting. They were told afterwards that if they resisted German entry into their territory they would have to do so unaided.

It can be argued that, since, both in France and Germany, the military experts were quite unwilling to launch a Franco-German war over Czechoslovakia in September 1938, there was never a real crisis at all, and that both sides threatened a war they neither intended nor expected, in the hope that the other side would give way. It may well be that Hitler, and even more so his generals, over-estimated the strength of the French, just as the French over-estimated the strength of the Germans. If Hitler was more than usually bad-tempered in the weeks after Munich, this was probably because he felt he had been manœuvred out of the unilateral exercise of force he had always thought desirable and feasible. There was thus little risk of general war in September 1938; all Chamberlain did was to organize an unconvincing pretence that to agree to Hitler's invasion of the Sudetenland, instead of unavailingly protesting about it, was a triumph for reason and orderliness.

To both Chamberlain and Hitler, however, it mattered a good deal that the Sudetenland had been handed over in this way. Chamberlain thought he had re-established the principle of negotiation in international affairs; but this merely proved that he did not understand the basis of Hitler's prestige: his claim to be the one man with the courage to right the German nation's wrongs by solitary defiant gestures in the teeth of foreign opposition. Munich annoyed Hitler by revealing publicly what had previously been undisclosed; namely, that the vicious conspiracy of the democratic powers to keep Germany bound in chains by the Versailles *Diktat*, against which he had been fulminating for a decade and a half, had never really existed.

Chamberlain underlined his major purpose by concocting the Anglo-German Declaration (or, more accurately, Chamberlain-Hitler Declaration) which, in memorable fashion, he brandished aloft on emerging from his aeroplane at Heston on returning to England. The declaration asserted that the Anglo-German naval agreement and Munich were

symbolic of the desire of our two peoples never to go to war with one another again,

but its vital sentence from Chamberlain's point of view was:

We are resolved that the method of consultation shall be the method adopted to deal with any other questions that may concern our two countries.

The news that Hitler had agreed to the Munich meeting had been made public towards the end of a long gloomy speech by the Prime Minister in the Commons on 27 September, explaining the unfruitful course of the negotiations up to that point. Hitler's message was passed to Chamberlain while he was still speaking, and his reading of it to the House produced a tumult of joy among the members, some of whom were alleged to have cried out, 'Thank God for the Prime Minister'. So nearly inevitable had

European war seemed, so intense and so personal had been the drama of
the Prime Minister's two sudden flights to Germany, that nerves were (as
Hitler had hoped) almost at breaking-point. Gas masks had been issued to
the population, the air raid precautions service had been mobilized,
trenches had been dug in the parks, and in imagination every one was
already hearing the 'crash of bombs' and 'the cataracts of masonry and
fire and smoke' that Churchill, over four years before, had prophesied for
the first hours of war, and which the public had by now seen with their
own eyes on the newsreels of events in Shanghai, Abyssinia and Madrid.
So miraculous did the deliverance of Munich seem, and so entirely the
work of Chamberlain, that there was an almost world-wide tendency to
attribute semi-divine qualities to him. A Norwegian newspaper thought
he deserved the Nobel Peace Prize. A Conservative M.P. was certain he
would 'go down in history as the greatest European statesman of this or
any other time'. The *New York Times* found him 'a heroic figure' and the
New York Daily News expressed a fairly widespread opinion when it
wrote:

In Chamberlain's actions in the last couple of weeks there is something
Christlike. . . . Chamberlain showed more of the spirit of the founder of
Christianity than any English-speaking politician we can remember since
Abraham Lincoln.

The unaccustomed limelight which illuminated the hitherto unloved
Chamberlain from the moment of his first flight to Germany (and the sheer
physical strain of his labours) provoked him during the crisis to make public
utterances of quite extraordinary ineptness. He prefaced one of his journeys
with a quotation from Shakespeare ('out of this nettle danger we'll pluck
this flower safety') without understanding that the words were an advocacy
not of concession but of reckless defiance. On 27 September he had said
in a broadcast:

How horrible, fantastic, incredible it is that we should be digging trenches
and trying on gas-masks here because of a quarrel in a far-away country
between people of whom we know nothing,

oblivious of the fact that more than three hundred years earlier, so far from
thinking it a far-away country which did not concern them, the Commons
had fiercely demanded intervention by King James I in a quarrel involving
the freedom of this same land of Bohemia. Before he went to Munich he
reverted to the nursery, and recalled that he had been told there, 'if at
first you don't succeed, try try and try again'; forgetting that the point of the
jingle was that Robert Bruce learned never to surrender. On the evening
of his return, he told the Downing Street crowds that, like Disraeli, he
had come back from Berlin bringing 'peace with honour', not understanding that, in 1878, Disraeli had inflicted a major diplomatic defeat on his
Russian opponents and conceded them almost nothing. He then concluded

his exhibition of incomprehension by announcing to the populace, 'I think it is peace for our time'.

The contention, therefore, that Chamberlain had few illusions about Hitler, and that the Munich affair was a calculated holding operation designed to give Britain time to rearm must, notwithstanding the distinguished names of those who have advanced it, be dismissed as at variance with the evidence. Chamberlain knew Hitler was a bully, and he knew that the stronger Britain's armaments were the more Hitler would be impressed; but he behaved, from the moment he became Prime Minister until the spring of 1939, consistently and patiently in the belief that he could convert and tame Hitler, and was prepared to go to almost any lengths to achieve this object. This is proved by Chamberlain's indifference to the fact that Hitler broke the Munich agreement within days of its signature. The various limitations imposed by the agreement on unrestricted German seizure of the areas claimed from Czechoslovakia were ignored; Chamberlain made no protest. Britain gave the new and enfeebled Czechoslovakia the guarantee which had been refused when Czechoslovakia was strong, and Inskip told the Commons in October that the Government would 'take all steps to see that Czech integrity' was preserved; a month later, under Hitler's patronage, and in contravention of the Munich terms, Hungary and Poland were allowed to seize border territories from Czechoslovakia on the grounds that they contained Magyar and Polish inhabitants. Chamberlain positively refused to protest; he insisted that the British guarantee had been only against 'unprovoked aggression' and not against what he chose to describe as merely 'the crystallization of frontiers'. Britain also gave post-Munich Czechoslovakia a loan of £30 millions; the unused portions of this were duly handed over to Germany when Hitler finally liquidated the Czech State in March 1939. Throughout that intervening period, Chamberlain continued to pretend in the Commons, and in less public confrontations with other politicians, that Munich had been what he had intended it to be: the beginning of a new era of Anglo-German co-operation presided over by himself. Critics of Munich, he said, were 'fouling their own nest'.

There was only one resignation from Chamberlain's Cabinet, that of Duff Cooper, Secretary for War from 1935 to 1937 and since that year First Lord of the Admiralty. Duff Cooper's Commons speech justifying his resignation made the essential point that Czechoslovakia was, by the Munich agreement, being invaded after all. He condemned the notion that Hitler could be converted by 'sweet reasonableness' and that his word could be trusted:

The Prime Minister has confidence in the good will and in the word of Herr Hitler, although when Herr Hitler broke the Treaty of Versailles he undertook to keep the Treaty of Locarno, and when he broke the Treaty of Locarno he undertook not to have further territorial aims in Europe.

When he entered Austria he authorized his henchmen to give an authoritative
assurance that he would not interfere with Czechoslovakia, and that was
less than six months ago. Still the Prime Minister believes he can rely on the
good faith of Hitler; he believes that Hitler is only interested in Germany, as
he was assured.

The Prime Minister may be right. I hope and pray that he is right; but I
cannot believe what he believes; I wish I could.

When the Munich agreement was debated in the Commons in the first
week of October, Conservative opposition was limited to the abstention
from the voting of nineteen members of the party. They included three
future Prime Ministers in Churchill, Eden and Macmillan, and Churchill's
son-in-law, Duncan Sandys.

---

32 · United Against Fascism?

The reluctant abandonment of pacifism by the more thoughtful among
those not actively engaged in party politics widened the gap between the
parties and the leaders of educated opinion from 1936 onwards. Only two
groups supported Chamberlain: the large number of the feckless, who were
confirmed in their indifference to foreign affairs by the popular Press, and
that large number of Conservative M.P.s whose continued presence
in its ranks could cause their party at this time still to be regarded as
'the stupid party'. Effective opposition to Chamberlain in the political
arena was therefore precluded by the aura of suspicion which still surrounded Churchill, and by the relative youth or inexperience of such men
as Eden, Duff Cooper and Macmillan. The Liberal Party counted for
nothing, despite the energetic hostility to appeasement of its leader, Sir
Archibald Sinclair. A cross-party alliance against Chamberlain was vaguely
hoped for by Dalton, and might have gained the support of Ernest Bevin
and Walter Citrine, the leaders of the T.U.C. Attlee, however, wanted no
truck with anybody either to the Right or to the Left of the thin pink line
of official Labour policy; and, worse still, he so disliked Chamberlain that
he opposed rearmament, and later conscription, largely because Chamberlain was in favour of them. Once again it was shown how the careers of
Lloyd George, MacDonald and Baldwin had deprived all those who were
not complacently of the Right of any vehicle for effective political action.

In the later 1930's, neither Chamberlain nor Attlee was a party leader in the sense that Gladstone, Disraeli, Salisbury and Asquith had been. Compared with them, Chamberlain and Attlee were leaders of small, small-minded, cliques. Chamberlain's Government by 1939 was without Churchill, Eden, Duff Cooper, Macmillan, Amery, Cranborne, and so far from being National was not even genuinely Conservative. As for Attlee, the Labour movement noticed him very little, and the general public did not notice him at all.

Already, in 1934, the absence of organized means of mobilizing opinion against the Government had given rise to attempts to form what was variously called a Popular Front or United Front for the purpose of prose-cuting what was called 'the fight against Fascism'. The true origins of this movement are to be found in the entry of the U.S.S.R. into the League of Nations and the signature of the Franco-Russian alliance of 1935. This produced 'about-turn' orders to the national Communist Parties. As agents of Soviet foreign policy (they had few other functions) they were now re-quired to become passionate in their advocacy of collective security through the League, indefatigable in proclaiming the Soviet Union's love of peace, and ceaseless in their endeavours to act as the 'spearhead' of the international fight against Fascism in collaboration with other anti-Fascist groups, however *bourgeois*.

With rigorous tenacity, the Labour Party leaders rejected collaboration with the Communists and therefore with Popular Front propagandists, throughout the remaining years of peace, even when, as happened later, they advocated a diplomatic and military alliance with the U.S.S.R. This obstinate parochialism on Labour's part served it well in the long run; one important reason for its substantial electoral victory in 1945 was that it was free from Communist taint. In the short run, however, the decision not only to anathematize Communists, but to ban all individuals or organ-izations which associated with them in 'Front' activities, reduced the Labour Party's power to lead public opinion almost to disappearing point.

The outbreak of the Spanish Civil War emphasized still more the un-representative character of the two main political parties. The only real difference between Chamberlain and Attlee was that the former did not care if Germans and Italians broke non-intervention agreements, while Attlee did care. Both men nevertheless believed in non-intervention as the ideal policy, whereas a large body of opinion viewed the civil war as a battleground between Fascism and Freedom in a way in which they never quite saw the conflict with the totalitarian States over Abyssinia or over the breaking of the peace treaties. The fight between Franco and the Republi-cans was, for most observers outside the inner party caucuses, a straight fight between Evil and Good in which it was impossible, if not criminal, to be neutral. A minority thought Franco Good and the Republicans Evil, being influenced by Franco's alliance with the Roman Church, and by the alleged anti-clericalism of the Republicans; such supporters of Franco also pointed to the increasing aid given to the Republicans by the Soviet Union. To the majority of those who interested themselves in the matter at all, however, Franco represented either or both of two evils. One was the wickedness of Right-wing militarists and politicians in general: Franco was alleged to be doing in Spain what all Right-wing extremists wanted to do everywhere, and Chamberlain, of course, was his natural ally. The other image of Franco was that he was the agent through whom German and Italian Fascism was promoting its own bestial policies; such a view at once allotted to the Soviet Union its desired position as defender of popular freedom wherever Fascism threatened it. The unanalytical generosity which had idealized the Greek rebels of the 1820's and the motley crew who had contrived the Italian Risorgimento was now re-created out of sympathy for the mixed bag of Liberals, Democrats, Socialists, Anarchists and Communists who fought so tenaciously and heroically against Franco and his Italian and German allies. The defence of Madrid, the German bombing of Guernica, holy city of the Basques, obscured altogether that there were heroism and suffering on the other side too. Young Englishmen fought and died in an International Brigade formed to assist the Republicans; and among less hardy resisters of Fascism there proliferated committees and organizations to send milk to Spanish mothers, medical aid to Spanish wounded, to care for refugee Spanish children and to produce evidence of breaches of international law committed by Franco's men against Republican prisoners. M.P.s and public-spirited persons of all parties paid visits to Spain and sat together in unaccustomed proximity on public platforms making speeches and appeals and giving lectures on their experiences.

All attempts to create a coherent political organization out of this coming-together in a deeply-felt cause were unsuccessful. A new attempt at Unity on the Left was launched by Cripps and the dissident Labour men in his Socialist League early in 1937. Since, however, the essential feature of all such moves was association with the Communist Party it collapsed in the face of the unshakeable opposition of the Labour Party Executive. As far as the Labour leadership was concerned there already was a 'united front' whose component parts were the Labour Party, the trade unions and the co-operative societies. The facts that the Labour Party was divided and ineffective in the Commons, that the trade unions were incapable of political decision and the co-operatives little more than purveyors of consumer goods to members who thought of nothing but their 'divi', were considered irrelevant. Cripps made one more effort to form a Popular Front in the first months of 1939 but this merely led to his expulsion from the party. It may, therefore, be said that, apart from its never very complete conversion to the idea of rearmament, the Labour Party failed completely either to lead or to represent intelligent non-Conservative opinion in the 1930's.

The cumulative wrongs of the 1930's, ranging from the shame of unemployment and the survival of the slums at home to the bombings and persecutions abroad, ended by giving to the thinking of the period a quality of almost Puritan earnestness, compared with the frivolity of the twenties. There was a thirst for information and instruction about contemporary social and political questions, and an anxious search for ways and means of righting the world's manifest wrongs, which contrasted sharply with the complacent indifference to known facts which marked so many of the country's official political leaders. The National Government did not care about unemployment at home and did not object to Fascism abroad; and the Labour Party had no policy except to intone the words 'collective security' and sit back and wait for the distant day when everybody should at last decide to vote for it. Yet, beneath the blinkered gaze of the political leaders, was a whole ferment of idealism which, because it did not conform to the ancient patterns of party, they chose to ignore. Neither party grasped that general standards of education had risen, continuing to regard the bulk of the population as politically illiterate. The Conservatives had little idea that anybody who had not attended a public school could know very much about public affairs, and those members of the Labour party who had not themselves been to public schools judged the general educational level of the rest of the country from their recollections of the Board Schools of the 1890's.

Yet this was, above all, the decade of the political pamphlet, the instructive paperback and the book club. The first 'Penguins' appeared in 1935, cost sixpence each, and soon found a ready market, not simply for reprints of standard works, but for a stream of serious studies of contemporary problems, such as the condition of the working class at home or current events in Germany, Italy, Spain and Czechoslovakia; and almost every crisis produced its punctual 'Penguin Special'. Symptomatic of the times also was the enormous sale of a stiff volume called *Mathematics for the Million* by Lancelot Hogben, which he followed by *Science for the Citizen*. Equally typical were the foundation of Mass Observation in 1936, indicating a new and more scientific interest in social behaviour, and the appearance of the first opinion polls.

While few of these publications and activities were the work of Socialists or persons avowedly connected with the Labour Party their total effect was always to discredit the National Government and the Conservative Party, for it was hardly possible to uncover the details of any problem, foreign or domestic, without it at once becoming apparent that the complacent Chamberlains, Runcimans, Simons, Hoares and Inskips had nothing to be complacent about. The long-term effect of this flood of writing on the condition of England and on the unchecked spread of Fascism was considerable; it was a major factor in causing the defeat of the Conservatives in 1945.

Equally effective in the long run, and more so in the late thirties themselves, was the foundation of the Left Book Club in May, 1936. It was not the first of the book clubs, but it was by far the most significant since all the choices (and they were often weighty and sometimes scholarly volumes) were selected for their relevance to the 'struggle for democracy against Fascism'. The choices were selected by Harold Laski, the far-Left Socialist teacher of political theory at the London School of Economics; John Strachey, also a far-Left Socialist who had for a brief period been a supporter of Mosley; and Victor Gollancz, who published the books and combined business acumen with what proved to be an unquenchable thirst after righteousness. The Club was so successful that soon there were additional choices and alternative choices, a monthly *Left News* to go with the monthly book, and a network of Left Book Club groups all over the country. In theory these groups met to study the book of the month; in fact they rarely did so, constituting themselves instead as Popular Front 'cells' whose members had a tendency to address one another as 'Comrade'. The club held annual rallies in London, which filled the Albert Hall or the Empress Hall and which were addressed by a startling variety of speakers. Apart from Strachey, Stafford Cripps, Laski, and the Communist, Harry Pollitt, there was Norman Angell, who had preached about the futility of war in a book called *The Great Illusion* as long ago as 1908; there was Sir Richard Acland whose career took him out of the Liberal Party into a party of his own creation called Commonwealth, thence to the Labour Party, thence to nuclear disarmament, thence to teaching, thence to teacher training and thence to a pretension to expertise in the art of religious instruction; and Hewlett Johnson, the 'Red' Dean of Canterbury, who was regular in his insistence that Russia was the greatest Christian country in the world. Lloyd George was lured to one meeting, improving the occasion by referring to the Chamberlain Government as having 'feeble, feckless fingers, without grip or grasp'. For lighter relief there was usually Paul Robeson to sing, and to preface a Russian folk song by saluting the U.S.S.R. as 'the fatherland of the international proletariat'. The Left Book Club groups organized meetings about help for Spain and usually contrived at one time or another to invite the Communist-run Unity Theatre group to put on a performance of Clifford Odets' *Waiting for Lefty* in which a group of trade unionists spend the greater part of the play waiting for a Communist organizer who is shot the moment he arrives, thus proving that the capitalists always get their man.

There was much that was naïvely idealistic and indeed naïvely or wilfully ignorant about the amateur Marxism of the Left Book Clubs, and there was much superficial nonsense about joining in the workers' struggle by people whose undisputed *bourgeois* respectability guaranteed that their knowledge of the working class was very slight. Their superficiality was denounced in one section of George Orwell's *The Road to Wigan Pier* which, though originally published as a Left Book Club selection, was apologized for by Gollancz, both before publication and in an introduction. Nevertheless, though the book is usually read as a document on life in the depressed areas, its biting sarcasm at the expense of petty *bourgeois* Socialists is probably at least as accurate a piece of observation.

It was not only the Left Book Club members who conceived a deep infatuation with Marxism. Poets did it as well, notably the trio formed by W. H. Auden, C. Day Lewis and Stephen Spender. They wrote much that was stirring or reverent about 'the workers', and Spender produced a volume for the Left Book Club called *Forward from Liberalism* in which he declared himself to be a Communist without producing much evidence that he knew what this meant. Pseudo-Marxism led, naturally enough, to admiration for the great Soviet Union. Russia appeared to have two virtues which the England of the thirties conspicuously lacked: it had avoided a Depression and it had a Planned Economy. Strachey's Left Book Club writings and utterances were full of praise for the way in which Russia provided Socialists with a model of how to Plan for Plenty, and how to end the capitalist phenomenon of 'scarcity in the midst of plenty'. It was therefore ironical that when Strachey became Minister of Food in the 1945 Labour Government it certainly fell to him to plan, but for scarcity; he was the first man to introduce bread rationing in this country.

An interesting feature of the Left-wing flirtation with Russia was its attitude to the Purges of 1936 onwards; just as the Conservatives condoned Fascist terror, the Left condoned Communist terror. The Purges were said either to be justified by the existence of spies and saboteurs, or to have been misrepresented; no noteworthy Communist sympathizer transferred his allegiance because of them. This was perhaps a little less dishonest than it seems; there was a real lack of reliable information about the Purges, then as now.

What was more important, however, was that the rulers of Britain had so failed some of their own best minds, that a foreign State, about which few people knew any hard facts, but which at least claimed to oppose Fascism, and at least seemed to have an organized economy, should seem preferable to what could be offered by a British Government. In like fashion, though it is easy to accuse middle-class intellectuals of superficiality in their talk of joining the working class in resistance to capitalism at home and Fascism abroad, they were virtually forced into this attitude because the Labour Party, which ought to have been the guide and beneficiary of their wholly genuine desire to combat social injustice, found nothing better to do than proscribe some of them and ignore the rest.

33 · Prague and Danzig, 1939

During the twelve months after the Munich agreement, European diplomacy fell into inextricable confusion. In London, Paris, Berlin, Rome, Prague, Warsaw and Moscow nobody knew what to do next. No Government had clear objectives and almost all finally abandoned, as the year went on, even the pretence of adhering to such principles as they had hitherto proclaimed. By September 1939, Britain had abandoned the entire policy towards eastern Europe which she had followed since 1920, Hitler had thrown overboard his anti-Communism, Stalin his anti-Fascism; the Czechs turned themselves into pro-Germans, the Poles into anti-Germans, and Mussolini, after one last fling in Albania, transformed himself from a ranting advocate of heroic war into the practitioner of a craven pacifism. France alone remained consistent to her now established policy of inaction, and did not abandon it until finally pushed into war less by Hitler than by the British.

Hitler was as perplexed as anyone. Munich, without satisfying his desire to 'smash' Czechoslovakia, had so weakened it that it was in danger of falling apart in ways that did not please him. Once 'self-determination' was applied to the Sudetens it was demanded by the Slovaks, and also by the Ukrainians living in the eastern tip of the country, known as Ruthenia or the Carpatho-Ukraine. The first official manifestation of this was the appearance, in October 1938, of the hyphen that transformed Czechoslovakia into Czecho-Slovakia. Hitler was greatly exercised by the fact that Hungary wanted both Slovakia and Ruthenia and that Poland wanted Ruthenia in order to gain a common frontier with Hungary. Hitler did not want to strengthen either of these two States, especially as, for a time, Mussolini was known to be toying with the idea of forming a common front with them. Hitler thought, for a time, of letting Poland have Ruthenia as a *quid pro quo* for a German seizure of Danzig and a strip of territory to link East Prussia with the rest of Germany, after which there might then be a joint German-Polish onslaught on the Russian Ukraine. It was not until later that he decided to embark on a specifically anti-Polish campaign. Nor is there evidence that he was contemplating a war in the west in 1939. He still seems to have been thinking in terms of turning on France and Britain no earlier

than 1943; and, even then, his aims for Britain may have been limited to
the traditional German dream of forcing her, while continuing to enjoy
her overseas Empire, to allow Germany to rule the continent. Nor, of
course, is there the slightest evidence that Chamberlain had changed
Hitler's mind about Britain. On the day of the Munich agreement, Hitler
told Mussolini 'the time will come when we shall have to fight side by
side against France and England'[1] and on 9 October 1938 he announced
in a public speech that the Declaration he and Chamberlain had signed
was being endangered by Eden, Duff Cooper and Churchill:

If these men were to obtain power we would know clearly and beyond doubt
that their aim would be to unleash immediately a world war against Germany.

Nevertheless, the British continued to feed Hitler with evidence that
he need not fear them, despite their increased rearmament. Halifax made
overtures for a 'general understanding' in December 1938, and in February
1939 Nevile Henderson thought there was a good chance of Hitler having
the sense, in view of the growing strength of England, to turn towards
'Normalcy' rather then 'Adventure'. On 10 March 1939, Chamberlain
said that Europe was 'settling down to a period of tranquillity' and Samuel
Hoare piously declared, in a speech at Chelsea on the same day, that the
three dictators and the Prime Ministers of Britain and France were in a
position to 'transform the whole history of the world':

These five men working together in Europe, and blessed in their efforts by
the President of the U.S.A., might make themselves the eternal benefactors
of the human race. Our own Prime Minister has shown his determination to
work heart and soul to such an end. I cannot believe that the other leaders of
Europe will not join him in the high endeavour upon which he is engaged.

Parallel with these amiable gestures and sentiments there had been
further advances to Mussolini. The Anglo-Italian agreement of the
previous April was put into effect in November 1938, even though the
Spanish question had still not been settled. In January 1939, Chamberlain
and Halifax paid an official visit to Rome; but it produced no results,
because Mussolini was currently organizing an agitation against the
French for the return of Corsica and Nice, and was considering the occupation of Albania. The obstinate conviction of Chamberlain and Halifax
that they had much to gain by detaching Mussolini from the Axis was as
mistaken as Hitler's view that he had much to gain from keeping him in it.

In mid-March 1939, Hitler's patronage of independence movements in
Slovakia and Ruthenia provoked a new crisis. The new Czech President,
Hacha, tried to suppress these movements. On Hitler's orders, Slovakia
then proclaimed its independence under German protection, and Ruthenia
also proclaimed its independence, with the immediate result of a Hungarian
ultimatum to Prague and the absorption of Ruthenia into Hungary. Hitler
and Hacha therefore met in Berlin and, on 15 March 1939, as German

[1] Robertson, op. cit., p. 159.

troops marched on Prague, turned what was now left of Czechoslovakia, namely the Czech provinces of Bohemia and Moravia, into German protectorates. Hacha's agreement had been hastened by the threat that non-compliance would lead to the immediate German bombing of Prague.

The final destruction of the Czechoslovak State in this way had effects on general opinion out of all proportion to its significance. It was a logical outcome of all that had happened since the *Anschluss* in March 1938; and it was as naïve to express surprise at Hitler's entry into Prague when it occurred as to pretend a generation later that it was neither 'sinister nor premeditated'.[1] This is as if a man should be exonerated from a charge of murder on the grounds that he did it on one day with an unexpectedly-discovered carving knife, after originally planning to do it on some other day with a carefully prepared phial of poison.

Nevertheless, the general view was that the occupation of Prague proved, for the first time, and beyond shadow of doubt, that Hitler was a ruthless aggressor. Even *The Times*, notorious for its advocacy of appeasement, was moved to protest:

For the first time since Nazism came to power German policy has moved unequivocally and deliberately into the open. There is nothing left for moral debate in this crude and brutal act of oppression and suppression.

The *Daily Telegraph*, accustomed as it was to using somewhat stronger language against Germany, was fiercer still:

'A monstrous outrage' is the mildest term that can be applied to the events in central Europe. The tale of them has sent a thrill of horror and indignation throughout the civilized world,

and the *Yorkshire Post*, in recording its opinion, found it necessary to use the words 'ruthless', 'determined', 'unscrupulous' 'contemptuous' and 'cunning' within the space of six lines.

Chamberlain himself yielded, though belatedly, to this outburst of anger. On the day Prague was occupied, he contented himself with saying in the Commons that he felt 'bitter regret', adding rather sulkily that he

could not believe that anything of the kind was contemplated by any of the signatories of the Munich agreement.

He went on to say, however, that the British guarantee of post-Munich Czechoslovakia did not now apply, because the country had been brought to an end by 'internal disruption'. Two days later, in a speech in Birmingham, he changed his tune. After a swift dismissal of the charge that what had happened was his fault because of the Munich agreement, he virtually apologized for his 'somewhat cool and objective' remarks in the Commons, and attacked Hitler for his breach of 'repeated assurances, given voluntarily to me':

[1] A. J. P. Taylor, *Origins of the Second World War*, p. 202.

Surely as a joint signatory of the Munich agreement I was entitled, if Herr Hitler thought it ought to be undone, to that consultation which is provided for in the Munich declaration. Instead of that he has taken the law into his own hands.

The events which have taken place this week . . . must cause us all to be asking ourselves 'Is this the end of an old adventure or is it the beginning of a new?' 'Is this the last attack on a small state or is it to be followed by others? Is this, in fact, a step in the direction of an attempt to dominate the world by force?'

This was language both foolish and dangerous. Foolish, because to imply that the establishment of a protectorate over Bohemia and Moravia might be 'a step in the direction of an attempt to dominate the world by force' was either absurdly ahead of the facts or absurdly in arrear of them. Dangerous, because of Chamberlain's implication that there was, in his mind, a major distinction between Hitler's breach of the two great European Treaties of Versailles and Locarno and his breach of 'repeated assurances given voluntarily to me'. This meant that Chamberlain's personally conducted foreign policy would henceforth be coloured by his angry resentment at having been humiliated. The contrast between what Chamberlain had said about Munich and what Hitler had now done was so clear that, in view of Chamberlain's narrowness of outlook, it is certain he would neither forget nor forgive. He would be even more disposed to action by the view of the Chiefs of Staff that British rearmament had now reached a point which made the risk of war less dangerous to contemplate than it had been earlier. This would not mean that Chamberlain wanted war; but it would make him more confident than ever in his own rectitude if he believed that it was now backed by sufficient armed strength.

Chamberlain made his first precipitate move at once. On the day of his Birmingham speech, 17 March 1939, there came an entirely erroneous warning that German troops were about to enter Roumania. Chamberlain immediately proposed a joint guarantee of Roumania by Britain, France, Russia and Poland. Before much progress had been made, there were two further alarms. On 23 March Hitler annexed the Baltic port of Memel which, though in Lithuania, was populated by a large number of Germans clamouring for reunion with the Fatherland. This was followed by further false rumours, this time of an imminent German attack on Poland; and Polish reservists were called up. On 3 March, therefore, Chamberlain made this statement in the Commons:

. . . certain consultations are now proceeding with other Governments. In order to make perfectly clear the position of H. M. Government in the mean-time before those consultations are concluded I now have to inform the House that, during that period, in the event of any action which clearly threatened Polish independence, and which the Polish Government accordingly considered it vital to resist with their national forces, H.M. Government would feel themselves bound at once to lend the Polish Government all support in their power.

On 6 April, an Anglo-Polish agreement was signed making this under-taking permanent.

There was more to follow. On 7 April 1939, Mussolini invaded Albania, long an Italian client-State. Two features of the invasion gave it that extra element of brutality which the world now regarded as typical of Fascist behaviour. The chosen date for the invasion was Good Friday; and the King of Albania's wife was forced to flee to Greece, taking with her her two-day-old son. On 13 April, Chamberlain accordingly concluded treaties of mutual assistance with Greece and Roumania, and a month later with Turkey. On 26 April, the Government announced the introduction of conscription in peacetime for the first time in British history. All males between twenty and twenty-one were to do six months' compulsory military service; the numbers involved were expected to be 20,000 a year.

Chamberlain thus moved at a breath-taking pace after the so-called 'Rape of Prague'. In a matter of weeks, he had conducted a revolution in foreign and military policy more radical and more nearly instantaneous than had so far been achieved by any of his predecessors or his dictator contemporaries. At one bound he had committed Great Britain to the defence of Poland, Roumania, Greece and Turkey against both Germany and Italy, without reliable evidence that any one of them was about to be attacked, with only two Army divisions available for dispatch to con-tinental soil if the guarantees were ever invoked, and with a compulsory service system which would provide only 20,000 additional trained men at the end of twelve months. This was indeed 'the very midsummer of madness'. This phrase of Chamberlain's, used to damn and to bury the collective security system of the League in 1936, was even more appropriate to his helter-skelter rush to improvise a rickety collective security system of his own in 1939. For not only did all this brave dispensing of guarantees by a Government that lacked the power to fulfil them not make sense; as an attempt to frighten Hitler it failed totally. Huffing and puffing were Hitler's speciality. On the day the Commons were approving the guarantee to Poland (3 April) he was giving orders to his generals to prepare to invade Poland on 1 September. In a blistering speech to the Reichstag on 28 April he denounced the Anglo-German Naval Treaty and also his 1934 non-aggression pact with Poland. And, although it is commonly said that Hitler had no reliable sources of information about the state of opinion in England, he produced an analysis of it, which no historian can improve on:

the opinion prevails there that no matter in what conflict Germans should some day be entangled, Britain would always have to take her stand against Germany. Thus a war against Germany is taken for granted in that country.

There is no means of knowing whether he regarded this statement as accurate or not; but he immediately produced evidence that he did not care. He went on to demand the return of Danzig to the Reich, and a route through the Corridor and a railway line possessing the same extra-territorial status for Germany as the Corridor itself has for Poland.

Yet of all Hitler's demands this was the least unreasonable. It was less drastic than the demand for an *Anschluss* with Austria; and, whereas the demand for the so-called 'return' of the Sudetenland had little or no justification either in history or in 'self-determination', a demand for Danzig had both. Nor would the return of Danzig or the granting of an extra-territorial railway line through the Corridor subject Poland to the economic and strategic amputation to which the annexation of the Sudetenland had subjected Czechoslovakia. Yet Poland's rejection of this demand had already been underwritten unconditionally and to the limit. No statesman made any real effort to put Hitler to the test on the matter. It was taken for granted that it there existed an irreversible decision to invade Poland if the demands were not granted.

In Britain, support of the guarantee to Poland had been almost universal; only the *Daily Express* condemned it. Yet suspicion of Chamberlain was so great that there was immediate parliamentary pressure, both from the Tory dissidents, led by Churchill, and by the Labour Party, to make his attitude to Germany even stiffer. In the debate of 3 April, on the Polish guarantee, Greenwood and Dalton, for the Labour Party, demanded 'an extension of the anti-aggression *bloc*' to include not only the Balkan States but 'the small West European democracies as well'. Both they and Churchill demanded the inclusion of Russia in the Prime Minister's apparent scheme of resistance. Churchill rightly said,

To stop with a guarantee to Poland would be a halt in no-man's land. . . . Having begun to create a Grand Alliance against aggression we cannot afford to fail. . . . The worst folly . . . would be to chill and drive away any natural co-operation which Soviet Russia . . . feels it necessary to afford.

It was Lloyd George, however, who showed the clearest appreciation of the dangers towards which Chamberlain was now advancing. He could not, he said,

understand why, before we committed ourselves to this tremendous enter-prise, we did not seek the adhesion of Russia. . . . It is for us to declare the terms on which we are prepared to assist Poland and unless the Poles are prepared to accept the only conditions on which we can successfully help them the responsibility must be theirs.

It was militarily impossible for Great Britain to 'guarantee' Poland; only Russia could do this. Yet Chamberlain was not interested in acting in consort with Russia. Hence, it was folly to give the Poles an unconditional guarantee. But because Chamberlain had at last begun to abandon appease-ment, the Churchill group and the Labour Party felt it essential, in view of his past record, to drive him on, lest he be tempted to revert to his former pro-Germanism. It did not occur to them that what Chamberlain needed above all in the mad midsummer of 1939 (assuming that peace was the objective) was to be put under restraint. Yet Chamberlain was no longer opposed in the Commons; he was pushed from behind, by men who, so far from realizing that he had handed over the fate of Britain and the Empire to the rulers of Poland, imagined that if they did not urge him on he would sacrifice all Poland to Hitler as he had just sacrificed Czechoslovakia. Already, Chamberlain had done the world his greatest disservice; from Munich onwards any attempt to find a negotiated settlement to anything would be described as 'appeasement' and be branded as cowardice.

WHAT, NO CHAIR FOR ME? Low speculates on Stalin's possible reactions to the exclusion of the U.S.S.R. from the Munich conference. 30 September 1938.

Before giving his guarantee to Poland, Chamberlain had already discovered that it would be difficult to make it real enough to deter Hitler effectively. Russia had already been making difficulties about associating with Poland in a collective treaty; and Poland did not want to associate with Russia at all. The reason in both cases was the same: the effect would be to range both on the anti-German side, with the consequent risk of a German attack from which, from elementary considerations of geography, they would be the first to suffer. The Russians suspected that Britain and France were secretly hoping to turn Hitler against the U.S.S.R., and regarded the Munich agreement as evidence of this. The Poles were convinced that, once Russian troops entered Poland, they would never completely withdraw; if only because eastern Poland consisted of territory taken from Russia by the Treaty of Riga in 1920.

Chamberlain did not want 'the adhesion of Russia' either, because he too did not want to associate Britain formally with Hitler's ideological foe; he wanted to frighten Hitler out of a war, not provoke him into one. He was also convinced that an agreement with Russia would be morally embarrassing, since he adhered to the conventional Anglo-Saxon doctrine that whereas the higher aims of peace might justify association with a Nazi or Fascist State almost nothing could justify association with a Communist one. Moreover, both he and his military advisers believed Russia to be incapable of fighting an offensive war against Germany. Since the British and the French were themselves thinking only of fighting a defensive war against Germany, and were not planning to do any fighting at all in or around Poland, this opinion may perhaps be regarded as based less on strategy than on a deep ideological dislike of a link with Russia.

The problem was complicated by the fact that Colonel Beck, the Polish Foreign Minister, was much more afraid of another Munich than of a war; he was convinced that if he made no concessions, and prevented Britain and France from making any, Hitler would climb down. The British were so obsessed with the notion of a Giant German Bully terrorizing the 'small States' of Europe that they failed to realize that Poland did not consider itself a 'small State' at all. Czechoslovakia was not the only 'far-away' country of which the British 'knew nothing'. Poland was even farther away and even more unknown. Czechoslovakia had no Great-Power tradition behind it, but Poland certainly had. Poland had once been one of the four largest States in Europe; Poland had hurled back the Bolsheviks in 1920; the Poles had been treated with such serious respect by Hitler that he had signed a non-aggression pact with them in 1934 and did not denounce it until April 1939; Danzig and the Polish Corridor were Germany's major grievance after 1919, and yet only now, after six years of power, was Hitler openly venturing to raise the matter. Consequently, though Poland was less efficiently armed than Czechoslovakia had been and, unlike Czechoslovakia, had no defensible natural frontier, Beck was determined not to suffer the fate of Benes. Hence, while Chamberlain was planning a kind of armed Munich instead of the unarmed one he had organized over the Sudetenland, Beck was planning to have no Munich at all. Nor, indeed, could Chamberlain even ask Beck to compromise once he had given Poland his blanket guarantee; he would simply be accused of reverting to his old habit of sacrificing 'small States' to save British skins. Chamberlain's one chance of getting Beck to be reasonable had been to make the guarantee conditional upon Beck making concessions to Germany. Once the guarantee was given, however, Chamberlain was trapped by his own past and by Beck's intransigence. This was what Lloyd George had in mind when he demanded that 'conditions' be imposed on the Poles; after all, Lloyd George knew more about Danzig and the Corridor – and the Poles – than most British politicians.

Under parliamentary pressure, and in view of the evident failure of the Polish guarantee to unnerve Hitler, the British Government now turned, despite its own distaste and Polish disapproval, to the negotiation of an agreement with the U.S.S.R. The discussions were difficult and slow, and in the end spectacularly unsuccessful. Most of the blame for the delays was inevitably laid at the door of the British Government. This was partly because in 1939 people were unaccustomed to the pedantic toughness of Soviet negotiators. It was also the result of assuming that in view of the anti-Bolshevik propaganda of the Nazis and the anti-Fascist counter-propaganda of the U.S.S.R., the Russians were not only waiting for an invitation to join Britain and France against the aggressors, but bravely eager to accept it. Unfortunately, the British and French found that yet another of their inventions of 1919–20 had returned to plague them. They had created Finland and the Baltic States, not to mention Poland, as a *cordon sanitaire* to keep Russia out of Europe; but now that they wanted Russia back in Europe the *cordon sanitaire* was very much in the way. The U.S.S.R. wanted all these States to be 'guaranteed' against Germany whether they wanted such a guarantee or not. This involved the passage of Soviet troops through their territory while the war was on, and the grave possibility that Soviet troops would stay there after the war was over. The British and French were once again caught by their *Munichois* past. They had sold Czechoslovakia; therefore they must now save Poland; therefore they could not sell the Baltic States. But Russia would regard a German attack on those States as an attack on Russia; hence Russian insistence on this point, and the coyness of the British. They would defend the Baltic States, and indeed any 'small State' anywhere between the Channel and the Soviet frontier. But they would not defend the Soviet Union. The discussions became so involved that Molotov, who had become Commissar for Foreign Affairs on 3 May 1939, suggested, at the end of July, that efforts at a political agreement be suspended and military talks be held instead. With evident reluctance the British agreed, and sent a mission to Russia, by sea. Headed by Admiral the Honourable Sir Reginald Plunkett Ernle-Erle-Drax, it reached Moscow on 11 August. The day afterwards, news reached Berlin that the U.S.S.R. was ready to receive a German representative in Moscow for the opening of discussions 'on all issues'.[1]

Hitler had realized for some time that it might be worth seeking to weaken Poland's resistance, whether diplomatic or military, by causing her anxiety about her eastern frontier. For their part, the Russians probably resembled everyone else in desiring to stop Hitler without the painful necessity of actually doing any fighting themselves. On any short-term calculation, the U.S.S.R. had more to gain by alliance with Germany than by alliance with the West. The Russians feared Germany; and for that reason were unwilling to be pushed into an anti-German posture by France

[1] Robertson, op. cit.

and Britain. Furthermore, collaboration with Germany might enable Russia to regain at least some of the territory lost at Brest-Litovsk and Riga, whereas the Western Powers had made it clear that this could not be achieved by collaboration with them. Finally, whereas the West was asking the Russians to accept the risk of war, Hitler, by asking merely for Russian neutrality, offered them the one thing they wanted most: the chance to stay out of the war altogether.

On 23 August 1939, the Russo-German non-aggression treaty, usually referred to as the Ribbentrop-Molotov Pact, was duly signed, after preliminary negotiations lasting about a week. It provided for Russian neutrality, for German disinterestedness in Finland, Latvia and Estonia, and for the division of Poland into spheres of interest. The speed with which Hitler had pushed on the negotiations was due to his having by now decided that the attack on Poland, if such an attack were necessary, should take place on 25 August, not 1 September. The Ribbentrop-Molotov Pact was the culminating act in his war of nerves. For five months now, M.P.s of all parties had been saying in the Commons that, without the U.S.S.R., Britain could not defend Poland. Hitler's reply was to ensure that Britain would be denied that essential Soviet aid, and would therefore give way.

The plan failed. Within twenty-four hours, Chamberlain reaffirmed the British guarantee to Poland, wrote personally to Hitler informing him of Britain's determination to support Poland, and ratified the Anglo-Polish treaty of mutual assistance.

This was not the only irritating news Hitler received. He had already been upset by the marked lack of enthusiasm that Mussolini was showing for war. Although the German-Italian military alliance, grandiosely described as 'the Pact of Steel', had been signed on 22 May, Mussolini had inserted the proviso that Italy would not be ready for war for another four years. Hitler expected that the Russo-German Pact, in addition to disheartening the British, would revitalize Mussolini. But he now received information that, though the Duce was 'unconditionally' still the Führer's ally, Italy could not assist in the war unless Germany provided all Italy's needs in war material.

Accordingly, Hitler cancelled the orders he had given for the attack on Poland to begin on 25–26 August; but, if he was to invade at all that year, he had only until 1 September.

Time was therefore still short, and on both the British and German sides, too short for clear thinking. Hitler still wanted to break the Poles without a war, the British to save them without one; Hitler thought the British would give in, the British thought Hitler was 'wobbling'. There was a scurrying to and fro between London and Berlin by Nevile Henderson, and by a Swedish emissary called Dahlerus, acting as a semi-secret, semi-official, agent for Göring, who was believed to be working for peace.

The result was a renewed and even more tense guessing game than before. Hitler had said that he would not negotiate with the Poles; the Poles refused to negotiate with Hitler. Chamberlain and Henderson, bent on peace, got as far, by late on 29 August, as persuading Hitler to negotiate with Poland after all. Unfortunately, Hitler demanded the dispatch of a Polish representative with full powers ('a plenipotentiary') within twenty-four hours; this demand, said Henderson, was little better than an ultimatum, to which Hitler replied, with both truth and indignation, 'My soldiers are asking me "Yes" or "No".' Henderson urged the Poles to comply, reminding them of their extreme vulnerability to the Germany Army and Air Force; on the other hand, the British Government insisted that Hitler should agree to negotiations being conducted in the normal way, i.e. without a preceding time limit and through the Polish ambassador in Berlin. It was, in fact, the delay caused by the British Government's apparent quibble over the difference between sending a Polish plenipotentiary at once, and negotiating, without a time limit, through the Polish ambassador, that led to the outbreak of war. Hitler's time limit having expired on 31 August without the arrival of a Polish plenipotentiary, the invasion of Poland began in the early hours of 1 September.

In view of Hitler's proved ability, over several years and in several crises, to change his tactics again and again and yet still convince those around him that he was in full command of events, the 'if's' of the last days of August, 1939 are many. It has been suggested that war might have been avoided had he made his demand for a Polish plenipotentiary twenty-four hours earlier. But this might well have worked only if the demands he actually made – and there is no means of knowing what exactly these would have been when it came to it – were such that either the Poles accepted them voluntarily, or accepted them under British pressure. To assess how much British pressure there would then have been on the Poles is impossible because, alarmed and impatient though they now were about Polish obstinacy, there is no certainty that the British would have dared to present the world with anything that looked like a second Munich. Even Henderson, who is on record as having found it infuriating, earlier in the month, that his Government was unable to 'say boo to Beck', and who regarded most of the Poles, as 'an utterly uncivilized lot'[1] also told Halifax after Hitler's call for a plenipotentiary that Hitler was determined to

achieve his ends, by a parade of strength, if that sufficed, but by force if it did not,

and that the result could only be

either war, or once again victory for him by a display of force and consequent encouragement to pursue the same course again next year or the year after.[2]

[1] Quoted, Gilbert, *Britain and Germany Between the Wars*, p. 148.
[2] Henderson, *Failure of a Mission* p. 268.

Thus the British quibble about the difference between a plenipotentiary and an ambassador was the fine point on which the whole issue between Hitler and the rest of Europe had in the end been concentrated. Here, on the brink of war, Hitler was still insisting that the only technique that would satisfy him was that of inducing submission through fear of force. Hitler had gained nothing since 1933 by fear and the threat of force that he could not have gained without them. Yet, essential gangster that he was, nothing could have deterred him but counter-terrorization. The obstinate reluctance of the British and French to realize this had led them in September 1939 to a situation in which they were compelled to fight the kind of war of nerves that he was used to fighting, but which they were almost certain to lose because their record convinced Hitler, until it was too late, that they were shamming.

The failure of the British to deal with Hitler without recourse to war may be ascribed to the failure of their rulers to understand his true character. This mistake is liable to be increasingly shared by some historians. It is distortion to represent Hitler as merely a 'typical' German politician whose only novel quirk was his anti-Semitism. He was not simply a new sort of front man for a traditional ruling class. He hated Right-wing aristocrats and politicians quite as much as he hated Left-wing politicians and trade unionists; and he hated and despised the ruling class of all countries.

British upper-class politicians, with their characteristic ignorance of social classes other than their own, either at home or abroad, had remained under the impression that, as a Right-wing revolutionary, Hitler must in the end develop into an orthodox Right-wing Conservative of the traditional gentlemanly sort, provided only that he were treated as one. This explains the regularity with which visiting Englishmen (including Chamberlain) had returned from Berlin asserting that Hitler was a man who could be trusted to keep his word. They thought that if they said this, not only would other Englishmen believe it, but so would Hitler. Their tactics failed. Each of the successes they conceded him increased his hold over his own country, and particularly over the Army. There was no hope of a democratic rising against Hitler in the thirties; but if just one of his more spectacular gambles had failed, it was always possible that the Conservative-military forces might have overthrown him, as they indeed tried to do in 1944 and as, in 1943, the Italian Conservatives overthrew Mussolini. But at every turn since 1933 British policy had been so directed that it continually inflated Hitler's prestige and his egoism; at every turn he had been allowed to dictate the course of events until, by the autumn of 1939, it proved impossible to convince him that Britain and France had either the will or the power to resist him.

Nor did Britain and France rush to arms even when the Germans invaded Poland. On the evening of 1 September they did not declare war, but sent Hitler a warning, threatening to do so if he did not desist. Hitler inquired whether the warning was an ultimatum. On 2 September the British replied that it was not, but that no conference could meet until he had withdrawn his forces from Poland. Chamberlain, on informing the Commons on the same day that negotiations had been continuing, met with a hostile reception. Urged by Leopold Amery to 'speak for England', Arthur Greenwood, leading the Labour Opposition in the absence of Attlee, who was ill, reminded Chamberlain that, although the German invasion had been going on for thirty-eight hours, the British Government was still not honouring its treaty with Poland; and Halifax warned Chamberlain that Hitler was likely to make a peace offer only after he had conquered a great part of Poland. An ultimatum was therefore at last delivered in Berlin, and Britain was officially at war with Germany by 11 a.m. on 3 September 1939.

Fifteen minutes later, Chamberlain broadcast the news on the B.B.C. His words were as maladroit as ever:

You can imagine what a bitter blow it is to me that all my long struggle to win peace has failed. Yet I cannot believe that there is anything more or anything different that I could have done that would have been more successful.

He reverted to this theme when he spoke to the Commons shortly afterwards:

Everything that I have worked for, everything that I have hoped for, everything that I have believed in during my public life, has crashed in ruins.

Perhaps for some of his hearers on that day his words recalled T. S. Eliot's lines,

> This is the way the world ends
> Not with a bang but a whimper.

PART VII:
WAR FOR EUROPE
AND ASIA

34 · Bewildered Crusaders, 1939-40

In contrast to Chamberlain, Churchill had already, on 3 September, 1939, produced the first of his always carefully composed wartime orations. It contained two characteristic sentences:

Outside the storms of war may blow, and the land may be lashed with the fury of its gales, but in our own hearts, this Sunday morning, there is peace. Our hands may be active, but our consciences are at rest.

The words did not reflect the nation's mood in the autumn of 1939. Uppermost in people's minds was a stunned fear, born of years of half-ignored dread. They were not to be roused by references to storms and gales; their thoughts were on the fear of gas attacks and on the Wehrmacht and the Luftwaffe. Nor was there rest for those who had consciences. Poland had been guaranteed; but nothing had been done for Poland, and nothing was going to be done. On 16 September the Red Army invaded Poland from the east; two days later, the invading German and Russian Armies made contact, symbolically enough, at Brest-Litovsk. On 28 September, the fourth partition of Poland was arranged. By 5 October, Hitler was able to review German troops in a ceremonial parade at Warsaw to mark the end of the campaign. Chamberlain had tried to stop Hitler by concessions at Munich in 1938; he had tried to stop him by a declaration of war in 1939. On both occasions, the effect on Hitler had been nil, and in early October 1939, the second case looked worse than the first. Prague still stood, its citizens still inhabited it; but Warsaw was in ruins and Chamberlain's guarantee was buried deep beneath the rubble.

Thus, even though the momentous psychological effort of declaring war had been undertaken, it seemed to have made little difference. The general malaise was increased by the twin phenomena of the black-out and the evacuation scheme. When Grey had spoken of the lamps going out all over

RENDEZVOUS. Europe's defender against Communism greets the standard-bearer of the international workers' fight against Fascism over the body of defeated Poland. *Cartoon by Low*, 20 September 1939.

Europe in August 1914 it had been for the most part a figure of speech. In 1939 it was literal truth. England blundered home after nightfall along streets that were hardly lit at all, in buses and trains with windows half-painted over, with blinds drawn, and with interior illumination suitable for sick rooms for the dying. The wholesale evacuation, to country towns and villages in 'safe' areas, of schoolchildren and expectant mothers from the great industrial centres turned millions into the least likeable of refugees, those who had fled from a disaster that had not occurred. With a painful shock, the immemorial country towns and country houses of England discovered for the first time what the other half of the population looked like, sounded like, smelt like and wetted the bed like. For their part, town children took quick dislike to the tree-clothed beauties of the English rural landscape, with its lack of cinemas and fish-and-chip shops; and the expectant mothers wandered disconsolate about the country lanes until, after a week or so, they could endure it no more, and went back home.

For stimulus, the politicians could offer only abstract nouns. There was understandable haste to insist that the rapid destruction of Poland was a minor irrelevance. In his 'storms and gales' speech Churchill had said:

This is not a question of fighting for Danzig or for Poland. . . . It is a war to establish on impregnable rocks the rights of the individual, and it is a war to establish and revive the stature of man.

Chamberlain's version was:

It is the evil things we shall be fighting against – brute force, bad faith, injustice, oppression and persecution.

Nevile Henderson, writing in December 1939 an account of his stewardship in Berlin in his *Failure of a Mission*, insisted likewise:

We are not fighting about Danzig, or the Corridor, or what should be the line of demarcation between the German Reich and independent Czech or Polish republics. The shifting sands of Eastern Europe are not our real concern. We are crusaders, at war on behalf of Christian ideals versus pagan doctrines.

Yet over it all brooded the huge doubt: Churchill apart, for his line had been all too clear for all too long, how could these men who, for years had been praising and flattering Hitler and almost snarling at Englishmen who criticized him, suddenly transform themselves into crusaders against him or, more important, turn fundamentally bored and frightened Englishmen in general into fellow-crusaders?

Nor was the national mood helped by the *volte-face* at the other end of Europe. It was awkward enough for Conservatives that Hitler had suddenly proved wrong their belief that he was Europe's bulwark against Communism; but for considerable numbers on the Left it was the prospect of fighting Hitler with the U.S.S.R. as an ally that had seemed the one guarantee that it would not be a war of the bad old 1914 sort, but a peoples' crusade against Fascism. Now that Russia was in league with Hitler, a whole decade of innocent illusions had been destroyed. At first, some Leftists could find no alternative to joining the Communists and adopting their proposition that the workers of the world were being endangered by a revival of aggressive *Entente* Imperialism. Others gave up in despair; a despair deepened by the absence of any discernible answer to the question how any war could be won with both Nazi Germany and Soviet Russia on the opposing side. It was reported from California, where a small colony of England's literary pacifists and former friends of the people were now living, that W. H. Auden had come to the conclusion that 'life was false to formula'. It was a highly unoriginal discovery, but it certainly applied to the war of 1939–40: no formula could make much sense of it. Confusion was even worse confounded when, by November 1939, the Government, having still made no move against Germany, began to consider going to the rescue of yet another small state, Finland.

In September and October, the U.S.S.R. had persuaded Estonia, Latvia and Lithuania to admit Russian troops on to their soil and had opened negotiations with Finland for the cession to Russia of various areas of strategic importance. The Finns resisted Russian demands, and Soviet

forces invaded Finland on 30 November. The Russians made small progress during the winter of 1939–40 owing to determined Finnish resistance,
and it was not until March 1940 that Finland capitulated and ceded to
Russia the territory required.

When the Russians first attacked Finland the League of Nations twitched
itself out of its *rigor mortis* and formally condemned Russian aggression;
the United Kingdom sought to provide material aid to Finland, and permitted the departure of volunteers. By mid-February, when it was too late,
direct military aid was being contemplated. All through the winter,
Churchill, whom Chamberlain had made First Lord of the Admiralty
when war began, agitated for naval and military action at the Norwegian
port of Narvik. It was through Narvik that the Germans were obtaining
Swedish iron-ore, on which they were greatly dependent now that they
could get none from Lorraine; and it was also the point at which troops
might be disembarked for action in Finland. The Cabinet would not consent, and Churchill had to content himself with glowering rhetoric:

All Scandinavia dwells brooding under Nazi and Bolshevik threats. Only
Finland, superb, nay sublime, in the jaws of peril, shows what free men can
do. . . . If the light of freedom, which still burns in the frozen north, should
be finally quenched, it might well herald a return to the Dark Ages. . . . But
what would happen if all these neutral nations were. . . . to do their duty in
accordance with the Covenant of the League and stand together with the
British and French empires against aggression and wrong?[1]

After the fall of Finland, however, it was agreed that mines were to be
laid in Norwegian territorial waters, as originally proposed by Churchill in
the middle of December. The date fixed for the operation was 8 April 1940
and plans were made, if the Germans took counter-measures, to capture
Narvik, Trondheim and Bergen.

On 7 April a substantial German naval force was at sea. It was allowed to
proceed to Norway because the Commander-in-Chief, Home Fleet, was
convinced its intention was to move into Atlantic waters. The consequence
was that although the British had overwhelming naval superiority, and
troops at Rosyth and in the Clyde on the point of departure for Scandinavia, the Germans were able to seize Norwegian ports and aerodromes
without interference, particularly as their merchant ships had for days past
been proceeding to Norway not empty, as had been assumed, but full of
supplies and troops. In the two days, 9–10 April 1940, Germany obtained
complete control of Norway; at the same time Denmark was invaded and
occupied also.

Owing to German air superiority in Norway, British counter-measures
were unavailing. Troops were landed on 14 and 17 April at Namsos and
Andalsnes, but had to be withdrawn after a fortnight. A similar attempt
at Trondheim was equally unsuccessful and only at Narvik farther north

[1] House of Commons, 20 January 1940.

was it found possible to effect a foothold, and then not until the end of May.

The swift triumph of Hitler's hazardous gamble in Norway brought about the downfall of Chamberlain, after two days of memorable parliamentary debate on 7-8 May 1940. The starting-point of the revolution, however, was a remark which Chamberlain had made in the course of a speech to a Conservative Party gathering on 4 April:

... when war did break out German preparations were far ahead of our own and it was natural then to expect that the enemy would take advantage of his initial superiority to make an endeavour to overwhelm us and France before we had time to make good our deficiencies. Is it not a very extraordinary thing that no such attempt was made? Whatever may be the reason ... one thing is certain: he missed the bus.

Had this simple, homely phrase been used earlier in the year it might have been noted merely as one more example of the kind of thing Earl Winterton doubtless had in mind when he said in the Commons on 7 May:

There are too many leaders of opinion in this country addressing the nation as if it mainly consisted of maiden aunts and old women in trousers.

Coming as it did only a day or two before Hitler's most spectacular triumph so far, and one achieved at the expense of the Royal Navy, it was never forgiven.

The mood of the Commons and (it is for once probably true to say) the mood of the nation as a whole was summed up in the words of the Tory Imperialist, Leopold Amery on 7 May: *We cannot go on as we are.* He proved remarkably successful in expressing the country's wearied disgust with a Government whose every move had seemed stamped with futility and failure. He quoted against them Cromwell's words to the Rump:

You have sat too long here for any good you have been doing. Depart, I say, and let us have done with you. In the name of God, go.

Amery insisted later that he used these words as his climax only because he felt himself

swept forward by the surge of feeling which my speech had worked up on the benches round me.

He was not, he asserts, aiming at

a dramatic finish, but for a practical purpose: to bring down the Government if I could.

So accurately had this relatively isolated Tory spoken for England that when he sat down,

I knew I had done what I meant to do. I had driven the nail home. What is more I felt, by the look on the face of the Ministers who had come in to crowd the Front Bench, that they knew it too.[1]

[1] Quotations from L. S. Amery, *My Political Life*, Vol. III, p. 362.

From all sides the Government was attacked for dilatoriness and facile optimism. Herbert Morrison declared:

. . . before the war and during the war we have felt that the whole spirit, tempo and temperament of at least some ministers have been wrong, inadequate and unsuitable . . . they lacked courage, initiative, imagination, psychological understanding, liveliness and self-respect in the conduct of foreign policy, so I feel that the absence of those qualities has manifested itself in the actual conduct of war.

He specified the three inadequate ministers as Chamberlain, Hoare and Simon, and went on to announce that Labour would divide the House. He appealed to members

in all parts of the House to realize to the full the responsibility of . . . a vote which, broadly, will indicate whether they are content with the conduct of affairs or whether they are apprehensive about the conduct of affairs. . . . I ask that the vote of the House shall represent the spirit of the country.

It was this that provoked Chamberlain to make his last, and fatal, political misjudgement. He intervened to say that Morrison had thrown out a challenge to the Government in general,

and the attack which he has made on them, and upon me in particular, makes it graver still. . . . I do not seek to evade criticism, but I say this to my friends in the House – and I have friends in the House. No Government can prosecute a war efficiently unless it has public and Parliamentary support. I accept the challenge. I welcome it indeed. At least we shall see who is with us and who is against us, and I call on my friends to support us in the Lobby tonight.

The remark gave Lloyd George an opening he was too experienced to resist:

It is not a question of who are the Prime Minister's friends. It is a far bigger issue. The Prime Minister must remember that he has met this formidable foe of ours in peace and war. He has always been worsted. He is not in a position to put it on the grounds of friendship. He has appealed for sacrifice. . . . I say solemnly that the Prime Minister should give an example of sacrifice, because there is nothing which can contribute more to victory in this war than that he should sacrifice the seals of office.

A little later, Duff Cooper, too, expressed regret at Chamberlain's reference to his 'friends' and announced that he would vote against the Government. Another Conservative, Commander Bower, indicated that he would do the same, and echoed Amery:

My view is that the dead hand must go. This sort of thing cannot go on any longer.

In spite, therefore, of a vigorous defence of the Government by Churchill who, as First Lord of the Admiralty, might be thought to have had more responsibility for the Norwegian fiasco than any other minister, the Government's majority when the House divided was only 81 instead of a normal figure of over 200. Apart from many Conservative abstentions, some forty Conservatives voted against the Government; among them were Amery and Duff Cooper, Harold Macmillan, Quintin Hogg and John Profumo.

Chamberlain realized at once that there must be a new Government. He found that the Tory rebels, who appointed Amery as their spokesman, would not serve unless Labour and Liberal men were brought into the Government, and that Labour would not enter any Government of which he was Prime Minister. For a short time there was the possibility of the succession going to Lord Halifax; Attlee might then be in charge of the political scene as leader of the Commons, and Churchill control the war as Minister of Defence. Churchill carefully showed no signs of being willing to serve under Halifax; Halifax thought a Prime Minister in the Lords would be undesirable; and news of a German invasion of Holland gave sharper edge to the feeling that a manifestly resolute leader was now essential. On 10 May 1940, Churchill was summoned to the Palace, and by midnight had made his first appointments, constructing a War Cabinet of five: himself, as Prime Minister and Minister of Defence; Attlee, as Lord Privy Seal and in effect Deputy Prime Minister; Chamberlain, as Lord President; Lord Halifax, as Foreign Secretary; and Arthur Greenwood, as Minister without Portfolio.

When Lloyd George had become Prime Minister in 1916 he confessed to feelings of anxiety; Churchill, in 1940, to none.

. . . as I went to bed at about 3 a.m. I was conscious of a profound sense of relief. . . . I could not be reproached either for making the war or with want of preparation for it. I thought I knew a great deal about it all, and I was sure I should not fail.[1]

Churchill enjoyed many advantages as wartime Prime Minister compared with Lloyd George. There could be no suspicion, as there had been in 1916, that his accession to power was the consequence of a backstairs intrigue; his elevation was the result of the freely and openly expressed demand of the Labour and Liberal Parties and of the more vigorous elements in the Conservative Party. He achieved his position, unlike Lloyd George, without dividing his own party: he would not jettison Chamberlain, much as Labour would have liked him to, and Chamberlain willingly agreed, as Asquith had not, to serve under his successor. Although the Labour Party felt that it was they who had promoted Churchill, and gave him the loudest cheers when he first took his place in the Commons as Prime Minister, he owed his appointment first and foremost to the action of unimpeachably patriotic Tories; yet the most loyal of Chamberlain's followers were compelled at least into acquiescence on seeing their chief at the new Prime Minister's side. Moreover, although, as an even more impetuous amateur strategist than Lloyd George, Churchill vexed and

[1] Churchill, *The Gathering Storm*, p. 589.

harassed his Chiefs of Staff and made grave errors of judgement, he understood and admired the military way of life. This preserved him from Lloyd George's sometimes dangerous radical suspicion that generals were *ex officio* fools or enemies of the people. Above all, both for good and for evil, Churchill brought to his task not the meretricious emotions of a wizard of mass-oratory but the true emotions of a man of feeling; and by the spring of 1940 the English found themselves in a position from which they could only extricate themselves by a surge of genuine emotion. In his first speech to the Commons as Prime Minister on 13 May 1940 he said:

I would say to the House, as I said to those who have joined this Government: 'I have nothing to offer but blood, toil, tears and sweat.'

The words did not pass into history because they were very meaningful in the context of a hand-round of Government jobs. They are memorable because of the response they elicited from a people who, at long last, had a political chief who sought, not to dope them with sedative complacencies, but to inspire them to resolute and unsparing exertion. For nearly twenty years England had been governed by bloodless politicians who had appeared to possess neither sweat-glands nor tear-ducts and to assume that everybody in the country was of like nature. Amery's 'We cannot go on as we are,' and Winterton's reference to 'maiden aunts and old women in trousers' had made clear the nation's need. Churchill's reply had come at once.

Chamberlain did not long survive his displacement as Prime Minister. During the summer he underwent several operations for cancer, resigned from the Cabinet on 3 October and died on 9 November 1940. Nothing in his training or his temperament had fitted him for the hazardous tasks of coping with the international turmoil of 1937–39; it was a misfortune for his country and himself that as a merely goodish second-class mind he had shown himself head and shoulders above the third-class men with whom Baldwin had chosen to surround himself. Obstinate, aloof and obtuse as he was, conscious of his rectitude and, justifiably enough, of his exceptional integrity, he had at every turn been outmanœuvred by the supple, sinister minds with whom he had been dealing abroad, while arrogantly despising political critics at home and persistently underrating the intelligence and temper of the nation at large. He was enclosed so firmly, and apparently so smugly, within the limits of his narrow, though clear, administrative mind that his public personality was more unattractive than that of almost any other prominent politician of the time; and the affectionate loyalty with which he was regarded by those who were close to him was, to the rest of the world, incomprehensible. Nothing became his political career so much as its close. His swift acceptance of office under Churchill (who had no doubt at all of Chamberlain's levelheaded competence) spared his party and country much bitterness, and his quiet doggedness during the critical summer of 1940, as he grappled with a fatal illness, enabled him at the last to secure the general respect and sympathy which, except during the short-lived hysteria of Munich, had always hitherto seemed properly denied to him.

Between 10 May and 15 May, Churchill filled the rest of his Government posts. Labour was well represented: Herbert Morrison went to the Ministry of Supply and later to the Home Office; Ernest Bevin became Minister of Labour and National Service; A. V. Alexander went to the Admiralty, where he had served in MacDonald's second Government; Hugh Dalton was appointed to the Ministry of Economic Warfare. Other significant appointments were those of Lord Beaverbrook, who had last held office as Minister of Propaganda in the summer of 1918, and who now took the vital post of Minister of Aircraft Production; and of Lord Woolton, a prominent figure in the world of retail trading, who became Minister of Food. Duff Cooper and Amery also received appointments, Eden became War Minister, and the liberal leader, Sir Archibald Sinclair, became Air Minister. Junior posts were found for Viscount Cranborne, who had resigned with Eden in 1938; for Harold Macmillan; and for the bustling Labour M.P. for Jarrow, Ellen Wilkinson, author of *The Town That Was Murdered*. No post was found for Sir Samuel Hoare, who was shortly afterwards sent as British Ambassador to Franco's Spain, and frequently referred to thereafter as 'the M.P. for Madrid'; and Sir John Simon, the other chief target of Opposition and back-bench Tory criticism, was carefully side-tracked into the position of Lord Chancellor where it was thought he would be 'innocuous'.[1]

The new Prime Minister had thus equipped himself with what was, potentially, the ablest administration to conduct the nation's affairs since 1908. Its achievements were considerable. It gave the lift to the national morale without which the trials of 1940-41 might not have been surmounted, and then piloted it, with zest and skill, through the worst of the strategic and diplomatic hazards of a world-wide war; it so organized and sustained the civilian population that the stresses imposed by total war were endured with unexpected equanimity; and it provided the blueprints and in some cases the administrative framework, of most of the social reforms implemented after its dissolution in 1945.

It achieved so much because, in practice, it adopted the system of separated spheres of responsibility that Lloyd George had proposed to Asquith in 1916, and which true friends of both men ever after wished they had been able to agree upon. In effect, Churchill concentrated on the strategy and diplomacy of war, leaving Attlee, John Anderson[2], Woolton,

[1] Attlee's word, according to Dalton, *The Fateful Years*, p. 313.
[2] See also page 412.

Bevin and Morrison to deal with the home front and the plans for post-war reconstruction. Churchill was always indisputably at the helm; but his part in the civilian aspects of the Government's work normally took the form of unpredictable incursions into matters of detail, suddenly triggered off by the impact upon his lively mind of an item lighted upon by chance in a lengthy Cabinet paper which he had probably only glanced at or skimmed through. This ability to seize on particular points and make a great (and sometimes salutary) fuss about them (which he applied also to matters of defence) was of considerable value in keeping his colleagues and subordinates up to the mark. It was impossible to guess in advance what the Prime Minister would want to probe into; almost anything, from the look of the flag displayed by the Admiralty in Whitehall to the name to be given to local authority canteens, or the propriety of a particular sequence in an Army training film that was also to be exhibited to the general public, might be the subject of a minute, a reprimand, a long speech in Cabinet, or a dramatic order to halt or drastically revise carefully prepared plans well after the eleventh hour. Nevertheless, it was to the waging of war and the conduct of inter-Allied diplomacy that Churchill devoted himself most whole-heartedly; over less grandiose problems, like the control of food and materials and of civilian labour, his mind merely flashed intermittent lightning, perhaps striking terror or creating confusion or, on other occasions, casting sudden illumination. It was as a consequence of the merely sporadic nature of his contacts with anything save the war itself that Churchill proved so out of touch with the workaday civilian world when the war ended.

To his chosen role as the nation's war leader, Churchill brought exceptional physical vigour, an agile, wide-ranging mind and resolute pugnacity. The unifying force, giving coherence and relevance to these otherwise potentially disruptive qualities, was an epic sense of history which, though permanent in him throughout his life, was also appropriate to the world around him only in wartime. His political career had been the disappointment it was until 1940 precisely because he tended to inflate everything that happened into an epoch-making event that would reverberate through history, and which therefore required men to behave, for example, over the success of the Bolsheviks in 1917, or the outbreak of the General Strike, as though they would be answerable throughout all succeeding ages for the smallest deficiency in aggressiveness. When least under control, this tendency inflicted him with a kind of historical elephantiasis; as when he fulminated against the modest proposals for a measure of self-government in India in 1931, or represented the abdication of Edward VIII as an act that would have throne-shaking effects in the future, or claimed that the election of a Labour Government in 1945 would prelude the creation of an Anglo-Saxon Gestapo. In wartime, however, this ability always to think and act, and above all to speak, in grand historic terms, communicated to all concerned in the higher direction of the war, and to many whose task was merely to obey orders, something of his own sense of being a privileged participant in a struggle of epic grandeur. It was his rhetorical skill in representing all the tasks and all the setbacks of total war, however severe, as pregnant acts within the working out of a high poetic drama that made Churchill, above all in 1940 and 1941, so effective a leader: with it, he shielded from weariness and defeatism not only himself but all who were in any way within reach of his voice or personality.

At close quarters, Churchill's cast of mind made him difficult to work with. To the essential business of conducting this great clash of arms at the grand climax of human history, all mundane affairs, like reasonable hours of work or methodical attention to the rules of procedure, were regularly subordinated. What protected Churchill from the fury that his often unreasonable methods would have aroused, had he been a lesser man, was everyone's awareness of his infectious courage, his extraordinary energy, his warmth of feeling, and his disarming ability to transform himself on the instant from an outrageous and hectoring taskmaster into a twinkling-eyed jester.

In the management of his Government he was protected, not only by his own outstanding personality, but by the unusual character of his principal colleagues. Attlee admirably counter-balanced Churchill's theatrical sense of destiny by his self-effacing matter-of-factness; it was perhaps symbolic that, whereas Churchill had planned the Gallipoli campaign as part of a grand strategy in 1915, Attlee, as a major in an infantry regiment, had actually commanded troops during the landings and thus knew that warfare involved flies and lice and dysentery and was not solely a matter for rhetoric. In the routine sense of the word, neither Sir John Anderson, a civil servant, nor Ernest Bevin, a trade union organizer, nor Lord Woolton, a pillar of the retail trade, was a career politician like the men who had intrigued so steadily, first against Asquith and then against Lloyd George, during the first German war. Eden was Churchill's devoted 'Heir Apparent' and, as Secretary for War and then Foreign Secretary, as loyal and devoted despite recurrent 'shouting matches' as, in his own particular sphere, was Sir Alan Brooke, when he succeeded Dill as C.I.G.S. And just as Eden was, throughout the period, a 'young' Conservative at odds with the established leaders of the 1930's, so, from the opposite party position, Dalton, though hardly less admiring of Churchill, had little of the conformist Labour politician about him.

In consequence, the Churchill Government was less trammelled by political orthodoxy, whether of the Left or of the Right, than any other twentieth-century British Government. It was the only one with a genuine claim to the title 'National', and the extent of Churchill's ascendancy over it has possibly prevented it from receiving, as a team, the recognition properly due to it.

35 · 'A Colossal Military Disaster', 1940

On 10 May 1940, the day Churchill became Prime Minister, the war in western Europe at last began, with a German invasion of Holland, Belgium and Luxembourg. By 4 June most British troops had been withdrawn from continental soil and, by 25 June, land fighting on European soil had virtually come to an end. The Germans took Copenhagen on 9 April, Oslo on 10 April, The Hague on 14 May, Brussels on 17 May and Paris on 14 June.

When war had officially begun in the previous September, Hitler kept to his promise not to fight on two fronts. He gave instructions that nothing should be done on the Western Front to provoke the French to attack, so that, as intended, he could complete his plans for Poland undisturbed. No decision to fight in the west was made by Hitler until 27 September 1939, and even then it was received with the greatest apprehension by his generals. The German professional view (and Hitler certainly shared it in the first week of September 1939) was that the efforts made in Germany since 1933 had produced an army capable of defeating Poland but not France.

The future might have been different had the French taken advantage, in September 1939, of the absence of fifty-nine divisions of the best German fighting troops in Poland. In the west at that time, only forty-six German divisions faced eighty French divisions and the four divisions of the B.E.F. The Germans' Siegfried Line was not strongly held and had been hastily constructed. The French and British had superiority both in tanks and aircraft, and the rate of output of the aircraft industry in the two countries greatly exceeded the German output.

The decision not to take the offensive in the autumn of 1939 was a French decision and a calculated one. General Gamelin of France, the Supreme Commander of the Allied forces, was convinced, from experience of the First World War, that an offensive strategy was bound to fail. The most he would contemplate, therefore, was to sit tight along the Maginot Line which guarded the French frontier with Germany, and dispose his main forces in readiness to move forward against a future German attack either across Belgium into Flanders or through the thickly wooded Ardennes. During the waiting period, both French and British forces would be built up, so that when the Germans did move forward they would break in pieces against the Allied Armies advancing along one heavily-manned continuous front.

By contrast, Hitler and his generals eventually decided, in February 1940, to concentrate the main weight of the attack on an all-out *Blitzkrieg*, using tanks, supported by aircraft, mechanized artillery and motorized infantry, to pierce the Allied line and split the Anglo-French Armies in two. It was the desperate gamble of men conscious of military weakness; and against a determined, competently-led opponent it might well have failed.

To breach the Allied line in this *Blitzkrieg* required that the greatest German pressure be directed across the Meuse between Namur and Sedan. Gamelin, however, believed the main German thrust would come from the north. He disposed his forces accordingly, leaving the weakest of his armies guarding the precise area, between Namur and Sedan, on which the Germans were to concentrate their main thrusts. Gamelin considered that if the Germans did in fact attack in that region they would first have to bring up masses of artillery. This would give him time to adjust his forces accordingly. He did not believe that the technique of the *Blitzkrieg* would be employed on the Western Front.

The German plan of attack included, naturally enough, the violation of Dutch and Belgian neutrality, and, to meet this, the Allies made their first forward moves. The B.E.F., under Lord Gort, moved into Belgium. On its left, the French Seventh Army moved into Holland and on its right the French First Army also moved into Belgium. Connecting the French First Army with the Maginot Line, were the French Ninth and Second Armies.

These moves were exactly suited to facilitate the execution of the German intention. On the left of the B.E.F. the French Seventh Army was soon in retreat, with most of its strength lost, owing to the swift capitulation of the Dutch. On the B.E.F.'s right, the Germans speedily reached and crossed the Meuse, breaching the First Army's front, and overwhelming the poorly-armed and badly-led Ninth Army. Farther south, at Sedan, the French Second Army also broke; its commanders refused to believe that the advancing German tanks were more than a preliminary indication of an attack that was yet to come, and, when the full *Blitzkrieg* burst swiftly upon them, the men cracked, not having been trained to cope with it.

By 20 May, only ten days after the German offensive had begun, German Panzers had reached the sea at the mouth of the Somme beyond Abbeville. On 25th May, Boulogne fell; on the next day, Calais. The French and British Armies in Belgium were now completely cut off from the French Armies in the south. On 28 May, his army having been defeated, King Leopold ordered the cessation of Belgian resistance. As early as 19 May,

Gort had warned London that it might be necessary to consider the evacuation of the B.E.F. through the Channel Ports. On the same day, Gamelin had similarly warned his own authorities that evacuation of certain forces might become necessary.

Nevertheless, even at this stage, all might not have been lost. The Panzer corridor which the Germans had now created between the Allied Armies was, as they fully realized, extremely vulnerable; and they were much disturbed when Gort launched a strong counter-attack against it at Arras on 21 May. They feared their armoured forces might be cut off before their infantry could come up to support them. Unfortunately, Gort received no assistance from the French; similar, though less dangerous, counter-attacks from the south by a French armoured division under Colonel de Gaulle had likewise produced no permanent effect through lack of support. On 25 May, with the Belgians in the north obviously at the end of their powers, Gort ordered the abandonment of all attempts to counter-attack to the south. There was now instead, to be a fighting retreat, preparatory to evacuation by sea. Had Gort not, by this decision, been able at once to switch additional troops from the south to the north, where the Belgians were collapsing, the Germans might have cut the B.E.F. off from the sea. General Blanchard, the French Commander in the north, also issued orders, later the same day, for a general retreat upon a bridgehead around Dunkirk.

On 26 May, Admiral Ramsay, at the head of the Navy's Dover Command, began to put in hand his prepared plans for the dispatch of ships to Dunkirk to evacuate the B.E.F.; and on the evening of that day almost 28,000 men had already been brought back to Dover. The view in London had been that only between 30,000 and 45,000 men would be saved altogether. General Ironside, the C.I.G.S., thought that nothing but a miracle would prevent the loss of all Britain's trained soldiers and that he would never see Gort again. In the event, by 3 June, over 224,000 British troops, out of a total strength of just under 400,000 when the campaign began, had been brought back, together with 142,000 French troops.

Many factors contributed to what was thought of as the 'miracle' of Dunkirk. The pursuit of the retreating B.E.F. by German armour was halted on 23 May because the B.E.F. was concentrating within an area unsuited to tanks, and putting up a grim resistance which was likely to cost the Germans heavy losses which, after the strains imposed on their vehicles by the advance from the Meuse, they could not afford. Furthermore, it was considered prudent to halt and regroup the German armoured divisions for the main attack across the Somme, against what were still presumed to be strong and formidable French Armies. Relevant also was the absence from the Dunkirk perimeter of two armoured German divisions engaged against the still stubborn defenders of Boulogne and Calais. The

B.E.F., under Gort's general direction, was thus able to fight a series of courageous and ultimately successful actions to hold the enemy back and keep the corridors of retreat open; in these engagements, Generals Brooke, Alexander and Montgomery were all prominent.

Contributory, also, was the decision that the Luftwaffe rather than the Army should be given the main responsibility for destroying the retreating Allied forces. The Luftwaffe had been much weakened by its successful support of the German Army's advance; and although it inflicted heavy damage during the days of evacuation, it concentrated on Dunkirk and the beaches instead of consistently bombing the heavily over-loaded shipping and the congested ports of disembarkation on the Kent coast. Like the German Army, the German Air Force was unable to drive its advantage finally home; both were overstrained by their previous successes, and both were unprepared for the opportunities which had so unexpectedly opened to them. For this reason, the somewhat limited number of patrols the R.A.F. thought compatible with its prime duty of reserving itself for the ultimate defence of the United Kingdom provided at least adequate air cover.

Combined as it was with the determination and courage of the men of the B.E.F. as they held off the German attacks on their ever-shrinking bridgehead, the greatest contribution was made by the Navy. As a result of the still-continuing Norwegian campaign,[1] the Germany Navy had lost half its destroyers and nearly a third of its cruiser strength and, short though the British themselves were of destroyers, the Germans did not effectively challenge British command of the Channel during the evacuation period. Under Admiral Ramsay's skilful direction, cross-channel steamers and small ships of all sorts were called into service to supplement the Navy's own vessels, and were organized to help transport troops from the Dunkirk beaches. The crews of many of these small ships, most of them civilians unfortified by service discipline, performed individual miracles of resource and endurance. They were liable to attack from dive bombers, from German guns and German E-boats, or to be run down in the dark by vessels of their own crowding armada. The smaller ones might be swamped when suddenly overcrowded by too many embarking soldiers, and the larger could be terrifyingly delayed off-shore by men who could only be taken on slowly because they had to wade out to their necks in order to get on board. Out of the total of nearly 700 British vessels of all sorts and sizes which took part, just over 220 were sunk. Included in this total were six destroyers; at least four others were damaged. The Dunkirk evacuation was thus more than a matter of 'little ships'. It was also a major naval engagement.

[1] The British captured Narvik on 28 May; but all operations in Norway were ended on 10 June 1940.

· · · · ·

With the elimination of the northern Armies, the French were now heavily outnumbered on a thinly-held front from the Somme to the Maginot Line. The Germans attacked on 5 June, and by 14 June had reached Paris, from which the French Government withdrew, declaring it an open city. By 17 June, the Maginot Line had been outflanked and the French Armies had virtually disintegrated. On that day Marshal Pétain became Prime Minister and asked for an armistice. Signed on 22 June, the terms provided for the German occupation of three-fifths of France: the whole area north of a line from Geneva to Tours and the whole of the Atlantic coastline.

The war in the west had been won; and in the six weeks long ago prescribed in the Schlieffen Plan. Where Moltke had failed, Hitler had been allowed to succeed.

The events of May 1940, culminating in the Dunkirk evacuation and the fall of France, destroyed the uncertain foundations on which British foreign policy had been so hazardously based since the signature of the *entente* in 1904. Ever since that date, Britain's chance of preventing German domination of western Europe had depended upon the ability of the French to hold the Germans off until the British could themselves mobilize an army of continental effectiveness, since the British were unwilling to have a large army in peacetime and often, in the 1930's, doubted the need to send an expeditionary force to Europe at all. Thus, everything would turn on the strategic competence of the French High Command and on the morale of the French Army, and most perilously so in the first weeks of general war, when the British military contribution to the struggle would be so small in comparison that the C-in-C of the B.E.F. could have little say in the formulation and execution of strategy.

Yet this was to stake everything on the myth that France produced brilliant soldiers endowed with exceptional understanding of the arts of warfare; whereas the facts suggested that the French had been conspicuously unsuccessful soldiers and strategists ever since Waterloo. The French had been unable to cope effectively with the Habsburgs in 1859 or the Mexicans in 1863. They had produced wrong strategic plans for the campaign in the Crimea, for the war of 1870, and for the war of 1914; and, true to their tradition, produced the wrong one for 1940. In the light of how the French had fared in 1870 and were to fare again in 1940, it is possible to view the nervousness of Sir John French in August 1914 as grounded in a great deal of wisdom, Lloyd George's passionate search for an Allied (i.e. French) generalissimo in 1917 as flirtation with military catastrophe, and Haig's determination not to be left to work alongside Pétain in 1918 as a decision both prudent and prescient. And Gort's decision to do in 1940 what Sir John French had been prevented from doing in 1914, and disengage his forces from the main French Armies, saved over a quarter of a million troops (and their leaders, such as Brooke, Alexander,

Montgomery) who would otherwise have been herded into German prison camps. Jokes about the badness of British generals obscured the truth that French generals were no better. Throughout the 1930's, and during the war itself, the brilliant political cartoonist, Low, persuaded most of the population that a drooping-moustached, bullet-headed old man, apparently always just emerging from a Turkish bath, and entitled Colonel Blimp, was a representative British commander. In truth, Colonel Blimp was not unrepresentative of the higher ranks in the Army, and of the General Staff, before 1938. But the truer cause of the catastrophe of 1940 was not the prejudices of retired British colonels but the incompetence of French generals and marshals still in uniform.

To prevent the calamities of 1940 it was not necessary to have created a vast British peacetime army. Intelligently equipped and led, the forces at the disposal of the French and British were adequate for an offensive in September 1939 and for the defensive in May 1940; the attempt to fix the blame for what happened on the pacific temper of the British electorate during the previous twenty years is beside the point. Virtually all the leading politicians, both the appeasers and their opponents, had had the wrong priorities: Germany could not be halted by strengthening the defences of the United Kingdom and leaving the French to do the bulk of the land-fighting. The delusion was persisted in because it seemed to eliminate the need for genuine political co-operation (which the British did not like), for joint military planning (which was not welcome to the French) or for intelligent examination (a process unacceptable to both sides) of how, by adopting new methods of mobile warfare, the mass slaughter of 1914–18 could be avoided. Yet strategic and tactical errors by Frenchmen on the outbreak of war could bring disaster to both countries within six weeks, as nearly happened in 1914 and actually happened in 1940.

The heavy reliance of the British on the French left them with few other resources for defeating Germany. The Royal Navy and the R.A.F. were, to the end, competent chiefly for the defence of the United Kingdom itself, and their role in this respect was fulfilled with resounding success in the months immediately after Dunkirk. All, however, that these arms (given a lack of troops) could contribute to an offensive (and to be on the defensive against Germany solved nothing) were the blockade and aerial bombardment. But the experience of the First World War showed that blockade was effective only as a means of facilitating the victory of armies on the ground; by itself it was too slow. As for aerial bombing, a cool appraisal of the situation might have led, well before real hostilities opened in 1940, to the view that mass-bombing, though an effective preliminary to the invasion of small countries with few large centres of industry and population, was unlikely to be effective against great States, either as a wrecker of industrial power or as a destroyer of morale.

The withdrawal from Dunkirk and the fall of France, though not destroying the capacity of the United Kingdom to defend itself, did therefore destroy its capacity to wage offensive war against Germany on the ground. More than that: it ended Britain's traditional role as the arbiter of Europe. This had been carried out, against the French, with the aid of the Dutch or of the Austrians and the Prussians; and, against the Germans, with the aid of the French. But with all Europe under German control, and with Russia in alliance with Germany, nothing but massive action by the United States could now drive Germany back from western Europe; and, although Hitler doubtless had plans for dismantling the British Empire after victory, so also had the United States. And when, in due course, Russia was forced into the war by Hitler, Britain was destined to find herself in alliance with two greater partners, neither of whom wished her well as an imperial power. It was clear that the United Kingdom would emerge from the war a victorious but enfeebled pensionary, much as the Dutch had emerged, in relation to their British allies, after the wars against Louis XIV. All this was implicit in the events of May and June 1940.

36 · The Few, the Tools and the Job, 1940

Much was written at the time, and much has been written since, about the heartening effects of the successful evacuation of the B.E.F., and of the 'Dunkirk spirit' which it is said to have engendered. Yet the evacuation was regarded less as a victory for the skill and courage of the armed forces than as a miraculous deliverance; and followed, as it soon was, by the fall of France it was seen principally as a prelude to air bombing and invasion. And although Mussolini's declaration of war just before the French armistice caused more disgust than trepidation, it served to underline the total nature of Europe's subjugation and the magnitude of the apparent threat to the British homeland and its imperial communications. Yet, at long last, the issue was drastically simple: all the complications of the international scene, with its confusing vortex of unnerving choices and unassessable contingencies had at last been swept away, leaving only the stark question of survival. It was so stark, and there were so few grounds for optimism, that Churchill at once inaugurated a tremendous propaganda campaign to exalt the national morale and to prevent it sagging beneath the weight of too much responsibility. Emotional rhetoric flowed from Westminster and over the nation's radios. Immediately after the evacuation, and before the fall of France, he set the tone of the next few months. Instead of the complacencies of the Chamberlain era there was a grim summons to resolution. Our thankfulness over Dunkirk must not, he said,

blind us to the fact that what has happened in France and Belgium is a colossal military disaster,

and he turned at once to the possibility of air attack and invasion. No absolute security against invasion had ever existed in our history:

We are assured that novel methods will be adopted, and when we see the originality of malice, the ingenuity of aggression, which our enemy displays, we may certainly prepare ourselves for every kind of novel stratagem, and every kind of brutal and treacherous manœuvre

His peroration was as famous as it was overdone:

. . . we shall not flag or fail, we shall go on to the end, we shall fight in France, we shall fight on the seas and oceans, we shall fight with growing strength and confidence in the air, we shall defend our island whatever the cost may be, we shall fight on the beaches, we shall fight on the landing grounds, we shall fight in the fields and in the streets, we shall fight in the hills, we shall never surrender. . . .

This was indeed invigorating; but it contained something else:

even if . . . this island or a large part of it, were subjugated and starving, then our Empire beyond the seas, armed and guarded by the British Fleet, would carry on the struggle until in God's good time the New World, with all its power and might, steps forth to the rescue and liberation of the old.

This oblique appeal to the U.S.A. for aid, paralleled in more desperate terms by Paul Reynaud on behalf of France on 10 and 13 June, was less noted at the time than the stirring call to national resistance. The Churchillian emphasis on the 'severity of the ordeal' ahead was repeated on 18 June when in the course of assessing the 'dread balance sheet' of dangers and hopes he called upon Englishmen to

show themselves capable of standing up to it like the brave men of Barcelona. . . .

Suddenly, Britain had shrunk. The Land of Hope and Glory had become, like Republican Spain or Poland, a small vulnerable outpost of freedom likely at any minute to be crushed by the monstrous might of Fascism. This was to overdo the shock treatment. Britain, to counter the threat of a German invasion, had the world's largest Navy and the world's best air defences. Elizabeth I, who lacked such advantages in 1588, had been at once more realistic and more masculine:

. . . and think foul scorn that Parma or Spain, or any prince of Europe should dare to invade the borders of my realm.

Moreover, Churchill once again signalled an S.O.S. to the United States:

if we fail, then the whole world, including the United States and all that we
have known and cared for, will sink into the abyss of a new dark age . . . Let
us therefore address ourselves to our duty, so bear ourselves that if the British
Commonwealth and Empire lasts for a thousand years men will still say, 'This
was their finest hour'.

Churchill's eloquence undoubtedly had a tonic effect. On 14 May, Eden,
as Secretary for War, had called for men between 17 and 65 who were not
engaged in military service to join a Local Defence Volunteer force. By
23 July, when the name of the force was changed to Home Guard, recruitment had to be suspended because over 1,300,000 men had enrolled. Considering how heavily manpower was already absorbed in industry, with
much overtime, and in air raid precaution services, this readiness to undertake the chores of part-time soldiering was remarkable. The Home Guard
was for long deficient in weapons. Its earliest members wore no distinguishing mark but an armband, and spent much time doing military drill by
shouldering broomsticks. The outward semblance of these would-be
defenders of their native soil against the swarms of paratroopers and fifth-
columnists with which the country was said to be threatened was thus for
some time as ludicrous as were many of the tasks that were allotted to them.
Nevertheless, the willingness of hard-working men to endure the frequent
parades and regular nightly guard duties 'protecting' vital points which
were not always vital, and which frequently lacked all means of communication with their headquarters had an emergency arisen, was one of the great
features of the months after Dunkirk. More vital was the success of the aircraft workers, under the promptings of Churchill's oratory, and the whirlwind organization of Beaverbrook as Minister of Aircraft Production, in
greatly increasing the output of new aircraft in the six months from May
to October. These examples, to name no others, show that the country
would eagerly respond to a lead, and suggest that its lethargy in previous
months and years was due mainly to the absence of leadership and to the
sedulous pretence of the pre-Churchillian National Government that there
was no real emergency.

The summer saw progress in the other aspect of the Churchillian
strategy, the move towards dependence upon the United States. In November 1939, Congress had passed a Neutrality Revision Act which allowed
arms to be sold to other States for cash provided they shipped them away
themselves. This, in effect, enabled the British to purchase arms for so
long as they could find the money and control the seas. In June 1940,
negotiations were opened for the dispatch of fifty old U.S. destroyers. In
return for the destroyers, which as it turned out were not needed and
arrived after the invasion threat was over, the United Kingdom gave the
U.S.A. long leases of naval and air bases in the West Indies, in Bermuda
and Newfoundland. Churchill thus described the deal:

Undoubtedly this process means that these two great organizations of the

English-speaking democracies, the British Empire and the United States, will have to be somewhat mixed up together in some of their affairs for mutual and general advantage. For my own part, looking out upon the future, I do not view the process with any misgivings. I could not stop it if I wished. No one could stop it. Like the Mississippi it just keeps rolling along.

It was perhaps impulsive of Churchill to be so eager to pay so high a price for what, after all, the United Kingdom did not urgently need. It was perhaps necessary to represent the country as being in sore straits, in order both to rouse morale at home and to help Roosevelt to overcome isolationist opposition in Congress. It was perhaps a good idea to woo the United States with a large generous gesture; and it was essential to secure United States assistance if Hitler was eventually to be defeated. But in 1940, the issue was, not the defeat of Hitler, but the defence of the United Kingdom against an invasion which never took place. The United Kingdom was not Poland or Republican Spain; nor was it the ramshackle France of the Third Republic. It was beyond the reach of a *Blitzkrieg*; and so little truth was there in the myth of German thoroughness that no plans for invasion of the United Kingdom had previously been drawn up, there was no German Navy large enough to protect an invasion force if it ever set forth, and if Göring's Luftwaffe tried to blast a way for invasion by smashing the R.A.F., the R.A.F. had long been preparing to fight it and was fortified by the invention of radar, to which the Germans had paid no attention.

Preliminary attacks by the Luftwaffe began in July 1940, the main attack in August. In practice, owing to the vulnerability of the heavy bomber, Göring had to confine his attacks to south-east England, employing at any one time about 400 bombers and the 700 fighters needed to protect them. The R.A.F. had available, on average, about 700 fighters and upwards of 1,400 pilots. Göring thus had too few fighters to achieve his two principal aims: to destroy R.A.F. installations on the ground and to destroy its fighters in the air. In the first week and a half of the main battle, the Germans lost 300 aircraft, and thanks to the efforts of the aircraft industry the R.A.F.'s available fighters had still not decreased. During the last week of August and the first week in September, the Luftwaffe succeeded in doing rather more damage on the ground, and inflicted relatively higher losses of aircraft on the R.A.F.; but this had been achieved by the diversion of more fighters to the task of protecting the bombers, so that the rather more urgent aim of destroying R.A.F. fighters in the air had perforce been neglected.

Nevertheless, the damage inflicted on fighter bases by 6 September was causing considerable anxiety. At this point, however, Hitler intervened. On 24 August some German bombers, not sure of their whereabouts, had dropped bombs on London, though causing only few casualties. In reply, the R.A.F. began a series of bombing raids on Berlin. On 7 September, Hitler therefore ordered intensive bombing of London as a reprisal.

Throughout the second week of September the bombing of London was particularly heavy, and created among the Germans the impression that victory could not be far off. In fact, the balance of resources was now swinging in favour of the R.A.F., which had more machines available by mid-September than in mid-July, whereas the Luftwaffe's effort was decreasing daily.

As the skies of south-eastern England were alive with battle by day and Londoners nightly endured what they came with a sort of melancholy pride to describe as 'the Blitz', everyone waited for the expected invasion. For reasons which are not very clear (with all western Europe in German control, intelligence was a difficult matter) it was concluded on the evening of 7 September, as London suffered the first day and night of 'the Blitz', that the German invasion was about to start. The Army and the Home Guard were summoned to a state of readiness. In fact, the Germans were rapidly running out of time. If a firm bridgehead was to be established on English soil before the winter, the preliminary orders for invasion could not be delayed after 17 September, and the pre-requisite air superiority was still not in sight. The Luftwaffe, therefore, made one last all-out gambler's bid on 15 September.

Two separate attacks were made on that day, in the morning and afternoon, so that, owing to shortages, some machines could do a double trip. The R.A.F. attacked German bombers and fighters with the utmost vigour on both occasions. At the end of the day, the British claimed to have destroyed 185 German aircraft and themselves to have lost only 25. The correct number of German machines destroyed was 60, though many more were damaged; nevertheless, the superiority of the R.A.F. over south-east England was now so manifest that operation Sealion (the code name for the German invasion) was 'suspended indefinitely'. Churchill had already claimed immortality on behalf of the pilots of the Hurricanes and Spitfires, in the Commons on 20 August:

The gratitude of every home in our Island, in our Empire, and indeed throughout the world, except in the abodes of the guilty, goes out to the British airmen who, undaunted by odds, unwearied in their constant challenge and mortal danger, are turning the tide of war by their prowess and by their devotion. Never in the field of human conflict was so much owed by so many to so few.

Although there was never again a danger of a German landing, there was no disposition to regard the slow *diminuendo* of the air campaign as a victory. Like Dunkirk, it was treated as a deliverance which secured no more than a temporary respite. Churchill's words on 8 October sounded more like an anticipatory threnody than a paean:

. . . do not let us dull for one moment the sense of the awful hazards in which we stand. Do not let us lose the conviction that it is only by supreme and superb exertions, unwearying and indomitable, that we shall save our souls alive. . . . . Long dark months of trials and tribulations lie before us. . . . Death and sorrow will be the companions of our journey; hardship our garment; constancy and valour our only shield. We must be united, undaunted, inflexible. Our qualities and deeds must burn and glow through the gloom of Europe until they become the veritable beacons of salvation.

From the point of view of maintaining morale at home, Churchill was right to speak in this continuingly sombre mood. The Germans had not run out of either hope or resource in their anti-British campaign, and they endeavoured throughout the winter of 1940–41 to inflict decisive blows on Britain's economy and morale. Göring still clung to the view that bombing would break morale, and the winter was given over to night attacks on numerous British cities, London, Coventry and Plymouth suffering most spectacularly. The British replied with what were called 'area attacks' on German cities, though, like the Germans, they tended to speak in terms of bombing 'military objectives'. Despite, or perhaps paradoxically because of, the death and misery these reciprocal bombings gave rise to, they increased morale on both sides by forging a comradeship of suffering and courage between civilians and the fighting services such as had not existed in the First World War. Tedium in wartime is corrosive of civilian as of military morale; but now the dreary austerities not only of the soldier's, but also of the civilian's, life were punctuated by the invigorating rigours of front line action. Yet the devotion of both sides to the wasteful slaughter of mass bombing could lead only to the search for more and more powerful bombs, until 1944 produced Hitler's V.1's and V.2's and 1945 the atom bombs that fell on Hiroshima and Nagasaki.

The other German device was the tried method of blockade by submarine. U-boats now had an increasing range, and magnetic mines were used, causing heavy losses until the invention of the 'degaussing cable'. Nevertheless, the effects of the Battle of the Atlantic were not at their worst until the second half of 1941. Again, German lack of preparedness and clear thinking told against them. A monthly average of just under 160,000 tons of shipping was sunk until March 1941. It was not until April 1941 that the figure of sinkings was raised to just under 200,000 tons. The Germans might have achieved more had they stepped up their campaign immediately after September 1940, instead of relying, for the third time in less than six months, on the Luftwaffe as an all-purpose weapon that could defeat a retreating army at Dunkirk, make good the lack of a navy to cover an invasion, and now provide a more terrorizing alternative to the silent U-boats.

But if victory against Britain had eluded Hitler, the declared British aim, as expressed by Churchill, of fighting on 'until the curse of Hitler is lifted from the brows of men' was further from realization than it had been twelve months earlier. Since it was Churchill's conviction that sooner or later the U.S.A. must become a much more active partner in the war, he wooed Roosevelt assiduously. During the twenty years between the wars the United States had contributed little to the task of preserving peace. In the Far East, there had been nothing more energetic than Stimson's doctrine of non-recognition; and in European affairs, Roosevelt had confined himself to the issue of appeals for peace, as if Washington were a sort of Protestant Vatican. Nevertheless, Americans had been highly critical of the policy of appeasement and of the inactivity of what they chose to christen the 'phoney war' from September 1939 to May 1940. On the evidence of these phenomena, they were of much the same mind as Hitler, and took a pessimistic view of Britain's will and capacity to survive. Thus, Churchill's speeches had been designed to counter United States doubts as well as revive morale at home; and, after Dunkirk and the Battle of Britain, the U.S.A. was disposed to take the British more seriously. Out of this new confidence, and after Roosevelt's re-election as President at the end of 1940, came a great burst of energy and a fine flowering of phrases to match. At a Press conference in November 1940, Roosevelt announced that 50 per cent of American armaments output was being made available to Britain; and negotiations began for supplying the R.A.F. with four-engined 'Flying Fortress' bombers. In December, plans were announced to step up the supply of cargo ships to Britain until it reached a total annual tonnage of three million. The Chairman of the Chase National Bank discovered, in the same month, that England was 'valiantly defending the ramparts of the democratic world including our own'; and the Mayor of New York thanked the British for enabling the United States to enjoy a peaceful Christmas. At a Press conference on 18 December, Roosevelt announced his intention of putting before Congress a 'Lend-Lease' enactment by which the United States Government would itself guarantee to manufacturers payment for all war materials ordered by the British. The materials would be made available to the United Kingdom on indefinite lease, being returned if undamaged and, if not, replaced in kind. In his message to Congress on 6 January 1941, Roosevelt called upon the United States to look on itself as 'an arsenal' for 'those nations which are now in actual war against aggressor nations' and he went on, in accordance with precedent, to present his policy in the glowing terms of a moral crusade:

In the future days, which we seek to make secure, we look forward to a world founded upon four essential human freedoms. The first is freedom of speech and expression – everywhere in the world. The second is freedom of every person to worship God in his own way – everywhere in the world. The third is freedom from want – which means economic understandings which will secure to every nation a healthy peacetime life for its inhabitants – everywhere in the world. The fourth is freedom from fear – which means a world-wide reduction of armaments to such a point and in such a thorough fashion that no nation will be in a position to commit an act of physical aggression against a neighbour – everywhere in the world.
That is no vision of a distant millennium. It is a definite basis for a kind of world attainable in our own time and generation.

The words found a ready response in Britain, for there was a ring of clarity in Roosevelt's eloquence which contrasted with Churchill's vaguely liturgical style, and in Wilsonian fashion the President had hit on phrases well suited for the ears of men who longed to be told what might be the due reward of their present adversity. Yet, no less than Woodrow Wilson, Roosevelt, by serving the mood of the moment, was laying up much dis-illusionment for the future.

Churchill, not to be outdone, gave his reply in a broadcast on 9 February 1941:

Here is the answer I shall give to President Roosevelt: Put your confidence in us. Give us your faith and your blessing and under Providence all will be well. We shall not fail or falter. We shall not weaken or tire. Neither the sudden shock of battle, nor the long-drawn trials of vigilance and exertion will wear us down. Give us the tools and we shall finish the job.

The words 'Give us the tools and we shall finish the job' need to be read in the context of more than one secret Anglo-American staff discussion in the first months of 1941, in which it was agreed that if America became involved in war against both Germany and Japan, priority should be given to the defeat of Germany. Nor does Churchill's rapturous excitement when the United States was forced into war by the Japanese attack on Pearl Harbor later in the year fit the notion that he wanted America to supply the tools and to leave Britain alone to do the job:

So we had won after all! . . . We had won the war. England would live; the Commonwealth of Nations and the Empire would live. . . . We should not be wiped out. Our history would not come to an end. We might not even have to die as individuals. Hitler's fate was sealed. Mussolini's fate was sealed. As for the Japanese they would be ground to powder.[1]

---

37 · Which Way to Lebensraum? 1941

In spite of having lost the Battle of Britain, Hitler's propaganda line in the winter of 1940–41 was still that the war in the west had been won, and his Italian and Japanese friends were being given to understand that all that remained necessary was a combined and crushing aerial and under-sea

---

[1] Churchill, *The Grand Alliance*, p. 539.

blow which would 'finally' dispose of British resistance. From October 1940 onwards, his thoughts were concentrated on plans for an attack on Russia. His intentions were known to the British, and warnings were conveyed to Stalin through Sir Stafford Cripps, who had been appointed ambassador to the U.S.S.R. in May 1940, in the unfulfilled expectation that a plain-living, high-thinking Christian and Socialist might soften Stalin's attitude to Britain. Stalin showed no interest in Cripps's warnings and gave every indication of being shocked when the Germans invaded Russian territory in June 1941. It was an event which was at once held to have purged the Soviets of their previous sins of appeasement (in fact the word, though invariably applied to pre-Churchillian British politicians, was hardly ever applied to Stalin) and made Russia by far the most popular of Britain's allies.

Churchill instantly broadcast his intentions on the radio:

The past, with its crimes, its follies and its tragedies, flashes away. I see the Russian soldiers standing on the threshold of their native land, guarding the fields which their fathers have tilled from time immemorial, and I see them guarding their homes where mothers and wives pray – ah, yes, for there are times when all pray for the safety of their loved ones, for the return of the breadwinner, of the champion, of their protector – I see the 10,000 villages of Russia where the means of existence are wrung so hardly from the soil, but where there are still primordial human joys, where maidens laugh and children play.

If the world's first great anti-Communist could use language appropriate to the thinking of a late nineteenth-century member of the *Narodniki*, it was not surprising that others, less convinced than Churchill of the naughtiness of the Communist system, should react in similar style. Almost at once, there began a persistent demand for the opening of a 'second front' in Europe to relieve the terrible pressure on the nation's Russian comrades. The brick walls which, twenty years later, bore the chalked slogan BAN THE BOMB began to bear the words OPEN A SECOND FRONT NOW, and, from the summer of 1941 onwards, too few voices were raised publicly in the necessary counter-assertion that from 1940 to 1945 there had been no occasion on which the British had not been conducting at least one, and usually more than one, front against the Germans.

By the end of 1941, the invasion of Russia had resulted in the German capture of Smolensk, Kiev and Kharkhov and of Kertch in the Crimean Peninsula. Nevertheless, lengthening lines of communications and the unexpected persistence of Russian opposition gave the Germans no sight of victory; and early in December 1941, as the Russian winter began, the offensive against Moscow was slackened.

Hitler's invasion of Russia is regarded as his fatal mistake. Yet it was surely the moment to which all his career had been moving. His landlocked mind, a phantasmagoric rubbish-dump of Mitteleuropean myths and delusions, was almost bound to produce those traditional backstreet café recipes for German salvation, the extermination of the Jews and the Slavs. For him, the defeat of France could only be a preliminary, and the overthrow of Britain no more than the elimination of a stumbling-block. The real mistake Hitler made was to have overestimated the importance and difficulty of the preliminary defeat of the west and, in consequence, to have attacked Russia at a time when his resources were already seriously strained and his armed forces already widely dispersed. If he had screamed less in the first place, he might have functioned against Russia as he had for a time intended, in collaboration with Poland, and thus perhaps eliminated the need for fighting in the west at all. If he had been less convinced, as by now he unfortunately seemed to have reason to be, of his own strategic insight, he might even in 1941 have concentrated his efforts on securing Japanese assistance, instead of keeping them in the dark and diverting them to an attack on the British and Dutch in South-east Asia. For this was to impose on the Japanese the necessity of an attack on the U.S.A., without which armed intervention by that country might still have been long avoided.

There had been an alternative for Hitler to adopt during the six months after the Battle of Britain. With France defeated, and Italy a belligerent, an energetically-led drive from Cyrenaica towards Egypt and the Suez Canal could hardly have failed. Success here would have given him control of the Middle East, enabled him to turn Russia's southern flank and would have deprived the United Kingdom of its supplies of essential oil. The Italians outnumbered the British in North Africa by over three to one; and if Hitler had sent German forces to North Africa in the autumn of 1940, instead of in January 1941, after an Italian débâcle, the Axis might well have succeeded in taking the Nile Delta instead of stopping just short of it as eventually happened.[1] As it was, the offensive campaign which the Germans mounted when they arrived was largely the independent decision of the German commander, Rommel. His original orders had been to stand on the defensive.

There were practical obstacles to all-out German action in North Africa. The transportation of large quantities of men and material to the area was dependent upon the protection of the Italian fleet; and the British inflicted heavy damage on the Italian Navy, at little cost to themselves, at Taranto, in November 1940, and again, in March 1941, off Cape Matapan. Attempts by Hitler to secure active support in the Mediterranean from the puppet French Government led by Pétain from Vichy, and from Franco's Spain, met with no response; and these various difficulties made a full-scale Mediterranean campaign as unalluring as it was unfamiliar to a mind

[1] As late as September 1941, Hitler's military advisers urged him to transfer his main offensive effort from Russia to the western Mediterranean. See Feis, *Churchill, Roosevelt, Stalin*, p. 25 footnote.

ignorant of oceans and other continents, and large enough only to contain the misty but essentially central-European notion of Lebensraum.

It was not certain, in the autumn of 1940, how far nearly two decades of Fascism had succeeded in imbuing the Italians with that heroic belief in war as the highest human activity which Mussolini had so sedulously propagated. General Wavell was C-in-C. Middle East and his available forces in Egypt and Palestine numbered only about 65,000. Against them were ranged 215,000 Italians in North Africa, and a further 200,000 in Italian East Africa (Eritrea, Abyssinia and Italian Somaliland); and the Italians had nearly 650 aircraft compared with the British total of about 400. The shortage of equipment was considered so serious that Churchill ordered the dispatch of tank reinforcements to the Middle East by way of the long sea route round the Cape. But in mid-September, with the Battle of Britain at its height and invasion of the United Kingdom thought imminent, the Italians advanced in strength to Sidi Barrani, sixty miles inside Egypt.

Reinforced at this particular moment with the fifty heavy tanks from the United Kingdom, Wavell speeded up his preparations for offensive action against the Italians and appointed General O'Connor to command the Western Desert Force. All that was planned, at the outset, was a five-day attack followed by a withdrawal, owing to British uncertainties about supply problems in a desert campaign; but, as the battle approached, both Wavell and O'Connor began to think in bolder terms.

On 9 December 1940, O'Connor attacked the Italians at Sidi Barrani. After three days they were in retreat. At once, the switch was made to an all-out offensive. The coastal fortresses of Bardia and Tobruk were taken on 5 and 22 January 1941 respectively, and on 7 February the British reached Benghazi, the capital of Cyrenaica, and surrounded and cut off the entire Italian force opposed to them. At a cost of less than 2,000 casualties, the Western Desert Force had advanced 500 miles and captured over 130,000 prisoners and hundreds of guns and tanks. Meanwhile, in January 1941, the British had invaded Eritrea and, in February, Italian Somaliland. By April, Addis Ababa, the Abyssinian capital, had been taken; a month later the Italians surrendered, leaving only small pockets of resistance in the mountains. Italian casualties in the campaign were just under 300,000, British battle casualties less than 2,000. On 5 May 1941, Haile Selassie, whom Mussolini had driven out in 1936, was restored to his imperial throne after his years of exile in Bath.

Few victories have been more complete than those of the British in Cyrenaica and Italian East Africa. They constitute a wry comment on the anxiety created by Italian ambitions in 1936, and in 1941 itself they were a firm reply to those who doubted the British will to hit back at their enemies. O'Connor's victories were overshadowed, in the minds of those at home, by the ever-present miseries of the continuing Blitz and by the continuing impregnability of Hitler's Europe; and they were soon submerged by the sequence of reversals in North Africa itself in the next eighteen months. Nevertheless, at a moment when the British were at their weakest in Egypt and when their enemies seemed strongest, they had successfully defended an area vital to their conduct of the war as a whole and had done so, not in traditional British fashion by grimly hanging on, but by a spectacular offensive on a terrain requiring battle techniques with which they were unfamiliar.

Having destroyed the Italians in Cyrenaica, Wavell and O'Connor now looked forward to advancing into Tripolitania and driving them out of North Africa altogether. This was made impossible by a decision to send armed assistance to Greece.

In October 1940, desperate to provide evidence that Italy possessed its full share of the aggressive spirit, Mussolini had launched an attack on Greece from Albania. The Greeks fought back, and were themselves soon on Albanian soil; and signs emerged that Hitler was about to intervene. Greece, however, was one of the States upon whom Chamberlain had showered guarantees in the mad midsummer of 1939, and Churchill was convinced that, since Hitler was clearly planning to attack Greece from Bulgaria, British forces must be sent to oppose him. The stiffening of Greek resistance would, it was thought, create a resolute anti-German front in the Balkans, consisting of Jugoslavia, Greece and Turkey. This would guard the Black Sea and the Caspian, and cause Russia to doubt the wisdom of continuing to support Germany.

Although the scheme came appropriately enough from the architect of the Gallipoli campaign, it is untrue that this was a purely Churchillian device imposed upon the military against their better judgement. Sir John Dill, then the C.I.G.S., General Maitland Wilson, who commanded the British forces in Greece, and both Wavell and Eden (who was at this stage Secretary for War) were all in favour of the operation at the time and prepared to defend it in principle later on. There was certainly much to be said for the idea that it was better to put a strong barrier between Hitler and the Near East at this stage than to chase the Italians on to Tripoli. Unfortunately, whereas the expulsion of the Italians from North Africa was a military possibility (though General Wilson doubted even this), a successful campaign in Greece was not, and for reasons which led to a repetition in miniature of the larger catastrophe in France. The help the British could offer was small, and the army being assisted adopted a mistaken strategy. Worse still, the need to dispatch three divisions to Greece meant the virtual disbandment of O'Connor's Western Desert Force immediately after the conquest of Cyrenaica. The outcome was that before the end of April 1941, Greece had been overwhelmed, Cyrenaica lost and Egypt again threatened; and it was nearly two years before British forces at last entered Tripolitania.

British troops began disembarking in Greece in March and, by the time

the Germans declared war on Greece, on 6 April 1941, about three divisions
of British and Commonwealth troops had been landed. Within ten days,
the Greek forces on the Albanian frontier had been cut off by the German
forces advancing from Bulgaria and between 24 and 30 April British forces
were evacuated by sea. In the following month, the British were driven
from Crete also, by a German airborne invasion.

The abandonment of the offensive in North Africa led to the establishment
of a static command in Cyrenaica; O'Connor's battle-trained troops were
dispersed and he himself transferred to command in Egypt. On 12 February 1941, five days after the British took Benghazi, Hitler had sent General
Rommel, and in due course the German Afrika Korps, to Tripoli, in the
first place to arrange for its defence, and eventually for the re-conquest of
Cyrenaica. Contrary to Hitler's orders and Wavell's expectations,
Rommel advanced upon Cyrenaica as early as the end of March. At this
moment, General Neame, the new British Commander, had few suitable
forces in Cyrenaica. The Germans recaptured Benghazi, and O'Connor

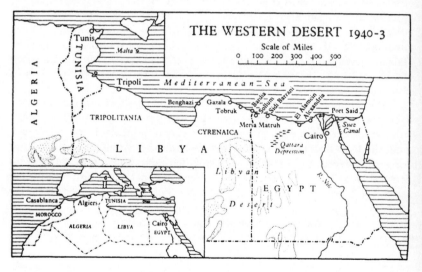

was sent from Egypt to advise Neame; on a dark night in early April 1941
they motored into the midst of an advance German detachment and were
taken prisoner.

As, by April 1941, Rommel brought German-Italian forces back to
Sollum within reach of the Egyptian border, Wavell decided that all he
could do for the moment was to try to contain him by holding on to Tobruk,
the port Rommel had by now by-passed. With this uncaptured on his flank,
his communications were highly vulnerable; as it was, Rommel at all times

had serious supply problems, and wrestled perpetually with the danger that he would run out of fuel.

Since the Greek venture had swiftly produced catastrophe, Churchill was insistent on retrieving the situation by victory in the desert. An attack at Sollum, east of Bardia, was therefore launched, with inadequate preparation, inexperienced leadership and hastily improvised forces, in June 1941. The attack (code-name Battleaxe) failed, and Wavell was replaced as C-in-C Middle East by General Auchinleck. Churchill, who had been quite unjustifiably angered by Wavell's refusal to launch Battleaxe earlier and still more by its failure, was further upset when Auchinleck himself produced massive arguments for not attempting an immediate offensive.

The changeover from Wavell to Auchinleck was not greatly for the better. 'The Auk' was an Indian Army officer with as little knowledge of armoured warfare as any other available replacement for Wavell, and with little knowledge of the men from whom he would have to select his principal subordinates. Auchinleck's choice of General Cunningham as Commander of the new Eighth Army, which now came into being to replace the much smaller Western Desert Force which O'Connor had commanded, was unfortunate. Cunningham had led the victorious attack on Italian East Africa, and his reputation therefore stood high; but he, too, had no experience of armoured warfare and, owing to Churchill's insistence that an offensive must on no account be delayed, had to learn what he could about it within eleven weeks.

One factor, however, soon came to be regarded as more than compensation for these largely unsuspected deficiencies; the enormously increased volume of men and equipment which had now been sent to Egypt. As the date of the offensive approached, there was a great lift of optimism. This was sanctioned and encouraged by Churchill when, just before the advance, he caused Auchinleck to be sent a message which declared:

For the first time British and Empire troops will meet the Germans with an ample equipment in modern weapons of all kinds. . . . The Desert Army may add a page to history which will rank with Blenheim and with Waterloo.[1]

The truth was somewhat less exhilarating. Taking over large supplies of complicated weapons and equipment was not quite the swift and unsophisticated process Churchill imagined. The British command had little experience of moulding tanks, guns and infantry into the kind of 'panzer' division which Rommel knew how to handle, and was given far too little time to acquire the tactical skills required for the conduct of large-scale mobile warfare in the featureless wastes of the Western Desert, with unfamiliar and untried equipment, against highly expert and resolute opponents.

Given the code-name Crusader, the operation began on 18 November

[1] Churchill, *Second World War*, Vol IV, p. 434.

1941, with, as its objectives, the recapture of Cyrenaica, an advance into Tripolitania, and the destruction of Rommel's armour. Cunningham's first objective was the relief of Tobruk and, to begin with, there was good progress; but Rommel countered with great skill, and the battle seemed to disintegrate into disconnected engagements in which the Germans gained the upper hand. Cunningham became so unnerved that he thought of breaking off the battle altogether and of retreating to Egypt. Auchinleck at once intervened, insisted that the battle be persisted in, relieved Cunningham of his command and replaced him, originally as a temporary measure, by General Ritchie. This decision proved the turning-point, and dogged determination once again made good some of the deficiencies in battle-technique. Tobruk was relieved on 10 December 1941 and, a fortnight later, the British were back in Benghazi; back, that is to say, where they had first arrived over ten months before. This achievement was due to Auchinleck's firm offensive spirit and his realization that Rommel, with Tobruk still in British hands at the moment when Cunningham wanted to give up, had been hardly less near to exhaustion than the British. Near-defeat had been turned into something that, if not a Blenheim or a Waterloo, at least looked like a victory. Rommel rapidly disengaged himself, to contemplate the loss of 36,000 prisoners, nearly all his tanks and most of his aircraft.

Nevertheless the cost to the British had been much greater than expected and the campaign had fallen short of its objectives. Rommel's forces, depleted though they were, were still intact and were being reinforced; and Tripolitania was still in enemy hands. Worse still, Auchinleck, like Wavell before him, now found that events elsewhere required part of the force at his disposal to be withdrawn to other theatres of action. In December, the Japanese had started on their desperate gamble for control of south-east Asia; the British entry into Benghazi, on Christmas Eve 1941, was followed on Christmas Day by the surrender to the Japanese of the British garrison at Hong Kong.

38 · Storm over Asia, 1941-42

The entry of Japan into the war was spectacularly signalized by an un-heralded and devastating attack on the American Pacific Fleet at Pearl Harbor in Hawaii on 7 December 1941. The entirely unprepared U.S. Fleet lost five battleships and 177 aircraft, and the Japanese secured naval and air supremacy in the Western Pacific.

Until Pearl Harbor, the United States had been something of a con-tinental Shangri-la, protected from history by the great oceans that guarded its flanks, and because Canada to the north and Latin America to the south were made innocuous both by their similar distance from other continents and by economic and political under-development. From time to time, Americans had sent out uplifting messages to the farther world, speaking of peace, freedom and equality to distracted hierarchical Europe, and of open doors, territorial integrity and independence to China and her despoilers. They had done so sure in the knowledge that they were the one people who had cut themselves free from history's wrongs and the one great power which, having been born of anti-Imperialism, was not Imperialist. Only once had they entered history's stream, led there by President Wilson, and had returned to Shangri-La determined never to repeat their error. But now, the Japanese had dive-bombed Shangri-La's defences; the United States at last discovered that power was vulnerable; and that the easy virtue of crying 'holier-than-thou' was not the way to keep it.

Japan's intervention was thus not quite the simple display of fiendish treachery it was instantly designated. It was a logical outcome of policies long pursued, not only by the Japanese, but also by the United States and the United Kingdom. Throughout the century, they had all been engaged on a triangular contest for control of China and the Western Pacific. Both the United States and the United Kingdom had endeavoured to fend the Japanese off by concessions and by phraseology. Their reliance on these unpropitious devices and their jealousy of each other had encouraged Japan to embark on a policy of aggression which, by 1941, had reached a point where it could be continued, if at all, only by an all-out attack on the British and Dutch Far Eastern Empires; and attack on those areas was feasible only if American striking-power at sea was eliminated first.

Just as fear of Russian pressure on China had led the British to espouse Japan's expansionist aims in Korea in 1902, so, in 1905, the United States likewise gave support to Japan's designs in Korea in return for a Japanese promise not to attack the Philippines, which the United States had acquired from Spain as a result of the war in 1898. By 1906, the desire of the United States not to be involved in trouble over the Philippines led them to take the further step of conceding to the Japanese a free hand in Manchuria. In 1909, President Theodore Roosevelt prophetically expressed the view that Manchuria was so vital to Japan that she could only be kept out of it by war;

and a successful war about Manchuria would require a fleet as good as that of England plus an army as good as that of Germany.[1]

This was unthinkable. Yet, anxiety to avoid trouble over the Philippines, Korea and Manchuria went hand in hand with a firm belief that the United States had a special mission to defend the Chinese Empire from the marauding inroads of European Imperialists. Accordingly, United States powerlessness to oppose Japan was increased by an antagonistic attitude to the United Kingdom, which was otherwise a natural ally against Japan. The United States protested against the dispatch of British forces to Tibet in 1904 on the grounds that it was United States policy to preserve the integrity of the Chinese Empire. This was hardly consistent with countenancing Japanese designs on the rather more obviously Chinese province of Manchuria five years later. Thus, Japan had every reason to believe that the United States had an attitude but no policy in the Far East, since they refused to acquire the power which alone made policy possible. The contrast with the Japanese, who had exploded the myth of Russia's threat to China by a policy based on what was not, after all, a great deal of power, was striking; but, whereas the Japanese took the significance of the contrast, the United States did not.

Increased pressure by Japan on China during the first German war produced nothing more energetic than the first enunciation, by Secretary of State Bryan, of the doctrine of non-recognition, later resurrected by Stimson in the Manchurian crisis of 1931–33. At the Washington Conference of 1921, the United States concerned itself as much with the problem of the British Navy as of the Japanese, and once again sought to buy security for the Philippines by agreeing to Japanese naval supremacy in the Western Pacific. Beside this, the reiteration of the principle of the 'open door' in China (i.e. equal trading rights for all nations and no annexations) was an exercise in meaninglessness comparable to reliance on 'collective security' or the Kellogg-Briand Pact. The consequent failure to co-operate with the British, when the Japanese attacked Manchuria and the International Settlement in Shanghai in 1931, followed naturally. In

[1] Quoted, Louis J. Halle, *American Foreign Policy*, p. 235.

short, the United States had helped, ever since the opening of the twentieth century, to perpetuate a power vacuum in China and the Western Pacific which constituted a temptation to the Japanese which was too great for them to be expected to resist.

Japan was not solely encouraged by the complacency of the United States and the uncertainty of the United Kingdom. The preoccupation of Europe with its two great civil wars, and with chaotic recovery from the first and claustrophobic preparation for the second, presented them with opportunities such as have been presented to few Governments in history. Not only did these wars divert British and United States attention; they paralysed Japan's nearest and potentially most dangerous rival, Russia. The Japanese aircraft that dived from the skies over Pearl Harbor on 7 December 1941 had been dispatched on their mission not only because of half a century's lack of policy in the United States. Among the many who helped to propel them into the skies, Grey and Bethmann-Hollweg, Chamberlain and Hitler must be included.

Yet all had not gone well with the Japanese since they had begun full-scale war in China in 1937. That war had been embarked upon because their control of Manchuria had roused China's national spirit against them; and although by 1940 they had captured Peking, Tientsin, Nanking, Shanghai and Hankow, forcing Chiang Kai-shek's Government far inland to Chungking, they were in secure control only of the chief towns, the ports and the railways. They were harassed by guerrillas, and Chiang was receiving supplies intermittently from the United States and the United Kingdom by way of the Burma Road. As the rest of the world devoted its resources increasingly to its own war, the Japanese found it difficult to import basic war materials; and it became more and more attractive to envisage the seizure of almost unprotected Malaya and the Dutch East Indies, with their supplies of rubber, tin and oil. As a prelude, pressure was put on Pétain's Government at Vichy, in July 1941, to permit Japanese occupation of French Indo-China. Military, naval and air bases were quickly established and the Japanese were thus clearly poised to attack. At once, Roosevelt imposed an embargo on the export of fuel oils to Japan; Britain applied economic sanctions also.

Japan, therefore, faced the situation that the British and the Germans had faced in 1939; whether or not to accept the inevitability of a war to which all things were tending, or, by a cool attempt to assess ultimate consequences, to make an abrupt change of course. The long-term risks were enormous; but present risks were negligible and present tensions ever more difficult to bear. Moderate elements in governing circles were overborne by those who saw in immediate war the only escape from an intolerable situation. But, given that war was a desperate gamble, speed and daring were essential. To attack Pearl Harbor, massively and without warning, was as necessary a preliminary to the Japanese plan for seizing Malaya and the

Dutch East Indies as the violation of Belgium had been·to the execution of
the Schlieffen Plan.

Pearl Harbor sowed for the Japanese an immediate harvest of victories.
It was followed at once by the destruction from the air of the small U.S.
fleet stationed in the Philippines and by the destruction, also from the air,
of two British capital ships, the *Prince of Wales* and the *Repulse*. These,
having just been rather pointlessly sent to Singapore, were sent north to
investigate reports of Japanese landings on the Malayan coast in the Gulf
of Siam. The loss of these vessels gave the Japanese complete naval
superiority in South East Asia and the Western Pacific.

There were immediate Japanese landings at the American bases of Guam
and Wake, in the Philippines, at Hong Kong and in Malaya. In January
1942, attacks began on the Dutch East Indies and on Burma. Guam fell on
13 December 1941, Wake Island a week later. Hong Kong surrendered on
25 December. Manila, the capital of the Philippines, fell on 2 January 1942,
and United States forces were driven into the Bataan Peninsula where they
finally succumbed in early April, the island fortress of Corregidor alone
holding out for another month. On 15 February 1942, Singapore itself surrendered. By 8 March the Japanese were in Rangoon, and all Burma was in
their hands by the end of May 1942, with the consequent closing of the
Burma Road by which aid had previously been reaching Chiang Kai-shek.
More menacing still, from the British point of view, the Japanese now
loomed threateningly over the Burmese frontier with India. The last
chance of saving the Dutch East Indies went when the Japanese won a
naval battle in the Java Sea on 27 February 1942. Not until May and June
1942, with the aircraft-carrier battles of the Coral Sea and Midway, was the
Japanese run of victories halted. By then they were masters of all South-
east Asia from North Burma to New Guinea.

The defeat of the British in the Far East was the most complete and the
most calamitous of the war. Yet, just as past United States policy had been
a long preparation for Pearl Harbor, so almost the whole past history of
British policy in the Far East had been ripening to this bitter moment of
fruition. So far from anticipating that the Japanese could plan to conquer
Malaya and Singapore by a landward advance, it was a firm belief, until
within a few months of the outbreak of hostilities, that an attack by land
was militarily out of the question. In consequence the Japanese needed, not
their own estimate of a hundred days to attain their objectives, but only
seventy.

Although the Malay States with their tin, rubber and rice were, in the
inter-war years, almost the only British dependencies to constitute a clear
exception to Lloyd George's savage dictum that the British colonial
empire was 'one vast slum', they lacked adequate landward protection; and
the function of the Army in Malaya had been conceived almost exclusively

as that of a defence force for the naval base. When reinforcements were dispatched to the area, in the spring of 1941, they were allowed few opportunities for realistic training, being confined to the roads for fear of disrupting the rubber plantations and the rice fields. There was the usual shortage of equipment and experienced officers and N.C.O.'s, and a total absence of tanks. There were so few aircraft that troops were scattered all over northern and central Malaya for the defence of airfields. The intelligence services proved incompetent, there was no sense of urgency among civilians; and, to add to these disadvantages, the Japanese virtually destroyed the Air Force and now commanded the seas.

JAPAN'S ADVANCE IN S.E. ASIA
1941-2
Scale of Miles
0   400   800   1200   1600   2000

Early in January 1942, Wavell, now Supreme Commander in the area, endeavoured to get the Japanese held back in Johore pending the arrival of reinforcements switched from their original purpose of strengthening Auchinleck in North Africa. It was too late; on the last day of January 1942, British forces withdrew to Singapore, having been driven out of Malaya in fifty-four days. Japanese superiority in staff work and training again told heavily. They deceived the defenders of the island as to the direction of their main attack, and by 12 February had seized the main water supply. Judging further resistance useless, the British surrendered on 15 February. There were over 166,000 casualties, of whom more than 130,000 were taken prisoner.

The prospects when the Japanese attacked Burma were even worse. The likelihood of a landward attack through the jungle had always been considered remote, the best Indian troops were in the Middle East, and the army in Burma was even less fitted for offensive action than the army in Malaya. The whole country contained only sixteen obsolete aircraft. Here, as in Malaya, British forces were not greatly outnumbered by their Japanese opponents; they were simply inferior to them in skill, training and determination.

The loss of these territories so rapidly was later made the occasion for further reproving lectures to the British people about their lack of military ardour in the years before the war. This disaster would, so the theory implied, have been prevented had the British people not grown soft and undisciplined compared with their toughened opponents. Such strictures arise from historical ignorance. There could be no decline in the will to defend the empire in the Far East against a military opponent because such a will had never existed and had not been thought necessary. The limit of Britain's major military intentions outside Europe had long been confined to the defence of the North-West Frontier of India against the Russians and the defence of Egypt and the eastern Mediterranean against anybody. Nor would the British have had to defend the Far East against military attack had they not simultaneously been engaged in defending Egypt and preparing for an attack in due season on the continent of Europe while suffering from a fierce U-boat blockade. But for these circumstances, no Japanese attack would have taken place. The proposition that the British Empire should have been capable of defence simultaneously at all points against the onslaughts of first-class Powers was written down in nobody's scheme of things. The British Empire was not that sort of Empire, and was not intended to be. That it would be vulnerable in the extremely unlikely event of its being attacked at various points by heavily armed military States all at once was a remote contingency against which it would have been unstatesmanlike to over-insure. The reluctance to believe that the Japanese would attack through the jungles of Malaya and Burma was probably not as reprehensible as the similar French disbelief in the possibility of a German *Blitzkrieg* in western Europe. The poor quality of the troops who faced the attack was not much more than a reflection of the prior needs of other theatres. No fact more glaringly obvious can be found in the history of the half-century before 1942 than that the British Empire, in any serious sense, was militarily indefensible, having been created in an age when it did not need to be defended.

39 · To Alamein and Stalingrad, 1942-43

Even before the flimsy defences of the Far East had finally collapsed under Japanese pressure, defeat had come again in North Africa. Heavy air and U-boat attacks on the British fleet in the central Mediterranean, the sinking of the aircraft-carrier *Ark Royal* and a sustained aerial bombardment of Malta were undertaken by the Germans after the loss of Benghazi in December 1941 to clear the way for the dispatch of reinforcements to North Africa. On 21 January 1942, Rommel went over to the offensive, recaptured western Cyrenaica, and in a fortnight drove the British back to Gazala, only forty miles west of Tobruk. The British had been out-generalled and out-manœuvred and it was an error on Auchinleck's part not to remove General Ritchie from his command. Nevertheless, Auchinleck made some attempt to re-train the army and re-think the problems of mobile warfare during the three months' pause which followed Rommel's successful offensive. Unfortunately, he was being besought by Churchill to attack Rommel at the earliest possible moment, and, partly in consequence of this, the disposition of Ritchie's forces was designed neither for all-out defence nor for all-out offence. Rommel on his side had good reasons for renewing the attack as soon as possible. Hitler's thoughts were now on the imminent summer offensive against Russia and he was seeking to limit Rommel's ambitions in the desert. This could only have the effect of spurring Rommel on.

He advanced on 26 May 1942, swinging towards and beyond Tobruk. The direction of Rommel's movement was unexpected; there was considerable destruction of British armour and a helter-skelter retreat. By 20 June, the bulk of the Eighth Army was back behind the Egyptian frontier.

Tobruk was left far behind; its defences had not been repaired since the British had destroyed them in December 1941 and its significance was now largely symbolical. Unfortunately the British were, at this stage, desperately short even of symbols; and the surrender of 33,000 British and South African troops at Tobruk on 21 June 1942 was perhaps, after the surrender of Singapore only four months before, the lowest point to which British fortunes sank during the war.

Only when the defeated Eighth Army had retreated as far as Mersa Matruh, 150 miles east of Egypt's frontier with Cyrenaica, did Auchinleck at last relieve Ritchie of his command. Appointing no successor, Auchinleck took operational control himself. He believed that British forces would run the risk of destruction by holding fast to Mersa Matruh, and he planned to retire still farther back, to El Alamein, only sixty five miles west of Alexandria. By this time, however, Rommel felt himself within sight of final victory in North Africa, and inflicted on the already disorganized British yet another severe defeat at Mersa Matruh in the last days of June, even though the British tanks outnumbered the German. Rommel and the Eighth Army were soon driving towards El Alamein.

At El Alamein, the British had a good defensive position holding a comparatively narrow forty-mile gap between the sea and the high cliffs of the Qattara Depression. Within the limited time allowed him by Rommel's pauses to regroup, Auchinleck endeavoured to provide the army with a more flexible order of battle, while at the same time avoiding the temptation to organize for a heroic last stand to save Egypt, since if this were to prove unsuccessful, it would be the end of the campaign. For his part, Rommel was hampered by Hitler's failure, obsessed as he was by his drive against Russia, to provide him with the extra tanks that might have made victory certain; but he believed that once he had got even part of his forces behind the British defences they were bound to retreat.

The first battle of Alamein began on 1 July 1942, and lasted until 17 July. Auchinleck directed the British with both calm and intelligence and, as the to-and-fro attacks and counter-attacks raged, Rommel was gradually forced to realize that he had lost what at the end of June had seemed, and not only to him but to Middle East Headquarters in Cairo as well: the almost immediate prospect of winning all Egypt and the Middle East. The thwarting of Rommel at the first battle of Alamein in July 1942 was thus a turning-point, parallel to the successful thwarting of the Germans by the Russians at Stalingrad during the succeeding six months.

At the time of first Alamein, however, the German defeat at Stalingrad was not in sight; nor was the attainment of Britain's aim of clearing the Axis out of North Africa. In consequence, what mattered most to national morale and also to what was felt to be the standing of the British with their new Russian and United States allies, was not that Rommel had failed to reach Alexandria, but that he had nearly done so, and might still do so.

Worst of all, Tobruk had fallen. Throughout the worst months of 1941-2 Tobruk, beleaguered but defiant, had seemed the one stable factor in a wearisome alternation of slow advance and rapid retreat, of hopes raised and hopes deferred. All the other strangely-named North African hummocks and escarpments and battle areas had had only brief moments of fame, but Tobruk, with a pronounceable name of two short syllables that sounded like the barking of a gun, was strong as a rock. Its loss was unprepared for, and regarded, with the Prime Minister's approval, as inexplicable. The strong suspicion that, in accordance with what was regarded as the most abiding feature of the British military tradition, someone had blundered, was irresistible. The Commons and the Press blamed Churchill, and in the relative secrecy of the high places, Churchill blamed Auchinleck.

The disasters in the Far East, the retreat in North Africa, the mounting toll of the U-boats, and what seemed the ineffectiveness of the British Army compared with the wide-screen epic being enacted on the vast Russian front, boiled up into a censure motion on the Prime Minister's conduct of the war, debated in the Commons on 1 and 2 July 1942. Aneurin Bevan expressed the feeling of a good many rank-and-file Englishmen in and out of uniform at that time:

The Army was ridden with class prejudice, a state of affairs which must be changed. The Army itself never had better material, but it was badly led and needed purging at the top. . . . There was no dismay in the country, but anger and humiliation; people could not stand that Sebastopol had held for eight months and Tobruk had fallen in twenty-six hours. . . . The Government should make their political dispositions, change the direction of the war, purge the Army and R.A.F. of elements not trusted at the moment, and get at the enemy where he really was – twenty-one miles away, not 14,000.

Bevan's views were more succinctly expressed by a contemporary *Daily Mirror* headline, 'RUSSIA BLEEDS WHILE BRITAIN BLANCOES'.

In addition to this notion that the Army commanders were incompetent was the belief, in more sophisticated circles, that the Prime Minister was interfering excessively with the conduct of military operations. In a debate on war strategy in May 1942, the Conservative M.P., Commander Bower, had deftly brought both themes together by expressing the view that an inquiry might reveal that Singapore had been 'lost on the playing-fields of Harrow'. As Minister of Defence with superintendence of the Chiefs of Staff Committee, Churchill was personally involved in all that had happened since May 1940; and now, after two years, there was little to show save defensive victories, evacuations and retreats, some of them glorious, some of them inglorious. The Churchill touch had little magic in it in the first nine months of 1942, and there were many to applaud Aneurin Bevan's gibe that the Prime Minister had 'won debate after debate and lost battle after battle.'

That all this issued in no real political crisis was due to two things. One was that the English, though angry and humiliated, were as determined on victory as ever. But so, quite obviously, was Churchill; and it stood him in good stead in 1942 that he had always prophesied, carefully, if perhaps excessively, that there would be much to endure before the tide finally turned.

Churchill's frequent demands for offensive action in North Africa greatly embarrassed the C.I.G.S., Sir Alan Brooke, and added to the difficulties of Auchinleck; but they were not simply the petulant interference of a frustrated would-be Generalissimo. Increasingly, the waging of war was reverting to the service of political purposes rather than those solely of self-defence, and to the demanding diplomatic strategy of new and global international relations. The whole trend of Russian and United States thinking in 1942 was towards the view held by unofficial Englishmen that it was high time the British Army got to grips with the enemy in western Europe where it would hurt him most. Churchill could hardly resist these pressures, or speak effectively to the Americans and Russians, while the Eighth Army seemed to be bungling its task in North Africa. His impatience was both political and temperamental; but it was also strategic and diplomatic.

Added to this, the whole German attack was reaching its climacteric. While Rommel was apparently within striking distance of Alexandria and Cairo, the German summer offensive of 1942 in southern Russia looked like overrunning the Caucasus within a matter of weeks. If this offensive succeeded – and German forces reached within a hundred miles of the Caspian Sea – both Persia and Iraq would be imperilled. This meant that British troops would be needed there and that they would have to come from the Eighth Army; it was thus imperative for Rommel to be defeated beforehand. Hence, while Auchinleck sought to postpone attack until his army was retrained and reinforced, Churchill sought to bring the attack on before that army was compulsorily weakened by the draining demands of the defence of Persia. In consequence, Auchinleck tried, in the third week of July 1942, to launch an offensive, immediately after the first battle of Alamein, without adequate preparation; he had to call it off after four days. In the first days of August, therefore, Churchill arrived in Cairo, and ordered Auchinleck's replacement as C-in-C Middle East by General Alexander. Two days later, after the accidental death of the commander originally designated, General Montgomery was appointed to command the Eighth Army.

Churchill's critics had asked for a shake-up in the Army Command. Now he had provided one. Crisp of speech, forthright in manner, untrammelled by doubt, Montgomery gave, at precisely the right moment, that impression of no-nonsense competence for which everybody was looking and which was held to have been absent before his arrival. He claimed to have found defeatism and a contemplation of retreat in the Middle East and to have whisked such ideas away with a few brisk movements of his purposeful new broom. In short, sharp sentences he diminished the great Rommel to the status of a bounderish fast bowler from a dubious rival prep school. With the assured abruptness of a religious Fundamentalist disposing of Agnostic doubt, he asserted the rightness of his strategic and tactical proposals and his confidence in speedy victory, and did so in phrases of crystal clarity. A lean, astringent and dedicated professional, and for fastidious tastes too cocky by half, Montgomery was as appropriate to the needs of the autumn of 1942 as Churchill had been to those of the summer of 1940.

Montgomery held an attempted offensive by Rommel at Alam Halfa at the beginning of September and then devoted the next weeks to absorbing great reinforcements of men and material. He did not launch the second battle of Alamein until 23 October so that, in fact, Churchill got an offensive out of Montgomery later, rather than sooner, than he would have done out of Auchinleck. With an overwhelming superiority in men and tanks, the Eighth Army flung itself forward and, after a slogging twelve days' resistance, the long German retreat began on 4 November. Before the battle began, Montgomery informed his men that it would be 'the turning-point of the war'. When it ended he announced, 'this is complete and absolute victory'. On 11 November Churchill told the Commons it was 'a British victory of the first order'. To remove all possibility of misunderstanding, an announcement from Downing Street asked that church bells should be rung everywhere before morning service on Sunday 15 November 1942. Since June 1940, this had been one of the countless customary actions which lay under Government prohibition: church bells were to be rung only should the authorities need to give warning of imminent or actual German invasion. But on 15 November 1942, to celebrate second Alamein, the bells were once again to ring out.

The purpose of Churchill's exasperating proddings during 1942 became apparent when the Allied plan (code name Torch) for landing troops (chiefly American) in French North Africa, was put into effect on 8 November, only five days after the German defeat at Alamein. That 'British victory of the first order' had surely all along been intended to occur before there was any possibility of the long-prepared, large-scale United States action farther west being deemed the cause of Rommel's retreat. It was also urgently required as a demonstration to both the United States and Russia that, in the North African theatre, really serious damage could be done to the Germans. Second Alamein was perhaps as much a political as a military victory. First Alamein had saved the Nile Delta, but Second Alamein proved what had so far not been demonstrated: that the British could actually defeat the Germans and force them to retreat. It is by no means without relevance that Churchill made one of his most significant wartime remarks in public only two days after Torch began. At the Lord

Mayor's banquet at the Mansion House on 10 November, in a speech whose general context did not require him to make the point at all, he announced:

Let me, however, make this clear, in case there should be any mistake about it in any quarter. We mean to hold our own. I have not become the King's First Minister in order to preside over the liquidation of the British Empire.[1]

As it was, this was not the most politic of remarks to come from the leader of an Empire already caught in the toils of an alliance with the two greatest anti-Imperialist powers in the world. Before second Alamein he could not have made it at all.

The postscript in North Africa was not short. Montgomery proved unable to encircle and destroy the Axis forces as O'Connor had done, even though Rommel's bases at Bizerta and Tunis were being threatened by Anglo-American forces from the west before the end of November. Nevertheless, by 13 November 1942, Tobruk was recaptured, and on 20 November, Benghazi; but Tripoli was not reached till 23 January 1943. On 7 April 1943 the two Allied forces linked, and on 12 May the North African campaign concluded with the surrender of a quarter of a million prisoners.

The early months of 1943 saw also the climax in Russia. The Germans had encircled Leningrad, but not taken it; they had not reached Moscow; and their drive to the Caucasus had been stopped by the Russian defence of Stalingrad in the rear of it. The Germans who, under General Paulus, attacked Stalingrad were, like those in North Africa under Rommel, ordered to resist to the end. All through the winter of 1942–3 the Stalingrad battle raged; on 2 February 1943 the 22,000 men who still survived of Paulus's original force of 300,000 surrendered.

The Torch landings equally marked a turning-point. From September 1939 to May 1940 the war had been an obvious repetition of the war of 1914. From June 1940 until the end of 1942 the only continuous theme had been the defence of the United Kingdom and the British Empire, conducted, physically at any rate, entirely by the forces of the United Kingdom and the Commonwealth. The great German drive on the Caucasus turned even the Russian front into the most massive threat to the British Empire in its history, when visualized in conjunction with the triumphs of the Japanese in the Far East. Now, Stalingrad and the two battles of Alamein had averted this global cataclysm and the three menaced powers, Britain, Russia and the United States, were compelled to adjust their plans to the entirely different purpose of an overall offensive. At once, the role of the British Empire diminished: offensive power, in men and resources, belonged primarily to the Americans and the Russians. The period during which the United Kingdom had saved all three empires by its exertions and its example alike was past. It was now a different war: a war of offence

[1] See p. 367.

in which it was never to play a dominating role. The two battles of Alamein were the last purely British battles of major consequence. The Western Desert campaign, though retarded and interfered with by political considerations and by the requirements of other theatres, had been an independent British campaign. There was to be no more independent British action. This was indeed the 'hinge of fate'.

PART VIII:
A GRAND ALLIANCE?
1941-1945

40 · Political and Strategic First Principles, 1941-42

The alliance of Britain and the United States and the U.S.S.R. in the prosecution, from December 1941, of an offensive war against Germany, Italy and Japan required the creation and pursuit of a world-wide strategy; and from the historical point of view the significance of the last three years of the war lies less in the success of the members of the alliance in defeating the enemy than in their failure to solve the problem of their relations with one another. This latter problem was with them from the beginning; and its initial subordination to immediate strategic needs created, even at best, a habit of disagreement grudgingly endured rather than of genuine collaboration.

The sources of disagreement were as manifold as the problems that required attention. Initially, the purely strategic issues appeared the most divisive. There was the larger problem of priority as between the European and the Far Eastern theatres, and the lesser but more vexatious problem of whether to conquer Europe by an immediate landing in France or after first undertaking a diversionary attack from the Mediterranean. There was the problem of how, whichever method was adopted, to ensure that it diverted a sufficient number of German divisions from the hard-pressed Russians. There was the problem also, as time went on, of what contribution Russia might make to the eventual defeat of Japan, with whom, throughout the fight against Germany, Russia was officially at peace.

Political problems, many of them arising out of what were superficially purely strategic ones, included the extent of the territorial rewards the Russians from the outset demanded that their allies allow them when victory was achieved. There was the future of defeated Germany, and of what it was hoped would be a victorious China; for China under Chiang Kai-shek had been fighting Japan since 1937 and, at any rate to Roosevelt, was the fourth member of the alliance. The destiny of the lesser States when liberated from the Germans (and to Roosevelt and Stalin, France was merely one of these almost till 1945), both as regards their boundaries and their form of government, was yet another problem, and so was the nature of the international machinery which would replace the League of Nations when the war was over.

The task of grappling with these varied and interlocking problems fell almost exclusively upon Roosevelt, Churchill and Stalin, who were in constant communication throughout the war and met in frequent conference. Their personal power in their respective countries was exceptionally great and, in consequence, much that happened was a reflection of their personal characters and methods.

Roosevelt derived unique prestige from his success in leading the United States out of the Depression and from being re-elected in 1940 and 1944, not only for a third but for a fourth term as President; and as President he was Commander-in-Chief of the American forces. In addition, he was temperamentally inclined to take action without making use either of his official colleagues or of the State Department, which was technically responsible for foreign affairs. This was partly because the Secretary of State, Cordell Hull, was given to woolly generalities, and partly because the Department was short of persons with expert knowledge of foreign countries. Thus, when Roosevelt's special envoy, Robert Murphy, arrived in North Africa in 1941 to prepare diplomatically for the arrival of American forces, he found there were virtually no Americans in official employment with knowledge of North Africa, or of French or Arabic. He had to enlist a miscellany of business-men, engineers and lawyers. In like manner, Roosevelt's whole conduct of the diplomatic and political aspects of the alliance was that of a brilliant, but fundamentally uninstructed, amateur, playing by ear.

Fortified as he was by little real knowledge of the world outside the United States he had thus perforce to rely heavily on the inherited attitudes he shared with other enlightened Americans, and on his own buoyant personality. The two together gave him that essential quality of a war leader, unshakeable optimism: the optimism of the American tradition, the optimism of one who could know for certain that his country was safe from defeat, the optimism of an unusually brave, successful and genial human being. For dealing with the mercurial Churchill and the hard, suspicious Stalin, these qualities contributed much to the maintenance of an alliance that was rarely harmonious for more than a week at a time. Unfortunately, Roosevelt's optimism steadily declined into evasion; a refusal to face the accumulating evidence that victory would complicate and not solve the problems of international life.

Churchill, though British constitutional law made him less powerful in theory than Roosevelt, was politically more powerful, if only because he did not have to submit himself to the polls at four-yearly intervals. Nor, like both Roosevelt and Stalin, was he a Commander-in-Chief. Nevertheless, he did his best to behave as one, and in view of the greater experience of both himself and the British Chiefs of Staff he enjoyed a considerable, if declining, influence over Anglo-American strategy, and Roosevelt was regarded by his own staff as unduly susceptible to Churchill in this respect. At least until the spring of 1944, the strategy pursued by the Anglo-Americans was Churchillian in broad conception, though never so in important details. As well as his strategic and tactical fecundity, he contributed a certain measured pessimism, by which he sought to moderate the almost irresponsible gaiety with which Roosevelt assumed that, just round the corner from military victory, was an instant future of smiling Anglo-American-Russian co-operation in beneficent governance of a harmonious, happy world, which would know neither empires nor spheres of influence, and neither armaments nor tyrannies.

Churchillian pessimism arose out of a combination of realism and emotion. He was the only one of the trio with a real feeling for the peoples of Europe. Stalin despised them, Roosevelt saw them only through vague mists of benevolence tempered, in American fashion, by a certain boredom. It was, therefore, with almost no success that Churchill tried to protect Europe from the consequences of Stalin's 'realism', and from Roosevelt's determination to withdraw U.S. troops as soon as possible after Germany's defeat. To restrain Roosevelt and mollify Stalin, to guide a strategy he could not hope to direct, to maintain an alliance which was essential for victory but whose very existence was a threat both to Europe and to the British Empire, was a task which exercised to the limit and, in the end, defeated Churchill. He had the capacity to plead a cause and to argue a case; to rage and then to melt; to scowl and then to grin; to propose with eloquence, but not to sulk too much when either Roosevelt or Stalin disposed otherwise. This combination of courage and comradeship saved the alliance; but it could save neither Europe nor the Empire in the end.

Stalin's contribution to the alliance was his control of the Russian Army. His adherence to agreed time-tables for the launching of offensives was usually punctilious. He was thus indispensable, for, even in the early months of 1945, the Russian Army was still engaging far more German divisions than were the Allied forces in the west; and it was their realistic appreciation of the magnitude of Russia's military contribution to victory which led the United States generals to discount Churchillian gloom about the Red Army's westward progress across Europe. And if subsequent history has cast Stalin for the role of villain in the story, previous history had given him little opportunity to play any other part, even had his temperament been different; and that, too, was a product of Russian history, much as Roosevelt's attitude sprang from the history of the United States. For, alone among the three powers, Russia was not (as the innocent jargon of the 1930's put it) a 'satisfied' power. Whereas neither the British nor the Americans had territorial claims requiring satisfaction, Russia had legitimate claims and ambitions which were never adequately, and certainly never generously, recognized during wartime. Victory in a world-wide war was bound to lead to Russian demands for the reversal of her defeats in 1905 and 1917, and for the cancellation of the Treaty of Portsmouth, which shut her out of Manchuria and Korea, and of the Treaty of Brest-Litovsk which, together with subsequent Allied hostility, deprived her of European territories she had long controlled. That Russia would, legitimately, seek ways and means of guaranteeing the security of her long and vulnerable western frontier against further attack ought to have been self-evident from the start: to believe that the U.S.S.R. could leave this to a non-Communist international organization, such as the United Nations was certain to be, was naïve.

In consequence, Stalin was bound, by national history as well as by evident personal character, to be acquisitive and suspicious. It was hardly relevant that he publicly eschewed the twin ideologies on which Russian attitudes to the West had been based for a century. He told Benes he was not a Pan-Slav; he abolished the Comintern and refrained, with what seems in retrospect astonishing correctness, from *sub rosa* ideological attacks on his allies, criticizing them sourly enough for cowardice or deceit, but never for being greedy imperialist-capitalists; and he treated non-Russian Communists with a contempt so large that it embraced both Tito in Jugoslavia and Mao Tse-tung in China.

His suspicion of outsiders was ingrained in him by Russia's long historic sufferings at the hands of foreigners, and by the more recent ostracism and invasion which Russia had endured since the 1917 revolution. His obsession with power was likewise personal, since, on the death of Lenin, he had intrigued to get power, and, in the 1930's, murdered in order to keep it; but it was also the basic principle of Marxist-Leninist Communism. Most observers in the 1940's, and many even later, confused themselves by supposing that Communism was chiefly to do with political economy. What was really peculiar to it, however, was its rigid, pedantic, suspicious obsession with the technique of acquiring power by the fastest possible means and of retaining it in unshakeable permanence. Communism had long ceased to be greatly concerned about ends; it was mainly pre-occupied with means – the means of getting and keeping power. Ruthlessness and suspicion followed inevitably from this, for in such a scheme of things all men were enemies, all ideals were cheats and no holds were barred. Yet, however clearly Churchill and Roosevelt might have realized it (and Roosevelt did not realize it at all, and even Churchill hoped almost to the end that the Bear could perhaps be wooed), there hung over them both the inescapable circumstances that without Stalin they could not defeat Germany, and that, even when Germany was defeated, he would still be needed for the defeat of Japan.

Divergence was apparent even before the United States had become a belligerent. Meeting at sea, in August 1941, Roosevelt and Churchill, at the instigation of the former, had concocted what came to be known as the Atlantic Charter, laying down the principles on which they 'based their hopes for a better future for the world'. They disclaimed all aggrandisement for themselves; they wanted no territorial changes which did not 'accord with the freely expressed wishes of the peoples concerned'; they expressed their respect for the right 'of all peoples' to choose their own form of government, and their desire to see 'sovereignty and self-government' restored to all peoples who had been deprived of them. All twenty-six of the United Nations then nominally or really at war with the Axis signed adherence to the Charter on New Year's Day, 1942; and it was on the original foundation of the Charter that the organization of the United Nations was eventually created.

Here at once, was divergence between a war and a moral crusade; and evidence of an apparently noble, but fundamentally arrogant, desire to force facts and peoples to conform to principles conceived without reference either to real facts or real people. In practice, the Charter was anti-British and anti-Russian, as well as anti-German and anti-Japanese. For neither Roosevelt nor Cordell Hull was it enough to want to overthrow Germany and Japan, even though, when the Charter was drawn up, the United States had not fired a shot or dropped a single bomb. As far as they were concerned, the right of all people to choose their own government was intended to involve the abandonment by Britain of all her colonial possessions; and, as far as both Churchill and Roosevelt were concerned, it amounted to a demand that, after defeating Germany, Russia would renounce the control over the Baltic Republics and eastern Poland she had lost at Brest-Litovsk but regained by agreement with Hitler. It was in response to this pressure that Churchill, fortified by the victory of second Alamein, had announced his intention not to preside over the liquidation of the British Empire. And it was because Churchill, no less than Roosevelt, was thus early insisting to the Russians that their future retention of the Baltic States was contrary to the Atlantic Charter, that Western relations with Russia began as they were to continue, in an atmosphere of mutual recrimination punctuated by such brief periods of goodwill as were dictated either by joint military peril or joint military success. The U.S.S.R. acceded to the Charter along with the rest, but with reservations which referred, realistically and reasonably enough, to the consideration

that the practical application of these principles will necessarily adapt itself to the circumstances, needs and historic peculiarities of particular countries.[1]

[1] Feis, *Churchill, Roosevelt, Stalin*, p. 24, footnote.

The urgencies of war, however, meant that the major matters of concern during 1942 would be strategic. At Washington, in December 1941, two weeks after Pearl Harbor, the British and Americans agreed to set up a Joint Chiefs of Staff Committee, and it was confirmed that the defeat of Germany would take precedence over the defeat of Japan. This in itself was a decision that failed to please all sections of American military thinking; and worse followed when the British insisted that it was impossible to project an invasion force into western Europe at any time during 1942. The shipping situation in itself seemed to rule this out: in the first six months of 1942, with the whole of the North American coast now open to U-boat attack, four and a half million tons of shipping was sunk and only 21 U-boats destroyed. Moreover, Churchill and the British Chiefs of Staff were convinced that any early landing in France would be on far too small a scale to cause the Germans to withdraw a significant number of troops from the Russian front. Yet the obvious alternatives were unsatisfactory: either inaction in Europe all through 1942, with its consequent effects on Allied morale, or a diversion of effort to the Pacific, which would likewise not help Europe and be of no assistance to the Russians; and how long Russia could hold out without some diversion of German forces to other fronts was, all through 1942, a matter of serious doubt.

Churchill opposed a landing in France in 1942, was prepared to consider it only provisionally for 1943, and almost till June 1944, when it actually occurred, was extremely anxious about its dangers. He insisted that it was wiser to wear the Germans down before attempting an invasion, and, whereas the United States wanted to make a frontal assault on the Germans at the earliest opportunity, Churchill wanted to out-manœuvre them first, with invasion in the west only as the final act. In consequence, as early as December 1941, he had tried to persuade the Americans to invade North Africa as a prelude to eliminating Italy and eventually to the Allied control of the entire Mediterranean. This would release a great deal of shipping compelled to use the lengthy Cape route to the East; it would facilitate an attack on German forces in the Balkans, possibly bring Turkey into the war and thus make it infinitely easier to get supplies to Russia. It would also, of course, establish Britain's position in the Middle East unshakeably for the rest of the war; and it was this aspect of the plan which the Americans found least attractive. Worse still, from Churchill's point of view, the ill-success of the Eighth Army in North Africa in 1942 made the whole thing look suspiciously like a plan to get the Americans to prop up British power in the Mediterranean and in particular in Egypt where, according to the principles of the Atlantic Charter, the British had no business to be in the first place.

In the end Churchill prevailed; Roosevelt finally gave way to him in July 1942 because he preferred some action to none at all. The consequence was immediate anger from Stalin, who believed that he had been definitely promised a second front in Europe during 1942. He was further angered by the temporary cessation of the convoying of supplies to Archangel owing to the severity of enemy naval action. Accordingly, Churchill went to Moscow, in August 1942, to try to placate him; and it was *en route* that he had stopped at Cairo to purge a Middle East Command,[2] whose offensive failures had made it so hard for him during the preceding months to argue that real damage could be done to the Germans in North Africa. Perhaps, too, he hoped that if he arrived in Moscow fresh from a purge of allegedly inefficient generals, Stalin, an expert at purges, would be duly appreciative. In fact, Stalin was extremely dissatisfied. He listened to Churchill's arguments, but insisted that he did not agree with them, and made unpleasant observations to the effect that British soldiers should learn, like Russian soldiers, not to be afraid of Germans. Such remarks were a sore trial to Churchill, who never excelled at the returning of soft answers; but Stalin, while not relenting at the political level, saw to it that the closing stages of their meeting were conducted in an atmosphere of conviviality. Churchill's revelation of the Allies' intention shortly to invade North Africa doubtless also helped to relax the tensions.

The Torch landings in North Africa in November 1942 were followed, as has already been related, by the surrender of all the Axis forces in North Africa in May 1943. In July of that year, Sicily was invaded, and the Italian mainland itself two months later. Mussolini was dismissed on 25 July 1943, and the Germans immediately took over the task of resisting the Allied forces. Not until May 1945 did they surrender in Italy; and by then there had still been no Allied advance into the Balkans, and Turkey still remained neutral. Almost no part of the campaign proved easy, with the possible exception of the conquest of Sicily; and Churchill's talk about Italy as Europe's 'soft underbelly' proved wide of the mark.

Yet even this may have been the consequence less of the inherent strategic unwisdom of an attack in this particular theatre than of those persistent United States doubts which led to its being conducted with insufficient drive and often with inadequate resources, because the claims of other theatres were regarded as more urgent. The landings in North Africa were made too far west in the first place, because the Americans were as nervous about the dangers of an amphibious landing in the Mediterranean as they were apparently eager for one across the Channel. The British pressed for substantial landings in Tunis; the Americans insisted on concentrating their initial landings at Casablanca, Oran and Algiers farther west, so that at least one of their major bases should be outside the Mediterranean. The delays occasioned by this caution (the Germans rushed reinforcements into Tunis) meant that the campaign was sufficiently long drawn out to prevent an invasion of France in 1943. The decision to go on

[1] See p. 358.

to invade Sicily was made grudgingly, and after the diversion of resources to
the Far East necessitated by the fear that the Japanese, once entrenched in
their Pacific strongpoints, might be impossible to dislodge if they were long
left in possession of them. The invasion of Italy was put on the programme
only when it was discovered that the invasion of Sicily had brought about
the overthrow of Mussolini on 25 July 1943 and his replacement by
Marshal Badoglio. The lack of men and landing-craft proved even more

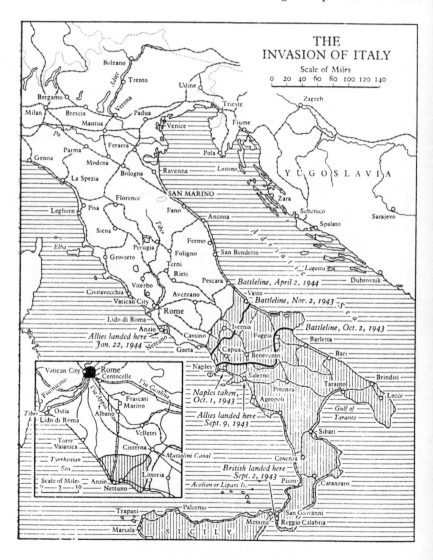

THE
INVASION OF ITALY

serious at this point. The only hope of preventing the Germans from pouring more divisions into central Italy was the dispatch of Allied forces to the mainland the moment Mussolini's downfall made an Italian surrender an imminent probability. The opportunity was missed; no landing in Italy was made until early in September 1943, by which time the Germans were as far south as Naples. The delay of three months (which took a year to make up for) was due to the Americans having thirteen divisions operating in the Pacific and fewer than four (owing to shipping problems) available for use in Italy. Thus the Allied advance from Calabria was slow, and a landing at Salerno south of Naples came near to disaster; and there was thus no hope of Churchill's realizing his hope of a swift capture of Rome and a subsequent link-up with the Balkan patriots.

The conflict between American and British policies continued through 1944. The German divisions sent into Italy coincidentally with the Italian surrender in September 1943 fought with their usual tenacity, and the winter of 1943–44 found the Allies stuck fast a hundred miles south of Rome. Here again, both the main offensive of 1944, and the landing farther north at Anzio to assist it in January, would have been entirely subordinated to the requirements not only of the projected invasion of Normandy ('Overlord'), but also of the additional landings ('Anvil') the Americans now favoured in the south of France, but for a great exercise of persuasion by Churchill. Rome was not taken until 4 June 1944, only two days before the Overlord landings began; and once more progress was baulked. Churchill argued strongly for a vigorous advance into northern Italy as a prelude to the move into Jugoslavia and Hungary that he had envisaged nearly two and a half years before. The United States Chiefs of Staff refused to agree. Their plan to supplement Overlord by Anvil was to take first place; there were to be no large-scale operations either in northern Italy or in the Balkans. Roosevelt supported his generals, adding the further point that he was not prepared to risk the criticism he would meet at home if the frontal attack on Germany met with reverses while there were U.S. troops in the Balkans. Churchill was made so despondent by this that he went so far as to tell Eisenhower he was thinking of resigning ('I may lay down the mantle of my high office'). The Mediterranean and Italian operation had, from first to last, been his particular contribution to the grand strategy, and he could not bear to see it drain away without the fulfilment of its larger purposes. 'I pray God you may be right,' he told Roosevelt fervently.

As it turned out, the forces already in Italy proved sufficient to drive out the Germans across the Po, while Anvil proved more successful than the British had feared; but, even as late as February 1945, when he met Roosevelt at Yalta, Churchill had still not quite given up. When it was agreed that three divisions be transferred from northern Italy to fortify Montgomery's advance into northern Germany, the Prime Minister

appended to his concurrence the proviso that victory over the Germans in
Italy should be followed at once by an Allied drive into Austria to forestall
the Russians.

His persistent advocacy of a Mediterranean onslaught against the Axis
has caused Churchill to be accused of strategic amateurishness on the
grand scale and of being a Machiavellian Imperialist. On the other hand,
since the full execution of his design would (or, more accurately, might)
have brought Anglo-American forces into the Balkans and Hungary in
1945 and thus prevented their subsequent domination by the Russians, he
has been highly praised for his political prescience by comparison with the
unthinking Americans. These interpretations are wide of the mark.

The presumption of political prescience is largely, though not entirely,
an exercise in hindsight. When the North African landings were first proposed in the winter of 1941-2, the issue was not that of taking long-term
precautions against a Russian victory, but immediate ones against a Russian
defeat. The notion that it was all a 'Churchiavellian' dodge to get the
United States to defend the British Empire is unacceptable, since as allies
of the United Kingdom the United States were under a moral obligation to
defend their ally's vital interests; that they interpreted their moral obligations in terms of liberating Britain's colonial subjects is a comment on
American policy, not on British. Furthermore, the opening of the Mediterranean to Allied shipping, the preservation of Allied access to Middle
Eastern oil, and the safeguarding of Russia's southern flank were not purely
British objectives. The Allied campaign in North Africa broke the Italians,
and cost the Germans a quarter of a million men. It gave the Americans
invaluable training in the arts of amphibious operations and thus contributed to the success of Overlord; it provided valuable training also in the
difficult techniques of Allied military co-operation in the field. Control of
northern Italy brought the aircraft factories of southern Germany and the
oilfields of Roumania within reach of Allied bombers; and the Italian
campaign engaged more German divisions than Allied divisions.

There were thus positive gains from action in the Mediterranean theatre,
despite the fact that it was never backed by adequate American support,
and the decisive factor in forming a judgement on it is that its ultimate
objective of the penetration of central and south-eastern Europe (assuming
it to have been militarily feasible) was finally denied to it by the United
States insistence on depriving Alexander in 1944 of seven divisions for the
Anvil operation in southern France.

That this central European thrust would perhaps have had political
effects for the better on the eventual destiny of that area was not a matter of
primary concern even to Churchill until 1944. That his basic concern was
strategic may be realized when it is seen for what it was: an attempt to
realize more fully the strategy for which both he and Lloyd George had
pleaded in the first war against the Germans. Churchill's advocacy of the

Gallipoli campaign, Lloyd George's vain search for a diversionary attack from Italy at a time when the aim was equally not to forestall, but to assist, the Russians, were the historical and strategic antecedents of Churchill's Mediterranean strategy in the Second World War, and a continuation of the old controversy between the 'Westerners', like Haig and the French, and the supporters of what were called 'sideshows'; only now it was not Haig and the French but the Americans who were 'Westerners'. In both wars, the opponents of an exclusively Western strategy had been properly concerned with the conservation of British manpower, and with the fact that, as a predominantly naval power, the British ought first and foremost to use the mobility conferred by naval power to seek to out-manœuvre the continental enemy. In the longer perspective which will be accessible to the historian of the future, it may well be thought that the downfall of British imperial power in the first half of the twentieth century was ascribable to the strategy which put its emphasis on British military action in western Europe rather than on the despised Mediterranean sideshows.

---

41 · Casablanca, Moscow, Cairo, Teheran, 1943

When Churchill and Roosevelt and their Chiefs of Staff met at Casablanca, in the first week of January 1943, their major strategic decision was that the conquest of Tunisia was too far ahead (it was not completed till May 1943) for an invasion of western Europe to be possible until 1944. Three main lines of action were planned; an intensification of the battle of the U-boats, the appointment of an Overlord planning organization in London under a Chief of Staff to the Supreme Allied Commander (C.O.S.S.A.C.): and, as a sort of time-filling operation, the invasion of Sicily. It was characteristic of the dilemmas which faced the planning of operations in any one theatre that the U.S. Joint Chiefs of Staff wanted the proportion of Allied resources allotted to the Pacific to be increased from 15 per cent of the total to 30 per cent; they threatened to reduce U.S. commitments in Europe if something was not done to meet their demands. The bulk of the U.S. fleet and much U.S. landing-craft were now allocated to the Pacific; yet it was precisely the lack of shipping and landing-craft that delayed both Overlord and the conquest of Italy. Furthermore, Stalin's anger on learning

of the Casablanca decision still further to delay Overlord was exacerbated
by U.S. attempts to get him to allow preliminary staff talks about possible
Russian action against Japan. Stalin wanted his allies to start a second
front in Europe; instead, they were asking him to start one in Siberia.
To complete his discomfiture in 1943, Allied supply convoys to Russia
round Norway had once more to be suspended during the summer owing
to the severity of German U-boat, surface fleet and air attacks.

The fact that, all through 1943 at least, the Russians would be left
to do most of the fighting against Germany lends point to the circumstance
that Roosevelt's penchant for personal diplomacy resulted in the absence
of the foreign office chiefs of both countries from the Casablanca conference. Thus there was no discussion either of the political implications
of a Russian advance into eastern Europe, or even of the policy to be
adopted in the event of the Mediterranean campaign achieving its desired
Churchillian objective of defeating Italy. Here, as always, Roosevelt betted
on the chances of getting along with Stalin, and on the notion that political
problems could be 'fixed' when the time came, without previous examination of them.

This spirit of cheerful amateurishness was startlingly illustrated by
Roosevelt's sudden announcement to the Press at the end of the Casablanca
conference that the Allies were committed to 'the unconditional surrender'
of Germany, Italy, and Japan. This meant, he said, 'total elimination' of
their 'war power' and

the destruction of the philosophies in those countries, which are based on
conquest and the subjugation of other people.

This pronouncement has been much criticized on the grounds that it
encouraged the enemy powers to continue their resistance to the bitter end.
Yet, the formula did not prevent the Italians seeking to surrender only
seven months later. The delay in meeting their request was due to the
presence of the Germans on Italian soil and the absence of the Allies from
it, so that for some considerable time Marshal Badoglio had nobody to
surrender to. It had no appreciable effect on the decision of the Japanese to
ask for an armistice in 1945; they surrendered because they had lost the war.
The German fight to the end was due to the character of Hitler and to fear
of the Russians. The notion that some statement of terms might have
encouraged revolt in the enemy states is a facile dismissal of the difficulties
and terrors of resisting any Government in wartime, let alone an authoritarian one. The theory that had Germany been offered terms it would have
surrendered sooner and thus could have been preserved as a barrier against
the Russians is a vindication of Hitler's propaganda line that because Russia
was a Communist State he should be allowed to do whatever he liked, with
all that that involved in political tyranny, racial hatred and moral corruption.
To suppose that there was an alternative to demanding unconditional

surrender is to display unawareness of what living in the world of the 1930's and 1940's was really like, and to fall into the grotesque error of implying that there were no real issues in the Second World War. The fact was that the Governments of Germany, Italy and Japan had proved impossible to live with. They had deliberately spread dissension, fear and cruelty into three continents in the years before 1939, and each had made war without a shadow of moral justification for doing so. It may have been wrong of the Allied Powers to allow the situation to deteriorate in the 1930's to the point where nothing but global war to the end could solve the problems posed by these Governments. But not to destroy them utterly once the war had been fully embarked on would merely repeat the errors that had caused the war to break out. Neither Russia, the United States nor Great Britain had desired war at any time; all had made positively abject efforts to avoid it. Only Germany, Italy and Japan had deliberately fought wars. It is no sort of history to pretend that the two great wars of the twentieth century were accidentally-contrived contests about nothing. Nor did the unconditional surrender formula ever really imply that *all* Germans were equally guilty.

The valid objection to the unconditional surrender formula was that, as almost the only precise statement of political intention to which Roosevelt ever committed himself during wartime, it was both irrelevant and inadequate. It was irrelevant because, with the important exception of Stalin, for whose benefit it had principally been made, nobody expected him to say anything else, and inadequate because the real political problem was what was to be done about the enemy *after* surrender; and to this problem no consistent thought was ever given. The United States and the British were rarely of one mind, and never of one clear mind, about the future either of the enemy Powers or of the States the Germans and Japanese had conquered or made satellites; they differed in their estimates of the future roles of France and China; they fumbled only intermittently with the problems of post-war world security; and both Roosevelt and Cordell Hull wanted the liquidation of the British Empire. Yet, whenever difficult European or Far Eastern problems were discussed, it was in a desultory fashion only, because it was felt that, given post-war Allied co-operation, no difficulties would be too great to be overcome.

This was particularly noticeable during the Moscow Conference of October 1943, presided over by Molotov, and attended by Eden for Great Britain and Cordell Hull for the United States. It was already clear that there would be serious trouble between the U.S.S.R. and the Polish Government in exile in London. Both the British and the Americans were perturbed by the signature of a mutual treaty of assistance between the U.S.S.R. and the Czech Government in exile under Benes. There was no United States or even Soviet co-operation with Eden's efforts to heal the serious rift in Jugoslavia between the Royalist anti-Germans under Mihailovich and the Communist anti-Germans under Tito; and no United

States support (nor even Soviet opposition) for British efforts to prevent Greece passing into the hands of the Communist resistance movement. There was agreement that Germany should be disarmed and occupied and perhaps federalized or even dismembered, but nothing precise was settled, and Roosevelt's reaction to State Department fears that dismemberment of Germany would unduly increase the influence of Russia was to give Hull no instructions on the matter. All these serious items were neglected while the ministers concentrated on their joyous anticipation of the unanimity and victory that would follow the launching of Overlord in the following spring, and on their relief that the U.S.S.R. had promised to join the war against Japan three months after Germany's defeat.

All that emerged by way of signpost to the post-war world from what was regarded as a thoroughly satisfactory conference was the Four Nation Declaration of 30 October 1943. (At Russia's insistence China was represented at the conference.) This flatulent document did no more than say that everything was going to be all right after the war because everybody would consult everybody else, and because the Great Powers were not going to quarrel. The four powers would, when the war was over, continue their 'united action . . . for the organization and maintenance of peace and security'. They

recognized the necessity of establishing at the earliest possible date a general international organization based on the sovereign equality of all peace-loving States.

They would, pending the establishment of this organization,

consult with each other, and, as occasion requires, with other members of the United Nations, with a view to joint action on behalf of the community of nations,

and, after the termination of hostilities, they would

not employ their military forces within the territories of other States except for the purposes envisaged in this declaration and after joint consultation.

In fact, the unease in the American State Department about this escape from reality into a cloud of high-flown generalities was considerable. On returning from Moscow, however, Cordell Hull informed a joint session of Congress:

As the provisions of the four-nation declaration are carried into effect, there will no longer be any need for spheres of influence, for alliances, for balance of power, or any other of the special arrangements through which, in the unhappy past, the nations strove to safeguard their security or promote their interests.

Churchill, like everybody else, appeared to swallow his doubts and to wager his all, in public at any rate, on the future co-operative zeal of the Russians. At the Mansion House on 9 November 1943 he said :

There is no doubt that the full and frank discussions between the three Foreign Ministers, Mr Molotov, Mr Eden and that gallant old eagle Mr Hull, who flew on a strong wing, have had the effect of making our Russian friends feel as they have never felt before that it is the heartfelt wish of the British and American nations to fight the war out with them in loyal alliance, and afterwards to work with them on the basis of mutual respect and faithful comradeship in the resettlement and rebuilding of this distracted and tormented world.

He was wily enough, however, not to risk the prophecy that the 'heartfelt wish' would be realized. In fact, Stalin had already anticipated Churchill. On 6 November, in a speech on the 26th anniversary of the October Revolution, he described the decisions of the Moscow Conference as 'historic' and on the subject of peace aims he declared:

Together with our Allies we must: (1) Liberate the peoples of Europe from the Fascist invaders and help to rebuild their national States, dismembered by the Fascist enslavers – the peoples of France, Belgium, Jugoslavia, Czechoslovakia, Poland, Greece and other States now under the German yoke must once more become free and independent; (2) grant the liberated peoples of Europe the full right and freedom to determine their own form of government, and . . . establish lasting economic, political and cultural collaboration among the peoples of Europe.

This was the most precise of the major statements about the future that was made in public after the Moscow Conference. It appears almost unequivocal; and since, in fact, time has shown that post-war co-operation between the members of the wartime grand alliance offers in the long run the only real chance of peace, it would have been both unwise and dangerous at this stage to behave as if it were impossible.

The Moscow Foreign Ministers' conference was followed, late in November 1943, by the fulfilment of Roosevelt's long-cherished wish for a personal meeting with Stalin. The three leaders met at Teheran, after a previous Anglo-American consultation in Cairo, which was attended also by Chiang Kai-shek. Both meetings were dominated by the mind and spirit of Roosevelt.

The Cairo meeting between the British and Americans included one more episode in the debate between the Americans' 'Western' attitude and Churchill's Mediterranean strategy. While the Americans were determined to concentrate on Overlord and Anvil, Churchill, as usual, pressed the case for vigorous action in Italy and then in the Balkans. Worse still, from Churchill's point of view, the President, contrary to the U.S. insistence that strategy should not be influenced by political considerations, was as anxious as his generals to divert resources to an invasion of Burma in order to bolster up the sagging war effort of Chiang Kai-shek's China. Churchill got the Burma proposals dropped; but this only made certain that Anvil, likewise a U.S. proposal, would have priority over the campaign in Italy. It was at Cairo, also, that Roosevelt secured as an Allied war aim the return from Japan to China of all Japan's possessions on and adjacent to the Asian mainland, including Manchuria and Formosa. Although the Moscow

Declaration had envisaged a world-wide international peace-keeping organization, Roosevelt still placed most faith in his frequently mooted idea that the U.S.A., the U.S.S.R., Great Britain and China should act as the globe's Four Policemen after the war. The plan required China to be wished into unity and greatness, and Russia to be wished into brotherly harmony with her three other peace-keepers; Roosevelt did not worry that Stalin had refused to have Russia represented at the Cairo conference as soon as he learned that Chiang Kai-shek would be there.

At Teheran, Roosevelt used all his personal gaiety on Stalin; and, whenever a problem arose that might disturb the harmony, he made sure it was Churchill and not he who did the arguing with Stalin. Verbal in-fighting with each other was a habit Churchill and Stalin had acquired at their Moscow meeting in August 1942, and at Teheran Roosevelt seems to have adopted the device of sitting back good-humouredly as Churchill and Stalin argued, and of laughing most loudly whenever Stalin got in a particularly good thrust against Churchill. The aim of this bonhomious diplomacy was to demonstrate to Stalin that, so far from ganging up with Great Britain against the U.S.S.R., the U.S.A. was rather better at seeing the Russian point of view than the Imperialist British were. In consequence, the Teheran conference made Churchill anxious, Roosevelt happy and Stalin unusually amiable; but virtually no firm decision on any concrete political problem was reached at Teheran. Churchill asked Stalin to be reasonable in his attitude to Poland, but Roosevelt was untidily imprecise and asked that nothing be done about it that might embarrass his chances of getting U.S. Poles to vote for him in the Presidential election that was due in the autumn of 1944.

There was more desultory chat about what to do with the Germans. Stalin was bloodthirsty on the subject, proposing the liquidation of up to 100,000 senior German Army officers, and growling when Churchill said he objected to murder for political purposes. Roosevelt merely contributed a funny remark. The sense of the talks, in general, seemed to adumbrate the permanent break-up of Germany, the domination of Poland by the U.S.S.R., and the disappearance of the French colonial empire. Roosevelt disliked empires and Stalin thought the French too weak to deserve to keep one. The effects of this on Europe, given that Roosevelt made no secret of the intention to withdraw U.S. troops as soon as possible, would be its domination by the U.S.S.R. Roosevelt, in so far as he seriously feared this at all, behaved as if he hoped to avert it by treating Stalin as a close and trusted friend.

The fault in this policy was that whereas Roosevelt displayed goodwill in order to persuade Stalin not to quarrel with the West, Stalin took Roosevelt's goodwill to mean that the West would not quarrel with Russia. To show neither military nor political interest in the future of Poland was to invite the U.S.S.R. to attempt a domination of eastern and south-eastern

Europe that the U.S.A. was to regard as objectionable only when it was too late to prevent it. The Russians could legitimately deduce from their contacts with their Western allies during the war that only Churchill and the British were concerned about the Balkans and eastern Europe, and that Roosevelt manifestly neither shared nor encouraged that British concern.

Since they had taken no concrete political measures to guard against Russian domination of half Europe after the war, the only chance left for the Anglo-Americans was that during 1944 their military chiefs would show altogether exceptional powers of drive and organization. One of the agreements made at Teheran was that Stalin would launch a new eastern offensive to coincide with the Overlord landings. It was already recognized that Berlin was almost certain to fall to the Russians, and this, therefore, would seem to impose upon the Western invasion force the political necessity of getting far into northern Germany as fast as possible. But 1944 was to see military indecision added to political indecision.

42 · From Normandy to the Ardennes, 1944

General Eisenhower had been appointed Supreme Allied Commander for Overlord in the autumn of 1943, and Montgomery was transferred from command of the Eighth Army in Italy to take charge both of British troops assigned to the invasion force and of the actual operation during its initial stages. Eisenhower's first action was to postpone the projected date of the first landings from May 1944 until June 1944, because of delays in providing landing-craft in quantities that would permit landings on a front broad enough to be effective. The Anvil landings were also postponed. The lack of landing-craft was due partly to planning miscalculations, and partly to the U.S. Navy's wish to concentrate shipping and landing-craft on the war in the Pacific, which it regarded as the United States' only important theatre of operations; an attitude attributable in part to mortification at British lukewarmness about an invasion of Europe in 1942. Postponement of the initial landings until June made the whole operation more hazardous owing to the lesser reliability of the weather; and, politically, the loss of a month of summer campaigning was considerable. From the point of view of the accumulation of material, however, the postponement was an advantage, since, against the most strongly defended coastline on which an amphibious assault had ever been launched, massive material superiority was considered essential.

The assault phase of the operation was assisted by the stratagem which led the Germans to believe that, taking advantage of the shortest sea route, the Allies would attack in the Pas de Calais area, where there were usable ports to try for. The Pas de Calais was heavily bombed to help reinforce this impression, and large numbers of troops who would not be needed in the first phases of the invasion were deceptively concentrated in Kent. Allied air strength prevented German reconnaissance from discovering that the main body of the invasion force was positioned for landings in Normandy. Even after the landings had taken place, Hitler persisted in the belief that they were diversionary, and held back Rommel's armour in case it were needed northwards to counter the 'real' attack on the Pas de Calais.

The decision to land on the Normandy beaches would not have been possible but for the inventiveness of the British in producing devices which would compensate, in the initial stages, for the absence of port facilities. The failure of an attempted landing at Dieppe in August 1942 had made it clear that to assault heavily fortified ports was suicidal. Hence stimulus was given to the production of prefabricated harbours, referred to as Mulberry, constructed of concrete caissons and floating piers which could be towed across the Channel, each protecting an area about the size of Dover harbour. Since armoured protection was vital from the start, amphibious tanks and tanks capable of flailing their way through mine-fields, as well as a pipeline under the ocean (Pluto), were among the contributions which made possible large-scale landings away from the heavily defended northern French ports.

The D-Day landings on 6 June 1944 were undertaken by the First (U.S.) Army under General Bradley and the Second (British) Army under General Dempsey, both at this stage being under the over-all command of Montgomery. Not surprisingly, the objectives laid down for D-Day were not in fact achieved, partly owing to deteriorating weather. Nevertheless, within forty-eight hours, the Second Army was in command of a bridgehead over twenty miles wide and up to ten miles deep, and was soon strongly attacked by German armour outside Caen. Protected by this British engagement of German armour, the First Army was able to unite its two originally separated bridgeheads, capture the Cherbourg peninsula by 26 June, and thence to break out eastwards. By the end of July, the British Second Army had at last taken Caen, and a sizeable area west and south of it; by mid-August the Germans had lost the whole area west of the river Orne and north of the river Loire. On 25 August Paris had been reached, by 31 August, Amiens; by September, Brussels and Antwerp. The Germans had suffered half a million casualties and lost nearly ninety per cent of their tanks. The delayed Anvil landings took place on 15 August and the invaders were in Grenoble on 24 August, Lyons by 3 September and as far north as Nancy on 15 September.

The Germans were thus, in the autumn of 1944, in a military situation in the west comparable to that in which they had been under Ludendorff in the autumn of 1918. But this time they had, in the east, not the relatively simple problem of holding down a defeated Russia with an army of occupation, but an advancing Russia against whom they were compelled to employ around 150 divisions, along a front stretching from the Finnish Lakes to the Black Sea. By the end of August 1944 the Red Army was far inside the

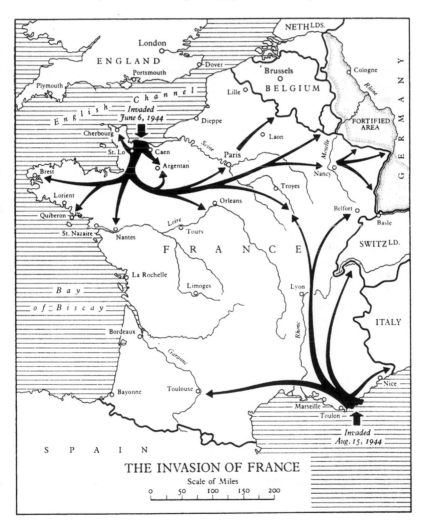

THE INVASION OF FRANCE

Scale of Miles

0   50   100   150   200

Baltic States, where Hitler had, in now customary fashion, ordered a strategically disastrous resistance to the end, and was also on the frontiers of East Prussia, and sweeping through Southern Poland. By 1 September 1944 the Russians had taken the Roumanian capital, Bucharest, and had reached the Roumanian frontier with Bulgaria.

The Germans had thus lost the war. Yet Hitler's optimism, which had conjured up the improbable successes of 1940, had now so little contact with reality as to constitute a form of mental derangement. Frenzied calls for a fight to the death, hysterical demands that his followers stand firm against the hated enemy, and that they should prefer death to the shame of surrender, are the stock-in-trade of the street corner rabble-rouser; but this particular rabble-rouser controlled the most military-minded nation in Europe, through Himmler's Gestapo and Goebbels' propaganda; and he held the Army's patriotic and capable generals captive also because of their sense of vocation and their oath of loyalty to him. If the war was fought to the point where the Germans had to surrender unconditionally, and in circumstances which put great areas of their own country, not to mention south-eastern Europe, under Soviet control, the chief responsibility lies not with the United States President, the United States Chiefs of Staff or General Eisenhower; it rests upon Hitler.

Hitler's generals did what they could to achieve some correspondence between his intentions and the real situation of his fighting forces. Rundstedt, his C-in-C in the west, disgusted by Hitler's insistence on unyielding and aggressive defence, declared before the end of July 1944 that there ought to be peace, and was removed from his command. His successor, Kluge, was even more oppressed by the German Army's plight, warning Hitler, as early as 21 July 1944, that a breakdown of the Army was imminent. Suspected by Hitler of trying to treat with the Allies, he was dismissed after less than a month in command. He committed suicide, leaving behind a letter urging the Führer to make peace.

Hitler, however, had his secret weapons. The threat of the fearful havoc these would wreak had been a constant feature of his psychological warfare against the British throughout most of the war. Now they were to go into action, and turn imminent defeat into victory. Revenge Weapon Number 1, jet-propelled pilotless planes, variously referred to as flying bombs, doodle-bugs, buzz-bombs and V.1's, began to descend on London and south-east England in the middle of June 1944; by the end of the month 2,000 V.1's had been launched, of which about a half actually reached London. They continued to descend until March 1945. On 8 September 1944, the first of the more sinister V.2's arrived. The V.2 was a 50-feet long, 15-ton rocket with a one-ton warhead, and a speed faster than that of sound. During the winter of 1944–5 over a thousand V.2's landed in England, most of them on London. The delay in perfecting these weapons, and the success of the R.A.F. in locating and bombing their launching sites before the summer of

1944, greatly reduced the effectiveness of this new campaign against British civilian morale. As it was, the Government greatly feared that the V.2 attack would compel the evacuation from London of the more important Government departments. But the sporadic character of the flying bombs' arrival and the unpredictability of their place of impact – varying dementedly from a crowded West-End street to a Sussex village – were perhaps more unnerving than the more damaging but more comprehensible Blitz. The V.2's, being fewer in number and inaudible until after they had done their damage, came to be accepted merely as one more wartime hazard. Their approach could excite no terror and their infrequency was a source of comfort. Nevertheless, the introduction of this manifestly pointless warfare against the civil population makes retrospective criticism of the Allied demand for unconditional surrender seem somewhat naïve; just as Allied persistence in 'strategic' bombing cast an air of dubiety over the post-war notion that only Nazis committed 'crimes against humanity'.

The threat of military and national disaster, to which Hitler was now bent on leading Germany, produced the Bomb Plot of 20 July 1944, in which a good many senior officers were involved. A group of staff officers had been seeking to assassinate Hitler ever since the débâcle at Stalingrad; the man selected for the actual planting of the bomb was Colonel von Stauffenberg; but the operation had been postponed until after the invasion of the west had begun. It was hoped that if the invasion had gone badly for the Allies, the death of Hitler would encourage them to offer moderate terms; or, if things went well for the Allies, the effect would be to stave off a final German catastrophe. The failure of the plot was due in part to bad luck and in part to the circumstance that, while the Army was prepared to jettison the Nazi system after Hitler was dead, it was not prepared to do so while he was alive. Therefore, since Hitler was so much alive that an hour or so after the explosion of Stauffenberg's bomb he was standing on a railway platform shaking Mussolini by the hand, the plot merely caused the death of the conspirators and a wholesale purge of suspicious elements throughout Germany that was greater in scope even than the purge of 1934. It was a brave thing to attempt to destroy Hitler; but it is difficult to understand, let alone fully sympathize with, the mentality of senior officers who, despising and detesting a political and military chief who had long been leading their country to certain ruin, and whose title to power was of the most dubious validity in the first place, were nevertheless prepared to follow him merely because he happened to be alive.

By early September 1944, strategic differences between the British and Americans involved not only the continued Churchillian desire for a drive towards the Danube from Italy, but Montgomery's desire for a concentrated drive towards Berlin rather than the slower advance into Germany on a broad front which was advocated by Eisenhower, whose headquarters at this date were still far back in the Cherbourg peninsula. Montgomery pressed his idea even more strongly after the 21st Army Group of British and Canadian forces, now his sole command, had captured Antwerp and Brussels. Strategic theories apart, however, support for Montgomery would have meant withholding resources from the 12th Army Group farther south, consisting entirely of U.S. forces, led by General Hodges and General Patton; and there was much dissatisfaction with Montgomery among U.S. generals, because of his often freely expressed self-confidence. It was partly to avert clashes of personality that Eisenhower had taken personal command of the land battle after the Normandy breakthrough. The broad front strategy may well have been decided on because Eisenhower thought it more likely to preserve unity among his subordinate commanders. To suggestions that it would be politically expedient to get to Berlin before the Russians, he was, like most U.S. commanders, deliberately deaf. Strategy must not be distorted by political considerations, and the U.S. command felt it had no reason to distrust the Russians.

Convinced that Eisenhower was denying him the means to speedy victory, Montgomery hit upon the imaginative device in September 1944 of seizing the crossings of the Dutch rivers and canals by calling upon the additional strength of the Allied Airborne Army. The British 1st Airborne Division was to seize the key point of Arnhem, and American Airborne divisions were to take Eindhoven and Nimwegen. The main ground forces under Montgomery's command would move north to link up with these airborne landings and the whole operation, when completed, would cut off the German forces in west Holland and establish a bridgehead in north Germany by outflanking both the Rhine and the Siegfried defences. The venture failed. The British airborne troops were dropped too far from their objective at Arnhem; a German armoured division happened to be in the vicinity, a sudden change in the weather made the dropping of reinforcements impossible, and the northward advance of the ground forces was not pushed on as hard as it might have been. Allied forces from the south reached only as far as the south bank of the river on which Arnhem stood; and, of the 10,000 men dropped by the British, little more than 2,000 eventually got south to the Allied lines.

The narrow failure of Montgomery's imaginative effort to use the Allied Airborne Army to outflank the main German defences left the Anglo-American forces as a whole without a dynamic strategy. Eisenhower, by promising all things to all his commanders, in fact denied to any of them the resources for an effective thrust into northern Germany. Eisenhower was perhaps proving better at commanding his commanders than at commanding the army itself. His difficulties were considerable: allowing Montgomery to use the airborne forces had upset the United States army commanders; but his refusals to let Montgomery have his way led to protests which only a man of Eisenhower's tact could have handled. Yet his success in surmounting these particular hazards delayed the army's progress and gave the Germans time to stage a recovery.

By all the rules the Germans were beaten by the autumn of 1944, but, like Louis XIV after 1710, the Prussians themselves after 1760, and the British after May 1940, the Germans were now in the desperate situation that breeds desperate recovery. For the first time since a united German Reich had been created in 1871, the Fatherland was in real and not just imaginary danger. The enemy was at the eastern and western gates and no mercy could be expected from either direction. Yet there could be no surrender. The Jews and the Slavs, and the other subjugated peoples, had suffered too much for that to be possible. It was useless now to attempt to overthrow Hitler: that would merely deprive Germany of its only means of organized self-defence. Nor, at this particular moment, could there be contemplation as there had been before and was to be later, of playing the desperate card of surrender to the West in the hope of splitting the grand alliance; for, in the last week in September 1944, the United States Press revealed that there was an official plan in Washington to 'pastoralize' Germany; all its industries were to be destroyed.[1] It did not require much imagination to grasp that such a scheme would condemn millions of Germans to death. Accordingly, over-all munitions and aircraft production hardly decreased at all in the last quarter of 1944, in spite of Allied bombing. Moreover, half a million new recruits were found for the army, and, although this would almost certainly prejudice future weapon production, Hitler was concerned solely with the winter. He resolved to repeat, by Christmas 1944, the miracle of 1940, by a great offensive through the Ardennes. Not only would it repeat that old feat of splitting the Allied armies in two; it would reach out to Antwerp and deprive the enemy of his only large modern port and of his enormous petrol dumps. This sudden stunning blow would crack the crazy unnatural coalition that was ranged against him, and force it to see that in fact the German Reich could not be destroyed, For, although Hitler's mental and physical powers were now rapidly deteriorating, it was chiefly his capacity to understand his own weaknesses that had collapsed; his capacity to diagnose the weaknesses of his opponents was undiminished. He told his stupefied, but subservient, generals in December 1944 that there had never in history been

a coalition like that of our enemies, composed of such heterogeneous elements with such divergent aims. . . . On the one hand a dying empire, Britain; on the other a colony bent upon inheritance, the United States . . . America tries to be Britain's heir; Russia tries to gain the Balkans, the narrow seas, Iran and the Persian Gulf; England tries to hold her possessions and to strengthen herself in the Mediterranean. . . . Even now these States are at loggerheads. . . . . If now we can deliver a few more heavy blows, then at any moment this artificially bolstered common front may suddenly collapse with a gigantic clap of thunder.[2]

[1] See p. 388.
[2] Quoted, Chester Wilmot, *The Struggle for Europe*, p. 158.

All that was missing from this accurate analysis of the internal contradictions of the grand alliance was the realization that, since he alone had called this monstrosity into being, it would endure for so long as he did.

On 16 December 1944, to the incredulous amazement of both soldiers and civilians in the Western world, thirty German divisions launched an attack from the Ardennes against the U.S. First and Third Armies, along a seventy-mile front that was very weakly held. There was an immediate break through, a breakdown in communications, and a confusion made up of resistance at some points and headlong flight at others. Eisenhower reacted quickly and surely, however; American armour denied the Germans the vital road centre of Bastogne; Montgomery was given the task of co-ordinating the counter-measures on the northern side of the great bulge; and the Germans did not reach the Meuse. Nevertheless, they penetrated to a depth of sixty miles, and they were not decisively turned back until 27 December; and it was not until the first week in February 1945 that the Allies were back on the line they had held at the beginning of December, 1944.

The chief beneficiaries of the Ardennes offensive were the Russians, since it deprived the German Army in the east of badly needed reserves. The Russian drive through Poland had been held up in the autumn of 1944 by transport difficulties and by a concentration on Roumania, Hungary and Jugoslavia. Hitler, however, refused to divert additional resources to the defence of the Polish front, preferring his Ardennes offensive and the defence of Budapest. The Ardennes offensive contributed in another way to the rapid march of the Red Army into Poland early in 1945: the moment the Ardennes offensive began, the United States urgently requested Stalin to launch his own offensive in the east as soon as possible. Stalin promised to do so, and kept his promise.

The result was that by the time Churchill, Roosevelt and Stalin next met, at Yalta in February 1945, Hitler had lost the war in the east. Warsaw had been taken, at last, in January; in February the Oder was crossed north of Frankfort, bringing the Russians to within forty-five miles of Berlin. Farther south, another Russian army had taken Breslau in Silesia; and when Budapest was finally captured in mid-February 1945, yet other Russian forces were only eighty miles from Vienna. By contrast, Anglo-American forces had taken hardly any German territory at all, and were not to cross the Rhine at any point until the first week of March 1945.

43 · Quebec, Moscow, Dumbarton Oaks, 1944

The period between the Teheran conference in November 1943 and the next (and last) Churchill-Roosevelt-Stalin meeting at Yalta, in February 1945, had thus, for the Anglo-Americans, but not the Russians, been one of unfulfilled military promise. It was also one of deepening diplomatic doubt and of persistent evasion of the clearly emerging problems of the post-war future. The problems that would matter most were, first, what was to happen to defeated Germany and, second, what were to be the relations between the three Great Powers and the liberated peoples of eastern Europe. The United States deliberately refused to face these problems because it believed, correctly, that it would prejudice Allied unity to do so; and in the United States' view, that unity had at all costs to be preserved, since it was essential to make sure of full Soviet participation in what was expected to be the long and difficult task of defeating the Japanese. That Japan would in fact surrender as early as September 1945 was not guessed during 1944 and could probably not safely have been relied upon even after Germany's surrender in May 1945. Nor can it be overlooked that the United States legitimately regarded the Pacific as their main theatre of war. Conciliatory attitudes to Russia were, in the United States view, dictated by a military necessity which, if pressed, no one at the time could have called in question. Also contributory to the evasion of difficulties about the future of Europe, was the decision to rely for their solution on the establishment of a United Nations. On this, however, there was clear guidance from the past. The League of Nations had solved nothing; and there was no evidence yet that setting up a United Nations Organization would solve anything either. Even more irrelevant was the attention that Roosevelt, with the co-operation of Cordell Hull, continued to pay to schemes for dismantling the British, French and Dutch colonial empires.

More anxious than ever about the incoherence of Allied political and military strategy, and about the long-term consequences of United States disinterestedness in the Soviet advance in eastern Europe, Churchill succeeded in holding a further conference with Roosevelt in September 1944, at Quebec. The now overwhelming preponderance of the United States

contribution to the war in the west prevented Churchill from gaining much
from the meeting. Its most startling product was the so-called Morgenthau
plan, devised by the U.S. Treasury, for destroying, dismantling or handing
over as reparations all German heavy industry in the Ruhr and the Saar,
with a view to 'converting Germany into a country either primarily agricultural or pastoral'[1] After initially opposing it, and in spite of the furious
disapproval of Eden, Churchill agreed to the Morgenthau plan. The prospect of continued American Lend-Lease after the end of the German war
and of a substantial U.S. loan may have lured him; and he may have sensed
the difficulty of opposing the plan without being accused by both Roosevelt
and Stalin of wanting to be soft with the Germans, so as to use them against
Russia after the war.

The plan was much more objectionable from a moral and from a propagandist point of view than the demand for unconditional surrender, for
that had always been coupled with the proviso that the Allies were not
making war on the German people. Yet there was a certain transatlantic
logic about it. If the U.S. wished to keep no troops in Europe once Germany was defeated, how else, save by the total destruction of Germany's
war potential, could a second German recovery, necessitating a third
United States intervention in Europe, be effectively prevented? Moreover,
Roosevelt, in much the same way as Woodrow Wilson, was an avenging
angel as well as a crusader for freedom. Just before the Quebec conference,
Roosevelt had written:

> It is of the utmost importance that every person in Germany should realize
> that this time Germany is a defeated nation. I do not want to starve them to
> death but, as an example, if they need food to keep body and soul together
> beyond what they have, they should be fed three times a day with soup from
> Army soup kitchens . . .[2]

There was speedy retreat from this crude programme. By mid-October,
Roosevelt decided that what precisely should be done to the Germans
might once again be left for future discussion.

On the matter of eastern Europe, Churchill got so little co-operation
from Roosevelt that he paid another visit to Stalin in Moscow in October
1944. By this time, Stalin had imposed terms on the Finns, the Roumanians
and the Bulgarians; had acquired an apparently influential say in the future
of Jugoslavia by sending tanks to Tito, who had hitherto received most of
his help from the British; and was apparently on the verge of imposing
terms on Hungary. In none of these areas did the Soviet allow their allies
any influence, and from all of those which had been given terms Russia was
demanding heavy reparations.

It was for this reason that Churchill tried to strike a bargain with Stalin
in Moscow in October 1944, by which Russia should have 90 per cent of the

[1] See also p. 385.
[2] Quoted Feis, op. cit. p. 366.

influence in Roumania, 75 per cent of the influence in Bulgaria, and 50 per cent in Hungary and Jugoslavia; while Britain should have 90 per cent influence in Greece, where Churchill was currently engaged in trying to prevent the country coming entirely under local Communist control. It was a curious but basically sound way of trying to arrange these matters; and, moreover, as far as Greece was concerned, Stalin adhered to it. When, in the winter of 1944–5, the British intervened by force to suppress the Greek Communists and preserve the Greek monarchy, Stalin merely contented himself with asking for information.

The United States disapproved; the whole scheme smacked of the wickedness of spheres of influence, and Churchill's apparent predilection for the monarchical system, in Greece as in Italy, was regarded as offensive to republican principles.

The rest of Churchill's percentage scheme fared less satisfactorily. Bulgaria, Roumania and Hungary came under 100 per cent Russian influence; and if, in time, Jugoslavia's position came to approximate to the 50–50 suggestion, this was the unforeseeable achievement of Tito himself.

Yet there were no serious problems here. Of the States figuring in Churchill's scheme, Stalin had offered the West 90 per cent of the influence in Greece, which alone among these States had from start to finish been indisputably a Western ally, and 50 per cent Western influence in Jugoslavia which, though Communist, had been more or less enabled to become so by Western aid, and which had likewise been associated with the Allied cause. Bulgaria, Roumania and Hungary, on the other hand, had throughout been Axis satellites; they were technically enemy powers and their enmity had been directed exclusively against the U.S.S.R. Thus, harsh treatment by Russia and even exclusive treatment by Russia were not to be thought of as of the gravest concern at a period when the war was still not won, though the way in which the Russians had denied their two Western allies even a nominal say in policy in these countries did not promise well for the future. What had caused much more anxiety was Stalin's evident determination to pursue the historic Russian tradition of hostility to Poland. In retrospect, it might truthfully be said of Europe after 1919 that it was the Polish ulcer that destroyed it.

Stalin's first demand about Poland was that it allow the U.S.S.R. to retain most of the eastern territories which Russia had lost in 1918, and regained in 1939 in collaboration with Hitler. This meant that Poland's eastern frontier should correspond more or less with the Curzon Line of 1919. His other demand was that Poland's future Government be dominated by nominees of Russia. Both demands were regarded by the West as conflicting with the Atlantic Charter, with the Four Nation Declaration of October 1943, and with the status of the Polish Government in exile in London, set up in 1939 at a time when Germany and Russia were Poland's joint conquerors. It was equally at variance with the fact that Britain had entered the war on behalf of Polish independence; and with the loyalty owed by British and American Governments to the many Polish soldiers who had fought in the Western Desert and Italy, and the Polish airmen who had, among other things, played their part in the Battle of Britain.

Unfortunately, Stalin had a strong case over Poland. Its first international actions after its revival by the victors of 1919 had been to invade the Soviet Union. It had ranked as Europe's prime anti-Bolshevik outpost until 1934 and from then, almost until the outbreak of war, as Hitler's senior satellite, next to Italy. Yet, as late as January 1944, the London Polish Government, through its Prime Minister, Mikolajczyk, was insisting that after the war it should not only receive back the largely non-Polish territories it had lost to Russia in 1939, but also extend its territory westward at the expense of Germany; and the Commander of the Polish forces in Italy, General Anders, declared, a month later, that Polish soldiers would 'refuse to consider the possibility of abandoning any scrap of Polish territory to the Bolsheviks'. Stalin's attitude was thus inevitably hostile; he had already withdrawn recognition of the London Polish Government, in October 1943, and he told Churchill at Teheran that a public statement by the Prime Minister that all territorial changes should be postponed until a peace conference had met would be taken as evidence of injustice and unfriendliness towards the Soviet Union. Yet, Stalin fully supported Poland's westward expansion; and, since both the British and the Americans agreed to this in principle, their attempts to oppose Russian annexation of eastern Poland could only appear as unfriendly as Stalin thought them to be. Churchill and Roosevelt were at fault in their excessive concern about the unfavourable reaction of public opinion to the acquisition by Russia of what was, at best, Polish territory only by virtue of a Polish act of aggression in 1920.

Even on the more debatable issue of the political complexion of Poland's ultimate form of Government, Churchill's view was unrealistic. It was all very well to advance the allegedly profound theory that Poland must not become a Russian-dominated Communist salient pointing to the heart of Europe; from the Russian angle, it was even more important that Poland should not become a Western dominated, non-Communist salient pointing towards Moscow, because whereas in the past Russia had never threatened the rest of Europe by way of Poland, Poland actually had threatened and invaded Russia more than once. Nor could the British and Americans object if Poland's future Government turned out to be Communist; Russia already had a Communist Government, yet Russia was their close ally. To pretend that the London Poles represented democracy was itself a largely unwarrantable assumption. To seek to create a truly independent Polish State was to engage upon the pursuit of the unattainable. It would have been more sensible of Churchill to have realized this as soon as Russia entered the war, and to have purged himself quickly of the excessive emotionalism about Poland to which all west Europeans were so susceptible.

In July 1944, Stalin set up in the areas of Poland from which the Red Army had now driven the Germans, a Polish National Council, formed from Poles sympathetic to Russia. He assigned to it the administration of the liberated Polish territories. In the same month the Red Army reached the Vistula, opposite Warsaw. The commander of the organized Polish underground army in Warsaw, General Bor, was anxious to take over the city just in time to anticipate the advancing Russians, and had received orders from Mikolajczyk to proclaim a general rising when the moment seemed suitable. On 29 July, a broadcast calling the Polish people of Warsaw to arms was sent out from a radio station in Moscow, and Bor's 40,000-strong force came out into the open against the Germans in Warsaw on 1 August. It failed because it was not until January 1945 that the Russians in fact entered the city.

Stalin did not merely content himself with claiming, not without reason, that there were serious military obstacles to an immediate capture of Warsaw; he also went out of his way to pour scorn on the Warsaw patriots. The destruction of General Bor's force was regarded as having been deliberately connived at by Stalin in order to ensure that when Warsaw was captured it would come under the exclusive control of the Red Army and the Communist, Russian-dominated Polish National Council. Since, however, Stalin's attitude to indigenous Communist Parties, long before and long after the Warsaw rising, was one of contemptuous hostility, it may be guessed that Stalin's objection to the Warsaw patriots was based less on ideology than on power politics. The only Poles Stalin would be prepared to support were Poles who would subordinate Polish interests to Russian. General Bor's rising was anti-Russian as well as anti-German; not surprisingly, therefore, Stalin did not like it, and would take no military risks to assist it. The Russians also refused to agree to Western aircraft landing on Soviet territory after dropping supplies on Warsaw, and Stalin blamed the disaster, which was now certain to befall the rising, on the irresponsible Poles in London, implying thereby that Britain and the United States were themselves also to blame. Moreover, Stalin asserted, the Warsaw rising had damaged Soviet prospects of taking the city, by leading to the concentration of German troops in that area. In the end, Stalin did in fact agree to the dropping of supplies by Soviet as well as Western aircraft. The Polish general commanding those Poles who were attached to the Red Army was allowed to send four infantry battalions across the Vistula to help the men of Warsaw, but they were repulsed with heavy losses; and the Soviet force facing Warsaw on the eastern side of the Vistula made no move forward. On 2 October 1944, the survivors of the Warsaw patriot force surrendered to the Germans.

Whatever suspicions Stalin might have harboured about the ultimate intentions either of the London Poles or of the Warsaw rebels, and whatever the difficulties that prevented an immediate attack on Warsaw, his handling of the crisis was a political blunder. The Warsaw rising became one of the war's great myths, appearing to represent the ultimate in heroism among the victims of Nazi terror; the Germans of the July Bomb Plot seemed temporizing bunglers by comparison. Yet not for one moment did Stalin permit himself a word of sympathy for their plight, a word of public regret for his inability to help them, or a clear gesture of co-operation with those in the West who wanted to help them, and whose motives at this moment were solely those of common humanity towards people suffering greatly in the common cause. Even on the grounds of brute political realism, Stalin might have asked himself whether Soviet security was not better served by keeping the sympathy of his two great allies than in venting his spite on Poles who, for all their manifold follies, would in the end have had to fall in with Russian wishes if they were to have a future at all. If it became an article of general faith that Stalin had deliberately allowed the Warsaw rising to fail, he had only himself to blame; nor did it escape notice that the hold-up of Russian forces outside Warsaw was accompanied by a rapid Russian advance into south-eastern Europe, giving the U.S.S.R. an irremovable control of that region. The Cold War, like the Hot War out of which it came, was started in Warsaw.

It was not surprising that when Churchill met Stalin in Moscow in October 1944, Poland was not included in their percentage table. By this time, Churchill realized there would have to be an accommodation with the Communist Poles of the National Council, which now nominally controlled liberated Poland from Lublin. Mikolajczyk was therefore compelled by Churchill to join the Moscow talks; but bound by his extremer colleagues in London, he refused to consider the Curzon Line as a suitable eastern frontier and would consider no plan for a future Polish Government except one based on an equal coalition of all the Polish political parties, among whom the Communists of Lublin would be but one out of five. Mikolajczyk said the eastern territories contained five million Poles, and that he had not come to Moscow to partition Poland. Stalin declared that since the majority of the inhabitants of the eastern territories were White Russians and Ukrainians, Mikolajczyk was in effect demanding the partition of White Russia and the Ukraine. Churchill suggested Mikolajczyk accepted the Curzon Line as a tentative frontier and proposed that Poland could not only expand westwards into Germany as far as the river Oder, but also acquire the important industrial centre of Stettin. Mikolajczyk insisted that Poland should have Lwow instead, with its important oil wells. But this was in what Stalin regarded as the Ukraine, and he refused flatly. He also refused Churchill's idea of the Curzon Line as a merely interim frontier. In the end, Mikolajczyk, yielding to the hard facts, agreed to ask his colleagues to agree to the Lublin Poles having one third of the places in a coalition Government and to the Curzon Line as a frontier, with Lwow going to Russia. Churchill's hopes of a settlement revived. Unfortunately, he was conducting his negotiations, as usual, without the slightest assistance from Washington. Roosevelt was mum, in case an anti-Polish decision lost him Polish votes in the imminent Presidential election.

The other major diplomatic activity of 1944 took place at Dumbarton Oaks, where a three-Power delegation met in September to draw up the organization of what was later to become the United Nations. Since the concern here was constitution-drafting, nearly always a sophisticated exercise in wish-fulfilment little connected with reality, considerable progress was made, until the Russians, with their pedantic concern for the facts of power, threw some real spanners into the still largely imaginary works. The Russian delegate, Gromyko, proposed that all sixteen constituent republics within the Soviet Union should be given separate membership of the Assembly. The request so startled the conference that it had to leave the matter in suspense; for it was such a shocking intrusion of power-politics into the agreeable pastime of making a fantasy world that they could not comprehend it. The motive of the Russians was blindingly clear. They believed that many of the separate States of the Western world, for all their legal title to independent sovereignty, would be most unlikely ever to vote against either the United States or the United Kingdom. The demand of the U.S.S.R. to have sixteen votes instead of one was an obvious attempt to redress what they uncharitably, but again not unreasonably, assumed in advance would be an unfair balance against Russia. They were also calling attention to the profoundest of all truths about international relations, namely that the whole conception that the world is divided into truly independent sovereign States is little more than a legal fiction.

The U.S.S.R. was even more unaccommodating about the right to a veto in the Security Council. The permanent members of this were to be the U.S.A., the U.S.S.R. and the United Kingdom, with the probable addition of France and, owing to an insistence which the United States was subsequently to regret, China. There were to be six semi-permanent members. It was decided that each of the five permanent members should have the right to veto any action by the Council to which it objected; a sensible enough accommodation to the fact that, in the real world, peace depended on the Great Powers not being at loggerheads. But the U.S.S.R. wanted the Great Powers to be able to use the veto even in disputes in which they were themselves involved; and this so contradicted everything that the non-Communist Powers felt were the fundamentals of free discussion that once again decision had to be postponed; and the conference ended without, as had been intended, a complete constitution for the world organization having been drawn up.

Like their demand for sixteen places in the Assembly, the demand of the Russians for unlimited use of the veto sprang from their ingrained suspicion that the non-Communist world could not be relied on to deal justly with them. They failed to grasp that their attitude was itself an incitement to even greater hostility; never before had Russia's standing with the rest of the world stood as high as it did in the middle of 1944. By their ruthless attitude to the Poles, and their obstructive disbelief in the existence of good intentions in any part of the world west of the Curzon Line, the Russians were doing their best to throw away the unparalleled esteem the Red Army had so rightly won for them.

Cordell Hull was so naïvely puzzled by the Russian attitude at Dumbarton Oaks, and by developments in south-east Europe, that he asked Averill Harriman, the U.S. ambassador in Moscow, if he could tell him why Soviet policy had apparently 'changed' since Teheran. Harriman's reply, drawn up with the assistance of George Kennan, explained the simple fact that the U.S.S.R. was not prepared to subordinate its interests, least of all the matter of its western frontiers, to the wishes of other powers or to an untried international organization almost all of whose members would be anti-Communist. Real agreement with the Soviet Union could only emerge if the U.S. showed definite interest in European problems as they arose. Kennan added a warning:

An international organization for the preservation of peace and security cannot take the place of a well-conceived and realistic foreign policy . . . and we are being . . . negligent of the interests of our people if we allow plans for an international organization to be an excuse for failing to occupy ourselves seriously and minutely with the sheer power relationships of the European peoples.[1]

The military situation made it almost too late to act upon this warning. When the three war leaders met at Yalta, a few months later, it was altogether too late. And so, what, if said earlier and heeded sooner, might perhaps have helped to make the fruits of victory seem less bitter, must stand instead as a coroner's verdict on the always ghostly body of United States wartime diplomacy.

[1] See Feis, op. cit., p. 434, et seq.

44 · Yalta, 1945

In spite of the obvious imminence of the defeat of Germany, almost no strategic or political problem had been settled at the end of 1944. In February 1945, therefore, Churchill and Roosevelt met Stalin at Yalta in the Crimea, pausing on the way to confer at Malta about their own strategic plans.

Malta saw the last flare-up of the controversy about how to advance into Germany. The British again took the view that Eisenhower was attaching too little importance to the necessity of a strong thrust into northern Germany across the Lower Rhine. This, however, was to over-estimate German strength after the failure of the Ardennes offensive and the prospects of the Russians' massive attacks in the east which had opened in January 1945; but the state of Anglo-American relations was such that the British apparently thought it impolitic to reveal that their chief anxiety about north-west Germany was to ensure that the Russians did not get there first and seize its ports and naval bases. In the event, Eisenhower's plan for 1945 fully provided for a vigorous thrust across the Lower Rhine.

When the triumvirate met at Yalta there was close Russo-American discussion about the rewards Russia should receive for joining the war against Japan. These included the return of all territories lost by Russia in 1904, particularly Port Arthur and Dairen; together with the Kurile Islands and a sphere of influence in Manchuria. Outer Mongolia was to retain its independent (i.e. non-Chinese) status. This generosity to Russia at the expense of China was a plan to recreate (and in any real sense create for the first time) that Russian domination to the immediate north of China proper which had caused an international crisis at the beginning of the century. It was hardly in line with China's position as Roosevelt's most favoured ally, or with his disapproval of Britain's retention of Hong Kong. Churchill gave reluctant agreement to the arrangement (when told of it after it had been made) chiefly because it cut away the ground from any objections Roosevelt might yet advance to the restoration of British power in South-east Asia. Roosevelt's own calculation was that by offering Stalin as much as he did he might secure future Russian goodwill towards Chiang Kai-shek, and

avoid Russian attempts to undermine post-war China by patronage of Mao
Tse-tung's Chinese Communists.

The Polish problem was now even grimmer than when Churchill and
Stalin had met in October 1944. Russia was demanding that Poland's
western frontier should be advanced to the line of the river Neisse, and
thus embrace almost all German Silesia. Stalin's justification was that only
if Poland was strong could Russia regard it as an adequate bastion against
Germany. To the argument that it weakened Poland to deny her Lwow he
retorted that Lwow had been taken from Russia against her will. To the
argument that if Poland extended westward to the Neisse line it would
contain six million Germans the answer was that they could be expelled
from the area. Yet again, Roosevelt left it to Churchill to object, and
deliberately engineered one last, and, as it proved, useless evasion. It was
agreed that Poland should lose Lwow to Russia and get 'substantial' compensation in the north and west. Final delimitation of her western frontier
should wait upon a peace conference. All that Roosevelt and Churchill had
denied Stalin therefore, was the specific mention of the Oder-Neisse line
on paper.

There was even less success over the question of Poland's form of government. The best to be got was an agreement that the Lublin Committee
should be broadened by the inclusion of democratic Polish leaders from
outside the territories already liberated. This meant, in effect, recognition
of the Lublin Committee as the only official Polish Government; and when
Roosevelt suggested that the eventual free elections that were promised
should be subject to international supervision, Stalin's reply was that this
would of course be a matter for the Lublin Government; and to all subsequent efforts to inject non-Communists into that Government, which was
shortly afterwards moved by the Russians to Warsaw, Stalin likewise
replied that this was Poland's official Government and the West was really
trying to liquidate it. By the time of the German surrender, the U.S.S.R.
had handed over to the Polish Communists the administration of all former
German territory east of the Oder-Neisse line, together with most of East
Prussia except Koenigsberg. In May 1945, sixteen leaders of the Polish
groups in London were lured to Warsaw, under what was thought to be a
promise of safe conduct, and were then promptly imprisoned as terrorists,
spies and diversionists.

The decisions made at Yalta on the German question went no further
than an agreement on zones of military occupation, which had first been
discussed at the Quebec Conference in 1944. Britain was to have a north-
western zone, the Americans a southern, and the Russians an eastern zone.
There would be a Control Council containing representatives of each of the
three allies, including the commanding generals of each of the zones. The
Control Council was to be concerned with matters affecting Germany as a
whole, each commanding general with matters affecting his particular zone.

POLAND'S FRONTIERS

Scale of Miles

0   50   100   150   200

EAST GERMANY

Gdynia

EAST PRUSSIA

Vilna

Szczecin (Stettin)

Berlin

P O L A N D

Warsaw

Brest-Litovsk

Wrocław (Breslau)

Lublin

Lwow

Ceded to U.S.S.R.

Gained from Germany

Prewar Frontier

Postwar Frontier

CZECHOSLOVAKIA

RUTHENIA (to U.S.S.R. 1945)

HUNGARY

RUMANIA

At the instigation of Churchill, the compliance of Roosevelt and the reluctant agreement of Stalin, France was accorded a zone and a place on the Control Council.

Since Berlin was situated well inside the Russian zone it was to be governed by commandants appointed by each of the zonal commanders. To carry out their functions on this Kommandatura, the British, French and Americans needed uninterrupted access to Berlin through the Soviet zone. This question was not thought to require much attention; it was regarded purely as a matter of military ways and means, to be dealt with when the state of the roads and the railways was better known.

Roosevelt again intimated that, subject to any responsibilities which might have to be assumed by virtue of her membership of the United Nations, the United States did not intend keeping troops in Germany for more than two years. Yet no decision was made about Germany's ultimate political future. Stalin argued passionately for a great measure of dismemberment, much as Clemenceau had asked for it in 1919, and for similar reasons, while Churchill demurred, exactly as Lloyd George had demurred in 1919. Roosevelt fumbled uncertainly and indifferently with the problem. Once again, because the search for a decision looked like sowing dissension, he preferred to call the search off.

After vehement references to the sufferings caused to the Russians by the German invasion, Stalin demanded that Germany pay in reparations (not in cash but in kind) the equivalent of twenty billion dollars, the Soviet Union receiving 50 per cent of this. This was not quite the abandoned Morgenthau plan for pastoralizing Germany, but something like it. The bulk of the payment, in the Soviet view, should take the form of the handing over of industrial equipment – factories, power plants, etc. – in order to reduce Germany's industrial capacity by four-fifths; the rest should be in the form of delivery of goods over ten years.

To this Churchill objected strongly. It would create conditions of near-starvation in the industrial areas (the biggest concentration of which was in the future British zone) and the result would be that Britain and the United States would find themselves supporting Germany so that it could pay reparations to the U.S.S.R. With even greater vehemence, Stalin suggested that if the British did not want the U.S.S.R. to receive reparations from Germany, they might as well say so. Churchill's preference for only partial dismemberment of Germany, and his resistance to reparations, seemed to Stalin a deliberate British attempt to keep Germany strong enough to resist Russia. Caught between these conflicting arguments, Roosevelt temporized as usual and said the decision should be left to a Reparations Commission. Stalin then hustled the President into the dangerous decision that the Russian figure should be passed on to the Reparations Commission 'as a basis for discussion'. Once again, there was great United States impatience with the British for being so awkward with the Russians.

On eastern Europe, all that emerged from Yalta was a regurgitation of the Four Nation Declaration made at Moscow in 1943. Faced with mounting evidence that in all the eastern states, including Hungary and Jugoslavia, Russia aimed to place all power in the hands of either the Red Army or local Communists under Russian influence, one more paper barrier was solemnly erected. The Yalta 'Declaration on Liberated Europe' pledged the three Allies

to concert during the temporary period of instability in Liberated Europe the policies of their three Governments in assisting the peoples of Europe liberated from the domination of Nazi Germany and the people of the former Axis satellite States, to solve by democratic means their pressing economic and political problems.

They would

form interim Governmental authorities broadly representative of all democratic elements and pledged to the earliest establishment through free elections of Governments responsive to the will of the people.

They resoundingly reaffirmed their faith in the Atlantic Charter and their

determination to build, in co-operation with other peace-loving nations, a world order under law, dedicated to peace, security, freedom and the general well-being of all mankind.

In fact, the Russians rarely bothered to consult their allies about eastern Europe, and Stalin was later to reject Anglo-American interference in Poland on the grounds that he, too, was not certain that the Governments set up either in Greece or Belgium were 'really representative' but had not thought it his business to interfere. Stalin made similar play of the circumstance that Russia had not been consulted over the form of Government to be set up in Italy. Between the political realities of 1944 and 1945, and Roosevelt's last message to Congress, on 1 March 1945, there was no correspondence:

I think the Crimean conference was a successful effort by the three leading nations to find a common ground of peace. It spells, or it ought to spell, the end of the system of unilateral action and exclusive alliances, and spheres of influence and balances of power and all the other expedients that have been tried for centuries and have always failed.

Indeed, so confident was Stalin that things were going his way, that he removed at Yalta the obstructions Molotov had set up at Dumbarton Oaks to prevent agreement on the United Nations. He dropped the demand for sixteen Russian seats in the Assembly and contented himself with asking for three only, one each for Russia, White Russia and the Ukraine. Eagerly, Roosevelt agreed. This might have been taken as a sign that Stalin was already looking forward to the voting support of Poland, Hungary, Jugoslavia, Bulgaria and Roumania; and that, having obtained so much substance at Yalta, he did not need to worry about the shadows. He also accepted the United States' limitation of the use of the veto.

On 12 April 1945, Roosevelt died of a cerebral haemorrhage; in July 1945, Churchill ceased to be Prime Minister of the United Kingdom. Thus, the Yalta conference was the last great meeting of the Grand Alliance; the Potsdam conference, attended by Stalin, by Roosevelt's successor, Harry S. Truman, by Churchill and Attlee before the British election results were known, and by Attlee and Bevin afterwards, was no more than an untidy postscript. By that time, almost all knowledgeable persons in high places, though hardly any of the general public, knew that the alliance was already on the verge of dissolution.

Basic to the breakdown was the gap which had existed from the beginning between the Russian and the American conception of the purposes of the war. To the United States the real enemy was Japan. To Russia the sole enemy was Germany. To the United States, the war outside the Pacific was a second crusade, another ideological war on behalf of a new world order of liberated Democratic States, sovereign but equal, who, though independent, would be bound together by the rule of law, enshrined, like the constitution of the United States, in a quasi-religious written document. To Russia, the war was not an ideological crusade on behalf of Communism. It was a simple patriotic war of national survival

and national self-defence. The United States had not been invaded and
devastated; European Russia had. The United States had never looked like
losing the war; in 1941 and 1942, Russia's defeat had seemed probable. In
consequence, whereas the United States fought to impose a system on the
world but not to acquire territory, Russia fought, not to impose a system,
but to acquire as much territory and control in eastern Europe as seemed
essential to the creation of a great bastion of defence against a world which
appeared, on past evidence, to hate her and which had breached her territory in war five times since the opening of the nineteenth century. Russia
could not afford to fight for ideals because, unlike the United States, Russia
had been fighting for its life, and asking, not to convert the world, but to
compel it to leave Russia alone. From start to finish, while the United States
fought for the Atlantic Charter, the U.S.S.R. fought for a protective Iron
Curtain.

His generous and persistent devotion in trying to break down this
Russian suspicion of the outside world showed that Roosevelt understood
the heart of the matter; and if, in pursuing this aim, he shouldered
Churchill aside, he was again in the right. Britain had taken the lead in
organizing European resistance to Russia in the Near East from the end of
the eighteenth century till the end of the nineteenth, and had pushed Japan
forward against Russia in the Far East at the beginning of the twentieth.
Churchill had called for an anti-Bolshevik crusade the moment Lenin had
come to power. On three occasions, Britain had allied with Russia; once
against France and twice against Germany; but always with the determination that, when war was over, Russia should be confined as far to the east
of Europe as possible. By contrast, the United States had no record of
hostility to Russia and no territorial aims in Europe that could endanger
Russia.

Yet, if Roosevelt had discovered the right policy to adopt towards Russia
and was the right person to pursue it, he adopted the wrong method. He
attempted to woo the Russians for a kind of post-war system that made
sense to the Americans but no sense to the Russians. The Russians thought
in terms of armies, frontiers, spheres of influence and alliances; the
Americans in terms of documentary protestations of high principle. To a
nation that conceived itself to have been founded on a Declaration of
Independence and a written Constitution, it was natural to imagine that
the States of the world could be united on the foundation of an Atlantic
Charter, a Four Nation Declaration, a Declaration on Liberated Europe,
and a United Nations Charter. The Russians could only think in concrete
terms.[1] To talk of withdrawing U.S. troops from Europe two years after a
German defeat could give Russia no other impression than that the United

---

[1] 'A declaration I regard as algebra, but an agreement as practical arithmetic. I do
not wish to decry algebra, but I prefer arithmetic.' Stalin to Eden, 1941. Quoted, *The
Reckoning*, The Earl of Avon, p. 291.

States did not care. If the United States really wanted any part of Europe to be run in conformity with United States ideals, the United States would seek to bring this about with its army, just as Russia was to shape eastern Europe with the Red Army. Moreover, since the United States was Russia's ally, it was bound to recognize that Russia needed eastern Europe as its sphere of influence, just as Russia sedulously recognized western Europe and Greece as the spheres of influence of the Anglo-Americans. Any departure from this simple arrangement was seen, first as disloyalty to the alliance and then as the prelude to sinister plans for future aggression. A firm and early declaration by Roosevelt that the United States proposed actively to collaborate with Britain in the future control of Europe would have had some prospect of making an impression on Stalin; getting him to sign pieces of paper about free elections gave him to understand that the United States would be happy with anything that happened provided it could somehow be made to fit the words in the pieces of paper. It was always difficult to assert that Russia had violated the Atlantic Charter, because its words were capable of an infinite diversity of interpretation. Everywhere in eastern Europe, democracies were established, everywhere there were elections; and the only sense in which they were not free elections was that traitors, deviationists, spies and lackeys of the Axis were rounded up first, so that they could not destroy the democracy the Red Army, at such heavy cost to itself, had achieved for these States.

Churchill's attempts to bridge the gap between his mutually uncomprehending allies met with little success. Although he had considerable understanding of the Soviet Union, his understanding of the United States was clouded by emotional presuppositions, and by his personal regard for Roosevelt. He correctly took it for granted that not only victory over Germany, but even the survival of the United Kingdom, had always depended on the United States; in consequence, he would impute no selfish motive to the United States and erect no obstacles in the way of Anglo-American co-operation, whatever the provocation. He was psychologically incapable of seeing that Roosevelt could smile and smile and be, in the friendliest possible way and from the highest possible motives, a villain. For Roosevelt, the only position to which the United Kingdom was entitled was that of a European off-shore island in the eastern Atlantic. He would support its Imperial strategic interests in the Mediterranean and the Far East only as a grudging concession to the fact that British support was needed against Germany and Japan. Even as an off-shore European island, Britain depended on the existence of a stable and friendly western Europe; but, throughout the war Roosevelt seemed determined to leave it in the lurch, by deliberately contributing nothing but paper protestations to the achievement of post-war European stability. Yet, although Churchill realized all this, he proved unable to do more than plead, argue, grumble and then relent. He would not quarrel with Roosevelt, his friend and brother-in-arms, even when Roosevelt behaved like a Big Brother, ever ready to denounce Churchill (though in the most comradely fashion) as an Imperialist-deviationist.

Churchill's failure was perhaps due to the dilution of his tenacity and pugnacity by magnanimity. The example of what the first two qualities could achieve when entirely free from magnanimity was before him, almost daily, from June 1940 to the end of the war, in the person of Charles de Gaulle. Persistently, De Gaulle insisted that he alone had the right to speak for France, in outrageous defiance of the fact that for a long time it was a right that few Frenchmen themselves would have accorded him. In the closing stages of the war, he secured for France the status of a victorious ally and a place on the German Control Commission, even though the contribution of France to the Allied victory was negligible. Throughout the war, Churchill had found him impossible to get on with, and for most of it Roosevelt and Stalin had attached only the slightest importance either to him or to his country. Yet, returned to France in the baggage train of the Allies no less than Louis XVIII in 1814, and with no Talleyrand to aid him, he nevertheless proved powerful enough to establish himself in the end as effectively as either of the two Napoleons. This was what could be achieved by a dedicated personality steadfastly refusing to accept the inferiority apparently imposed by fact. In single pursuit of his aim, De Gaulle was so continuously unco-operative that on one occasion he caused Churchill to go white with fury, to shake his fist at De Gaulle, and, with clicking dentures, to exclaim in Churchillian French, '*Mon Général, il ne faut pas obstacler la guerre!*'[1] Yet Churchill, unlike De Gaulle, had every right, by virtue of the British contribution to the war effort, to 'obstacler' both the political and strategic direction of the war. But he was so obsessed by American greatness that he tended to maximize Britain's weakness before 1941 and to minimize the scale of his country's contribution to the war thereafter. He was so warmed by Roosevelt's friendship that he allowed even himself to be diminished to the size of a jolly 'character', a rascally Imperialist old lag who, if not watched like a hawk, would lure the innocent American people into dying for the British Empire or into quarrelling with their great Soviet ally for purely British interests. Churchill might have insisted, at the outset, on setting up, parallel with the Joint Chiefs of Staff Committee, a high-powered Anglo-American body to work out political strategy and have got it to work continuously, and independently of the periodic summit meetings of the war. For the great meetings at Quebec and Moscow, at Casablanca, Teheran and Yalta were hurried and informal, indecisive and inconclusive. The agreements they produced were susceptible of a variety of interpretations, and produced misunderstandings that were deeper and more permanent than the purely personal sense of comradeship they established in the minds of those who made them. As

[1] See Robert Murphy, *Diplomat Among Warriors*, p. 219.

Truman found when he succeeded Roosevelt, all those convivial nights-before among the mutually toasting leaders were likely to be followed by stony mornings-after in the brick-hard presence of an unyielding Molotov. And, whereas the Russian Foreign Minister knew what he wanted, his Allied counterparts were at the mercy of Roosevelt's vague benevolence and Churchill's muffled but ineffective pessimism. The rapidity with which the United States later more than compensated for its failure to match the realism of the U.S.S.R. in wartime suggests that, if Churchill had been rougher with Roosevelt, the United States might have seen, long before the war was over, that the vital issue of how to live in peace with a victorious Russia could not be solved simply by creating a United Nations, or through an attempt to complete the War of American Independence by dismantling the British Empire.

45 · Victory without Peace, 1945

In March 1945, the allied forces in the west crossed the Rhine at last. Montgomery drove north of the Ruhr in the direction of Lübeck and, as he himself hoped, Berlin. General Bradley's American First Army thrust south of the Ruhr, and by the end of the month 300,000 German troops in that area had been encircled.

At this point, Eisenhower decided to switch the direction of his main thrust. Instead of giving Montgomery the chance to get to Berlin, he chose to put greater weight on Bradley's advance along a more southerly route, to Leipzig and Dresden, which would link up with the Russians on the Elbe, well south of Berlin. In view of the increasing intransigence of the Russians, Churchill strongly criticized the failure to concentrate on Berlin. The likelihood that at the end of the war the Red Army would be in actual occupation of every East European capital seemed to him to be fraught with danger. The United States insisted that the psychological effect of capturing Berlin was less valuable than the prospect of effecting the destruction of the German Armies by an advance into the heart of the country. Moreover, since the Red Army was, by mid-March, less than thirty miles from Berlin, it seemed probable that an attempt by the Anglo-American armies to race the Russians was a waste of time. Furthermore, much German

industry had been moved from the Ruhr to the centre of the country, and
there were fears that the Germans might be preparing for a last stand in the
mountainous regions of Bavaria.

Eisenhower's view prevailed. Moreover, even though the American First
Army progressed at such a rate that by 11 April it was in a position to move

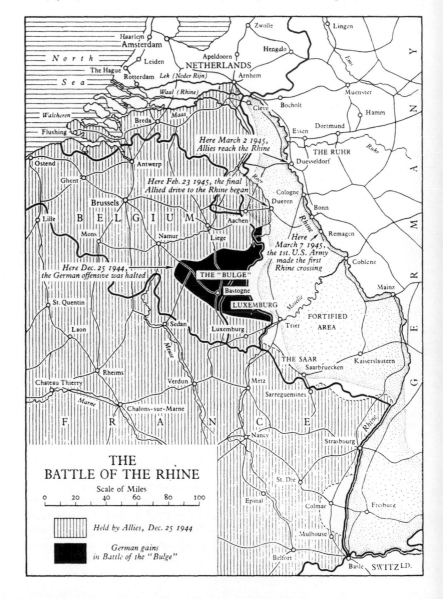

THE
BATTLE OF THE RHINE

Scale of Miles

0   20   40   60   80   100

Held by Allies, Dec. 25 1944

German gains
in Battle of the "Bulge"

on Berlin from the south, Bradley refrained from doing so, even though the Russians did not reach the centre of Berlin till 2 May. Churchill continued to press for a rapid advance farther east but Eisenhower still refused; and personally informed Stalin that he was halting his forces on the Elbe. Farther south, he refrained from sending U.S. troops into Prague, so that it was the Russians who entered the city, soon after the final German surrender on 7 May. In Austria, because U.S. troops were halted at Innsbruck, Vienna also was liberated by the Red Army.

The assertion that Eisenhower's holding back of the Western armies was a grave mistake which left Russia in control of far too large an area of eastern Europe has substance only in that it made it possible for the Russians to claim all the credit for liberating that area. It is therefore necessary to recall that the actual post-war zones of occupation, and the division of Berlin between the Allied forces, had been fixed at Yalta. Any attempt to prevent the Russians taking over the zone allotted to them would have been a much grosser breach of the alliance than anything yet done by the Russians. It would have been an impossible policy to adopt towards an ally whose help in the still unfinished war against Japan was regarded as essential. In the political circumstances prevailing in 1945 it was out of the question for Western forces to advance to a line well inside the agreed Russian zone and then refuse to withdraw from German territory until the Russians did likewise. Eisenhower's action, though allegedly based on purely military considerations, was founded squarely on the declared United States policy of co-operating fully with the Russians till the end of the war with Japan. Nor can it have seemed at all sensible to push farther forward into Germany, with the risk of sustaining unnecessary casualties, a United States Army that was to withdraw from Europe at the earliest possible moment.

If the Americans erred in this matter, their mistake was political, for by early April the strategic situation had changed markedly in favour of the West. The German Western Front had broken completely, whereas on the Eastern Front the Russians were long held up on the Oder-Neisse line and did not succeed in breaching it until 16 April. It was this reversal of the military situation which impelled Churchill to demand that the Armies of the West press ever eastwards to assert, by the sheer weight of their armed presence, a claim to be the liberators of Europe, the conquerors of Germany, and the future custodians of both. In the very last stages of the war, Eisenhower would certainly have yielded to political pressure had it come from Washington as well as from London. Roosevelt was, in the last weeks of his life, deeply disturbed by the blank refusal of the Russians to allow any Western participation in the affairs of eastern Europe, and by the announcement that Molotov was not going to attend the imminent San Francisco conference to draw up the United Nations Charter; but the President's death and the succession of Truman meant that United States

policy adhered to the end, though with ever-increasing doubt, to the line
Roosevelt had adhered to from the beginning: the British were potential
trouble-makers and the Russians essential allies for the future, both for war
against Japan and for peace thereafter.

The success of the West, and the check to the Russians on the Oder-
Neisse line, had much to do with the increased hostility of the U.S.S.R.
Stalin bristled with suspicion over an abortive secret plan to secure a
cease-fire from the German forces in Italy. The incident convinced him
that his allies were aiming at a separate peace. He hinted that the contrast
between German resistance in the east and the lack of it in the west foreshadowed a secret anti-Soviet compact between his allies and the Germans.
All history suggested such an eventuality; and, while the Americans came to
think that Stalin was ignoring them because he no longer needed them,
Stalin jumped even more swiftly to the conclusion that, now that the West
no longer needed him, it would resume the anti-Soviet line it had so firmly
trod right up to 1939.

Hitler's last flash of optimism derived from the same historical deduction. The death of Roosevelt, whom he rightly saw as the true architect of
this unnatural coalition against him, together with the realization that U.S.
forces were already inside what had been fixed as the Russian zone, had convinced him, in mid-April, that he was about to be saved by the inevitable
collision between the rival invading forces. By 22 April, however, as the
Russians began shelling the building in Berlin beneath which he had his
underground bunker, he began to take steps to complete his revolution of
destruction by destroying himself. This he did, on 30 April 1945. There
died with him, and as an act of voluntary self-sacrifice, Eva Braun, whom
he had made his wife the day before, and his Propaganda Minister,
Goebbels, who in his turn saw to it that his wife and their children also
died with him. Hitler naturally took care to leave behind him a political
testament. It was one more propaganda setpiece: everything that had
happened was the fault of 'cliques' and 'tools' and 'International Jewry',
and the Germans would go on hating their enemies through the centuries
until at last from its ruined cities a new and glorious National Socialist
movement would restore the Fatherland's majesty and might.

Göring having at the last apparently tried to supplant him, and Himmler,
the head of the Gestapo, having tried to negotiate with the Western Allies,
Hitler nominated Grand Admiral Dönitz as his successor. Instantly,
together with the aristocratic pro-Nazi, Count Schwerin-Krosigk, whom he
appointed Foreign Minister, Dönitz launched a propaganda drive to create
the image of a Germany suffering tragic and heroic martyrdom in the cause
of Europe's salvation from Bolshevism. Dönitz broadcast from Hamburg
radio:

It is my first task to save the German people from destruction by the Bolsheviks, and it is only to achieve this that the fight continues. As long as the

British and Americans hamper us from reaching this end we shall fight and defend ourselves against them as well.

Schwerin-Krosigk did even better, on the same evening: using, in the process, words that his country's Western conquerors were soon to find all too familiar in their own mouths:

> In the streets of still unoccupied Germany a great stream of desperate and famished people is rolling westwards, pursued by fighter-bombers, in flight from indescribable terror. In the east, the iron curtain behind which, unseen by the eyes of the world, the work of destruction goes on, is moving steadily forward.
> As more and more of the German East, which should be the larder of the hungry people of Europe, falls into the hands of the Bolsheviks, famine is bound to overtake Europe quickly. Bolshevism is going to thrive in this soil of starvation and need. A Bolshevized Europe will be the first step on the road to world revolution the Soviets have been following for twenty-five years. The achievement of that goal or a third world war are the inescapable alternatives.

Hitler himself could not have improved on this. But it was too late. On 29 April, over a million Germans had surrendered to General Alexander in Italy. All the German armies in the north-west surrendered to Montgomery on 4 May, and on the following day the German forces in Austria and Bavaria surrendered to the Americans. The unconditional surrender to representatives of all three Powers took place at Rheims on 7 May, after a request to be allowed to surrender only to the Western Allies had been rejected.

Truman and Churchill had wanted the announcement of the cease-fire to be made simultaneously in all three Allied capitals. Stalin refused. Throughout the last three months of the war, the Soviet Press had made only meagre reference to the rapid progress of the Anglo-American forces into Germany, and the surrender at Rheims was likewise accorded little notice. For Russia, the war was not regarded as ended until, on the following day, the surrender was ratified in Berlin at a ceremony presided over by Marshall Zhukov. Britain and America celebrated victory on 8 May. Soviet Russia would not celebrate victory until 9 May, after submission had ceremonially been made to the commander of the Red Army.

By the time of the German surrender, the tide of war had already turned against the Japanese. In achieving their great western Pacific conquests, and creating the defensive ring of bases that guarded them, they had strained their resources to the limit. By contrast, the United States, in spite of the demands of the European theatre, had an economic and industrial potential the Japanese could not hope to match. Japan's only hope was to resist so fanatically and make the Americans pay so dearly for every inch of ground recovered, every island-base eliminated, that they might come to regard a compromise peace as a better solution. But, although some Japanese-held islands were only recaptured after bitter frontal assaults

(Guadalcanal and Saipan among them), others, thanks to growing U.S. air and sea power, could be by-passed. Hence, by August 1944, the U.S. had penetrated far beyond the outermost of the Japanese-held islands and had recovered New Guinea, the Gilbert and Ellice Islands and Guam. During the autumn of 1944 and the spring of 1945, the Philippines were regained; and bases for air attacks on the Japanese mainland were secured by the capture, at enormous cost to both sides, of Iwojima in March 1945 and Okinawa in June. Nevertheless, the ferocity with which these places had been defended seemed to confirm the estimate that final victory would be achieved only after another eighteen months of fighting, and at a possible cost of over a million British and American casualties. The difficulties which British and Indian troops had met with in the slow reconquest of Burma by May 1945 seemed to confirm this pessimistic forecast.

On their side, however, the Japanese, who never lost their sense of the possible to the extent that the Nazis had done in Germany, began to make overtures for peace at the end of June 1945, through the still-neutral Russians.[1] Since Stalin had only until 8 August to earn his promised rewards for declaring war on Japan within three months of the German surrender on 8 May, there was no evident Russian haste to pass the proposals on. Nevertheless, United States Intelligence was aware that the Emperor was determined upon surrender, provided only that it was not unconditional surrender.

Thus, by the summer of 1945, both major contestants were agreed in dreading the war's prolongation; but with the sinister difference that whereas the Japanese would move slowly in order, if possible, to negotiate themselves out of the incalculable consequences of an unconditional surrender, the Americans now sought to fulfil a prepared time-table that offered prospect of swift and total victory. The sequence of events from June to August 1945 was perhaps more important for the future than any that had occurred since the war began.

When Truman became President he discovered for the first time that the United States was in the last stages of perfecting an atomic bomb. Plans were made to explode a trial bomb in Mexico in July and to have another ready for use on a Japanese city by the beginning of August. The Mexican explosion was successfully undertaken on 16 July 1945, during the three Power conference at Potsdam. On 18 July, Truman informed Churchill that he proposed to order the use of the bomb on Japan if there was no response to an ultimatum. On 24 July, he informed Stalin, with careful lack of emphasis, that the Americans had just come into possession of a weapon whose destructive power was exceptional. On 26 July, Truman and Churchill issued a proclamation to the Japanese from Potsdam. Although it called for 'unconditional surrender of all the Japanese armed forces', it

---

[1] Lord Avon asserts that these overtures 'were not significant because they were not from any quarter in Japan where power then lay'. *The Reckoning*, p. 547.

was presented as giving Japan an 'opportunity' to end the war and in fact set out conditions of peace. These were the elimination of 'the authority and influence of those who have deceived and misled the Japanese people', and the loss of all Japan's overseas possessions. There would be an Allied occupation, though only of 'points in Japanese territory', and the Japanese people would be neither enslaved nor destroyed. In short, the proclamation demanded no more and no less than had always been demanded: the cessation of armed resistance and the overthrow of the authoritarian system of government that had launched the war. Two items were, however, missing. There was no warning that failure to accept and grasp this 'opportunity' would result in the dropping of a fearsome new weapon: nor did it refer to the position of the Japanese Emperor. It nowhere stated that the Allies had no intention of treating the Emperor as a war criminal; and here was a matter on which information would have been both sought and given had no atomic time-table been drawn up with the first week of August in mind. As a device for getting the Japanese to make peace before an atomic bomb was dropped on them, the proclamation, whether through accident or design, was hardly to be taken seriously. The Japanese Government ignored it, and on 6 August, the first day on which weather conditions were favourable, an atomic bomb was dropped on Hiroshima. Exploding at a height of 2,000 feet, it completely burnt three-fifths of the city and caused about one hundred thousand deaths. Fatal radiation effects were felt up to a thousand yards from the centre of the explosion and fatal burning effects up to three miles from it.

On 8 August, Stalin presented the Japanese with a declaration of war, and proceeded at once to occupy a large part of Manchuria. Truman having ordered the dropping of both of the only two bombs in existence, the second was exploded over Nagasaki on 9 August. On 10 August, the Japanese announced their willingness to surrender, subject only to an undertaking that this would not prejudice the prerogative of the Emperor as a sovereign ruler. The Allied reply demanded the subjection of the Emperor's authority to the Allied Supreme Commander and left Japan's eventual form of government to be decided in accordance with the will of the people. These terms were accepted, and on 15 August, Japan's surrender was announced; it was formalized on the American battleship *Missouri* in Tokyo Bay on 2 September. President Truman commented thus:

We had won the war. It was my hope now that the people of Germany and Japan could be rehabilitated under the occupation. The United States, as I had stated at Berlin, wanted no territory, no reparations. Peace and happiness for all countries were the goals towards which we would work and for which we had fought. No nation in the history of the world had taken such a position in complete victory. No nation with the military power of the United States of America had been so generous to its enemies and so helpful to its friends. Maybe the teachings of the Sermon on the Mount could be put into effect.[1]

[1] Harry S. Truman, *Year of Decisions, 1945*, p. 369.

The process by which, in August 1945, a United States President found
himself in a position to drop two atomic bombs on Japan as a preliminary
to implementing the principles of the Sermon on the Mount was a complicated one. Although by this time Hitler had been dead for months and the
British had virtually no influence on what was happening, the bomb was in
fact a British-sponsored invention conceived out of fear of Hitler.

The discovery that when an atom of uranium was bombarded with neutrons the result was the fission of its nucleus, and the creation of a chain
reaction instantaneously liberating vast stores of energy, had been made in
the Kaiser Wilhelm Institute for Chemistry in Berlin in December 1938 by
Dr Otto Hahn. Previous work on 'splitting the atom', done in England
by Lord Rutherford in 1919 and by Cockcroft in 1932 had not resulted
in an increase of energy, but rather the reverse, and it was doubtless for this
reason that Rutherford had almost always dismissed the notion that atomic
energy had practical possibilities. Hahn's work on uranium was thus a
decisive step forward, and the fact that it had been made in the capital of
Hitler's Third Reich was a determining factor in the sequence of events
that led, in the short space of five and a half years, from this abstruse
laboratory experiment by a theoretical chemist in Berlin to the blasting of
Hiroshima and Nagasaki. When, in 1945, Hahn heard of the bomb being
dropped, he did not at first believe it.

Hahn's researches were published early in 1939, and soon the theoretical
problems involved were being discussed in laboratories all over the world.
Attempts to produce a chain-reaction were made in Russia, the United
States and, most notably, in France where, from the spring of 1939 onwards, a team of scientists under Joliot-Curie, son-in-law of the famous
Curies, was determined on creating a nuclear chain-reaction that could be
used in industry. The possibility of the development of a nuclear weapon
was referred to in Britain in the scientific journal *Discovery* in September
1939; and already by that time the British Air Ministry had made attempts
to secure advance supplies of uranium from Katanga in the Belgian Congo.
The Joliot-Curie team in France took out a patent for a uranium bomb in
1939; and in the same year two refugee scientists, the Hungarian Szilard
and the Italian Fermi, warned the United States of the danger of a nuclear
weapon being perfected by the Germans. Einstein added his warning also.

In Britain, however, during 1939–40, scientific endeavour was needed
most for air defence, and for this reason there was a heavy concentration
of available talent on the development of radar. It was felt, on the scientific
evidence available by the end of 1939, that the creation of a workable bomb
was not yet a practical possibility, either in Germany or Britain, and that to
divert resources and talent to this problem would be dangerous. It was also
realized, thanks to further work by Niels Bohr, the Danish physicist, that it
was only the rare uranium 235 isotope which was subject to fission when hit
by neutrons. The nucleus of normal uranium 238 merely absorbed the

neutrons; at best, use of uranium 238 might produce nuclear power, but not a nuclear bomb. How much uranium 235 would be needed to produce a bomb and how to separate it out from uranium 238, nobody yet knew.

The solutions to the first of these problems were produced during 1940 in the Universities of Birmingham and Liverpool, and were the work of the British scientist Chadwick, the discoverer of neutrons, and three refugees from Europe, Rotblat (a Pole), Frisch (a Viennese) and Peierls (an anti-Nazi from Berlin). The contribution of Peierls, Frisch and Rotblat, as well as that of Niels Bohr and many other European refugee scientists, provides the only clear evidence that there was an international Jewish and intellectual 'conspiracy' against Hitler, although it was a 'conspiracy' his own acts had brought into being. They were all victims of, or refugees from, the Nazi system; all were deeply concerned lest the Third Reich produce a nuclear weapon first; and those who were in England were allowed to pursue their nuclear researches at this stage because, as enemy aliens, they could not be employed on radar research, which was so secret that only British nationals by birth were allowed to take part in it. Nuclear research was still 'pure' research, in the official view.

Frisch and Peierls discovered theoretically that the amount of uranium required would be smaller than at first thought, and that the explosive power generated would be much greater; and duly informed Sir Henry Tizard, chairman of the Air Ministry's principal scientific committee. He, in turn, empowered Sir George Thomson to set up a group to study the implications of the Frisch-Peierls findings. It met first in April 1940, and christened itself the Maud Committee.[1] By the summer of that year Government-sponsored research on the main problems of preparing a nuclear weapon was in hand at Liverpool, Birmingham, Cambridge and Oxford universities. Nevertheless, it still seemed unlikely that a nuclear weapon would be perfected in time to affect the war with Hitler. Nor did it seem that anything so monstrous as to be morally indefensible was being meditated. A uranium bomb, despite the fact that nuclear energy was a million times more effective than chemical energy, was not a hydrogen bomb capable of devastating whole regions. It was not in essentials any more (or any less) objectionable than the area bombing of German cities later carried on by Bomber Command; and fire bombs, if used in sufficient quantity, could be hardly less effective than one uranium bomb. In 1940, it was possible to think in terms of using the bomb against German forces massed for some future invasion, and in terms of the danger of the Germans perfecting such a weapon first. It was, therefore, with little sense of inflicting an entirely new kind of horror on the world that the teams working under the Maud Committee carried on their investigations. They were

[1] The curious tale of how it came to be called the Maud Committee may be read in *Britain and Atomic Energy* by Margaret Gowing or *The Birth of the Bomb* by R. W. Clark.

working to produce the blueprint of something that might not, in the end, prove practicable, and which might never in fact be made. And over all their activities between April 1940 and July 1941 there hung the physical menace of the Nazi tyranny that then gripped all Europe, and a sense of the isolation and vulnerability of the British Isles, which cannot now be discounted merely because hindsight and subsequent historical research reveal that Britain was less vulnerable than she seemed, and was soon to acquire massive allies. The uranium bomb was, in a very real sense, conjured up by Hitler.

By July 1941, however, the Maud Committee had made substantial progress. Its final report was that there was a good chance after all of a uranium bomb (with a destructive effect equivalent to that of 1,800 tons of T.N.T.) being produced before the war was over. It indicated what problems remained to be solved, and offered an estimate of the resources in money and materials that would be required. At the end of August 1941, Churchill authorized the inauguration of work on the complicated processes of actual manufacture. A Government organization called the Directorate of Tube Alloys was set up within the Ministry of Supply in October 1941, the responsible Cabinet Minister being Sir John Anderson. Anderson, a distinguished former Civil Servant and Governor of Bengal, had been made Lord President of the Council by Churchill in 1940, and scientific development was one of his responsibilities. The most well-known product of his scientific stewardship was the Anderson air-raid shelter, but, in spite of his rather grim Victorian appearance, he was in fact a trained scientist; by a strange coincidence he had written a Ph.D. thesis at the University of Leipzig in 1900 on the chemistry of uranium. He seems, doubtless in consequence, to have been almost the only person connected with the higher direction of the war to have grasped in advance that the uranium bomb was not just one more explosive.

The entry of the United States into the war, only seven weeks after Tube Alloys was set up, terminated Britain's independent scientific contribution to victory almost as drastically as it did her independent military action. Already, as the result of an official mission led by Sir Henry Tizard in the second half of 1940, the United States had been put in possession of all the results of Britain's radar research; and the United States was given prompt details about the contents of the Maud Report also. This revealed that the British were so far ahead of the leisurely United States efforts that, as early as October 1941, Roosevelt offered to make the vast engineering and industrial resources of the United States available, so that atomic development might from the start be a joint Anglo-American undertaking both for war and peace. Unfortunately this was not at once seized upon by Churchill as the basis for a formal agreement; and over this, as over matters more exclusively diplomatic, Britain suffered much from the slovenly generosity of both Roosevelt and Churchill in behaving as if their personal sense of comradeship was an all-sufficient substitute for proper agreements properly negotiated. Once the United States was in the war it became more and more evident that the bomb would be made in America; yet it was not until June 1942, eight months after Roosevelt's first communication to Churchill, that the two men, meeting at the President's home at Hyde Park, discussed together the terms on which Britain should partner the United States in the Manhattan Project which shortly afterwards, under the direct control of the U.S. Army, began to construct the bomb. Their discussion was so nebulous that it is evident that it never got beyond the indefinable and ultimately meaningless proposition that there should be 'equal partnership'. British scientists sent to the U.S. from Tube Alloys found themselves excluded from access to information about the development of the project, no doubt partly on the ground that they were not U.S. nationals. Relations between Roosevelt and Churchill got steadily more strained in consequence of the persistent exclusion of the British, and the outcome was that at the Quebec conference of August 1943 the production of a uranium bomb was made an entirely United States project. Most of the British physicists concerned were then absorbed into the American teams. In much the same way as Stalin later insisted that rival Polish elements should be submerged by the Communists of the Lublin Committee, so Roosevelt had rival British scientists submerged in the American Manhattan Project. Independent British work on the bomb came to an end. In this matter, as in the later problems of Western-Russian partnership over eastern Europe, the absence of systematic and efficient negotiation led to power falling unresistingly into the hands of the stronger partner.

Both the early development and the eventual employment of atomic bombs in the war were based on miscalculations. The fear that Germany might develop atomic weapons was, as it turned out, groundless; and the belief that, if the bomb were not used, the Japanese would go on fighting for another eighteen months was groundless also. How much calculation there was in the complete exclusion of Russia from participation in the bomb's development, or in the fact that the bomb was used at a moment which made Russian intervention against Japan a formality, and U.S. reliance on Russian help in the Far East unnecessary, is not a matter about which it would be wise to guess. It was, however, depressingly relevant to post-war international relations that Russia was without atomic weapons until 1949, had no hydrogen bomb till 1953, and had general inferiority to the U.S. in nuclear power until the mid-1950's. The result was also to augment the doubts in the minds of many scientists. While retaining a proper pride in the quality of the research that had gone into atomic development, they saw, more clearly than the politicians and soldiers at the time, how terrifying were the powers that had now been released, how difficult it would be to agree on international control if one of the greatest powers was denied access to information, and how contrary to scientific tradition it was that fundamental research should be appropriated by one part of the civilized world and denied to another. Yet, just as there were nuclear physicists, among them men such as Pontecorvo and Klaus Fuchs who had been at work in the earliest days of the Maud Committee, who could claim that they were justified in handing over nuclear information to the Russians so, too, the soldiers and the politicians of 1944–45 could justify the denial of this information to Russia. In hastening to erect his Iron Curtain well before the war in Europe was over, Stalin gained Poland and East Germany, but, by doing so in a way that alienated the West, he may perhaps be held responsible for denying his country effective nuclear power until after his death in 1953. Certainly, the two factors put together, the Russian insistence on an Iron Curtain and the United States insistence on a Western monopoly in atomic weapons, condemned the world to a peace in which, for at least a decade, nobody could seriously believe.

PART IX:
BEGINNING AND END,
1945-1951

46 · The 1945 Election

On 31 October 1944, Churchill told the Commons that he thought it would be wrong to 'continue this Parliament beyond the period of the prolongation of the German war'; and the Labour Party Conference declared in December 1944 that a General Election should take place as soon as the international situation permitted. When the Germans surrendered, however, Churchill proposed the continuance of the wartime Government until the defeat of Japan and, when Attlee proposed an autumn election instead, Churchill decided to hold an election immediately. On 23 May, therefore, the Coalition Government resigned, to be replaced by a Conservative 'Caretaker' Government, though Churchill continued to refer to it as a 'National' Government, since it contained a handful of Simon's so-called Liberal Nationals. On 15 June, Parliament was dissolved, and polling took place on 5 July; but as a large proportion of the electorate was overseas in the armed forces the results were not declared until three weeks later. Since nobody could know in the interval who would be Britain's Prime Minister by the end of the month, Attlee accompanied Churchill and Eden when the Potsdam conference opened on 17 July.

When the results were announced on 26 July it was found that Labour had won 393 seats, the Conservatives 213 and the Liberals only 12. It was the most clearly defined electoral result of the century. The defeat of no fewer than 294 of the 306 Liberal candidates, 64 of whom lost their deposits, meant that for the first time since 1885 the classical two-party system existed in fact and not solely in constitutional theory. Although Labour's majority in the House was smaller than the Liberal majority in 1906, its mandate was more emphatic: it had no commitment to another party, such as the Liberals had to the Irish Nationalists, and no rival for the anti-Conservative vote, such as the Liberals had had in Labour in 1906. Yet the electoral system had its eccentric mathematical last word: there were just

under 2,250,000 Liberal votes, and when these were added to the just under
10,000,000 Conservative votes the total recorded against Labour exceeded
by about 240,000 Labour's own total of 12,000,000. In spite of this, the
result was the most decisive verdict in favour of radical change that the
British electorate had ever delivered.

The electorate had arrived at this dramatic decision in 1945 in almost total
ignorance of the tense diplomatic situation abroad and of the economic and
financial condition in which the country was certain to find itself when the
war terminated. In 1945, the British people passed a vote of no confidence in
the past and proclaimed a quiet, determined wish for a social revolution.
Their mood at the time was most accurately expressed by the poem 'For
Johnny', written by John Pudney about the death of a crashed R.A.F. pilot:

> Do not despair
> For Johnny head in air
> He sleeps as sound
> As Johnny underground
>
> Fetch out no shroud
> For Johnny in the cloud
> And keep your tears
> For after years
>
> Better by far
> For Johnny the bright star
> To keep your head
> And see his children fed

Undeflected by celebrations of victory, deluded by no notions of grandeur, undeterred by assertions that a Labour Government would be a prelude to totalitarianism, the electors kept their heads; and, remembering the
unremedied poverty of the thirties, voted to have their children fed, and
fed as they had been in wartime, in ways which ensured equal justice even
in times of shortage. Suddenly, too, their traditional deference to the upper
classes was abandoned. Early in the war, a United States Vice-President,
Henry Wallace, had proclaimed that 'the century of the Common Man' had
arrived. In the 1945 election, the British people assented to that proposition.
    The electors did not turn against the Conservative Party merely because
they believed it to have been indifferent in the 1930's to the problem of
poverty and subservient to the dictators. They rejected it for the positive
reason that they wished to make permanent in peacetime the social and
economic equality which had been achieved under the compulsions of war.
The principle of conscription itself had, in the most important sphere of the
war effort, done much to create a classless society; exemptions from service
in the forces had been based solely on the national need, not on privilege.
Privilege deriving from education or class might still be a factor in officer
selection in the Army and the Navy (and ratings and other ranks were

certain of this, whatever the facts) but in all three services, and above all in the R.A.F., commissioned rank had increasingly demanded the possession of technical competence. And even demobilization had been scrupulously and skilfully designed by Ernest Bevin's Ministry of Labour to combine consideration for those who had served longest with regard for the needs of national reconstruction.

The civilian population had similarly been welded into equality. As a result of the Emergency Powers Act of May 1940, Bevin, as Minister of Labour and National Service, had acquired absolute authority over the life and work of everyone in the country between the ages of sixteen and sixty-four. Later, by a Restriction on Engagement Order and by various Essential Works Orders, he compelled all workers to be engaged through labour exchanges so that employers might not poach skilled labour, and forbade employers to dismiss workers or workers to leave their jobs without reference to the Ministry. Strikes and lockouts were prohibited, trade union privileges were waived, wages and conditions in a wide range of industries, including agriculture, the docks and the catering trades, were improved by various worker-employer bodies established by Bevin, and it became virtually impossible in any trade or industry to pay wages less than those fixed by wage agreements, whether or not a particular firm or employer had been a party to such agreements. By 1943, the armed forces were well on the way to their eventual total of just over 5,000,000, and there were 5,250,000 workers in the munition factories; in addition, 7,750,000 women were working full time on the war effort, either in industry or in the forces, and 1,000,000 more were doing voluntary service. This takes no account of the large numbers who, whether or not they were employed in industry, were enrolled in part-time Civil Defence work, the Home Guard, or in street or factory fire-watching duties in the evenings or overnight. Yet this regimentation of the labour force was maintained with remarkably little opposition. This was in part because the idea of armed resistance to the Nazis had all along been rather more acceptable to the organized working class than to the middle and upper class, and in part because, once Russia had become an ally, the war had been rather naïvely regarded as a working-class struggle in whose prosecution the upper classes were suspected of dragging their feet. It was also partly because Bevin and his Ministry officials had shown an unusual concern for the welfare of the large number of conscripted civilians for whom they were responsible. A considerable industrial welfare service was called into being, works canteens were developed, and the lodgings of workers who had been sent to work away from home were subject to regular inspection; even a radio programme, 'Music while you Work' was introduced specifically for the purpose of assisting the war effort.

Food rationing, under the deliberately benign guidance of Lord Woolton and his Ministry of Food, was similarly organized in a way which seemed

to combine the elimination of privilege with the principle of social benevolence. The value of the meat ration during the war varied from between
1s. and 2s. a head, and usually part of the ration had to be taken in corned
beef. The bacon ration per person varied from a quarter to half a pound,
the tea ration from two to four ounces; the cheese ration had been as high
as eight ounces and as low as one. Almost everything else that could be
eaten was liable to be allocated by a complicated 'points' system. Individuals might be allotted sixteen to twenty points monthly; in 1943 sixteen
points would have permitted the purchase of one tin of condensed milk, a
pound of sweet biscuits and one tin of Irish stew. The composition of the
loaf of bread (there was no bread rationing during the war) was fixed: it
could not contain more than 12½ per cent of white flour, and barley and
potato might be incorporated in it. To save shipping space, people were
urged to eat potatoes instead of bread; sausages were, by regulation, required to contain 7½ per cent soya flour, 55 per cent 'cereal filler' and only
37½ per cent meat. Prices were controlled, and kept low by Government
subsidies; to economize on transport, manufacturers and fruit and vegetable growers were required to sell their products only in particular zones.
Soap was severely rationed, and a twelve-ounce packet of good soap powder
would take up half a normal monthly ration.

Clothing was rationed and could be bought only against coupons; to
conserve materials, elaborate regulations established 'utility' garments with
a minimum of 'trimmings'; new furniture, also produced to a 'utility'
standard laid down by the Board of Trade, was available only on a 'units'
system and then solely to newly married couples, to the bombed-out, or in
anticipation of the birth of a child; and its price was restricted to 133⅓ per
cent of comparable pre-war prices.

Yet there had to be set against food rationing the works canteens and the
British Restaurants set up by local authorities, in which food coupons did
not have to be surrendered. (By contrast, meals in restaurants were subject
to strict limitations as to price and quantity.) There was also the extra milk
and the orange juice and cod-liver oil which were made available for
children, as well as the greatly increased provision of school meals. Nor did
the Food Ministry exercise over young children's ration books the bureaucratic pedantry that might have been expected; and the family with young
children was able to increase its over-all entitlement to rationed foods by
virtue of their offspring's ration books. The most remarkable feature of the
social scene during wartime was that the health of young children improved
rather than deteriorated; and the whole operation of mobilizing and feeding
the working population and its children was conducted with an efficiency,
sanity and humanity which seemed to prove that the impression of failing
initiative and communal heartlessness which hung over the twenties and
thirties was due entirely to the poor quality of the nation's leadership in
those years.

If, uppermost in the civilian mind, was this consciousness of having lived during wartime in a social system which seemed to subordinate the privileged and wealthy to the community as a whole, the members of the armed forces adopted a different attitude which nevertheless tended in the same direction. The most frequently iterated Other Rank remark in the early forties was, 'Things are going to be different after the war'. The men in the services may have known relatively little of what civilian life was like in wartime, but they had an indelible recollection of what it had been like before the war, and were determined that the world to which they returned would be a better world. They also thought that, on the whole, Britain had not had a very good war. Neither during nor after the Second World War was there the bitter contempt for generals displayed in the thinking and the writing about the First World War; yet, until the advent of Montgomery, with his astute realization that he could best project his own image by 'putting every soldier in the picture', the Army rank and file mostly took the view that its commanders were incompetent Blimps, who owed their elevation chiefly to their social class, and contrasted this with the classlessness and courageous efficiency they assumed to characterize the Red Army. The soldier, like the civilian at home, had a passionate admiration for the Russians. Much of this was attributable to the ranker's psychological defence-mechanism of bloody-mindedness which enabled him to compensate, by anarchistic conversation in the N.A.A.F.I., for the state of total subordination in which he spent his days; but even this contributed to the anti-Conservative vote on 5 July 1945. Invited, at long last, freely to express his true opinion about those who had for so long been set in authority over him, the ranker put a bloody-minded cross on his ballot paper and the Conservatives were out.

The Churchill Government's inept handling of the Beveridge Report on Social Insurance also contributed to the Conservatives' downfall. The Report had originated from a decision taken by the Churchill Government in 1941, when Labour's Arthur Greenwood was still in the Cabinet as Minister in Charge of Post-war Reconstruction. Published in December 1942, it was a major State paper and a landmark in the history of social security throughout the world. Beveridge had been deeply involved with the problems of social security ever since, as a Civil Servant, he had worked with Churchill and Lloyd George in the days before 1914. He now produced a detailed scheme of comprehensive social insurance which seemed to show that what had hitherto been a matter of verbal or emotional aspiration (like Labour's reference in 1929 to the 'morality in the nature of things') could, if the nation so desired, be translated into practice, and that a start could be made even before the war was over. It was presented as much more than a universalization and augmentation of the security payments, such as pensions, unemployment and sickness benefit, which had come into existence since 1908. It was deliberately presented by its author as part of a social revolution:

Now, when the war is abolishing landmarks of every kind, is the opportunity for using experience in a clear field. A revolutionary moment in the world's history is a time for revolutions, not for patching. . . .
Organization of social insurance should be treated as one part only of a comprehensive policy of social progress. Social insurance fully developed may provide income security; it is an attack upon Want. But Want is only one of five giants on the road of reconstruction, and in some ways the easiest to attack. The others are Disease, Ignorance, Squalor and Idleness.

The Plan proposed the total abandonment of the Poor Law mentality which, surviving through all the previous reforms of the century, had caused all payments to the old, the widowed, the sick and the unemployed to be regarded fundamentally as charitable disbursements, to be kept as low as possible in order to deter idleness and improvidence. Beveridge insisted that the Plan was

first and foremost a plan of insurance – of giving, in return for contributions, benefits up to a subsistence level, as of right and without means test, so that individuals may build freely upon it.

In the last part of the Report, Beveridge insisted that the Plan involved three further assumptions. The first was that there should be non-contributory children's allowances for each child after the first, paid for out of taxation and not out of insurance contributions. The second was that there should be a national health service to give every citizen whatever medical treatment he required, and in whatever form he might require it. The third was that there should be, not what was later rather loosely called a policy of 'full employment', but at least an end to the mass unemployment that had plagued the Britain of the thirties.

Beveridge concluded:

Freedom from want cannot be forced on or given to a democracy. It must be won by them. Winning it needs courage and faith and national unity; courage to face facts and difficulties and overcome them; faith in our future and in the ideals of fair play and freedom for which century after century our forefathers were prepared to die; a sense of national unity overriding the interests of any class or section. The Plan for Social Security is submitted by one who believes that in this supreme crisis the British people will not be found wanting, of courage and faith and national unity, of material and spiritual power to play their part in achieving both social security and the victory of justice among nations upon which security depends.

It would be fair to say that these words reflected the mood of the Britain of the latter years of war as fully as Churchill's had done in its earlier years. Beveridge enunciated what the British people really conceived themselves to be fighting for. Merely fighting to 'win' had little meaning for them. It was always a mistake to suppose that they were fighting to preserve the kind of England that had gone to war in 1939; they wanted to abolish it.

This was something Churchill's passionate patriotism nevertheless failed to comprehend. His reaction to the immediate best-selling success of the Beveridge Report was to warn the Cabinet off it, in a note circulated to his colleagues as he left, in January 1943, for the Casablanca conference. He told them:

A dangerous optimism is growing up about the conditions it will be possible to establish here after the war.

and then enumerated the hopes that were currently being entertained. They included the abolition of low wages and unemployment, great advances in education, housing, health and agriculture, and expensive plans for colonial welfare, all without a fall in the value of money or a rise in the cost of living. He concluded

The question steals across the mind whether we are not committing our forty-five million people to tasks beyond their capacity to bear.

We must all do our best and we shall do it much better if we are not hampered by a cloud of pledges and promises which arise out of the hopeful and genial side of man's nature and are not brought into relation with the hard facts of life.[1]

This cautious pessimism was entirely appropriate; but it was not until well after 1945 that the British people were finally prepared to concede that Churchill had been right to fear that victory would have been won at the cost of national bankruptcy. But he failed to realize that if the mass of the people had known, even before 1945, that years of hardship still lay ahead of them, they would have insisted, no less than they did in fact, on social arrangements that protected the weakest members of the community from destitution and which sought to limit the privileges of wealth. They would still have voted for rationing by the Government rather than for rationing by the purse.

The Government therefore laid up trouble for itself when it tried to prevent knowledge about the Beveridge Report being disseminated among the troops. There existed by now an Army Bureau of Current Affairs, which circulated to the Army pamphlets on contemporary problems which were intended for use in a 'current affairs hour' for other ranks. This was supposed to occur fortnightly, under the guidance of the unit education officer. Indeed, A.B.C.A. may be regarded as largely responsible for the passion of post-war educationists for discussion techniques in teaching in general, and for introducing civics, current affairs and social studies into the newer secondary schools. It may be regarded also as an attempt to spread to the rank and file of the Army the awareness of the contemporary world which had been stimulated in the lower middle class by the Penguin paperbacks of the thirties. The A.B.C.A. pamphlet for December 1942 contained a detailed and commendatory account of the Beveridge Report; but shortly after units had received their copies they were ordered to send

[1] W. S. Churchill, *Closing the Ring*, pp. 861–2.

them back again. As this fact was known in every orderly room and unit headquarters throughout the British Army it soon became known to every soldier, since orderly room and headquarters soldier-clerks were to the Army in general the equivalent of the political journalist's 'well-informed sources'; and as many military clerks had themselves been journalists, the news soon became a national sensation, and in due course the pamphlet had to be reissued. This incident, bearing as it does the marks of one of the Prime Minister's typical incursions into the lesser realms of administration, was a major political blunder.

Its effects were aggravated by the Commons debate on the Report in February 1943. Sir John Anderson gave the Report faint praise for its 'practical idealism' but then implied that he thought it was not practical, by declaring that at least some of the financial assumptions on which it was based 'might prove ill-founded'. Kingsley Wood, the Chancellor of the Exchequer, who had been one of Neville Chamberlain's favourite Ministers, poured much cold water:

We should not overlook the strong and urgent claims by other legitimate interests which must be taken into account when considering priorities, among them post-war housing, education, and schemes to benefit the younger generation, and civil aviation. We must also not overlook the heavy burden which present high taxation placed on the community, and especially on the middle and upper-middle classes.

As a result, the Government gained no credit for the fact that Sir John Anderson accepted, in principle, the proposals for a comprehensive medical service and for children's allowances. A conciliatory speech by Herbert Morrison asserting that the Government was united in being 'definitely committed to the principles of the Report, with certain reservations', made a poor impression also. Worse still, from the point of view of the future, almost all the Conservative M.P.s who contributed to the debate referred to the Report in language which was, at best unenthusiastic, and at worst hostile. Among the few Conservatives who commended the Report was Quintin Hogg. He was almost alone in seeing the essentials of the matter. After observing that Sir John Anderson's speech could not 'kindle the smallest spark of imagination' he said:

While not burking the economic question, nor imagining that after the war there would be anything but a grim world in which people could only be offered self-sacrifice and struggle for many years, he considered this an argument for, not against, the proposals, since people could only be asked to look forward to self-sacrifice and restriction if offered at the same time a complete measure of social justice guaranteeing equal sacrifice.

Ninety-seven Labour M.P.s voted against the Government in the division, thus creating some embarrassment for the Labour Ministers, who naturally voted on the Government side; and it is perhaps not surprising that between the Beveridge debate in February 1942 and the dissolution in

1945 the Conservatives lost ten by-elections, even though, by agreement, official Labour candidates were not put up against them. Three of the seats were lost to the short-lived Commonwealth party, founded in 1942 by the West Country Liberal M.P., Sir Richard Acland, to contest by-elections in which 'reactionary' candidates would not otherwise be opposed.

Churchill's conduct of the election campaign was calculated to speed a popular retreat from Conservatism. He opened with the broadcast, on 4 June 1945, of what may well have been the silliest election speech ever made by a British Prime Minister. He tried to claim that the Caretaker Government he had formed the previous month was a National Government because Labour had withdrawn 'on party grounds alone', as if the electorate could be stampeded in 1945 as it had been in 1931, and in total unawareness of the fact that the label 'National Government' had been a fraud from 1931 to 1939 and by 1945 had become, for half the electorate, little better than a term of abuse. He then embarked on a Grand Guignol portrayal of the evils of

this continental conception of human society called Socialism, or in its more violent form, Communism.

It was, he informed his embarrassed listeners,

an attack not only upon British enterprise but upon the right of an ordinary man or woman to breathe freely without having a harsh tyrannical hand clapped across their mouths and nostrils.

Then, in a supreme effort to persuade them of the frightful consequences of making Clement Attlee Prime Minister, he went on:

I declare to you, from the bottom of my heart, that no Socialist system can be established without a political police. . . . No Socialist Government conducting the entire life and industry of the country could afford to allow free, sharp, or violently worded expressions of public discontent. They would have to fall back on some form of Gestapo, no doubt very humanely directed in the first instance.[1]

There was only the most perfunctory attempt to explain what Conservative policy really was, and the conclusion took the form of a rabble-rousing tirade which ended:

On with the forward march! Leave these Socialist dreamers to their Utopias or nightmares. Let us be content to do the heavy job that is right on top of us. And let us make sure that the cottage home to which the warrior will return is blessed with modest but solid prosperity, well fenced and guarded against misfortune, and that Britons may remain free to plan their lives for themselves and those they love.

[1] The following comment, made during the year 1910 by C. F. Masterman, one of Churchill's colleagues in Asquith's government, could well apply to this speech: '(Churchill) is in the Greek sense a Rhetorician, the slave of the words his mind forms about ideas. He sets ideas to Rhetoric, as musicians set theirs to music. And he can convince himself of almost any truth if it is once allowed thus to start on its wild career through his rhetorical machinery.' See *Winston Churchill, The Liberal Phase* in *History Today*, December 1964, pp. 823-4.

It is hard to imagine a speech less related to the realities of 1945. It was beyond the wit of man to persuade the electors that the Labour Party was an organization favouring continental semi-Communist theories which would lead to the setting up of a British Gestapo; and it is hard to conceive how anyone could talk, in 1945, of demobbed rear gunners, or able-seamen or corporals going back to their semi-detacheds or their tunnelbacks, or even their back-to-backs, in the dingy streets of suburb and provincial town, as warriors returning to 'cottage homes'.

Churchill's only other important contribution to the campaign was to make a great fuss about Professor Laski. Most unfortunately, Laski happened to be that year's chairman of the Labour Party, and his mis-guided attempts to intervene in the political developments of the summer of 1945 were a source of great irritation to Attlee and in the end a personal disaster for Laski himself. Laski had announced, when Attlee accompanied Churchill to Potsdam, that Attlee would not be committed to its decisions because they would have first to be submitted to Labour's National Execu-tive or to the Parliamentary Party. This was a fatuous statement, indicating that though Laski was an academic expert on government he did not know much about it in practice. Churchill tried several times to make a national issue of this; and conjured up blood-chilling prospects of a Socialist Government of puppets dancing to the secret instructions of a non-parliamentary conspiracy run by an extreme Left-wing professor. The argument was too involved to impress the man in the street; and Labour's more educated supporters were liable to be on Laski's side, as a tribute to his great influence as a scholar and to his work in the thirties as a Left Book Club selector. Attlee, for his part, dealt in quietly waspish fashion, not only with Churchill's various fantasies, but also, in due course, with Laski. Laski later sued a newspaper for libelling him during the campaign, and lost his action.

The election result caused almost universal astonishment. Churchill was sufficiently mortified to include a brooding reference to his defeat as soon, in the first volume of his war memoirs, as he came to write about his appointment in 1940:

. . . . I acquired the chief power in the State, which henceforth I wielded in ever-growing measure for five months and three years of world war, at the end of which time, all our enemies having surrendered unconditionally or being about to do so, I was immediately dismissed by the British electorate from all further conduct of their affairs.[1]

His successor, too, was taken aback, and, when he appeared at the Palace to kiss hands, Mr. Attlee looked, according to King George VI, 'very surprised indeed'. The surprise of his prospective colleagues took the form of an attempt to prevent him becoming Prime Minister at all. A small

[1] W. S. Churchill, *The Gathering Storm*, p. 589.

intrigue was worked up by the tiresome Laski, who persisted in the view that, even after five months and three years of acting efficiently as Deputy Prime Minister to Churchill, Attlee was still the 'little mouse' Dalton had thought him in 1935. Laski preferred Morrison because he was a more vivid personality who had shown considerable powers of leadership in the thirties as the head of the controlling Labour group in the L.C.C. Ernest Bevin, however, was as devoted to Attlee as he was hostile to Morrison; and Attlee brushed Laski's intervention aside with unemotional celerity.

The only surprise in Attlee's Cabinet-making was that he put Bevin in the Foreign Office and made Dalton Chancellor of the Exchequer, instead of vice-versa as they had expected. It was for some time asserted that the change was suggested to Attlee by King George VI; an alternative explanation was that Bevin would, if immersed in foreign affairs, have fewer opportunities for quarrelling with Morrison. In the event, since Bevin was a skilled negotiator and Dalton an economist of some distinction, the switch was justifiable on its merits, despite Bevin's interest in public finance and Dalton's long acquaintance with the affairs of Europe. Morrison became deputy Prime Minister as Lord President of the Council; Stafford Cripps was successively President of the Board of Trade, Minister of Economic Affairs and, in 1947, Chancellor of the Exchequer in succession to Dalton; and Aneurin Bevan became Minister of Health. These five were the dominant figures in the Government, and since all of them, except Aneurin Bevan, had served in Churchill's wartime Government, they constituted a powerful and able team.

A less satisfactory feature of the Government as a whole was that it contained little new or young blood. This was largely because 253 of the 393 Labour members had entered the Commons for the first time in their lives in 1945, and many were almost entirely unknown to their leaders. Thus, almost every important member of the Government had been born in the 1880's or even earlier than that. Aneurin Bevan, having been born as late as 1897, could claim to be positively youthful. One result of having a Cabinet whose average age was over sixty was that Bevin who died in 1951, and Cripps, who died in 1952, had killed themselves, Attlee had developed ulcers, and most of their senior colleagues, after in many cases being continuously in office for the ten most gruelling years in English history, were plainly exhausted. The balance was not redressed by the appointment of Attlee's two successors to the party leadership, Hugh Gaitskell and Harold Wilson (both actually born in the twentieth century) to ministerial posts in 1947. Except in its financial policy, the Government lived very much in the past, and very much on the Labour movement's past, and it eventually lost the allegiance of those electors who were not committed Labour supporters.

Yet, given that it was a Government of the Left, it was unusually strong almost to the end. This was ascribable to the unusual character of the

Prime Minister, for he was fortified, not only by the fierce championship of Ernest Bevin, but also by his own mental and emotional asceticism. Few men can have combined the efficient exercise of the duties of Prime Minister with such an avoidance of histrionics, and with what seemed an almost saint-like ability to make himself personally unnoticeable. He contrived this feat, too, without being dismissed for long as merely dull; for he possessed a devastating and deflating common sense, in whose presence pretension and attitudinizing seem to have wilted. He neither projected himself, nor allowed others to project themselves in his presence; and the extremes of feeling seem to have been expressed, for him, at one end of the scale with the word 'rubbish' and at the other with the deflating phrase, constantly employed, 'it was a very interesting experience'. Yet, despite the contemporary quip that Mr Attlee was such a modest man because he had so much to be modest about, he had more faith in his own competence than he allowed his contemporaries to suspect. In consequence, he secured more affectionate respect from his supporters and less dislike from his opponents than any other major political figure of his time. His greatest deficiency, his lack of interest in ideas, was a major asset between 1945 and 1950; it was only from 1951 onwards that the Labour movement came painfully to realize that he had led them to an end from which they could not discover how to fashion a new beginning.

---

47 · Economic and Financial Problems, 1945-50

The first problem which faced the new Government was not how to start on the road towards the ultimate objective of turning Britain into a Socialist Commonwealth, but how to avoid financial ruin. The Cabinet discovered at once that the country had virtually no money with which to finance the post-war reconstruction it had been elected to carry out.

During the first weeks of the Government's existence, Keynes, now the Treasury's chief adviser, produced an analysis of the country's financial situation which prompted Dalton to advise his colleagues in mid-August that it was necessary to begin negotiations for an American loan at once. Urgency was added to the situation by the abrupt termination of United States Lend-Lease on 21 August, seven days after the surrender of Japan.

Keynes's Treasury delegation accordingly began talks in Washington on 11 September 1945.

The burden of the United Kingdom's case was that it was entitled to a loan, and on generous terms, owing to the fact that it had contributed a greater proportion of its resources to the cost of the war, and suffered proportionately greater losses, than had the United States. British war casualties were about three times greater than those of the United States; Britain's national wealth had declined by about 20 per cent; Lend-Lease to Britain had amounted to about 1 per cent of U.S. national production, whereas Britain's aid to the U.S. represented about 15 per cent of Britain's national production; civilian consumption in the United Kingdom had decreased by 16 per cent during the war, but in the United States it had increased by 16 per cent. The cost of financing the war, between 1939 and the start of Lend-Lease in the spring of 1941, had reduced Britain's gold and dollar reserves from £864 millions in 1938 to £3 millions. That they had risen to £453 millions by the autumn of 1945 was due mainly to expenditure by U.S. forces in the sterling area, which would now be rapidly reduced. Britain had sold £1,118 millions of foreign investment during the war, and the country's overseas debt had risen from £760 millions to £3,355 millions. As for the future, it was tentatively estimated that the country faced a balance of payments deficit over the next five years amounting to at least £1,250 millions.

The British therefore asked in the first place for a free grant-in-aid of 6,000 million dollars (£1,500 millions). After three months of hard negotiation, the British delegation had to be content with a loan of $4,400 millions (£1,100 millions) to be repaid in fifty annual instalments, starting on 31 December 1951, with interest at 2 per cent. $650 millions of the total represented the sum due to the United States at the end of the war in respect of Lend-Lease. No part of the loan could be used to reduce Britain's debts to other countries and, more important, the British were compelled to submit to the United States resolve to remove all currency restrictions on the movement of world trade. This meant that in 1947 the British would have to permit sterling to be freely convertible into other currencies. Thus, if the United Kingdom bought goods from countries which preferred to buy from the United States, these countries could insist on the United Kingdom paying for its purchases in dollars. This would be very likely to happen, since the United States had peace-time goods to sell much sooner and in larger quantities than the United Kingdom had. The British point of view was that sterling would not for a long time be strong enough for convertibility to be tolerated. In fact, convertibility lasted only from 15 July 1947 to 20 August 1947; during that brief period the drain on the gold and dollar reserves rose from its previous average of $75 millions a week to $237 millions in the week when convertibility was suspended. Convertibility was not in fact permanently established until the end of 1958.

When the loan Agreement was debated in the Commons, members of both parties rebelled against it. On the Labour side, 23 voted against it and 44 abstained; and on the Conservative side, despite an urgent appeal by Churchill, 72 M.P.s voted against and 118 abstained. Labour objections were perhaps best summed up by the Conservative who said that any mention of American finance was, to the Labour Party, like waving a bull at a red flag. There was a resentful feeling that the future of Socialist Britain was being tied to American capitalism. Conservative objections were concentrated on attempts to prove that a similar financial link with the Commonwealth would be possible. Robert Boothby declared that the agreement was 'our economic Munich' and that the Government was selling 'the British Empire for a packet of cigarettes'.

The objections of the rebels on both sides were instinctive rather than economic. There was no immediate bearable alternative to a loan in 1945: and although, since the American terms were unpleasant, it was proper to complain about them, there was no escaping the fact that without the loan, economic recovery from the war would have been so difficult, attended with such scarcity and marked by so little social improvement, that the consequences might have been politically disastrous. Perhaps the true significance of Britain's new dependence on the United States and the international financial agencies to which the British were henceforth committed was not fully revealed until the Suez crisis of 1956. The military operations against Egypt had to be stopped because Britain could not otherwise have obtained from the U.S.-dominated International Monetary Fund the loan made urgently necessary by the steep fall in gold and dollar reserves which the crisis had brought about. At the end of 1945, however, the general public were little concerned about the loan; they did not appreciate the need for it, saw no reason why the United States should not make Britain a loan, took it for granted that the Americans would impose difficult terms, and assumed that the whole operation was a relatively unimportant matter of coping with a purely temporary embarrassment.

What seemed more relevant to daily life by the beginning of 1946 was the consequences of a dramatic world food shortage, particularly in wheat and rice, accentuated by various natural disasters, including droughts in Africa, the Argentine and Australia. Output had been reduced in the producing countries during the war, but it had been thought that accumulated stocks would be adequate until normal harvests could be resumed. These expectations proved false, and Sir Ben Smith, the Minister of Food, a jovial and rotund ex-trade union official, presented to the Commons in February 1946 a tale of woe which one M.P. claimed to be reminiscent of the first chapter of the Book of Job. He indicated that the wheat available for the importing countries in the first half of 1946 would be $5\frac{1}{2}$ million tons below requirements and that Britain had therefore accepted a reduction in her own imports of 250,000 tons. Not only would this mean a return to the 'darker, wartime loaf' but a reduction in available animal feeding stuffs, with a consequent scarcity of bacon, poultry and eggs. There was a rice shortage, which aggravated the wheat shortage; it would also cause India to cut down the export of groundnuts and would thus produce a shortage of vegetable oils, which was already worse than it might have been because of a bad whaling season in the Antarctic resulting from exceptionally bad weather. This would necessitate a reduction in the ration of butter, margarine and cooking-fat. The Food Minister's unhappy position was not improved by the fact that dried egg from the United States, which had been available during the war, had now almost disappeared from the shops with the ending of Lend-Lease. His reply was that the country was too short of dollars to buy American dried egg, and for good measure he then forecast a world shortage of sugar. The only consolation he had to offer was a reminder that the country had just received its first shipload of bananas for six years. To add further to the gloom, the Minister of Agriculture urged everyone to grow food in their gardens and allotments because the need for self-help was 'as great as in the darkest days of the war'.

Throughout the spring of 1946 the situation worsened: the wheat deficit proved to be, not 5½ million, but 8 million tons. In April, the Ministry of Food tried, without success, to deal with the bread shortage by reducing the size of the loaf: people merely bought more loaves. In May, Sir Ben was replaced as Food Minister by the former Left Book Club selector, John Strachey, who, having written much in the thirties about Socialist planning for plenty, at once became involved in planning for scarcity and introduced bread rationing in July 1946. The most the operation achieved was to prevent consumption going up. The ration was always adequate, and its retention until July 1948 was attended by much Food Ministry mismanagement and much tedious coupon-handling by the public. Rationing was accompanied by the rule that bread could not be served as an accompaniment to a main meal in any catering establishment. Naturally enough, the Government was criticized from all quarters. It was criticized for failing to anticipate the crisis, for the increase in the number of Civil Servants required to operate bread rationing, and for the poor quality of the bread (angrily described as 'cattle food'). But it was also criticized for spending dollars on American films and tobacco; and, while some critics saw no reason why British imports of wheat should be limited so that starving Germans could have bread, others thought too little was being done to help famine-stricken Europe and Asia. And the country had barely assimilated the implications of a world food shortage before it was plunged, by the winter of 1946–7, into an even more dramatic fuel shortage.

There had been a sharp fall in coal production during the war, owing to the ending of the export trade; manpower was diverted to the forces and there was a decline in productivity. Recovery after the war had been very slow, in spite of fuel economy campaigns and the development of opencast mining. The demand for coal was already insufficient to meet the requirements of the great increase in electricity generating stations and of the expanding export trade. The situation became disastrous when the winter of 1946–47 proved the hardest for fifty years. Not only was there not enough fuel to meet the exceptional cold; transport was immobilized as well. At one time there were sixteen degrees of frost in the London area; as one blizzard immobilized shipping off the south-east coast, another swept the north. Many places were under frost and snow from December to March. By the latter month, three hundred main roads were still blocked; sheep were frozen by the thousand and acres of winter corn had been ruined. When the thaw did come, in March 1947, it arrived in the shape of a ferocious storm which inundated a great part of the Fens and produced floods in thirty-one counties.

These four months of meteorological misery were marked by something like complete industrial breakdown. Factories had to shut through lack of coal, and by early February two million men were out of work. In December, coal supplies to factories were cut by 50 per cent; in February, coal supplies to all industrial users in the south-east, the midlands and north-west were stopped altogether, and it became an offence to use electricity in the home between 9 a.m. and midday, and 2 p.m. and 4 p.m. Some power stations themselves were closed because of lack of coal. There was very little gas also. To save fuel, street lamps were switched off, London Tube escalators were stopped, the B.B.C. suspended both the TV service and the Third Programme, and the publication of weekly magazines was forbidden. Vegetables became scarce because it was impossible to get them out of the ground; there was an inevitable shortage of candles; and it was impossible to buy a warm coat to keep out the cold because few people had enough clothing coupons to spare.

The luckless Minister of Fuel and Power, who had put through the nationalization of the coal industry as from the first day of 1947, was Emmanuel Shinwell, who had considerable administrative ability. He was removed from his post, and from the Cabinet, in October 1947. His place in the Ministry, though not in the Cabinet, was taken by Hugh Gaitskell. (Shinwell went to the War Office, but returned to the Cabinet as Minister of Defence in 1950). Shinwell later sought to show that the crisis was mishandled by Dalton and Cripps. Attlee had appointed a committee in October 1946 under Dalton's chairmanship to cope with the problem of a likely coal shortage but it was, according to Shinwell, slow to act. Shinwell further criticized both Dalton and Cripps (the latter was then Minister for Economic Affairs) for not realizing that the crucial problem was less a shortage of fuel than a failure to tackle the problem of transport.[1]

[1] E. Shinwell, *The Labour Story*, pp. 182–4.

He in turn was criticized for not anticipating the shortage much earlier in the year.

Perhaps the most remarkable feature of the food and fuel shortages of 1946-7 is the relative good humour and patience with which they were endured by the mass of the population. The people at large had still not quite lost the habit of subordinating personal comfort to the need to combat national adversity which Churchill had first inspired in the period of Dunkirk. The middle class was becoming increasingly disgruntled and the Conservative Party was naturally doing what it could to activate this disgruntlement; but, for something approaching 50 per cent of the electorate, Labour was still 'their' Government, to whom they were prepared to give the benefit of the doubt. Moreover, the feeling persisted that, whatever the discomforts of the shortages, they were at least being fairly shared; the failings or misfortunes of Sir Ben Smith and Emmanuel Shinwell induced little desire to return to what was still regarded as the party of Baldwin, Chamberlain and the means test. In addition, well into 1948, there was continuing evidence of economic recovery, of purposeful change, and of social and financial policies which were creating a real rise in living standards in spite of all the shortages.

In handling the scarcities that resulted from the aftermath of war, from the requirements of the export trade, and from the need to conserve dollars, the Government had at its disposal the innumerable controls which the central administration had acquired during the war itself. Not only was food rationing maintained; it was rationed even more stringently than in wartime. The introduction of bread rationing for the first time was followed, at the end of 1947, by the rationing of potatoes, which had likewise not been rationed during the war; and by 1948 most rations were below the wartime average. Clothes rationing did not end until 1949; the points system lasted till 1950; as late as 1951 the meat ration was as low as tenpennyworth per head per week, Only in May 1950 did it become permissible to spend more than five shillings on a restaurant meal or to take more than three courses. In addition to this elaborate mechanism for sharing deliberately limited supplies as fairly as possible, prices were kept artificially low by Government subsidies, the cost of which was £265 millions in 1946 and as much as £485 millions in 1949. By this means, part, though by no means all, of the burden of the rising cost of food was transferred from the industrial wage-earner to the general taxpayer. Although there were mounting complaints that consumers ought to pay the economic price of food, the Labour Government maintained subsidies both in order to keep wage demands down (and thus the price of British exports) and as a means of redistributing the national income in favour of the industrial wage-earner.

In addition to the rationing of food and clothing, there was rationing of building materials. Licences for new building were hard to obtain because the Government determined to concentrate scarce and costly resources on new schools and factories, on the repair of property which had suffered war damage, and on local government housing. Only one house could be built by private builders for every four council houses built by local authorities. The amount which could be spent on the alteration and decoration of property was strictly limited, and furniture was also still rationed. Investment in new industrial building and in housing and school building, however, was facilitated by Dalton's 'cheap money' policy which kept interest rates low.

Controls were not, however, merely a response to the twin factors of scarcity and the demands of social justice. They were just as much concerned with the transfer from a wartime economy to a peacetime economy, and with the need to develop a large and rapid increase in the export trade. After 1945, Britain's economic position was gravely weakened by the loss of two advantages which had assisted her recovery of prosperity during the thirties, namely, the income from her foreign investments and the low prices of imported food and raw materials. She had incurred a heavy burden of foreign debt, and the income she had been accustomed to receive from shipping and from financial services to the foreigner could not, for the present, cushion the country against its difficulties in the chaotic world of the late 1940's. In addition Britain found it difficult in this period either to export to, or import from, many of her former customers, still suffering as they were from the aftermath of war; and this created a quite new dependence on the United States. The dollar gap which bedevilled the period was largely caused by the fact that British exports to the United States were never large enough to pay for imports from that country. It was for this reason that the Loan negotiated in 1945 was almost spent by the middle of 1947.

While the process of re-establishing export markets was in train, the home market was deliberately kept short. This helped to explain, for example, why over 70 per cent of the output of private cars in the late forties was exported. The Government, in addition to becoming a great bulk buyer of food, became a bulk buyer of supplies for industry, and allocated them according to a list of priorities, with the needs of the home consumer coming very low down, if not at the bottom; and there was an elaborate system of controlling imports in general. The Capital Issues Committee of the Treasury strictly controlled the spending of money on new capital equipment.

By these means, the Government succeeded in a rapid and smooth transition from wartime to peacetime production; the volume of exports in 1947 was 37 per cent above the level of 1938, and when the Conservatives took office in 1951 it was 74 per cent above it; yet perhaps the only external factor working in the Government's favour was the lack of competition in this period from its earlier twentieth-century rivals, Germany and Japan; so that although in 1938 Britain's share of the world's export trade in manufactures had been 18·6 per cent by 1950 it was 25·6 per cent.[1]

From the point of view of the industrial wage-earner the great virtues of the Labour Government were that it appeared to have exorcised the old spectre of industrial depression and to have abolished unemployment. Neither feature of the post-war economy received the unqualified approval of the economists, many of whom considered that employment tended to be 'over-full'. It also became accepted doctrine in educated circles that the Government's restraints on private enterprise restricted initiative, and that over-full employment led to inflation and removed the incentive to hard work which had been provided in earlier days by fear of the sack. The working class was widely accused of enjoying all the privileges, such as high rates of overtime pay and subsidized council housing, while the middle and upper classes were paying high taxes and finding the cost of private enterprise houses greatly inflated by the Government's preference for local authority building. The complaints of the professional and middle classes occupy a large place in the mythology of the period, tending to create a picture of a Britain that was nearly starving, sunk in misery and seething with sour discontent. This impression is reinforced by the necessity, in any account of the period, of noting the recurrent financial crises and the permanent problem of the balance of payments; it is therefore necessary to recall that the industrial wage-earner was not an economist, that he cared much less about the balance of payments than he would have done about a slump, which would have affected him so much more quickly and catastrophically, and that he saw little or no connection between his own working day and the concern of the financial expert with the dollar gap.

In a much publicized phrase, Emmanuel Shinwell answered back on behalf of the wage-earner in the course of a speech to the T.U.C.'s 1947 conference:

We know that you, the organized workers of the country, are our friends – indeed, it could not be otherwise. As for the rest, they do not matter a tinker's cuss.

This frame of mind, though valuable for rallying the faithful, ignored how much Labour's victory in 1945 had been assured by the conversion of sections of the community who were not members of the organized working class. Politically, Labour depended for success on their votes, or at least upon their abstention from voting Conservative.

The Government as a whole was aware of this, and therefore more sensitive to economic considerations. The convertibility crisis in the summer of 1947, coming as it did on top of the bread rationing affair and the fuel crisis,

[1] See G. C. Allen, *British Industries and their Organization*, Chap. 8.

made the Government seem highly vulnerable. The extreme dollar shortage produced by the disastrous month of convertibility, and the imminent exhaustion of the American Loan, led to a formidable programme of cuts. The miners' day was lengthened by half an hour, food imports were cut, the meat ration was reduced, and the private motorist found himself virtually prevented from obtaining petrol. There was a flurry of intrigue in the Cabinet: Cripps and Dalton tried without success to persuade Bevin to take Attlee's place as Prime Minister. Attlee's counter-measure was to pacify his two chief economists by making Cripps (who had hitherto been President of the Board of Trade) into a Minister of Economic Affairs on 29 September 1947. His replacement at the Board of Trade was Harold Wilson, who thus entered the Cabinet at the unusually early age of 31.

The management of the national economy was, however, shortly to pass entirely into the hands of Cripps. While in the House of Commons lobby, *en route* to introduce an emergency Budget on 12 November 1947, Dalton paused to talk about his speech to a newspaper correspondent. The newspaper published details of Dalton's Budget proposals before he had had time to announce them to the Commons. In view of the strict tradition that the contents of the Budget should not be revealed before they are officially laid before the House, this breach of the rules, technical offence though it merely was, compelled Dalton's instant resignation, and Cripps became Chancellor in his place. (Dalton re-entered the Cabinet in May 1948 as Chancellor of the Duchy of Lancaster).

The situation presented the kind of challenge which Cripps appeared most fitted to overcome. The American Loan was almost gone, and although American aid through the Marshall Plan[1] was already in prospect it could not affect the situation till well into 1948, and even then somewhat unpredictably. The export trade was increasing, but not increasing fast enough to make, as yet, any real impact on the adverse trade balance. As Cripps saw it, salvation could come only through the organized reconversion of the whole nation to the lost Victorian gospel of Work and Sacrifice. Industries were given targets; working parties were set up to advise upon methods of industrial modernization; there was a proliferation of joint production councils; Regional Boards of Industry were set up, together with a National Production Advisory Council. Cripps preached eloquently about the productivity drive at fortnightly Press conferences, and the Treasury established an Economic Information Unit which organized an insistent publicity campaign in the national Press, organized exhibitions, and distributed thousands of leaflets to the factories. The purport of all these devices was best expressed in the most memorable poster of the Crippsian era, which shouted from the hoardings, WE'RE UP AGAINST IT: WE WORK OR WE WANT.

The Productivity Drive was an attempt to persuade the nation to labour

[1] See p. 477.

without seeking for any reward except that of achieving a favourable balance of trade. It was for this reason that the reign of Cripps came to be known as the era of 'Austerity'. Not only were business men to improve methods of management: workers were to realize that it was greedy to ask for higher wages. This would not only put up the price of exports: it was a selfish attempt to take a larger slice of the national 'cake' at the expense of others. It was also immoral in another sense: until the export drive had succeeded, we were 'living on tick'. The unfortunate result of this vast exercise in economic planning by exhortation was that what had previously appeared a temporary situation, caused by the aftermath of a dislocating war, began to look extraordinarily like a permanent reconstruction of the European Middle Ages, but by economists instead of medieval schoolmen. Man's life on earth was the working out of a primeval curse, the War taking the place of the Fall. The pleasures of the world (things in the shops) were temptations to be resisted because they prevented men from working out the salvation that would ensure future bliss – not in heaven but in an equally unimaginable state where there was an eternally favourable balance of payments. Damnation was an ever-present prospect; Satan lay in wait, ever ready to lure the idle squanderer of his substance, not into the fires of hell but into the bottomless pit that would open up the moment the nation's gold and dollar reserves disappeared. Cripps presided over this weird theologico-economic cosmogony, combining the organizing ability of an Innocent III with the propagandist fervour of a St Bernard of Clairvaux.

The ceaseless exhortations to greater effort and the continuance, and from time to time the aggravation, of cuts in consumer goods, were violently castigated as setting the nation on the road to serfdom, and as illustrating beyond question that 'Socialism' made men equal only by making them all equally miserable. In fact, Cripps, with impartial grandeur, was in some ways as much a scourge of labour as of industrialists. In his 1948 Budget he scourged the proud by making a once-for-all levy on capital; but in his 1949 Budget he did not spare the humble. He cut the food subsidies, declared there must be a ceiling on the social services, and said that the process of redistributing income could go no further until there was more income to distribute. In 1948 he even organized an increase in unemployment by cutting down the building industry's programme to increase the mobility of labour. Perhaps his greatest achievement in this disciplining of his own side was his success in securing the trade union movement's agreement to wage restraint at a time of rising prices, even though 1948 did see some increases in the pay of engineers, railwaymen and post office workers. This was a remarkable achievement. The function of the trade union movement was essentially that of securing a larger share of the national cake; yet Cripps temporarily, but at a critical period, made them converts to the gospel that the cake was not big enough for it to be morally right to press for the larger slice they existed to obtain. The obverse of this triumph was 'voluntary absenteeism' among mineworkers, and the occurrence of unofficial strikes, which inevitably earned an excessive share of the newspaper headlines.

Yet, such was the primeval curse that all seemed lost by the summer of 1949, when a foreign exchange crisis put all in jeopardy, just when the British balance of payments position seemed better than it had been since before the war. In the first three months of 1948, the dollar deficit was £147 millions; twelve months later it was only £82 millions; but by the summer of 1949 it was up again to £157 millions. In September 1949, after momentarily divorcing morality from economics by denying that he was intending to do so, Cripps devalued the £, so that instead of being worth $4.03 dollars it was now fixed at only $2.80. This, though perhaps an excessive devaluation, was a more realistic figure; it put up the price of imports, but it cheapened and therefore encouraged British exports. It was, like the abandonment of the Gold Standard in 1931, regarded as a grave national humiliation and the prelude to uncontrolled inflation; and there was great Conservative outcry. The event was attended by no more consequences for evil than the devaluation of 1931, and should have been undertaken sooner than it was. There were immediate cuts in dollar imports, however, and this increased the general feeling that austerity was for ever.

Yet, by 1950, it would be true to say that the battle had been won, for in that year the balance of payments position was better than at any time since the 1920's. Unfortunately, there was no evidence, when the General Election took place on 23 February, that the country really was in fact at last within sight of solvency, so that Labour's majority in the new Parliament was reduced to a mere half-dozen. Worse still, the economy was once more plunged into crisis by the outbreak of the Korean War in June 1950. The world-wide shortage of materials pushed up the cost of all Britain's imports, and the Government's decision to embark upon a larger rearmament programme created anew the necessity for cuts and economies, and produced a damaging split in the Government.[1] The real gains so painfully achieved between 1945 and 1950 were thus almost entirely eclipsed in the public mind, and the Conservatives were returned to power in 1951.

[1] See p. 494.

48 · Nationalization

Between 1946 and 1949 the Labour Government put through a large programme of nationalization. The Bank of England was nationalized in 1946.
The coal industry was nationalized and placed under the control of a Coal
Board in 1947, and in the same year civil aviation was nationalized under
three Airways Corporations (reduced to two, British European Airways and
British Overseas Airways, in 1949). Public transport was nationalized in
1948, under a British Transport Commission, with six executive boards
administering Docks and Inland Waterways, Railways, London Transport,
Road Haulage and (some) Road Passenger Transport. By the Electricity
Act of 1947 the generation, supply and distribution of electricity came under
a British Electricity Authority under which were twelve area boards. The
gas industry was similarly placed under a nationalized Gas Council, with
twelve area gas boards, in 1948; and an act of 1949 established the short-
lived Iron and Steel Corporation of Great Britain, which (like road haulage)
was denationalized by the Conservatives in 1953.

These changes gave the Government considerable control over a large
area of the economy in the important spheres of power, transport and civil
aviation. The most important subsequent addition to Labour's list was the
establishment of the United Kingdom Atomic Energy Authority in 1954.
The passing of the relevant legislation was accompanied (with the exception
of iron and steel nationalization) by only formal political opposition from
the Conservatives, and criticism soon concentrated on matters of finance
and administration. But while nationalization facilitated the Labour
Government's control of the economy it failed to convince the public at
large that it was anything more meaningful than a new form of top-level
management. Coal nationalization was certainly a political necessity, and
without it labour relations in the industry would probably have been as bad
in the forties as they had been in the twenties; but transport nationalization
brought neither the dramatic and much overdue improvement in the wages
and working conditions that railwaymen deserved, nor a noticeable improvement in the service to the public. The nationalization of the Bank of
England and of civil aviation were matters of little popular interest. From

the point of view of the electorate as a whole, nationalization of electricity
and gas merely made the areas of administration larger than before; and
whatever eventual benefits were secured from a national plan of increased
electricity generation, they were masked, like the modernization of the coal
industry, by the over-all scarcity of resources, and by the spectacular
calamity of the 1947 fuel crisis.

The Government's decision that the nationalized industries should be
managed by public corporations was due to the persistent advocacy of
Herbert Morrison. Although the chairmen and members of the boards
were nominated by the appropriate departmental Minister, and were
ultimately accountable to him, the day-to-day operation of the nationalized
industries was left strictly in the hands of the board. This meant that
employees of the nationalized industries were not Civil Servants, and their
wages, salaries and conditions of employment were negotiated by their
appropriate trade union or professional organization in much the same way
as if the industries remained in private hands. It meant also that the public
corporations were 'for the most part, free from direct parliamentary
pressure and the indirect pressure of the constituents of M.P.s'.[1] It was
soon discovered that when an industry became nationalized it was more,
and not less, difficult to raise questions about it in the Commons. The
public corporation thus avoided the pitfalls which would have beset any
attempt to run the mines and the railways and the electricity industry, for
instance, on Civil Service lines, and prevented the gross overloading of
Parliamentary and Government time which would have resulted from
making departmental ministers responsible for their detailed operation.
Nevertheless, public corporations were soon regarded as effective devices
for running nationalized industries with the minimum consultation either
of workers or consumers. Even though consumer councils were established
for gas and electricity, for instance, their selection, their effectiveness and
even their existence were wrapped in what seemed deliberate obscurity.
Thanks, also, to Morrison's insistence that the Labour Party did not
believe in 'workers' control' of the nationalized industries, the idea that
the 'management' of these industries was an esoteric technique, from
which both employees and the public at large should be rigorously excluded,
was elevated by the Attlee Government to something very like a principle
of the constitution. Even when the public corporation did succeed in creating some sort of alliance between management and employees, it often had
the effect of creating the suspicion that they existed to provide employment
for those engaged in them rather than a service to the general public. The
expression 'public ownership', so frequently applied to the public corporations, is largely deceptive; and they soon seemed little more 'public' than
the public schools. It is because these corporations widened the gap
between the great industries they managed and the public they were

[1] Herbert Morrison, *Government and Parliament*, p. 253.

supposed to serve, and did not greatly narrow the gap between management and worker, that nationalization so rapidly became an electoral liability to the Labour Party.

The other source of electoral weakness in the nationalization programme was that both the mines and the railways were out of date and in need of more capital investment than was allotted to them. Lack of capital investment hampered the much-needed development of electric generating power, as did the chronic shortage of coal in the post-war period. This situation was aggravated by the Labour Government's readiness to cut back capital investment every time there was a financial crisis, a policy which was in many ways self-defeating. In consequence, the nationalized industries became a byword for failing to provide efficient service, above all during the fuel crisis, and for annually producing alarming financial deficits in spite of the theory that they were to operate on a strictly commercial basis. The Government made little or no attempt to remind the public that the financial losses and the poor service were an inescapable burden, created by past sins of omission (like the neglect of the mines) or of commission (like the over-capitalization of the railways), as well as by the years of war and the exigencies of post-war shortages. Regarding nationalization above all as a dogma, the Labour Government retained the habit of defending it as a dogma and, in the face of increasingly hostile Conservative propaganda, let the case for nationalization go by default.

It was not, however, until the Bill to nationalize the iron and steel industry was introduced that the Conservatives staged a full-scale attack; significantly, the basis of their opposition was that the industry was efficient, thus implying that the State should resort to nationalization only as a rescue operation for industries which, though of national importance, had become unprofitable and out of date, or were, like electricity, partly under State control already. Yet, nationalization of iron and steel would give the Government control of a great manufacturing industry on which the vital motor-car, shipbuilding and engineering industries depended; if the Government had really believed in State ownership of the means of production, nationalization of iron and steel was a matter of urgency. However, partly because of the complexity of the problem, and partly because of the Government's fear that it would arouse excessive controversy, preparation of the Bill did not begin until 1947, and it was not introduced until the end of October 1948. By that time, general disillusionment with nationalization had proceeded so far that the Bill aroused neither public support nor public interest. Nor was it possible, in 1948, to whip up enthusiasm by what were already coming to be regarded as anachronistic references to pre-war Jarrow, particularly as labour relations in the industry had for some time been satisfactory. Hence what, if mounted sooner, might have rallied support as a courageous attack on one of the citadels of economic power, appeared instead to be the rather tedious manœuvre of a

Government of doctrinaires. The Conservative opposition to the Bill in the Commons was continuous, lively and sarcastic.

Conservative vigour on the issue derived also from preparatory action taken by the Government in anticipation of Conservative rejection of the Bill in the Lords. In October 1947, a new Parliament Bill was introduced in the Commons to amend the Parliament Act of 1911, which had left the Lords with a two-year suspensive veto over all Bills except Money Bills. Under Labour's Parliament Bill, a Bill to which the Lords objected would become law in spite of them provided it was passed by the Commons in two sessions in the course of one year. The Conservatives, under the leadership of Lord Salisbury, had used their majority in the Lords with most astute moderation since 1945, but the Labour Party objected on principle to the fact that the 1911 Parliament Act could reduce the effective legislative life of a non-Conservative House of Commons to the first three years of its five-year term. The Government was also determined that the Iron and Steel Nationalization Bill should be on the statute book, and the formal take-over of the industry begun, before the end of the 1945 Parliament, which was due not later than June 1950.

The new Parliament Bill was introduced in the Commons in October 1947. It reduced the duration of the Lords' veto from two years to one as from the date of the Bill's introduction in the Commons. Thus, although the Lords naturally used their two-year veto power under the 1911 Act to delay the new Bill from October 1947 until December 1949, its provisions were deemed to apply to all Bills introduced after the first of these two dates, even though it did not receive the Royal Assent until the second.

While this protracted manœuvre was in progress, the Iron and Steel Bill was also introduced, receiving its second reading in the Commons in November 1948. To be covered by the Parliament Act of 1949 it would, therefore, have to pass through all its stages twice within twelve months; despite the use of the guillotine, however, the persistence of Conservative Opposition delayed its third reading until May 1949. Churchill declared, with characteristic choice of language, that it was 'an operation in restraint of trade' and that the Government were rushing this 'partisan, factious' proposal through because they feared that the General Election would 'end in obloquy and censure their dismal reign'.

Lord Salisbury carefully steered the Conservative peers from a head-on clash. It had been the declared policy of the Conservative majority in the Lords not to reject measures included in Labour's 1945 programme, on the grounds that the election result gave the Government a clear mandate to put them through. Salisbury was careful to avoid a frontal assault even on the Iron and Steel Bill, though he declared that it was a move in the direction of 'Communism'. It was realized that the worst thing the Conservatives could do would be to act in such a way as to revive the ancient cry of 'The Peers versus the People'; at this date the result might have been the abolition of the second chamber altogether. Under his leadership, therefore, the Conservatives amended the Bill to postpone its coming into operation until after the latest legal date for the next General Election. Thus, while not actually opposing the Bill, the Conservatives were insisting that the electorate be given another chance of expressing their opinion. The Government used its majority to secure the rejection of the amendments in the Commons on 26 July 1949; but the Conservatives used their majority in the Lords to pass a resolution two days later reaffirming their amendments.

If the Government had persisted in the original terms of the Bill, it would still, even under the new Parliament Act, not have become law until early 1950. This would make the original starting date for the take-over of the industry, May 1950, impossible. The Government therefore altered the vesting date to January 1951, and the date of appointing the Board which would run the industry to October 1950. The effect of this was to concede the victory to the Conservatives. Their use of the Lords to prevent the nationalization of the industry during the lifetime of the 1945 Government had been successful. The Lords accepted the Bill as thus amended by the Government, and it received the Royal Assent on 24 November 1949.

49 · Social Insurance and the National Health Service

The social insurance legislation of the first Attlee Government followed naturally from the work of the Churchill wartime Government, and since Labour implemented a scheme which had been approved by a predominantly Conservative Government on the basis of a Report drawn up by a convinced Liberal, the National Insurance Act of 1946 must be regarded as a harvest towards which all three major parties had contributed.

Publication of the Beveridge Report in 1942 had been followed by a draft Bill published by the Churchill Government as a White Paper in 1944, and by the establishment of a Ministry of National Insurance in the same year. In June 1945, Churchill's Caretaker Government took the first step towards implementing the Beveridge recommendations by passing the

Family Allowances Act, which was to come into operation as soon as possible after the war. Dalton provided the funds in his first post-war Budget, and the first allowances were drawn in August 1946.

The granting of Family Allowances was a somewhat mystifying piece of social policy, being based on emotional and sociological attitudes that were rapidly becoming outdated. Their introduction carried the implication that wages were generally insufficient to enable a working-class family to support more than one child; yet the amount of the allowance per child (5s.) was so small, even at 1945 values, that it was financially worth while only for very large families; and there was no stopping to inquire whether it was right social policy to encourage large families among the poorest sections of the community. The scheme sprang partly from the demographic forecasts of the thirties, which had predicted a continuous decline of the birthrate; and from sociological evidence of the same period that working-class mothers had often been able to feed their children only by half-starving themselves. This gave added point to the successful campaign of the feminist M.P., Eleanor Rathbone, to make Family Allowances the legal entitlement of the mother and not the father; it was a provision that also accorded with the middle-class view that working-class fathers were thriftless characters too much given to beer and tobacco. The final eccentricity of the scheme was that the allowances were treated as taxable income, so that for income tax payers the scheme represented a great deal of administration for the disbursement of a large number of very small sums of money.

The next step was the passage through the Commons of the National Insurance (Industrial Injuries) Bill. The Labour Government's Bill was not substantially different from the original Bill, framed by the Coalition Government, and introduced in the first place by the Caretaker Government just before the 1945 Election.

Like the old Workmen's Compensation Acts, the new Act, which became law in 1946, provided for compensation for injury or disability resulting from 'accidents arising out of or in the course of employment', with additional supplements in respect of dependants. It was, however, following the Beveridge principle, compulsory and universal for all persons employed under any contract of service or apprenticeship, and without income limit. The central fund from which payments would be drawn would be financed by equal contributions[1] from employer, employee and the State. The scheme thus made compensation for industrial injury a social service administered by the Ministry of National Insurance; under the Workmen's Compensation Acts employers had themselves been responsible for the payment of compensation. This had usually led to a worker's claim becoming a disputable issue at law, with the result that there had often been a temptation for the claimant to accept a lump sum offered by his employer

[1] In 1946, the rate of contribution was 4d.

rather than risk the uncertainties of litigation. The Compensation Acts had the further disadvantage that, while making the employer legally liable to pay compensation, they had placed upon the employee the onus of proving that his injury or disability arose out of his employment. Under the new Act, accidents arising 'in the course of' employment would be deemed to have arisen 'out of' the employment. Even after this beneficent change the precise definition of the phrase 'arising out of and in the course of employment' was still a source of difficulty. Disputes on this, and on all other points, would in future be dealt with by the officials of the Ministry of National Insurance, from whom there was a right of appeal to a tribunal composed of a workers' and an employers' representative and a lawyer chairman. A final appeal could be made to a Government-appointed Commissioner. This arrangement, by which the executive was given judicial as well as administrative functions (a common feature of legislation in this country since 1919), was criticized by members of both parties, one Labour member declaring that a system under which a workman would have to go to a State doctor after an accident in the service of a State employer, and then to a State official to decide whether he was entitled to compensation, was 'not a Socialist dream but a Marxist nightmare'.

The main National Insurance Bill was made law in 1946. The entire adult population was compulsorily insured for sickness benefit, unemployment benefit, retirement pensions, widows' pensions (with allowances for orphans), maternity grants and allowances, and death grants. The population was divided into three categories: the employed, the self-employed and the non-employed. All were required to pay a weekly contribution (which, in the case of employed persons, included the industrial injury element), by means of a stamp on a single insurance card; this in itself was a great simplification of the previous system which, owing to the piecemeal development of health, unemployment and pensions insurances since 1912, had necessitated different insurance stamps for different types of insurance. The contribution paid by all three categories included an element which was allocated to the National Health Service. Following the method first adopted by the 1911 Act, the contributions of employed persons to the Insurance Fund were supplemented by contributions from employers and by contributions from the Exchequer.

The only aspect of the Bill which was considered really controversial at the time was the decision not to allow the friendly societies to continue to administer the payment of sickness benefit under the new scheme as they had done under the old scheme since the National Health Insurance Act of 1911.[1] One hundred and ninety-nine Labour M.P.s threatened to vote against the Bill if the Government insisted on excluding the friendly societies and on issuing sick pay from local offices of the Ministry of

[1] See p. 37.

National Insurance. It was claimed that 8,000,000 insured persons were receiving sickness benefit through friendly societies and that if the societies lost this work it would be their death-blow; it would also rob the insured person of the individual human touch which such societies could offer. James Griffiths, the Minister in charge of the Bill, managed to talk the objectors into acquiescence chiefly by pointing out that the majority of the 8,000,000 belonged to the large, centralized friendly societies which were as impersonal in their operations as any Government department. Accordingly, the friendly societies ceased to participate in National Insurance, although Beveridge himself had wanted them to do so. The exclusion of the commercial insurance companies had been intended from the outset; this had led, in 1942, to a demand that insurance agents be paid compensation for loss of business.

There were, doubtless, by 1946, overwhelming administrative arguments for the concentration of social security payments in the bureaucracy. Yet, together with the proliferation of corporations and boards which characterized nationalization and the creation of the National Health Service, it was a further move away from a democratically organized society towards a collectivized one. Working-class friendly societies had been of incalculable value in the education of the working class in the realms of insurance, social welfare and finance during the nineteenth century; and they had stood in much the same relation to State social insurance as the churches had stood in relation to State education. They pioneered these services long before the State took a hand in them; but when the State did intervene it steamrollered both of them aside on the grounds that they were incapable of providing an efficient and comprehensive service. Yet it is permissible to wonder whether it would not have been more democratic if social insurance had been constructed on the basis of universalizing the self-insurance they had pioneered, rather than on the basis of tripartite contributions by employee, employer and State to a fund administered exclusively by State officials. The pretence that people were 'insuring' themselves under the National Insurance scheme obscured the reality that benefits were paid for by a poll tax on the individual worker, by a payroll-tax on employers, and by a subvention from the proceeds of general taxation. The system suffered also from the depressing assumptions that underlay family allowances: namely, that the earnings of the working class were destined always to be insufficient to enable them to raise a family or save enough to insure themselves against sickness, unemployment and old age. State insurance was a device for financing the sick, the unemployed and the old by means of a regressive tax on both employer and employed, in the confident expectation that the bulk of the working class, unlike the bulk of the middle class, would never get adequate earnings and never be able to insure themselves by their own efforts. Thus, social insurance, though not a characterically Socialist device, derived from the Socialist belief that the working class would always be exploited, and from the Victorian belief that they could never learn to help themselves.

At the time, these doubts could not be raised; and only one M.P., the Conservative, Sir Waldron Smithers, celebrated as a life-long defender of last ditches, actually voted against the Bill on Third Reading. He said it was 'Socialist mass bribery'. Other doubts were expressed by some Conservatives. In view of the foreseeable increase in the proportion of elderly people, it was suggested that the old would get a better deal out of the Act than the young who would have to support them; while the prospective increase in the Exchequer's contribution to the fund over the next thirty years would have to come out of increased production, the proportion of persons productively engaged would fall. As things turned out, the expectation that the old would do best out of the scheme proved false, chiefly owing to inflation.

The completion of the system of State financial provision for those 'distressed in mind, body or estate' came with the National Assistance Act of 1948. This destroyed the last remnants of the Poor Law and created a National Assistance Board, analagous to the old Unemployment Assistance Board, but with wider powers and more comprehensive duties. The financial aid it provided to those who were outside the National Insurance scheme, or whose requirements could not adequately be met by it could, like welfare payments under National Insurance, be claimed as a right. National Assistance was to be a comprehensive service of financial assistance provided by the State for people in need. The Act also legislated the workhouse out of existence. In future, workhouses were to be replaced by residential homes provided by new local authority welfare committees; and though, in practice, this meant for some time that existing workhouse buildings were used, the word itself disappeared from the public vocabulary as a result of this Act as quickly as the expression 'the dole' disappeared as a result of the National Insurance Act.

The intention, in 1945, was that National Assistance should be a rarely-used last defence against destitution since, theoretically, the National Insurance Act covered the whole population, and benefits under it were adequate. In practice, many elderly people had to resort to National Assistance. Persons insured for the first time in 1948 were not entitled to full pension benefits for ten years, and there were still many old people whose only legal claim on the State was the non-contributory pension provided by the 1908 Act (which had been raised to 10s. in 1919 but remained subject to an upper income limit of £89 5s. a year). In addition, the continuous inflation of the post-war period rendered the insurance benefits less adequate than intended; temporary unemployment might now afflict types of employee whose working income was sufficiently high to make insurance benefit inadequate, particularly in an age of hire purchase and mortgages.

In consequence, the Assistance Board played a larger role in the treatment of the poor, and a very much larger role in providing aid for the old, than was anticipated. About 68 per cent of the $1\frac{1}{2}$ million recipients of National Assistance in the late 1950's were old people. Since its payments were uncovenanted disbursements of public funds it necessarily imposed a means test; and this helped, particularly among the old, to recreate something which, for all the efforts of sympathetic officials, looked more like the old pre-war system than was generally admitted by the politicians. With their long memories, the old were often unwilling to avail themselves of their rights under the N.A.B., associating it with the humiliating Poor Law of their younger days. Yet, even though it inquired into means, the N.A.B. did not, like the U.A.B., impose a household means test, nor did it, like the Poor Law, take account of the means of the applicant's relatives, even those not living in the same household. The N.A.B., in making its decisions ignores the resources of all the other members of an applicant's family, save that it assumes the liability of husband and wife for each other, and of parents for children under 16.

The most impressive part of the social security programme was the National Health Service, set up under the Act of 1946. The purpose was to provide, virtually without charge to the individual, hospital and specialist services, as well as general practitioner, ophthalmic and dental services for all. Included in the scheme also, were midwifery, maternity and child welfare services, together with the provision of drugs, medicines, spectacles and dentures. The cost would be borne chiefly by the Exchequer out of general taxation; though, as noted above, part of the contributions under the National Insurance Act were allocated to the Health Service. The Act also envisaged the establishment of local Health Centres from which general practitioner and dental services were expected principally to operate, and which would also house clinics operated by the local authorities and the hospitals; but this part of the Act was stillborn. It was decided, because of the general shortage of materials, that it was impossible to build the Centres.

The Act was thus a major act of nationalization. Like the development of State education, where voluntary Church schools gradually gave way to State-maintained schools, it turned voluntary hospitals into State-maintained ones. Just as nationalization had taken a number of gas and electricity undertakings out of the control of local authorities, so the Health Service ended local authority control of a number of hospitals. And just as nationalization took the running of mines out of private hands, so the Health Act took the doctors' and dentists' surgeries out of the realm of private enterprise into that of public service.

The moulding of all the manifold activities involved in the care of the sick into an entirely novel organizational framework raised problems whose rapid solution was not facilitated by the combative nature of Aneurin Bevan who, as Minister of Health, was in charge of the Bill and of the negotiations with the medical profession. All other acts of nationalization were logical developments from pre-existing traditions of State control or of large scale integrations. No other Minister had had to interfere with the entrenched privileges and prejudices of a highly qualified body of middle-class professional people who, by the nature of their functions, were accustomed to ordering everybody about (politicians included) and who had always been at pains to surround themselves with an impenetrable cloud of awe and mystery. It was fortunate for Bevan that this absolute freedom of the medical profession had already been somewhat eroded by the existence of salaried medical officers of health employed by the local authorities, by the wartime Emergency Hospital Service and by the fact that, during the war, thousands of younger doctors had not found it impossible to carry out their professional duties when serving as salaried (and even uniformed) servants of the State under military discipline. The bulk of the opposition to Bevan came from the general practitioners within the British Medical Association, who, until a very late stage in the negotiations, were threatening to boycott the whole scheme on the ground that their proposed method of payment included the provision of a basic salary. They said that this would make them Civil Servants, which, they implied, would be lowering to their dignity, and make them playthings of politicians and helpless victims of red tape. They also claimed that it would interfere with what was pompously called 'the doctor-patient relationship' whereas every normal person had known for years that what really interfered with the doctor-patient relationship was poverty. The attitude of the B.M.A. to the introduction of the Health Service is a salutary reminder that, when they considered their sectional interests were being threatened, doctors could be just as obstructive as dockers and miners. It was noticeable, however, that the highly qualified specialists raised little objection to a properly financed hospital service, since they would in future get paid for their hospital work. Previously they had done it in an honorary capacity in order to increase their standing as private consultants.

Under the scheme as finally drawn up, the Minister assumed responsibility for the hospital and specialist services; but their administration would be in the hands of regional hospital boards appointed by the Minister in consultation with university medical schools, the medical profession and the local health authorities, and they were promised a high degree of independence. Each board would appoint hospital management committees to manage each hospital or group of hospitals; and the regional boards, following the pattern of the nationalized industries, would be the employers of all persons engaged in the hospital service. As one of his concessions to the profession, Bevan excluded a number of 'teaching' hospitals from this organizational scheme, by allowing them their own separate governors.

Similarly, the medical and dental schools were to be under their own governing bodies or under the universities of which they formed a part. In order to prevent the spread of private nursing-homes, Bevan also agreed to proposals from the specialists that single bedrooms or small wards in hospitals could be made available for those prepared to pay extra for the privilege of privacy; and no bar was put on the provision, where possible, of rooms or blocks where patients paying their own fees could be treated privately.

Management of practitioner and dental services would be in the hands of local medical executive councils, 50 per cent of whom would be nominees of the Ministry and the local authorities, the other 50 per cent being chosen by the local practitioners. The executive council would publish a list of doctors and dentists within the scheme, and the patient was free to make his own choice from the list; in the same way, the executive council would publish lists of the pharmacists from whom drugs prescribed by the doctors could be obtained without charge.

After lengthy and bad-tempered negotiations, which lasted from the passage of the Act in 1946 until within a month of the scheme's coming into operation on 5 July 1948, the doctors secured that as a general rule the whole of their remuneration should come out of a capitation fee in respect of each patient on their panels; those doctors who wanted a basic salary could have it if they could demonstrate to their executive council that they would otherwise suffer hardship.

The final problem was the abolition of the system by which a doctor's practice had been regarded as a piece of private property to be bought and sold. Doctors joining the scheme would be compensated (normally on death or retirement) for the loss of the right to sell their practices and, for the future, a compulsory superannuation scheme would be introduced.

The National Health Service was a major reform which deserved to have been introduced without the noisy obstructiveness of the B.M.A. and Bevan's celebrated remark, made the day before the scheme was launched, that he regarded the Tories as 'lower than vermin'. The National Insurance scheme was open to the criticism that it was financed by a regressive tax which took no account of ability to pay and provided cash benefits which related only to the barest necessities of life and which, in this particular respect, gave the working class too little and the middle class virtually nothing. The National Health Service was open to no such objection; nor could it be objected that a comprehensive State system of providing skilled care for the sick and the suffering offended any moral principle. This did not, of course, prevent the objection in fact being made; but rarely on the English side of the Atlantic. The ending of the gross social anomaly that the great hospitals of the land should depend for finance on rag days and flag days was indisputably an improvement; no longer was the community's inhumanity to be advertised publicly in the streets by the announcement,

'This Hospital is maintained solely by Voluntary Contributions', or revealed even more embarrassingly by the private interview with the almoner on which depended just how much a hospital patient would contribute to the cost of treatment. True, the attitudes inculcated by the strong traditions of the past were harder to eliminate than the old system of management; but gradually it penetrated into the tradition-bound minds of the medical and nursing professions that the care of the sick was a public duty rather than an act of charity by the skilled or the powerful towards the weak and the poor, or a relationship in which the rights were all on one side. Later economic policies inhibited hospital modernization, so that nearly twenty years later most of them were still hideous and under-equipped. Hospital administration suffered, like all forms of public administration, central and local, from the inability to recruit staff of good quality owing to the general high level of employment, and to the low rates of pay obtaining in all branches of public service. With the passage of time, too, Government neglect of the hospital services led to the encouragement, through middle-class insurance schemes, of private hospital and nursing-home treatment, with the consequent danger of importing back into the hospital system the division into a first-class service for the affluent and a second-class service for the bulk of the population which was allowed to continue unchecked in the field of education. Yet, in spite of these developments, the abolition of the doctor's bill, the specialist's fee and the hospital bill which resulted from the National Health Service Act constituted a social advance from which almost every class of society could derive benefit.

Immediate criticism of the scheme, after it began, was over its cost. Within twelve months of the scheme coming into operation, 5,250,000 pairs of spectacles were issued; it became almost as difficult to make an appointment with a dentist as it was to buy a motor-car, and no less than 187 million prescriptions for drugs and medicines were written out. The annual cost of the Health Service soon soared past £500 millions a year and it became one of the largest of the country's industries and the largest single item in the Budget after the defence forces. It was for this reason that charges were introduced by the Labour Government for spectacles and for dental treatment and, later, by the Conservatives, for prescriptions. The fiscal practice of taxing people who suffered from ophthalmic or dental defects, or were in need of medicines and drugs, was morally indefensible.

50 · Education, Housing and Town Planning

In 1939, the broad basis of the State educational system was still that provided by the Education Acts of 1870 and 1902, though, in detail, the situation was one of considerable diversity and confusion. Many State-educated children were still attending elementary schools catering for all ages from 5 to 14. A minority went, as scholarship holders or as fee payers, to the secondary schools, which, after the Fisher Act of 1918, rapidly developed Sixth Form work and sent some of their ablest pupils to the Universities. Reorganization of elementary schools to permit the separate education of children over 11 in a technical or modern (sometimes 'senior' or 'central') school had been proceeding slowly ever since the Hadow Report of 1926, which had been initiated by Sir Charles Trevelyan, President of the Board of Education in the first Labour Government. But, by the outbreak of war, 46·5 per cent of all children receiving elementary education were still in all-age schools. As for the school-leaving age, this had still remained at 14, though 15 had been recommended in the Hadow Report.

The standardizing of the practice of making a clear break at the age of 11 throughout the State system was the main feature of educational development during Labour's period of office; but the necessary legislative action had already been taken by the Churchill Government in 1944 and had been preceded by the publication, in 1943, of a Report drawn up by a committee headed by Sir Cyril Norwood.

The 1944 Education Act, known as the Butler Act because it was piloted through all its stages by R. A. Butler, then President of the Board of Education, was the most complex Act of its kind. It provided for the raising of the school-leaving age to 15 on 1 April 1945, or not later than two years thereafter. The school system would be reorganized in three main stages: nursery schools, at which attendance would be voluntary, for children under 5; primary schools for the 5 to 11 year age-group; and secondary schools for all children over 11. Provision of school meals and school milk became compulsory. Fees in secondary schools (i.e. in what were henceforth to be called secondary grammar schools) would be abolished. As an earnest of its serious intentions about secondary education, the Act defined the purpose of compulsory school attendance as that of ensuring that all children received 'efficient full-time education suitable to their age, ability and aptitude'. Previous acts had compelled attendance only for 'efficient elementary instruction in reading, writing and arithmetic'. Local government responsibility for the carrying out of the Act would be concentrated in future almost exclusively in the hands of the county and county borough councils. The President of the Board of Education would become a Minister of Education, not merely because he had never had a Board of Education to preside over, but chiefly to raise the status both of the post and the department it controlled.

The most difficult administrative problem was the position of those schools, most of them elementary Church schools, which received financial assistance from the State and were therefore subject to varying degrees of control by the local authorities. These schools, previously called 'non-provided', were now given the choice of becoming either 'aided' or 'controlled'. A school would be 'aided' if it could meet half the cost of modernizing its premises in accordance with the standards required to implement the new Act. It would then appoint its own staff and retain control of religious instruction. If it could not afford the cost of modernizing its buildings it would then become 'controlled'. The local education authority would finance it entirely, and its only major surviving freedom would be that a limited number of teachers of the relevant religious denomination could be appointed to its staff.

The religious issue was also dealt with by imposing on maintained schools the duty of teaching non-denominational religion. Each county authority, after consultation with all religious groups (except the Roman Catholics) was to draw up an Agreed Syllabus of Religious Instruction for use in the schools in its area. Thus Religious Instruction became the only subject of study which, by statute, could not be left out of the school curriculum. Further to win over the churches, the Act made the daily 'corporate act of worship', which had previously been normal but not mandatory, a statutory duty. It was, therefore, with some truth that Dr Temple, the Archbishop of Canterbury, declared, during the Bill's second reading in the Lords on 6 June 1944, that it 'wrote religion into national education in a way never done before'.

In practice, the never-ending rise in building costs made the chances of Church schools retaining their aided status, and therefore their denominational character, more difficult than was imagined at the time. This was a particular anxiety to the Roman Catholic community, whose religious susceptibilities could not be met by the device of an Agreed Syllabus, and which was unique in the country in having substantially increased the number of its schools during the previous forty years.

One other feature of the system as it developed was the creation of a specially privileged educational parallel to the self-governing teaching hospitals in the Health Service. One hundred and sixty-five old-established secondary grammar schools which had previously been either aided or independent were allowed the privilege of receiving their grants direct from the central Government and not from their local authority, and were allowed to charge fees for 50 per cent of their places.

The test of the new system would be less its administrative tidying up than the fulfilment of the claim, made by all three parties at the time, that it would provide secondary education for all; and on this particular point there was much incoherence. The Norwood Report, finding a tripartite system already developing in the State system, went on to deduce that what was characteristic of educational organization was characteristic also of human personality:

The evolution of education has in fact thrown up certain groups, each of which can and must be treated in a way appropriate to itself. Whether such groupings are distinct on strictly psychological grounds, whether they represent types of mind, whether the differences are differences in kind or in degree, these are questions which it is not necessary to pursue. Our point is that rough groupings, whatever may be their ground, have in fact established themselves in general educational experience, and the recognition of such groupings in educational practice has been justified both during the period of education and in the after-careers of the pupils.[1]

The tripartite division of secondary education into grammar, technical and modern schools or courses, was thus based on assertions about the developing child which the authors of the Norwood Report did not think it 'necessary to pursue'; and the claim that the existence of these different 'groupings' had been established by the 'evolution of education' was without foundation. Treatment of children over 11 years of age before 1943 had been so haphazard that it could prove nothing. The Report nevertheless confidently divided the nation's children into three distinct groups. Some children loved learning for its own sake: these would go to a secondary grammar school and would thereafter enter the learned professions or take up higher administrative or business posts. The second type of child had evolved in the technical school:

He often has an uncanny insight into the intricacies of mechanism whereas the subtleties of language construction are too delicate for him. To justify itself to his mind, knowledge must be capable of immediate application, and the knowledge and its application which most appeal to him are concerned with the control of material things.

The authors of the Report evidently thought it 'uncanny' that a child should understand 'mechanism', and apparently associated this peculiarity with a lack of 'delicacy'. Naturally, such persons would enter 'certain crafts – engineering, agriculture and the like'.[2]

[1] H.M.S.O. 1943, 'Curriculum and Examinations in Secondary Schools', p. 2.
[2] Op. cit, p. 3.

The third group would consist of the majority of children. These could deal with 'concrete things' (apparently the Committee could clearly distinguish in its mind between a 'modern' child who could 'deal with concrete things' and a 'technical' child who desired to 'control material things'). These children were interested 'only in the moment'; their ability was 'in the realm of facts'; they were interested in 'things as they are' and they were 'essentially practical'. Their mental make-up showed no pronounced leanings at an early stage. They should be taught in a way that was 'practical' and 'concrete':

> The aim would be to offer a general grounding and to awaken interest in many aspects of life and citizenship before the pupil passed on to the specialized occupations which modern conditions demand with increasing insistence, and not to provide any special training for particular occupations.[1]

It was hard to avoid the conclusion that the Norwood Report was trying to say that the secondary modern child, being good at nothing in particular, should be taught nothing in particular.

When considering how the segregation of children into these three groups could be arranged, the Report did not, however, advocate a rigidly tripartite division. It thought secondary technical schools might have to be separate from the others, but grammar and modern courses might be run in the same school; and it gave a hesitant nod of approval in the direction of 'multilateral' schools containing all three sorts, subject to reservations about the undue size of such schools. It gave no clear directive about methods of selection at 11-plus, insisted that such a selection should be provisional, and thought all types of school should pursue a more or less common curriculum during the first two years, so that it would be easy to switch children from one type of school or course to another. It was doubtless because of the flimsy basis of the Report's tripartite theories, and of its refusal to show clearly how to organize it in practice, that the Butler Act itself said nothing about tripartism and contented itself with the formula about 'age, ability and aptitude'.

Faced with the requirement that they must give secondary education for all, but with little guidance save the ambiguities of the Norwood Report, the local education authorities soon realized that tripartism was impossible, since there were very few secondary technical schools. Accordingly, they had to organize the education of children over 11 in much the same way as they had done before the Act; in the future, as in the past, some would go to grammar schools and some would not, the difference being that the latter group would now also be described as receiving secondary education, and would eventually get buildings with the same physical facilities as those previously enjoyed by grammar schools (laboratories, assembly halls, gymnasia, etc.). In addition they would, from April 1947, stay at school until they were 15 instead of 14. In some counties, the word 'secondary

[2] Op. cit., p. 21.

modern' would be used; in others it would not; but whatever the local title, the Norwood label was the one which stuck in the popular mind.

Since, in many areas, it would be some time before all-age schools were reorganized, and in others the buildings used for non-grammar school education would for some time be below the standard which would give them what the Norwood Report had called 'parity of esteem' with the grammar schools, the selection of children at 11-plus for grammar or non-grammar school education became a matter of immense importance; and, once made, the selection was likely to be irreversible save in most exceptional circumstances. Moreover, the Act also compelled new methods of selection for the grammar school by abolishing both the pre-1944 fee payer and the pre-1944 junior county scholarship, which had let the clever elementary school child into the grammar school for nothing. Most counties therefore devised a selection examination based on English, Arithmetic and an Intelligence Test. Its results were supposed to prove that some children were suited for a grammar school and that others were suited for a secondary modern school. In fact, the 11-plus was something quite different; in each county it was a competitive examination to fill the number of grammar school places the county happened to have available. In some counties this might be as few as 15 per cent of the total secondary school places, in others as many as 45 per cent.

The selection problem would have been less acute had the secondary modern schools been able to convince parents that no child suffered by attending them. From the outset, however, they suffered from the crippling disadvantage that the grammar schools alone were geared, by tradition, organization and staff, to the task of preparing their pupils for public examinations; therefore, only by going to a grammar school could a child be sure of obtaining access either to a university or to one of the professions. This made secondary modern schools inferior to the grammar schools in that they offered their children fewer opportunities; and, despite strenuous denials by education officials and other interested parties, it became the general opinion that a secondary modern school was where a child went when he or she failed the 11-plus. Thus, the hierarchical system which the Norwood Report and Butler Act were supposed to have abolished, was perpetuated.

The secondary modern schools were not only branded as schools for the failures and the less able; worse still, they lacked, and never found, the clear (if cramping) sense of purpose that the grammar schools derived from the knowledge that most of their pupils would pass public examinations and enter upon professional or semi-professional careers. These were grave burdens to impose on those who taught in the modern schools, and whether or not a secondary modern school developed into a vital and self-confident institution depended very much on the policy of the local authority responsible for it, on the zeal and imaginative understanding of the head master and staff, and on the character and age of its buildings. The essential defect of the Butler Act in practice was that it condemned a majority of the population of State schools to the status of second-class children by the time they were 11, and did so by methods which, though alleged to be scientific, were in fact haphazard.

As time went by, local authorities sought to devise ways and means of making the 11-plus less final in its verdict and of ensuring that those who did not go to a grammar school at 11-plus were not permanently disadvantaged thereby. From the beginning there were moves in London and elsewhere to solve the problem by means of comprehensive secondary schools; but less than sixty of these schools existed fifteen years after 1945, and their creation was attended by violent controversy. It was said that they would destroy grammar school education; but by providing yet another type of school offering wider opportunities than the secondary modern schools, the comprehensive idea was damaging to them also.

Anger over the 11-plus contributed much to the disenchantment of the lower middle class with the social revolution of the late forties. Parents resented the exclusion of their children from grammar school education by an examination whose justice was doubtful but against whose life sentence there seemed no appeal; and, although escape routes and alternative ladders to higher education were being devised all the time, they were not very accessible between 1945 and 1951. The Labour Government was insensitive to this grievance; the parents concerned were written off as 'snobs' who wanted their children to go to grammar schools only in order to prevent them mixing with 'ordinary' children. In consequence, the prospect that Labour would try to eliminate the 11-plus by setting up comprehensive schools gave rise to fears that, having succeeded in keeping some lower middle-class children out of grammar schools by the 11-plus, Labour's ultimate intention was to abolish grammar schools altogether.

The over-all result of the Butler Act was that State education became, even more than before 1944, a system to which people entrusted their children only if they could not afford to send them to independent schools. Independent schools, whether good or bad, large or small, famous or dubious, day or boarding, were all extremely expensive, if only because, under the Butler Act, they were now subject to Ministry inspection; but, even at their worst, they did at least go through the motions of trying to prepare their pupils for positions of responsibility and opportunity in life. Independent schools of all sorts, and public schools in particular, were given a new lease of life by the 11-plus, and their flourishing condition by the mid-fifties belied both Labour's claim to have achieved a social revolution and the claim of the middle class that high taxation and the welfare state had ruined them.

Labour's failure to understand the weakness of its education policy was due to ignorance. Almost all members of the Cabinet were either products of public schools (Attlee went to Haileybury, Cripps to Winchester, Dalton to Eton) or of the board schools of the 1880's and 1890's. They were thus either unacquainted with State education, or unaware of the great strides which had in fact been made since 1902. It became a commonplace of Government propaganda that the new schools of the 1940's were vastly superior to the grim regimented elementary schools of the beginning of the century, but the proper comparison should have been with the schools of the 1930's. The schools of the 1940's and 1950's were much less purposeful than the schools of the 1930's, whose pupils were often less miserable and less discontented with their schools than post-war propagandists made out. Every effort was made to divert attention from the deficiencies of the educational system under Labour by pointing to the improved physical well-being of working-class children; in the words of George Tomlinson, Minister of Education from 1947, 'our children are bigger and bonnier than ever'. This was true and it was admirable; but the excessive emphasis on these consequences of full employment, better living standards and (perhaps) school meals and milk, sometimes gave the impression that the Labour Party regarded the State education system as a kind of elaborate freedom from hunger campaign.[1]

Another cause of Labour's failure was that men such as Bevin and Morrison and Shinwell, having had little formal education, tended to dislike it. Indeed, the Labour Party as a whole may be said to have nourished a secret fear of academic education. It seemed to them to be associated with the middle and upper classes in the way that the Church had been associated with the Bourbons or the Romanovs, and tainted by the association. For their part, the Conservatives did not like State education either; it was a service they did not use, but had to pay for, and it tended to be the means of introducing into the universities young persons with an embarrassing tendency to take examinations seriously. With such ill-equipped political leadership, chiefly by individuals in whose eyes the system was for other people's children but not their own, it may be asserted that the State system of education progressed as much as it did in the 1950's in spite of the political parties, and not because of them.

Re-housing and the re-planning of cities had a high priority in the minds of all who visualized a great programme of post-war reconstruction. Among most thoughtful people it now seemed impossible to permit the survival of so much deplorable nineteenth-century working-class housing all over the country, or to allow the continuance of the suburban sprawl which had been created, in particular, between the wars. It was at last becoming recognized that the cities and towns of Britain were hideous but that it was now essential to abandon, because it was literally uncivilized, the purely

---

[1] See also G. D. H. Cole, *The Post War Condition of Britain*, p. 336, where this preoccupation with food as an element in state education is clearly visible.

nineteenth-century fiction that the only place where an Englishman could live graciously was 'in the country'. Sidney Smith's proper witticism that the country was 'a kind of healthy grave' had long been regarded as absurd, owing to generations of indoctrination by schoolmasters and litterateurs suffering from an overdose of the Lake Poets, and from a snobbish infatuation with the cult of the English 'country house'. But during the war there grew up a strong desire to make English cities places to live in rather than to flee from.

Unhappily, economic conditions made it more difficult to build new houses after the war than before, and more difficult still to replan the cities; and, under pressure of manifest hardship, the building of houses for the working class had priority over town planning. The housing programme suffered from the high cost and scarcity of materials and from an initial shortage of labour; and even when the labour force was raised to the pre-war level, as it was by 1948, output per man hour was one-third less than before the war. This reflected the lower standards of efficiency associated with full employment, the primitive organization of the building industry, and the Government's restriction of private-enterprise house building.

In consequence, re-housing proceeded at a pace much below the national requirement. The average number of new houses built per annum during the housing boom of 1934–9 was 358,000. In 1946 only 51,000 were built; in 1947 the figure rose to 127,500, and in 1948 to over 206,000; but in the next three years the figure settled back again to approximately 170,000 a year. Out of these totals, only just over 20,000 a year were built by private builders for sale; all the rest were council houses. The result was that the working class was frustrated by the inevitably long queue of candidates for council houses and by the difficulty, for all but married couples with children, of getting on the queue at all; while the lower middle class faced a steep increase in the purchase price of private-enterprise houses. The result was the enslavement of the entire younger generation of skilled and professional classes to the twenty to twenty-five year mortgage. A chronic shortage of housing, with the consequent inflation of its costs, was therefore to remain a major social problem for years to come, imposing real hardship on the most productive and enterprising sections of the community, young people in their mid-twenties. It also kept open old class-war wounds, by creating a contrast between the mortgage-bound, rate-paying middle class and the subsidized council house tenant, who was rarely required to pay an economic rent, or a rent proportionate to his capacity to pay. The whole problem was aggravated by the tendency to early marriage, and the consequent increase in the number of separate families requiring to be housed.

Town and Country Planning had been an ideal to which statutory lip-service had been paid ever since the first Act with this title had been passed in 1909. The Act of 1947 theoretically applied to the whole of Great Britain.

Every county authority was required to draw up a development plan for the use of all the land within its area for the next twenty years. The result was a plethora of county development plans which, in practice, provided employment for the town and country planners, but relatively little town and country planning. From the point of view of the general public, the effect was to increase the power of local authorities to stop them using, buying or selling land in the way they wanted to, in case such actions conflicted with development plans which, though not being carried out, might be carried out one day, when the finance was available and all the objections of the various vested interests had been successfully overcome. Local authority control of the use of land in such a way as to conform with its development plans was also difficult because of the inflated cost of building land; and no satisfactory way of dealing justly both with the owners of such land and with the community at large was evolved.

The New Town Acts of 1946 was, therefore, by far the most imaginative and revolutionary contribution which the Government made to the improvement of urban living. The Ministry was given power to designate an area as the site of a new town, and to establish a corporation to develop it and administer the town as it grew, until, in due course, it could hand over to a new or existing local authority. Fourteen New Towns were established under the Labour Government. The original intention behind eight of them was that they should be near enough to London to be alternative centres for industry and residential purposes, but sufficiently far away not to become commuter towns; it was a first principle of their conception that they should not be suburban dormitories. The first of these New Towns was Stevenage, whose Corporation was set up at the end of 1946; Crawley, Hemel Hempstead and Harlow New Towns were projected in 1947, Hatfield and Welwyn in 1948, Basildon and Bracknell in 1949. In other parts of the country, Cwmbran and Newton Aycliffe were created by the expansion of trading estates established in the 1930's, and Corby was associated with the steel works of Stewart Lloyd, also begun in the 1930's. The remaining New Towns created by 1950 were East Kilbride, Peterlee and Glenrothes. None of the New Towns had, by 1950, advanced far towards the total population originally planned for each, and there was an inevitable, but somehow characteristically English, laggardliness in the provision of civic amenities. Even when fully realized, the New Towns programme would not greatly affect the location either of industry or population, and it failed to prevent the further expansion of the London suburbs or an increase in the number of long-distance commuters. Nevertheless, it offered the one opportunity that had been presented in the age of industrialism to create towns consciously, and with reference both to the grim lessons of the past and to the needs of twentieth-century society. Outside the New Towns, however, the only noticeable evidence that an architectural renaissance had been expected after the war was to be found in the purely domestic field of improved council house planning by some local authorities, particularly the London County Council, and in new school building, for which Hertfordshire soon became internationally celebrated. In general, it remained as true after 1946 as before it that whoever wished to find pleasure in English architecture had largely to confine his attention to buildings erected before the accession of Queen Victoria.

Among the other legislative achievements of the first Attlee Government were the Trades Disputes Act of 1946 which repealed the Trades Disputes Act of 1927[1], and the Representation of the People Act of 1948. This was intended to establish the principle of one man, one vote, by the abolition of the additional votes electors had hitherto acquired by virtue of occupying business premises, or by possession of a university degree, which enabled them to vote for M.P.s representing the universities. The business vote was abolished and the twelve university seats disappeared. This was strenuously opposed by the Conservatives. Churchill declared that it was wrong to deprive universities of a right which had come down to them for 350 years for the sake of 'a small fleeting electioneering advantage'. The Government further angered the Opposition by abolishing the separate City of London constituency and amalgamating it with Westminster. Most of the few electors in the City constituency (there were only 4,600) had voted by virtue of the now abolished business vote; but the Sheriffs of the City appeared before the bar of the House to petition unavailingly against the constituency's disappearance, and the pointless pageantry of it all helped to work up a feeling that the most sacred traditions of the land were being ruthlessly destroyed by a Government of doctrinaire levellers. The Government also undertook a redistribution of constituency boundaries, and reduced the number of M.P.s, which had been 640 in 1945, to 625. The six months' residential qualification for a vote was abolished, and two electoral registers were to be drawn up and published annually. The parliamentary register would henceforth be used also for local government elections, in which the franchise had hitherto been confined to ratepayers.

[1] See p. 200.

51 · India ; Palestine

The constitutional position in India at the outbreak of war in 1939 was the consequence of the India Councils Act (the Morley-Minto Reforms) of 1909, and the Government of India Acts of 1919 and 1935. There was now an elected Indian Assembly to which the central Government of India was responsible in all but defence and foreign affairs; and in the provinces there was already responsible government, though provincial governors in special circumstances retained the power to veto legislation. It had been intended in 1935 to create a federal structure for the whole sub-continent, but the Indian Princes would not co-operate. They thus remained technically outside British India, but subject by treaty to the Government of India as the 'paramount power'.

The outbreak of war in 1939 had led to an immediate attempt by the Indian National Congress party, which controlled a majority of the provincial governments in India, to make its co-operation in wartime dependent on the granting of Indian independence at once. That dominion status was the ultimate goal of Indian constitutional development was no longer seriously questioned by the majority of British politicians; but the stumbling block was the existence in India of religious minorities whose rights would be inadequately protected if power were transferred to Congress which, though it still claimed to represent all Indians, was by now an exclusively Hindu organization. The great boast of the British was that they had found India a warring sub-continent of rival communities and had given it the rule of law, with equal rights for all creeds. Indeed, by arranging elections on a communal basis, they were accused of perpetuating India's political disunity. The last thing they wanted to do, however, was to hand back India to communal strife, least of all in time of war, when Britain alone could undertake India's defence.

In August 1940, the Government offered, immediately the war ended, to admit Indians to the Viceroy's executive council and to set up a representative council and a representative body to draft a new constitution. Congress replied by allowing Gandhi, to whom it always turned when it needed to harass the British by mass-protest, to organize another civil disobedience campaign. This led to the imprisonment of Nehru, the political leader of

Congress, and thousands of ordinary Congress members. They were not released until the end of 1941.

The entry of Japan into the war made it simultaneously more necessary and more difficult for the British to secure Indian support. In 1942, Stafford Cripps was dispatched to India in the hope that he might secure from Indian politicians the friendly co-operation he had failed to get from the Russians in 1940. He offered not only dominion status but the right to leave the Commonwealth; and the drawing up of the constitution of free India would be entirely in Indian hands. All this would, however, still only happen at the end of the war, though the British hoped for the establishment of an interim Government containing leaders of all the principal sections of Indian opinion. With the Japanese actually bombing Indian towns at the time, however, Congress declined to accept what Gandhi is alleged to have called 'a post-dated cheque on a bank that was obviously failing'. The Cripps Mission was perhaps dispatched by Churchill primarily to please the United States and the Labour members of his Cabinet and with no lively hopes of its success. Congress shortly afterwards announced that if the Japanese invaded India its policy would be one of non-violent non-co-operation; in August 1942 it decided to organize a nation-wide campaign to force the British to 'Quit India'. Gandhi approved this decision fervently. The British reply was once more to arrest Gandhi and all the principal Congress leaders. When widespread disorders followed, Congress was declared an illegal organization without this producing any nation-wide resistance to the Government. By the end of 1943, India was comparatively quiet.

When the Labour Government took office in 1945 it was as determined to grant India its independence as, in 1905, the Liberals had been determined upon self-government for the Boers. This determination followed from the inherited Labour dogma that the British were exploiting the Indians, from the anti-Imperialism of the United States and of the Atlantic Charter, from the need to reduce Britain's financial commitments and from the difficulty of holding on to India with what was now a conscript army. There remained, however, the apparently insoluble problem posed by the existence of Mohammed Jinnah's Muslim League. From Westminster, this looked a relatively simple matter of how, in a predominantly Hindu India, to erect safeguards for a communal minority. Jinnah, however, was aiming not at safeguarding the rights of the Muslim minority but at the creation of an independent Muslim State of Pakistan. This was a reminder that the British were only the most recent of India's conquerors; and that, though the Muslims had perforce to submit to the British, they were determined, once the British left, not to become subject to the Hindus over whom they had themselves also once ruled. Moreover, the clearer it became that the British were bent on leaving India the more uncompromisingly would Congress demand to rule all India, and the more resolute would be Jinnah's efforts to prevent this. Thus, Jinnah demanded that the British divide India and then quit, while Nehru, for Congress, demanded that the British quit India and leave its subsequent political structure to them. Thus the political unity of India disintegrated, as traditional Conservatives had always prophesied, the moment the British made a definite offer of independence. Inasmuch as he was the product of a Westernized education, and was a Fabian as well as a high caste Brahmin, Nehru found religious communalism distasteful; and in that he was a Hindu politician, he was bound to resist the claim of the Muslim League, on the eve of independence, that Congress did not represent the whole of India.

As Hindu and Muslim political speeches grew more violent, disorder spread, and the prospect of sanguinary civil war increased. The chances of the British being able to limit, let alone prevent, bloodshed in India were now negligible. The Indianization of the Army and the Indian Civil Service had already ruled this out. Demobilization of British troops, and the abandonment of European recruitment into the administrative service, meant that a *de facto* transfer of power was already far advanced. The British were, in any real sense, already ceasing to rule India; and Indians were pursuing policies which threatened to produce, if only through the mere processes of delay, a transfer, not of power, but of anarchy and mass-murder.

In 1946, the British Government sent out one more mission to India, once again headed by Stafford Cripps. The mission would set up a constitution-making body and a representative executive council, and the Indians themselves were to decide the form the constitution should take. An interim Government was set up in September 1946; but it was boycotted by Jinnah until he realized the inadvisability of permitting the establishment of a Hindu-dominated Government at the centre of Indian affairs. The Muslim League continued, however, to refuse to co-operate in the drafting of a constitution; and this created the additional problem for the British Government that Congress was very ready to accuse it of using Muslim intransigence as an excuse for delaying independence. Accordingly, Attlee announced on 20 February 1947 that the Government proposed to take steps to transfer power 'into responsible Indian hands by a date not later than June 1948'. He indicated that the Government did not exclude the possibility of partition, and appointed Lord Mountbatten of Burma as Viceroy, replacing Lord Wavell; the latter had offended Congress by his obvious concern lest their intransigence accelerate the already obvious slide into civil war.

Attlee's attempt to force Indians into compromise by giving them barely fifteen months' notice of Britain's intention to quit was a failure: it merely intensified the determination of Congress to work for an undivided India and of Jinnah to work against it. Violent communal outbreaks in Calcutta and East Bengal in 1946 were followed, in the early months of 1947, by bloodshed in the Punjab, the North-West Frontier Province and Assam.

Almost as soon as he arrived in Delhi in March 1947 Mountbatten realized, perhaps more clearly than had been realized previously on the British side, that there was no hope of resisting Jinnah's demand for a separate Pakistan. The facts that Pakistan would consist of two widely separated areas, that the process of division would cut across the subcontinent's administrative, military and economic systems and that the partition would lead to mass-expulsions of minorities with all its attendant horrors, were a source of anxiety to the British and to Nehru, but not, apparently, to Jinnah. Hence, Mountbatten and, eventually, Nehru accepted that the choice was between the greater bloodshed that would follow an attempt to impose unity under Congress and the lesser bloodshed that would follow partition. Mountbatten also soon realized that the run-down of British civil and military personnel was now so far advanced that Attlee's original date of June 1948 for the transfer of power was too late. Nevertheless, both Congress and the Muslim League were still insisting that the actual division should be done by the British; at the very moment of achieving freedom, the politicians of India were refusing to accept responsibility for their own destiny and passing the problem back to the British who, by now, had little or no real power in India.

The new date for the transfer of power was now fixed for 15 August 1947; the decision was reached in London in May 1947. This time the shock treatment seems to have worked. A plan of partition was agreed upon, and details of the administrative procedure to be followed were worked out by Mountbatten's staff.

The last constitutional problem to be tackled was that of whether or not the two new States should accept the status of dominions within the British Commonwealth. Although Congress had always demanded complete independence, it decided in favour of accepting dominion status at this late stage, being afraid that Pakistan might decide to accept it, and thus secure a more favourable relationship with Britain. Dominion status was also important to the British Government as likely to disarm the Conservative opposition, which had always declared itself in favour of India's eventual attainment of this status. The mid-century conception of a multinational Commonwealth, maintaining the continuity of the British Empire but transforming it into a world-wide association of peoples regardless of race, colour or creed, that even republics could join at the cost of acknowledging in some ill-defined and non-effective way an hereditary monarch as their 'Head', was born of the political fears of Attlee and Nehru in the summer of 1947.

It is generally agreed that, in organizing the division of India's territory, peoples, its assets, its Army and Civil Service in seventy-two days, Mountbatten showed unusual skill and energy. One of his achievements was to persuade virtually all the princes in India to come to terms with the emerging Governments of the Indian Union and of Pakistan. These princes were nominally independent sovereigns, though in treaty relationship with the United Kingdom Government as the 'paramount' power. Congress demanded that, when the British withdrew, paramountcy should pass to the successor authorities. From a strictly legal and moralistic point of view, the proper substitute for paramountcy over the princes was the restoration of the princes' former independent status; on the other hand, the princes owed the survival of their great wealth and despotic powers entirely to the British presence in India. The preservation of their independent status after the British withdrawal would thus be incompatible with true Indian liberation. In addition, the States were so numerous and many were so small that their perpetuation in an India whose separation into an Indian Union and Pakistan was divisive enough, would have produced administrative chaos and war. Although the position of many of the States was complicated by the fact that the ruler was not of the same religion as the majority of his subjects, almost all the princes agreed to accommodate themselves either with the Indian Union or with Pakistan. The one large State where there was no success, owing to its strategic importance and its common frontier with India and Pakistan, was Kashmir, which long after the British withdrawal was to remain a cause of hostility between the two nations.

The major problem proved to be the division between India and Pakistan of the two great provinces of Bengal and the Punjab, and the British were compelled to draw the relevant frontiers themselves. In the initial stages, the partition of Bengal passed off with relatively little trouble, but the partition of the Punjab produced a bloodthirsty triangular struggle involving Sikhs, Hindus and Muslims which it proved impossible to control. The bloodshed in the Punjab led to the flooding of Bengal with Muslim refugees and to widespread bloodletting in Delhi. The communal murderings in Calcutta, however, were limited by the intervention of Gandhi.

The Indian Independence Act became law at Westminster in July 1947, and on 15 August, Mountbatten, the last viceroy of India, was sworn in as the first governor general of the Indian Union, and Jinnah became governor-general of Pakistan. The politicians in both Britain and India congratulated each other and themselves upon the completion of legal and ceremonial acts of such undoubted significance in the history of the world; but the immediate connection between the historically significant acts of the politicians and the realities of the situation was, on this occasion, even smaller than usual. Labour politicians saw themselves as having effected a peaceful transfer of power to a group of responsible politicians in India; and it could be claimed that there was no precedent in history for the voluntary abandonment of power by a great imperial nation at the conclusion of a victorious war. They saw themselves as having carried through this transfer while preserving British investments and commercial undertakings in India, and as having secured for the first time in imperial history the friendship of India's political leaders; they saw themselves as launching upon the world an entirely new kind of multi-racial Commonwealth of Nations. For their part, the *bourgeois* Congress politicians and the astute leaders of the Muslim League could congratulate themselves on having achieved far more than, in their hearts, they had really thought possible even up to the eleventh hour. Yet the immediate reality was that while politicians, British and Indian, had been manœuvring for a solution that redounded to their own credit, they had allowed the sub-continent to descend into ultimately leaderless civil war. Among both British and Indian politicians there had been a complacent but quite unjustifiable expectation that their mere political solutions would automatically pacify the Indian masses. Independence was in fact accompanied, and followed, by communal killings involving, at a fairly conservative figure, half a million people; and the murderings and burnings were succeeded by a mass migration of refugees fleeing from possible destruction at the hands of the communal majority in the state they inhabited. This involved a further 12 million people.

The misery which independence initially brought to the Indian people was in part the consequence of the natural tendency of politicians to take one another too seriously. Labour saw itself as a great liberator of the Indians; Congress and the Muslim League saw themselves in the same light; but each group in its different way was out of touch with the real India, the Labour leaders through ignorance, the Indians because, having used and exploited mass prejudice to further their struggle against the British, they imagined they could turn it off like a tap the moment the British conceded victory to them. The main contributory cause was the speed of the operation. Yet although the rapidity of the transfer was the responsibility of the Labour Government, it had little choice in the matter; delay, however it might have been required by the necessity of maintaining order and of securing a juster and more economically sensible settlement, would have been regarded as one more sign of British insincerity and have produced even more disorder. This would have left behind the kind of legacy of hatred of the British which was bequeathed to Egypt and Cyprus; and one major benefit the events of 1947 conferred upon the British was that hatred of them seemed to have vanished with the running down of the British flag.

The wider significance of Indian independence was its effect in proclaiming the doom of the whole principle of European political dominance in Africa and Asia. Henceforward, wherever in these continents European political rule survived, it could never again be accepted as part of the established order of things.

Abandonment of India and Pakistan was logically accompanied by abandonment of Ceylon and Burma. Ceylon became an independent, self-governing State within the Commonwealth in 1947, without incident. The emergence of independent Burma was somewhat less smooth. The Japanese invasion had sharpened the national consciousness of a sufficiently large number of Burmese politicians for the British to become convinced that the wish for speedy independence expressed by the Anti-Fascist People's Freedom League would be too difficult and costly to resist. Accordingly, the British agreed to the election of a constituent assembly in April 1947; and this decided upon the creation of an independent republic outside the Commonwealth in 1948. The only reason for Burma's withdrawal from the Commonwealth was its desire to be a republic, which, before the decision to allow India to combine republican institutions with membership of the Commonwealth, seemed a contradiction in terms.

The spectacular problems which faced Ernest Bevin, as Foreign Secretary, in his dealings with Palestine were only partly the consequence of the Balfour Declaration's optimistic aim of reconciling the establishment of a Jewish National Home in Palestine with the protection of the non-Jewish inhabitants. They were also a legacy bequeathed him by Hitler.

In consequence of Hitler's anti-Jewish mania, between 1933 and 1935 the British increased the rate of permissible Jewish immigration into Palestine; being at once faced with Arab rebellions, they reduced the rate of entry between 1935 and 1939, just at the time when the Jews were in direst need. Yet, although the number of Jews admitted to Palestine was always small in relation to Jewry's needs, the proportion of Jews to Arabs in Palestine rose from just over one in ten in 1922 to just under one in three by 1939; and there was every expectation among the Arabs that by the early 1960's the Jews would outnumber them.

The British therefore set up the Peel Commission in 1937. It reported in favour of the partition of Palestine. This came to nothing because it would have had to be enforced against the wishes of both Jews and Arabs; and a full-scale military operation in Palestine was thought impossible in view of the dangerous international situation in 1938. In May 1939 the Government issued a White Paper which fixed the Jewish immigration rate for five years, promised no increase on this rate without Arab agreement, and undertook that the independence ultimately required by Palestine's legal status as a mandated territory would not be granted without the consent of the Jews. This at least served to keep the Arab world moderately contented during the desperate period when Wavell, Auchinleck and Alexander were protecting it against Hitler. But it did little to protect European Jews against Hitler: the annual rate of permitted immigration of only 10,000 a year was only half of the number which had entered Palestine in 1936. The results of British policy included much illegally organized immigration, a ten-month British ban on all immigration in September 1938, and the frequent turning back of immigrant vessels at a time when the ultimate destiny of so many Jews was likely to be Hitler's gas chambers. This led to charges of inhumanity against the British to which there were several rational answers but no very convincing ones. Terrorist organizations grew up among Palestinian Jews; one, known as the Stern gang, murdered the British Minister in Cairo, Lord Moyne, in 1944, and the United Nations mediator in Palestine, Count Bernadotte, in 1948. The Irgun Zwei Leumi, the parent body from which the Stern Gang originated, having called off terrorism at the beginning of the war, resumed it in 1943; its most spectacular action was to blow up a considerable part of the King David Hotel in Jerusalem in 1946, causing over a hundred deaths.

With that overbearing egotism which was his least attractive characteristic, Ernest Bevin informed the House of Commons that he would stake his political future on solving the Palestine problem. Unfortunately, he was in this, as in most areas of foreign policy, operating from a position of weakness, and beset by more contradictory pulls and pushes than he could control. The War Office was anxious to keep Palestine because of the possibility of losing the use of the British base in the Canal Zone of Egypt; the Colonial Office was unwilling to abandon its thirty-year administrative task in Palestine and hoped for a united Palestine with provincial autonomy; the Foreign Office did not want any kind of partition because it would upset the Arabs, upon whose goodwill it was felt that supplies of Middle East oil ultimately depended; while the Treasury was in haste to liquidate the entire commitment, for the good reason that by the middle of 1947, with its convertibility crisis, the country could not afford the cost of administering Palestine. The urgency of finding a solution quickly was increased by other complications. There was a growing fear that a disordered Middle East would be an incitement to interference by the Soviet Union. At home, there was a growing feeling of bewildered anti-Semitism and distaste for the whole Palestine commitment, particularly after the hanging, by Jewish terrorists, of two young British sergeants as a reprisal in August 1947. Worst of all, the assumption by the United States, through the so-called Truman Doctrine of March 1947, of responsibility for the defence of the eastern Mediterranean, made that country's nagging hostility to British treatment of the Jews more inescapable than ever. The turmoil, at a time when the British were themselves living under conditions of austerity, cost them £100 millions during the years 1945-6-7. The pressing complexity of the situation was calculated to strain the patience of the most saintly and supple of Foreign Secretaries, and Bevin's exasperation was at times indiscreetly vocal, chiefly against the United States, but also against the Jews.

In February 1947, therefore, Bevin referred the problem of the Palestine mandate to the United Nations. Inevitably, this immediately served to undermine British authority in Palestine still further, and in September 1947 it was announced that the British Government proposed to abandon the mandate altogether. This was perhaps an attempt by the Cabinet to try a second time, the shock tactics that had apparently served so well in India; but it was also a decision which, had there been time to reflect single-mindedly on anything in the hectic state of the world of 1945–6, might have been made earlier. The Palestine problem was essentially one which affected two widely disseminated peoples, Jews and Arabs; even the security of the Middle East was not, as it is so often treated in this connection, an exclusively British interest; and there was no special moral obligation on the British taxpayer, in the relatively indigent state in which the country then found itself, to spend millions of pounds sterling trying to keep order against terrorists subsidised, as they largely were, by American dollars. The curse of anti-Semitism was a crime for which all civilized nations and not the British by themselves, were required to do penance. In the understandably impassioned atmosphere created by the world's tardy awareness of what Hitler had done to the Jews, it was overlooked that Britain and Britain alone, not solely for selfish reasons and certainly to its own hurt, had brought the Jewish community in Palestine into existence in the first place. Bevin was widely accused of being anti-Jewish and pro-Arab throughout the dispute, and it does seem that he started from the basic proposition that the Jews were making harmonious relations between British and Arabs extremely difficult. Nevertheless, the only British action which would have seemed to the Arabs to be pro-Arab would have been that of forcibly ejecting the Jews from Palestine altogether.

In November 1947, the United Nations Assembly voted in favour of the partition of Palestine. The unwillingness of the British to use their army to enforce, on behalf of the United Nations, a partition they had always shrunk from trying to enforce on their own account, was reinforced, during the first months of 1948, by the need to withdraw troops from Palestine in view of the worsening situation created by Russian policy in Berlin. By the time the Palestine mandate ended, in May 1948, Britain's capacity to maintain order was as exiguous as it had been in India in the summer of 1947.

When the moment came for the final British withdrawal, the United Nations, not unexpectedly, had failed to decide how partition should be carried out. The world therefore looked on while the Jews proclaimed the existence of an independent State of Israel, and made good that claim, despite the immediate attack upon them of the armies of the Arab states, chiefly Egypt, Syria and Jordan. By 1949, when the full-scale fighting ended, the Jews had established a State somewhat larger than that originally assigned to them in the U.N. plan of partition.

52 · Struggle for Europe, 1945-49

The chief fact which slowly acquired general recognition during the interminable international negotiations of the years 1945 to 1947 was that, in all respects save one, the U.S.S.R. was, after all, a typical Great Power like the others. The British Left ended the war as convinced as Roosevelt had been that friendly relations between the U.S.S.R. and 'Imperialists' like Churchill were impossible; but believed that, once the Conservatives were driven from office, everything would be different. Ernest Bevin, who recovered from the error with a rapidity which alarmed his party, declared before the 1945 election that 'Left would understand Left'; and Cripps, who, having actually been to Moscow, might have been expected to know a little better, thought a Labour Government would 'have the broad sympathy of the Russian people'. It was gradually revealed, however, that the governing factor in Soviet policy was less that it had a Communist ideology than that it was a true-to-type sovereign state concerned with its own political and economic advantage, and determined to protect its security by whatever means it thought fit. The only important respect in which the U.S.S.R. was unique among Great Powers at that time was its lack of experience of, or faith in, any kind of international co-operation. When seen in this light the U.S.S.R. is revealed as having, at this time, one of the most reactionary Governments in the world. In so far as any historical precedents were held to apply on the subject, the U.S.S.R. would regard them as justifying this attitude. The League of Nations had been founded by anti-Bolshevik interventionist States; when the U.S.S.R. joined it, it failed, from their point of view, to resist Fascism, and turned to appeasement instead; and its only notable act after 1935 had been to condemn Russian aggression against Finland. If Czarist experience was taken into account, international co-operation immediately after the Napoleonic wars, through the Holy Alliance or the Congress System, could be dismissed as the collaboration of tyrants, and what the much-vaunted Concert of Europe had principally concerted during the rest of that century had been European resistance to Russian claims upon Turkey and Constantinople.

In consequence, the U.S.S.R. pursued after the war the foreign policy which had been precisely foreshadowed by its diplomacy during the war.

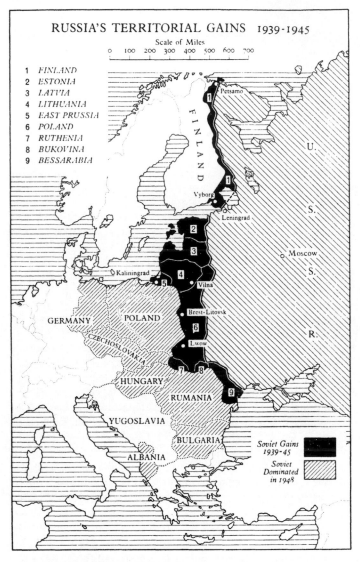

RUSSIA'S TERRITORIAL GAINS 1939-1945

Scale of Miles

0   100   200   300   400   500   600   700

1   FINLAND
2   ESTONIA
3   LATVIA
4   LITHUANIA
5   EAST PRUSSIA
6   POLAND
7   RUTHENIA
8   BUKOVINA
9   BESSARABIA

Soviet Gains
1939-45

Soviet
Dominated
in 1948

It would seek political, economic, military and ideological control of
every State on its borders with a view, if possible, to eliminating any base
of operation against it from central Europe, the Mediterranean or the
Middle East. In Europe, the area of its control was to be pushed steadily
westward, and there would be no relaxing of pressure unless and until
counter-pressure made further expansion impolitic. By contrast, any

attempt by either the United Kingdom or, at a later date, the U.S.A., to act similarly in regions contiguous to their own borders or relevant to their world-wide interests, was at once stigmatized as aimed at creating an anti-Soviet *bloc*. It was a reconstruction, on a world scale, of the situation created by the Kaiser's Reich, when alliances or agreements made by others were regarded by the Germans as 'encirclement', while their own alliances were to be regarded as inherently innocent. Ernest Bevin early expressed, again in that strangely self-centred manner of his, how exasperating he found this Soviet attitude, in a House of Commons debate on foreign affairs on 7 November 1945:

I am not a criminal if I ask to be on good relations with nations bordering the British frontier. What am I doing wrong? I am doing nothing to injure any-body, and I am not prepared to accept that position from any country in the world. What H.M. Government are willing to give they claim the right to do with France, Holland, Belgium, Scandinavia, or other countries – not a Western *bloc* for war purposes. They are our cultural friends, our historical associates, they acknowledge the same democracy as we do, and therefore I say that I am entitled, on behalf of H.M. Government, to have good neigh-bours in my street, just as any other country in the world is entitled to have good neighbours in any other street. I think I am perhaps a little energetic about this, but I am a little resentful, and I think the House will agree that I am entitled to be.

In general, the House of Commons tended to agree that Bevin was entitled to be resentful about the Russians, though, as this extract illus-trates, his injured feelings were expressed with scant regard for the rules of sentence construction. Only the Left wing of the Labour Party disapproved of Bevin's rather bucolic protestations of injured innocence. As he himself put it in the Commons on 21 February 1946:

I would like to say this to some of my friends on this side of the House, I have been told that when the Opposition cheer me I am wrong. But you cannot carry out a foreign policy on a very narrow and limited basis. Neither can you alter history by a slogan.

It was certainly true that the Opposition tended to cheer Bevin; both Churchill and Eden usually referred to him in tones of respectful sympathy and his officials are said to have been greatly impressed by his 'soundness' and his skill as a negotiator. Perhaps R. A. Butler made the point most woundingly for the Labour Party as a whole when he said in the Commons, on 23 November 1945, that Bevin sparkled among his contemporaries like 'a diamond lying on a vast heap of coke'.

The feeling that Bevin's resistant attitude to the U.S.S.R. was a result, not of Soviet policy, but of his adoption of a Conservative and Foreign Office view of the world, was increased by the general misunderstanding in British circles of the real point of Churchill's celebrated speech at West-minster College, Fulton, Missouri, on 4 March 1946. The speech was intro-duced by President Truman and was clearly intended to be a major pronouncement. Its most celebrated passage was that which caused the expression 'Iron Curtain' to pass into common usage:

From Stettin on the Baltic to Trieste on the Adriatic an iron curtain has descended across the continent. Behind that line lie all the capitals of the ancient states of central and eastern Europe – Warsaw, Berlin, Prague, Vienna, Budapest, Belgrade, Bucharest and Sofia.

The deeper intent of the speech, however, was to make one more appeal for the United States to interest itself in Europe such as he had been making ever since 1940. With some skill, Churchill contrived to do so in language which Americans could appreciate:

From what I have seen of our Russian friends and allies during the war I am convinced that there is nothing they admire so much as strength and nothing for which they have less respect than military weakness. For that reason the old doctrine of the balance of power is unsound. We cannot afford, if we can help it, to work on narrow margins offering temptations to a trial of strength. If the Western democracies stand together in strict adherence to the principles of the United Nations Charter, their influence for furthering those principles will be immense and no one is likely to molest them. If, however, they become divided or falter in their duty, and if these all-important years are allowed to slip away, then indeed catastrophe may overwhelm us all.

This was, in fact, an appeal for an Atlantic Alliance; and it was this, at this stage, that constituted the difference between Churchill and Bevin, since Bevin still believed he could wrestle with the Russians successfully on his own. The Fulton speech had a hostile reception in the United Kingdom. Mr Tom Driberg, from the Labour back benches, asked Attlee in the Commons on 11 March 1946 whether he would make it clear that the speech did not represent the policy of the Government; another Labour M.P. asked Attlee to proclaim the Government's entire disapproval of 'the tone and temper of the speech'. Attlee replied in a sentence intended perhaps to sting in two directions at once:

The Government is not called upon to express any opinion on a speech delivered in another country by a private individual.

Between 1946 and 1947, however, the catalogue of Russian obstructiveness and the shadow of its oppressive power seemed to grow longer and longer, while, for the most part, the United States looked on, still largely isolationist and anti-colonialist in outlook. Negatively, it wished to avoid embroilment in the clash of Anglo-Russian imperial rivalries which, after all, was nothing new in world history, and did not seem greatly to concern the U.S.A. Positively, it was more interested in encouraging the dismantling of the French and Dutch colonial empires in south-east Asia than in giving diplomatic, let alone financial, support to its former allies. Truman could effect little change in U.S. policies in the immediate post-war years. His elevation to the Presidency had been accidental, his qualifications were considered negligible and Congress was recalcitrant; these things counted a good deal more than his own obvious and sharp dislike of Soviet methods. Shrewd and uncomplicated, and with both feet firmly on the ground, he felt no call to attempt the politically impossible.

Bevin was therefore compelled to play the role of Russia's deeply injured well-wisher largely on his own until the middle of 1947. In contravention of the Potsdam agreement, the Russians treated the eastern zone of Germany as if it were within their full legal sovereignty. They drained it of resources for their own use, regardless of the fact that western Germany normally depended on the east for its food supplies; and only the Communist Party was allowed to function. In Poland, as already related,[1] the Russians created a purely Communist State, and never wavered from their obvious determination that the Oder-Neisse line should constitute its permanent eastern frontier. They proved endlessly obstructive over the peace treaties with Finland, Roumania, Bulgaria, Hungary and Italy, insisting on heavy reparations payments, particularly from Italy; and they refused to sign a peace treaty with Austria at all during this period. Nevertheless, the Russians were fairly accommodating in Austrian affairs and, to everyone's surprise, Austria remained a non-Communist state without noticeable Russian hostility. Finland also was allowed to choose its own political paths, Russia being content, through its reparations demands, to divert its economy to Russian needs. This, indeed, was the basis of Russia's attitude to all the Iron Curtain countries: their economy was to be operated to help make good Russia's deficiencies in machinery. This would necessitate an authoritarian and usually unquestioningly pro-Russian Communist Government; and wherever local Communists clung to the patriotic ideas they had absorbed during the struggle against the Germans, they were replaced by nominees of Moscow who put Russia's needs first. It was inevitable that in western Europe there should be protests at what was regarded as 'enslavement' of the Iron Curtain countries in contravention of the various promises of political freedom enunciated so loudly in wartime documents from the Atlantic Charter onwards and, indeed, in the peace treaties themselves; but it was recognized that in practice little could be done except to make unavailing protests.

From the British point of view, much more alarm was felt at the evidence of Russian pressure in the direction of the Mediterranean and the Middle East. Not until May 1946 did the U.S.S.R. withdraw its troops from northern Persia, despite an Anglo-Russian treaty of 1942 providing for their withdrawal within six months of the end of hostilities. The Russians had used the interim in endeavours to secure the annexation of Persian Azerbaijan to the territory of Russian Soviet Azerbaijan. In Turkey, the Russians likewise made demands for the return of Kars and Ardahan, and for the replacement of international control of the Straits by a bilateral Russo-Turkish agreement. The Russians also displayed an interest in the

[1] See p. 396.

possibility of establishing military bases on Turkish soil to protect the
Straits, and for a short time were disposed to claim part of Italy's former
colonial territories in North Africa. Most embarrassing for the British was
evidence that the U.S.S.R., through its Communist satellites in Albania,
Bulgaria and Jugoslavia, appeared to be actively encouraging Communist
attempts to create disorders in Greece, where British troops had been
maintained since Churchill's intervention there in 1944,[1] propping up a
succession of incompetent but anti-Communist Governments, and
endeavouring to arrange for free elections. Bevin was faced, as Churchill
had been, with much criticism from the Labour Left wing, which took the
view that Greek Communists had proved their patriotism by their resistance
to the Germans, that they were not mere puppets of Moscow and that,
even if they were, this did not matter. Worse still, the U.S.S.R. abandoned
its previous acceptance of British interference in Greece. At the first
meeting of the Security Council, in London, in February 1946, the Soviet
representative Vyshinsky declared:

The war is over, and the presence of British troops on Greek soil is not justified by any substantial reasons, and can only endanger the national and internal situation in Greece. On the basis of these conceptions, the Soviet delegation insists on the quick and unconditional withdrawal of British troops
from Greece.

Bevin's explosive reply, unfortunately, was appropriate to a mass meeting
of angry strikers in the days of the Triple Alliance; and by reducing
Security Council discussion to the level of a slanging match it helped to
justify the cynical comments that the business of the United Nations was
'open disagreements openly arrived at'. He began by implying that
Vyshinsky's criticism justified Britain sending even more troops to Greece,
presumably to stop an immediate Soviet attack; and, in a later attack on
Vyshinsky, worked himself into something like a frenzy:

The basic charge, in which the honour of my country and of the Commonwealth – I repeat, the honour of my country and the Commonwealth – are
involved, is that we have deliberately put troops into Greece to support certain elements in that country, with the object or likelihood of disturbing and
endangering world peace. Does M. Vyshinsky believe that? If he does, then
I ought not to be sitting at this table. The British Government after all these
years of war and bloodshed, to be engaged in a policy of using troops to disturb or endanger the peace of the world in any way at all or anywhere – you
ought to tell me to leave this table because I am not fit to be with you. You
are established to maintain world peace and I am branded at the first meeting
as the one person in the world endangering it. The British Government are
entitled to an answer. I met my Cabinet this morning and they ask for an
answer. Have we, by responding to the Greek Government and leaving troops
there, endangered world peace? The Soviet Government should tell me
whether I have. If they say so I am not fit to sit with them or with any other
peace-loving nations, because the basis of this Organization is an assembly of

[1] See p. 389.

peace-loving States. I claim that Britain is as much a peace-loving State as anybody round this table or in the Assembly. I am entitled to a straight answer.

Subsequent events in Greece were shaped not by Bevin but by the instability of Greek politics. The Governments whose free elections the British presence secured were unstable and corrupt. As the United States was later to discover in other parts of the world, politicians placed in power under foreign protection on the grounds that they were anti-Communists often had little but their anti-Communism to commend them; and if such politicians were provided with loans or aid by the protecting Power, the money was swiftly absorbed, but rarely remedied the economic ills it was designed to cure. The presence of foreign troops in a small State and the supplying of economic aid are indeed almost guarantees of political instability and irresponsibility; there is no comfortable half-way house between liberty and subjection, and Soviet control of Iron Curtain countries was as effective as it was in this period because it recognized, as, for instance, the British realized in Egypt in the days of Cromer, that troops and money are inadequate guarantees of stability unless there is also direct administration by the protecting Power's own agents.

Moreover, by 1947, with chaos following the fuel crisis, with the American Loan running out and the convertibility crisis soon to be upon them, the British could not afford troops and money for the Greek commitment. Not only was the whole policy unpopular with the Government's supporters; the Treasury was in revolt against the expense. Yet, there remained the firm conviction that if Greece were allowed to go Communist, Turkey, with its ill-equipped army, would follow suit and the Soviet Union would then control the Straits, the Aegean, the eastern Mediterranean and the entire Middle East. In short, the British Government believed itself, in 1946, to be facing, as an immediate prospect, what it had believed itself to be facing as a long-term prospect, in the days of Canning, Palmerston and Disraeli. By 1947, furthermore, the safeguards against Russia the British had acquired by occupying Egypt after 1881, by the partition of Persia in 1907 and by the control of Palestine, Jordan and Iraq after 1919 were all in danger of crumbling. Accordingly the Government informed the United States, at the end of February 1947, that Britain could afford no further aid to Greece and Turkey after 31 March 1947, and that the strategic consequences of this situation were likely to be disastrous.

In March 1947, therefore, President Truman appeared before Congress to request authorization for a grant of 400 million dollars for Greece and Turkey in order to save 'democracy':

I believe that it must be the policy of the United States to support free peoples who are resisting attempted subjugation by armed minorities or by outside pressure.

Economic and financial aid for such countries was essential if they were not to succumb to a way of life which

. . . relies upon terror and oppression, a controlled Press and radio, fixed elections, and suppression of personal freedoms.

Such totalitarian régimes, he declared:

undermine the foundations of international peace and hence the security of the United States.

The enunciation of what quickly came to be called 'The Truman Doctrine' is usually taken as the true beginning of the Cold War. It was soon looked back on as a summons to a world-wide crusade to save the true democratic faith from the depredations of the infidel Communist. In fact, immediate reactions on both sides of the Atlantic, save among Churchillians, were hostile. The view in the United States was that the country had been landed with a difficult problem by the renegade British who had fallen down on their responsibilities and were now luring the United States into the risk of war with the U.S.S.R. for the sake of British imperial security. The view in the United Kingdom was that Bevin was reverting to the bellicose anti-Russianism of Churchill, and handing over the defence of Europe to United States capitalists, and encouraging the United States, which had atomic bombs, to threaten the U.S.S.R., which had none. Only in retrospect would Bevin and Truman be regarded as having performed a combined act of high statesmanship. Bevin would be praised for the astute timing and the calculated 'shock tactics' of the British S.O.S. to Washington, and Truman would be praised for his brave bluntness in at last facing Congress with the international realities. A genuinely historical judgement, whether on the details of Bevin's methods of procedure, or on the wisdom of Truman's decision to advocate what was, after all, only a matter of dollars for Greeks and Turks, in terms that implied that Russia was directly threatening United States security, is hardly yet possible, most of all perhaps because the real acts and intentions of Stalin's Russia at this time are, and are likely long to remain, matters either for conjecture or for myth-making. What can be said is that the Truman Doctrine tended to impose on United States foreign policy the ideological rigidity that previously had been peculiar only to the U.S.S.R.

One section of the Labour Party had, ever since the war, consistently advocated that the Government's foreign policy be founded on co-operation with social democratic Governments in Europe, and after the announcement of the Truman Doctrine, this group began to talk as if western Europe could be integrated into a Third Force of progressive Governments who, living on equal terms with the U.S.A. and the U.S.S.R., might one day federate with the peoples of eastern Europe in a truly 'Socialist' continent. The prospects of this actually happening were remote;

but it had been as evident to Bevin as to Churchill, who strongly advocated the creation of a European federal union in a speech at Zurich in September 1946, that the strengthening of western Europe politically and economically, was urgently necessary. The perpetuation of a power vacuum could only be a temptation to the U.S.S.R.; and the creation of some kind of European system into which an eventually renovated Germany could be assimilated was equally desirable.

The first move Bevin took in this direction was the Treaty of Dunkirk in March 1947, by which the United Kingdom and France bound themselves in military alliance against Germany. The purpose of the treaty may be regarded, less as a bolting of the stable door upon a German horse that was not only prostrate but mutilated, than as an official British recognition of the return of France to the status of a Great Power.

The next step came, originally in a somewhat muted way, as a result of a speech by General Marshall, the U.S. Secretary of State, at Harvard on 5 June 1947. He referred to the economic dislocation of Europe, and suggested that the European States could not expect aid from the United States unless they themselves were first to agree 'on their requirements and on the part they themselves will play'. Whether the extreme caution of Marshall's speech was a deliberate attempt to avoid the rather frightening bellicosity with which the Truman Doctrine had been presented, and to what extent it was contrived as a positive development of that policy, is far from clear. It may well have been actuated by the realization that one-third of the electorate in France and Italy voted Communist, and that Communists were holding Cabinet posts in the Governments of both countries; and it was certainly a rational response both to the clear evidence of renewed financial crisis in the United Kingdom, and of its rapid retreat from the eastern Mediterranean, India, Burma and Ceylon. What is also of interest in Marshall's speech was his careful avoidance, in contrast to Truman's speech about Greece and Turkey, of ideological fanfares:

Our policy is directed not against any country or doctrine but against hunger, poverty, desperation and chaos.

No country, including Russia and her satellites, which was willing to assist in the task of recovery would be excluded.

Bevin seized upon the speech eagerly. The story is that he learned about it from a news broadcast and from the columns of the *Daily Herald* on the morning of 7 June 1947. Immediately, he told the glad news to Attlee, informed the United States of Britain's deep gratitude, and communicated with the French Foreign Minister asking for his co-operation:

By noon that day the first steps had been taken that led to the formation of the sixteen-nation Organization for European Economic Recovery and the vast and historically decisive plan for Marshall Aid for Europe.[1]

[1] Francis Williams, *Ernest Bevin*, p. 265.

The result was the expenditure by the U.S.A. of 17 billion dollars during the four years beginning in 1948, the first really effective steps towards west European co-operation, and a degree of economic recovery in that area which at the beginning of 1947, would have seemed improbable.

The most significant fact, however, was that after some preliminary havering, the U.S.S.R. declined to participate in the Marshall Plan and also prevented the satellites, in particular Czechoslovakia, not then entirely under Communist control, from participating. From the United States point of view it is, therefore, possible to say that though the Cold War seems in retrospect to have begun with the Truman Doctrine, it began in earnest only when the U.S.S.R. rejected Marshall Aid. From the Soviet point of view, however, the Truman Doctrine had damned American dollars in advance as a means for the pursuit of anti-Communist power politics. From the point of view of western Europe, Soviet abstention from the Plan was, economically at any rate, an almost unmixed blessing. Had negotiations for the implementation of the Recovery programme been conducted with the Russians and their satellites in attendance, the delays and the demands would almost certainly have been so prodigious that Congress would have turned against the whole scheme.

From the beginning of 1948 onwards, British and United States foreign policies in Europe were more closely co-ordinated than in the days of Churchill and Roosevelt, though the objectives now being pursued were, basically, the Churchillian ones of restoring western Europe and of setting limits to Soviet hegemony. For the next five years, hopes of accommodation with the U.S.S.R. were so completely cast aside that when, on the death of Stalin, the post-1948 policy of 'containment' looked likely to be replaced by 'peaceful co-existence', the prospect of reverting to what had been taken for granted as recently as the beginning of 1947 was regarded in the United States as something like treason.

The most deeply-felt Soviet blow to the West since the affair of the Polish Underground in Warsaw took place when, in February 1948, there occurred a sudden but unresisted Communist *coup d'état* in Prague. A Communist Government took over and a Communist replaced Benes, who had resumed his former position as President of Czechoslovakia at the end of the war. This was almost certainly a Communist reaction to the threat by the non-Communist groups that, if the Communists ever ceased to be the largest party in the state, Czechoslovakia would take part in the Marshall Plan. The inclusion of Czechoslovakia within the Russian orbit with such an economy of effort caused alarm as well as distress in the West. The discovery shortly afterwards, in circumstances suggesting either suicide or violent death, of the body of Jan Masaryk, the Czech Foreign Minister, also created a strong impression. Jan Masaryk was the son of Czechoslovakia's founder-president, Thomas Masaryk, and a notable and popular figure in wartime London.

The most spectacular Soviet counter-measure against the West was the blockade of Berlin beginning in June 1948. The agreement at Yalta had been that the separate zonal occupation of Germany should be solely for the purposes of its convenient demilitarization and denazification. The zones had not been devised as a prelude to partition, and German affairs were to be administered jointly by the victors by means of the Control Commission in Berlin. Agreement on the Commission proved impossible, chiefly because the U.S.S.R. maintained its insistence on large-scale reparations.[1] The administration of Germany on a zonal basis therefore acquired a permanent character; and while the U.S.S.R. developed Communist institutions in the East, steps were taken during 1947 in the western zones to develop a traditional parliamentary system. In 1948, the West decided on currency reform in their zone, in order to restore the German economy, which was being stifled by lack of confidence in the value of the mark. The U.S.S.R. refused to take part in the currency reform and was greatly embarrassed when its implementation led to shops in the western zone filling with goods and to a great revival of production. The effects were most noticeable in divided Berlin, where the traffic between the eastern and western sectors became uncontrollable; the Soviet blockade of West Berlin followed accordingly. The likely result of this Soviet blocking of all access to the city (far inside the Soviet zone as it was) by road, rail or canal was that, unable to supply their sectors of the capital, the Western Powers would have to abandon them. Their stock of food when the blockade began was sufficient only for thirty-six days, and the coal supplies would last only forty-five.

The United States reacted with determined efficiency and, with British co-operation, organized the dispatch of supplies by air. The Berlin Airlift continued through the winter of 1948–9 and by the spring of 1949 was ferrying in 8,000 tons of supplies daily. Twenty-three per cent of the total of nearly 2 million tons of freight were carried by British airmen, at a cost to the U.K. Exchequer of over £8½ million. Finally, after 321 days, the U.S.S.R. called the blockade off; and railway communications with the western sector were ceremoniously resumed with the dispatch from the East of a train whose locomotive was decorated with Picasso's dove of peace.

The most important long-term result of the Berlin Blockade was the West's decision, in August 1948, to establish a German Federal Republic, with a federal Parliament and Government at Bonn and with Konrad Adenauer as Chancellor. In October 1949, the Russian Zone (with West Berlin still islanded in its midst) became the German Democratic (i.e. Communist) Republic. There were some observers who viewed with satisfaction this undoing of Bismarck's unifying handiwork, productive as it had

[1] See p. 398.

been of so much misery for Europe as a whole. Others felt alarm at the bestowal of sovereign status on the Federal Republic, fearing that it could hardly survive with credit unless it proclaimed its resolve, not only to 'liberate' the territories of the Democratic Republic, but also those German lands to the east of the Oder-Neisse line which the Russians had bestowed upon Communist Poland. These fears played their part in stimulating the movement for a Western European Union which might prevent the possibility of the German Federal Republic one day trying to provoke a war on the matter of German unity.

The movement, therefore, for closer European co-operation gained momentum between 1947 and 1949. It was a natural reaction to the universal fear inspired by Soviet foreign policy; it was rendered more urgent by the need to assimilate Federal Germany quickly and harmoniously, so that it became an accession to Western strength rather than a disruptive force working for purely German ends; and, above all, it was essential if military support was to be secured in permanence from the United States. Americans could not be expected to abandon for ever their long-standing distaste for sending either their dollars or their sons to Europe, unless its Governments gave clearly decipherable evidence of their stability, unity and capacity to help themselves.

Bevin had already, in March 1948, made the first move in the direction of a common European defence policy by the Treaty of Brussels, signed by Britain, France, Belgium, Holland and Luxembourg, in which they pledged themselves to joint military action in the event of war. A consultative Council of Foreign Ministers was set up by the treaty, and it was a logical step from this to the creation of a wider military alliance with the United States. This came with the North Atlantic Treaty of 4 April 1949, to which the signatories were the five Brussels powers, the United States, Canada, Denmark, Iceland, Italy, Norway and Portugal.[1] The signatories agreed to regard an attack on any one of them as an attack upon them all, and the agreement covered all the territories, islands, vessels and aircraft of any of the signatories in Europe, North America and the North Atlantic; also covered were French Algeria and the Allied armies of occupation in Europe. The North Atlantic Treaty Organization (N.A.T.O.) set up by the treaty included a North Atlantic Council, with an international staff of permanent officials, and a Defence Committee, which established the Supreme Headquarters of Allied Powers in Europe (S.H.A.P.E.) at Paris, and a similar Headquarters in the United States to cover the defence of the North Atlantic. The Treaty thus created the most closely integrated military alliance in peacetime that had ever existed in modern times. It was the first military alliance to which the United States had fully committed itself since the alliance with France in 1778 during the War of Independence; and, by a strange paradox, it also involved the United Kingdom, at a time

[1] Greece and Turkey joined in 1952, Federal Germany in 1954.

when it was regarded as an imperial power in retreat, in the widest military alliance in its history. N.A.T.O. involved one other paradox. Its creation was an open acknowledgement that the United Nations Organization had not even begun to draw the nations of the world together; yet the implementation of N.A.T.O. would involve its members in a greater surrender of their sovereign capacity for defence to an international organization than had ever before been known. The sharp reaction in the United Kingdom when, at the end of 1950, the British Home Fleet came under the command of an American Admiral holding the appointment of N.A.T.O. Supreme Commander, North Atlantic, showed how little this was realized.

53 · Struggle for Asia, 1950-53

The revolutionary nature and the elaborate machinery of N.A.T.O. created, in the course of time, the impression of a fully effective organization for European defence. Yet, by 1951, there were only 12 N.A.T.O. divisions and 1,000 aircraft in western Europe whereas the Soviets commanded over 240 divisions and 20,000 aircraft; and it would be difficult to assert that N.A.T.O. constituted in the strictest sense a credible deterrent to Soviet expansion. The perpetuation both of N.A.T.O. and of the division between east and west which it expressed resulted from events outside western Europe, none of which directly concerned the United Kingdom.

The determining events of this period in international affairs were the collapse of Chiang Kai-shek's Kuomintang régime over the whole of mainland China and the establishment in its place of the Communist People's Republic of China under Mao Tse-tung in 1949; the explosion by Soviet Russia of an atomic bomb in that same year, despite expert U.S. predictions that this would not happen until 1952; and the outbreak of war in Korea in June 1950. Until these events, the idea of permanent U.S. involvement in Europe and a policy of active resistance to Communism were making headway only slowly against the traditional policy of isolationism. The Berlin Airlift and the establishment of N.A.T.O. were manifestations of the relatively cautious but eminently sophisticated notion of 'containment' which the Truman administration, under the influence of Dean Acheson and George Kennan, had been slowly evolving since the death of Roosevelt. The basic proposition behind containment was that the U.S.S.R. would have to be lived with, and eventually brought to the conference table; but that this could only happen at some time in the future, and after it had been made clear to the Kremlin that further pressure against the West would be resisted and, owing to America's sole possession of atomic weapons, too risky.

By 1950, however, although containment could claim some success in halting Soviet expansion and subversion in western Europe, in all other respects it appeared a calamitous failure. The overthrow of the United States wartime and postwar protégé, Chiang Kai-shek, on whom billions of dollars had been lavished, was a national humiliation comparable to the Japanese attack on Pearl Harbor, and it was at once seen as providing evidence, much nearer to American hearts than anything that had happened in Europe, of a vast Communist conspiracy against the American way of life. The fact that, in December 1949, Mao Tse-tung visited Moscow, and later announced the existence of a Sino-Russian Military Alliance, at once obliterated any awareness there may have been that until that date Stalin had given Mao as little friendship and support as he had given to Tito in Jugoslavia.

The impression of conspiracy was deepened both by the Soviet explosion of the atomic bomb and by the real and false treason sensations of the first half of 1950. In January, after two long trials, a State Department official, Alger Hiss, who had been one of Roosevelt's advisers at Yalta, was found guilty of perjury in denying, as he did with great persistence, that he was involved in Communist plots to send U.S. documents to the Russians. In February, the eminent atomic physicist, Klaus Fuchs, who had been engaged in atomic research in Britain since 1941, was found guilty of passing atomic and thermo-nuclear secrets to the Soviets. In the same month, a U.S. Senator, McCarthy, launched a virulent campaign designed to prove that the State Department was riddled with Communists. The sensations in the United States, and to a lesser degree in the United Kingdom, continued throughout the next two years. As the combined Sino-Russian threat in the western Pacific increased, McCarthy, serving the Republican opposition to the Truman administration as Titus Oates had served Shaftesbury's Country Party in its attacks on Charles II, did all he could to work up anti-Communist hysteria, blackened reputations indiscriminately, and accused the U.S. Government of having deliberately conspired to turn the western Pacific into a Red Lake dominated from the Kremlin. United Kingdom opinion reacted violently against McCarthy; but his campaign, combined with Russia's new possession of atomic power, introduced a new climate of fear. Bewildered anxiety was further increased when yet another atomic scientist working in Britain, Bruno Pontecorvo, disappeared across the Iron Curtain in October 1950, and when, in the spring of 1951, two Foreign Office officials, Burgess and Maclean, whose behaviour was under investigation, decamped to the Soviet Union in even more mysterious circumstances. The sudden outbreak of war in Korea, when superimposed on an already almost hysterical political situation in the United States, created what may properly be regarded as the most potentially dangerous crisis in the history of human affairs.

The destiny of Korea had been at issue between China, Russia and Japan at the opening of the century, and had been a causal factor both of the Russo-Japanese War and of the Anglo-Japanese alliance. It had been wrested from China by the Sino-Japanese War of 1894–5; it had been assigned to Japanese domination in 1905 by the Treaty of Portsmouth and was annexed by Japan in 1910, in both cases with the reluctant approval of the United States. As a result of the Cairo and Potsdam conferences, Korea was promised eventual independence; but the surrender arrangements imposed on the Japanese required their forces in Korea north of the 38th parallel to surrender to the Soviet Union, and all forces south of it to surrender to the United States.

As happened in Germany, however, a division intended to have purely administrative significance acquired the characteristics of a political and ideological frontier. The Korean scene itself mirrored that of wartime Poland. A Western-style Government in exile came into being outside Korea, while a Communist administration appeared on the spot in the wake of the Russian advance. The former, led by a lifelong Korean patriot called Syngman Rhee, was established at Seoul, in the South, under United States patronage; in North Korea a Democratic People's Republic emerged under Kim Il Sung, a Korean who had served in the Red Army. The two Governments ruled on either side of the 38th parallel by the end of 1948.

The Truman administration and its service experts decided by the spring of 1949, that it was neither feasible nor necessary to defend the island of Formosa, to which Chiang Kai-shek's Kuomintang régime was now confined, or to maintain United States occupation forces in South Korea, particularly after Soviet forces had withdrawn from North Korea in December 1948. The United States withdrawal from the South was therefore completed by the end of June 1949. The strategic calculation behind these decisions was that the Soviet Union would not launch a war until after they had begun to acquire atomic weapons in quantity (i.e. after 1952) and that, if they did attack in the meantime, they would do so in Europe and be met by an all-out United States air offensive, to the conduct of which Formosa and Korea would be irrelevant.

On 25 June 1950 the North Korean Army, which numbered 90,000 men and had 150 Russian-built tanks, attacked South Korean forces across the 38th parallel and advanced rapidly towards the capital, Seoul. The United Nations Security Council was at once summoned, and called on the North Koreans to withdraw their troops. On 27 June it called upon all members of the United Nations to give South Korea assistance against attack. This resolution therefore 'legitimized' the action Truman had previously taken to assist South Korea with air and naval forces from occupied Japan, which was under the control of General MacArthur as United States Commander in Chief, Far East. At the same time, Truman had ordered MacArthur to send the United States Seventh Fleet to prevent any extension of the conflict to Formosa. The Korean War thus instantly worsened United States, Chinese relations by, in effect, placing Chiang Kai-shek's régime in Formosa under United States protection. It was not until 28 June 1950, however, that United States ground troops were ordered to Korea; had they not been sent then, the whole of the South would have speedily fallen into North Korean hands. Truman took this action only after U.S.S.R., though refusing to call the North Koreans back, appeared to indicate it would not itself interfere in Korea if United States ground forces were sent; from the outset, therefore, though the United States committed itself to the expulsion of the North Koreans, it did so only after seeking some assurance that its action would not automatically lead to a full-scale general war.

Between the end of June and the end of September 1950, under MacArthur's resolute, and sometimes strategically reckless, leadership, the whole of South Korea had been cleared of North Korean forces; and, in late September, MacArthur began preparing to project his forces across the 38th parallel into North Korea. His overpowering personality thus transformed the war from one of containment to one of liberation: his military success opened up the prospect of releasing the whole of Korea from Communism and not merely the South of it. United States opinion reacted instantly in favour of this total solution in Korea. The sacrifice of American lives would not be justified by a mere return to a *status quo* that left Communist North Korea still an entrenched and menacing forward post of Soviet expansion immediately north of the 38th parallel. Accordingly, the Truman administration sought and obtained, from the U.N. Assembly, authority to secure a united, democratic and independent Korea. In this policy, the British Government concurred, Bevin declaring that the artificial division between North and South Korea must be ended. MacArthur's military energies had opened up opportunities; the politicians jumped into them.

But once MacArthur's forces had entered North Korea in early October 1950, they could hardly be halted thereafter until they had reached the Yalu river, Korea's northern frontier with the great Chinese province of Manchuria (and, in the easternmost part of its length, with the U.S.S.R.). The result was an immediate response by the People's Republic of China. By mid-November at least 300,000 Chinese infantrymen (officially described by Peking as Chinese People's Volunteers) had crossed the Yalu River; barely had some units of American forces reached that river when the

THE KOREAN WAR

Scale of Miles

0   50   100   150

Mukden

Vladivostok

U.S.S.R.

C   H   Yalu R.

Sinuiju

NORTH KOREA

Pyongyang

Kosong

38th. Parallel   Panmunjom

Inchon   Seoul

SOUTH KOREA

Taegu

Pusan

JAPAN

Quelpart I.   Tsushima Is.

Nagasaki

major part of those forces were flung back from it. By 15 December 1950 they had retreated 120 miles in ten days, and were back at the 38th parallel. The only post-war case of a Communist State being 'liberated' had ended after two months.

The shock created by the retreat which the Chinese now imposed upon MacArthur's forces was world-wide. As it reeled back in the face of the onslaught of the apparently underfed, underclad, under-equipped Chinese hordes, the army of the most highly industrialized nation in the world suffered deeply in its morale, and opinion in the United States itself veered dangerously between a sense of national humiliation and fear, and an angry desire to avenge the humiliations by all-out atomic warfare. Somewhat incautiously, Truman himself said, at a Presidential Press Conference, that there had always been 'active consideration' of the use of the atomic bomb. In fact, his military experts were still convinced that war with China must be avoided and that the real enemy was Russia. As General Bradley later said in public:

Red China is not the powerful nation seeking to dominate the world. Frankly, in the opinion of the Joint Chiefs of Staff, this strategy would involve us in the wrong war, at the wrong place, at the wrong time, and with the wrong enemy.[1]

It was at this point, in the first week of December 1950, that Attlee flew to Washington for four days of talks with Truman, a visit precipitated by fear that the U.S. was about to authorize the bombing of Manchurian air fields. The outbreak of the Korean War had already (see p. 436) produced great economic difficulties for the United Kingdom, but its political repercussions were perhaps even more enduring. The public and political reaction to the war was a curious compound of fear of incalculable atomic consequences, of jingoistic dislike of the strategic and oratorical *braggadocio* with which MacArthur had conducted his campaign, of a more rational conviction that it was foolish to brand Communist China as an international pariah, and of a contemptuous indifference to the whole affair as a hypocritical example of American aggression under false United Nations colours. There was, also, a half-unconscious resentment at the fact that, for the first time since the Thirty Years War, a major international conflict had arisen in which Britain was too weak to play any significant part.

Attlee's flight to Washington was dramatized, therefore, as a statesmanlike attempt to re-assert Britain's status as an ally with the right to be consulted, and to give to the blustering amateurs of the State Department and the Pentagon the benefits of the ripe wisdom and matured political skills with which, as the world's senior great power, Britain was uniquely endowed.

So insidious was the poisoned memory of Munich that there were many in the United States who believed Attlee differed from Chamberlain only in that, unlike his ill-starred predecessor, he did not come armed with an umbrella. The British were 'dragging their feet', were 'soft on Communism' and hell-bent on another Munich. The theory was all the more difficult to refute since the United Kingdom had afforded diplomatic recognition to Red China in 1949 and was known to favour its admission to the U.N., against which the United States had felt compelled to set its face.

Since, however, Attlee had flown to Washington and not, as he would have done if another Munich were in mind, to Peking or Moscow, the outcome of his visit was a strengthening of both his own and Truman's official policies. Truman made it clear that concessions to Red China immediately after its troops had expelled U.S. forces from North Korea were out of the question; the logical consequence of acquiescing in Communist aggression in Korea was to acquiesce in it in Europe. From his side, Attlee accepted this diagnosis, but pressed in return for the abandonment of any attempt to unite all Korea under a non-Communist Government by 'liberating' the

[1] Quoted Rees, *Korea, The Limited War*, p. 274.

North. There must be re-imposed upon the operation its original limited objective of containing Communism at the 38th parallel. Perhaps this decision by these two rather humdrum men, the one so intellectually limited and ordinary compared with Roosevelt, the other so inarticulate and subfusc beside Churchill, was as significant for the world as any made by their two so much greater predecessors. Both men were driven from power by the decision; the Republicans won the next presidential election largely because Truman was accused of appeasement at the behest of the British; and the Labour Party was rent with dissension because Attlee was accused of tagging along behind American imperialism.

In the six months from December 1950, the Chinese undertook three major offensives to drive U.S. and U.N. forces out of South Korea. By early January 1951, Seoul was once again in Communist hands, and by that time the U.S. retreat from the Yalu had measured 275 miles. A bitter war of attrition followed; the slow, slaughtering U.N. advance back towards the 38th parallel was rendered slower and more difficult by the fact that, owing to their lack of elaborate administrative and supply services, the Chinese could usually produce a numerical superiority of front-line fighting troops in the neighbourhood of 5 to 1. The indifference of the Chinese to their high casualty rate added a further element of horror.

By April 1951, the situation reached a new danger point. As the U.K. and the Commonwealth countries endeavoured to produce cease-fire resolutions for the U.N., attempting to lure Red China to the conference table with the bait of possible discussions about Formosa and a seat in the U.N., the temper of U.S. opinion was raised to new heights of rage against the 'appeasers' in the State Department and in London. Spokesmen of the Republican Opposition talked in terms of treating Europe as neither possible to defend nor worth defending against inevitable Russian control, and of concentrating totally on all-out resistance to Communism in Asia. Thus, though the Truman administration did at least insist on contributing additional ground troops to N.A.T.O., its *quid pro quo* to its critics was a pledge never to abandon Formosa. The dangers intensified as, under General Ridgway's competent leadership, U.N. forces once more approached the 38th parallel; for now General MacArthur, still Supreme Commander in Tokyo, renewed his demand for an advance beyond it. In direct contradiction to General Bradley's dictum, he believed not only that Red China could be crushed, but that now, in Korea, was the place and the time for the final showdown with the forces of Communism. He said so, publicly, in what may well have been a bid, not simply to fight a war he patriotically believed in, but also as a move, in association with the Republican Party, towards his own candidature for the Presidential election of 1952. MacArthur's demands constituted a threat to the office of President and caused the liveliest anxieties in the British Foreign Office; and on 11 April 1951 Truman took the politically daring step (though it was fully supported by the U.S. Chiefs of Staff) of dismissing MacArthur from his Command.

The move was a success. MacArthur, as the greatest of American fighting soldiers, the conqueror and re-creator of Japan, and the symbol of the United States' passionately patriotic loathing of Communism, received a hero's welcome in New York, and in a farewell address to Congress reduced strong men to tears by his impressive and dignified statement of his strategic aims. There was no pausing to recall that his headstrong tearaway disregard of realities had been the direct and foreseeable cause of the greatest military defeat in U.S. history. Nevertheless, much hysteria was purged by the full-throated emotional deification he received on his return, and by the subsequent Senate inquiry into the situation surrounding his recall. Thereafter, as a national hero, MacArthur acted out the last words of his own valedictory message to Congress.

I now close my military career and just fade away – an old soldier who has tried to do his duty as God gave him the light to see that duty.

The recall of MacArthur, and his replacement by the soundly efficient Ridgway, removed all that there had ever been of the heroic in the Korean War. In July, as the battlefront stabilized itself in the vicinity of the 38th parallel, truce talks opened. Together with the war itself, they were to continue until July 1953, and were used by the Communists chiefly as a means of maintaining the struggle through the medium of their obstructive distortion of traditional diplomatic procedures. What eventually brought them finally to agree to abandon their attempt to break United States' determination to hold on to South Korea is uncertain. It may have been a combination of economic factors, uncertainty about Soviet policy on the death of Stalin in March 1953, or the warning conveyed by the new Eisenhower administration through Indian channels that if the truce were much longer delayed the war would be widened, and use of atomic bombs once again be contemplated.

In British minds, the thirty-seven months of the Korean War, with its four million casualties and the devastation of Korea from end to end that accompanied it, seemed an exercise in ultimate brutality and futility, which left the frontier between the Communist and non-Communist world exactly where it had been in 1951. This unwillingness to seek for a justification for the war reflected the minimal part played by British forces in the actual operations and its disproportionately adverse effect on the United Kingdom's economy. Britain contributed little more than two infantry brigades, one armoured regiment, two R.A.F. squadrons and the Far Eastern Fleet to the Korean fighting; and whereas U.S. total casualties numbered 142,000 (of whom over 33,600 were killed), U.K. casualties were 4,286 of whom 686 died. Nor were the British impressed by what they properly regarded as the fiction that this had been a United Nations opera-

tion in defence of collective security of the sort they were still being criticized for not having undertaken against Japan in 1933, or Italy in 1935, or
Hitler at any time before 1939. In fact the U.N. was able to act at all only
because, at the time of the original North Korean invasion, the U.S.S.R.
was boycotting the Security Council for its refusal to eject the Kuomintang
delegate and replace him by the admission of Red China. Not only did the
absence of the U.S.S.R., let alone that of China, cast doubts on the validity
of the U.N.'s actions; so also did a resolution passed, during the Korean
War, designed to bypass a Great Power's veto in the Security Council.
This attempted to establish that, where such a veto otherwise prevented it,
U.N. action to deal with a threat to peace could be authorized by the
Assembly. It was on the basis of this dubiously legal resolution that the
Assembly condemned the Anglo-French attack on Egypt in 1956; this
provided a painful illustration of the fact that the distortion of the U.N.
Charter to facilitate action in the despite of a Communist Power was a device
that could be used in the reverse direction. Time was to enfeeble still further
the view that the Korean War established the principle of collective action
against aggression. The multiplying, throughout the 1950's, of the number
of emergent African and Asian members of the UN made it unlikely that
the mounting of a predominantly U.S.-Commonwealth operation to keep
the peace would ever again receive U.N. support.

Moreover, a long-term assessment of strategic and political realities can
be undertaken only by realizing that ideological attitudes have at no time
been the basic factors in international relations. To believe that they are, is
not, as is commonly supposed, a sign of deep understanding of the 'real'
causes of international antagonisms; it is to fall victim to propaganda. Just
as, in the 1930's, men were often more deceived by Nazi and Fascist propaganda the more they detested these systems, so the more strenuously men
adopted anti-Communist attitudes after 1945 the more slender their grip
on reality and the greater their liability to error. Ideologies are normal
instruments for the conduct of political warfare at home and psychological
warfare abroad; and they are, no less than the physical devices for serving
political and external power, such as tanks, missiles, rockets, subject to
modification, obsolescence and discard. Hitler's anti-Communism was a
psychological weapon which he used till 1939 (and then only in public),
which he then totally discarded and which, because it was a weapon he
needed once more, he took out of mothballs in 1941, first to fight the Soviet
Union and then, unsuccessfully, to divide the West from its support of
Russia. Similar considerations apply to his Germanism: he used it or, as
over the Italian Tyrol, ignored it, according to the requirements of policy.
In like manner, Stalin's Communism did not lead him to support either
the Communists of Jugoslavia or China, unless and until it happened to
suit the needs of policy; just as he supported Communism in Greece only
after 1945, when for the first time it seemed convenient or possible to do so.

The history of Soviet attitudes to the League of Nations, to Britain and the U.S.A., shows that these attitudes were as changeable and indeed reversible as if the Soviet system had possessed no distinctive ideology at all. And on the non-Communist side of the Iron Curtain it became a commonplace that support of freedom, democracy and the Western way of life repeatedly involved American or British support of régimes which suppressed freedom, evaded or denied democracy and whose way of life was distinguished by political corruption and economic injustice.

From the outset, therefore, the pressures to treat the problem as ideological drove the Truman administration to a largely unrealistic assessment of the whole western Pacific situation. In real terms, the proper destiny for Korea was that of an autonomous State preserving its long-standing links with China. This had been its position in 1890; and every attempt made after that date to detach it altogether from China was wrong. In 1900 Russia and Japan had wanted it, and Japan had got it by 1910; by 1950 it was, in real terms, partitioned by the U.S.S.R. and the U.S.A.; and that was wrong too. The only real identity of aim that ought to have existed over Korea in 1950 was the common interest of both China and the U.S.A. that this unhappy country should in no circumstances pass under Soviet control, for this was contrary to the wishes of the Koreans, the Chinese and the Americans. U.S. policy, by refusing to recognize Mao Tse-tung, by neutralizing Formosa and bolstering up Chiang Kai-shek, by rushing pell-mell to North Korea's frontier with Manchuria, compelled the Chinese to fabricate an anti-American ideology that had little basis in historical fact. Russia was the most successful perpetrator of aggression against China even if, temporarily, Japan had been the most violent. Commercially and financially, the British had been the chief offenders against nineteenth-century China. Besides these three powers, the U.S.A. had been benevolent, unaggressive and unacquisitive, and alone consistently committed (though in practice very feebly) to the twin aims of Chinese territorial integrity and the commercial open door. All these truths were obscured by anti-Communist hysteria; as was the plain fact that no Chinese Government, whatever its ideology, would fail to react to the appearance of a vast non-Asiatic military force on its Yalu river frontier.

Thus, General Bradley's view that to fight an all-out war against China in or about North Korea was the wrong war, was grounded in reality. The North Korean People's Army was dominated by its Russian military advisers, and it has been suggested that up to 5,000 Soviet personnel were involved: clearly the North Korean Army was the instrument of Soviet Communism, itself the instrument of Russian Great-Power expansionism. Yet the choice by the U.S.S.R. of this vicarious method of expansion, and its studied avoidance of any direct involvement in the war ought to have been noted not only as a cunning but also as a diffident method of conducting what was alleged to be a programme of world-domination. Curiously,

MacArthur probably realized this most clearly. He drew from it, however, the conclusion that neither Russia nor China, who likewise did not officially go beyond labelling its men in Korea as volunteers was strong enough to resist an all-out United States attack at this stage. His argument that time was working against the U.S. if its true aim was the destruction of Eurasian Communism was probably true; and, in repudiating MacArthur, the U.S. may well prove in retrospect to have repudiated the policy he stood for, and to have lost the last opportunity there was (assuming it to have existed even in 1951) to implement that policy without involving something approaching total annihilation.

Yet had there been no resistance to the invasion of South Korea in 1950, there could have been neither the policies of containment (favoured by the Democratic Party under Truman, Kennedy and Johnson) nor even the odd mixture of brinkmanship and moral crusading pursued by the Republican State Secretary, John Foster Dulles, under Eisenhower. There could only have been more and more unresisted Soviet expansion, becoming ever more provocative until the point was reached when, as in Europe in 1939, failure to contain the opponent while there was no general war resulted in a situation in which total war seemed the only alternative to a craven, and otherwise perpetual, policy of surrender. The Korean War would have been avoided only if the United States had long before 1950, even long before 1945, succeeded in demonstrating to the U.S.S.R. that such action would be resisted. The way in which the Korean War was allowed to escalate was a tragedy for all who were involved in the fighting and the directing of it. But, because it was fought, more was saved for the world than the ruined towns and wastes of Korea.

Perhaps, too, distant, frightened and generally ungrateful Europe was saved at Seoul, Inchon and Pusan, and even on the Yalu river, for here it was that it first began clearly to be understood that a crusade to liberate some from Communist rule would probably lead to the annihilation of all. Above all, it preserved Europe by confirming the United States in its commitment to N.A.T.O.; it led to large rearmament efforts in western Europe, and consolidated U.S. determination to promote the economic recovery of that area. Nor were only western Europe and the United States preserved and tutored in the bloody school of Korea; so also were the Russians and Chinese. The Korean armistice in 1953 was followed in 1954 by a settlement not dissimilar in Indo-China; surveying their handiwork, all the Chinese had got in Korea was a reputation for anti-colonialism, a heap of corpses and no calculable chance of securing Formosa. Nor might there have been, after Stalin's death in 1953, quite the readiness there was in the Kremlin to repudiate his policies in public, or quite the same readiness to talk the language of co-existence; and without the Korean experience the West might well have been debilitated by Krushchev's exuberant bear-hug hardly less than it had been between 1941 and 1950 by the basilisk stare of his hardfaced predecessor. As it was, the diversion of Soviet and Chinese energies from western Europe to the emergent peoples of the world indicated clearly enough that the struggle for power in the world would continue, but that the pattern for the latter decades of the twentieth century would probably be less like the pattern of the decade after 1945 than men then visualized.

---

54 · Dying Fall, 1950-51

The problems in diplomacy, defence and finance imposed on the Labour Government by the Korean War were difficult enough in themselves; they were aggravated by the political situation created at Westminster by the election of February 1950, which reduced its majority in the Commons to a bare half-dozen. This result has usually been regarded as indicating rather more disillusionment with the Government's performance than is perhaps justified by the fact that in an election which produced the highest percentage turnout (84 per cent) since December 1910, Labour received 46·1 per cent of votes cast, compared with the figure of 47·8 per cent of a smaller total of votes cast in 1945. Labour was thus more successful in retaining electoral support over its five years in power than the Liberal Government had been between 1906 and 1910. A remarkable feature of the election campaign, in view of the exceptionally high turnout, was its extreme sobriety. Churchill, with obvious nostalgia for the rumbustious past, said it was 'demure'; but wiser counsels prevailed in the Conservative Party in 1950 than in 1945 and this time he made no references to the Gestapo.

The major significance of the election was the evidence it provided of the revolution that had taken place within the Conservative Party since 1945. In the early years of the Attlee Government, Conservative performance in Opposition had not been good, in part because Churchill's prime function at this time was that of a leader of international opinion. This reduced the amount of time he was prepared to devote to the chores of Opposition in a House he had grown accustomed to commmanding. Nor was he as assiduous as he might have been in cultivating and encouraging the new young talent that emerged in the party in those years. The success of the Conservatives in gaining the support in 1950 of over 2·5 million more votes than in 1945 was due to the labours of Lord Woolton and R. A. Butler.

Woolton, the wartime Minister of Food, was a northern business-man with an early training in social problems and therefore an untypical Conservative. Gathering round him a group of able young men at Central Office, he set to work to reorganize the constituency associations, to raise funds on a large scale, and to imbue party workers generally with the notion that henceforth Conservative success at the polls would have to be worked for – and paid for – and could no longer be relied on to emerge from the operations of divine providence and the voluntary contributions of men of wealth. At the same time, R. A. Butler established himself as the first successful political educator of the party since the days of Disraeli and Young England, directing and encouraging the working out of policy statements on most major issues. The Conservatives shed during these years the legacy of Baldwin and Chamberlain; and with men such as Macmillan, David Eccles, Maudling, Angus Maude, Edward Boyle, Iain Macleod and Peter Thorneycroft in its Parliamentary ranks, the Conservative Party ceased to be either 'the stupid party' or a party of old men. Throughout the 1950's, in consequence, it was Labour that appeared by far the more elderly and traditional of the two parties, so that by 1964 it was only by appropriating to itself the essentially Conservative claim to be a 'modernizing' party that Labour was able to struggle uncertainly back into office.

In 1950, however, Labour was still making the running, and the Conservative revival then was analagous to its revival after 1832. In effect the party's policy statement *The Right Road for Britain* was a kind of Tamworth Manifesto accepting the rival party's basic legislative achievements (this time, the welfare state and its major acts of nationalization) as the foundation on which it would in future operate. Equally reminiscent of the age of Peel, the Conservatives challenged their rivals most successfully in the realms of public finance, appealing against the whole theory and practice by which Labour had sought to control and restrict the national economy. In particular it was rapidly becoming apparent that the Attlee Government was so accustomed to the economics of scarcity that, when the balance of payments problem appeared at last to have been solved in 1950, it made no attempt to end rationing and, instead, devoted surplus foreign exchange to Government bulk-buying of large quantities of not very urgently needed foods from Europe. The Government seemed wedded to food subsidies and food rationing, regarding them as indispensable instruments of social welfare. Nor did Labour succeed in discovering any coherent attitude towards the private enterprise sector of the economy; not until the 1960's did it bring itself to stop thinking of the private entrepreneur as a parasitic profit-sucking capitalist.

Yet even this failure to adjust to changing economic circumstance might have been less damaging but for the disarray into which the Government fell because of the breakdown in health of its principal members and the collapse of party unity under the strain of the Korean War. These factors combined to deprive the Government, between October 1950 and April 1951, of Cripps, Bevin, Bevan, Wilson and John Freeman, and at a critical moment in the latter month incapacitated Attlee with an ulcer, so that it was a weakened and divided Government that endeavoured to carry on through the rest of 1951, its efficiency being still further reduced by the sheer physical effort involved in trying to defend itself in the Commons with so small a majority.

The last stage in the Government's history opened in September with the announcement of a £3,600 millions expanded defence programme as a response both to the Korean War and to the associated necessity of making N.A.T.O. appear, to the U.S.A. and the U.S.S.R. alike, as something more than the mere organizational framework for the defence of Europe.

It was soon evident in Labour Party circles, however, that the rearmament programme met with the disapproval of Aneurin Bevan. Matters were made worse when, after Attlee's return from his Washington talks with Truman, the programme was stepped up and was now planned to cost £4,700 millions over the next three years. This was, in fact, less than the United States had demanded, and probably the lowest figure which would enable the Truman administration to rebut the Republican charge that the U.S. administration was pouring out money for the defence of a Europe that refused to defend itself. Quite apart from the increase in the cost of imports resulting from the demands of the Korean campaign, the British economy now had to bear the strain of devoting 14 per cent of its national income, and almost the whole of its increased wealth for the next three years, to the needs of defence. The result was to hamper the country's economic growth for a number of years, and to create a tradition of 'independence' in the realms of defence which was probably, in the long run, in excess both of the country's needs and its capacity. Taken in conjunction with the Labour Government's decision in 1949 to manufacture its own atomic bomb, the decision also to manufacture almost all Britain's defence equipment and weaponry meant a disproportionate allocation of domestic resources to armaments. Thus the 'independent deterrent' which was to feature in controversy for another decade and a half, together with the whole notion that the United Kingdom should strive to arm itself because otherwise it could neither resist Russian threats, nor effectively influence the international policy of the United States, was born of the Attlee Government's response to the internal political difficulties of the Truman administration during its great debate with MacArthur and the Republicans during the Korean War.

Yet if the size of the programme and the methods by which it was carried out were open to criticism, the need for rearmament at this particular juncture is less debatable. It would have been politically difficult in 1951, if not impossible, for Truman to have secured approval from Congress for U.S. aid for British rearmament, even had Attlee asked for it, because the whole object of the exercise was to demonstrate that the United Kingdom was not composed entirely of cowardly appeasers whose moral fibres had been rotted by 'socialized medicine'. Nor, at that time, could a convincing demonstration of the will for self-preservation against Soviet expansion or subversion have been provided by anyone else in western Europe. The recovery of Western Germany had barely begun, and there were still far too many Communist voters in France and Italy for the lead to come from them. Once again Britain had to adopt the postures of leadership; but, this time, the British people themselves barely recognized that they were leading, and felt only that, because the impossible MacArthur was working for total war in Korea, and a precarious Labour Government was still in office in Westminster, the whole dreary business of cuts and shortages, which had seemed to be ending, had started all over again. With a meat ration now reduced to eightpennyworth a week, with prices once more rising, with a million men in the services, and conscription extended to two years, the British people soldiered unhappily on; and the real surprise of the 1951 election was perhaps not that the Labour Party lost, but that it received more votes than in 1950.

By the spring of 1951 Bevan, however, had decided to join issue with the party leadership over the rearmament question. He paralleled, in civilian dress and from the opposite end of the political spectrum, the almost exactly contemporary insubordination of MacArthur towards Truman; and, like MacArthur, he opposed on the basis both of principle and of personal ambition. In October 1950, Cripps's uncertain health caused him to resign from the Government; eighteen months later he died. As a senior member of the Government, Bevan considered himself eligible to be Cripps's replacement at the Treasury. Instead, Attlee appointed a much younger man, Hugh Gaitskell, who had succeeded Shinwell at Fuel and Power after the 1947 fuel crisis, and had then worked under the eyes of Cripps as Minister of Economic Affairs. His appointment was, so Attlee told Shinwell, 'an experiment'. It was, however, a comment on Attlee's confidence not only in Aneurin Bevan but in the much more senior Cabinet Minister, Herbert Morrison, who acted as Deputy Prime Minister. Attlee's next move was even more pointed. On 17 January 1951 he moved Bevan from the Ministry of Health to the Ministry of Labour. This was certainly not the case of the English Truman dismissing a Welsh MacArthur; but it gave notice that if Bevan was to oppose the rearmament programme, he would do so not as the architect of the National Health Service, but as a mere Minister of Labour. When the increased January programme was debated in February, Bevan, though supporting it in principle, spoke of it as liable to create a campaign of hate and hysteria. This would be hard to control, like the McCarthy anti-Communist scare which, he said, had accompanied (though its origins in fact preceded) the armament of the United States for the Korean War.

In March, Attlee administered another rebuff. Bevin, a victim of severe heart trouble for several years past, gave up the Foreign Office and died a month later. Attlee replaced him by Morrison though, once again Bevan considered himself a candidate. Clearly the future held little prospect for Bevan unless he came out boldly in favour of the Left Wing of the movement; the Old Guard on the Right had nothing to offer him. The likelihood of a head-on clash was increased by the fact that Attlee was now immobilized in hospital with a duodenal ulcer, leaving Cabinet business in the not always very soothing care of Herbert Morrison.

Bevan's bid to capture power, and to convert the party to a Leftward policy which he never succeeded in defining to the satisfaction of any but his always small body of personal supporters, proved as inept in execution as it was incoherent in principle. Given warning that Gaitskell's budget would, as one of its economy measures, compel recipients of National Health Service spectacles and dentures to pay half their cost, he announced in a public speech, a week before Budget Day, that he would never be a member of a Government that imposed charges on National Health Service patients. He proceeded to maintain this objection in Cabinet under the threat of resignation, but failed to secure any support, since Gaitskell proved immovable. The flamboyant Bevan never understood that this rather mild-looking economist was an unusually tough and obstinate man who was, moreover, as emotional in his own way as Bevan himself.

Gaitskell accordingly presented his Budget as planned and Bevan at once resigned. But he still failed to explain satisfactorily what he was resigning about. After beginning by protesting at the National Health charges, he let the point be lost in larger issues, so that the anomalous device of taxing people for needing spectacles and dentures, like the later impropriety of taxing them for requiring drugs, rapidly became accepted as normal. Yet it was a thoroughly bad tax for all that it was partly offset by increases in retirement pensions, and in the allowances for dependent children payable to widows, the sick and the unemployed. Similarly, the higher income tax rates which were introduced were offset by increased marriage and child allowances. The purpose of the National Health charges was presumably propagandist, like the earlier attacks on food subsidies by Gaitskell's mentor, Cripps. It was a warning to the lower classes not to take the welfare services for granted and not to expect too much from them; and was thus a pointer to the developing tradition of the succeeding thirteen years of Conservative rule that, although welfare services would certainly survive, they would be maintained only at a low standard. Bevan did not foresee this, or if he did, failed to say so.

Instead, he claimed in his resignation speech, on 23 April 1951, that rapid rearmament would do more damage to the Western cause than 'the behaviour of the nation the arms are intended to restrain'. It would produce 'unemployment in many of our important industrial centres', and he further declared, 'the foundations of political liberty and Parliamentary democracy will not be able to sustain the shock'. This, in his view, would lead to the triumph of Communism after all, since the 'real' weapons of the 'totalitarian' States were not military but social and economic. Rearmament, therefore, in Bevan's view, would dislocate the economy and lead to Communist subversion from within. Finally, he appealed to, and expressed, the curious topsy-turvy Jingoism which had already become a characteristic feature of Left-wing thinking in the post-1945 period. As the process of dismantling the Empire got under way the Bevanite faction and the Labour Left in general could not resist the desire to cheat. They revealed that, though they were ready enough to discard the physical attributes of Imperial power, they still wanted to retain the moral and spiritual attitudes that Imperial power had created and nourished. Like the Papacy in 1870, they laid unprecedented claims to leadership over men's minds and souls at the precise moment when temporal power was passing away:

This great nation has a message for the world which is distinct from that of America or that of the Soviet Union. Ever since 1945 we have been engaged in this country in the most remarkable piece of social reconstruction the world has ever seen. There is only one hope for mankind and that hope still remains in this little island.

It was indeed strange to suppose that, as the second half of the twentieth century began, the inhabitants of the world were still 'lesser breeds without the law', whose only hope of betterment lay in recognizing the superior fitness of Englishmen to instruct them in right behaviour. Nothing showed more plainly that Bevan, Neville Chamberlain, Curzon, Livingstone and Rudyard Kipling were after all brothers under the skin, and that the Anglo-Saxon attitudes of the nineteenth century could survive in the oddest places.

Bevan's resignation, and that of Harold Wilson and John Freeman, had little impact on the general public who, throughout his political career, rarely understood what Bevan was talking about; the effects on the active section of the Labour Party, however, were disastrous. With his great capacity for attracting personal loyalty, his intellectual liveliness and broad social and cultural interests, Bevan could not but stand head and shoulders above his party contemporaries. Fertile in ideas, strong in his emotions, ever ready to challenge the innate tendency of the party to lose its revolutionary zeal and warmth of heart, he died in 1960 leaving behind him little (apart from the National Health Service) except a trail of destruction. The disunity he created helped towards the Party's defeat in the 1951 election, and his feud with Gaitskell prevented its recovery, either in 1955 or 1959. In attacking Gaitskell as he did, when he called him a 'desiccated calculating machine', he devised a phrase as arresting as it was inaccurate. Yet, as in so much that Bevan said, there was a truth whose implications he did not fully comprehend; that, by the 1950's, passionate conviction and a boundless faith in the virtues of dynamic emotion were no longer in themselves sufficient for the movement.

As if the incalculable potentialities of the Korean War were not enough, the depleted Government faced renewed and exasperating trouble in the Middle East. Egypt raised a demand for the substitution of Egyptian sovereignty over the Sudan for the Anglo-Egyptian condominium that had been established, after Kitchener's victory at Omdurman in 1898; and, from April 1951 onwards, there developed an extraordinary dispute with Persia, arising out of the demand by the Persians for the nationalization of the property of the Anglo-Iranian Oil Company. This began spectacularly with the murder, in April, of the Persian Prime Minister who tried to avoid being precipitated into such a policy, and his replacement by a new Prime Minister called Musaddiq. To the accompaniment of great displays of mass hysteria, and in the intervals between fainting fits, Musaddiq ordered the take-over of all the A.I.O.C.'s installations. Unable to continue its operations, the company removed its personnel from Persia and abandoned its large oil refinery at Abadan; a settlement was not reached until 1954. During the Government's last months the spectacle of the neurotic Musaddiq becoming, for a time at any rate, a hero to all who wished Britain ill, appeared to fill the cup of national humiliation. The particular target of criticism was the new Foreign Secretary, Herbert Morrison. Morrison might have considered a strong line against Musaddiq, but the service experts insisted that no resources were available for a rapid employment of force at Abadan, Attlee disliked the idea as morally wrong, and the United States, as usual, expressed extreme coolness at the idea of any forcible assertion of British power in the Middle East.

To end this year of trouble, Attlee decided to appeal to the country in October 1951. The economic situation was worsening and could not be dealt with by a Government so vulnerable in the Commons, so thinly endowed with new talent, so greatly encumbered by men whom office had staled or exhausted, and so unable to think of anything it could do quickly to regain wide popularity.

Yet, even now, the electorate seemed not to be experiencing the sensations of disillusionment ascribed to it by the majority of contemporary journalists and by most subsequent writers. The percentage turnout was still as high as 82·5; 1,376,000 more people voted than in 1950, only twenty months before, and almost exactly half of the additional voting strength still went to Labour. For the third election in a row, Labour gained more votes than their rivals; but this time the electoral system gave the Conservatives

321 seats and Labour only 295. The thirteen years of Conservative rule, lasting without interruption till 1964, had begun.

The achievements of the Government during its six years of office were considerable. The change-over in the deployment of manpower from wartime purposes to those of peace was much smoother than after 1918. Social strain was avoided by full employment, and economic recovery accelerated, despite much need for social investment, by a higher rate of industrial investment. The upward trend in both production and exports was continuous and there was remarkable progress in the aircraft industry, in the peaceful use of atomic energy, in engineering, in the chemical and electrical industries and, again in contrast to the inter-war years, in iron and steel and shipbuilding. To set against this were the association of full employment with a decline in labour productivity, the unchecked inflation caused by the excessive demands made on limited resources by the needs of the social services and, during 1951, by the rearmament programme, which recreated the balance of payments problem that, by 1950, seemed to have been overcome.

In the field of social services and welfare the Government effectively established principles which, however imperfect in application, transferred what had hitherto been left to the haphazard operations of individual self-help and private charity to the less capricious realms of statutory obligation. To the objection that the welfare state undermined initiative, there was the historically attested reply that the absence of a welfare state had undermined it even more and that, for example, the high rate of emigration from the United Kingdom in the half-century before 1914 testified less to the initiative of the working class than to the belief of many members of it that real opportunity did not exist in their own country; and lack of opportunity was for a large proportion of the population certainly a major feature of Britain as it was run between 1919 and 1939. And if the nationalization programme was too narrow in scope and too bureaucratic in operation to deserve being called Socialist, it was neither socially nor economically possible to run the coal industry or the railways without nationalization, and it would have made little sense not to organize electricity and gas or aviation on a national scale.

Nor was the insistence on a technique of managing scarce resources through rationing and food subsidies, and by control of labour and materials, merely the negative, cramping policy which it was declared to be by its opponents from the beginning, and which it showed distinct signs of becoming in fact by 1951. It was almost wholly to the good, and perhaps to the permanent good, of the nation's social and political health, that in those critical years it was held together within the restraints of a common purpose. In the end, Labour's attempts to bind British people together in an austere acceptance of a scarcity both of consumer goods and of economic liberty came to seem a wilful exercise in bureaucratic frustration; and in undertaking to 'set the people free' (which they were able to do as the Korean War petered out) the Conservatives undoubtedly appealed to the growing weariness of a people whose material satisfactions had been so few, ever since the opening of war twelve years before, and who felt that the sacrifices they had made in the intervening period had earned them little tangible reward. Yet the size of the Labour vote offers little evidence that this feeling was as general as is still usually asserted or that it was strong enough to make people turn away from Labour in the emphatic way they had turned against Conservatism in 1945.

In imperial affairs, despite failures of execution, the abandonment of India was an act of profound, if precipitate, wisdom. The greatest of the imperial powers acknowledged the fact that the Age of Vasco da Gama was coming to an end in Asia, and in doing so heralded an imperial retreat from Africa and Asia of wider significance as the prelude to a new era of history than the withdrawal of the Roman Legions; little though these consequences were foreseen at the time. Yet all this was of small electoral advantage to Labour. The urban masses had scant interest in India (working class Imperialism looked mainly to the White Dominions) while to the rest of the country the whole story, from the handing over of India, through the bungled exit from Palestine, to the spectacle of Anglo-Iranian Oil being expropriated by Musaddiq, was one of shameful 'scuttle'.

The foreign scene, heavy with fears of Communist 'aggression' and 'subversion', and seemingly under sentence of death from the Bomb, offered, in 1951, few gleams of hope. On the Right there was frustration at apparent powerlessness, and on the Left a Bevanite conviction that Labour had sold itself to Wall Street and the Pentagon. The wisest single act of the Government in foreign affairs, its recognition of Red China in January 1949, aroused little or no enthusiasm from the Left, and smacked of appeasement when viewed from the Right. Yet here again, assuming that foreign policy has any influence on elections at all, the essentially unexciting, costly, and nevertheless potentially dangerous, actions of the Government provided no real revulsion against it. Indeed, the *Daily Mirror* was expressing, as well as attempting to influence, the opinion of its large and largely Labour readership when it sought to discredit Churchill and the Conservatives during the election campaign by publishing a large picture of a pistol, with the cautionary caption 'Whose Finger on the Trigger?'

It remains true, however, that the Government, like the party, had run out of ideas by 1951. It had done its duty to the past: it had nationalized; it had cured unemployment and it had done for the social services what had needed doing for years. It had solved many post-war problems by preserving the techniques of control it had inherited from the years of the war itself. But it had no policy for the 1950's: and though Bevan was right to see, in his intuitive way, that the party had come to a dead end, his own ideas were largely a revival of old factions, a beating of worn-out drums, an effort to summon up the ghosts of the hunger marchers and the brave days of the Popular Front.

And the past, even the immediate post-war past, was manifestly dying. Within four months of Labour's fall from power, George VI died in February 1952, and the Coronation of Elizabeth II in 1953 created a sense of new beginnings – and indeed of youthfulness – that few changes of monarchs had previously signified. In 1953 Stalin died, and within twelve months of his death the morose Soviet refusal to enter into even standstill agreements with the outside world was terminated by the Geneva Conference on Indo-China in 1954. By that time, too, it was likely that the imminent possession of hydrogen bombs by both the U.S.A. and the U.S.S.R. had ended the technological inferiority of the latter, from which had sprung much of its international ill-will. In 1955, both Churchill and Attlee gave up their respective party leaderships; and, as the long Conservative reign continued, the six years of Labour rule from 1945 to 1951 began to take on something of the character of a dim-remembered aberration, like a quiet sort of Puritan interregnum, whose origins were unnatural, whose ending was inglorious and whose course was a social and political experiment that had never been fully worked out.

One event in 1951, however, the Festival of Britain, and in particular its most noteworthy feature, the South Bank Exhibition, served as an indication of what might have emerged from the otherwise cold social climate of the forties. The Festival was intended both to celebrate the centenary of the Great Exhibition of 1851 and to display the character and achievements of mid-twentieth-century Britain. The choice of the South Bank site was only an afterthought but, in the event, highly significant. The 27-acre site was created by the clearance of an area of depressing slum property between Waterloo and Westminster Bridges, bisected by the Charing Cross railway bridge. It was thus an overdue act of modernization; and the association of the Exhibition with the building of the Festival Hall by the L.C.C. was a fitting tribute to the work for London and the Labour Party of Herbert Morrison. As Lord President of the Council, he was the Minister answerable to Parliament for the Festival. The smallness and awkwardness of the site were characteristic of the problems which afflicted all schemes of social improvement in the crowded United Kingdom, as were the shortage and cost of all the necessary materials. The skill of the chosen architects and designers nevertheless produced, in these unpromising surroundings, a complex of piazzas, buildings and architectural features which gave an unexpected impression of space, light and gaiety; and, for the first time in modern history, Londoners had the opportunity to walk, or even just stand and gaze, by the side of their own river. The more earnest purposes of the Exhibition, to display aspects of English achievement and character, were the least conspicuous part of it. Yet, although the contents of the Lion and Unicorn Pavilion, designed to prove that there was much endearing eccentricity in the English, were rather precious, the attempt to cut loose from the more normal tendency of the English to represent their country as an Old Curiosity Shop full of the relics of the centuries was a sign of spiritual health. Equally outside tradition were the various large mobiles, the Skylon which pointed upwards for no other purpose than that of pointing upwards, and the finely designed Dome of Discovery. And, although the most permanent effect of the Festival was probably that of popularizing the kind of interior design thereafter known as 'contemporary', its chief impact was visual. It was perhaps the first time that ordinary Englishmen were confronted with visible evidence that architecture was concerned with the subtle relationships between buildings and spaces. In spite of the disapproval of the more traditionally-minded leaders of taste and culture, the South Bank Exhibition was a popular success. If, coinciding as it did with the Korean War, it was something of a testimony to the escapism of an island race, it was also a demonstration that, after all, it did possess the capacity, if it would will the means, to create for itself a pleasing and harmonious physical environment.

A month after the Exhibition closed in September 1951, Labour was defeated at the polls, and the new Conservative Government decided that the Exhibition would not open for a second season. All its buildings were therefore demolished or removed from the site.

Books

The list indicates the works upon which this book is principally based. A. J. P. Taylor's *English History, 1914–1945* is not included. This book was completed before Mr Taylor's volume was published and is therefore in no way derived from it.

PART ONE: R. C. K. Ensor's *England 1870–1914*; Roy Jenkins's *Mr Balfour's Poodle*, and *Asquith*; A. P. Ryan's *Mutiny at the Curragh*; G. D. H. Cole's *History of the Labour Party*; *The Common People* by G. D. H. Cole and Raymond Postgate.
On foreign policy, books consulted included A. J. P. Taylor's *The Struggle for Mastery in Europe 1848–1918*; G. W. Monger's *The End of Isolation*; *The Old Diplomacy* by Lord Hardinge of Penshurst.

PART TWO: C. R. M. F. Cruttwell's *The Great War*; *Kitchener* by Sir Philip Magnus; Correlli Barnett's *The Swordbearers*; Alan Moorehead's *Gallipoli*; Roy Jenkins's *Asquith*; Lord Beaverbrook's *Politicians and the War*; Lloyd George's *War Memoirs*; *The First World War* by A. J. P. Taylor.

PART THREE: C. L. Mowat's *Britain Between the Wars*; Alan Hutt's *The Post War History of the British Working Class*; H. G. Nelson's *Land and Power, A Study of British Foreign Policy 1916–19*; Elizabeth Monroe's *Britain's Moment in the Middle East* (used also in Part Nine); Beaverbrook's *Downfall of Lloyd George*.

PART FOUR: The works of Mowat and Hutt already cited; Robert McKenzie's *British Political Parties*; Julian Symons's *The General Strike*; Alan Bullock's *Life and Times of Ernest Bevin, volume one*; Robert Blake's *The Unknown Prime Minister, The Life and Times of Bonar Law*; *Stanley Baldwin*, by G. M. Young; *My Father: The True Story* by A. W. Baldwin; *John Maynard Keynes* by Roy Harrod. Beatrice Webb's *Diaries 1912–24* and 1924–32 were frequently consulted for the whole of the period to 1932.

PART FIVE: In addition to the works named above, J. K. Galbraith's *The Great Crash*; G. D. H. Cole's *Condition of Britain, 1936*; Sir Harold Nicolson's *George V, His Life and Reign*.

PART SIX: This is based chiefly, though never exclusively, on E. M. Robertson's *Hitler's Pre-War Policy*; A. J. P. Taylor's *Origins of the Second World War*; Hugh Dalton's *Call Back Yesterday*; Keith Feiling's *Life of Neville Chamberlain*; Sir Nevile Henderson's *Failure of a Mission*.

PART SEVEN: W. S. Churchill, *The Gathering Storm;* Basil Collier's *Defence of the United Kingdom*; David Divine's *The Nine Days of Dunkirk*; *On Their Shoulders* by Brigadier C. N. Barclay; *The Desert Generals* by Correlli Barnett; The *Memoirs* of Field Marshal Earl Alexander of Tunis.

PART EIGHT: Principally, *Churchill, Roosevelt, Stalin* by H. Feis; *The Struggle for Europe* by Chester Wilmot; 1945 *Year of Decisions*, by Harry S. Truman; *The Reckoning* by the Earl of Avon; also *The Birth of the Bomb* by R. W. Clark, and *Britain and Atomic Energy* by Margaret Gowing.

PART NINE: G. C. Allen's *British Industries and their Organization*; Andrew Shonfield's *British Economic Policy since the War; Labour's First Year*, by J. E. D. Hall; *Ernest Bevin* by Francis Williams; *The Post War Condition of Britain*, G. D. H. Cole; *The Last Years of British India* by Michael Edwardes; *Korea, The Limited War* by David Rees; *The Age of Austerity*, edited Michael Sissons and Philip French; *The New Look* by Harry Hopkins; *From My Level*, Sir George Mallaby.

Figures relating to election results, and dates and details of ministerial appointments are taken from *British Political Facts 1900–1960* by David Butler and Jennie Freeman. Extracts from Press and Parliamentary reports and summaries of Acts of Parliament for the period from 1937 onwards are based on the material in the relevant numbers of Keesing's *Contemporary Archives*.

Index